PHILIP ZIEGLER was born in 1929 and educated at Eton and Oxford. He was a diplomat before becoming an editorial director at the publishers William Colliaimed biographies of William IV   batten and Harold Wilson, as well   )eath.

From the reviews of *Edwar*

'Written with the style, grace and polish that one has come to expect from Ziegler … the great strength of the book lies in its grasp of Heath's psychology and of the psychology of political leadership'
VERNON BOGDANOR, *Times Literary Supplement*

'Brilliant and timely … Ziegler writes the story like a good novelist, and as readably'   WILLIAM WALDEGRAVE, *Spectator*

'The finest political biography of the year was Philip Ziegler's meticulous and beautifully written *Edward Heath*, which got beneath the skin of a sometimes perverse, often pompous and always enigmatic prime minister'   ROD LIDDLE, *Sunday Times*, Books of the Year

'Ziegler has not lost his silken narrative touch … this is a deliciously readable and unfailingly fair book'
FERDINAND MOUNT, *London Review of Books*

'As gripping as a tragic novel, with all the comical inevitability of a cautionary tale'   CRAIG BROWN, *Mail on Sunday*

'Characteristically scrupulous, elegantly composed and impeccably judicious'   JOHN CAMPBELL, *Independent*

'[An] elegant, compelling and devastating study'
ROBERT HARRIS, *Sunday Times*

'Beautifully done, presenting a picture of a modern King Lear thwarted and humiliated by his inability to influence events'
ANTHONY HOWARD, *Sunday Telegraph*

EDWARD HEATH
The Authorised Biography

———◆———

PHILIP ZIEGLER

Harper
Press

HarperPress
An imprint of HarperCollins*Publishers*
77–85 Fulham Palace Road
Hammersmith
London W6 8JB

This Harper*Press* paperback edition published 2011
1

First published by HarperPress in 2010

A catalogue record for this book is available from the British Library

ISBN 978-0-00-724741-7

Typeset in Minion

Printed and bound in Great Britain by Clays Ltd, St Ives plc

MIX
Paper from
responsible sources
FSC
www.fsc.org   **FSC® C007454**

FSC is a non-profit international organisation established to promote the
responsible management of the world's forests. Products carrying the FSC
label are independently certified to assure consumers that they come
from forests that are managed to meet the social, economic and
ecological needs of present or future generations.

Find out more about HarperCollins and the environment at
www.harpercollins.co.uk/green

To Clare

CONTENTS

LIST OF ILLUSTRATIONS

Unless otherwise stated, all photographs come from the collection of Edward Heath, currently at Arundells, and are reproduced by kind permission of the Trustees.

ix

SECTION TWO

Golfing in 1970.
With the Queen and Nixon at Chequers.

Visiting Ulster in 1971.
Signing the Treaty of Accession in 1972.

Greeting Henry Kissinger at Number 10. (Lord Armstrong)
Manoeuvring the grand piano into Number 10.

First encounter with a panda.
With Deng Xiaoping.

A book-signing.
On the rostrum.

The inner circle. (Sara Morrison)
At Arundells. (Lady Armstrong)

As a Knight of the Garter.

The last birthday party. (Lady Armstrong)

CARTOONS

The author and publishers wish to thank various illustrators and publications for permission to reproduce the cartoons on the following pages.

Page 168 Cartoon by Jak/*Evening Standard.*
Page 181 *Daily Telegraph* 17 October 1967. Nicholas Garland/*Daily Telegraph.*
Page 187 *Evening Standard* 12 October 1968. Cartoon by Jak/*Evening Standard.*
Page 259 *Evening Standard* 18 May 1971. Cartoon by Jak/*Evening Standard.*
Page 505 Ingram Pinn/*Financial Times.*
Page 555 'Trog'.
Page 576 *Independent* 20 June 1989. Nicholas Garland.

FOREWORD

Edward Heath changed the lives of the British people more fundamentally than any prime minister since Winston Churchill. By forcing through the abolition of Resale Price Maintenance he cleared the way for the all-conquering march of the supermarket and transformed every high street in the country. By securing Britain's entry into Europe he reversed almost a thousand years of history and embarked on a course that would inevitably lead to the legal, political, economic and social transformation of his country. Both these reforms he forced through by a combination of determination, patience and persuasive powers, against the inertia or active hostility of a large part of the British population, including many of his own party. There may have been others who could have done as much, there may have been others who desired to do so, but it is hard to conceive of any other individual in the second half of the twentieth century who would both have been able and have wished to achieve this transformation.

Yet Heath today is largely forgotten: a meaner beauty of the night eclipsed by the refulgent moon of Margaret Thatcher. This is because, in spite of all he did, he was seen by others, indeed portrayed himself, as a disgruntled loser. Lady Thatcher, though she too was shipwrecked in the end, is remembered as a winner. It is the winners who remain prominent in people's minds. Heath brought it on himself, but the importance of his contribution to British history deserves greater attention. Opinions may differ as to whether what he did was right; the immensity of his achievement in doing it is open to no question.

ACKNOWLEDGEMENTS

The Sir Edward Heath Charitable Foundation invited me to write this biography and gave me unrestricted access to Sir Edward's massive archive. To the Trustees of that Foundation my first acknowledgement is therefore due.

Lord Armstrong of Ilminster, Chairman of the Foundation, knew Heath as well as any man alive. His help and advice have been invaluable during the four years that I have been at work on this book. Perhaps equally important, he from the start made it clear that though my biography was 'official' in the sense that it was authorised by the Foundation, neither he nor the Trustees wished to exercise any sort of control over my conclusions. For better, for worse, this is *my* book.

At the time of writing the Heath papers were still at Arundells, his house in Salisbury. My work there would have been immeasurably more difficult and far less pleasant if it had not been for the constant support of James Elder, Heath's last political secretary, Heath's devoted factotum, Stuart Craven, who did so much to make his final years tolerable, and his housekeeper, Pamela Finch.

All biographers must owe a debt to those who have covered the same ground before them. In their biographies of Heath, George Hutchinson, Margaret Laing and Andrew Roth did me the priceless service of recording the words of witnesses who are no longer accessible today. John Campbell, in his important biography of 1993, unwittingly rendered me a still greater favour. Heath heavily annotated his copy of the book. His observations – usually angry – provide a most valuable indication of his attitude on many questions.

It seems invidious to pick out two names from the host of people who have helped me in the writing of this book but I must record my particular gratitude to Lord Hurd and the Hon. Mrs Sara Morrison. Douglas Hurd has been endlessly patient in answering my innumerable queries and kindly obtained from the Foreign Office elucidation of problems that might otherwise have baffled me. More than anyone else, Sara Morrison convinced me of what from time to time I doubted – that the subject of my biography was a fully functioning human being, bleeding if pricked and dying if poisoned.

Whether or not I have quoted from them verbatim, many people have talked to me about Edward Heath or have helped me in other ways in my research. I am most grateful to The Hon. Edward Adeane, Mr Robin Aisher, Araminta Lady Aldington, Mr Andrew Alexander, Lord Baker of Dorking, Mr Stuart Ball, Mr Peter Batey, Mrs Joey Bieber, Professor Vernon Bogdanor, Field Marshal Lord Bramall, Lord Bridges, Mr Richard Burn, Lord Butler of Brockwell, Mr David Butler, Sir Michael Butler, Dr. John Campbell, Lord Carrington, Mrs Margaret Chadd, Sir Christopher Chataway, Sir Robin Chichester Clark, Mr Anthony Churchill, The Rt. Hon. Kenneth Clarke, Mr Michael Cockerell, Mr Alistair Cooke, Mr Brian Coleman, Mrs Penelope Craig, Lord Croham, Esmé Countess of Cromer, Miss Kay Davidson, The Very Revd. Hugh Dickinson, Professor David Dilks, Dr. Jeffrey Easton, Lady Antonia Fraser, Sir Martin Gilbert, the late Lord Gilmour, The Rt. Hon. John Selwyn Gummer, Mrs Penny Gummer, Lord and Lady Healey, Mrs Muriel Heath, the late Sir Nicholas Henderson, Professor Peter Hennessy, Lord Heseltine, Lord Howe, Lord Howell, Mrs Tatiana Hurd, Mr David Irving, the late Earl Jellicoe, Mr Mick Jones, Sir Anthony Kenny, the late Lord Kingsland, Mr Henry Kissinger, Sir Timothy Kitson, Mrs Kate Knowles, Lord Lawson, Professor Roger Louis, Ros Lady Lyons, Mrs Pamela McCarthy, Lord McGregor, Mrs Sarah Macnab, the late Sir Donald Maitland, Lord Marlesford, Mr David Marsh, Mr David Mathews, Mr Tom Miller, Mr Charles Moore, Lord Moser, Mr Geoffrey Munn, Mr Peter Nicholson, Sir Michael Palliser, Mr Bernard Palmer, Lord

Patten of Barnes, Mr Robert Ponsonby, Lord Prior, Sir Peter Ramsbotham, Mrs Susan Rathbone, Elaine Lady Rawlinson, Mr Andrew Roberts, Mr Christopher Roberts, Caroline Lady Ryder, Mr Anthony Seldon, Mrs Nancy-Joan Seligman, Sir Stephen Sherbourne, Mr Richard Simmonds, Mr Michael Sissons, Lady Soames, Miss Margot Strickland, Mr Robert Taylor, Dr. Richard Thorpe, Sir Crispin Tickell, Lord Tugendhat, Sir John Ure, Dame Joan Varley, Mr Hugo Vickers, Mr Michael Wade, Lord Waldegrave of North Hill, Lord Walker of Worcester, Mr Wilfred Weeks, Lord Wright of Richmond, The Hon. Lady de Zulueta.

Archives can seem remote, even intimidating places but archivists are almost always the most helpful and generous of people. In particular I would like to express my gratitude to Geoffrey Baxter of the National Archives, Mary Bone of the Royal Institute of International Affairs in Chatham House, Sue Crabtree of the Templeman Library in the University of Kent, Sue Donnelly of the British Library of Political and Economic Science in the London School of Economics, Clemens Gresser and Jonathan Dixon of the British Library, Colin Harris and Helen Langley of the Bodleian, Alan Packwood and Sophie Bridges of the Churchill Archive Centre, Jonathan Smith of Trinity College Library, Cambridge and Sheridan Westlake and Jeremy McIlwaine of the Conservative Party Archive. Like so many other British writers I have found the London Library an indispensable support.

My agent, Caroline Dawnay, has been endlessly helpful and encouraging and has proved, if proof were needed, that a professional relationship need not preclude real friendship. Richard Johnson, who recruited me for HarperCollins some twenty years after I first defected from it, sadly retired before this book could be delivered. His extremely capable successor, Martin Redfern, has admirably filled the gap. Benjamin Buchan has done a strikingly efficient job of sub-editing and has saved me from innumerable blunders that would otherwise have shamed me.

As always my warmest thanks must go to my wife Clare. Her marriage to a biographer has meant that she has been forced to share her life with many unlikely companions but none can have been more testing than Edward Heath. Her perception and generous understanding of the vagaries of human nature have been as valuable to me in the writing of this book as they have been in every other facet of my life.

ABBREVIATIONS USED IN TEXT

ACAS	Advisory Conciliation and Arbitration Service
ACP	Advisory Committee on Policy
AEU	Amalgamated Engineering Union
CBI	Confederation of British Industry
CPRS	Central Policy Review Staff
CPS	Centre for Policy Studies
DTI	Department of Trade and Industry
ECSC	European Coal and Steel Community
EEC	European Economic Community
EFTA	European Free Trade Area
EMU	European Monetary Union
ERM	Exchange Rate Mechanism
FCO	Foreign and Commonwealth Office
HAC	Honourable Artillery Company
IRA	Irish Republican Army
JCR	Junior Common Room
NATO	North Atlantic Treaty Organisation
NCB	National Coal Board
NEDC	National Economic Development Council
NIBMAR	No Independence Before Majority African Rule
NIRC	National Industrial Relations Court
NUM	National Union of Mineworkers
NUR	National Union of Railwaymen

OUCA	Oxford University Conservative Association
PEST	Political, Economic and Social Toryism
pps	Parliamentary Private Secretary
RPM	Resale Price Maintenance
RUC	Royal Ulster Constabulary
SDLP	Social and Democratic Labour Party
SDP	Social Democratic Party
SET	Selective Employment Tax
TGWU	Transport and General Workers' Union
TUC	Trades Union Congress
UCS	Upper Clyde Shipbuilders
UDI	Unilateral Declaration of Independence
UNCTAD	United Nations Conference on Trade and Development
VAT	Value Added Tax

ONE

The Child and the Boy

Two future British prime ministers were born in 1916. Both belonged to what may loosely be called the lower-middle class and found their way by scholarships to grammar school and Oxford, where both were strikingly successful. Both served at one time in the civil service and took a precocious interest in politics. Both prided themselves on their knowledge of economics and were endowed by nature with prodigious memories. One was prime minister from October 1964 to June 1970 and from February 1974 to March 1976; the other occupied 10 Downing Street for the intervening years. In all other ways, few men can have been less similar than Harold Wilson and Edward Richard George Heath.

In fact, for those who take an interest in such arcane distinctions, the Wilsons were in origin slightly grander – or at least less humble – than the Heaths. They had been lower-middle class for several generations; the Heaths had only recently taken their first steps from the working classes. Ted Heath's first identifiable ancestor, his four times great-grandfather, Richard, had been a fisherman living in Cockington in Devonshire at the end of the eighteenth century. His son William followed the same calling but with scant success. By 1819, when William was 56 and presumably too old for an active seafaring life, he found himself with fourteen children and no job and was forced to lodge a petition with Trinity House as having 'no property or income whatever'. Undiscomfited, *his* son, Richard, also took to the sea, joined the Coastguard Service and, in 1831, was transferred to the new coastguard station in Ramsgate, Kent. Before migrating he had married a Somerset girl. Their son, George, Ted's great-grandfather, was the last of the seafaring Heaths; he served with the merchant navy and ended his working days in charge of Ramsgate pier.[1]

George married a local girl. Their son, Stephen, the first terrestrial Heath, did not notably improve the family's prosperity. He went into the dairy business and at first did well, but then, according to his son William, 'lost all his money and went on the railway',[2] with the un-glamorous task of moving passengers' luggage between the station and the hotels. He survived this setback with equanimity and lived to the age of seventy-seven, invariably genial, frequently inebriated and loved by his grandson, Ted. He too married a Kentish girl, as did William, Ted's father. Ted, therefore, was of solidly Devonshire and Kentish stock, with no tincture of more exotic blood in the five generations before his birth. In 1962 Iain Macleod, seeking Heath's endorsement when a candidate for the Rectorship of Glasgow University, asked hopefully whether he could not scrape up some Scottish connection, however tenuous. His only claim, Heath replied, was that he had been educated at Balliol, a college which owed its existence to John de Balliol and Dervorguilla of Galway: 'I do not know whether on this somewhat flimsy basis you will be able to build up a case which will secure the Nationalist vote.'[3]

William Heath was far more like his exuberant and outgoing father than his more unapproachable son. He was a 'quiet and unassuming' man, said Heath in his memoirs,[4] but this does not correspond with the testimony of many of those who knew him well. He was 'a dear man', said Nancy-Joan Seligman; 'heaven', said Mary Lou de Zulueta; 'a great hugger and kisser, even a bottom-pincher, to the occasional embarrassment of his son', recalled Margaret Chadd.[5] He loved parties: other people's would do but it was best of all to be at the centre of his own. His jollity was not allowed to interfere with his work, however: he was enterprising, energetic and conscientious. By train-ing he was a carpenter; he ended up as a builder with his own firm, small but still employing several workmen. Ted Heath took considerable pride in his father's advance into the middle classes. In his biography, John Campbell mentioned that Heath had had to be dissuaded from suing *Isis* for describing his father as 'a jobbing builder'. Heath scrawled angry denials against several of Campbell's assertions but here he merely noted that it was the *Sunday Express* and not *Isis* which had used the phrase.[6] William had all the fierce conservatism so often to be found in the small and struggling businessman. During the First World War he had been assigned to the Vickers armaments factory at Croydon and forced to join a union. 'It was terrible,' he remembered. 'The union was all right, it was the way it was run. There was a clique of people in control and unless you were in the clique you couldn't get anything past.'[7] In his own life as a builder he resolved to have as little to do with unions as could be contrived, and he inculcated in his son a conviction that, whilst unions as an institution were acceptable, even desirable, they should never be allowed to run riot or to consider themselves above the law.

William Heath was a man of intelligence, common sense and limited education. The few letters to his son which survive in the archive at Arundells, Heath's house in Salisbury, are sound in content but wayward in grammar and spelling; in one short letter we have 'emportant people', 'busness', 'we planed our week', 'untill', 'they have wrote to him' and a dearth of question marks and apostrophes. Possibly he suffered from what would now be diagnosed as dyslexia; certainly he left school at the age of twelve and never had time to continue his formal education. He never doubted its value, however, and was resolved that his children should have a better start than he did. In this ambition his wife wholeheartedly supported him.

Without Edith Heath, indeed, it is unlikely that Ted would have been launched so successfully on his vertiginous career. She was a Pantony, another Kentish family, and her father had been gardener in a big house a few miles from Broadstairs. She became lady's maid to a rich, exacting but benevolent mistress and absorbed uncritically the values of propriety, decorum and unostentatious good-living which she found in the home of her employer. In his description of Edith Heath, John Campbell used the phrase 'strait-laced';[8] Heath underlined it, usually an indication of disagreement. It seems apt enough. Certainly she tolerated, if perhaps silently deplored, her husband's conviviality, but she kept a house that was resolutely clean and well ordered and dedicated herself, to an extent for which William had neither the time nor the inclination, to instilling in her elder son the habit of hard work and a burning hunger to succeed. 'She was the driving spirit,' a childhood friend of Heath's remarked. 'His father was a nice guy but without the drive his mother had. She was the one who encouraged ... the ambitions.' Heath felt her to be beyond reproach. 'My mother was a wonderful woman,' he wrote in his memoirs. 'My lasting memory is of her beauty and calmness ... At home we adored her for these traits and also because she was so supportive of us.' Some felt her resolution verged on the implacable and detected in her not so much tolerance as contempt for the looser standards of her husband. Certainly she was strong-minded and convinced that her values could not be questioned, but she was sensitive and generous, ready to endure the shortcomings of anyone except herself and her beloved son. She missed no opportunity to inculcate her most cherished values in her children. As a Christmas present when he was eight Ted was given a leather commonplace book in which various improving thoughts had already been inscribed. The first was: 'To get you must give, but never give to get.' Some time later she added: 'Make new friends but keep the old. One is silver, the other is gold.' Ted made little effort to improve on these but the book was still in his possession when he died.[9]

Different though they were, both physically and psychologically, William and Edith Heath were happy in their marriage. Edith may have been the stronger character and certainly it was her standards that prevailed at home, but she was wise enough to ensure that her husband never felt himself excluded or ignored. 'In a marriage, nobody's boss – I don't believe in that,' he told one of Heath's biographers, and everything suggests he approved heartily of the way his wife was bringing up his children. They started life in St Peter's-in-Thanet, a village now absorbed into the Kentish holiday resort of Broadstairs. Teddy – the use of 'Ted' seems to have become habitual during the Second World War, he was never known as 'Edward' –

was born on Sunday, 9 July 1916. His middle names were Richard and George. Almost immediately the family abandoned St Peter's to move inland to Crayford, where William Heath had been assigned to war work at the Vickers aircraft factory. Only a few months old, Teddy was spared the worst rigours of what must have been a miserable winter. Wartime privations were at their worst. 'We had a ramshackle house,' William Heath remembered, 'and the wind used to whistle round it like a pack of wolves. I remember begging in the street for coal and potatoes ... It was a terrible time.' 'Begging', presumably, involved asking for an additional ration from under-supplied shopkeepers rather than soliciting from passers-by. William Heath was never unemployed and quite well paid – but the last two years of the war were exceptionally difficult. It may have been these problems which deterred the Heaths from adding to their family; at all events it was four years before Teddy acquired a brother, John.[10]

The difference between the two boys was quickly apparent. By the time he was eight or nine Teddy was conspicuously diligent and hardworking, with formidable powers of concentration and a distaste for anything bordering on frivolity. John, on the other hand, was amiable, messy, easygoing and almost entirely without ambition. He viewed his elder brother with a mixture of awe, incredulity and derision. Many years later the journalist John Junor had a conversation with John at a party and found him 'a very dull chap indeed. Pleasant but commonplace.' This was the general verdict. Ted Heath always denied hotly that he had been his mother's favourite or had been given any special treatment. The evidence of those who knew the family well – Nancy-Joan Seligman, Araminta Aldington – is that, on the contrary, Edith Heath, without ever being consciously unkind to her younger son, lavished most of her loving attention on Teddy. She always put his needs first, said John's widow, Muriel; it was taken for granted in the household that the normal rules of conduct were suspended for his benefit. 'She spoiled Teddy rotten,' recalled Margaret Chadd; whenever he came to stay with the Chadds he left his pyjamas all over the floor and assumed that somebody else would pick them up. The inevitable result was that John, finding that nothing was expected of him, responded by achieving nothing. At school one day he overheard two masters extolling Teddy's virtues: 'Of course his brother is nothing like ...' one of them added. John accepted without undue dismay the fact that he was 'nothing like ...'; Teddy took it for granted that he too was 'nothing like ...'; nothing like John nor like the generality of his schoolfellows. He grew in confidence while John resigned himself to rubbing along in contented obscurity.[11]

Teddy began his schooling at a dingy little church school in Crayford. He learned enough to be well able to cope with the next stage of his education but his life did not really take off until the family returned to Broadstairs in 1923. Broadstairs then as now was an amiable little seaside resort, busy in summer, under-occupied in winter, with few buildings of distinction but many of quiet attractiveness. It prided itself on its connections with Charles Dickens: a suitably bleak Bleak House still looms over the seafront; plaques abound asserting that the author wrote this or that book while in residence; Heath's favourite was a discreet notice proclaiming 'Charles Dickens did not live here'. Though neighbouring Margate and Ramsgate were better equipped to handle yachts of any size, Broadstairs was rich in boats. In spite of their maritime antecedents, however, the Heaths were neither rich nor enthusiastic enough to own a boat themselves.

Once back in Broadstairs Teddy began to attend St Peter's Church of England School. James Bird, the assistant headmaster, described how he presented himself 'neatly dressed and completely self-possessed' and handed over a transfer form from his school in Crayford which lauded his attainments in reading and arithmetic. John's first wife, Marian, who wrote a mildly malicious account of her brother-in-law after her marriage broke up, quotes Mr Bird as saying that Teddy 'was not a good mixer. He was inclined to be aloof.' It was not her intention to paint a sympathetic portrait of her former husband's family but in this case she seems to have been recording faithfully. To another biographer Bird spoke of Teddy's 'general cleanliness and wholesomeness and a certain aloofness – even as a small boy he was self-contained and purposeful'. It is not an entirely attractive picture. The headmaster's report that he was 'a good boy ... earnest, painstaking and thoroughly well-behaved' is almost equally daunting. That Teddy was a good influence at St Peter's can be taken for granted; whether he got much fun out of it or gave much fun to others is more doubtful. Once his mother went up to his room and suggested that he was working too hard and should come down to join the family. 'Mother,' Teddy replied severely, 'sometimes I think you don't *want* me to get on.' Self-discipline and a conscious distrust of emotional display were as evident at the age of ten as sixty or seventy years later. On a radio programme his interviewer Mavis Nicholson once asked him whether the Heaths had been demonstrative as a family. 'As we were by nature a close-knit family it wasn't necessary to demonstrate great emotion towards each other,' he replied. 'If people are demonstrating their emotions, there must be something lacking in the background.'[12]

Emotional austerity did not preclude an early and intense love of music. A cousin of his mother's first introduced him to the piano, he began to take lessons, and his parents, at what must have been considerable financial sacrifice, invested in an instrument for him to play on. He was not the most amenable of pupils. 'I was always in too much of a hurry,' he confessed, and he was irritated by his teacher's insistence that he should master one piece before moving on to another. 'What I was after was the musical experience, the opportunity to express feeling and emotion in pieces of different kinds, according to my moods.' It would be an over-simplification to say that in music Heath found expression for the emotion of which he had deprived himself in his everyday life, but even at the age of ten or eleven he was indulging on the piano a freedom which he would not have allowed himself in personal relationships. It was his father who encouraged him most vigorously. If Teddy got bored of practising, William would urge him to fresh efforts: 'Stick to it! Once you've mastered it, nobody can ever take it away from you. Your music will be a joy for life.' His brother at one point also began to play the piano but, according to his first wife at least, was switched to the violin on the grounds that it would be nice for Teddy to have somebody to play duets with. John got no pleasure out of either instrument and renounced them at the first opportunity.[13]

The local church of St Peter's-in-Thanet had a large choir of twenty-four boys and twelve men, and Teddy, who had a good if not outstanding treble voice, joined it and was soon singing solos. After a few years he began to take an interest in the organ and before long was assisting the regular organist and understudying Miss Price, the lady who habitually played at the children's services. 'He is a great worker, very quick to learn, conscientious, and for his years a very capable musician,' wrote the vicar, Alfred Tatham. Teddy was 'thoroughly dependable; I have always found him a very present help in trouble'. Much later, Tatham's widow remembered Teddy sitting beside Miss Price: she 'was a very poor performer on the organ and I always thought you kept her straight'. For those oppressed by the vision of Heath's unwavering rectitude it is only fair to say that he seems to have been a genuinely kind and helpful child. Mrs Matthews, the widow of a former vicar, remembered him as being 'one of the nicest boys I have known'. When Mrs Matthews, by then aged 86 and wavering in her mind, invited him to a party to celebrate the return of her son, who in fact had been killed in action thirty years before, Heath scrapped the run-of-the-mill letter submitted by a secretary, wrote a long and friendly letter in his own hand and also wrote to Mrs Matthews' surviving son to express his sympathy.[14]

It was Mr Tatham who prepared Teddy for confirmation. His schoolfriend Ronald Whittall, who underwent the same ordeal, said that Tatham was the first man to have had a serious influence on either of the boys: 'He opened our eyes to religion, to Christianity, and from that point on Teddy took his religion very seriously. I believe that it's a deep-seated sense of religion which may – rightly or wrongly – make him think he's a man of destiny.' Extravagant though it may seem, the evidence suggests that Heath saw himself as a man of destiny several years before his confirmation; certainly, from the age of nine or ten he was hoarding every scrap of paper with the zeal of someone who is well aware that one day a momentous tale would need to be told. His religion did mean a great deal to him, however: partly because the Church and music were in his experience so closely related, more because the Christian faith and Christian values had been deeply inculcated in him when he was a child and he rarely saw cause to question them. The same interviewer who had asked him whether the Heaths were demonstrative as a family asked him whether he prayed. 'Yes.' 'Is it very helpful to you?' 'Yes.' 'Why?' 'Because it is a spiritual communion.' To an unbeliever such an answer might not seem to take matters much further but to Heath it was wholly satisfactory. He never doubted that, through prayer, he was in direct communication with God, and though religious problems did not preoccupy him, his faith provided a bedrock on which he believed he could construct his life. His mother at one time hoped he might enter the Church, then discovered how badly clergymen were paid and changed her mind. Even if she had not done so he would never have taken holy orders: he 'did not feel a true calling', he wrote in his memoirs and – a somewhat vainglorious reflection for a young man on the brink of life – such work would not have given him an opportunity 'to shape the affairs of my country'.[15]

By the time Teddy was confirmed he had already moved on to Chatham House Grammar School, a Local Education Authority school in the heart of Ramsgate. Chatham House was built of an aggressively red brick and from outside was entirely charmless. Its interior was little, if at all, more prepossessing. It was, however, an excellent school. It was geared to equip its pupils to make a living in a competitive world: accountancy was an optional subject and the emphasis in economics was on the practical rather than the theoretic. At the same time, however, it encouraged an interest in literature, regularly put on plays in which a high proportion of the boys performed some part, and organised vigorous debates, both within the school and against other schools in the vicinity. The fees were twelve guineas a year but about half the boys were on scholarships. Teddy sat for one of these and was successful. At the final interview the headmaster, H. C. Norman, asked him what he wished to be in later life. 'An architect,' said Teddy; an ambition which he had never admitted to his parents and which seems to have passed rapidly from his mind. The Kent Education Committee provided a further grant to cover travel and the cost of lunch, so the only expense left for the family was a guinea a year for music. William Heath was happy to provide for this, though making it a condition that Teddy would not take up music as a career.[16]

Teddy went to Chatham House in the autumn of 1926. A combination of precocity and the date on which his birthday fell meant that he was far younger than the average age of his class: ten years five months, against thirteen years one month. In spite of this he managed to come eighth out of twenty-eight – 'most promising', said the headmaster.[17] At no point in his time at Chatham House did he excel academically, though the occasional complaints – geography: 'He must work very much harder'; French: 'Much lacking in accuracy' – were outweighed by enthusiastic comments or references to his comparative youth. His performance in general seems to have been creditable but somewhat graceless; in 1931 the English master remarked gloomily: 'He must remember that he writes to be read and that the Examiner is, after all, only a human being.' Being too young for his class proved a problem when most of his fellow pupils were about to take School Certificate. The headmaster noted that, though his work had been 'most promising' (a formula which he invoked seven or eight times during Teddy's career at Chatham House), it would still be 'tempting providence to let him sit this year. He is too immature for an exam of this standard.' This evoked a protest from William Heath – inspired, one suspects, and possibly even written, by Teddy's mother. Teddy, wrote William, was 'most depressed at the thought of not being allowed to sit … He is young, I agree, but even the young sometimes exceed our expectations.' He would undertake to have Teddy coached in French – his weakest subject – during the holidays. The headmaster gave way and Teddy did exceed expectations though not extravagantly so; he gained his School Certificate but had to wait another year for the Matriculation which opened the way to university.

Throughout these years it is clear that Teddy was considered by his parents, and up to a point by the boys and masters as well, as being outside the common run. Only rarely were these pretensions slapped down. Shortly after he arrived at Chatham House his father – once again, no doubt, put up to it by Mrs Heath – wrote to say that the school food did not agree with him. Could he please take his dinner at a nearby café? Only if he had a doctor's certificate saying he needed a special diet, ruled the headmaster: 'There is nothing in the school dinners which should be unsuitable for a boy in ordinary health.' He was, however, excused football and cricket, on the grounds that such games might damage his hands and thus impair his music. He got on perfectly well with the other boys and was never bullied or ostracised, but he does not seem to have made close friends or to have spent much time visiting their houses. He led a 'one-dimensional life', recalled his contemporary, Keith Hunt. 'He took no interest in games and played as rarely as possible. He often had special classes just for himself.'[18] His behaviour was almost always immaculate. Only once in his first three years did he suffer a detention, for some unspecified but, no doubt, innocuous crime. He was invariably punctual. Almost his only recorded offence was 'running along a passage in which running is forbidden'. His penalty was self-inflicted; he banged his head so hard against a projecting pipe that he had to have several stitches in the resultant wound. 'I cannot discover that anyone was to blame but the boy himself,' wrote the headmaster severely, presumably fearing that, even in 1929, an indignant parent might sue the school for negligence. Why Teddy was running is not explained: it is depressingly likely that it was merely to ensure that he was in good time for the next class.

In part this remoteness from the preoccupations of his contemporaries must have been fostered by the fact that music was his favoured pastime, and that the instrument he chose inevitably took him away from his fellow schoolboys. But he did not exclusively practise on the organ, and music also brought him further into the life of Chatham House. He won the Belasco Prize for the piano and increasingly began to experiment with conducting. By the time he left he had established a unique position as a leader among the school's musicians. 'I cannot speak too highly of the tremendous amount of work he has done,' recorded an awe-struck music master. 'He has been a help to me and an inspiration to the boys. As a conductor of choirs he has been outstanding ... I am grateful to him for all he has done for me.' This note, giving the impression that the master viewed Teddy more as a collaborator than a pupil, marked all his reports during his triumphant last year at Chatham House. In their eyes – and not only in their eyes; in the last year he won a prize for character awarded by the votes of all the boys of the fifth and sixth forms – he was a remarkable force for good in the school. 'It will be long before his ability, character, personality and leadership have failed to leave their mark on Coleman's,' testified a grateful housemaster. The headmaster was still more lavish in his panegyric: 'The purity of his ideals, his loyalty to them, and his sense of duty have made him outstanding among boys who have helped build the School. That his mental and moral worth may have the reward they deserve is my wish for him.'

It would be easy to assume from all this that Teddy Heath was a ghastly little prig, who should have been shunned by any boy of spirit. He was not: on the contrary, the recollections of contemporaries make it clear that he was on the whole well-liked as well as respected. Inevitably he was prominent among the school prefects: he was 'a bit of a stickler', one master remembered. 'He was very down on kids who had their hands in their trouser pockets, or weren't behaving well in the street in their school cap and blazer. He thought that breaking a school rule amounted to disloyalty to the school.'[19] But though he was allowed to use a gym-shoe to beat recalcitrant schoolboys, he rarely availed himself of the opportunity. 'Discipline and organisation,' he told a television interviewer in 1998, were of paramount importance, but need not involve harsh rule. 'I carried out my responsibilities, of course,' he replied loftily, when asked if he had often resorted to physical punishment. His popularity was established when the school held a mock election in January 1935 to choose one of the boys as prime minister. Teddy stood as the national government candidate and fought an enterprising campaign: persuading the local MP to write a letter in his support and taking advantage of a sudden snow storm to arrive early at school and tramp out a gigantic 'VOTE FOR HEATH' on the lawn in front of the main entrance. He won a landslide victory.[20]

The energy he spent on enterprises of this kind slightly alarmed the headmaster. 'He must not jeopardise his own interests by giving *too* much time to sidelines – either in or out of school,' warned Mr Norman. As well as music, Teddy in his last two or three years proved an enthusiastic actor, playing important roles in most of the school's productions and featuring as the Archangel Gabriel in the annual nativity play. He also took eagerly to debating, proposing successfully, at various times, that sweepstakes, Sunday cinemas and capital punishment should be abolished and that the House would, in defiance of the recent vote in the Oxford Union, be prepared to fight for King and Country. 'Its present flourishing condition is largely due to his efforts,' the master in charge of the Debating Society appreciatively recorded.

Another extramural activity which profoundly influenced his thinking was a school trip to Paris in the spring of 1931. 'It was the most exciting event of my life so far,' wrote Heath some forty years later. 'It was this which embedded in me a lifelong curiosity about every other part of the world and a determination to see for myself before I formed judgments about other people's customs, traditions and way of life.'[21] This somewhat portentous declaration perhaps overrates the significance for a fifteen-year-old schoolboy of a brief shuffle round the more obvious sights of Paris leavened by a furtive escapade to the Folies Bergère. In fact the expedition was more memorable for Teddy because it included his first visit to an opera, *Carmen* at the Opéra Comique. This experience heralded an addiction to opera-going which persisted throughout his life. The Parisian trip, however, failed to herald any similar addiction to the French language; Heath's French remained appalling, in accent, syntax and vocabulary, and some of the most important conversations of his life had to be conducted through an interpreter.

The trip to Paris was organised by a Dr Woolf, who included Teddy in the party even though all the other boys were from another school. Teddy – keen, cheerful, friendly, intelligent, deferential without being obsequious – had a capacity for gaining the interest of older men in a way which even the most prurient would have agreed was free of any undertone of sexuality. Another such patron was Alec Martin, a future chairman of the auctioneers Christie's and a considerable authority on painting. Martin owned a large house in the neighbourhood for whose upkeep William Heath was responsible. He met Teddy, decided the boy was worth cultivating and took to asking him over when there were guests. He remained a friend until he died in 1971. From him Teddy learned to look at and enjoy pictures; he was never to be an expert but he had a good eye and a shrewd collector's instinct. Martin advised him on his purchases and left him two valuable paintings by Sargent. Through Martin, Teddy met several distinguished painters. One of whom he missed out on, though, was Walter Sickert. In 1934 Sickert bought a home in St Peter's-in-Thanet. Teddy used to bicycle regularly past his house and often saw paintings hanging on the clothes line to dry, including the celebrated if artistically insignificant portrait of King Edward VIII, painted from a photograph. In this case, though, his charms failed to prevail. Once he took a group of carol singers to Sickert's house and, after the singers had done their bit, rang hopefully at the front door. After a long pause the door opened a crack. 'Go away!' said Sickert.[22]

Another elderly admirer brought into his life by his father's building activities was the rich Jewish solicitor, Royalton Kisch. Kisch was an expert on roses and a considerable amateur musicologist. From the start he decided that Teddy had limitless potential and he was accustomed to say from time to time: 'That boy will one day be prime minister.' Arnold Goodman was a frequent visitor who well remembered the youthful Heath as a feature of Kisch's home. 'Although he was clearly a very intelligent boy and intensely interested in politics,' wrote Goodman, 'I never shared Kisch's view about his future.' He told one of Heath's biographers that he thought Teddy 'an eager, questing person who was looking for founts of experience; founts of sophistication, founts of knowledge ... He was not at all a man on the make.' What most impressed Goodman was that, when Kisch was a very old man and Heath had become a public figure, Heath went on regularly visiting his old benefactor. 'Seemingly he never forgot a friend,' wrote Goodman, adding dryly that this was a quality 'complemented, some critics may say, by too firm a recollection of his adversaries'.[23]

Musical, interested in painting and politics, religiously minded, reasonably well read: by most standards Teddy, when the time came to move on from Chatham House, was a formidably well-rounded individual. He had his limitations. 'You were always a poor judge of a good film,' wrote a friend in 1935. 'Mickey Mouse seems to be the only "actor" who interests you.'[24] He was intellectually unambitious and of limited imagination. Though his essay on Keats was judged to be 'fairly well done' there is no evidence that poetry held any joys for him. He paid little attention to the appearance of the buildings or countryside around him. But he was still better informed and had far wider interests than most of his contemporaries. His masters took it for granted that whatever college at Oxford or Cambridge he favoured would be grateful to receive him and would smooth his way with scholarships. The colleges proved to be less enthusiastic.

First, in 1934 he tried for music scholarships at St Catharine's, Cambridge and Keble, Oxford. Both were denied him. Next he applied for a Modern Greats scholarship at Balliol. Charles Morris, the Tutor for Admissions, asked him what he wanted to do in life. Architecture was by now long forgotten; his most ardent wish, he replied, was to be a professional politician. 'I don't think I ever heard any other schoolboy answer a similar question in these terms,' admitted the Tutor. He was rejected on other grounds. Though his economics were close to being of Exhibition standard, his general work was not so good and his French was lamentable. 'You will understand,' the Tutor wrote consolingly to Norman, 'that it is not so much a question of a candidate being weak in some subjects as of his being sufficiently better than the other candidates.' Balliol would be happy to accept him as a Commoner. He was still very young, however. If he were to stay on for another year at Chatham House, he might well get an Exhibition. Norman discussed the matter with Teddy's parents and established that, though they were prepared to keep him at school for another year, they did not think they could possibly afford to send him to Oxford without some kind of scholarship. May 1935 was pencilled in for the next attempt.[25]

Teddy, however, grew restive. In January 1935 he wrote directly to the Tutor for Admissions at Balliol. The letter was cautiously phrased but suggested that he was well placed to win a scholarship worth £80 a year to Cambridge. If he was to get an Exhibition or scholarship to Balliol, how much would it be worth? If the purpose of the letter was to enhance his value in the eyes of Balliol, it was unsuccessful. The reply was discouraging. 'It seems to me that you can hardly afford to take the risk of letting the possibilities at Cambridge go by in favour of an examination in May which (so far at any rate as this College is concerned) has only got one £100 award.' If an Exhibition worth £40 would give Heath the support he needed, then his chances were obviously better, but even at that level an award was far from being a certainty.[26]

Teddy concluded that a bird in the hand was worth more than a – probably pretty speculative – bird in the bush, and decided to stick with Balliol. He duly tried again in May 1935. The bird turned out not to be in the hand after all. Perhaps his extracurricular activities had proved too distracting, perhaps he had grown stale. He did no better in economics and decidedly worse in literature: his essay earned a derisory gamma+. 'On balance he does not appear to have made any marked advance,' the Tutor for Admissions concluded depressingly.[27] Once more his parents were consulted. In the intervening twelve months William Heath had grown slightly more prosperous, the acclaim for Teddy at Chatham House had become still more fervent: the Heaths decided that, whatever the sacrifice involved, their son must accept the place at Balliol which the college was still happy to offer him. The new term began in October 1935. 'It will be my last letter to you before you go up,' wrote his former schoolfriend, Ken Evans, on 1 October, 'so take my warning. Don't get drunk at the first dinner, it looks bad.'[28] He was clearly joking. No one who knew Teddy Heath in 1935 could have believed that the advice was necessary.

TWO

Balliol

Balliol in the 1930s was not quite the intellectual powerhouse which it had been before the First World War, but it was still one of Oxford's leading colleges and as likely as any other to produce the next generation of political leaders. For Heath it had another salient advantage; it was not even slightly smart. Its uncompromisingly ugly architecture and the – by contemporary standards – unusually polyglot or at least polychrome nature of its student body meant that it was derided by the more conventionally snobbish of the undergraduates. The year Heath went up, Korda's epic *Sanders of the River* was playing in Oxford cinemas. At one point a canoe-load of ferocious black warriors scudded furiously down the river in pursuit of the fleeing hero. It became a ritual that shouts of 'Well rowed, Balliol!' should ring round the auditorium at this point. Such mockery only enhanced the self-esteem of the members of Balliol, whose bland consciousness of their own superiority ensured that they would assume that any hostility was based on jealousy.

As well as being cosmopolitan, Balliol prided itself on being socially inclusive. Half the undergraduates came from public schools, a handful from patrician families. In some colleges this led to the formation of uneasy cliques; no doubt some such social divisions were to be found at Balliol but they were deplored by the great majority of the undergraduates and practised only surreptitiously. 'What little snobbery there was tended to be intellectual rather than social,' wrote

17

Heath, 'and, to my delight as well as my surprise, I soon found myself mixing easily with freshmen from almost every conceivable background.'[1] Any undergraduate who let his snobbishness obtrude would have had to reckon with the formidable Master of Balliol, A. D. Lindsay. Lindsay was a former Professor of Philosophy at Glasgow University whose resolute radicalism was tempered by openness of mind and a tolerance of almost any point of view except the bigoted and the stupid. He liked Heath from the start: 'v.attractive chap', he wrote in the 'handshaking notes' which he kept to remind himself of the salient points about all the undergraduates.[2] 'No background' was a slightly cryptic additional comment; if it meant that Heath almost unconsciously distanced himself from his roots, it would have been justified. Heath never made a secret of his origins or in any way appeared ashamed of them, but he felt family and university to be two widely distant sectors of his life and saw no reason to mix them. Throughout his life he tended rigidly to compartmentalise his interests, his activities and his personal relationships. During his four years at university his parents visited him only once or twice, his brother John seems never to have come. He was not ashamed of his family; it was just that it had no place in his Oxford life.

'The College is delightful,' Heath told his old headmaster. 'Of course, not an architectural wonder, but it has its own, to me, very pleasing atmosphere. The dons are very nice ... Here too everybody mixes very well, unfortunately not always the case.'[3] Heath did not strive consciously to adapt to his new surroundings but, in the words of his tutor, the future Lord Fulton, he was not one of those working-class undergraduates who remained 'conspicuously loyal to their social background'.[4] It was while he was at Oxford that his accent evolved into the slightly uneasy compound which endured until his death: plummy upper-middle-class varied by disconcerting vowel sounds that betrayed a more plebeian background. When Nigel Nicolson, an Oxford contemporary, referred to his 'cockney accent', Heath remarked indignantly that he had not a trace of London blood in his make-up. 'I think it is a mixture of rural Kent and Wode-housean Oxford,' suggested his sister-in-law. Whatever its origins, Heath was aware of the fact that his accent was noticeably different from that of most of those with whom he consorted. Either he was unable to change it or, more probably, had no wish to do so. More than most politicians, he genuinely disdained cheap popularity and eschewed anything that might be interpreted as an attempt to win favour by pretending to be something other than what he was. He would not ostentatiously parade his social origins but nor would he excuse them or conceal them. Nicolson said he thought Heath's accent 'counted against him a little'. Given the progress that lay ahead, it can not have counted much.[5]

Not that everything was easy. Heath was certainly one of the poorest undergraduates at Balliol. A few came from similarly humble homes but most of those had scholarships or grants to help them. Heath had a small loan from the Kent Education Committee and another from Royalton Kisch, but beyond that every penny that he spent was an extra burden on his hard-pressed parents. He had no car and could not afford the train fare, so he never went home during the term; he bought no books unless they were essential for his work; he did not get a single gramophone record or anything on which to play it until his second year. 'I like to have things of my own,' he told a *Guardian* interviewer in 1970, 'pictures of my own, even if they are poor pictures.'[6] The hunger to acquire, which became so marked later in his life, must have been fuelled during that bleak first term at Balliol.

Relief came soon. He had barely installed himself before he learnt that an organ scholarship worth £80 a year would be coming free in December. He was encouraged to apply. 'I feel you may think it strange that somebody already up here should compete for an award which would allow someone else to come up,' he wrote apologetically to Mr Norman, 'but I feel from the financial point of view that I must.' He duly won the scholarship and was installed as organ scholar by the first term in 1936. The award made all the difference between penury and modest comfort. The duties – playing the organ at evensong on Sundays and at the 8 a.m. morning service on weekdays – might have seemed oppressive to an undergraduate used to late nights and heavy drinking, but neither Heath's finances nor his inclinations led him into such excesses. According to David Willcocks, the eminent organist and conductor, who heard him play the organ in Salisbury Cathedral shortly after the war, he was 'an intellectual rather than a musician' but played 'reasonably fluently'. The praise is hardly ecstatic, but Heath was quite good enough to get pleasure out of it and to satisfy the dons of Balliol. He enjoyed still more his involvement in the Balliol concerts, which were held in Hall every other Sunday evening, and with the Balliol Players. For the latter, he composed the music for their production of Aristophanes' *The Frogs*. The performance was directed by an American Rhodes Scholar called Walt Rostow, who was to attain fame, or perhaps notoriety, as foreign affairs adviser to Lyndon Johnson. Heath was 'one of the two or three most promising men I met at Oxford', Rostow remembered: 'a rare example of purposefulness, amiability and reserve'.[7]

The reserve was a characteristic noted by several of his contemporaries. Another American Rhodes Scholar, the future ambassador, Philip Kaiser, found him 'agreeable and congenial' but 'not a gladhander ... there was a little bit of a quality which comes out more prominently in the person presented today [1970] – essentially self-protective, in a certain obliqueness about him which came through in a rather charming way in those days'. He was 'somebody one noticed', remembered another contemporary, Julian Amery. 'One found him in all kinds of groups, but he was in a way rather detached from any of them.' But his presence in those groups was more generally noticed than his remoteness from them. Denis Healey, who knew him well and was secretary to the Junior Common Room when Heath was president, found him affable and companionable, well-liked by every element of the college. Hugh Fraser, who was one day to stand against Heath for the leadership of the Conservative Party, thought him 'extremely nice, agreeable, friendly' though he noted a certain lack of ebullience: 'There was nothing madcap about him.' Nicholas Henderson, another future ambassador, denied even the lack of ebullience; Heath was 'as gregarious, as boisterous, as friendly as anyone at Oxford'. Henderson's father had a house in Oxford where his son held occasional parties. Heath was their 'life and soul', one of the most popular and sought-after of the undergraduate guests.[8]

Oxford was predominantly masculine; it was an inward-looking society in which Sebastian Flyte and Harold Acton flourished extravagantly while the rugger hearties threw stones through their windows or ducked them in Mercury. Heath was neither aesthete nor hearty. Such evidence as exists suggests that he recoiled nervously even from those intense but sexless emotional relationships which were so often to be found among the undergraduates. In August 1939, an unidentified 'Freddy' wrote to remonstrate. 'Now, Teddie, I am going to be very frank,' he began. 'Please tell me what it is you don't like about me. I hate being on anything but really friendly terms with people, especially when as nice as you. Your attitude towards me last term was obvious ... It upset me quite a bit ... I remember you behaved in the same way last year about Michael ... If it is just jealousy, you have no justification for it ... we all want to be your friends.' Without the context it is impossible to say how much or how little such letters mean, but it seems clear that Freddy was demanding a greater and more demonstrative commitment than Heath was willing, or perhaps able, to give.[9]

Nicko Henderson recalled that, brightly though Heath had shone at parties, he could not remember ever seeing him talking to a girl. In Oxford in the 1930s there were not many girls to talk to, but there are enough anecdotes from this period, indeed from every period of his life, to show that he was ill at ease with women. An old acquaintance from Chatham House urged him to venture into the brave new world of feminine society. 'I think it very doubtful if one can make friends of the old schoolboy type if one has left school,' he chided his backward friend. 'I am certain that female friendship is the natural thing to take its place. I think that it's unnatural for adults to form new friendships of the previous type: it obviously has had for part of its basis an emotional admiration which is transferred to one's opposite sex.'[10] Heath had never been strong on 'emotional admiration'; certainly he had no intention of transferring it to the opposite sex.

He did not actually dislike women, indeed he was happy to consort with them if they were attractive and intelligent, but his appreciation of their attractiveness was purely aesthetic and his expectation was that they would not have much to say that was worth listening to. The consorting, if it took place, had to be at arms' length; he shrank from physical contact with both men and women, but whereas an effusive gesture from a man would have been distasteful, from a woman it was repugnant. Nigel Nicolson remembered walking with Heath along the banks of the Cherwell and arriving at the spot known as Parsons' Pleasure where undergraduates traditionally bathed in the nude. Heath was shocked. 'Why,' he said, 'anyone might come along. *Girls* might come along.' Denis Healey mentioned to Heath that a mutual friend was spending the weekend with his girlfriend in Bibury. 'You don't mean to say that they are sleeping together?' asked a dismayed Heath. Healey replied that he had no idea but thought it probable. 'Good heavens,' said Heath. 'I can't imagine anyone in the Conservative Association doing that!' Certainly he felt no inclination to allow women into those sanctums of Oxford life from which they were still excluded. When the admission of women to the Union was debated in 1938 Heath declared: 'Women have no original contribution to make to our debates and I believe that, if they are admitted to the floor of this House, a large number of members will leave.'[11]

Most young men, even if little preoccupied by sex, find it desirable to affect more enthusiasm than they actually feel. Heath was not wholly above such posturing. 'I hope you enjoyed the Carnival,' wrote a friend, 'and did not run after young ladies like you did last year, and call to them from windows.' He was alleged to have taken a fancy to a pretty young blonde, Joan Stuart, though he 'never got his arm beyond her shoulder – not even around her waist'.[12] The limits which he imposed on his relationships with women were well exemplified by the case of Kay Raven. Kay was the friendly and attractive daughter of a Broadstairs doctor, socially a notch or two above the Heaths but by no means in another world. From Heath's point of view, indeed, she was alarmingly accessible. He felt at home with her, enjoyed their games of tennis, talked to her about music, but that was that. To his family she seemed the perfect match; Mrs Heath talked confidently of her son's eventual engagement. Kay would happily have concurred. When Heath went up to Balliol she missed him greatly and began to bombard him with letters; 'quite honestly, though I don't mean to be sentimental, it does help to write and makes Oxford seem as though it was not really on another planet'. The response was not what she had hoped for – Heath's replies seem to have been friendly but distancing. 'I have a feeling you may be fed up with me and my wretched corres- pondence,' she wrote a fortnight later. 'That is what is on my mind, Teddy. I may just be rather depressed.' She *was* rather depressed; her father noticed it and cross-examined her, and Kay evidently admitted that she was in love. She had promised Heath that she would not talk to her parents about their relationship. 'I am afraid that through this I have broken my word, but I told him that I didn't want Mummy to know. I am awfully sorry that this has happened, the curse of living at home is that parents are so observant … it does not mean, of course, that we are committed to anything, that would be foolish seeing how young we both are. It is damnable your being so far away.'

Heath probably thought there were certain advantages in distance; he was genuinely fond of Kay, he got as close to loving her as he was ever to come with any woman except his mother, but at least once the war was over he seems never to have contemplated accepting the total commitment which is or should be involved in marriage. Perhaps he felt he had outgrown Kay, perhaps he did not feel financially secure, probably most of all he had a deep-seated preference for living his life on his own, without the responsibilities and distractions of matri- mony. Kay continued to hope but the hopes grew increasingly more wistful; eventually she accepted that she would have to settle for friendship and that Heath was going to find it difficult to find time even for this in an increasingly crowded life.[13]

What most conspicuously filled that life was politics. Heath was a Conservative by nature almost from childhood. His father had taught him that the freedom of the individual was the highest goal and that socialism and liberty were incompatible. Heath found much that was appealing about the Liberal Party but, supremely practical in dis- position, concluded that it had no real chance of capturing power and should therefore be avoided. That left the Conservatives. But though he never doubted that it was to the Tories that his allegiance was due, he found certain elements in the party snobbish, self-interested and out-of-date. The true Conservatives were 'compassionate men who believed in opportunity, and a decent standard of living for all'.

Baldwin, the then prime minister, he felt had the right instincts but was stuck in the past, slave of a class system which held the country back. Chamberlain was even worse: 'infinitely boring', a 'small-time businessman'. His heroes were Churchill, Macmillan and most of all – if only because he held high office while the other two were in the wilderness – Anthony Eden. He heard of Eden's resignation in early 1938 when he was in the rooms of Philip Kaiser. 'I remember that Ted said very little that night,' recalled Kaiser. 'It affected him, Eden was important to him … a great thoughtfulness settled on him … He thanked me and then walked out.' But he never thought of leaving the party. He had nowhere else to go. He would stay with the Conservatives and give his support to those of its leaders who wanted to change it. In the end, he had little doubt, he would contribute to that change himself.[14]

Lindsay's Balliol was on the whole a left-wing college. Though Heath became president of the Junior Common Room, his immediate successor was Denis Healey; Kaiser followed Healey but the president after that was Roy Jenkins. When Heath joined the Oxford University Conservative Association (OUCA), its membership in Balliol was so sparse that he was immediately appointed secretary of the college branch. He soon found that Balliol was not unusual in its politics; in the mid-1930s most of the more politically conscious undergraduates were to the left and a fair number of them, believing that no other effective force was combating the growth of fascism, were Communist as well. Heath therefore joined an organisation that, if not moribund, was at least unfashionable. His energy and persuasive powers were quickly recognised and in June 1937, against inconsiderable opposition, he was appointed president of the OUCA. His biographer George Hutchinson wrote that he built up its membership from 600 to around 1,500. The previous president, Ian Harvey, a Conservative politician whose career was prematurely ended when he was arrested cavorting with a guardsman in the bushes of St James's Park, claimed that the achievement was really his, Heath was only moving further down a path that had already been prepared for him. There may be some truth in this, but Heath was rightly considered a president of outstanding ability, under whose leadership the OUCA prospered at a time when it might well have suffered an almost terminal decline. He canvassed vigorously when Professor Lindemann, the future Lord Cherwell, stood as Conservative candidate in a by-election in 1936 and, as a reward, was asked back to the Professor's rooms when Churchill came down to support his friend and scientific adviser. It would have been surprising if Heath had not been impressed by the grand old warrior. 'I was struck not only by the force and clarity of his arguments but by his sheer presence,' wrote Heath in his memoirs. He 'reinforced my determination to help articulate and later implement a new brand of Conservatism'.[15]

It was in the Oxford Union, not the Conservative Association, that Heath first attained real prominence. He did not seem a particularly promising candidate for such a role. Physically he was unremarkable. Asked by David Frost how he would describe himself, Heath said that he was 5 feet 10½ inches tall and 'fairly lean'. He flattered himself; even as an undergraduate he verged on the portly. 'Glad to hear you are getting some exercise,' wrote a friend in 1936. 'If you keep it up you should get rid of that fat.' Though he kept the fat within the bounds of respectability for another forty years he habitually ate and drank too much and remained inelegantly solid. His face, recalled Philip Toynbee, was 'soft and unformed'; his most impressive attributes were his striking blue eyes which in repose could seem detached, even glaucous, but when animated blazed with vehement excitement. His voice was powerful but unmelodious, his oratorical technique more that of the battering ram than the rapier. 'Teddy Heath was born in the summer of 1916, some two years before the Tank,' said the Oxford magazine *Isis*, when it nominated him its '*Isis* Idol'. 'Lacking the thickness of skin of this early rival, he soon outstripped it in charm of manner, and has since proved its equal in force of utterance and ability to surmount obstacles.' There was, indeed, something relentless about Heath's public speaking; his weapons were a powerful memory, a mastery of the facts and a capacity to marshal and deploy them to best advantage. He saw the need to leaven this mass with a little humour but while he could be genuinely witty, particularly when in a small group of people whom he knew well, his more considered efforts to amuse often seemed laborious and were occasionally embarrassing. In 1938 Alan Wood, in another Oxford magazine, *Cherwell*, said that Heath was 'the Union's best speaker' and that he succeeded 'by the simple process of knowing more about the subject than his opponents'. He eschewed the flamboyant and rarely made any emotional appeal. Why did he think there was no place for public political passion, he was once asked. 'I've always distrusted rhetoric and I still do,' Heath replied.[16]

For his first few debates Heath wisely kept silent, content to listen and learn. His most important lesson came from the then Home Secretary, John Simon, who spoke for half an hour without a note while successfully dealing with every point of substance that had been raised. Heath, who had hitherto always written out in full every speech that he delivered, resolved that Simon's was the proper way. For the next sixty years he regularly astonished his listeners by his ability to deliver long and carefully crafted speeches with apparent spontaneity. He had still not mastered the art, however, by the time he delivered his maiden speech in the Union, defending Britain against the charge that it was a declining power. His speech was praised by *Isis* as 'extremely forcible and able', but there was no feeling that a new star had been born. Solid worth rather than fireworks marked his contributions, though the tank to which he had been likened by *Isis* often figured in his performances. Ian Harvey, then President of the Union, praised his confidence but warned that 'he must be careful not to appear too aggressive'.[17]

He first established himself as a major player in October 1937, when he led the opposition to a motion approving the Labour Party's programme which was introduced by the then chairman of the party and future Chancellor of the Exchequer, Hugh Dalton. To Dalton's indignation and against the normal temper of the house, the motion was defeated by forty votes; a result for which Heath's speech was held to be largely responsible and which led to him being elected secretary to the Union at the end of the term. But though on this occasion he defended the National Government and took an impeccably Conservative line, it was becoming increasingly evident that he was not disposed blindly to accept party policy. He abhorred the doctrinaire and looked always for common ground that he could share with his political adversaries. He wrote a long essay for Roy Harrod on the Popular Front. 'I think this is an excellent paper,' wrote Harrod. 'I feel there is a little too much tendency to tell the Socialists that they are really only Liberals or bound to become Liberals.'[18] Throughout his life Heath believed that any Socialist open to reason was really only Liberal, and that any Liberal was close to the Conservative – or at least his own branch of Conservatism. He was constantly disillusioned by the discovery that most Socialists, indeed most Conservatives, were *not* open to reason and refused to join him on the common ground where he was rationally ensconced. Each time he believed that such obduracy could not be repeated, only to be disappointed once more when the next occasion arose.

Appeasement was the issue on which he found himself most starkly at variance with orthodox Conservative policy. As late as 1937, Heath – assuming the fascist leaders to be as much susceptible to reason as any Socialist or Liberal – considered that war could and should be avoided. 'I don't agree with you on pacifism,' his friend Tickner told him. 'It fails. The Socialist parties in Germany and Austria adopted it.'[19] Within a few months he had been convinced that Tickner was right. He was appalled by Chamberlain's abandonment of the Czechs at Munich and in October 1938 proposed the motion 'that this House deplores the Government's policy of Peace without Honour'. The motion was carried, with support from many Conservatives as well as Socialists. A fortnight later a by-election became necessary in Oxford. Heath put his name forward as a possible candidate, pointing out as his principal qualification that he was opposed to the Munich agreement and would therefore be a better Foreign Secretary than the present incumbent, Lord Halifax. Unsurprisingly, the Oxford Conservatives preferred the almost equally youthful but more orthodox Quintin Hogg. The Master of Balliol, Sandy Lindsay, then announced that he would stand as an Independent Progressive candidate in the by-election. Although Lindsay was a prominent Socialist, Heath had no hesitation in joining Jenkins and Healey in canvassing for his cause. Heath much later told Basil Liddell Hart, the military historian and strategist, that a speech Liddell Hart had made to the OUCA had been the decisive factor in convincing him that he must canvass against the official Conservative candidate (Liddell Hart responded by saying that Heath was the one man who might induce him to support a Conservative government). He cannot have taken much convincing; even if his performances in the Union had not made his views unambiguously clear, his loyalty to Lindsay both as an individual and as Master of Balliol would surely have proved decisive.[20]

It was the issue of appeasement which won Heath the appointment he most wanted, President of the Union. He had tried the previous year and had been defeated by another Balliol man; thanks to his music scholarship he was able to stay on for a fourth year and try again. In November 1938 he moved: 'That this House has no confidence in the National Government as at present constituted.' He won the debate and, the following day, the presidency. Enough of Britain's most eminent politicians had in their day been President of the Union to ensure that his appointment was widely noticed. He only had one term in which to make his mark but he used it with energy and imagination: reorganising the structure and workings of the society, enlarging its social role and thus its membership, and holding the first-ever dance in its hallowed headquarters. Even more remarkably, perhaps, he introduced these reforms without annoying those traditional elements which, in Oxford perhaps more than anywhere else, can be relied on to rise in rage at any disturbance of their cherished practices. Leo Amery, who had been persuaded to come to Oxford for a debate on conscription, remembered dining with 'Heath of Balliol, a very nice youth'. A very nice youth would have been the verdict of most of his contemporaries. *Isis* paid a remarkable tribute to his performance. 'No president for many years has provided a more interesting series of debates and visitors; no president has done more to re-establish the prestige of the Union not only as a debating society ... but as a club ... He will not soon be forgotten.'[21]

One of the more controversial debates while Heath was President was on the motion: 'That a return to religion is the only solution to our present discontents.' Heath tried to persuade Bernard Shaw to oppose the motion, failed, and made do with Stephen Spender. He did not speak himself; probably as much because he did not know what he wanted to say as for any other reason. Though the debate was generally deemed a success, he found it thoroughly unsatisfactory. 'Over sixty people wanted to speak, not six of them were worth hearing,' he wrote in *Isis*. The typical undergraduate who spoke in the Union was obsessed by politics: 'All the superficiality, the shallowness, the sterility of undergraduate thought, were revealed unmercifully as speaker after speaker tried to find something to replace the political *clichés* with which he can normally get away.'[22] The lofty tone of these remarks suggests that Heath thought himself above such trivia, but at that moment in his life he would have found it difficult to express his real views on the subject with any force or clarity. He does seem to have been undergoing something of a spiritual crisis at the time. The following year he indulged himself by writing a diary in what was for him an uncharacteristically introspective vein. 'The only principles I have ever had firmly implanted have been religious,' he wrote, 'but these never had any intellectual backing. I never even realised what the grounds of belief are and how they compare with anything else. The result was that the religious beliefs I had were undermined at Oxford. I felt that they were silly, that I couldn't defend them against other people. Only now am I beginning to realise their justification. I may be slowly coming through the valley of bewilderment.'[23] He had not descended very far into that valley, nor were the heights to which he was to climb of imposing altitude. Heath never thought much about religion. His time at Oxford was almost the only occasion when he found his implicit faith challenged by clever and articulate contemporaries; that threat removed he reverted to the comfortable and unchallenged convictions of his youth. They underpinned but did not notably affect his political beliefs. 'In all this time in the House of Commons,' he wrote in 1996, he had found that there were 'comparatively few issues on which one has to sit back and say, "Well, now, does this correspond with the values of my own faith?"'[24]

Faith or not, he asked himself more often than was true of most politicians how far his attitude on any given issue corresponded with the moral principles by which he regulated his behaviour. Many of those principles were formulated while he was at Oxford, although it was the travels that he undertook in the vacations that did most to shape his views. In the summer of 1938, with a small group of fellow undergraduates of whom he was by far the most right wing, he went on the invitation of the republican government to visit Catalonia, the last major Spanish province which Franco had not yet overrun. It was an exciting visit. In Barcelona the party was advised to take shelter in the hotel basement since an air-raid was beginning. They decided that the risk was slight and that it would be more interesting to stay above ground and watch events. According to his memoirs, a bomb hit the hotel, skittled down the lift-shaft and killed all those who had taken shelter. Somewhat perplexingly, his version of the event in a book published some twenty years earlier says that the bomb 'went straight through our hotel, without, however, causing any great damage'. By the time he came to write his memoirs he was not above occasionally gingering up the narrative with somewhat romanticised anecdotes, but it is curious that he should have published two versions of the same incident, apparently so contradictory.[25]

There were other moments of danger. On the road from Barcelona to Tarragona their car was machine-gunned by one of Franco's aircraft and they had to crouch in a ditch until the danger had passed. When they reached the British contingent of the International Brigade, Heath met and talked to a young volunteer called Jack Jones. They were to see much more of each other, on different sides this time but in more peaceful surroundings, nearly forty years later when Heath was prime minister and Jones leader of the Transport and General Workers' Union (TGWU). Though Heath regretted the powerful influence of the Communist Party and recognised that, in a civil war, atrocities were likely to be committed by both sides, he was as satisfied as any of his party that the republican cause was the better one. It was, as he saw it, a battle between legitimate government and militaristic fascism; the republican government was 'introducing progressive social reforms and encouraging a bracing democratic atmosphere'; Franco was providing 'a convenient testing bed for the hardware of the Nazi war machine'. Heath returned to Britain resolved to canvass for the republican cause, even though he accepted that it was probably lost. He was moreover convinced that the Spanish civil war was merely the preamble to a greater European war for which Britain must urgently prepare.[26]

He had had few illusions about this since the summer of 1937 when he had spent two months in Germany working on his German. In his biography, John Campbell writes that Heath 'never learned a second language'. In his copy of the book Heath wrote against this remark 'Wrong!' He does, indeed, seem to have spoken German with some fluency at this time. He read it too; he claimed that Thomas Mann's *Buddenbrooks* had given him a unique insight into the German character: 'What a superb book it is,' he told Professor Winckler, in whose home in Bavaria he spent several weeks as a paying guest.[27] But he was not a natural linguist, and by the time he found himself negotiating with German politicians over Britain's entry into Europe he would have found it impossible to sustain a serious conversation in their language. To his surprise, he was invited to attend a Nazi Party rally in Nuremberg and found himself within a few feet of Hitler and meeting the other Nazi leaders at a cocktail party: Göring, 'bulky and genial'; Goebbels, 'small, pale and insignificant', and Himmler, 'I shall never forget how drooping and sloppy Himmler's hand was when he offered it to me'. He was horrified by the ferociously nationalistic zeal which permeated the whole affair: 'I was utterly convinced now that a conflict was inevitable, and that it was one for which we must prepare immediately if we were to save Europe from the evil domination of National Socialism.'[28]

He went back to Germany in August 1939. His companion was Madron Seligman, a Balliol contemporary who was, and would remain, his closest friend. Seligman was Jewish, educated at Harrow and from a family of rich aluminium manufacturers. A fine sportsman and a lover of music, Seligman could have made himself at home in any sector of Balliol society. For a time, remembered Roy Jenkins, he had links with the 'Rugbeian pi group' which went in for 'low living, social concern and high moral tone'. Though Heath avoided association with any clique, this was a group with which he too had much in common. He and Seligman became, if not inseparable, then at least intimate to a degree which Heath was never to permit himself with any other friend. The two discussed where they should spend their last months of liberty before embarking on their respective careers. Seligman favoured Spain. Heath acquiesced and filled in a visa application. To the question why he had visited Spain the previous year he wrote: 'To observe the Civil War'; to 'What is the purpose of your present visit', he wrote: 'To observe the peace.' Perhaps the Spanish authorities found this unduly flippant; perhaps they disapproved of his republican sympathies; the visa was refused. Instead, the two set out for a tour of Danzig and Poland, travelling by way of Germany. Seligman's Jewish blood, Heath told Winckler, provided the couple with 'many amusing moments'. The words were curiously chosen: it was less than a year since the pogroms of *Kristallnacht* and since then the plight of the German Jews had inexorably worsened. Seligman was protected by his British passport, but if they had got their timing wrong and war had broken out while they were still in Germany he would have been in great danger. Even as it was it must have been always unpleasant and sometimes distressing. The English were not well liked in Germany in 1939 and an Englishman of Jewish appearance was doubly unwelcome.[29]

They travelled to suit Heath's budget rather than Seligman's, which meant that discomfort was added to their other woes. The train from Berlin to Danzig was filled with drunken Austrians and they had to try to sleep in the luggage rack: when they had a meal with the consul next day, according to Seligman, Heath was half asleep and 'didn't utter a word the whole way through lunch except to say how bad the food was'. By the time they reached Warsaw it was obvious that war was imminent; they were sped on their way and hitch-hiked towards the frontier with the Polish army as it moved up to defend its country. Once in Germany things were still worse; the – far more formidable – German army was moving the other way and they had to battle against the tide. Suspicion of foreigners, particularly English-speaking foreigners, was even worse than it had been on the way out and several times they thought they were on the point of being arrested or beaten up. Eventually they arrived at Paris and called at the Embassy, to be told: 'Unless you get out now you will never get out at all!' The advice was perhaps unduly alarmist but the situation was indeed dire: Heath got back to Dover a week before war broke out.[30]

*   *   *

His Oxford career was over. He had reason to feel proud of his achievements. He had attained heroic status within the university – 'That's Teddy Heath. He's going to be prime minister one day', a new arrival among the women undergraduates – the future Mrs Anthony Barber – was excitedly informed. More important, his name was known in Westminster; visiting politicians had noticed him as a potential recruit to their ranks. Only in one way was he disappointed. He had read Modern Greats (PPE) and he would have liked to crown his triumphs with first-class honours. He knew that the time and effort which he had devoted to the Union, the OUCA, the Balliol JCR and his musical duties had made his task doubly difficult. 'He would have done even better had he not been a man of wide and very active interests,' wrote Lindsay. 'I have the greatest admiration for Mr Heath's energy, initiative and sense of responsibility.' Such praise from Lindsay was most welcome but Heath had still hoped for more. 'You seem to have got a very nice Second in the Schools, and I dare say that all things considered you are quite satisfied,' wrote one of his tutors at Balliol consolingly. Heath did not think his Second was very nice and he was far from satisfied. He believed that, with just a little more application, he could have gained the coveted First.[31]

In this he was probably wrong. The notes which Lindsay made on the undergraduates, based on the reports of the various tutors, show that Heath was not felt to be distinguished academically. One don was 'not impressed, uninspired work', others contributed 'fairly intelligent, decent, slow mind'; 'No outstanding work; second class'; and even 'stupid, lacks thought'. This was not the whole picture; some said that he was 'v. intelligent' or 'can do v. good work'; but the overall picture was not that of a student for whom first-class honours could be expected.[32] The economist Redvers Opie taught both Harold Wilson and Heath at Oxford and left notes on his pupils. Wilson had 'exceptional intellectual ability and a remarkably comprehensive mind'; Heath, on the other hand, 'was usually given a beta mark and criticised for trundling out run-of-the-mill views'.[33] When he was writing his memoirs Heath got hold of Harold Wilson's marks in Finals so that he could compare them with his own. He found that he had one beta+ while the rest were betas or beta–. Wilson got one beta+ and the rest alphas. The figures were not quoted in Heath's memoirs.

If Heath had achieved all he did at Oxford and nevertheless gained first-class honours it would indeed have been a triumph. If, though, he had failed to become President of the Union and, in spite of the extra effort put into his work, had still gained only a Second, it would have been a sad waste. No one can doubt that he made the right decision and put his energies where they counted most.

THREE

War

New graduates leaving Oxford at the end of the summer term of 1939 must have been aware that whatever career they planned was likely to be interrupted. It was still possible, however, that war would not come. If it did, it might last only a few months. The only sensible thing to do was to prepare for a peacetime future with a tacit awareness that all such plans would probably come to nothing.

For Heath the first and most important decision was whether he should pursue music as a career. As organ scholar at Balliol he had put in a more than adequate performance in college chapel; as a pianist too he was competent beyond the standards of the talented amateur. He had no illusions, however, that he would ever achieve greatness as an instrumentalist. To choose as his life work something – however enjoyable – in which he knew he would never progress beyond the second-rate would have been unacceptable to Heath. If music was to be his career it would have to be as a conductor. Heath already had more experience in this field than most musicians of his age. He had been largely responsible for conducting the Balliol Choral Society, one of the oldest and most distinguished of Oxford choirs. Since childhood, too, he had been involved with the Broadstairs carol singers and, even though less than twenty years old, he had taken over the running of their annual carol concert in the mid-1930s. The Mayor of Oxford's Christmas Carol concert, conducted by Dr Armstrong, seemed to him a model of its kind and, despite the far smaller resources available, he decided that Broadstairs could do something similar. He conducted his first carol concert there in 1936; it was judged a great success and the tradition was established of an annual concert under Heath's baton, which continued for some forty years. But did such modest achievements provide a base from which a professional career could be mounted? Heath consulted Sir Hugh Allen, Heather Professor of Music at Oxford and a man of vast influence in musical circles. If Heath made some money and went into politics, the possibilities were limitless, judged Allen. Probably he would end up as prime minister. If instead he became a conductor he would have to dedicate himself totally to it, and even then it would be a fierce struggle to get to the top. 'I believe you can do it, but if so you must be prepared to be just as big a shit as Malcolm Sargent.'[1]

Heath might not have been put off by the thought of having to emulate Malcolm Sargent's shittishness but the need to dedicate himself exclusively to the task was a serious deterrent. He knew that his heart was in politics. If a career in music would rule out politics for ever, it could not be right for him. It would have taken more encouragement than Allen was prepared to offer to make him reach a different conclusion. Thomas Armstrong, himself an organist of great repute and one-time Principal of the Royal Academy of Music, many years later heard Heath's recording of the Beethoven Triple Concerto. 'I sometimes wonder', he wrote, 'whether HPA[llen] was right, after all, and in spite of all you've done, to steer you away from a professional career in music.'[2] Heath may sometimes have wondered the same thing, but he can never seriously have doubted that he had reached the best, the only possible conclusion.

A life in politics, therefore, was his firm objective. But the concept of the professional politician, without private means, who lived on his salary as an MP or worked his way up through the party organisation, was almost unknown in 1939. Heath would have to make his name, and with luck his fortune, in some other walk of life before he could begin to look for a seat in the House of Commons. The two safest professions for people of a musical bent, one friend told him, were 'the BBC and school teaching'. The BBC would require 'submission to an intolerable bureaucracy', teaching was ill-paid and probably involved severing one's ties with London.[3] Neither appealed to Heath. A more attractive possibility, which offered a better chance of making money quickly, was the Bar. Heath had an excellent memory, a clear mind well adjusted to grasping the essential points in any problem, a well-honed capacity for debate and argument: all qualities required of a successful barrister. If he went to the Bar and prospered he could reasonably expect to have established himself within ten or, at the most, fifteen years; the route from the Bar to the House of Commons was a well-trodden one. Before he had left Oxford he had begun on the essential preliminary of eating his dinners at Gray's Inn.

Even that course, however, posed financial problems. To spend another two years in study, unless supported by a scholarship, would have placed an unfair additional burden on the parents who had sacrificed so much for him. He had already been summoned to Gray's Inn for an interview and had been led to believe that, if he turned up and made a good impression, a scholarship would probably be his for the asking. Before anything could be clinched, however, an opportunity arose to go to the United States on a debating tour. The chance was too good to miss, but it meant that he had to forgo the all-important interview. At the end of 1939, he heard that the scholarship had been awarded to someone else. 'I had been relying on this to enable me to finish being called to the bar,' he wrote in his diary. 'Of course, it would have been wonderful to think that after the war this money would have been waiting for me … Now this is impossible. I may have to give up the whole idea of law and go into something else … The temptation to get into politics in an era of reconstruction will be enormous.' At least one of his friends thought that his loss of the scholarship was a blessing in disguise. 'You have done very well for a C[hatham] H[ouse] S[chool] boy, something out of the usual,' wrote A. C. Tickner. 'The bar seems rather too conventional a finish for you. Hence my disappointment.' If Heath had envisaged a spell at the Bar as anything more than a stepping stone on the way to a life in politics, Tickner's disappointment might have been justified; as it was, the main cause for Heath's chagrin at the loss of the scholarship was that it seemed to make more remote the time when he could hope to make his move into the House of Commons.[4]

The trip to the United States which cost him his scholarship had been arranged under a scheme by which two debaters from English universities crossed the Atlantic each year to go on a tour of American universities. Heath was to have been accompanied by his Balliol contemporary Hugh Fraser. When war broke out both young men volunteered for military service. Fraser, who had been training as a territorial, was at once called up. Heath was told that he would not be wanted for several months. The way was open, therefore, for him to go as planned to America. Instead of Fraser he was to share the platform with Peter Street, a former treasurer of the Oxford Union.

One Balliol contemporary doubted whether this was a good idea:

> Were I you I would go to the war rather than to the USA, because, while the propaganda in America might be a more valuable contribution to Britain, there might be a number of people who would place an uncharitable construction on your absence from this country. After all, it is more important to do what the public think right than what you might think right! That sounds cynical, but it is true in politics. A good war record is of great assistance to a politician ...

If 'going to war' had been a possible alternative Heath would certainly have taken it but there seemed little point in hanging around awaiting call-up when a far more interesting and potentially valuable way of using the time presented itself. If people chose to suggest that he was in some way running away or shirking his duty then they were welcome to do so. He and Street consulted the Foreign Office, were encouraged to go ahead with the tour and did so with alacrity.[5]

The Foreign Office did, however, issue one caveat. Public opinion in the United States was in a delicate state and there were many people who would be quick to resent what they might see as an attempt to push them into the war. Two brash students, holding forth about the duty of the Americans to join the British and the French in defence of Poland, might do considerable harm. Any such debate was to be avoided: like Basil in *Fawlty Towers*, they were not to mention the war. The difficulty about this was that the American students with whom they were to debate thought that the war by far the most interesting topic. The University of Pittsburgh dismissed the twelve possible subjects proposed by the British team and announced that the debate would be on the motion: 'That the United States should immediately enter the war on the side of the allies.' When Heath and Street demurred they were told that this was the published motion and that nothing else would be accepted. To refuse to appear would seem both churlish and chicken-hearted, to speak would be to brave the wrath of the Foreign Office and perhaps to provoke an international incident. In dismay, Heath appealed to the British Ambassador, Lord Lothian. Not for nothing was Lothian known as one of the most ingeniously devious of politicians: they should agree to speak, he ruled, but only on condition that one proposed and one opposed the motion. That way nobody could claim that the visitors were trying to manoeuvre America into the war. The fact that the more eloquent and well-briefed of the speakers seemed always to be the one who favoured intervention could in no way be blamed on the British representatives.

Heath did not delude himself that his efforts had any marked impact on American public opinion. The most usual question – not easily answered – was why, if the war was being waged in support of Poland, Britain and France were not also at war with the other aggressor, Russia. They met very little out-and-out pacifism but did not feel that they had done much to shake 'the final and all-compelling assumption that America must stay out of the war'.[6] Some universities were content to abide by the choice of subject made by the visitors. At Brooklyn College the debate turned on what should be done after the war to secure a lasting peace. This was a topic on which Heath had already thought deeply and which had preoccupied him during his recent trip to Europe. In the debate he envisaged various possibilities, not mutually exclusive, but inclined to the view that the best hope was a federal Europe, a 'United States of Europe … in which states will have to give up some of their national rights … There seems to be a better view for the future if we lean towards a federalism that can be secured either by joining with a small national group and/or big group, because this seems to be the most foolproof sort of thing you can get.'[7] It was the first public airing of a view which, though from time to time modified, was to dominate his thinking for the rest of his life.

On his way back to England he mused on the differences between the New World which he had just visited and tired old Europe. America was a new country and 'though it lacks dignity is filled with pulsating life'. Britain's rulers, on the other hand, were 'out of touch, uninspired, content to deal with new problems in an old way. The opposition is just as lifeless and tied to dogmas and formulae of which everyone is heartily sick.' What was needed was a new breeze which would sweep away 'stuffiness, dead convention, stultifying distinctions, all those things which paralyse our national and individual life'. But it would not be enough to produce some prophet who would 'talk in vague generalisations'; he must be able to conjure up visions in other people's minds, but also 'to think things through right to the bitter end, a leader who is practical and strong'. Who that leader might be and where he would spring from, he did not surmise. Given the astonishing self-confidence that was already so apparent it would be surprising if, at the back of his mind, he did not cherish a hope that it might one day be him. At the moment the Tory Party seemed a spent force. Could it be revived? Was he right in thinking that his future lay with its left wing rather than with 'the Liberals, whose practical policy and mode of thought is much more in keeping with my own than those of many Conservatives; or the Socialists, most of whom are from my own "class" and are perhaps more concerned than many Conservatives with domestic problems?' It was the issue that he had faced when he joined the Conservative Association at Oxford, and he reached the same conclusion. But the question still was how they were 'to secure greater equality of opportunity and of wealth and abolish class distinction'. The Socialist recipes – confiscation of wealth, high taxation, nationalisation – repelled him: 'If one has government control and planning it becomes national socialism and political control too often follows.' But what was the alternative: spending to make work, deficit spending, the American New Deal?

Such a policy would be risky but at least it would be positive and would offer the possibility of fruitful advance.[8]

He knew that such speculation was largely academic. Political activity would be at a low ebb until the end of the war and, anyway, he expected that he would quickly be called up and would have many more immediate preoccupations. His younger brother, John, was already with the infantry in France, yet Heath was kept hanging about. 'I'm horribly bored,' he told a Balliol friend some time in the early summer of 1940.

> I've been waiting now since February … without anything really to do. Each time I've heard from them or pressed them I've been told I should be wanted in only a couple of weeks, with the result that it was impossible for me to get a temporary job to pass the time. I was called up once actually for the Buffs [John's regiment] but two days before I had to report I received another notice saying 'owing to unforeseen circumstances' my calling-up notice was cancelled … I'm rather anxious to get in and get on with it … There is so much to do and, as ever, so little time to do it. What a struggle it will have to be, but what a magnificent opportunity.[9]

From Balliol, Lindsay had promised to do what he could to get Heath into military Intelligence, but either his attempt aborted or he forgot about it. When Heath finally came before the Board he found that he had been assigned to the Royal Artillery. He had every hope that he would be commissioned as an officer within a few months, but the basic training that had to be undergone by every gunner lay ahead of him. 'I don't think I regret what's coming,' he told his diary resignedly. 'It may well be for the best.' There would be hardships, of course: uncomfortable clothes, lack of privacy, gruelling hard work, difficult hours, 'bad food served absolutely revoltingly', but there would be good things too: fitness, discipline, relief from responsibility for a while. Living cheek-by-jowl with 'people of whom he knew nothing, unintelligent people, uneducated people, unstimulating and unstimulatable', was the thing that frightened him most. Yet he recognised that 'if I could feel at the end that I knew them and what

41

they expected from life it would be a good thing'. He prayed that there would be at least a few men 'reasonably like people I'm accustomed to'; but at the same time he told himself that he should welcome the chance to escape from his background and the class with which he had been assimilated: 'I have a desire, perhaps when analysed not very rational or even sane, to get "hard" like other men; to take the knocks they can take, to go wining and whoring with them. Yet whenever I meet them I feel repelled by their lack of intelligence and concern only with things like pay, leave and food. Perhaps my nature's different.'[10]

When the call-up did eventually come in August 1940 Heath found that his nature was not so very different after all, or at least that physical exhaustion and a common resentment of the iniquities of the lance-bombardier in charge of his barrack room produced a sense of camaraderie and mutual tolerance among the recruits. By good fortune he found a fellow music-lover, a future director of the New York City Ballet, among the other novice gunners at the training camp near Storrington in Sussex; still more remarkably they found that the composer Sir Arnold Bax was a habitué of the local pub. Even without such resources, however, Heath would have found life at Storrington tolerable, almost enjoyable. It was comforting for him to know where he stood in relation to other people, exactly where his duties began and ended. He could not have endured for long his lowly status, the total absence of responsibility, but for the three months of basic training it suited him very well. Given his record, he would have had to do something badly wrong not to be selected for a commission; he made no such blunder and was duly sent as an officer cadet to Shrivenham in Wiltshire. His training there was as straightforward and as uneventful as at Storrington. In March 1941 he was commissioned into the Royal Artillery and posted to a Heavy Anti-Aircraft Regiment at Chester. For the next three years and two months he shuttled around the United Kingdom, occasionally helping defend Britain's cities against air attack, more often sitting around waiting for something to happen.

What quickly became evident was that Heath was a good soldier. Whether he had the qualities necessary for success at the highest level was never to be tested, but as a regimental officer he showed himself impressively calm, clear-headed, resolute and with marked organisational skills. One of his few faults, indeed, was a tendency to over-organise. When his battery was to move from the north prior to embarkation for France, for instance, he worked out every detail, even down to the seats the individual men would occupy, and produced a set of instructions so comprehensive that nobody could be bothered to read, let alone implement them. The results, as he ruefully admitted, were 'completely catastrophic'.[11] On this occasion he recognised his failing and resolved to correct it. But he never altogether conquered his conviction that every eventuality had to be prepared for, every problem foreseen. Time and again he was to be disappointed when things did not turn out as he had expected; each time it came as a disagreeable surprise.

At his level at least it was a fault generally on the right side: better too much organisation than too little or none at all. Successive commanding officers paid tribute to his talents. 'I consider E. R. G. Heath to be the most capable officer I met in any department during the four years in which I had command,' wrote Major Tyrell, when recommending Heath for a military MBE. 'He had personality, drive and ability of the highest order. He was quick to grasp essentials and to formulate plans and his determination, energy and enthusiasm guarantee that they shall not miscarry. I find it difficult to present a fair picture of a man in whom I could detect no weakness of character, whose intellectual scope and integrity I could but admire and for whom I feel nothing but respect and affection.' Colonel Chadd, who was to become a lifelong friend and make Heath godfather to his son, was equally complimentary. 'At his interview,' Chadd wrote, Heath told him that after the war, 'he hoped to go into politics. Within a very short space of time Ted was held in the highest possible esteem by all of us – officers and other ranks alike – and we were quite sure that one day he could be prime minister.' (Given that this was written in 1946 the officers and other ranks in question were remarkably perceptive.)[12]

Not everyone was so ecstatic. Tony Race, his site commander when he was posted near Liverpool, found him 'mature and confident' and admired his 'stamina and efficiency', but felt him to be 'a little withdrawn. He hadn't a warm personality.' But even this accusation – which was to become all too familiar over the years – was denied by his admirers. 'The men liked him,' claimed Chadd. 'He was never impatient with dullards or arrogant to people not so bright as himself.' When he took over a battery from a major who had commanded it for several years, he was viewed with some suspicion. 'We were none too happy,' remembered the orderly room sergeant, James Hyde:

> Up to then he had been an administrator. He hadn't done any fighting worth speaking of ... But I think it's right to say that within a fortnight or three weeks he exercised such a persuading influence ... that one found Heath was first class. So far as administration was concerned, he was perfect. The other reason he was first class – and this was to my surprise – was that he rapidly understood the men and their reactions ... Within a month or two it was Heath's battery. The men liked him because they thought he was a fair man.[13]

He became adjutant of his regiment in March 1942. 'I imagine life as an Adjutant must suit you down to the ground,' wrote Kay Raven. She wrote to him regularly throughout the war; letters beginning 'Darling Teddy' but rarely venturing beyond the chatty or the gossipy. She was now an officer in the WAAF and in 1944 Heath sent her a photograph. 'My batwoman asked me if "that was my steady – he looks just like a film star"! Knowing her tastes, you must be a cross between Charles Boyer and Bob Hope. So now you reside on my mantelpiece and greet me in my waking and sleeping.'[14] Whether he *was* her steady was a question which even he would have found it hard to answer. In a letter to Tim Bligh, a Balliol friend who was later to become principal private secretary to Harold Macmillan, he had evidently envisaged the possibility of marriage. 'I would like to point out,' replied Bligh, 'that there are more convenient methods of experiencing the grand passion, and as you should know we can justly claim the title of lady-killers *par excellence*.'[15] The reputation of lady-killer was not one to which Heath aspired, but even if he had considered marrying Kay it would have been a long-term project, not to be contemplated until the war was over. They met rarely, and when they did the meetings, for Kay, generally ended in frustration. 'I'm awfully sorry about spoiling it the other night,' she wrote after their leaves had for once coincided. 'It was the horror of months of going by and hearing nothing of you ... Perhaps it won't be so long before you are back again.'[16]

By that time Heath had already spent nearly a year in Europe. His last months in England had been marred by a gangrenous appendix, which should have been operated on months before and nearly cost him his life. By the time it was removed he was convinced he was going to die. He wrote, in high emotion, to his parents, 'It is not possible to thank you for all you have done, for your love, for my schooling, my career, and for the sacrifices which you have all the time made. Everything I have done I have owed largely to my early training and the standards you taught me.' The tribute was most sincerely meant. Fortunately it never needed to be dispatched. The appendix was successfully removed, though its condition was so revolting that the hospital had it pickled and put on exhibition as a reminder of what should never happen.[17]

Heath and his regiment crossed the Channel a month after D-Day and fought their way towards Belgium, taking part, on the way, in the bombardment of Caen and the battle of the Falaise Gap. For a time they lingered in Antwerp, then in September 1944 moved on to support the allied forces trying to relieve the airborne troops at Arnhem. Their most serious action, wrote John Campbell in his biography, was keeping open the vital bridge at Nijmegen. 'Nonsense!' Heath scrawled in the margin; it is hard to understand why he took exception to the comment, because the action was indeed both bloody and of critical importance.[18] The level of casualties among the gunners is usually lower than that in the infantry, but in the advance into Germany Heath frequently saw men die within a few yards of him and was constantly in danger. He never wavered. This officer, said his citation, 'showed outstanding initiative and devotion to duty ... His work was of a very high order and contributed largely to the success achieved.'

His last year as a soldier was spent in Germany. For three months he was in charge of a prisoner-of-war camp near Hanover. 'I hope my experience and knowledge of the German people helped me to run the show with understanding and fairness,' he told Professor Winckler.[19] He was put in charge of the reconstruction of the city and gave the rebuilding of the opera house top priority. Whether the German population was entirely in accord with his scale of values is uncertain. Since the Brigade Commander was equally insistent that the racecourse should be reopened rapidly it is possible that they felt their housing needs were being unreasonably overlooked.

In his memoirs Heath records in moving detail the execution by firing squad of a Pole found guilty by court martial of aggravated rape and murder. He was in charge and had to give the order to fire. 'I believe', he wrote, 'this made a mark on my mind which later crystallised the view to which I have adhered for nearly four decades of my political career, as to the justification for abolishing the death penalty in peace time.' He is never known to have referred to this incident until work on the memoirs was almost completed. Rupert Allason in his as yet unpublished biography of Heath casts doubt on the story. He points out that no record of such an execution exists in the files kept by the Court Martial Centre. Since the war was four months over when the incident is alleged to have taken place, the guilty man would have been hanged rather than shot. A major would not normally have commanded a firing squad. The situation is not as clear-cut as Allason suggests. A few executions by firing squad did in fact take place after the end of the war. There are no records of executions of soldiers of Polish origin serving in the British Army at the time in question but, given the situation in Germany at the time, the Ministry of Defence believes that the victim could have been a member of the Polish land forces serving under allied command. Another possibility is that the executed Pole was incorrectly described as a soldier. One Polish national, Piotr Kuczerawy, was executed in Hanover at a time when Heath's regiment was based in the city and it is possible that he found himself charged with this grisly task. Heath was in general a scrupulously truthful man and he had nothing to gain by inventing such a story. On the whole it seems likely that his story is substantially correct. Certainly the result was as he indicated; in the course of his political career he was consistent in his opposition to the death penalty.[20]

He might have been in a position to vote on the issue even before the supposed incident took place. Early in 1945 an Army Council Instruction invited anyone interested in fighting the anticipated general election to fill in a form requesting the necessary three weeks' leave. Heath applied for a copy of the form. Andrew Roth, one of Heath's biographers, suggests that he hoped to be adopted as Conservative candidate for the Isle of Thanet. He does not seem to have made any serious effort to press his candidature. In his memoirs he writes that he decided not to stand in the 1945 general election 'because I did not feel that I could abandon my colleagues in the regiment at such a time'. This is certainly part of the story: Heath was conspicuously loyal to those with whom he served and in the post-war years did much to help any former fellow servicemen who had got into trouble or needed a leg-up in their career. But there may have been another contributory factor; that in the circumstances of 1945, he was not sure he wanted the Conservatives to win.[21]

He never seriously contemplated joining any other party. The nearest he came to it – and that was not very near – had arisen from a chance encounter early in 1945 when he was on leave in England. Late at night, while waiting for a train at a provincial station, he went into the tea room. There he found Arthur Jenkins, father of Roy and a pps to Clement Attlee, whom he had met several times at Oxford before the war. Jenkins, it turned out, was waiting for Attlee and when the Deputy Prime Minister arrived Heath joined them. Jenkins explained who he was. 'Oh,' said Attlee. 'He's now commanding a battery in Germany,' said Jenkins. 'Oh,' said Attlee. 'From what he's been saying he's obviously still interested in politics.' 'Oh,' said Attlee. 'I think he'll make a damn good politician.' 'Oh,' said Attlee. 'I think we ought to try to grab him as one of our candidates.' 'Oh,' said Attlee. At this point Heath's train was announced. 'This', he concluded, 'was the nearest I ever came to becoming a Labour candidate.'[22]

Though he is said to have told his old acquaintance and future opponent, Ashley Bramall, that he was still uncertain whether he wanted to take up politics,[23] he never doubted that if he did so it would be as a Tory. But in 1945 the disillusionment which he had expressed on the journey back from the United States still lingered. He believed that the old Conservative Party survived unregenerate, governed, as it had been before the war, by 'stuffiness, dead convention, stultifying distinctions'. If, as almost everyone assumed would be the case, they were returned to power on the coat-tails of Churchill's popularity, then these attitudes would survive unchanged. A period of opposition would give the modernisers a chance to take control of the party and reshape its thinking and its principles. He did not expect, still less hope for, the landslide Labour victory of 1945, but there was some comfort to be drawn from it. Certainly he rejoiced that he had not personally been involved in the debacle.

He had one last searing experience before he returned to England and civilian life. In February 1946 he drove across a shattered Germany to Nuremberg, where the trial of the Nazi war criminals was in progress. In the dock were those leaders whom he had seen or even shaken hands with eight years before. Then they had been rulers of Germany, soon to be rulers of the continent; now they were reviled and tragic figures. In the meantime, Europe had been almost destroyed. Somehow it must be made impossible for this to happen again. 'My generation did not have the option of living in the past: we had to work for the future ... Only by working together right across our continent had we any hope of creating a society which would uphold the true values of European civilisation.' Heath's vision of a united Europe had been formed before the war but it was in Germany in 1945 that it found its full realisation.[24]

FOUR

In Waiting for Westminster

'I now so often have the feeling', Heath had written on the way back from the United States at the beginning of 1940, 'that I've a lot of energy, power, ambition, and so on, and yet nothing to which to harness it. Is this, I wonder, because I've got so many things I haven't thought out and that, when I've done that, I shall see the way to go? Or am I just blasé?'[1] Blasé was certainly not something which Heath could have been accused of being at any point in his life. To most people in 1940 he had appeared impressively clear-headed and decisive. His inner uncertainty, his doubt as to where he should go and how he should get there, were largely kept to himself: unconfiding by nature, he was least of all inclined to expose his weaknesses, even to those few whom he trusted fully. By 1946, to a large extent, those doubts had been resolved. He knew that he wished his long-term future to lie in politics; that the Conservative Party, for all its imperfections, was the only institution that offered him a chance to realise this ambition; that within that party his loyalties would lie with the left, reforming wing. The war had confirmed his belief in his own powers and helped him decide where those powers were to take him. He was tougher and more effective in 1946 than he had been six years before. It was perhaps symbolic of his evolution that the cosy 'Teddy' of pre-war years had now become a starker, sterner 'Ted'. Not all his old friends made the change, even among new acquaintances some still preferred the earlier form, but by 1946 'Ted Heath' had established itself as the address most usually employed. It was to remain so until his death.

His family never fully recognised the change. It was Teddy Heath who returned to the family home in Broadstairs. Even more than before the war he was the centre of attention. William Heath's business was prospering in the post-war building boom and it was no longer necessary to take in paying guests. For the first time, Teddy and his brother, John, had separate rooms. But John had slipped still further from centre stage. To his father's disappointment he had refused to join the family firm and had instead taken a job in a local radio shop. Within a year he had become engaged and was moving out.

The marriage lasted only a few years. John's wife, Marian, maintained that Teddy Heath was the be-all and end-all of his mother's and, to a lesser but still considerable extent, his father's life. There were only two comfortable chairs in the kitchen/living room: Teddy would commandeer one while his mother sat knitting socks in the other. 'She was always knitting socks.' William and John helped with the washing-up; Teddy was never expected to join in. Everyone had to dress for breakfast except Teddy, who was allowed to come down in his dressing gown. His mother waited on him hand and foot: 'I've seen her sitting there cracking nuts for him so that he wouldn't have to crack them himself.'[2]

Teddy was 'very clannish' and expected the family to do things together, wrote Marian. It was always he who had the final choice as to what was to be done. On one occasion she revolted and, even though Teddy favoured a family picnic, insisted that she and John should go on the river with some cousins. 'When I say we quarrelled, it was a case of Teddy and I crossing swords while the rest of the family sat around in awe-struck silence.' He did not share the same circle of friends as John and Marian and was often to be seen striding along the cliffs or seafront immersed in thought. Such friends as he had in the neighbourhood were noticeably more mature – except for an occasional game of tennis he had little to do with the young. 'My father was once invited to lunch with the Heaths,' wrote Marian, 'and was astounded to find Teddy walking in and out of the room without seemingly seeing anyone. He was so wrapped up in his thoughts and plans for the future.' He was not ungenerous – more often than not he paid if they went to the cinema or on some similar outing – but Marian was told by Mrs Heath to make nothing of it: 'Teddy hates to be thanked, he gets embarrassed,' she explained.

When John and Marian were married, Teddy was best man and made what Marian remembered as a 'most amusing speech'. There were no bridesmaids, so, he said, he felt in no way committed: 'I might add that he was the only one not to kiss the bride.' Kay Raven would certainly have been among the family friends at the wedding. 'She was looked on by all as Teddy's girlfriend,' wrote Marian. 'It was a strange relationship. Teddy never seemed very attentive, yet she didn't seem to mind.' She minded more than appeared but she had to put up with what she could get. John Heath never believed that there was any serious romance between his brother and Kay; so far as Teddy, at least, was concerned, it was 'a bit of a smoke screen' which provided him with a convincing reason for not forming a relationship with any other woman.

Broadstairs provided a convenient base to which he could retreat, but there was no question of Heath seeking a job in the neighbourhood. Politics were his long-term ambition and he hoped the wait would not be very long. His plan was to have found a seat before the next general election. By that time he would be 35 or thereabouts. But in the meantime he had to earn a living, ideally a living in a career which he could continue part-time when he had become a Member and which would pay enough to enable him to make some savings. Though he says in his memoirs that the scholarship to read law at Gray's Inn which he had nearly secured before the war was still available, it does not seem that any specific promise had been made. Even if it had been, he had decided that the law was 'rather dry' and that it would take him five or six years to earn a modest salary.[3] Academic life, even if he had been suited to it, was hardly the ideal jumping-off ground for politics. The Master of Balliol tried to fix him up with a job as personal assistant to the Regius Professor of Medicine at Oxford; Heath had his doubts about this, the Professor had still more and looked elsewhere. One problem was that Heath made no secret of his political ambitions and this discouraged possible employers who were looking for a longer-term commitment. He could have been Meetings Secretary at the Royal Institute of International Affairs at Chatham House – a post which would have brought him into close contact with many leading politicians – but when they realised that they might only have the benefit of his services for a few years, they lost interest.

The same was true when he looked to business and industry. 'At the moment I have six irons in the fire; two of them certainties if I want them and I hope to get them sorted out this month,' he told a friend in November 1946. One of the certainties was ICI, but when Heath told them that he hoped to be standing for parliament at the next election the certainty became unstuck and he was told he could not be considered. Another certainty or near-certainty was the North Central Wagon and Finance Company. This job would have carried with it alluring prospects of promotion to chairman within three years, but though this would have been lucrative it would have involved a move to Rotherham, unacceptably far from the political power centre. Unilever seemed more promising but here there appears to have been some misunderstanding. Heath thought that they were not disturbed by his wish to enter parliament, but the report on his application said that he had abandoned his political ideas without regret: 'Provided he really can subordinate his interests in politics as a career, I believe he would be very well suited to business.' The man who interviewed him could hardly have been more flattering. Heath, he said, was 'one of those rare men who is extremely competent intellectually yet a normal, pleasant, honest person ... I found him very likeable'. Under the heading 'Quality of Social Relations' the interviewer said: 'I rate this man very high. He strikes me as a well-balanced, human sort of person whom others would willingly work for and with.' He was offered a management traineeship. Possibly the true position about his political ambitions now came to light; certainly he turned the offer down.[4]

There remained the civil service. Heath knew that if he became a parliamentary candidate he would not be able to continue to work in Whitehall but that he would be free to pursue his career until that point was reached. If he never succeeded in finding a winnable seat he would at least have a respectable profession on which to fall back; if he did escape to politics he would have gained valuable experience of the workings of the civil service. He appeared before the Final Selection Board in August 1947. Just over 200 applicants survived to face this ultimate hurdle. Twenty-two passed in, and of these Heath was top. With this glittering success he could reasonably have expected to be able to choose his department. He was told that the Foreign Office was his for the asking (whether the Foreign Office had been consulted over this is unclear; they were a law unto themselves when it came to selecting future diplomats). The idea was appealing in many ways, but Heath realised that the long periods of exile which the career would involve would be incompatible or at least hard to reconcile with a move into politics. His wish was to join the Treasury, which he felt carried the greatest prestige and wielded power over all the Whitehall departments. Peter Masefield, his eventual boss in the civil service, thought that possibly his avowed political ambitions, though no bar to entry into the civil service, counted against him when it came to the choice of a department. Heath openly admitted that his main concern was to gain experience which would be of use to him when an MP; to the Treasury this may have seemed *lèse-majesté*. Whatever the reason, to his chagrin he was consigned to the fledgling Ministry of Civil Aviation. His first task was to work with the future Dame Alison Munro, deciding which of the 700 mainly grass airfields dotted around the country should be retained for future development. Heath was responsible for the airfields near London, Alison Munro for the rest of the United Kingdom.[5]

Soon he found himself working almost exclusively to the head of the Long-Range Planning Department, Peter Masefield. Masefield was a man of enterprise and imagination, a temporary civil servant who, in a couple of years, was to move on to take charge of British European Airways. Masefield took to Heath, pronouncing him 'pleasant, sound and highly intelligent ... And, with all, when you get to know him (which isn't easy) he is a sensitive and warm-hearted chap who has a direct approach and an endearing sense of the ridiculous.' Heath quickly found himself with a finger in a wide range of pies, from the development of the Comet to the planning of Heathrow (a name for which he accepted no responsibility). This last task was particularly stressful. 'Every time I arrive at Heathrow,' he wrote in his memoirs, 'I shudder to think that I was in any way involved in the creation of that monstrosity.' But for his efforts, it might have been more monstrous still. The first plans provided for no parking areas and no aircraft piers to avoid the need for buses. Heath championed both causes and won the day. 'He used to go and fight on the committee,' Masefield remembered, 'and come back and cry on my shoulder about all the spokes put in the wheel by bumble-dom.'[6] Another achievement with which Masefield credited him was persuading de Havillands, when the Comet was in the final stages of development, to substitute four-wheel undercarriage legs for the two-wheel version which they had been proposing to use. The 'Heath modification', as Masefield called it, made it possible for the Comet to land on many runways which would otherwise have been too weak to support the impact. 'That change', Masefield told Heath many years later, 'enabled 77 Comets to be produced and used throughout the world.'[7]

Masefield quickly recognised that Heath was an invaluable member of his team. 'But I fear I shall not have him here for long', he wrote regretfully, 'because, outside the office, he lives and dreams politics.'[8] He was right. Heath's first move was to try for a job in the Conservative Research Department, a body which, under Rab Butler, was busily rebuilding a new and more progressive Tory Party from the ruins left by the 1945 election. He knew that several of the cleverest and most ambitious of the young Conservatives – Iain Macleod, Enoch Powell, Reginald Maudling – were already at work there; he longed to be doing the same thing himself and was uneasily conscious of the fact that they were snatching a lead over him in the race up the greasy pole of political advancement. Michael Fraser, a wartime friend, was another rising star in the department; Heath appealed to him but was told there was no vacancy or any prospect of one in the near future. By then he was already embarked on the road which he knew he would one day have to travel: the quest for a constituency. Early in 1947 he added his name to the approved list of prospective candidates held by Central Office. He had high hopes that, with his talents and qualifications, he would quickly be selected. By the standards of some would-be candidates he did indeed have a relatively easy passage, but he still suffered some disconcerting setbacks along the way.

The first constituency to summon him for an interview was Ashford, in Kent. It went well, but when it came to the final selection the chairman said that they wanted a member who would apply himself wholeheartedly to the needs of the constituency. Would Heath promise that, if he was offered a job in any forthcoming Conservative government, he would turn it down? Heath would give no such undertaking; for him the main point of being in the House of Commons was the prospect it offered of serving in the government. Ashford rejected him, in favour of the *Daily Telegraph* journalist Bill Deedes. Deedes later said that he had been selected for the seat because he wore a tweed jacket for his interview while Heath wore a city suit. To this Heath retorted that, at the time, he didn't even own a city suit.[9] There may nevertheless have been something in what Deedes said. Though the reformers might be busily at work in London, in the shires the Tory Party was still a highly traditional if not reactionary body. The selectors in a largely rural constituency like Ashford would have wished their member, if not actually drawn from the landed gentry, at least to look and sound as if he were. Heath, with his suspect accent and unabashed lower-middle-class origins, was far from this ideal. The fact that he got through to the final round shows that any such prejudice was not held too seriously, but there could well have been an element of snobbishness in the final selection.

When Rochester and Sevenoaks followed Ashford in preferring another man, Heath began to feel discouragement, but in September 1947 the constituency of Bexley, in north-west Kent on the fringes of London, was looking for a candidate. It was a Labour seat, which meant that competition for it would not be so intense as it had been for Ashford or Sevenoaks; on the other hand the sitting member, Ashley Bramall, had a majority of only 1,851, so it would not need too significant a swing to restore the seat to its traditionally Tory incumbent. Geographically it was ideally placed, being on Heath's route from central London to Broadstairs. Best of all, the local party chairman, Edward Dines, was said to be looking for a candidate who was 'not rich or grand but from an ordinary family'. His other criteria for an ideal candidate – that he should be young, well educated, versed in political science and a 'local boy made good' – seemed equally applicable to Heath; Broadstairs was not actually Bexley but it was in the same county and, as the crow flies, not much more than fifty miles away. Best of all, Dines thought that the fact Heath was a bachelor told in his favour; marriage and family could have distracted him from his constituency work. Heath sailed through the preliminary stages and, with two other possibles, faced the selection committee for a second time on 18 September. Gladys Whittaker was one of the selectors. 'That half-smile of his is what I will always remember,' she said many years later. 'Of course, he was good on policy, but it is the smile that sticks in my mind. It was not the broad grin which we are used to from him now, but a shy kind of half-smile.' The shy smile proved decisive. Heath was selected. The approval of the choice of candidate by the Association was a formality. Heath was asked whether he proposed to live in Bexley. He replied that, given the shortage of housing in the constituency and the easy access to it from both Westminster and Broadstairs, he did not think that this was necessary or even desirable. His argument was accepted without demur and on 7 November he was adopted as candidate without a dissenting vote.[10]

This was only a start. The next general election might be more than two years away. Heath was confident that the tide was turning towards the Conservatives but far from sure that by then it would have moved far enough to gain him victory. 'The landslide was so great that it is bound to be some time before there can be a complete changeover,' he told Professor Winckler. 'People don't change their minds so quickly. It may take place before the next election; that will depend a good deal on the crisis and the economic situation, and how constructive the Tories can be. They have to win back a great deal of confidence before they can be certain of the result of an election.'[11] For him, the worst possible result would be if the Tories won the election but he failed to carry Bexley. Even if the constituency remained loyal he would be left fuming on the sidelines while his contemporaries established themselves in government. A swing great enough to return the Tories to power *should* also carry him into the House of Commons, but confident though Heath was in his own abilities he knew enough about the vagaries of politics to realise that the worst could happen.

That, however, was a problem for the future. Earning his living until the next election was his most immediate preoccupation. Though he was never entirely fulfilled by his work in the Ministry of Civil Aviation – 'I couldn't get anything done,' he said much later. 'I was so impatient. You mustn't go there hoping to change the world.'[12] – he had enjoyed his time there and would happily have stayed on for another couple of years. Masefield tried to persuade the establishment that this should be allowed but got nowhere: as an adopted candidate for parliament Heath must resign and resign at once. 'I am exceedingly sorry to lose Mr Heath,' Masefield concluded. 'His work during the past year has been of the utmost value and on several occasions has been favourably commented on by the Minister.'[13] For Heath it was back to the Oxford University Appointments Board. The first job vacant turned out to be that of sub-editor on the *Church Times*. He knew nothing of theology and had no experience as a journalist, promotion would be unpredictable because of the small size of the staff, the work seemed likely to be easy to learn but pretty dull: on the other hand the pay – £650 a year – was good, they were 'very pleasant people', and they did not seem to mind about the political connection provided his name was not publicly linked with the newspaper. 'I am still waiting to see your name emblazoned over the *Church Times*,' wrote a friend. He was to wait in vain. Heath's main task was editing other people's copy; when he did write pieces himself they were anonymous. The last thing he wanted, indeed, was to be too conspicuous. He had belatedly discovered that the Bexley selection committee had a rooted aversion to journalists. The *Church Times*, he protested, was too respectable to count as a real paper; the argument was accepted but he did not want to test the committee's tolerance too severely.[14]

John Trevisick, a reporter on the staff, felt that Heath had no real flair for journalism and tried to steer clear of serious writing. But he was quick to grasp the essentials of any problem and, when called on to do so, wrote with clarity and precision: 'I have vivid memories of Heath being roped in to cover the Anglo-Catholic Congress – a really tough job … But he turned in a workmanlike précis of what he had heard, thus reflecting his ability.'[15] His inexperience sometimes led him into blunders: he caused some consternation when, never having heard of the UMCA (the Universities Mission to Central Africa), he assumed it was a typing error and corrected it throughout to YMCA. But his real talent was for administration. Though his position in the hierarchy gave him no particular authority, another of his colleagues, Nicholas Bagnall, remembers that 'after a couple of months he had us eating out of his hands. He did it by force of personality, mainly by making it obvious how hard he worked himself.' The editor's secretary was so impressed by his prowess that she told Bagnall: 'Mark my words, Nicholas, that man will be prime minister one day.' Bagnall was not prepared to go as far as that: 'To the rest of us he simply didn't look like Downing Street material: not nearly devious enough, we thought.' Besides, the secretary in question, according to Bagnall, was in love with Heath. Heath, alarmed by her adoring looks, took Bagnall to a pub for a consultation. 'What on earth shall I do about this woman?' he asked. 'I don't think I was much help,' Bagnall recorded. (When, many years later, he told this story to Mrs Thatcher, she expostulated: 'Impossible! No one could love Ted Heath.')[16]

Whatever his secretary might have felt about Heath, the editor, Humphrey Beevor, looked on him with a jaundiced eye. 'Politically they were poles apart,' said another member of the staff, 'Heath to the right, Beevor to the left. Heath was an army man of steady disposition; Beevor was a navy type, a brilliant man but a man of moods.' He would fly into a passion over some trivial slip, and delighted in trying to catch Heath out on abstruse theological points – not a difficult task, since, though Heath soon mastered the technical jargon which beset religious reporting, his bent for philosophy remained obstinately under-developed. But though Beevor had little enthusiasm for his thrusting young sub-editor he was quite content to let him pursue his political interests in his spare time. When eventually the Board considered the matter, it was minuted that, though they too had no objection, they were concerned lest his activities as a would-be member of parliament took up an undue amount of his energies. They had some grounds for disquiet: one friend complained that, whenever he rang up the *Church Times* and asked to speak to Heath, he was told that he was out and that 'Mr Heath's private movements are unknown to us'. 'From the frequency of that remark,' the friend commented, 'I have gained the notion that the majority of your movements fall into this category!' Heath was constitutionally incapable of not giving value for money but it was clear to anyone that his heart was not wholly in his work. The Board agreed that he could stay on until he actually became involved in an election, but as early as August 1948 Heath told a friend on the Oxford Appointments Board that he had decided to leave as soon as another possibility offered itself. The trouble was, he said, that he was 'liable to be sent anywhere at any time. This means that I can never make an engagement and be absolutely certain of keeping it.'[17]

He wanted an employer who would offer regular hours, who would not be concerned by the fact that he would shortly be fighting an election, who might provide work on a part-time basis even after Heath became an MP and who would offer him new experiences that would be useful in his life as a politician. 'I must say that I think it will be hard to get what you want,' wrote his father apprehensively; then, with a return to his habitual cheerfulness: 'Keep trying. Mummy has a feeling that something is going to turn up for you.' Heath looked to the City of London and found the solution in Brown Shipley, a small but well-established merchant bank which specialised in financing deals in timber and wool. It was not ideal. The work would involve frequent visits to the north of England, which would provide useful knowledge for the future but would also make more difficult the nursing of his constituency. Worse still, Brown Shipley were only prepared to take him on as a management trainee at a miserable £200 a year and lunch in the staff canteen. This would involve a serious sacrifice. Heath felt it was worth it. The training would last only a few months, after which he could hope for employment as a full-time banker. Brown Shipley seemed delighted to have a potential Tory MP on their staff and were sure that they would be able to accommodate him in some way even if he did win his seat. He took the job, broke the news to a not particularly disappointed Beevor, and began work in the City in October 1949. Far more than at the *Church Times*, he seemed to fit in right away. 'All the partners knew him,' wrote the chairman, Ian Garnett-Orme, in 1970. 'He was obviously highly intelligent and very interesting ... He left a most awfully good impression here. Large numbers of people here went to help him in his election campaign. People don't do that unless they like a man.'[18]

That election campaign was now imminent. Heath had been nursing the constituency assiduously and with great success. The Bexley Conservative Association had a membership of only 600 when Heath took over, within a year it had grown to 3,500, by the election it was over 6,000. Every weekend was spent in the constituency. For the work of wooing the voter and making himself a well-known local figure, Heath renounced all the social pleasures that a young man of his age could have expected to enjoy. Even more painful, he sacrificed the raffish sports car in which he had been accustomed to cover the distance between central London and Broadstairs. He loved his glamorous dark-green MG two-seater but reluctantly accepted that it did not create the right impression in a period of stark austerity and traded it in for a more mundane Vauxhall saloon.

The local party agent who insisted on such a change was right in this case, but wrong about much else. Worst of all, he suffered from *folie de grandeur*, and plotted to replace the chairman and other senior officers of the association by nominees of his own. Heath's own position was not threatened in the short term but he would never have worked satisfactorily with the agent and would certainly have stood less chance of winning Bexley if no change had been made. He allied himself with the chairman, organised a counter-coup, and was triumphant. The agent resigned a few months later and it became clear that the finances of the local party were in disarray and that the fighting fund, which Heath had largely built up by his own efforts in preparation for the election, had been dissipated. With a general election probably only a year away, Heath found himself with an organisation in tatters and without the money essential to wage a successful campaign.

Things quickly improved. Central Office found an excellent replacement as an agent: Reginald Pye, a former rubber-planter in Sumatra, was hard-working, conscientious and level-headed. Quite as important, he liked Heath, appreciated his qualities and served him with total loyalty through twenty-five years and seven electoral campaigns. A good agent, especially if the MP concerned takes on responsibilities which make it hard to devote as much time as is desirable to the affairs of his constituency, is one of the most necessary elements of political life. From the moment Pye was appointed, Heath never had cause for serious concern about the running of his constituency. He was to prove as assiduous a member as he had been a candidate, but without the safety net of an efficient local organisation no MP can guard against the sort of lapse which leaves a sense of grievance among the constituents and can cost vital votes on election day. It was largely thanks to Pye that Heath was accepted, even by his political opponents, to be a model constituency member. It did not come easily. Though he genuinely enjoyed talking to the young about their ambitions and preoccupations, he lacked social graces and already showed some of the unease in company which was increasingly to mar his public life. 'The road to Westminster', he wrote in his memoirs, 'was not so much a long march as an interminable dinner-dance ... I made more speeches, presented more prizes and danced more waltzes than I had ever done in my life.'[19] Even for somebody more naturally sociable than Heath it must be a strain to be endlessly jolly while doing things that bore one with people whom one does not find particularly congenial. For Heath it must sometimes have been agonising. The prize was worth the price, but the price was a high one. It did not become smaller with the years. He developed a technique for coasting through social gatherings in overdrive, with fixed smile and a battery of bland banalities, but it never came easily and the self-discipline which kept the carapace in place became progressively more tattered as he grew in consequence and found the demands made on his time and energies ever less tolerable.

His colleagues in Brown Shipley were not the only people from outside the constituency who were ready to come to his help at election time. Among the many responsibilities which he crowded into an already amazingly cluttered life was the Territorial Army. Early in 1947 he was asked to re-form the 2nd Regiment of the Honourable Artillery Company (HAC) – a heavy anti-aircraft regiment. The HAC was the oldest surviving regiment in the British army and the second most senior territorial unit. Heath felt that the Territorial Army was a critically important element of Britain's defences at a time when the Cold War was setting in and a hot war seemed a serious possibility. He was eager to serve in it and took immense pride in his association with a unit as ancient and distinguished as the HAC. He flung himself into the recruiting of members with all the energy and conviction he had shown in building up the Bexley Conservative Association. It was a time-consuming task: almost every day he had to devote some part of his energies to the affairs of the HAC; every Tuesday night was given up to drill at the HAC's headquarters in Finsbury; once a year two weeks of his allotted holidays were spent at the annual training camp. For months before camp he would spend much of his exiguous spare time in preparation, while the months after would be devoted to consideration of what had gone right and what wrong. 'Believe me,' wrote a colleague in 1948, 'the success at camp was due to your leadership, inspiration and enthusiasm, and in saying this I am confident that I speak for the whole Regiment.' That he did speak for the whole regiment was shown by the number of volunteers who flocked to Bexley to help their commanding officer when the electoral campaign began.[20]

Such military preoccupations, particularly when linked to a body as traditional as the Honourable Artillery Company, might suggest that Heath was as conservative in instincts as the political label that he bore. He did indeed cherish a nostalgic affection for some of the more picturesque and time-hallowed practices of the past but by the time of the 1950 election he had acquired the reputation of being a reformist, even, in the eyes of some, a dangerous radical. 'Without sharing your desire for a larger opposition, I hope at least to see you here soon,' wrote Roy Jenkins from the House of Commons.

Whatever his father may have thought when he recommended Heath to Attlee as a potential Labour candidate, Roy Jenkins knew that Heath was a committed Tory, but he knew too that his Balliol friend was well to the left and that the two young men probably had more in common with each other than either did with the extremists of their own parties. At his adoption meeting Heath had told his future constituents that 'there is still a suspicion of our party in the minds of the people'. That suspicion, he privately believed, had more than a little justification. The country was growing tired of Labour, he told Professor Winckler at the end of 1947, 'but there is not yet, I regret to say, a very great revival of trust in the Conservatives. The Conservatives have still a lot of hard thinking to do about our present problems.'[21]

He regretted greatly that he was not himself in a position to contribute much to that process. He joined the Coningsby Club, a dining society where some of the more liberal Tories foregathered, but though this put him in touch with current thinking it was no substitute for joining in the policy making. Though he felt that the Labour Party was trying to do too much too fast, and was particularly sceptical about its belief that nationalisation was a panacea for all Britain's social and economic woes, he accepted that much of what it was doing was necessary and desirable. He openly supported the nationalisation of the Bank of England and privately felt that it was inevitable that the coal industry too should come under public ownership. The Tory Party's efforts to bring its policies up to date seemed to him belated but eminently desirable. He wholeheartedly backed Butler's Industrial Charter, which for the first time in Tory circles accepted that the trade unions were a vital and desirable part of society and should be worked with rather than treated as enemies. He was a one-nation Conservative before the term had gained – or regained – popular acceptance, and he made it plain to the voters of Bexley that these were his views.

The voters of Bexley liked what he said and seemed prepared to believe him when he rejected Ashley Bramall's claim that the Tories were bent on restoring a high level of unemployment as a means of curbing the just demands of Labour. But when the general election was called for 23 February 1950, it was anyone's guess who would win at Bexley. Everyone accepted that the Tories had gained ground since their disaster of 1945, but would Bexley necessarily follow the national trend and, even if it did, would the swing be sufficient to wipe out Bramall's majority? Heath had come in for his fair share of heckling and abuse at the innumerable meetings he addressed. 'Your candidate was born in Kent,' one local chairman had announced. No particular enthusiasm was evoked by this revelation. 'He was educated in Kent!' the chairman went on. Still the response was muted. 'And he lives in Kent!' the chairman concluded. 'And for all I bloody well care, he can die in Kent!' shouted a Labour supporter from the back. On the whole most of the meetings had gone well, but so too had Bramall's. There was a Liberal candidate in the field who nobody thought would win but who was expected to poll a few thousand votes. At whose expense would those votes be cast? More satisfactorily from the point of view of the Tories, there was also a Communist standing: any votes he garnered could only come at the expense of Labour. By the early afternoon of polling day Heath was reasonably hopeful, but the flow of Labour voters on their way back from work disquieted him and by the time the count began neither Heath nor Bramall would have put money on their prospects. As the count went on it became obvious that it was going to be a desperately close-run thing. Finally the result was announced: both the leading candidates had secured between 25,000 and 26,000 votes; Heath led by a mere 166. The Communist had polled 481 votes, thus losing the election for Labour. 'In the next election if you have any trouble finding money for your deposit I'll look after that,' a grateful Heath told him. 'You must stand again. It's your right to stand.'[22]

Bramall demanded a recount. It took place and Heath's majority shrank still further to a mere 133. A request for a further recount was lodged but refused unless the Labour candidate was prepared to meet the cost himself. This Bramall refused to do and the result was confirmed. Edward Heath at the age of 33 was Member of Parliament for Bexley. He would be joining a party still in opposition, for though the Conservative Party had made substantial gains, reducing Labour's lead from 142 seats to a mere five, Labour could still cling on to power.

From Heath's point of view this was almost better than an overall victory. He could not have hoped to have been offered any sort of job if the Conservatives had won, it seemed likely that they would be in power after the next election, in the meantime a short period in opposition would give him a chance to make his maiden speech and establish his parliamentary identity.

Margaret Roberts, a young research chemist who was later to marry a prosperous businessman called Denis Thatcher, was standing in the neighbouring constituency of Dartford. She and Heath spoke at each other's meetings during the campaign. 'I hope you gallup to the top of the poll,' read the telegram which Miss Roberts sent him on polling day. 'Among my fellow Conservative candidates in neighbouring seats, only Margaret Roberts failed to be elected,' Heath wrote in his memoirs. Whatever his feelings may have been when he wrote those words, at the time her failure caused him mild regret. For the rest, it was exultation.[23]

FIVE

The Young Member

Heath was no Pitt the Younger, entering parliament like a young lord taking possession of his ancestral home, but he found his first appearances in the House of Commons less stressful than did most of his newly elected colleagues. His political activities at Oxford, the year he had spent nursing his constituency, the assiduity with which he had cultivated useful connections at Westminster, all ensured that to some extent his reputation went before him; he was known to the leadership as a sound and useful man, potentially a suitable candidate for preferment. The first meetings of the House which he attended, he wrote in his memoirs, 'reminded me more than anything of the debating chamber of the Oxford Union. Nothing could be more natural. I was coming home.'[1]

The House had undergone a dramatic transformation since it had last met. A huge Labour majority had melted away; in spite of the fact that they had won 1½ million more votes than the Conservatives they had only 33 more seats and their majority over all other parties was five. Their front bench still contained the giants of the 1945 administration – Attlee, Bevin, Cripps, Morrison – but they had been in office since the formation of the coalition government in 1940; they were older, tired, in some cases seriously sick. Even that splendid firebrand, Aneurin Bevan, seemed to burn less fiercely; as for the backbenchers, they were demoralised and diminished, conscious that they were in for some gruelling sessions and probably defeat at the end of them.

The Tories had achieved electoral success which, if not as great as they had dreamed of, at least was vastly better than had appeared possible a few years before. One more push, it seemed, and victory would be theirs. Over the previous years, under the guidance of R. A. Butler, they had planned new Tory policies for a return to power, but it had seemed at times a dispiritingly academic exercise. Now there was a real chance that soon they would be able to put those policies into practice. This lent a new urgency to their deliberations and ensured that the members who had won their seats for the first time in February 1950 would have a chance to make their mark as representatives of a new Conservatism. The new entrants were, indeed, an outstandingly able and forward-looking group. Even the scions of the traditional Tory grandee families – Julian Amery, Christopher Soames – seemed to have a slight flavour of radicalism about them; most of the others came from minor public or grammar schools and offered some promise of a serious shift both in the social composition and in the thinking of the party. Heath was one of these, but not considered to be among those most obviously destined for stardom. Ian Trethowan, then a young parliamentary lobby correspondent, reckoned that Iain Macleod, Reginald Maudling and Enoch Powell were the three most exceptional of the new members, the men among whom a future leader of the party must be looked for. Heath, he considered, 'in those early years seemed a conscientious but rather plodding man'.[2] But, along with Angus Maude, Robert Carr, Harold Watkinson, it was clear from the start that, whether or not he attained the stratosphere, he had to be reckoned with as potentially a formidable figure within the Tory hierarchy.

He made no attempt to thrust himself into the limelight with a premature display of fireworks. As in the Oxford Union, he was content at first to watch and listen. He 'took the quiet but persistent way', remembered Anthony Eden. 'He attended the House regularly and modestly, but missed nothing. Pains and patience are needed to learn the way at Westminster. Heath had both.'[3] In his first five years in the Commons Heath only missed ten divisions, and he had been paired in six of those. He put a parliamentary question in May 1950 – on an issue relating to civil aviation on which he could reasonably be held to have some expert knowledge – but did not make a speech in the House of Commons until 26 June. When he finally spoke, however, it was to considerable effect and on the subject with which his parliamentary career was above all to be identified: that of Europe.

It can be argued that Heath would never have become so irrevocably committed to the cause of Britain in Europe if he had not been entrusted by Harold Macmillan with the negotiations for British entry in the early 1960s. He was by nature strikingly single-minded and, if he had been given some other task, would have pursued it with similar dedication. But from the time that he had fought his way across Germany in 1945 he had felt passionately that war in Western Europe must never be allowed to happen again. The only way by which he felt this could be achieved with certainty was by tying Britain, France and Germany into a union so inextricable that war would become not merely inconceivable but impossible. Britain had to be part of such a group, not just to cement it but to lead it; as the Empire disintegrated British influence in the world would inevitably be diminished; only by entering Europe would the British be able to retain that position in the world, economic as well as political, to which they were accustomed. When colleagues suggested that any European Union, if it were truly to be a force in the world, would have to involve a possibly unacceptable sacrifice of national sovereignty on the part of its members, he brushed the arguments aside. The word 'federalism' held no terrors for him and he envisaged a Europe where, in the long term, all important decisions, whether on foreign policy, economics, defence or social policies, would be made in common, without any individual member state being able to frustrate the ambitions of the others. 'The nation state is dead,' he would say. 'What has sovereignty to do with anything in the twentieth century?'[4] But though these were his private views, he was still cautious about pressing them openly unless he was certain that he was addressing a sympathetic audience. One can feel pretty sure that he did not express himself very forcibly on the subject when, in the summer of 1950, he was taken by another Conservative MP, John Rodgers, to lunch in the South of France with that arch-imperialist and enemy of British association with Europe, Lord Beaverbrook. 'I liked your young friend,' Beaverbrook told

Rodgers after the meeting. 'I think he should go far.' (Beaverbrook's favourable view of Heath did not survive the discovery of his true views on Europe. By August 1962 he was telling Alec Martin: 'If you meet that young man Heath, of whom I once formed a good opinion, please tell him to look westward.')[5]

In 1950, his dream of a united Europe with Britain at its heart seemed infinitely remote. The Labour Government had refused to take part in the conference that drafted the treaty setting up the European Coal and Steel Community (ECSC). Heath was dismayed. 'A very short-sighted and, for the United Kingdom, an immensely damaging decision,' he judged it. 'It was quite simply an abrogation of leadership.'[6] The Conservatives, if only to be seen to oppose, were formally critical of the Labour policy, but Heath knew well that many of his colleagues were sceptical about the merits of European union and that the heir-apparent to the visibly crumbling Churchill, Anthony Eden, was quite as anxious to preserve full British sovereignty as any Labour minister. But though he knew that he was swimming against the tide, Heath never ceased to press the European cause when any opportunity arose. In his constituency he was as likely to talk of Germany and the need to bring it back into the comity of nations as to offer more orthodox fare about cripplingly high taxes or stultifying controls. When he visited Germany in the Whitsun recess of 1950 he was both exhilarated and alarmed by the pace of recovery; what was already a high priority in his mind took on fresh urgency. And when in June 1950 the House debated the Schuman Plan, the blueprint for European unity conceived by Jean Monnet and accepted in principle by both Germany and France, Heath saw the opportunity to make his maiden speech on a subject about which he was an authority and which he had passionately at heart.

Heath was exceptionally good at expounding complex issues with clarity and objectivity; he could produce apparently impromptu after-dinner speeches or memorial addresses which were as amusing or as moving as the occasion could demand; but he rarely excelled with the parliamentary set-piece. His maiden speech was one of the exceptions. For fourteen minutes he pleaded with the Government to take the Schuman Plan seriously and to join in its formulation before it became set in a rigid structure which might not suit our national interests. This was an opportunity which might never recur; to bind Germany into a peaceful Europe and to ensure that the voice of Britain was heard loudly in the creation of this new union. 'It was said long ago in the House', he concluded, 'that magnanimity in politics is not seldom the truest wisdom. I appeal tonight to the Government to follow that dictum and to go into the Schuman Plan to develop Europe and to co-ordinate it in the way suggested.'[7]

The Government, of course, did not follow that dictum, nor did Heath expect them to. Even the most sceptical of Labour members, however, were impressed by his authority and obvious sincerity. His own colleagues were still more enthusiastic. The content of Heath's message was not really to Eden's taste but he still wrote appreciatively: 'Warm congratulations on a very capable and debating maiden speech. The House enjoyed it very much; so did I.' Heath wrote in his memoirs that this note gave him 'immense pleasure'.[8] His own career as leader of the party might have run more smoothly if he had himself written rather more such messages to backbenchers hungry for a little encouragement from on high.

It was, however, not as a pro-European but as a committed member of the liberal wing of the party that Heath made an early mark. More than most of his colleagues he was possessed by a strong social conscience. He had been brought up in an era of mass unemployment and he felt that any government which condoned it was committing a crime against the country which it ruled. Many years later, when Heath was prime minister, the then Minister of Housing and Local Government, Peter Walker, wanted him to appoint a 26-year-old as chairman of one of the New Towns in the north of England. Heath was sceptical but asked Walker to bring his protégé along to Number 10. 'Do you really know the north-east?' he asked the young man. He took him up to his flat and pointed out a painting by John Cornish of a miner slumped semi-conscious at the bar of a grim Durham pub. 'That's the north-east!' said Heath. 'If I appoint you, do you think you can see that man and his children have a rather better quality of life in the future than he and his family had in the past?'[9]

The instincts of youth were reinforced by his experiences during the war. The men beside whom he had fought in France and Germany were now the dockers and the miners who would confront him when he was prime minister. The sense of common purpose and national unity which had existed during the Second World War could and must be revived. There *was* such a thing as society. The issues which were in time to separate him so starkly from Margaret Thatcher were partly personal, but it should never be forgotten that they were also separated by a very real and deep ideological divide. Throughout his life Heath was repelled by the standards of unbridled capitalism and the defeatist philosophy of laissez-faire, with which, unfairly or not, he identified Margaret Thatcher. 'I fear that to place one's faith in some invisible hand, rather than to grapple with problems with determination, is a failure of the human spirit,' he told a young Conservative who questioned his political philosophy. 'What distinguishes man from animals is his desire and his ability to control and to shape his environment.'[10]

The ardently left-wing trade-union leader, Jack Jones, once described Heath as being 'very much a one-nation Tory'. It was Disraeli who had written that in England 'the Privileged and the People formed Two Nations', and ever since then liberal Conservatives had from time to time claimed that it was their role to fuse the two nations into one. Heath did as much as anyone to revitalise the concept. When a group of left-wing Tory members with whom he was associated were preparing a pamphlet summarising their beliefs, there was much debate about what to call it. All were agreed that 'A Tory Approach to Social Problems' summarised the contents of the paper but, as a title, lacked punch. Some advocated 'The Strongest and the Weak', but, Heath recorded, 'the irreverent feared that this might deteriorate into "Mild and Bitter"'. I do believe, he went on, 'that what I might call the "One Nation" approach is the only right approach to social and economic problems in this country today'.[11] 'One Nation' was the title adopted, and the 'One Nation Group' was the banner under which assembled a band of young or youngish Tory members, who were disturbed by the reactionary policies of some of their leaders and were resolved to push the party into the modern age. Heath claimed in his memoirs that the group had its genesis in a late-night talk between him, Angus Maude and Gilbert Longden after Duncan Sandys had made a particularly disastrous contribution to a debate on housing. Certainly he was recruited at an early stage but Maude, Longden and Cuthbert 'Cub' Alport seem to have been the originators of the movement. Robert Carr, Richard Fort, Enoch Powell, John Rodgers and Heath himself were soon added; Iain Macleod, according to Heath, was something of an afterthought: 'We were suspicious that he might remain under the influence of the party machine, with which he was closely involved, as part of the Conservative Research Department.'[12]

In fact Macleod played a highly important part in the group's deliberations and, though there was never anyone who could formally have been described as the leader, was both the most conspicuous and the most creative among its members. So much so that one member suggested that they should be called not the One Nation but the 'One Notion' Group, the notion being that Macleod should be drawn as vigorously as possible to the attention of the leaders of the party. They met, at first, at dinner in the guests' dining room in the House of Commons; then, when they had begun work on their policy papers, assembled two afternoons a week to discuss progress and inspect each other's contributions. Heath was charged with producing a paper on the financing and future of the social services, a subject which was bound to create dissent within the party when it returned to power. According to John Rodgers he was not considered one of the more significant contributors or potentially an important innovator: 'I believe that Enoch thought Ted wasn't an intellectual at all – he tended to brush him aside. It was true that Ted over-simplified, he didn't see the light and shade of an argument.' He would listen to the pontifications of Macleod, Maude or Powell and then surface with some such question as: 'Well, what are we going to do about it?' 'However,' Rogers added, 'I can't recall that he ever told us what we *could* do.'[13]

When *One Nation* was finally published in October 1950 it met with guarded approval from the party leaders. 'A healthy piece of constructive work,' R. A. Butler described it, praising the fact that it advocated not laissez-faire but 'private enterprise in the public interest'. Maude and Powell did most of the work in preparing the pamphlet, though Iain Macleod, co-editor with Maude, got most of the credit.[14] Heath definitely gained in reputation by his association with what was seen as an influential and distinguished group but he did not form any particularly close ties among its members. He was, indeed, generally taken to be something of a loner. After the easy camaraderie of Oxford and the army, with ready-made friends formed almost automatically by the way of life pursued in the two institutions, he found the shifting world of the House of Commons difficult to encompass and a bit alarming. He was quite clear about himself, his abilities, his position in the hierarchy, but found it hard to fit into any coherent, still less cosy pattern. 'One should never under-estimate the loneliness of a political career,' says John Selwyn Gummer.[15] Heath was never 'part of a gang'; it was not in his nature to be so: and a member who is not part of a gang in the House of Commons is confronted by a host of acquaintances and a paucity of friends. It is doubtful whether, in the House of Commons in 1950 and 1951, Heath could have named a single member whom he could properly have described as a close, still less an intimate, friend.

In January 1951 Iain Macleod wrote to the members of the One Nation Group to report that he had been approached by a Labour backbencher, Reginald Paget (celebrated as being the only Labour MP to have been master of the Pytchley Hunt), to discuss the possibility of a coalition. The suggestion was that Labour should retain the social services and economic ministries, while the Conservatives should take over foreign affairs and defence. 'It might be an idea if we could know each other's minds on this subject before the House meets,' suggested Macleod. 'It may be, of course, that we cannot reach agreement, but this, above anything else, is precisely the sort of subject on which the voice of a group is of importance, when the individual opinions count for little or nothing.' There is no reason to think the matter was taken any further. Paget was a lone voice in the Labour Party and he would have commanded little support for his initiative. The enterprise was clearly a hopeless one. If it had become a serious possibility, however, Heath might have been more interested than certain other members of the One Nation Group, Enoch Powell in particular. Heath never felt that the ideological divide between left-wing Tories and right-wing Socialists was insuperably wide and might well have been in favour of at least exploring the possibility of a regrouping which would link the moderates on both sides. The concept would certainly have provoked some lively discussion within the group and might well have put some strains upon its unity. Macleod saw another reason why it might have been difficult for the group to present a united front. 'It might be again', he suggested, 'that the position would be complicated by one of us being offered an important position such as PPS to the Assistant Postmaster General.'[16] Since there was to be no coalition, no such alluring invitation was issued, but within a few weeks of Macleod's letter Heath received an offer which had similar results. He was invited to become one of the Tory Whips.

He was uncertain whether he should accept. To become even the most junior of the Whips would be to rise above the ruck of back-bench MPs; he would be the first of his generation to do so and thus would have stolen a march on the others. So far, so good, but by many members the Whips' Office was seen as something of a dead end. Promotion might be gained within it, but it was not often that a former Whip became a senior minister. 'It had traditionally been the place for the less bright and imaginative of men,' wrote the political historian Anthony Seldon. The vacancy which Heath was asked to fill had been caused by the resignation of Sir Walter Bromley-Davenport, a hearty squire from Knutsford who was to become a member of the British Boxing Board of Control. On one unfortunate occasion, Sir Walter had been tempted to exercise his pugilistic skills in the House of Commons. Observing a man whom he thought to be one of his flock sneaking out of the House when he should have been waiting to vote, Bromley-Davenport kicked him heartily, bringing him to the ground. Legend has it that the target of his kick was not a Conservative MP but the Belgian Ambassador; in any case the victim, not unreasonably, took exception to this maltreatment. Bromley-Davenport, it was felt, had gone too far and must be replaced.[17] To be appointed successor to such a boor hardly seemed appealing to Heath. The Chief Whip, Patrick Buchan-Hepburn, insisted, however, that a change of style was intended. The new junior Whip was to be sensitive, a good listener, ready to argue with recalcitrant members rather than kick them. Heath seemed unconvinced. 'I don't think he was very keen to come into the Whips' Office to start with,' wrote Buchan-Hepburn in 1968. 'It curtailed his speaking in the H of C and in the days of the 18 majority there was not much time to speak outside either.'[18] The fact that a Whip was precluded from speaking in the House was, indeed, one of the most unfortunate aspects of Heath's promotion. His forced silence lasted for eight years; by the time that he resumed normal service in October 1959 he had largely lost the knack of handling the Commons in a difficult debate. At the best of times, he would never have been an Iain Macleod or a Michael Foot, have displayed the quicksilver ingenuity of Harold Wilson or the eloquence of Aneurin Bevan; as it was he had to struggle to be merely competent. Only when he was relieved of the burdens of office – and indeed of loyalty to his party's leadership – did he develop a style which was truly suited to his personality and the needs of the occasion.

His life as a Whip, however, gave him unrivalled knowledge of the strengths and weaknesses of his colleagues. 'He did know about people,' Buchan-Hepburn remarked perceptively. 'He took great trouble to know about them, and their backgrounds and what they wanted ... He enjoys people, but I don't know that he needs them – he's extraordinarily self-sufficient.'[19] His role as a Whip ensured him a wide acquaintanceship with the Tory members and all their vagaries but also denied him any chance of intimacy. This merely reinforced a predilection that was already obvious, but his new role gave him an obligation to behave in such a way. He did not formally sever his ties with the One Nation Group until the Tories were in power and he found himself on the front bench, but already he had begun to distance himself from their proceedings. The day that he accepted the role of Whip saw the extinction of the last chance that he would ever 'join a gang'.

He was in one way particularly well suited for the job, because he found the endless grind of House of Commons life perfectly acceptable and had no compelling wish to be elsewhere. He had the advantage of being what was termed in the Commons NHTGT – No Home To Go To.[20] His poky flatlet in Petty France, little more than a bed-sitting room, offered few attractions. He would have liked to go to operas or concerts but disliked spending money unnecessarily and was saving every penny that he could; what then could be more appealing than the warmth, light and animation of late night sittings at the House? Ned Carson, a young Conservative MP from Kent, once went into the Whips' Office after an indecently protracted debate and asked indignantly why Heath did not get married, go home and leave people like him free to go to bed. 'He looked up slowly, with a very blank face, and answered simply: "I don't want to get married".' Nor did he want to go home, or even particularly to go to bed. His dedication, his self-discipline, his mastery of detail, won the respect of his fellow Members. He was not outstandingly well liked but, as Buchan-Hepburn pointed out, that did not matter much in the House of Commons: 'Respect is the first thing, and confidence. Popularity comes very much second.'[21]

'He was shy to start with,' said Buchan-Hepburn, 'but quickly developed and became invaluable to me, and I am sure that from his own point of view it was very important for him to have those years in the Whips' Office – breaking down the reserve, getting on with all and sundry.' Heath would have agreed. He much enjoyed the organisational role involved in being a Whip. 'I loathe incompetence, inefficiency, bungling and waste,' he told Michael Cockerell on television in 1988. Even when he was the most junior of the Whips it was noticeable that the Office functioned more smoothly for his presence; once he had become Deputy Chief Whip in April 1952 procedures were revolutionised. The Whips, if only to be alert to incipient scandal, had always felt it necessary to know a lot about the private lives of the individual members; under Heath procedures were regularised, card-indexes established, the psychological strengths and weaknesses of each member analysed and recorded. The Bromley-Davenports of this world had barked commands and expected unquestioning obedience: Heath relied more upon reason and persuasion. 'Now be a good chap. It's not really a matter of your conscience this time, is it?' was the line Ned Carson remembered him taking. If it really was a matter of conscience he did his best to be sympathetic. As a result, when he did find it necessary to be tough, he was listened to with attention. 'I remember one occasion when he was stern in a tactful way and I was so surprised I went into the lobby at his bidding.' The deadpan and slightly black style of humour which was more and more to become his trademark matured during his years as a Whip. His object seemed to be more to disconcert than to amuse; its victim was often uncertain whether Heath's remarks were intended as a joke or were to be taken seriously. Sometimes both were true. John Peyton, a future minister in Heath's government, once let off steam to him about the failure of certain ministers to consult interested members about problems which affected them or their constituents. Some months later Heath, as Deputy Chief Whip, asked Peyton whether he would like to serve as a parliamentary private secretary. 'To whom?' asked Peyton. Heath looked at him in affected surprise: 'Do you not feel equally warmly towards all our colleagues?'[22]

It was not only his social life that was circumscribed by his work as a Whip. In 1951 he gave up command of the 2nd Regiment HAC. The historic rituals, the social consequence, the pomp of the Honourable Artillery Company had all appealed strongly to Heath; as well as the unstrained masculine comradeship of the mess and the training camp and the feeling that, as an effective element in the Territorial Army, his unit was making an important contribution to national defence. He knew that he had to retire but deplored the need. The blow was softened when Lord Alanbrooke, Colonel Commandent of the HAC, offered him the appointment of Master Gunner within the Tower of London. The post was almost entirely honorary but it enabled Heath to entertain dignitaries in the grand manner and at small expense and to dress up and preside over the firing of salutes on occasions such as the royal birthday. He relished such opportunities and even endured with equanimity the debacle when on one occasion the ammunition was damp and all four guns failed to fire. At one point the desperate troop commander was reduced to extracting a faulty shell and, for want of a more suitable repository, flinging it into the Thames. It was a singularly courageous action but not one recommended by the drill manuals. The officer concerned could well have earned a stiff rebuke, even dismissal, but Heath and Alanbrooke between them saw to it that the War Office was not troubled by any report of the incident.

More importantly from the point of view of his finances, once he became Deputy Chief Whip Heath felt he could no longer work part-time for Brown Shipley. As a tyro backbencher he had managed to spend most mornings in the City and even as a junior Whip he had kept up more-or-less regular attendance. The arrangement had suited Brown Shipley well: to have a promising young MP on their staff both lent the bank a certain prestige and gave them a potentially useful foothold in Westminster. In the summer of 1951 they had sent him on a visit to the United States and Canada; not to transact any particular business but so that he could get to know how Brown Brothers Harriman, Brown Shipley's associate in New York, transacted its affairs and to make contact with people who might be useful to him both as a banker and as a politician. One of those he hoped to meet was the influential Senator Paul Douglas from Illinois. A mutual acquaintance wrote enthusiastically to urge the Senator to set up a meeting. Heath, he said, was 'very able and exceedingly well informed and a very fine guy indeed ... He's much more "liberal" that most of our best Democrats, but withal a genuine and convinced Tory ... Recently he's been made an Assistant Whip which, I've just learned, makes him a Front Bencher and, should the Conservatives get in power, very likely a cabinet minister.' Heath's rise was not to be quite so meteoric but the judgment is of interest as showing how seriously he was already taken in political circles in the United States. A date was fixed for a meeting with the Senator but before it could take place Heath visited Ottawa, staying at the same hotel as Labour's foreign secretary, Herbert Morrison, and his parliamentary private secretary, Eddie Shackleton. On 19 September he met the pair of them heading hurriedly towards the exit. 'Have you heard?' asked Shackleton. 'Attlee has just called a general election!' 'And the bloody fool didn't ask me first,' added a disgruntled Morrison.[23]

*   *   *

'Nobody knows whether we can expect an election in the near future,' Heath had told a friend in August 1951. 'Personally, I don't think there will be one for the very simple reason that the Government has nothing to gain but a lot to lose. However, only time will tell.'[24] Time had told, and had showed that Attlee disagreed with Heath. Though Morrison turned out to have had good reason for his doubts, Attlee was not acting irrationally. His ministry was in tatters. Cripps and Bevin had retired through ill-health; Bevin's successor, Morrison, had made a disastrous mess of foreign policy in the Middle East; Heath's Oxford contemporary, Harold Wilson, together with Aneurin Bevan, had resigned in protest at the increased spending on defence. Attlee could have struggled on but he concluded that the best chance for Labour was to go quickly to the country and then to rebuild the government with new blood and a new mandate. The election was called for 25 October.

Heath must have felt reasonably confident as he hurried back across the Atlantic. On the national scene all the indications were that Labour would do worse than at the last election; in his own constituency he had consolidated his position. He had been an exemplary constituency MP; had dealt conscientiously with the problems of the voters; attended endless fetes, garden parties, dances, rotary lunches, meetings with businessmen; had escorted innumerable constituents around the House of Commons. Local elections had strengthened the position of the Conservatives. He had beaten Ashley Bramall once and was sure that he could do so again.

But it was not only the election that preoccupied him. Shortly before he left for the United States his mother had been diagnosed with cancer and had almost immediately been operated on at the Ramsgate General Hospital. Heath thought of cancelling his tour but the operation seemed to have gone well and the prognosis was that she would be home and well on the way to recovery by the time he got back. She was home, but she was in pain and obviously extremely weak. His sister-in-law Marian told Michael Cockerell that she and her husband were with Ted in the kitchen in the Broadstairs house when William Heath broke it to them that his wife was dying. 'Ted was absolutely devastated,' she said. 'I don't think I ever saw him before or after as he was on that day.'[25]

It took the realisation that he was about to lose his mother to make him fully take in how much she had meant to him. He was not dependent on her, in the sense that he turned to her for advice or for moral support, but the love which she had lavished on him over the years, the knowledge that in her eyes he could do no wrong and should be the beneficiary of any and every sacrifice, had created a bond between them which he enjoyed with no one else. Though he fought the election campaign in Bexley with all the energy and conscientiousness that his supporters expected of him, the thought of her suffering was with him every moment. Each evening he would drive back to the coast to be with her; he would sit at the piano in the room directly below her bedroom playing the old sentimental songs which his father had used to sing and which he knew his mother cherished: 'In a Monastery Garden', 'Love's Old Sweet Song', 'When You Come to the End of a Perfect Day'. She died on 15 October, ten days before polling day. Ashley Bramall suggested that there should be a day's truce in the electioneering on the day of her funeral. Heath gratefully accepted. Margaret Roberts, still battling away in the safe Labour seat of Dartford, wrote to commiserate: 'I am so glad your mother saw your initial success and the way in which you followed up with a steady ascent to great things.' The precipitous descent which she was one day to engineer lends a certain irony to this letter but, as Heath acknowledged in his memoirs, it was 'most generous' and, without doubt, sincerely meant.[26]

'As I think you know, I loved and admired her tremendously,' wrote the former Kay Raven. His relationship with his mother had not been the only one that had ended about this time. A year or so before, Kay had written to announce her engagement to a regular air force officer and former bomber pilot, Richard Buckwell. 'I hope you will be glad for me, you know I'm rather a loving kind of girl and must have been a horrid bore for you.'[27] For nearly fifteen years she had looked for something in Edward Heath that he was unable to supply; finally she had decided that life was too short and that she must move on. 'Apparently her family persuaded her to go on holiday with a group of young friends, and that was when she got engaged,' said

William Heath. 'She was keen on him. He wasn't, or if he was he never showed it.' It was Mrs Heath who seems to have been the most upset by the news; she had set her heart on Ted's marriage with Kay and burst into tears when she heard of the engagement.[28]

Ted Heath remained impassive. He was more moved than he cared to admit, however. For so many years he had taken it for granted that she was there, permanently available in case he should one day decide that the time had come for him to marry. It is conceivable that the death of his mother and the fact that he was now well launched on his climb up the political ladder might have impelled him to marry Kay; conceivable, but on balance improbable. By 1950 he was set in his bachelor ways; the thought of sexual intercourse or of procreation would have filled him with mild dismay; how could he fit a woman into his crowded life; what sacrifices might he not find imposed on him? But her engagement was still a blow to his pride, and the closing of a door which he had liked to feel was at least a crack ajar. He soon convinced himself that he had been in love and had been robbed of a cherished aspiration. Many years later Michael Cockerell, with that startling temerity which adds such zest to his television interviews, asked Heath whether he had been saddened by Kay Raven's engagement. 'Yes,' he replied. When asked if he had ever been in love, Heath again replied, 'Yes. Why shouldn't one love?' Almost incredibly, given his habitual reluctance to express emotion, he seemed on the point of tears.[29] He kept a photograph of Kay by his bedside, though it seems to have disappeared before he died. She became a convenient alibi; designed as much to deceive himself as anyone else, to be adduced whenever it seemed possible that he might become close to some other woman. He had loved and lost, once was enough: or that, at least, was the official story. Though he was to get to know many women over the next forty years and become attached to two or three of them, there was never again to be a suspicion of romance, let alone matrimony.

Perhaps inevitably this absence of female involvements meant that there were rumours that Heath was homosexual. In April 2007 one of the Conservative leaders in the London Assembly, Brian Coleman, alleged in the *New Statesman* that Heath regularly 'cottaged' along the motorways and had only desisted when he became a Privy Councillor and MI5 warned him that he must mend his ways. When asked for evidence of this Coleman was unable or unwilling to provide names but said that it was 'generally known' in the House of Commons that Heath was gay. General knowledge seems to have been based on little or no information. No man has ever claimed to have had any sort of sexual relationship with Heath, no hint of such an involvement is to be found among Heath's papers and everyone who knew him well insists that he was not in the least that way inclined. He had friendly relationships with a number of women over the years, but never, it seems, one in which there was any hint of a romantic, let alone sexual, element. It may be that, after Kay Raven decided to marry someone else, he determined never to allow himself to be in a position in which he could be let down (as he might have seen it) in that way again. He certainly had a weak sex drive and may have been to all intents and purposes asexual: a condition which is by no means rare but which those who are more conventionally endowed find hard to believe exists. He was perhaps the poorer for this deficiency, but at least it left him with more time and energy for the other activities which filled his crowded life.[30]

For the moment it was back to the political fray. His task in Bexley was made more difficult by the fact that this time there was no helpful Communist standing to whittle away at Bramall's vote; on the other hand there was no Liberal candidate either – a fact which on the whole seemed to favour Heath. The most controversial weapon which Labour employed in this election was the scare story, launched by the *Daily Mirror* ('Whose Finger on the Trigger?'), claiming that Churchill was a war-monger and that Britain would not be safe under his leadership. Bramall had little enthusiasm for this line of argument, Heath had no difficulty in rebutting it, and the voters of Bexley appeared unconcerned by the prospect of imminent annihilation. Heath's majority went up from 133 to 1,639, a swing slightly greater than the national average. Bexley was still a marginal seat but much less so than had been the case before. With the Conservatives enjoying an overall majority of sixteen, Heath could return to Westminster in the confidence that he left a secure base behind him. He could be confident too that, with the new Government enjoying so small a majority, a government Whip was going to have a great deal to do.

Until this time he had been a junior Whip with plenty of work but no financial reward; now he was appointed a Lord Commissioner of the Treasury, which signified nothing in the way of additional responsibilities but meant that he was paid an extra £500 a year (comparative values mean very little, but the equivalent of £10,000 today would not be far wrong). It was not princely, but it usefully replaced the salary he was no longer receiving from Brown Shipley. He earned his pay rise, for he was given responsibility for pairing – the system by which members could miss a division only if they could ensure that a member of the Opposition would also be away. This called for much negotiation and a certain amount of bullying. It also required tact and discretion. Sometimes Heath found himself telephoning the home of a missing MP in the small hours of the morning only to be told by an unsuspecting wife that her husband was in the House. 'Naturally we were able to demand a high degree of loyalty from colleagues in return for our concern, interest and discretion,' wrote Heath blandly in his memoirs:[31] a euphemism which did not conceal the fact that genteel blackmail was one of the weapons by which the Whips controlled their flock. Heath used such methods less than most: few complaints were made about the way he went about his business.

No one was surprised when, after a year or so, he was appointed joint Deputy Chief Whip and, a few months later, was confirmed as the only Deputy. A Chief Whip, Buchan-Hepburn told one of his successors, had 'to take the responsibility and be jolly rude at times'. Then the Deputy had to pick up the pieces. Heath 'became very good at that. He could be very nice to people.'[32] In due course Heath was to show that he could be surprisingly nice to people even when he was Chief Whip; for the moment he concentrated on building a network of relationships within the party. His new role meant that he became well-known, not only to the rank-and-file but also to the dignitaries of the party. Of these none was half as eminent or as remote from the hurly-burly of back-bench life as the Prime Minister, Winston Churchill.

When Heath had first been appointed a Whip Churchill had said to him: 'It will mean much hard work and it will be unremunerated, but so long as I am your leader it will never remain unthanked.' That was almost all that Heath saw of the Prime Minister for the next few years. Buchan-Hepburn remembered that, when Heath had gained greater prominence, Churchill used to claim that it was he who had discovered him. This was rubbish, claimed Buchan-Hepburn: 'He asked me more than once, even when Ted was Deputy Chief Whip, who he was.' But later 'he got to know him very well, and thought a lot of him'.[33] The relationship did not grow close until Heath had become Chief Whip and Churchill had ceased to be Prime Minister, but by 1953 at the latest Churchill would have had no doubts who the young Whip was. Several times Heath had to extricate him from dinner parties to come back to the House to vote when the Tory majority seemed dangerously low; once it was the other way round and Heath had to persuade him to honour an invitation to dine with the HAC on St George's Day on an evening when Churchill decided that his duties in Westminster precluded his attendance. In July 1953 Heath was one of the very few leading Tories who knew about Churchill's stroke and realised that the country was in effect being governed by a cabal of self-appointed substitutes. He was present when Churchill made his first speech after his illness at the Party Conference at Margate. By mistake the Prime Minister's private secretary had left in both the original and an amended version of a certain page. Churchill began to repeat himself. 'The Chief Whip and I looked at each other and shuddered. This must be the end of the road, I thought.' But then Churchill stopped, rallied, remarked blandly: 'I seem to have heard this somewhere before ...' and moved on to the next page. Heath was conscientious in presenting new Tory members to the old hero. Nigel Nicolson was already unnerved by the prospect and he was made no calmer when, as they approached the comatose figure in the smoking room, Heath murmured: 'Remember, Winston simply hates small talk!'[34]

The relationship was not purely official. The visitors' book for Chartwell, Churchill's country home, shows that Heath stayed there nine times between 1957 and 1961, once finding himself expected to play poker for high stakes with Aristotle and Christina Onassis. Churchill liked him well enough to give him two of his paintings. He was an unlikely habitué of Chartwell. The young men whose company Churchill usually enjoyed were more socially accomplished – Jock Colville, Anthony Montague Browne – or more raffish – Brendan Bracken – than Ted Heath. Heath's musical interests had only limited appeal to Churchill; his dedicated sense of purpose, though no doubt seeming admirable to the veteran statesman, was not calculated to amuse or stimulate. Nevertheless, Churchill clearly enjoyed his company. Mary Soames, Churchill's daughter, believes that it was probably her mother who was primarily responsible for the repeated invitations. Heath's social ineptness and his patent inadequacy when it came to handling women inspired in some a protective instinct. Clementine Churchill would not have been the only woman who took pity on him and resolved to make his task a little smoother than it would otherwise have been. He was appropriately appreciative and continued to invite Lady Churchill to lunches or dinners long after Churchill had died, taking pains to assemble small parties of old friends who would give her pleasure and impose no strain.[35]

As the Prime Minister visibly faded, Heath inevitably saw more of his designated successor, Anthony Eden. He felt for the Foreign Secretary none of the reverence that he held for Churchill but he admired and liked him and believed he would make a worthy incumbent of Number 10. He felt, too, that the sooner Eden got there, the better it would be, both for the country and for the party. Like many others, he wished that Churchill had retired after, or better still before, the defeat of 1945. He was not close enough to Eden to discuss directly with him his views about the succession; but Eden can have been in little doubt that Heath would prove a stalwart supporter. He for his part valued Heath highly and had no doubt that one of his first actions when he did finally become Prime Minister would be to appoint him his Chief Whip.

It was presumably as a reward for faithful service that Heath in August and September 1954 was despatched as deputy Conservative leader of a delegation to a Commonwealth Parliamentary Association Conference in Nairobi. He took advantage of the visit to travel widely throughout Africa, ending up in Cape Town. His reception reflected more his likely future than his actual status; wherever he went he met the leading figures of the country. It is a reflection of the times rather than of his own predilections that, except in Egypt, he did not talk at length with anybody who was not of European origin. Cairo provided the most interesting meeting. At dinner at the British Embassy Heath met Colonel Nasser, the young nationalist firebrand who was shortly to depose the President, Neguib, and take over the leadership himself. The two men sat in the Embassy garden in the small hours of the morning, talking about politics and the future of the Middle East. At that time the United Kingdom still had a substantial garrison in the Canal Zone; Heath was left in little doubt that it could only be maintained, and the Canal kept under British control, if the Egyptians could be persuaded that this was to their benefit. Heath was impressed by Nasser and thought that, though he would certainly champion Egyptian interests, he was in no way anti-British. Nasser talked of his wish to bring democracy to Egypt and of the problems he was encountering. 'I am sure that his intentions were sincere,' commented Heath, 'although perhaps at that stage he underestimated the task ahead.'[36] The favourable view that he took of Nasser was to be an additional cause for discomfort when the Suez Crisis split the Tory party and the country two years later.

Before that, however, much was to happen. In April 1955 Churchill finally resigned. His successor, Eden, almost immediately called a general election; he could have held on for another year or more but the economy seemed to be going well, the nation was glowing in the false dawn of the 'New Elizabethan Age', the temptation to go to the country, demand a fresh mandate and, with reasonable luck, secure a substantially increased majority proved irresistible. The gamble, in so far as it was one, paid off. The Tories cruised to victory, gaining an overall majority of 59. Heath, faced with a new and not particularly impressive Labour candidate, increased his own majority to 4,499. No longer did Bexley have to be considered a marginal constituency. Eden deferred a major cabinet reshuffle until the end of the year. As a preliminary, Buchan-Hepburn, who was to become Minister of Works, resigned as Chief Whip. He had no doubt who should succeed him. Nor did Eden: 'Ted Heath took over as Chief Whip; by what seemed a natural process,' he told Heath's biographer, George Hutchinson.[37] In December 1954 the next stage of Heath's career began.

SIX

Chief Whip

'Painless flagellation is what we are all looking forward to,' wrote Fitzroy Maclean – then a junior minister – when Heath's promotion was announced. Derek Marks of the *Daily Express* doubted whether this would work: 'I still think you have far too much sympathy with the chaps who smoke in the rugger team to make a very good head prefect.' Anthony Wedgwood Benn, as Tony Benn then still styled himself, from the opposition, thought he would bring it off: 'How you manage to combine such a friendly manner with such an iron discipline is a source of respectful amazement to us all.'[1] Benn caught exactly what was Heath's aspiration: he did not wish to over-emphasise the iron discipline but knew that it was a vital part of a Chief Whip's role; he believed that he could exercise it with restraint and liberality. Sir Thomas Moore, a veteran Tory MP and perhaps extravagantly uncritical admirer of Heath, told him that he had known six Chief Whips but that Heath was different because he had 'the capacity of making friends easily. That may make things much easier for you, or it may not … I believe that under that friendly smile you have the strength of character to make an outstanding success of this job.' Comforting though such assurances might be, Heath had no illusions about the scale of the problems which faced him. He believed he could overcome them. 'In this post,' the Archbishop of Canterbury assured him, 'you will spend your time controlling the uncontrollable and reconciling the irreconcilable! But, after all, that is the best kind of life.' Throughout his career, even when the facts pointed most vigorously to the contrary, Heath believed that the uncontrollable could always be controlled, the irreconcilable reconciled. This was how he saw his future role.[2]

The most essential quality in a Chief Whip is loyalty. This Heath had in abundance. He saw himself as the servant of the Prime Minister, appointed by him and there to do his bidding. He could argue, point out the dangers, but in the last resort what the Prime Minister decided was law. Macmillan quoted Asquith as saying that a Chief Whip should have a 'large capacity for self-assertion and self-effacement'. This was true, he considered, but there was one characteristic even more important: 'absolute and undivided loyalty'. Heath had given him this 'without reserve'. Loyalty did not imply supine acquiescence. John Wyndham, Macmillan's most private private secretary, said that Heath was 'tremendously loyal' and also 'tremendously frank. I think he regarded himself as a conduit for conducting information about what the party was thinking.' But tremendous frankness must be as far as it went. Unlike a minister, a Chief Whip could not allow himself the luxury of a conscience. 'The resignation of a government Chief Whip on a major issue of policy would be a mortal blow to confidence in the government,' wrote Heath in his memoirs. 'For a Chief Whip to resign ... would be an act not only of utter disloyalty, but of wilful destruction.'[3]

This austere creed meant that Heath sometimes found himself arguing against the causes which he held most at heart. He told Geoffrey Rippon, a future minister in his government, that if he went on supporting motions in favour of Europe he would have to resign as parliamentary private secretary. Many years later Rippon reminded him of this. 'The jowls flipped. "Did I say that?" said Ted doubtfully. "If I did, it did not fit in with what I was doing behind the scenes!"'[4] This may have been true, but in front of the scenes he never even hinted at his real feelings. He 'soundly berated' a group of Tory backbenchers who had put down a parliamentary motion calling for British membership of the Community, and when John Rodgers remained unconvinced, he told him: 'For God's sake don't rock the boat.'[5]

A Chief Whip could not afford to have intimates; even among his fellow Whips there had to be a certain distance. But he needed friends, many friends, people with whom he could communicate easily and with natural confidence. To those who knew only the withdrawn and often curmudgeonly figure of later years it is hard to conceive Heath as mixing affably with all around him. Yet Gerald Nabarro, a man temperamentally as far removed from Heath as it is possible to imagine, claimed that he had more friends than almost any other politician; Benn, when he called on Heath to discuss the possible renunciation of his peerage, described him as 'a most amiable and friendly soul'.[6] But even in those early days he did not always find it easy to establish a quick rapport. He had a 'heart full of kindness', wrote Woodrow Wyatt, but there was also 'an element of reserve and awkwardness' which held him back: 'The warmth in him has never got out properly.' Jim Prior was in time to get to know him better than any other member of the House of Commons. He had quality and vision, wrote Prior, and 'even if he never dared to show it, he had a softer side which we understood. This enabled us to share things with him.'[7]

In the mid-1950s the softer side was more readily accessible and the ability, vastly important in a Chief Whip, to persuade people 'to share things' was immediately apparent. But he was resolved not to commit himself totally to any relationship, not to take sides or adopt partisan attitudes, not to use his influence to help those whom he had befriended. His career is pitted with the complaints of friends who felt that he had failed to reward or even thank them for their loyal support; the tendency grew more marked as his power to help grew greater, but even now a former Balliol friend was disgruntled when Heath refused to back his candidacy for a Sussex seat on the grounds that, as Chief Whip, he never interfered in such matters.[8] Inevitably he found himself having to suggest names for jobs or jobs for names: Robert Carr wanted a list of members who might 'like to have small directorships'; Quintin Hailsham dropped into his 'shell-like ear' the news that Lord Rothermere was trying to find a job for Neill Cooper and that Louis Spears badly wanted a peerage.[9] He took whatever action he felt necessary on such requests, but without enthusiasm and with an almost perverse reluctance to further the interests of those whom he liked or to whom he felt obliged.

Throughout his career he made up his mind slowly and with some reluctance. Michael Hughes-Young, one of his Junior Whips, remembered interminable meetings: 'Ted would chew a subject over and over and over again, not saying much himself.' But when he had finally come down one way or the other he was hard to shift and would fight his corner with resolution. It was not only the prime minister who got the benefit of his blunt advice. 'I've seen him be very tough with ministers,' said Hughes-Young, 'just telling them flatly that they couldn't do it, it wasn't on.' He was, indeed, more likely to be tough with ministers than with backbenchers. 'When we were lunching together,' wrote Eden's press secretary, William Clark, 'you mentioned the problem you had trying to explain to the public that you did not run the House of Commons on the authoritarian lines of a public school.'[10] He never succeeded in dispelling the illusion. Indeed, it was not wholly illusory. Authority had to be exercised. But it was done with discretion and good grace. When John Rodgers, an old ally of Heath's and parliamentary private secretary to David Eccles, the Minister of Education, rebelled over a bill about shop-closing hours, Heath came to see him, 'his Whip's face firmly on, and saying: "You can't be a pps and attack the government like this: you must make your choice."' Rodgers chose and resigned, but two years later he was offered a ministerial job and was urged by Heath to accept. Another backbencher, David Price, had to be sharply rebuked for straying out of line. 'I really must express my sincere appreciation of your attitude during our interview this evening,' wrote Price. 'You *had* to carpet me; I realise that, but you couldn't have been nicer or more gentle about it.'[11]

Not all members were so ready to take correction. Sir William Anstruther-Gray, a Tory of the old school who probably took exception to Heath's social origins and relative youth as well as to the fact that he was being rebuked for missing a three-line Whip, retorted haughtily: 'I am not a member of the government, paid to take orders. I am a private member, returned by my constituents to support the party and prime minister *as I think best* ... I shall continue to work for the party and prime minister as I think best and, while on the subject, I shall *not* be available to vote on Thursday, 8th.'[12] Since the gravamen of the Chief Whip's complaint had been that Anstruther-Gray had given no warning of his absence, Heath probably let the matter rest – but a black mark would have been registered against the errant member. Not many others would have been similarly defiant. The notably independent-minded Hugh Fraser arrived at a dinner party announcing that the debate that evening was on a matter of trivial importance and that he had no intention of returning to vote. An hour later the telephone rang and the servant reported that it was the Chief Whip for Mr Fraser. Fraser left without waiting for the pudding. Heath was the last Whip to act as teller during crucial votes; on certain issues he stood by the Opposition entrance so that any rebel would have to file by directly in front of him.[13]

He was particularly hard on any behaviour that he thought might bring discredit to the House. When the Tory MP for Dorset North, Robert Crouch, touted for business on House of Commons writing paper, Heath summoned him and sternly pointed out the impropriety of his behaviour. Crouch promised to mend his ways but shortly afterwards died, leaving many unpaid bills and an indigent widow. Heath was active in raising funds so that Mrs Crouch was not left in too parlous a state.[14] If he felt a member was not and never would be up to the job he would not hesitate to plan for his replacement. He thought badly of the member for Oxford, Lawrence Turner, and did what he could to arrange a change. When Harold Macmillan was asked to drop in at the Cowley Conservative Club after a dinner in Oxford, Heath urged him to take up the invitation: 'It would be important that the prospective candidate, the Hon Montague Woodhouse, is at the Club in order to receive the benefit of this rather than Mr Turner.' Sometimes, in the eye of the victim at least, he seems to have behaved with some insensitivity. When Airey Neave, a junior minister, resigned in 1959, he was told bleakly that his political career was over. 'Airey deeply resented the way he felt he had been discarded and the way it had been done,' remembered Margaret Thatcher's future minister, Norman Fowler. Fifteen years later Neave got his revenge. Only somebody who had been present at the original interview could tell how justified his resentment really was. Another version has it that it was alcohol rather than illness that had forced Neave's retirement and that Heath's harshness was therefore justified. The story shows, however, that no Chief Whip, however tactful and emollient, could do his job properly without making some enemies along the way.[15]

More often, however, Heath was trying to persuade members *not* to retire at a time when it might prove damaging to the party. When the famous former fighter pilot 'Laddie' Lucas reported that he felt his employment as managing director of the White City stadium was stopping him from doing a proper job as an MP, Heath replied that there had been no complaints from his constituents and that 'as it would be very difficult for anybody else to hold his seat, it was his duty to carry on'. Lucas temporarily agreed but, two months later, wrote from holiday in Italy to say that he had finally decided to resign. 'Italy seems to have a fatal effect on everyone's ideas of both love and duty!' wrote Heath resignedly.[16] Sometimes he was more successful. Derick Heathcoat-Amory, then Chancellor of the Exchequer, told Heath late in 1958 that he wanted to retire and 'spend his declining years in some useful form of service' (a curious reflection on his estimation of his actual job). Heath persuaded him that it was his duty to soldier on, at least until the next election.[17]

Another desirable quality for a Chief Whip is to be invariably equable. Here Heath was less than perfect. He always suffered from a short temper and was apt to explode if opposed in any way which he felt pig-headed and unreasonable. 'He was fratchety as Chief Whip,' said one not particularly rebellious member. 'He can be very huffy if you don't agree with him.' Humphry Berkeley, a left-wing Tory back-bencher, was lunching with a friend in the Carlton Club in 1956, discussing the capital punishment bill which was then being debated in the Commons. Heath joined them and tried to persuade them to accept the compromise proposal supported by the Government, which retained the death penalty but only for four categories of murder. He failed, whereupon, according to Berkeley, he 'became abusive; he called us soft and then relapsed into a sullen silence, refusing to join us for coffee afterwards ... We were shocked at this display of anger and rudeness on the part of the Government Chief Whip.'[18] The anecdote is the more striking because Heath's personal conviction was that the death penalty should be abolished. It was another example of his belief that a Chief Whip could have no views of his own, or at least none that he would own to publicly. It was also uncharacteristic: the explosion of bad temper was not unheard of but, at this stage of his career at least, the sustained sulk was unusual. He must have been in an exceptionally fratchety mood that day.

'You'll remember asking last Saturday what I thought about a certain person's private affairs,' the veteran Tory politician, Harry Crookshank, wrote mysteriously. He recommended an approach to the Queen's private secretary.[19] It was but one of many such covert communications. Heath constantly had to enquire into the private affairs of one person or another, and usually found the task distasteful. Peter Baker, the member for South Norfolk, was an alcoholic whose businesses had failed badly. He tried to persuade Heath that he was now a reformed character but the Deputy Chief Whip, as Heath then was, insisted he should resign. Baker refused, though promising not to stand at the next election. 'What is to be done?' asked the Prime Minister. Nothing, replied Heath, 'short of guiding his hand to sign an application for the Chiltern Hundreds,* which would have been particularly dangerous as he is in a Nursing Home under the care of a doctor'. Eventually Baker was charged with forgery and sent to prison.[20]

Another scandal erupted in 1965, when Alec Home was Prime Minister. Anthony Courtney, a Tory MP, had been photographed in Moscow – presumably by the KGB – in flagrante with an attractive Intourist guide. Courtney went to see Heath and found him 'wholly unsympathetic' and showing 'a complete absence of that human quality of personal involvement which to me at any rate is the mark of true leadership towards a colleague in trouble'. He does, indeed, seem to have been unusually disobliging. If Courtney insisted on making a personal statement in the House, Heath said, he could not

* A sinecure appointment, the acceptance of which involved resignation of a parliamentary seat.

expect to get any support from the Government. He should go quietly. Heath always found it hard to understand or condone the sexual misdemeanours of others but in most cases he did his best to be sympathetic. On this occasion it seems probable that Courtney had been given a damning report by MI5 and that Heath had been advised to have nothing to do with him.[21]

'It was commonly believed', wrote the future Chairman of the Conservative Party, Edward du Cann, 'that his four years as Chief Whip had given him a healthy contempt for his fellow members of parliament in the Conservative party.' Certainly he had little respect for the Crouches and Courtneys of this world but 'contempt' is too strong a word to describe his attitude towards the rank and file of the party. His time as Chief Whip did, however, foster a conviction that members were cannon fodder, to be deployed according to the needs of the Government and without much consideration for their personal feelings. When Peter Walker was 22, Heath came to address his constituency party. He told its members that they should not be worried about Walker's youth: 'Be assured that when he gets into the House of Commons I shall, as Chief Whip, have no difficulty in guiding him.' He no doubt meant it as a joke but, like many of his jokes, it misfired: the audience was not particularly amused and Walker was furious. Joke or not, the remark conveyed something of Heath's true feelings: it was for him to guide, it was the duty of members to be guided. This cast of mind was not to make things easier for him when in due course he became leader of the party.[22]

There was a noticeable change of style when Heath took over as Chief Whip. Buchan-Hepburn had devoted what Heath felt to be a disproportionate amount of his time to ensuring that the requisite number of MPs passed through the appropriate lobby. Heath saw the importance of this function but felt that it was still more important to ensure that the Prime Minister and Cabinet were at every point fully aware of the feelings within the party. In his biography John Campbell observed that Heath had delegated less responsibility to his deputy, Martin Redmayne, than Buchan-Hepburn had been willing to grant him. 'Greater', wrote Heath in the margin. Up to a point this was true.

Redmayne was left in charge of operations on the floor of the House to an extent which Heath had never been. But this says more about Heath's order of priorities than his opinion of his number two. In his memoirs he praised Redmayne as an 'excellent deputy' who did a fine job looking after the daily machinery in the House of Commons, but in an unguarded interview, the text of which survives in his archive, he remarks that, as Chief Whip, he was much more concerned with policy than about 'chasing people in the House of Commons'. Martin Redmayne, he went on, 'did all the chasing, which he enjoyed. He was really a military type, he owned a sports shop, and he was really very dim.'[23]

The Chief Whip was not formally a member of the Cabinet but Heath was present at almost every meeting and increasingly behaved as if he belonged there as of right. He saw this as being a perquisite of his office, not a tribute to him personally. Against Campbell's statement that Willie Whitelaw had never sat in a Cabinet before 1970, he scrawled 'Chief Whip'. Under Eden, and later still more under Macmillan, Heath intervened in Cabinet not just to report on the feeling in the party but to make points of policy. In a discussion of the Tory manifesto in the summer of 1959 R. A. Butler urged the inclusion of a pledge to revise the laws relating to betting and gambling. 'I don't know about that,' said Macmillan. 'We already have the Toby Belch vote. We must not antagonise the Malvolio vote.' Everyone chuckled dutifully. 'Then', remembered Butler, 'the Chief Whip, ever business-like and forceful, intervened by pointing out that we had committed ourselves to such reforms.' That settled the matter. Eden appreciated his abilities and valued his advice: 'I have never known a better equipped Chief Whip,' he wrote. 'A ready smile confirmed a firm mind.'[24]

A majority of fifty-nine meant that the policing of the lobbies, however much Redmayne might have enjoyed it, could be reasonably relaxed. 'The party is not vociferous about anything,' Heath told Eden after a meeting of the 1922 Committee in February 1956, 'neither does it appear to be particularly enthusiastic about any particular course of action, it is quietly awaiting economic events and the budget.' In his penetrating study of back-bench opinion, Robert Jackson has shown that there was more unrest within the party ranks than Heath's comments suggest. The fact that the Government was unlikely to be defeated meant that backbenchers allowed themselves greater latitude in promoting personal or constituency points. Most of the issues related to domestic matters: purchase tax, licensing, the coal industry, rent control and government expenditure were all the subject of sometimes acrimonious debate. Between 1955 and 1958, Jackson reckons, there were thirteen revolts on domestic issues and eight on foreign affairs and defence.[25] None of these threatened the position of the Government. Apart from the Suez Crisis, the subject on which passions ran highest was the one that had provoked Heath's fracas with Humphry Berkeley in the Carlton Club, capital punishment. The ministers were insistent that their compromise proposals must prevail. Heath warned them that there were enough out-and-out abolitionists among the younger Tory members to mean that the Government would probably be defeated. He could not convince the Cabinet that it should modify its views. Loyally, he worked to persuade the recalcitrant backbenchers to withdraw from a cause which he himself had at heart. Sir Thomas Moore claimed that no Whip had tried to influence his vote on the issue, but as he was himself a defender of the death penalty he did not seem likely to reject the party line. Berkeley was only one of many would-be reformists to be approached. In the case of the young MP, Peter Kirk, it is said that Heath even threatened to use the ultimate sanction available to a Chief Whip: to denounce the erring member to his local constituency association. It made no difference; the Government lost by almost exactly the amount that Heath had predicted.[26]

The imposition of prescription charges late in 1956 provides an illuminating snapshot of the Whips at work. This was an issue on which people felt strongly but not with the passion provoked by capital punishment. Busily, the Whips canvassed opinions and did their sums. 'Price thinks we should exclude all OAPs.' 'P Forth hoped the Whips had taken note of the party's strong disapproval. *This will be very serious.*' John Vaughan-Morgan wanted a preliminary discussion in the 1922 Committee. Philip Remnant 'is still determined not to vote for the charges', but, a day later, 'I think he is weakening a little'.

Julian Ridsdale is 'very shaky and liable to vote against'. John Eden is 'all worked up, though I don't think he will oppose actively'. And so it went on. In the end Heath was able to tell the Cabinet that, at the price of a few conciliatory noises, their majority was secure. Nearly always the Whips were successful. On 28 June 1956 the 1922 Committee was almost unanimous in its opposition to an American take-over of Trinidad. On 4 July no Tory voted against it and only one abstained. 'This was considered a text-book case of brilliant whipping.'[27]

These were mere storms in a teacup, however, compared with the hurricane that was about to break. In July 1956 Nasser nationalised the Suez Canal. When the issue was first raised in the House of Commons, the Leader of the Opposition, Hugh Gaitskell, supported the Government, provided that the problem was handled through the United Nations. It seemed that a bipartisan approach might be possible, but Heath saw trouble ahead and warned Eden not to count on Labour support. As preparations went ahead for an attack on Egypt and the reoccupation of the Canal Zone, regardless of the United Nations and world opinion, it became clear that not only would Labour oppose such action but that the Tory Party was divided. Initially, Heath thought that this threat was small. Towards the end of August he told the Egypt Committee – the inner group which handled the crisis and which he regularly attended – that he was 'pretty sure about the party, though there might be some weaker brethren'. To William Clark he said that nobody would revolt and that 'it won't cause much bother in parliament because there are no leaders on the Conservative side to cause trouble'. Two or three weeks later the mood had changed. Heath reported that there were three groups: those who would support any action; those who would accept it, but only after reference to the United Nations; and those who were opposed to the use of force. 'The Chief Whip cannot estimate the strength of this group. It might be large enough to put us in a minority in a division.'[28]

Though Heath must have suspected what was going on, it was not until almost the end of October that Eden told him of the plot that was being hatched with Israel to circumvent the tortuous negotiations in the United Nations. Israel was to invade Egypt: Britain and France would then intervene to separate the contestants. 'This is the highest form of statesmanship,' Eden declared – 'rather unnervingly', in the view of his Chief Whip. If Heath was unnerved he concealed it well. His personal position was singularly difficult. He did not share Eden's conviction that Nasser could be equated with Hitler and that the nationalisation of the Canal was another Munich crisis over which the West could not afford to fail. He believed that an honourable if imperfect solution could be reached through the United Nations. He felt that military intervention without the endorsement of the United Nations would be at the best extremely dangerous, at the worst disastrous. His doubts were evident to a few insiders. According to the Secretary of the Cabinet, Norman Brook, the sceptics in the Cabinet were Butler, Walter Monckton, Macleod, the Earl of Selkirk, Chancellor of the Duchy of Lancaster, possibly the Lord Chancellor, Kilmuir and Derrick Heathcoat-Amory and certainly, though strictly speaking he was not a member, Edward Heath.[29] Yet he hugged his true opinions to himself. When, fifteen years later, Willie Whitelaw was asked what he believed were Heath's views on Suez, he replied: 'Do you know, I have no idea. He does keep his own counsel very much. I have a suspicion, but such a tiny suspicion that I couldn't venture it.' Certainly Heath did not see it as being his role to try to convert the Prime Minister; he was doing his duty if he brought home to Eden the misgivings in the party. An old friend from Oxford, Robert Shackleton, urged him to resign: 'You *must* agree Government policy is disastrous. I implore you to put first things first. The resignation of the Chief Whip would do more than any other single thing to rescue the country. I beg you to consider it.' It was just because his resignation would have been so seismic in its consequences that he would not consider it. And if he could not resign, then it was his duty to try to persuade every member of the parliamentary party to support the government.[30]

But when it was a case of working on members opposed to military intervention – in particular the eleven MPs, among whom Keith Joseph and Bob Boothby were the most prominent, who signed a letter demanding that British troops should be placed under the command of the United Nations – his approach was notably dulcet.

It was also on the whole successful. Just before a crucial vote on 8 November he was seen exhorting two young MPs, Peter Kirk and David Price, who were known to be planning to abstain. He warned them that, if they did so, they might destroy the Government and, incidentally, their own futures. His arguments prevailed. But he was less successful with Nigel Nicolson. 'I still believe it cannot be a bad thing for the party', Nicolson told Heath, 'that there should be at least one Conservative backbencher who is prepared to state he agrees with the very many eminent Conservatives outside this House who have expressed their distress at the Government's action.' Eventually Nicolson said that he would support the Government if the Chief Whip would assure him 'that the purpose of our invasion was "to separate the combatants", as the Prime Minister claimed and not to regain control of the Canal by a subterfuge. He held my gaze steadily and said nothing. I thanked him for his honesty, told him that I would abstain, and left the room.'[31] When Anthony Nutting, a junior minister at the Foreign Office, resigned in protest at the Government's action, a campaign to discredit him was launched, hinting that there were malign influences at work and that he had personal reasons for his behaviour, unconnected with the merits of the case. As often as not this sort of campaign would have had its origins in the Whips' Office. It is hard to prove a negative but it would have been wholly out of character if Heath had lent his authority to such an operation. Again and again in the course of his career he refused to make use of damaging gossip, even though he believed it to be true. The sort of disinformation used to blacken Nutting's reputation would have repelled him. If such a campaign was in fact mounted it was more probably the work of somebody in Number 10.[32]

But both wings of the party were in revolt. One group objected to intervention; the other, the 'Suez Group', was outraged when the government succumbed to overwhelming American pressure and agreed to withdraw from Egypt. The latter were more numerous, more clamorous and, in Heath's eyes, less worthy of sympathy. He treated them altogether more roughly. When Patrick Maitland said that he could not in conscience support the party, the Chief Whip exploded: 'I'm fed up with your bloody consciences. I'm going to get on to your constituency.' According to Maitland, he did so and was rebuffed. Maitland went public on the 'extraordinary and unexampled pressures – some of them altogether underhand', to which he and his fellow rebels had been subjected. That Labour hatchet-man, George Wigg, tried to raise the matter as a breach of parliamentary privilege but the Speaker ruled that 'the work of the Whips had never been thought to be a matter of privilege'. There were very few occasions during his term of office as Chief Whip that Heath could legitimately be accused of going too far, of straying beyond the boundaries of propriety. That it was the Suez Group who provoked such conduct perhaps reflects his uneasy conscience at having pressed the opponents of intervention to vote for a course of action which he himself felt to be morally wrong and politically inexpedient. He could not publicly condone their behaviour if they rejected his pleas but he could express his true feelings by the added vigour with which he denounced rebels from the other wing. He turned to John Biggs-Davidson, a rabid member of the Suez Group, and told him: 'You were a Communist before the war and now you are nothing but a bloody Fascist.' Some years later he was asked if he had really used such words. Heath reflected for a movement. 'I didn't say "nothing but",' he concluded.[33]

Whatever his personal views, he could not disguise the fact that a substantial element in the party, both inside and outside parliament, was deeply dissatisfied with the Government's conduct of the Suez crisis. On the whole he handled such protests with tact and moderation. When Lawrence Turner abstained on a critical vote on the grounds that 'the present Government has betrayed basic Conservative principles and been disloyal to everything for which the party stands', Heath replied mildly that he appreciated Turner's honesty but wished that he had expressed his views a little earlier so as to allow time for ministers to explain their position to him.[34] He was disconcerted to find how strongly anti-American even some of the less extreme members had become; there were reports from the smoking room that names were being collected for resolutions calling for the admission of Red China into the United Nations and the nationalisation of the Panama Canal.

Like the after-shocks that follow an earthquake, the Suez crisis continued to plague the Tory Party for the next two or three years. In mid-1957 the Suez Group once more caused trouble when it was proposed to resume paying Canal dues to Egypt. At one point it seemed as if as many as thirty members would abstain, though in the end only eight remained seated ostentatiously in their places. The venom was going out of the campaign, however, and by the end of the year the obdurate hard core who had forfeited the party whip were asking for talks which might lead to their return. Philip de Zulueta, the Prime Minister's private secretary, consulted Heath. The Chief Whip, de Zulueta reported, 'thought that you should not be forthcoming about this suggestion. He was anxious that it should still remain cold outside.' Heath was more forgiving when it came to the tribulations of Nigel Nicolson. Nicolson, a bookish intellectual of markedly liberal views, had never been happy in his constituency of Bournemouth where his stance over Suez had caused great offence. Early in 1957 a mutiny broke out. 'There is no doubt that the Association has every intention of getting rid of Nigel Nicolson in spite of reasonable pressure from me not to do so,' Heath told the party chairman. All he would do was discourage those right-wingers who were hungry for a safe seat from taking any action while Nicolson was still the member. Nicolson was duly deselected by his constituency and told the Chief Whip that he felt his situation would be impossible if he did not resign the seat immediately. 'Don't believe that for a moment,' Heath encouraged him. 'Nobody feels anything but respect for your attitude. You have done well and served the party most creditably.' Nicolson was moved and delighted: Heath, he told his father, 'was quite clearly speaking with real conviction, and not as a formal condolence'.[35] But a year later came another 'distressing but amicable interview'. A bill concerning obscene publications was passing through the House of Commons with support from both parties. The publishing house in which Nicolson was a partner, Weidenfeld & Nicolson, chose this moment to publish Nabokov's *Lolita*, a brilliantly written yet curiously distasteful masterpiece about the passion felt by a middle-aged man for a pubescent twelve-year-old nymphet. It threatened to cause a scandal, was denounced as corrupting, and, Heath believed, would complicate the passage of the bill. He asked Weidenfeld and Nicolson at least to postpone publication. George Weidenfeld, however, would not hear of it: *Lolita* duly appeared, caused the anticipated furore and had no noticeable effect on the progress of the bill. When Heath first approached the publishers about the book Nicolson asked him whether he had read it. Yes, said Heath; he had found it 'rather boring'. Some people have been sickened by *Lolita*, many were moved, excited or discomposed. Few can have been bored. Heath was genuinely at a loss, unable to see what all the fuss was about. Unlike *Lolita* and the bill, Nicolson's parliamentary career perished at the next election.[36]

Heath was one of the very few people who survived the Suez crisis with their reputation substantially enhanced. It had been a disaster for the Conservative Party, and but for him it would have been a catastrophe. The Lord Chancellor, David Kilmuir, described him as 'the most brilliant Chief Whip of modern times ... the most promising of the new generation of Conservatives'. The quiet skill with which he had handled the party had been exemplary: 'While never showing any weaknesses or forgetting his responsibility to the Government, Heath calmly and gently shepherded the party through a crisis which might have broken it.' The Chief Whip was the one man of whom he had not heard a word of criticism, wrote the Secretary of State for Scotland, James Stuart. 'There has been nothing but praise for the fair and impartial manner in which you have handled a most difficult situation.' Till the time of Suez Heath had been respected and well liked but something of a back-room boy; from 1957 he was clearly a coming man.[37]

Apart from the credit he personally had gained, there was for Heath one redeeming feature about the crisis. Until the end of 1956 many Tories had continued to believe that Britain, at the centre of a still worldwide empire, could go on playing the role of a great power while isolated from the continent of Europe. Now he believed even the most sceptical must see that Britain's future lay 'in our own continent and not in distant lands which our forefathers had coloured pink on the map'. Even Eden, in one of the last memoranda he circulated as Prime Minister, acknowledged that a consequence of the disaster might be 'to determine us to work more closely with Europe'. He was not to survive to implement such a policy himself. Heath had felt it essential that Eden should go from the moment when, on 20 December, he heard the Prime Minister deny that he had any foreknowledge of Israel's invasion of Egypt: 'I felt like burying my head in my hands at the sight of this man I so much admired maintaining this fiction.' A few hours later he met Norman Brook leaving the Cabinet Room. 'He's told me to destroy all the relevant documents,' Brook said. 'I must go and get it done.'[38] But no hecatomb of incriminating papers could eliminate the evidence, nor great Neptune's ocean wash the blood from Eden's hands. It was only a question of how many days or weeks he could survive. On 8 January 1957 he summoned Heath to the Cabinet Room and told him that he was going to resign.

The two obvious successors were R. A. Butler and Harold Macmillan. Heath liked them both and would willingly have served under either, but he believed that Macmillan was better qualified to rebuild the shattered party. More to the point, he knew that the majority of Tories in the country felt the same. Pat Hornsby-Smith was only one of many members who reported meetings of constituents at which the scuttle from Suez had been denounced and who had demanded 'new leaders who would back Britain'. The Tory voters, she claimed, were convinced that Butler was 'the villain appeaser'. The fact that Macmillan had been the most insistent in demanding that the British and French must withdraw was either unknown or forgotten: Butler was seen as craven-hearted, Christopher Hollis wrote in *Punch*:

> There was a man called Edward Heath
> Who looked a gift horse in the teeth.
> Ted Heath who, you must understand
> Is not the leader of the band,
> But is the chap who has to say
> What instruments the others play.
> He told a bean, who told a bean,
> Who told a bean who told the Queen,

> We really must have someone subtler
> Than Mr Richard Austen Butler.
> A proper man, and what is properer
> Than take a fellow out of opera
> And build him up as large as life
> The character of Mac the Knife?[39]

So far as Heath was concerned there was only one bean involved and he was Michael Adeane, the Queen's private secretary. Heath told him that, by a substantial majority, the party would prefer Macmillan and that he personally agreed. His was not the decisive voice, but he spoke for the backbenchers and must have carried a lot of weight. It was to Heath that fell the unpleasant task of telling Butler that he was not to be Prime Minister. 'Look after him, for he's a very solitary figure just at present, and he relies on you,' Butler's private secretary, Ian Bancroft, wrote to urge him. There was no way by which Heath could make palatable the news that, in spite of the confident predictions in almost all the morning papers that Butler would be the next Prime Minister, the Queen had sent for Macmillan. 'He looked utterly dumbfounded.'[40]

In his memoirs Heath pays the most fulsome compliments to the new Prime Minister. Macmillan possessed, he says, 'by far the most constructive mind I have encountered in a lifetime of politics'; he showed 'a generous spirit and unquenchable desire to help the underdog'; he was 'more than anyone else, my political mentor and my patron'. This may not have been the whole story. Several people have remarked that Heath was sometimes irritated by Macmillan's sedulously cultivated insouciance; Kenneth Baker goes so far as to suggest that he disliked him and sometimes made disparaging remarks about him. Nor was Macmillan without reservations in his championship of his Chief Whip. He once told his future biographer Alistair Horne that Heath did not possess the qualities of a prime minister. 'Hengist and Horsa', he went on, 'were very dull people. Now, as you know, they colonised Kent; consequently the people of Kent have ever since been very slightly – well, you know ... Ted was an excellent Chief Whip ... a first class staff officer, but no army commander.'[41]

So far as most people could see, however, the relationship was notably harmonious: certainly each man found the other extremely useful, if not indispensable. It was Heath whom Macmillan took with him to dine at the Turf Club on the night after he had taken over. 'Had any good shooting lately?' asked a fellow member when the Prime Minister entered the dining room; then, as he left some time later, 'Oh, by the way, congratulations'. The dinner took place in the course of discussions about the shape of the new Government. Changes were kept to a minimum but some new blood had to be introduced and many hopes were disappointed. 'It was a *most* difficult and exhausting task,' Macmillan wrote in his diary. 'Without the help of Edward Heath, who was quite admirable, we couldn't have done it.' Heath himself was one of the disappointed. He realised that he was bound to stay where he was – 'The Government is like a regiment,' he remarked. 'You can't change the CO and the adjutant at the same time' – but he still felt a pang of jealousy when Reginald Maudling was made Paymaster General with a brief to concentrate on Britain's relationship with Europe. It was the task which he coveted above all others.[42]

But he had no reason to complain that he was treated with lack of consideration. Heath, an unidentified minister told Andrew Roth early in 1958, 'is probably the most influential man around the Prime Minister today. The PM consults him about practically everything.' Should the Prime Minister accept an invitation to dine with the Progress Trust? He should. How should he reply to a rather cheeky letter from the backbencher Martin Lindsay? 'I have always found that a snub works and does not lead to increased heat.' Should he visit Northern Ireland? Yes. If he were able to visit Lord Brookeborough at his country home it would be a most enjoyable and worthwhile experience.[43] He was the central figure in the preparation of party political broadcasts, was closely involved in the selection or de-selection of MPs, and worked with the party chairman on political honours. When the time came to prepare a manifesto for the next election, the Steering Committee charged with drafting it consisted of Butler, Alec Home, Hailsham, Macleod and the Chief Whip; he was equally included in the inner group of Macmillan's most intimate advisers – Norman Brook, Philip de Zulueta, John Wyndham – who met informally for half an hour several times a week.[44]

He never hesitated to speak his mind. Early in 1958 the Government found itself inexplicably – in its own mind at least – unpopular. Things came to a head when the Liberal candidate won a by-election in Rochdale and the Tory was pushed into third place. The Steering Committee met to consider this disaster. Macleod identified the Liberals as the most dangerous enemy, who must be destroyed. Heath questioned whether they should be treated as enemy. They had much in common with the Conservatives, more so than with Labour. The Tories in the past had largely maintained themselves by absorbing other parties; if they were now to do a deal with the Liberals this would surely again be the final result. It was a line to which he was to revert several times over the next decades. On this occasion he met with a mixed reception. Home supported him; Hailsham strongly backed Macleod; as is usually the case with such debates it grumbled on until the circumstances which had engendered it no longer pertained and the issue became irrelevant.[45]

It was maintaining the cohesion and loyalty of the party, however, that was his chief preoccupation, and the gauge by which the success of his tenure as Chief Whip would be judged. Many of the stresses within the party related to the disintegration of the empire, which had begun with the granting of independence to India and Pakistan in 1947, had gathered speed after Suez and was now to be accelerated still further by Macmillan. Heath was far from being a dedicated imperialist, but he had to manage a vociferous right wing which bitterly resented the humiliation of Suez and was resolved that no further scuttles should be permitted. The first battlefield was Malta. In this case the proposal was not that Malta should become independent but that it should be wholly integrated with the United Kingdom. Maltese members would sit in the House of Commons; all tariffs or restrictions on movement between the two countries would be abolished. The hard-core Suez Group, supported in this case by many moderates, broke into a clamorous protest. A six-line Whip would be needed to get the proposals through, said John Peyton; William Teeling announced that he and his friends would not merely vote against it in the House but would hold public meetings up and down the country in protest. Heath reported to Alan Lennox-Boyd that the executive of the 1922 Committee foresaw 'very great trouble in the Party if the proposals for integration were proceeded with'. He calculated that a minimum of forty-eight Tory members would vote against the Government. In the event the Maltese Government declared that it would not take the matter further unless it were offered independence as an alternative to integration. With some relief the Colonial Office dropped this uncomfortably hot potato and the incipient mutiny died away.[46]

Cyprus provided a more typical battleground. Archbishop Makarios had been exiled in March 1956, but it was obvious to most people that sooner or later he must be allowed to return and that the Greek majority on the island was determined to have him as its leader. Negotiations were under way. The Tory right wing passionately rejected any such solution. Busily the Whips reported to Heath on feelings in the party. Wolrige-Gordon 'feels that God does not agree with our conduct of the Cyprus negotiations. We will have trouble with him when the debate comes.' Henry Legge-Bourke was 'more angry over the Cyprus settlement than he was over Suez'. Cyril Black said that Makarios's return would 'provoke an explosion in the House and the country among our own supporters'. The figures were remarkably similar to those on Malta; this time Heath had to report that a minimum of forty-seven Tories were probable rebels. It was Makarios's insistence on enosis – union with Greece – which particularly offended the disaffected Tories; in the end he was cajoled into abandoning this position and the worst of the bitterness went out of the dispute.[47]

The most serious threat to Macmillan, however, came over domestic issues. In the autumn of 1957 the Chancellor, Peter Thorneycroft, insisted on cuts in public expenditure which departmental ministers were not prepared to accept. Macmillan dallied over intervening in the dispute and, when he did so, found that positions were so entrenched that he must expect resignations from one side or the other. Heath told him that Thorneycroft's intransigence had largely forfeited the support of the party, even those parts of it that were disposed to accept the logic of the Chancellor's position. The Government could survive the resignation of Thorneycroft and the other Treasury ministers. Macmillan took his advice and left the country on a six-week overseas tour, referring airily as he prepared to board the plane to the 'little local difficulty' which the Government was confronting. Heath was right: there was no revolt, nor even serious misgivings. His handling of the crisis had been 'superb', wrote Macmillan in his diary; Dorothy Macmillan doubted whether anyone realised 'the overwhelming regard and affection my husband has for Mr Heath'.[48]

By now it was evident to most people that Heath would, one day, be a serious contender for the leadership. R. A. Butler, in July 1958, was reporting 'intense personal rivalries' between Heath and Macleod. 'They are the same age and look anxiously to the throne. The Chief Whip's status has been raised to God Almighty by the PM asking him to every meeting on every subject at every hour of the day and night.' But divine though his status might have been, Heath was uncomfortably aware that he had enjoyed the role quite long enough for his own good. If his career was to prosper as he hoped it might, it was essential that he should soon be given a department of his own in which he could establish his credentials. The opportunity was not to be long delayed. A debilitating attack of jaundice early in 1959 kept him out of action for a couple of months and led him to take things slowly for a few weeks after that, but by the time Macmillan called a general election for 8 October he was fully recovered. Given the disastrous circumstances in which Macmillan had taken over, and the unpopularity which the party had experienced at the time of the Rochdale by-election, it was remarkable that the Conservatives went into the election as clear favourites. Heath was by no means complacent about his prospects at Bexley. His old adversary, Ashley Bramall, had returned to the fray and the seat, if no longer marginal, was still vulnerable to an adverse swing. Harold Macmillan came to speak for him during the campaign, saying that Heath represented 'everything that is best in the new progressive, modern Tory party ... He stands for the new philosophy and modern thought in the party. You send him back, for he is a good man.' The Prime Minister undoubtedly meant what he said, and was glad of a chance to say it, but he would hardly have bothered to make the trip to Bexley if it had seemed that the constituency was secure. As it turned out, his efforts were unnecessary. Nationally, the Conservatives increased their popular vote by half a million and gained an overall majority of a hundred. In Bexley Heath's majority went up to 8,500.[49]

His last job as Chief Whip was to help Macmillan form a new Government. His own future was quickly settled: he was to succeed Iain Macleod in the critically important and taxing role of Minister of Labour. Mrs Thatcher, as Margaret Roberts had now become, who had at last secured herself a safe seat, wrote to congratulate him and thank him for the telegram he had sent her on polling day. 'As you once said to me,' she wrote, 'even *I* could not lose Finchley. I am very sorry that you will not now be Chief Whip. I trust that Mr Redmayne will be no harder a taskmaster than you would have been.'[50]

SEVEN

Europe: The First Round

Heath had wanted the Ministry of Labour, wrote Macmillan, 'and it was only right, in view of all his services, that he should step into independent ministerial command'. In fact he had wanted the Board of Trade but that had been promised to Maudling. He was well satisfied with the alternative, knowing that his success or failure in the role would be critically important to the economic and social performance of the government. The history of the unions in post-war Britain suggested that this task, though difficult, would not be unmanageable. Walter Monckton in 1951 had set a pattern of conciliation which had been broadly continued by Iain Macleod; the unions for their part had been controlled by moderates who were almost as anxious to avoid confrontation as the ministers with whom they dealt. But there were signs that all might not run so smoothly in the future. On one side the Tory right wing was growing restive: strikes, though still relatively infrequent, were becoming more common. There were calls for the abolition of the closed shop and the political levy, and the introduction of secret balloting. Sir John Laing, a giant of the construction industry, wrote to the Prime Minister demanding a return to the discipline enjoyed during the Second World War and citing examples from the Continent to show that this would be generally acceptable. 'I can see no prospect of reverting to the wartime policy of combining a prohibition of strikes with a compulsory form of arbitration on industrial disputes,' commented

Heath. 'The industrial conditions in Switzerland are so different from ours that a comparison is not very fruitful.' He did not rule out legislation, yet he felt that the TUC must be given a chance to put its own house in order before the Government tried to impose its will on them.[1]

But, on the other side, the union leadership was becoming less disposed to take any steps which might satisfy the Tory right. The scene was still relatively tranquil. Though the stalwarts of the wartime years had now departed, the TUC was still largely in the hands of moderates. George Woodcock, the General Secretary, and his deputy, Vic Feather, were eminently reasonable or, as their left wing saw it, feeble. So were the majority of members of the General Council. When Macmillan wrote in dismay to Heath about a rumour that the TUC was proposing a boycott of South African goods – 'There are terrible dangers, especially for the heavy machinery business. In their present mood the Union of South Africa might retaliate by boycotting mining machinery and all the rest of it' – Heath replied soothingly that all was under control. He would talk to Tom Williamson, 'one of the more level-headed members of the General Council', and was sure that the TUC would show restraint. So, for the moment, it did, but with Frank Cousins in charge of the giant Transport and General Workers' Union (TGWU) it was clear that the industrial scene was likely to grow more tempestuous. Arthur Scargill and his like were still a distant menace, but Scargill was already ensconced in his local branch of the National Union of Mineworkers (NUM) and still a member of the Young Communist League. The problems that Heath was to confront in the mid-1970s had their genesis fifteen years before.[2]

Heath was genuinely well disposed towards the unions; he adhered to the view which had been propounded in *One Nation*, that 'a strong and independent Trade Union movement is essential to the structure of a free society'. He set out to create a good working relationship with its leaders. Vic Feather warmed to him from the start. 'He was ready to depart from the formal procedures and see people informally,' Feather told Heath's biographer, George Hutchinson. 'He recognised that preconceived positions by the Minister are no good ... He played the traditional role of being neutral ... He understood the need for conciliation.' William Carron, the president of the Amalgamated Engineering Union (AEU), was likely to prove one of the most influential players in the game. Heath asked him out to dinner. Carron opted for lunch but refused to meet Heath in a restaurant as being too public a venue. Finally they settled for the Carlton Club. Carron can hardly have found the environment congenial but at least there were no lurking journalists. The lunch was a great success and went on till 4 p.m. In December 1959 Heath asked if he could borrow Chequers for a working party on industrial relations. Macmillan's appointments secretary thought this would be a dangerous precedent and was probably outside the designated purposes of the Chequers Trust. With benign hauteur Macmillan minuted: 'I expect Mr Heath's guests will be more-or-less house-trained. Please arrange.'[3]

Heath's first few months in office were uneventful; even when a rail strike began to seem a probability it was Ernest Marples as Minister of Transport who led in Cabinet. Heath said that, since the railwaymen had refused arbitration, he would have been entitled to intervene, but he thought 'it would be better to await developments'. The situation was complicated by the fact that the Guillebaud Committee was about to report on the issue and was certain to recommend a substantial pay increase. The 4 per cent rise on offer was therefore no more than an interim figure: two of the unions involved were prepared to accept it but the National Union of Railwaymen (NUR) stood out for an immediate 5 per cent. Heath made the disagreement between the unions an additional reason for holding his own fire but when it became clear that a national rail strike was otherwise inevitable he called in the unions and the British Transport Commission for direct talks. An element of charade was added by the fact that it was by now known to ministers that the Guillebaud Committee was going to suggest a figure far higher than the NUR was demanding (in the event it offered rises of between 8 per cent and 20 per cent). Heath argued in Cabinet that, given this, to refuse the NUR demand would present 'difficulties from the point of view of the Minister of Labour in his conciliatory role'. Some members of the Cabinet complained that this would be a surrender to blackmail and the Chancellor muttered darkly about the dangers of inflationary settlements, but the majority was anxious to avoid a pointless and damaging strike.[4] 'I am thinking of you all the time,' cabled Macmillan from Cape Town. 'Do not hesitate to let me know if there is anything you want me to do.' The press reaction had been reasonable, Heath replied, 'but there may be criticisms from some members of the Party'.[5] In the event, he was considered to be the hero of the hour and those sceptics who feared the long-term effects on negotiations with the unions for the most part kept their doubts to themselves.

Heath was convinced that the time was ripe for a high-level meeting between employers and union leaders, presided over by the Prime Minister, which would open the way for a new age in industrial relations. To his dismay his Cabinet colleagues were politely unenthusiastic – the project was too ambitious, it would be dangerous to convene such a meeting until the ground had been carefully prepared and a measure of consensus established. 'Further consideration was needed,' concluded the Prime Minister. Undeterred, Heath battled on and by the end of July 1960 was able to tell the Cabinet that both the British Employers' Confederation and the TUC were ready to enter into talks. He had arranged for a meeting of the Joint Consultative Committee in the near future.[6] By the time it took place he had moved on, but he had launched a process which was to be carried on by his successor, John Hare. Heath's relationship with the unions tends to be judged in the light of his performance as Prime Minister, particularly by the legislation which he championed intended to place the unions within the framework of the law. 'In the period from 1959 to 1964,' writes Eric Wigham, 'the Ministry of Labour moved from the field of talk into that of action and legislation. Perhaps it began with Edward Heath, the future Prime Minister with the laughing shoulders and cold eyes.' Cold eyes or not, Heath's most considered views on labour relations in these earlier days were delivered at the Swinton Conservative College in May 1960. What should be done to improve industrial relations, he asked. 'Some people would like to see the legal situation tightened up, but there is a grave danger in seeking legal solutions. How would they work in practice? What happens if thousands of men ignore the law and go on strike? ... In dealing with these problems, we are dealing with the whole of the industrial population of this country. Those who think it is purely a legal affair would do well to remember that the law deals with criminal and civil cases in which one person or a small number of persons is involved. Here we are dealing with very large numbers indeed, with a long history behind their problems, and holding very deep feelings. They need to be approached very carefully, both by industry and by ourselves.' It might have been better for Heath if he had had those words engraved and displayed permanently on his desk.[7]

In June 1960 Heathcoat-Amory finally retired as Chancellor. In the reshuffle that followed Heath was moved to the Foreign Office, to serve as Lord Privy Seal, with a seat in the Cabinet, under the new Foreign Secretary, Alec Home. When Heath became Minister of Labour his one stipulation had been that he should serve for the full period of the Government; now he was to be transplanted before he had been able to do more than start on what he thought was necessary. With Home in the Lords, however, he would speak for the Foreign Office in the Commons and, still more important, would be in charge of Britain's relationship with Europe. If any other Foreign Secretary had been involved Heath might have had doubts, but he liked and trusted Home and believed that they would work successfully together. Some people predicted dire consequences from the divided leadership but James Stuart, always one of Heath's most ardent admirers, reassured him. 'I quite like the idea of FO in the Lords', he wrote, 'because the Commons mustn't get into the way of regarding themselves as entitled to all important posts. Also, from your own personal future angle, it should be of great value to you to get the experience of another most important Department and to have to run important debates in the House.' For Heath it was the prospect of negotiating British entry into Europe that was above all enticing. He had no doubt that he must accept the challenge. But he left Labour with regret. 'I know you'll do a first-class job,' wrote Vic Feather, 'which is why I rather wish you'd had another year or so at the Ministry of Labour where you'd so quickly won the respect and confidence of the unions. Anyway, there it is – from one hot spot to another!'[8]

*   *   *

Though Europe was to be at the centre of Heath's time at the Foreign Office, it was by no means his only responsibility; indeed, for several months, it made relatively few demands on his time. In Cabinet Home tended to take the lead when any subject except Europe was under discussion but Heath would often accept responsibility when the countries of the Gulf, particularly Bahrain or Kuwait, were causing problems. He visited both states and considered himself something of an authority on the area; allegedly assuring the immensely experienced Sir William Luce, then Resident in Bahrain, that he understood how the Arabs thought and needed no advice on the subject.[9] Otherwise he filled in for Home whenever the Foreign Secretary was out of the country or otherwise engaged. When Madame Furtseva visited London she became increasingly discontented with her programme and finally went on strike when required to visit Henry Moore's studio – 'It would be quite inappropriate for a Soviet Minister of Culture to inspect the work of a sculptor who put holes in people.' Heath came to the rescue, took her to Wimbledon and the ballet and invited her to visit him in his new flat – the first time she had ever entered a British home. But though there were occasional compensations, the work was far less interesting and the responsibilities less serious than had been the case at the Ministry of Labour. Nor did his performance in the House of Commons do much for his reputation. 'He seems to lack authority and grasp of his subject,' said the MP for Berwick-upon-Tweed, Lord Lambton – a comment that reflects more on the amorphous nature of his job than the merits of his performance but still makes it clear how difficult it was for Heath to shine when presenting someone else's case on issues which were not under his control. In the *Sunday Graphic* in July 1960, the Tory MP Gerald Nabarro had tipped 'the tough, imperturbable Edward Heath' as a future Foreign Secretary. A few months later he had slipped back in the stakes so far as future promotion was concerned.[10]

The setback was only temporary. Heath's real work at the Foreign Office more than restored his reputation. When he was appointed Lord Privy Seal he was known to be well-disposed towards Europe and critical of the Labour Government's failure to move towards the Common Market, but he was not generally held to be – to use the phrases current some fifty years later – a Europhile, still less a Euro-fanatic. Once Macmillan had taken the decision to apply for British entry and had charged Heath with the task of negotiating acceptable terms, however, what he had always felt would be a most desirable step forward became for him the Holy Grail. Heath became totally committed to the concept of Britain as an integral part of Europe and fought for it tenaciously until the day he died.

To a remarkable extent the decision to apply for British member-ship was made by Macmillan alone. He had, of course, to take the Cabinet with him but it was he who led and the rest who followed. The crucial moment probably came in January 1961 when Macmillan returned from a meeting with the French President, de Gaulle, at Rambouillet to report that there were 'some grounds for thinking that it might now be possible to make some further progress towards a settlement of our economic and political relations with Europe'. There were, he said, 'powerful influences in favour of the development of a close political federation in Europe'. De Gaulle was resolutely opposed to any such development. He believed that the United Kingdom by and large shared his views and would be a useful ally in the battle against the federalists. While there was no guarantee that de Gaulle would welcome British entry it was at least possible that he would not oppose it. It might therefore be best to seek a settlement while de Gaulle was still in power. The Cabinet enthusiastically agreed that steps should at once be taken to see if the way could be made clear for British entry.[11]

But what did entry into Europe mean? In Britain, wrote Heath in 1967, 'a myth has become fashionable that we were concerned only with economic affairs … Nothing could be further from the truth. The main purpose of the negotiations was political.' Robert Marjolin, one of the two French Commissioners on the first European Commission, called on Heath in the House of Commons in March 1961. The EEC 'was not an end in itself but only a stage on the road to a wider political union', he said. The question was not whether the British wished to be associated with the Community as it was today but as it would be in the future. The UK, Heath replied firmly, 'had always made it clear that they regarded the … question as primarily political'. The historian

Keith Middlemas has suggested that Heath more than any other Conservative minister recognised the full implications of this concept and accepted 'how great and painful the adjustments would have to be'. Probably this is true, but he shared his vision with the Lord Chancellor at least. 'I am myself inclined to feel', he told Lord Kilmuir, 'that we have allowed ourselves to be over-impressed by supra-nationality, and that, in the modern world if, from other points of view, political and economic, it should prove desirable to accept such further limitations on sovereignty as would follow from the signature of the Treaty of Rome, we could do so without danger to the essential character of our independence and without prejudice to our vital interests.' Kilmuir replied that he thought it would be difficult to persuade parliament or the public to accept any substantial surrender of sovereignty. 'These objections ought to be brought out in the open now because, if we attempt to gloss over them at this stage, those who are opposed to the whole idea of our joining the Community will certainly seize on them with more damaging effect later on.'[12]

Heath accepted the argument, but with reservations. It might be undesirable to let this sleeping dog lie altogether, but there was no need to wake it too energetically. The emphasis when arguing the case in public should be on the immediate advantages to be gained from British entry and the damage that would be done by staying out; not on a hypothetical threat to national sovereignty that might or might not arise in the distant future. When the issue of sovereignty *did* arise, Heath played it down. Speaking at a private meeting in Chatham House in October 1961, he emphasised that any move towards feder-ation could only come about with the unanimous support of all the members: 'Therefore the position of those who are concerned from the point of view of sovereignty is completely safeguarded.' That he believed this to be true is certain; that he privately considered that when the time did come the arguments in favour of some surrender of sovereignty would prove irresistibly strong is no less clear. This was not the moment to argue that case, however. He did not seek actively to mislead the British public about his expectations, but he did not feel it necessary or desirable to spell out the full implications of British entry in any detail.[13]

Until July 1961, however, the British Government was not committed to make any formal application to join. Exploratory missions were despatched to the most important capitals: Macmillan and Home received an encouraging reception in Bonn, Heath went to Rome in August 1960 and was assured that the Italians would welcome British accession. It was in Paris, though, that the problems were going to be found. Heath went there in October and found the French 'predictably difficult'. Their stance was not that they opposed British entry but that they professed not to see how it would be possible. It was not as if the United Kingdom alone was applying to join. Largely to counter the EEC, Britain had been instrumental in creating the European Free Trade Area (EFTA), a loose association of seven fringe countries forming a rival trading bloc. Heath was able to tell the Cabinet that EFTA welcomed the British application, but only on the understanding that, in any negotiations, the British 'would have full regard to the interests of their partners'. Were such interests, the French wondered, compatible with membership of the EEC?[14]

Worse still, there was the Commonwealth. The French had defended the position of its former empire when the Common Market was established; such arrangements could hardly now be renegotiated to meet a still greater complex of individual needs. Macmillan hopefully proposed that, when explaining the British position to the Commonwealth, 'we should set the economic considerations in the context of the great political issues which were involved and the importance of reaching a settlement in the interest of Western unity'.[15] That was all very well, said the French, but would the Commonwealth countries necessarily put the need for Western unity ahead of their export markets? And, if they did not, would the British be prepared to abandon them? Heath was impressed by the calibre of the French negotiators but not by their readiness to compromise. Couve de Murville, the Foreign Minister, was coolly non-committal. His deputy, Olivier Wormser, was quite as cool but rather more ready to commit himself. His preliminary views on the question of Commonwealth exports were so unforthcoming that Maudling exclaimed: 'It seems to me to be pointless to be talking about any negotiations with them. They have in effect rejected in advance any proposals on the points of vital interest to us.'[16] Baumgartner, the Minister of Finance, was one of the few Frenchmen in a high position who seemed favourable to British entry; but, he warned Heath, his Cabinet was divided and 'he did not know what General de Gaulle's innermost thoughts were on this'.[17]

Nor did anyone else. The General kept his own counsel. Pierson Dixon, the British Ambassador in Paris, believed that de Gaulle was hostile to British entry but hedged his bets by saying that he would 'not be able to turn down a genuine offer from us to join'; Macmillan clung to his hope that the General would welcome the UK as an ally against creeping federalism in Europe. Jean Monnet, the great architect of European unity, maintained that in the last resort de Gaulle would accept British entry because his views 'were coloured and guided by thinking how history would judge his actions'. One thing on which everyone agreed was that, if a British application was in principle desirable, there was no point in deferring it in the hope that de Gaulle would make his intentions known. In May 1961 Heath told the Cabinet that the signals from Paris were more encouraging; the French seemed less unwilling to take into account British obligations to EFTA and the Commonwealth. Ministers were divided: Christopher Soames, the Minister for Agriculture, Fisheries and Food, Duncan Sandys, the Minister for Defence, and Heath were eager to start negotiations, Hailsham and Maudling saw no justification for such a step, Butler was characteristically uncertain. The Prime Minister had no doubts; it would have taken more than a few sceptics to check him. The decision to enter negotiations was announced in the House of Commons on 31 July. A fortnight later, on holiday in Brittany, Heath read in a newspaper that he was to conduct the talks. When he had left London a final decision on the matter had still not been reached. 'There was nothing that I wanted more than this.'[18]

A formidably competent team was quickly assembled. The original proposal had been that the leading official should be Eric Roll, a polyglot civil servant of Austrian birth, who was an academic economist by training and possessed the unusual ability to lip-read in three languages – an invaluable asset in international negotiations. Heath respected his talents but told Macmillan he doubted whether he should be the senior official on the delegation. Macmillan agreed: 'He thinks it specially important that the official in charge should be a man of standing and authority.' That man, at Heath's insistence, was Pierson Dixon: 'Knowing that French agreement was the key to success, he wanted to put the man who was closest to them in charge in Brussels.' The disadvantage of this was that, if Dixon was much of the time in Brussels, he would no longer be so close to those making policy in Paris. Probably it made little difference to the final outcome but it certainly placed an almost insupportable burden on Dixon himself and, on balance, was a mistake.[19]

But the real leader was Heath himself. The members of his team were united in their admiration for his achievements. He was out-standing, said Roll. 'He combined in a unique way the qualities of a first rate official having complete mastery of complex technical details with the necessary political touch in his contacts with Ministers and officials of other countries, with the press and with London. He was the sort of Minister British senior civil servants particularly admire and like to work with, always ready to listen to advice yet quite clear in the end as to what ought to be said and done.' Donald Maitland, the chief press officer seconded from the Foreign Office, wrote that, within the first few days, 'Heath managed to create an almost tangible team spirit among members of the delegation. He was relaxed yet totally in control, he let others speak, including the most junior, and he ensured that by the end of the evening we each knew what was expected of us.' The pressure on both Heath and his team was un-remitting. In the eighteen months after May 1961 Heath flew 100,000 miles and spent one night in five abroad. His team spent less time in aeroplanes but were more often away from home; when the negotiations finally ended Heath sent Donald Maitland's wife a bouquet of flowers with an apology for so often disrupting her family life.[20]

Jean Monnet was the European whom Heath most respected and to whose opinions he paid the greatest heed. In Monnet's view the way was wide open for British entry: 'The greatest difficulty was to take the decision which the British Government has taken.' The right tactic, he urged, was that Britain should accept the Treaty of Rome as it stood and then, having acceded, seek to change things from within. The idea had obvious attractions. Even de Gaulle could hardly have rejected an unconditional application to join and if Britain had become a member in mid-1961 it would have been in time to participate in the formulation of the Common Agricultural Policy instead of being confronted with a system largely devised to meet the needs of French farmers. But though left to himself Heath would probably have proceeded along such lines, he knew that there was no possibility that either the Government or the country would let him do so. Willy-nilly, he was doomed to fight for the interests of EFTA and the Commonwealth. He told Monnet that Macmillan would never 'let the substantial domestic opposition which he faced prevent him from carrying out his aim of taking the United Kingdom into the developing European Union'; but in fact Heath knew that such opposition could not be ignored and that his conduct of negotiations in Brussels would have to take account of it.[21]

When he expounded to the Cabinet the line that he intended to take in his opening statement on 10 October 1961 he said that he would stress that 'the aims and objectives of the Treaty of Rome were accepted by the Government'. That point made, however, he would 'deal in some detail with the three major matters – the Commonwealth, agriculture and EFTA – for which satisfactory arrangements would have to be secured if the UK were to join the Community'. If a united Europe had been eager for British accession such an approach would have been reasonable, but given the attitude of the French it guaranteed that there would be, at the very least, endless delays and difficulties, and possibly final failure. He told the Cabinet a fortnight later that the response to his speech had been 'reasonably favourable'. When speaking at Chatham House he was still more hopeful. Fears among the Six – France, Germany, Italy, Belgium, the Netherlands and Luxembourg – that Britain sought only to break up the union, or at least to impede its growth, had, he believed, been finally dispelled by his assurances. 'The fact is that they do want us there, I believe now, broadly speaking, and we shall know finally one day.' He would indeed. So far as five of the Six were concerned his optimism was well based, but if he found cause for comfort in the cool hostility of the French he was sadly deluding himself.[22]

In retrospect it is easy to say that Heath should have fought harder in London to be allowed to decide for himself which items were worth a battle and which were not. As it was he found himself proposing terms which he knew would be unacceptable and in which he did not even believe himself. This was particularly true of the transitional periods which Heath proposed should be allowed before the full rigour of the EEC's rules affected the Commonwealth exporters. 'It was no good talking only about a short transitional period,' he told the secretary general of the Italian Foreign Ministry, Cattani. 'The Commonwealth system would continue and must be protected from anything which would seriously damage the interests of its members. It would not be possible from the internal political point of view in the UK to accept arrangements which caused such damage.' Yet, as he admitted in his memoirs, the opening position that he was required to take up was 'always unrealistic, at times farcically so'. The result was that even Britain's staunchest allies among the Six wondered whether the will to join was really present; the French were exultant at such clear-cut evidence that the British were not serious in their application.[23]

Once it became clear that every commodity – from butter, through bananas, to kangaroo meat – was to be the subject of lengthy bargaining, it became obvious that the negotiations would be protracted, tedious and faintly absurd. It was his activities at this period that earned him *Private Eye*'s mocking nickname of 'Grocer Heath'. The noble concept which Heath cherished was almost lost in a welter of trivial haggling. Since, after every British offer, the Six had to retreat into conclave to agree on their response, the delays became almost intolerable.

The French rejoiced in this sluggish progress. It was their object to spin matters out so as to ensure that the Common Agricultural Policy would be operational before matters came to an end. Heath might reasonably have despaired at the snail-like advance of the discussions. Instead he remained alert, cheerful and resolute. 'A less resilient personality than the Lord Privy Seal', wrote Nora Beloff of the *Observer*, 'would have been driven to distraction by the long hours he was to spend pacing in ante-rooms.' He saw it as his function not only to remain abreast of every detail of the bargaining but to keep up the spirits of the British team. Morale was not always high. Both Eric Roll and Patrick Reilly, a future ambassador in Paris then working in the Foreign Office, believed that the extravagant demands of London, particularly those of the Ministry of Agriculture and Fisheries, had made it far more difficult for the other members of the Six to over-rule the French.[24] Heath himself felt that, after a bold start, the British delegation had disappointed their allies by failing 'to stand up to the French and to outwit and out-manoeuvre them'. Yet he had been left with so few cards to play that his ability to outwit or out-manoeuvre was very limited. 'It was a gallant and indefatigable effort,' wrote George Ball, an American diplomat who was as eager as anyone to see the negotiations succeed, 'but inevitably mired in technicalities. During the ensuing debate the British purpose became obscure; the political momentum was lost in niggling bargaining.'[25]

Heath was resolved that the purpose should not become obscure, that the flame should continue to burn. Late every evening in Brussels he would join the journalists in the basement bar of the Metropole Hotel. 'On these occasions,' remembered Maitland, 'he was thoroughly relaxed and totally in control. His mastery of detail was complete and his confidence infectious.' In London he used every avenue open to him to dispel what he felt to be unhelpful misunderstandings. The Labour Party, which for the most part had switched under Gaitskell's leadership to opposition to British entry, was beyond his power to influence but he used his old contacts with the trade unions to brief them at regular intervals. Would he be giving a similar report to the House of Commons? asked the trade union leader Frank Cousins. 'Mr Heath replied that in Parliament he could only give broad outline statements of what had been taking place and could go nowhere near so far as he had at the present meeting.' The one point that the union leaders made repeatedly was that there should be a specific reference in the Treaty of Rome to the maintenance of full employment. Heath replied that 'if they were successful in achieving the general aims of the Treaty, full employment would follow naturally'. Not wholly satisfied by this assurance, Cousins returned to the charge and Heath retorted that the trade unions in the Six were happy with the existing formula; the British could hardly insist on more.[26]

It was the sceptics in his own party who required the most careful handling. Paul Channon, R. A. Butler's pps, reported to his master that a meeting of the Foreign Affairs Committee was 'well-attended and extremely friendly. Members were much impressed by the clarity and knowledge of the Lord Privy Seal.'[27] The 1922 Committee proved more critical. At a meeting in June 1961 d'Avigdor-Goldsmid attacked the negotiations on the ground that the interests of the Commonwealth were being neglected while Alfred Wise spoke for EFTA. Was it really necessary to be inside the EEC to influence it? he asked. 'Has Britain had no influence up-to-date?' This sally met 'with a grumble of support'. Kenneth Pickthorn asked a question which preoccupied many members: 'Can we at any time self-determine ourselves out?' But though a majority of those who attended needed some convincing, the atmosphere was more one of enquiry than hostility. Opinion on the whole moved in favour of the Government. When a few months later Heath delivered a 'long and complicated speech' to the 1922 Committee it had 'a very favourable reception'.[28] Though he won the argument, however, some felt that he was doing himself harm in the process. Robert Rhodes James, at that time a Senior Clerk in the House of Commons, noted that 'an ominous note of thinly-veiled intellectual contempt for those in his party who opposed the application was sometimes clearly apparent in his speeches ... For the first time, one was conscious of a substantial hostility developing towards Heath in some quarters of the Conservative party.'[29] 'Substantial' is a strong word, probably too strong. No other reports of the period make the same criticism. But when Heath knew that he was right – and he almost always *did* know that he was right – he was not at pains to conceal his opinion. Some members did undoubtedly feel that they were being brushed aside and their views treated with scant respect. They did not yet feel hostility towards Heath, but their affection was limited.

Persuading the Commonwealth countries that it was in their best interests to see Britain safely embarked in the Common Market was a first preoccupation of the Government. Heath firmly believed, or at least convinced himself, that this was true. Ministers were despatched to the capitals most concerned to set at rest any mind that might still be uneasy. They went out as doves, remarked Robin Turton, a strongly anti-European Conservative MP, 'but returned not with an olive branch but with a raspberry'.[30] Heath went to Ottawa and received, if not a raspberry, then at least a very cautious welcome. When the Commonwealth leaders convened in London in mid-September 1962 the atmosphere was no more cordial. Heath's own performance, noted Macmillan in his diary, 'was really a masterpiece – from notes and not from a script. The temper was good, the knowledge of detail was extraordinary, and the grasp of complicated issues affecting twenty countries and many commodities was very impressive.' But though the premiers of Canada and Australia, Diefenbaker and Menzies, may have been impressed, they were not converted. Two days later Macmillan wrote ruefully: 'Poor Ted Heath ... who is only accustomed to Europeans who are courteous and well informed even if hard bargainers, was astounded at the ignorance, ill-manners and conceit of the Commonwealth.' But having let off steam and berated the British negotiators, the Commonwealth leaders took stock and concluded that they could live with the sort of settlement which Heath was envisaging. The worst was averted. 'The meeting had ended better than it had begun,' Macmillan told the Cabinet. Somewhat grudgingly, a green light had been given for the negotiations to continue. More than anyone else, Heath had been responsible for the change in the atmosphere. *France Soir* described him as being Macmillan's '*brillant poulain, le célibataire aux joues roses*'. '*Poulain*' – literally 'foal' – suggested a talented novice, a trainee. It was perhaps not exactly the description that Heath would have preferred but he accepted it as the compliment that was intended and kept the cutting among his papers.[31]

It had been his hope that, before the date of the Commonwealth Conference, every important issue in Brussels would have been resolved. It was not until July 1962 that he accepted a recess was inevitable and that negotiations would have to be resumed in the autumn. It was the fault of the French, he told the Cabinet. They had refrained from discussing their objections when the British had been present but had not hesitated to press them at meetings of the Six. 'A high proportion of the obstacles which we were still meeting could be attributed to French initiatives.' Almost as disturbing was the hostility to Europe which was growing in the United Kingdom. Gaitskell was not alone in his opposition. 'If they don't want us we certainly don't need them', was increasingly the attitude. But still Heath could not believe that, after so many weeks and so much bargaining, the negotiations could founder. Even the pessimistic Dixon, on the last day of the discussions before the adjournment, told Eric Roll that the French were 'rather resentful of our rewriting their sacred writings ... But they are chittering with interest; not, I judge, with hostility.'[32]

Through the autumn and early winter, the mood of optimism grew stronger. Frank Giles, the exceptionally well-informed *Sunday Times* correspondent in Paris, said that British entry was now very nearly a certainty. 'If the Archangel Gabriel himself were conducting the negotiations,' he wrote, 'he could (assuming, of course, that he was British) scarcely do better than Mr Heath.' The crunch would come in mid-January 1963, Heath told the Cabinet. The French had agreed that there could be a long ministerial meeting and, though they had not accepted that this should be the final stage, they seemed resigned to the certainty that substantial progress would be made. The French were isolated, he announced confidently on 10 January. All the other members were 'earnestly seeking to reach a settlement on terms acceptable to the UK'. The possibility that the French would not be deterred by the feelings of their allies, though it had been endlessly discussed, still seemed too fanciful a chimera to take seriously.[33]

What disturbed Heath most was that the negotiations in Brussels were only part, and not necessarily the most important part, of the relationship between Britain and Europe, particularly between Britain and France. In March 1962, in a memorandum to the Foreign Secretary dealing with the possibility of cooperating with the European countries on the development of nuclear weapons, Heath showed that he was painfully aware of the link between such matters and British accession to the Common Market:

What alarms me more than anything, is that, at the same time as we are trying to negotiate our entry into the EEC – in which we have all too few cards to play – we are giving every indication of wishing to carry out political policies which are anathema to the two most important members of the Community. This can only increase the mistrust and suspicion already felt towards us in the political sphere ... We must never forget that the countries of the Community are interested in two things: first, in jointly increasing their own prosperity – in which they regard us as a possible liability and the Commonwealth as an undesirable complication; secondly, in strengthening their defence against what they regard as the persistent and menacing threat from the Soviet Union ... What they see here is our apparent determination, with the United States, to prevent the French from developing their atomic and nuclear defence ... Our colleagues have instructed us to carry out a negotiation for our entry into the EEC at the same time as they – showing a complete lack of understanding of European attitudes and problems – are carrying out contrary policies in the political and defence fields. It is no wonder that these negotiations, already sufficiently difficult and complicated, threaten to become almost unmanageable.[34]

For 'our colleagues' read, above all, the Prime Minister. Macmillan negotiated with the Americans at Nassau an agreement for the exclusive provision of Polaris missiles to be carried on nuclear submarines; to de Gaulle, at Rambouillet in mid-December 1962, he made it clear that, though the French were welcome to jog along as junior partners, the so-called 'independent' deterrent would remain firmly in British hands. 'I only trust that nothing I have done at Rambouillet or Nassau has increased our difficulties,' Macmillan wrote apologetically to Heath. His trust was misplaced. 'I can well imagine de Gaulle's feeling', wrote Heath in his memoirs, 'at being asked to accept the terms of an agreement negotiated in his absence by the British and American governments. With more sensitive handling, we might, at the very least, have denied him this particular excuse for behaving vindictively towards the British.'[35]

Was the nuclear issue a decisive feature in de Gaulle's thinking or was it just one more piece of evidence that Britain could never become truly European? From early in the negotiations Heath had been in no doubt that de Gaulle disliked the idea of British entry; he told Macmillan that 'there was a genuine fear on de Gaulle's part of admitting Britain as a kind of Trojan horse which would either disrupt the present system or prevent French domination'. But it did not necessarily follow that he would block British entry whatever the outcome of the negotiations. Some of the British team involved in the negotiations were convinced that that had been his intention from the start. He was determined to keep us out, says the British diplomat, Michael Butler, 'because he feared the UK would gang up with Holland and Germany to create a Europe which was both too federal and too closely linked to the United States'. Any delay in making his position brutally clear was caused by his hope that the negotiations would break down without his intervention.[36] Yet Couve de Murville, whom Heath believed would not wilfully have misled him, told him just before the final sessions in Brussels: 'No power on earth can now prevent these negotiations from being successful.' De Gaulle, he claimed, had 'neither the power nor the intention to veto UK membership'. Eric Roll was convinced that the General 'made up his mind almost at the end'. The answer could be that de Gaulle did not ask himself till the last minute whether or not his mind *was* made up. He preferred not to contemplate the problem until it was thrust upon him. But if a decision had been forced upon him three or six months earlier he would almost certainly have acted as he did in January 1963. His mind may not have been made up earlier, but his mindset was inexorably fixed. Given his temperament it seems almost inconceivable that, whatever the course of the negotiations, whatever the feelings of the other countries involved, he would have allowed the British to enter the Community.[37]

A few days before the last round began Heath dined with the American diplomat George Ball in Paris. He was 'in ebullient high spirits', wrote Ball. He described his meetings with various French ministers and concluded that, though some serious obstacles remained, he was 'reasonably confident that the British application was in no serious trouble'. Then came de Gaulle's press conference of

14 January, at which he stated bluntly that Britain was socially, economically and politically unsuitable to be a member of the European Community. Swiftly, Couve de Murville made it clear that, so far as the French were concerned, the negotiations were over. Heath at first hoped that so arrogant a volte-face might 'rouse the Five to a new level of anger', but, as he told the Government in London: 'It begins to look as though none of them will have much stomach for the idea of carrying things to the point of breaking up the EEC.' The last meeting of 29 January confirmed this view. Paul-Henri Spaak, the Belgian Foreign Minister, condemned the French behaviour in the harshest terms. It was, he said, 'a day of defeat for Europe ... If the Rome Treaty did not explode, the Community spirit was gravely, perhaps mortally wounded.' But the Rome Treaty did not explode, nor was it near doing so. Gerhard Schroeder, the German Minister for Foreign Affairs, made the best of it when he praised 'the splendid effort which had been made by his British friends' and hoped that 'the impulse for European unity would not die away in Britain. For the day would come when it could be realised.' Heath in his reply spoke with moving dignity. There was no need for fear, he said: 'We would not turn our backs; we were a part of Europe by geography, history, culture, tradition and civilisation.'[38]

It was one of the worst days of his life. The journalist Nicholas Carroll recorded seeing him in his hotel just before midnight: 'The Lord Privy Seal, normally cheerful and tireless and the best-liked negotiator here, seemed frozen into profound depression; his cheeks grey, his eyes glazed with fatigue.' Christopher Soames recalled driving with him to the meeting when they already knew that the veto was to be applied. 'I remember sort of putting my hand on his knee and saying: "You mustn't mind too much, Ted. Nobody could have tried harder than you" ... and I got absolutely frozen dead-pan. I could never understand how undemonstrative he was.'[39] Impassivity was indeed his usual reaction to any setback. Carroll must have caught him with his guard down. But he rallied with remarkable speed. Within a few days he was raising in Cabinet the possibility of a new initiative confined to those members of the Six who favoured British entry, 'preferably of a political or military nature and linked with

NATO, which might strengthen our own position in Europe and serve as a counterpoise to the ambitions of the French government'. He gained little support for his ideas. Macmillan thought it would be dangerous to press for some new form of association which might seem incompatible with the course the British had so recently been espousing, and the Cabinet endorsed his views. The truth was that a substantial minority in the Cabinet was privately relieved that the effort to join the Six had shipwrecked and the rest felt that the whole European problem had best be left to simmer for a while, at least until the General had departed the scene.[40]

The debacle had done no harm to Heath's reputation. Evelyn Shuckburgh, from the UK delegation to NATO, spoke for the whole of the British team when he found some consolation in the fact that 'you personally have emerged from the whole affair with such a tremendous reputation and, indeed, with a position in Europe and at home which is in many ways unique. This is a really remarkable result to have achieved through a failed negotiation.' It *was* remarkable, yet, as was to happen so often in his career, Heath contrived to forfeit some part of the credit that was due him by the embittered intransigence of his behaviour. Philip de Zulueta told Macmillan a few months later that Heath was being 'a bad loser'. He was refusing to leave ill alone, constantly making speeches attacking the French, which left them irritated but unmoved and embarrassed the other Five. 'I am sure you ought to raise this with the Lord Privy Seal,' urged de Zulueta. There is no evidence that he did so, but Macmillan noted in his diary: 'Heath is so bitterly anti-French as to be almost unbalanced in his hatred of de Gaulle, Couve etc.'[41]

One reason why he harped so angrily on the past was that he did not have enough to do. For some eighteen months his activities had centred almost exclusively on Britain's relationship with Europe. During this time his other responsibilities in foreign affairs, ill-defined at the best of times, had largely been looked after by other people. Even if he eventually managed to re-establish his position the work would never be of adequate importance: he had been appointed to the Foreign Office above all to secure Britain's entry into Europe, and that avenue was now closed. He was marking time. It is the lot of those who mark time to pass unnoticed. Worse still, though nobody blamed Heath personally for de Gaulle's veto, he was associated in the eyes of the public and the party with a failure of British policy. In the first six months of 1963 his reputation went, not dramatically but noticeably, into decline. It seemed unlikely that it would recover until Macmillan overhauled his Cabinet or retired.

The moment was not long postponed. Heath had been losing confidence in his former hero since the summer of 1962. His responsibilities in Brussels had kept him to some extent remote from Westminster politics and he was even more taken aback than most of his fellow ministers when Macmillan, in the notorious 'Night of the Long Knives' in July 1962, savagely reshaped his Government and put six of his senior cabinet ministers out to grass. 'I knew nothing of what he had in mind,' said Heath some years later. 'After all, I was engaged in Europe. But it was ill-advised. The timing was wrong. And to do it on such a scale!'[42] The Profumo scandal, giving as it did the impression that the Prime Minister was old, inadequate and out of touch with contemporary life, further weakened his position. When ill health forced him to retire just before the Party Conference in October 1963 it caused surprise but little distress in the parliamentary party.

If the negotiations in Brussels had ended in success and Heath had been rewarded for his efforts by promotion to a senior department it is possible that he might have been a significant challenger in the jostling for position which followed Macmillan's resignation. Even as it was, he could not entirely be ruled out. Alec Home, the dark horse who was eventually to romp home the winner, told his Minister of State at the Foreign Office, Peter Thomas, that he thought the choice was between Maudling and Heath. Maudling, he felt, had the better chance, 'because Ted Heath's single-mindedness and lack of rapport with some backbenchers would disqualify him in many people's eyes'. Home said not a word to suggest that he might be a candidate himself. Macmillan himself thought Heath and Maudling were both too young, and the same went for Iain Macleod: their chance would come in five or ten years.[43] The Times disagreed. If Heath was really too

young – 'after all, he is a mere year older than President Kennedy' –
then R. A. Butler would be the best choice. But, considered *The Times*,
'that "if" needs to be questioned. Sooner or later the reins of Conservatism will be placed in the hands of a new generation. There
is much to be said for that being done now.'[44] David Bruce, the
American ambassador with an extremely sensitive understanding
of British political life, felt that, in the wake of the Profumo scandal, 'an unmarried man would be at a great disadvantage'. He too
felt that Heath's time would come but that in the meantime his supporters were likely to vote for Butler or Hailsham, who could be
expected to disappear from the scene more rapidly than Maudling
or Macleod.[45]

Heath's own views are hard to establish. He told his pps, Anthony
Kershaw, that he was not going to throw his hat into the ring. If people
wanted to vote for him he could not stop them, but he would give
them no encouragement. In his biography of Alec Home, D. R.
Thorpe states that, while Heath was staying with the chairman of the
1922 Committee, John Morrison, at his Scottish home on Islay in July
1963, the question of the succession came up. Morrison told Heath
that Alec Home was going to be urged to run and Heath agreed to
back him if he did. This Heath strongly denies. He told Hailsham that
he had played no part in the choice of a new leader except to tell the
Lord Chancellor, Lord Dilhorne, who it was that he personally supported. He had no discussions with Butler, Maudling or Macleod, and
the matter was never discussed while he was at Islay. At that time,
anyway, he pointed out, Macmillan's retirement did not seem imminent. It is almost incredible that during their days and, still more, long
evenings on Islay two men as passionately concerned with politics as
Morrison and Heath should not even have touched on the question
of who would be Macmillan's successor. Heath, however, had no high
opinion of Morrison's judgment or his discretion; he might well have
chosen to abort the conversation or to confine himself to a non-
committal grunt when Home's candidature came into question.
Whatever the truth, Heath did back Home and made no secret of his
loyalties.[46]

Why he did so is another matter. He knew Home well, had found him easy to work with and could be reasonably confident that, with the former Foreign Secretary in Number 10, his own career would flourish. Was that all there was to it? Jim Prior, who worked as closely with Heath as any Tory and was his strong supporter, suspected that there was more. 'Perhaps Ted had recognised that, although his own time had not yet come in 1963, he did stand a chance of being Alec's successor, and that he would be much more out of the running if either Rab Butler or Quintin Hailsham had been chosen. This seems the most likely explanation ... but it does also reveal Ted in a more scheming guise than I was to associate with him on virtually any other occasion.'[47] A more suspicious nature still might see Heath as even more guileful. Home was twelve years older than Heath, not believed to be hungry for office or likely to be particularly tenacious in holding on to it. He would be taking command at a time when the Tory ship was heading into storms, probably into electoral defeat. He would not be a caretaker prime minister but he would more nearly fill that role than any of his rivals. Heath would probably have backed him any-way, but a measure of self-interest may well have been among his motives. Certainly Home was a far happier choice from Heath's point of view than either Macleod or Maudling, one only two years older than him, the other two years younger. If either of these secured the succession Heath's prospects of reaching Number 10 would have been dim indeed.

In the event it became clear that Macleod had made too many enemies on the right and centre of the party to be in the running. In a ballot of Tory MPs, Maudling secured 48 first choices to Heath's 10, and 66 second or third choices to Heath's 17, but since Heath was not a formal candidate this meant little. Quite as important was the fact that Maudling was credited with six 'definite aversions' – in effect, blackballs – against Heath's one. Hailsham, at one time said to be Macmillan's favoured successor, piled up so many 'definite aversions' as a result of his ill-judged and extravagant performance at the Party Conference that he was ruled out. In the end the Queen, largely, it seems, on Macmillan's recommendation, sent for Home. It was the consummation Heath had hoped for. It was made even better by the fact that Iain Macleod and Enoch Powell took exception to the secretive and, as they saw it, undemocratic process by which Home was finally selected and refused to serve under him. By doing so they gravely damaged their own prospects of future promotion. On 19 October 1963, the Earl of Home, as he then was, became Prime Minister, renounced his peerage and stood for election to the House of Commons as Alec Douglas-Home. It remained to see what job he would offer Heath.

EIGHT

Minister

For his first twelve years as an MP Heath's style of living had been frugal. He lived in a tiny flat in an unfashionable area. As a Whip he had spent much of his time in the House, as Lord Privy Seal he was often in Brussels. He entertained little, and then largely on expenses. He spent most of his weekends at the family home in Broadstairs and for his holidays tended to patronise the houses of his richer friends. By the standards of a City tycoon his salary was pitifully small, but his commitments were even smaller. Each year he saved, and his money was invested for him by Brown Shipley, who took particular trouble to ensure that he was well looked after. Increasingly too he was advised by the investment maestro, Jim Slater, a man who had his problems from time to time but was generally considered to possess one of the shrewdest minds in the financial world. When he briefly rejoined Brown Shipley as a director after the Conservatives lost the election in 1964, Heath bought or was given 3,125 shares worth £7,000.[1] Though his stay with the merchant bank was brief, he made a most favourable impression: the chief foreign-exchange dealer said that Heath spent two days with him and 'mastered every subject that I expounded ... He understood it all: it takes some people years ... If everyone had fallen down he could have run the bank.'[2] If he had remained in the City he probably would one day have run the bank; certainly the directors felt that he was somebody with whom close contact should be maintained. 'When you get your pass sheet you will see that you have been credited with rather higher directors' fees for the current year,' he was told after he had resigned for the second and final time. 'This is intended as a gesture of our thanks for your very real help.'[3]

The money he thus earned he guarded assiduously. He was not mean – he was capable of surprising generosity and when he entertained he liked to do so in style – but he much preferred other people to pay for things. There are innumerable anecdotes of people who thought that they were being treated to a drink or meal and ended up paying the bill themselves. Every expense was carefully considered and often begrudged. When, in 1970, the Carlton Club put up its annual subscription to £55, Heath minuted that this was 'a monstrous sub for this useless club'. Surely he should be exempt? Enquiries were made and he was told there could be no exemption. 'You will have to ask Brown Shipley to pay the extra,' concluded Heath: which, seeing that it was at that time five years since he had ceased to be a director, cast a curious light on his relationship with the merchant bank.[4] Yet he never acquired any of the skills that might have made it easier for him to economise. He could not have sewn on a button and approached with caution the task of making a bed. He could not cook.[5] Once he volunteered to produce breakfast for the crew of *Morning Cloud*. He broke the eggs, put them on slices of bread in a frying pan, and could not understand why the unpalatable mess that resulted was so unsatisfactory.[6]

He kept his room in his father's house in Broadstairs and occasionally took his father and stepmother, and his brother John with his wife, out to lunch or dinner; but he does not seem otherwise to have contributed to the household expenses. For Heath, the heart had gone out of his family with his mother's death. He resented his father's remarriage and never established any real relationship with his kindly if unexciting stepmother Mary. William Heath's marriage day was a botched affair. Heath was an hour late in picking up his brother and, when they got to Ramsgate, could not find the Register Office. They arrived there only five minutes before it closed. 'It was the saddest wedding I've ever been to,' John Heath's wife, Marian, remarked. 'Looking back, I regret very much not taking the lead, as the boys might have followed in kissing the bride and giving good wishes. After a quiet celebration lunch, where no one proposed the health of the bride, we returned to London.' Heath's new stepmother had previously been married to a committed socialist, but since Heath would never have considered the possibility of discussing politics with her, this caused no problems. When asked what she thought of her stepson she replied: 'He frightened me. It was difficult to know what to say, because he dislikes small talk. If there is nothing much to say he likes to keep silent. I find he is a man with whom you can be happily silent, however.'[7] Many women were to make the same complaint over the next forty years, though there were few who learnt the art of being happy in the prevailing silence.

Heath spent his weekends at Broadstairs out of habit and because it was cheap. He preferred to take his holidays with his more sophisticated and richer friends. Madron and Nancy-Joan Seligman remained particularly close; he visited them frequently and almost every year spent holidays with them in France or Italy. He became part of an extended family and was accepted by the children as an honorary uncle, to be treated with affection and cheerful disrespect: 'If only Uncle Teddy and Daddy weren't so fat, we'd have won,' one of the boys complained after their boat had come last in a local regatta. But though he was thoroughly at home and at the time was closer to Nancy-Joan than to any other woman, it would not have occurred to him that he might confide in her; 'letting down one's hair' was a concept wholly alien to Heath's character.

The same was true of the Aldingtons. Lord Aldington, or Toby Low as he was when Heath first knew him, was a Tory MP who, after achieving modest distinction in politics, took over the family bank of Grindlays and became chairman of GEC and Sun Alliance. His wife Araminta, like Nancy-Joan Seligman, had the knack of making Heath laugh and tolerated his moods with equanimity. If he felt inclined to be surly or sulky then he was free to indulge himself: she would pay no attention and would be happy to resume more comfortable relations when the time seemed propitious. Aldington was one of the most important people in Heath's life. Heath respected his judgment, welcomed his advice and took advantage of his powerful connections in the world of business and the City. If ever it was necessary to cobble together some informal group which would support Heath by financial or other means, then Aldington could be relied upon to do it. Like Heath he was a consensus man; not so firmly convinced that in the end reason would prevail but always agreeing that reason should be given every chance of doing so before there was resort to other measures. Most important of all, he greatly admired Heath and supported him to the uttermost; to a man as naturally suspicious as Heath the knowledge that this powerful and well-connected figure was on his side was immensely comforting.[8]

Heath was no snob. He continued to make no effort to conceal his origins and, indeed, was not above using them to his advantage. When he was urged not to support Alec Home for leader on the grounds that the party needed someone from the middle classes, he replied that, since he was working-class himself, he could not see things in quite that way. But he liked great houses and the appurtenances of wealth: he told Sara Morrison that he found the very rich 'interesting'; he also found them attractive and curiously exciting; he had no expectation, or even wish, that he would ever achieve the same status himself but was more than ready to accept their hospitality and, with due restraint, anything else that might be on offer. He would never have pushed some cause that he believed to be wrong because somebody had done him a favour, but if people chose to lavish their gifts upon him he was quite ready to take advantage of it. One of the things that most vexed him when he was Prime Minister was what he saw as the unreasonable insistence of the Treasury that all the silver salvers, Ming vases and cases of champagne thrust upon him by foreign dignitaries must be declared and, if retained, paid for. Once his pps, Tim Kitson, remembers him hiding an obviously very valuable ivory model of a dhow, presented to him by Y. K. Pao, the Hong Kong millionaire, as a reward for launching a ship, in case it was spotted by one of his private secretaries and impounded on behalf of the authorities.[9]

Sara Morrison, though no plutocrat, embodied many of the assets that he thought most desirable. A daughter of Viscount Long and Laura, Duchess of Marlborough, she was grand enough to satisfy any criteria. He met her at Islay, the Scottish retreat of her father-in-law, John Morrison, chairman of the 1922 Committee and the future Lord Margadale. Her husband, Charles Morrison, was also to become an MP, and both the Morrisons were strong supporters of Heath. Sara was as politically conscious as either of them and a great deal more intelligent; born twenty years later she would have been among the leaders of the Tory Party. She was not in the least in awe of Heath, obviously enjoyed his company, told him, with sometimes alarming frankness, when she thought he was making a mistake, made him laugh, and, like Araminta Aldington and Nancy-Joan Seligman, was undiscomfited when he sulked or behaved with a rudeness which would have upset anybody with less self-confidence. She was to become closer to him than any woman since his mother – not romantically or even sentimentally attached but with a real affection and loyalty that endured in spite of all the vicissitudes that from time to time assailed them.

The Aldingtons, the Morrisons, lived in a world in which Heath knew he did not belong. He never wanted to join it but he was happy to indulge in the attractions of gracious living. His frequent stays in Brussels, too, taught him expensive habits. He enjoyed eating in the most sumptuous restaurants, preferred malts to other whiskies, champagne to other wines, Dom Perignon to other champagnes. He had a large appetite and a penchant for sweet things: when he had tea with the Cromers in the South of France he seized the largest pink éclair; when he was staying at the embassy in Washington, Lady Henderson put a large box of chocolates in his room. By the next morning all were gone.[10] He began to spend more money on his clothes; he bought a better car; proposed by Harold Macmillan and seconded by Michael Adeane, he joined the Beefsteak Club. 'I have known him for more than ten years,' wrote Adeane in his letter of support, 'have the highest regard for him as a friend and companion and am sure those members who don't know him already will find, if he is elected, that they have made a most agreeable addition to their number.'[11]

But the most significant change to Heath's way of life came in July 1963 when he moved from his mean rooms in Petty France to chambers in Albany, Piccadilly – for a sedate bachelor, probably the most eligible address in London. The main house had been built for the first Viscount Melbourne in the 1770s; in 1802 Henry Holland added a long walkway at the back lined with bachelor apartments. It had at times provided a London retreat for Lord Brougham, Palmerston, Byron, W. E. Gladstone, Macaulay, not to mention the fictional but hardly less celebrated Raffles. With Eric Roll, Pierson Dixon and a host of other dignitaries already installed there, Heath would have no shortage of eligible company: it provided status, silence, seclusion, instant access to the heart of London and, if he felt so inclined, which he rarely did, a brisk fifteen-minute walk to the House of Commons. Sets of rooms rarely came on the market and Heath had been on the waiting list for thirteen years when the death of Clifford Bax, brother of the composer Arnold, freed F2 Albany. Heath secured a seven-year lease for a remarkably reasonable £677 per annum. He at once called in the interior designer Jo Patrick and had his rooms decorated in a style that was assertively modern yet classically restrained.

The newspaper magnate Cecil King lunched there on several occasions and found the flat 'a luxurious one, with many good prints of soldiers in various uniforms, and he had acquired some excellent white porcelain horses depicting various manoeuvres of the horses in the Spanish Riding School'.[12] This was only the nucleus of what was becoming a distinguished collection of ceramics and modern paintings and drawings. Through shrewd buying and, still more, the generosity of friends, Heath was soon able to embellish his rooms with an Augustus John drawing, the first of a series of John Piper paintings, a Picasso lithograph and, in pride of place, two landscapes by Winston Churchill. For Heath the most important item in the flat was the Steinway grand piano. In 1963, as a consolation prize for the failure of the negotiations in Brussels, the city of Aachen awarded him the Charlemagne Prize for 'encouraging international understanding and cooperation in the European sphere'. The only Briton who had received it before was Churchill. The prize was worth £450 and Heath used the money to buy a piano which would both give him something of quality to play on and suitably grace his new home.

With his rooms decorated to his satisfaction, Heath began to entertain. He was, in general, a good host and an appalling guest. At dinner in other people's houses he was apt to relapse into morose silence or completely ignore the woman next to him and talk across her to the nearest man. Many hostesses have testified to his unreadiness to make the slightest contribution to the success of a party. Even at home he eschewed small talk and sometimes paid scant attention to guests who did not secure his interest. But he was lavish where food and wine were concerned and was usually jovial; not necessarily providing a relaxed or comfortable experience but at least making the guests feel that they were welcome. In Albany he did not often entertain guests for meals but frequently for drinks. His policy was never to ask a husband without his wife or vice versa; he cultivated assiduously every shade of opinion in the party and continued to invite the most inveterate right-wingers or bigoted Europhobes even though he can have derived little satisfaction from their company. Though he was determined that everything in Albany should be of the highest quality – whether in the vintage of the wines or the elegance of the furnishings – he never missed a chance to economise. His old friend and commanding officer, George Chadd, was now dealing in carpets: Heath expected him to provide the best for his new flat, but only at a substantial discount. Life was more expensive for Heath once he was living in Albany but he still contrived to live within his income and even to add to his savings.

Privately, Heath had coveted the job of Foreign Secretary. Harold Macmillan had told Home that he thought Heath was the obvious man for the job, and, other things being equal, the new Prime Minister would probably have taken the advice. Douglas-Home felt, however, that he must offer the twice-rejected Butler any post he wanted, and the Foreign Office was his choice. Instead Heath was given the job he had hoped for four years before: President of the Board of Trade. Regional development was one of his particular interests and he asked that it should be added to his portfolio; his full title was therefore Secretary of State for Industry, Trade and Regional Development (the order being dictated by the need to avoid the new minister being known as TIRD). It was a well-run and powerful department, ranking among the more important in the hierarchy even before the new responsibilities were added. The Permanent Under Secretary, Richard Powell, was by nature cautious and conservative, but unlike certain other Whitehall mandarins he saw his responsibility as being loyally to support his minister, not to outwit or obstruct him. The only disagreeable element was provided by the Minister of State, Edward du Cann. Du Cann was everything Heath was not: smooth, unctuous, habitually concealing his true feelings under a cloak of bland amiability. 'By taste, habit and disposition he was an intriguer,' wrote the journalist Hugo Young. Heath disliked him from the start and, unusually, admitted the fact in his memoirs. His 'ingratiating manner immediately led me to mistrust him', wrote Heath – a comment no doubt coloured by the role that du Cann was to play in Heath's downfall twelve years later.[13]

It was quickly made clear that in Heath's view, and it seemed in the view of Douglas-Home as well, the Board of Trade was to play an enlarged and invigorated role in the regeneration of industry and the British economy. One of his first important steps was to introduce in Cabinet a White Paper giving local authorities in South East England power to requisition land for building or for launching major development schemes. Priority, Heath emphasised, must still be given to the depressed areas in North East England and Central Scotland but the population in the South East was going to increase by 3.5 million over the next twenty years and steps must be taken to prepare for this expansion. To some of his colleagues the proposals seemed alarmingly interventionist; the Prime Minister struck a cautionary note when he said the matter 'required further examination'. Heath himself was undisturbed by charges that he wished to interfere in the economic life of the country in ways which should not be contemplated by a Tory government. Interference, he maintained, was not merely permissible, it was essential. He 'despairs of the efficiency and enterprise of British industry', noted the political journalist and academic David Butler after an interview with Heath a few months later, 'and is in a rather cynical and destructive mood. He is most worried of all about the machinery of government and thirsts after a Gaullist solution.' For the most part his ideas were well received. Douglas-Home was intent on showing that his was a reformist government, ready to tackle the problems of society and the economy. The new, upgraded Board of Trade was a vital, perhaps *the* most vital, weapon in this campaign: as the political correspondent Ronald Butt argues, it had been equipped for its role by being given a minister who was distinguished by his hunger for modernisation and who had 'a devoted personal following among younger Conservatives as well as industry and the City'.[14]

To one minister in particular the enhanced status of the Board of Trade and Heath's growing reputation as a determined modernist came as an unpleasant threat. Reginald Maudling at the Treasury resented any intrusion into his territory and made a point of emphasising that he alone retained overall responsibility for economic policy. But no amount of such assertions could alter the fact of Heath's new prominence. 'The rise of Heath', wrote Maudling's biographer, 'had a significant effect on Reggie's chances of winning the leadership ... From being the candidate of youth, Reggie was subtly transformed over the next two years into being the quiet life, steady as she goes candidate.' This coloured their relationship. A Treasury official noted that though 'on the surface they seemed to be like-minded colleagues, there was always an edge when Ted Heath came into the Chancellor's office, as he often did, and the temperature dropped'.[15] This tension – hostility would be too strong a word – made it inevitable that when Heath pressed for his most conspicuous and controversial piece of modernisation, the Chancellor, though a supporter in principle, in practice argued for caution.

The abolition of resale price maintenance (RPM) – the system by which manufacturers were empowered to fix prices which retailers must charge customers for their products in all their outlets – had theoretically been a Tory objective for many years. The critics of RPM argued that it restricted competition, kept prices high and safeguarded the inefficient or idle shopkeeper; its champions pointed out that it enabled the small neighbourhood shop, an important element in urban or village life, to survive in the face of what would otherwise be irresistible pressure from the supermarkets. The Board of Trade had always been in favour of abolition but had despaired of finding a minister who would have the determination and energy to force it through. The need for reform had been accepted in principle by a series of Conservative, and indeed Labour, governments, but the timing never seemed propitious. Of all the groups convinced that the abolition of RPM would gravely damage their industry, the publishers were the most vociferous; it was hardly surprising, therefore, that while Macmillan was prime minister the issue was not pressed with any great enthusiasm.

Heath too had in the past been opposed to abolition. In 1950 he had told the Bexley Chamber of Commerce: 'I agree in principle that a manufacturer should have the power to prescribe the retail prices for goods bearing his name.' Such a provision, he assured the local tobacconists, was necessary 'to protect employment, industry and the small trader'.[16] The issue, however, was not one about which he had thought deeply: he told the tobacconists what he knew they wanted to hear without considering the wider implications. In 1964, when he was responsible for making policy, it was a different matter. When the Labour MP John Stonehouse put down a private member's bill on the subject, Heath realised that he must act. The war between the supermarkets in which customers were bribed to use one chain or another by gifts of trading stamps had already undermined the principle of RPM; the more he considered it the more obvious it seemed to him that the Government must introduce its own Bill to settle the issue for once and for all. Flying up to Scotland with his pps, Anthony Kershaw, he produced some draft legislation and asked what Kershaw thought of it. 'It's fine, but there'll be the hell of a row!' Kershaw commented. Heath grunted and said nothing. 'He wouldn't reply to that sort of observation – he never would,' remembered Kershaw, 'he just docketed it away in his mind ... When he's made up his mind to do something he really is completely inflexible – he takes a long time and he talks to an awful lot of people, but after he's made it up you might as well talk to yourself.'[17] His officials in the Board of Trade were delighted by this unexpected resolution but, like Kershaw, predicted that there would be storms ahead.[18] Heath was unperturbed. At the end of 1963 he told the Prime Minister of his intentions. 'This is very difficult,' Douglas-Home replied gloomily, but he accepted Heath's argument that the abolition of RPM would be a bold modernising move that would redound to the credit of the Government and be generally popular with the electorate.[19]

The first cabinet meeting at which the matter was discussed, in January 1964, showed that Heath was not going to have an easy passage. No one denied that such legislation would, in principle, be desirable; it was the timing that caused concern. The abolition of RPM would alienate an army of small shopkeepers; small shopkeepers were traditionally Tory voters; a general election could not be too far ahead; the Government's position was already precarious. St Augustine's celebrated prayer – 'Give me chastity and continency, but do not give it yet!' – summed up the position of at least half the Cabinet. Heath would have none of this. 'The Government had committed themselves to a policy of modernising Britain and promising a more efficient use of resources,' he reminded his colleagues. 'This policy would fail to carry conviction if they were to tolerate the continuance of a practice so manifestly at variance with it.' In the end the Cabinet doubtfully agreed that legislation should be introduced, subject to the exemption of booksellers and, possibly, one or two other categories of retailer. On the main issue of proscribing RPM, said the Prime Minister, 'the Government intended to act with speed and decision'.[20]

Delay and indecision naturally followed. The uproar in the Cabinet was as nothing to the explosion of indignation that ensued, when all those Conservative MPs with marginal seats discovered that the small shopkeepers were likely to be turned against them. The Chief Whip, Martin Redmayne, bore the brunt of their resentment. He bullied one recalcitrant MP so ruthlessly that his victim emerged from the Whips' Office 'brick-red in the face, his teeth tightly clenched and tears of rage squeezed out from under his eyelids'. Like Heath over the death penalty and Suez, Redmayne had the ill fortune of having to whip up support for a policy which he personally opposed. Unlike most of his colleagues he disliked the principle of abolition as well as deploring the timing. Heath, he complained, 'showed an almost malevolent lack of interest' in the problems that the Chief Whip was having with the backbenchers. He made Heath's task more difficult by urging on the Prime Minister a series of exceptions to the Bill which cumulatively would have fatally weakened it. It was perhaps appropriate that, after the next election, he should have resigned his seat and become, inter alia, a director of Harrods.[21]

The backbench revolt was at its fiercest in the 1922 Committee. At the first meeting which discussed it it became clear that, while the membership divided more or less fifty-fifty on the merits of the proposal, everyone agreed that the timing was disastrous. The Committee devoted more time to the matter than they had done to any single issue since a particularly turbulent debate on MPs' pay ten years before. John Morrison, though counting himself a friend and ally of Heath's, was as appalled as any other member of the Committee. He told Douglas-Home that feeling ran so strong that the Government might be defeated: 'I think I ought to put it in writing before he, Ted Heath, succeeds in breaking us up entirely which, though I sincerely trust I am wrong, is in my opinion quite likely.'[22] The protests achieved little. Some concessions were made to meet the complaints of the backbenchers, particularly when it came to the onus of proving that any individual exception would not be contrary to the public interest, but Heath was emphatic that the Government must be 'seen to adhere firmly to the basic purposes of the Bill'. The Prime Minister remained stalwart. 'I think that your sympathetic handling of the Committee will enable us to hold our party together,' he wrote to Heath in early April 1964, 'but the folly of some is almost incurable … I am sure we were right, but we underestimated the reaction and the short-term damage which the sight of a party in disarray would do. But the thing to do is to plug on, and your skill and fortitude will get us through.' John Stonehouse, whose private bill had originally launched the operation, thought that Heath had gone too far in making concessions, he was 'a good man fallen among bureaucrats'. Scarcely any Tory member believed that he had gone far enough. The majority in the House of Commons once fell to a single vote. At one point Heath is said to have threatened resignation if the Bill was not fought through on its present basis; he himself denies that he went this far but admits that he was 'close to resigning'. At all events he got his way. The Bill passed, substantially unaltered. It was, said Heath, 'one of the most satisfying successes of my ministerial career'.[23]

It was won at a price. George Hutchinson, his cautiously obsequious biographer who at that time was the party's director of publicity, wrote that 'I have never myself heard a Cabinet Minister so much abused by his colleagues, so badly spoken of and so widely condemned in the party as Heath was then.' Part of this was due to the unpopularity of the policy he was promoting, part to the way in which he did it. What was unfortunate and damaging, wrote Robert Rhodes James, 'was for Heath to adopt a truculent, and at times abusive, attitude towards those Conservatives who opposed his proposals'. One senior backbencher told Ronald Butt that Heath had been 'arrogant' and 'autocratic', and when Butt suggested to another 'normally mild' Tory MP that Heath might be driven to resignation, 'he received the surprising reply "Who cares about that?"' Heath was as dismissive of members of the public as he was of Tory backbenchers. An avalanche of protesting letters arrived at the Board of Trade. The Department prepared four different replies to cover the different approaches of the correspondents: Heath refused to sign any of them. Edward du Cann, who made no secret of the fact that he thought the timing of the Bill 'tactless and politically stupid', used to ensure that the 'many hundreds of letters of complaint' were directed towards him rather than to Heath, so that he could make sure they were answered. Heath's devoted pps, Tony Kershaw, saw the damage that his master was doing himself and, as tactfully as he could, urged Heath to mend his ways. Please spend more time in the House, he pleaded. 'There is a feeling that you are ignoring the backbenchers, because you don't want to hear their criticisms. I think it is vitally important for you to do this, because if we lose the next election, and if it occurs fairly soon, it could be that you will be blamed for it. At the moment you are indisputably the second man in the Party, and while you must do whatever has to be done for good government, it is right also to preserve your personal position.'[24]

That personal position had undoubtedly been damaged. And yet at the same time his reputation had been enhanced. 'It was a very, very long-drawn-out issue,' recalled the Minister of Education,

Edward Boyle, 'and frankly, if it hadn't been for Ted Heath's very great determination and personality, I dread to think what would have happened.' Jock Bruce-Gardyne and Nigel Lawson, journalists and Tory politicians, agreed that no other Tory minister could have carried it through, indeed 'it is not easy to think of other contemporary politicians who would not have quailed and drawn back when confronted by the rage of backbenchers and the distaste and hostility of Cabinet colleagues'. It is a curious twist of fate that the attributes that made Heath so unpopular in early 1964 – truculence, obstinacy, indifference to criticism – were suddenly to seem so desirable when the Tories were looking for a new leader a little over a year later. When asked at his seventy-fifth birthday party what, apart from Europe, had been his greatest achievement, Heath said that it was the abolition of RPM. It had opened up competition, he said, and 'made possible the vast choice and low prices available today'. It had also, though he did not mention it and perhaps never accepted it to be the case, made it more likely that he would become prime minister in 1970.[25]

Whether the indignation of the small shopkeepers in fact cost the Conservatives many, or any, seats in the election that followed in October 1964 must be a matter for speculation. Certainly it scarcely featured in the campaign – probably because Labour and the Liberals were themselves generally in favour of the legislation and were immensely relieved that the Tories had grasped this nettle instead of leaving it to them. Some rancour, however, may still have lingered. 'It probably cost us seats at the general election,' Douglas-Home told the historian Peter Hennessy; 'it certainly cost the Tories some marginal seats', considered John Boyd-Carpenter, a minister who had been one of those members of the Cabinet most vociferous in pleading for the deferral of the measure and who saw in Heath's response the first signs of the 'inflexibility and unwillingness to listen which he was later to show as Prime Minister'.[26] If Douglas-Home and Boyd-Carpenter were right then Heath may indeed have cost the Tories the election. Labour's overall lead was only four; a handful of disgruntled shopkeepers could have tipped the scale in half a dozen marginal constituencies. The *Sunday Express* had no doubts on the subject. When the row over RPM was at its height it denounced the damage that Heath was doing to the Party: 'For this bland, chuckling man is the Tory Jonah. Whatever he touches goes wrong. Wherever he goes there is trouble … He carries chaos in his vest pocket.' But there were many more consumers in the electorate than there were shopkeepers and though they had less reason to air their views they may also have changed their votes because of the legislation. Heath insisted that the abolition of RPM, far from costing the Tories seats, had been responsible for the gap between the parties being so small. 'If other departments had thrown off their stale approach in that last year by bringing forward up-to-date proposals,' he wrote in his memoirs, 'we could have won.' On the whole the weight of opinion is against him, but he may have been right.[27]

A week before the election R. A. Butler was asked by the journalist George Gale what he thought of Douglas-Home's praise for the 'young, dynamic Heath'. 'That's interesting,' said Butler, 'I think Alec's a bit bored by him.' Possibly Butler was just making a little mischief, a pursuit in which he from time to time indulged. There is no other evidence to suggest that Heath was out of favour. He and Maudling were given equal billing in the election period: Maudling being responsible for the daily press conferences and Heath for the television programmes. 'I can't thank you enough for all you have done to guide and implement our TV,' wrote the party chairman. 'You have been super, under circumstances [which] were bound to be trying and tricky. Thanks a million.' If Lord Blakenham was being sincere he was in a minority. During the European negotiations Heath had been notably adept at expounding on television the complex issues which were being addressed in Brussels. Remembering this, the party managers had assumed that his skills could easily be translated to the very different arena of the political broadcast. These assumptions proved wrong. His performances were not disastrous but he was stilted and ill at ease. In one broadcast, said the political documentary maker and author Michael Cockerell, he flopped so badly that even a Tory backbencher who appeared with him and who was said 'to have sounded "like a man in a TV programme about indigestion" was judged to have performed better'. By the time the campaign was halfway over it was obvious that Heath's authority and drive would have been better suited to the press conferences, while Maudling's avuncular benevolence would have come through well on television. By then, however, it was too late.[28]

Starting from the assumption that his own achievements over RPM had produced one of the few positive features of the Tory campaign, Heath judged the party's approach to the election to be 'tired and shorn of new ideas'. In fact, given the way the tide had been flowing even a few months before, Douglas-Home did well to hold the swing to 3.5 per cent. Labour's share actually fell but a substantially increased Liberal vote, achieved mainly at the expense of the Conservatives, was enough to tip the balance and give Harold Wilson's party a tiny overall majority. Heath was worried about the inroads the Liberals might make into his majority at Bexley and told Lord Blakenham that he wanted to devote 'as much time as possible to my own constituency'. In the event the Liberals won a little over 6,000 votes and Heath's majority was almost halved, to 4,589 – comfortable enough, but not so large as to mean that he need have no concerns about the future. If any Tory candidate attributed his own defeat to the abolition of RPM he does not seem to have expressed his views in public; Maudling, who as Chancellor was seen to bear greater responsibility for the economic problems that had bedevilled the Tories' last year in office, was at least as much damaged as Heath by the election setback.[29]

The main loser was, of course, Alec Douglas-Home himself. The Tory Party judges failure harshly and, even though the result could have been much worse, an election had been lost. The nature of the defeat was particularly damaging to the former Prime Minister. Harold Wilson had fought a sparkling campaign and had contrived continually to contrast his own personality – dynamic, a man of the people, daring, innovative – with the dusty, tweed-suited, out-of-touch image of the Tory leader. Neither sketch was fair, let alone told the whole story, but there were sufficient grounds for them to give the Tory backbenchers the uneasy feeling that they were being led by the wrong man. That feeling was redoubled when it became clear that Douglas-Home, as Leader of the Opposition in the cockpit of the

House of Commons, was no match for the quick-witted and un-scrupulous Wilson. More and more members felt that a change was needed: the main factor inhibiting a revolt was doubt as to who the new leader ought to be.

Almost at once Douglas-Home took the first step to resolve that doubt. When parliament reconvened he announced that Maudling was to be shadow Foreign Secretary; Heath would take over as shadow Chancellor. It is unlikely that he intended to convey any clear message by these appointments – it was perfectly sensible to let Maudling widen his experience; indeed, it could well have been a stepping stone to the eventual leadership. The result was, however, that Maudling played a relatively unobtrusive role over the next nine months, while Heath was in the firing line with every opportunity to attract the attention of his party and the general public. He took his chance by launching a ferocious attack on Labour's budget and the Finance Bill that followed. In so doing he immensely raised the morale of the Opposition, enraged the Government and frequently outmanoeuvred and confounded the Labour Chancellor, Jim Callaghan. Knox Cunningham, an Ulster Unionist MP, regularly briefed Macmillan on what was going on in the House of Commons. Early in April 1965 he reported: 'Ted Heath made a first class speech in the budget debate. Our side were greatly pleased and at times the Government supporters looked glum'; a month or so later, 'Ted Heath made a truly excellent speech and got under the Chancellor's skin in the opening stages. It was a first rate performance'; at the beginning of July the Chief Whip announced a three-line whip for the whole of the follow-ing week. 'Such was the morale of the party that not a voice was raised in protest.'

Heath asked nothing of the backbenchers which he did not give himself. Night after night at midnight or later he would go over to John Cope and Mark Schreiber, the two young men who were in attendance in case some information was called for, and say 'I don't think there'll be much more happening tonight. You boys had better go off to your night clubs.' They would instead totter off to bed; he would as often as not stay on in the House for several more hours. Sometimes he expected too much even of the most willing assistant.

Leaving the House of Commons at 6.15 a.m., he turned to Peter Walker and said: 'I'll see you at 8.30, and you might prepare me a brief on Clauses 23 and 24.' 'He was somewhat shocked by my response!' said Walker dryly. His determination, assiduity and endless resourcefulness impressed many of those who had hitherto taken it for granted that Maudling was the heir apparent. Stratton Mills, a moderate Unionist MP, told Maudling's biographer: 'After seeing Ted I was much more impressed by his style and approach, his energy ... If Reggie had been handling that Finance Bill it would have been totally different. Callaghan ended up demoralised.' The government was equally struck by his performance. In a censure debate on home loans Dick Crossman noted in his diary that Heath 'made an extremely powerful oration, accusing us of welching on our pledges and deceiving the public. What was I to reply? What he said was quite true.'[30]

Yet, however ferocious his onslaught, he was scrupulous in sticking to the truth. Once, in the debate on the Finance Bill, a Tory backbencher made use of what Heath felt to be false statistics. Angrily he said to Peter Walker: 'If we cannot oppose bad legislation without being dishonest we shouldn't oppose it at all.' In the Lobby afterwards he berated the startled member for his sharp practice (unsurprisingly, the member in question was prominent in the campaign to unseat Heath as leader of the party a few years later). He also sometimes disconcerted the right wing of his party by accepting Labour propositions which they would have rejected either from conviction or for the sake of scoring points in opposition. When Callaghan introduced a capital gains tax Heath accepted that, at a modest level, such a tax might be useful 'if it enabled people to keep more of their earnings and also removed any sense of injustice'. Enoch Powell, who thought the whole idea 'economic and political nonsense', was outraged by what he saw as misguided liberalism.[31]

As if waging a full-scale war in the House of Commons was not enough, Heath had also been made responsible for the whole apparatus of policy planning. As chairman of the Advisory Committee on Policy (ACP) he took over from Butler the task of rethinking the principles on which Tory government should be grounded. The probability that Wilson, with his exiguous majority, would call a general election in the near future meant that the process could not be as thorough as Heath would have liked, but whatever the outcome of such an election might be, he intended that the work should carry on until the party had been truly modernised. Thirty-six policy groups were set up and most of their reports were ready by the summer of 1965. Heath was determined that the operation should remain under his individual control: he enjoyed, said John Ramsden, the Conservative Party historian, 'a more personal monopoly of authority in the party than any other leader since Neville Chamberlain'.[32] He brooked no interference. Maudling telephoned Brendon Sewill in the Conservative Research Department and asked to see the papers. Sewill agreed but then consulted Heath. 'Don't give them to that bloody man, he'll only take credit for them,' was the disobliging reply. Sewill was forced to prevaricate and go into hiding in case Maudling arrived in his office and demanded to read the reports.[33]

To the more traditional Tories such an enterprise seemed dangerously radical. Lady Douglas-Home was quoted in the *Daily Mail* as deploring the emergence of a 'shiny, bright new party' in which nobody would recognise the true Conservatives. William Anstruther-Gray, successor to Morrison as chairman of the 1922 Committee, announced at a meeting in Central Office that 'he didn't understand what all this talk of policy was'. It seemed to him to be 'quite unnecessary and deeply disturbing to the party'. William Whitelaw, who had recently been appointed Opposition Chief Whip, was not so averse to the idea of reform but he too felt the exercise was 'nothing but disaster'. He spoke, however, as somebody whose main preoccupations were to keep the party loyal to Douglas-Home and Douglas-Home prepared to continue to lead the party. Those objectives, he believed, were being undermined by the activities of the ACP: 'There is no doubt that as the policy groups continued and Ted Heath dominated to the extent he did, many people who had not known him before, came to believe that they wanted another Leader.'[34]

Shortly after the general election Tony Kershaw reported to Heath that there seemed to be no pressure for a quick change of leadership. This, he remarked, was just as well, 'because at the moment Reggie

Maudling is the alternative choice ... Any attempt by your friends to force the pace would probably be counter-productive ...' They should work on the assumption that there would be no change for two years. 'We must and should play it slow. We thought that a number of dinner parties would help. It would be very good, we thought, if you would also do this – it would dispel any austere-bachelor-technician image you may be surprised to learn you have.' A poll in the *Daily Telegraph* in February 1965 seemed to support Kershaw's view: three-quarters of the Tory MPs wanted Douglas-Home to carry on; if he did resign 35 per cent favoured Maudling as his replacement, 28 per cent still hankered after Butler, only 10 per cent wanted Heath.[35]

But things were changing. There had always been a small but robust section of the party which had thought it vital that there should be a change of direction and of management. 'We are sick of seeing old-looking men dressed in flat caps and bedraggled tweeds,' wrote a 44-year-old industrial manager. 'The nearest approach to our man is Heath. In every task he performs, win or lose, he has the facts and figures and looks a director (of the country) and most of all he is quite different from these tired old men.' As Heath's reputation grew in the ACP as a reformist and in the House of Commons as a powerful and relentless debater – so people began to see him as a future leader. As Douglas-Home time and again demonstrated that he was too gentle-manly, too courteous, too restrained to cope with the mercurial mischief of Harold Wilson, so the feeling strengthened that the change should be made as soon as possible. A new system of selection had recently been introduced which meant that the traditional sounding of opinion would be abandoned in favour of a secret ballot among all Tory MPs. So long as a general election seemed likely at short notice the would-be rebels, nervous about the notorious risks of changing horses in mid-stream, preserved their silence. In the summer of 1965, however, Wilson announced that there would be no election that year. The main reason for restraint had disappeared; the dogs of war were let slip.

What dogs and who let them slip? R. A. Butler had retreated from the political arena to become Master of Trinity College, Cambridge, but Maudling was quite as ready as Heath to replace Douglas-Home as leader if the opportunity was offered. Nevertheless, the weight of opinion suggests that it was Heath's followers who made the running. 'A number of Heath's henchmen,' wrote Humphry Berkeley, were urging members to write to Whitelaw or du Cann, the new chairman of the Conservative Party, expressing their misgivings about the present leadership. Macleod and Walker in particular, alleged du Cann, were lobbying against Douglas-Home – 'unknown to Heath, I dare say, though one could not be sure'.[36] Heath himself always vehemently rejected any such insinuation. He could make a good case in his own defence. To correspondents who urged him to press his candidature he replied that any speculation on such lines was playing into the hands of Harold Wilson; 'the best service any of us can give to the party is to give full and loyal support to the leader'.[37] But he cannot have been wholly unaware of what his supporters were doing, if not in his name then at least on his behalf. Nor could he deny that he was positioning himself so that *if* Douglas-Home did retire he would be well placed to challenge for the succession. Nigel Fisher claimed that some of the preliminary meetings 'designed to put him in an advantageous position should Douglas-Home decide to go' were held in Heath's flat in Albany. Over this period he at least twice entertained influential political journalists to lunch *à deux*. 'If there were a leadership contest now I think you'd probably win it,' said one of them. Heath considered the proposition. 'You may be right,' he concluded. He had no need to play a more active part himself; it was all happening without his personal intervention. As Chateaubriand said of the duc d'Orléans, he 'did not conspire in fact, but by consent'. The worst of which Heath can be accused is that he could have called off the dogs of war. He chose not to do so.[38]

Douglas-Home himself never blamed Heath for his behaviour. 'Ted was very unhappy in case people thought that he was trying to undermine me,' he told Heath's biographer, George Hutchinson. 'I am quite sure he was not.' His wife, Elizabeth, was less charitable. She made no secret of the fact that she felt Heath had been indelicately quick in letting himself be drafted as the next leader. 'The fact', commented Rhodes James, 'that the principal architects of Sir Alec's removal were also those of Heath's subsequent campaign for the leadership left an aftertaste of bitterness in some parts of the party.'[39]

The plotters were pushing at an open door. Douglas-Home had no intention of continuing to lead a party which was not substantially behind him. On 22 July 1965 he summoned Selwyn Lloyd to his office and said: 'I am going to let you down. I have decided to chuck my hand in and give up the leadership.' Later the same day he announced his intention to the 1922 Committee. 'The "rotters" eleven has won,' snarled one knight of the shires angrily, but the feeling of the majority was some relief and a regretful acceptance of the inevitable. At once interest switched to the election of a successor. Macleod, knowing only too well his unpopularity in certain sections of the party, accepted that he must be a non-starter. Maudling and Heath were the obvious front-runners. Christopher Soames urged Selwyn Lloyd to stand: 'He felt very much that the bulk of the party did not want either Maudling or Heath and there should be a third candidate.' Quintin Hogg agreed that 60 per cent of the party were looking for someone else; after his experiences at the last leadership election he had no intention of himself standing again but he, too, would have backed Lloyd. Lloyd, after some reflection, decided he would not stand unless there was something near a dead heat on the first ballot and a bitter conflict would otherwise ensue. Whitelaw agreed that this was a proper course of action. Harold Macmillan let it be known that he thought it should either be Heath or Maudling: 'That was the type of person they wanted, the age they wanted and it was no use kicking against the pricks.' Peter Thorneycroft at first insisted that, whatever happened, he would compete himself because 'he thought he was a better man than either of the other two'; after much persuasion he accepted that he would secure only a handful of votes and decided not to stand. Enoch Powell alone remained in the race, presumably so as to lay down a marker for the future. In effect it was to be a straight race between Heath and Maudling.[40]

Maudling was the favourite at the start. He had the greater experience, had for some time been treated as deputy leader, was widely popular in the House. But his very popularity seemed to count against him: Home had been popular but Home had failed to hold his own; perhaps someone rougher, more abrasive, would better suit the need?

The press for the most part favoured Heath. Cecil King, proprietor of the *Daily Mirror*, liked both men but he believed that Heath was 'a positive force – a leader … certainly the best available man to be Tory PM'. More remarkably he told Heath that Beaverbrook felt the same: a striking tribute given the differences between the two men over Europe, though Maudling too was stamped in Beaverbrook's eyes as a dangerous Europhile. Of the Tory grandees Lord Avon was non-committal; Macmillan was decidedly for Heath – 'I feel sure that Ted is the best choice. He is a stronger character than Maudling'. Home was equivocal; he told Michael King 'he would have preferred Reggie: he thought lazy men came off better in a crisis', but to Selwyn Lloyd he 'made it pretty clear that he himself was going to vote for Heath'. Probably the most important single voice was that of Iain Macleod. If he had stood he would have gained some forty-five votes; though he made no attempt to control the way his supporters cast their votes it was well known that he favoured Heath: almost to a man, the Macleodites plumped for Heath. But for those votes, Maudling would have won. 'It was in character,' du Cann wrote balefully. 'Macleod had let down Alec, now he let down Reggie. Macleod was to have his reward: Heath made him Shadow Chancellor.' Both Margaret Thatcher and Keith Joseph were warmly in Heath's favour. 'I was a Heath man,' said Joseph. 'He had been very good to me … listening to me. He had the right ideas on management. I remember the sheer excitement when he won.'[41]

Heath's team left nothing to chance. Heath had asked his young acolyte, Peter Walker, to manage his campaign. Walker doubted whether he was experienced or senior enough. 'Do you really want me to organise it,' he asked, 'or to be told by you what to do?' Heath offered him a free hand, and he accepted. His first proviso was that two of Heath's prominent senior supporters should be denied any role in the campaign on the grounds that their extreme right-wing views were likely to lose more votes than they gained. Heath agreed, and told them to stay out of London. 'They were extremely disgruntled but did as they were asked.' Walker, with the help of Charles Morrison, Ian Gilmour and the veteran former minister Geoffrey Lloyd, then conducted an extremely professional operation in the course of which every MP who could remotely be classified as doubtful was canvassed and urged, for the sake of the party, to vote in the right way. Additional support was wheeled out when there were special interests to be won over. Heath told Michael King that, while he had the support of almost all the younger members, he was not popular with the grand old knights of the shire, who still carried a lot of weight in the party. Tufton Beamish, a squirearchical but highly intelligent backbencher who could play the Tory grandee as convincingly as any pompous blimp, was assigned the task of winning over this sector of the party. Nigel Lawson's particular contribution was to ensure that Heath went conspicuously to church the Sunday before polling day. Maudling was no churchgoer, so the votes of a few of the devout might be secured for a Church of England stalwart. Maudling's campaign, on the other hand, was faltering and incompetent: Philip Goodhart, who was part of it, described it as 'the worst organised leadership campaign in Conservative history: a total shambles'.[42]

The day before the election the issue was still in doubt. Both sides were making big claims, Knox Cunningham told Macmillan, but 'I cannot say how the party as a whole is going'. His instinct told him, however, that only one ballot would be needed and that Heath would win. Maudling could not accept that this was so. Ever since Douglas-Home's appointment as Prime Minister he had assumed that he would one day succeed him. It could not be that the prize was to be snatched from him at the last moment.[43]

He was to be bitterly disappointed. On the first ballot on 27 July 1965 Heath won by 150 votes to Maudling's 133 and Powell's 15. According to the rules Maudling could have gone forward to a second ballot but he chose instead to concede. Whitelaw hastened to admit to him that he had given his vote to Heath: 'I hope that I would have been equally frank with him had he won.' Maudling did not appear notably cheered by this confession. Edward Boyle found him in the Smoking Room behind a glass of Scotch. 'What is there left for me to do save to sit here and get pissed?' asked Maudling. 'Which is precisely what he did.' Almost as disappointed, though for very different reasons, was the Labour Minister of Housing, Dick Crossman. 'I knew that Douglas-Home's departure was a real disaster for us,' he wrote in his diary, 'and I wanted Maudling instead of Heath because Heath would be the most formidable leader ... As a result we have curiously similar leaders in the Tory and Labour parties. Two wholly political politicians, much more tactically then strategically minded ... All the disadvantages of Harold Wilson seem to me incorporated in Heath – and most of the advantages as well – his drive, energy, skill in debate, his dedication to politics ...' It was not the only occasion that Crossman got things hopelessly wrong – Heath was one of the least tactical of politicians – but Crossman was right in seeing that he would prove a more formidable opponent for Wilson than Douglas-Home had been or Maudling would have been.[44]

The following day Heath spoke to the 1922 Committee. He made all the right noises – praised the conduct of the ballot, the selflessness of Douglas-Home. 'He pledged himself to maintain the unity of the party. He pleased the Committee by saying that pressure would be kept up on the Government during the recess.' When he entered, Knox Cunningham told Macmillan, 'he got a *not* very loud welcome, but when he finished he got loud applause'. So far so good; but Heath did not imagine that things would always run so smoothly between him and the more turbulent members of his party. He saw the problems ahead but also felt immense elation. Peter Walker had waited with him while Maudling was making up his mind to concede. He was obviously happy, remembered Walker, 'but already recognising the magnitude of his task. He had an immense desire to restore the fortunes of his country. Much of his political motivation is, in fact, simple patriotism.'[45]

NINE

Leader of the Opposition

Throughout Heath's years as Leader of the Opposition he was waging a war on two fronts: against the Prime Minister, Harold Wilson, and against a substantial element of his own party. On the whole his loathing for his Conservative opponents was the more intense.

Not that he had any love for Wilson. He would have been outraged if he had known that Crossman found him and Wilson 'curiously similar'. Both men were ambitious politicians dedicated to their careers, but where Wilson was intellectually agile, endlessly resourceful and almost entirely indifferent to questions of principle, Heath was ponderous, thoughtful, tenacious and obstinately convinced that there were certain values to which he must at all costs adhere. Asked in a 1985 television interview what he had thought of Wilson, Heath replied that he found him 'too preoccupied with immediate advantage'. 'You mean that he was a tactician rather than a strategist?' asked the interviewer. 'It wasn't even tactics. It was just opportunism. He wasn't my style.' The two men actively disliked each other. To a man as genial as Willie Whitelaw this was regrettable. 'There is a real, embarrassing animus between Heath and Wilson,' he told David Butler in 1969. 'Both are to blame ... It is embarrassing to be in the same room as them both.' Maudling, equally affable, was disconcerted to find that, when they called on Wilson for a meeting on Privy Councillor terms – that is, completely confidential and off the record – Heath 'froze as soon as Wilson came into the room'. Heath himself denied that there was any real animosity between them; the press, he claimed, had 'wildly exaggerated it'. But when in 1975 David Frost persistently asked whether he liked Wilson he could not bring himself to say more than that 'it was not a question of liking'. They 'worked perfectly well together when it was necessary'.[1]

Heath disliked Wilson more than Wilson, Heath; partly because his was the more unforgiving disposition, partly because Wilson, at first at least, regularly outshone him in the House of Commons. A presage of the future came on 2 August 1965 when Heath as Leader of the Opposition for the first time proposed the motion of censure on the Government. His followers flocked to the Chamber to see their gallant young champion flatten the Labour leader. The results were dire. He had 'so factual a brief, so exhaustively worked out', remembered Enoch Powell, 'that the House was almost dead by the time he got through it'. There was no drama, no passion, no sense of occasion. 'Ted didn't really think, I believe, that the House of Commons has a heart, let alone the British people.' Cecil King recorded in his diary: 'The general opinion in the Tory party is that he has got off to a poor start.' His speech had been 'not good'; and, worse still, 'far inferior to Reggie's'. Harold Wilson somewhat sanctimoniously disclaimed any wish to make a gladiatorial display of the occasion but expressed surprise in his memoirs that Heath's speech was 'less good than I expected, no light and shade'. Their encounters in the House of Commons tended to be more bullfight than gladiatorial display: the flashy matador confronting a sullen and angry bull. Sometimes the matador got gored, far more often the sword went home. 'I have witnessed many confrontations between rival leaders in Parliament,' wrote James Griffiths, 'but none which was so uneven as that between Wilson and Heath.'[2]

At times the battle took on an unattractively personal note. 'Is this a private row or can I join in?' asked the veteran Labour leader, Emmanuel Shinwell plaintively on one occasion.[3] On both sides there was a feeling that it went too far. Once, in Cabinet, Wilson showed some alarm at the recent local election results and urged his colleagues to 'kick Ted in the groin. We must be rough with him!' Tony Benn argued that this would be counter-productive and would forfeit the high position in the public mind which Wilson and his government now occupied. Most of those present agreed. Geoffrey Howe for the Conservatives urged Heath to avoid doing battle on grounds which would allow Wilson 'to excel in the exchange of abuse and mud'. The advice was probably otiose, he said, as well as being impertinent, but some of his colleagues had told him that 'I had a fair chance of not having my head bitten off.'[4]

He did not have his head bitten off. Heath knew that the advice was sound and, if only in self-protection, avoided slanging matches with Wilson whenever possible. But he was bound constantly to confront him in debate and usually came off worst. As for his set orations, they were rarely more than competent. This was not for want of effort. 'He drafts and drafts and drafts,' said Anthony Kershaw, 'takes out a comma and puts it back in, crosses out a phrase and puts it back.' But he was not interested in how his speeches sounded, only that their meaning should be clear. Iain Macleod was baffled how someone so musical, with a highly developed sense of harmony, should be unable 'to make a speech that anyone can listen to: no feeling for words at all, no feeling for the rhythm of language'. The curious thing was that speaking, apparently extempore, after dinner or at a memorial service, Heath would be funny, moving, rousing, could hit exactly the note required. Ian Trethowan remembered him making 'the wittiest speech I can recall in 35 years of listening to political oratory', but that was on a private occasion and most of those present were friends or, at least, Tories of more or less similar views. Before an unknown or hostile audience, in the House of Commons or some other such assembly, he became laboured in his delivery, cautious in his content. Describing a speech to the 1922 Committee – a body which, in May 1968, was certainly critical if not actively hostile – Knox Cunningham told Macmillan that Heath 'did not pause for applause and did not get it. He uses his new style – grave and serious with few smiles. It is quite effective, but his gestures are stilted and the intense seriousness tends to become monotonous.'[5]

In mid-1968 Andrew Alexander of the *Daily Telegraph* wrote to the new chairman of the Tory Party, Tony Barber, to plead that something drastic should be done about Heath's speeches 'or he will soon end up being totally ignored. Nowadays in Fleet Street the news that EH is to make a big speech is received with, at best, a yawn, at worst – and more commonly – derision.' He did improve. A few months later, when Heath had been fortified by some excellent by-election results and the Government was in serious trouble, Alexander admitted that, though he could not match Wilson's 'cool mastery of the House', he was capable of producing 'a first class speech'. Early in 1970 Cunningham was telling Macmillan that: 'There was a splendid row between the Prime Minister and Ted – Ted got the best of it. At the end the Prime Minister got laughed at and didn't like it.' Three months later: 'Ted did well. He was rather playful at the start and neither the Chancellor nor the Prime Minister liked it.' He would never have allowed himself to be playful two years before.[6]

One of the reasons Cunningham gave for Heath's new-found confidence was that he had recently returned from Australia after achieving sensational success in the Sydney-to-Hobart yacht race. Heath's career as a yachtsman was curious yet characteristic. It was curious in that he undertook it at all given that, until the age of fifty, he had rarely even stepped on to a sailing boat; characteristic, because, once he had decided to undertake this venture, he applied himself with total dedication and was not content until he had established himself as a seriously important figure in the international yachting world.

His reasons for beginning, he said, were partly medical. His doctor told him he was working too hard and taking too little exercise: he must find a diversion which would remedy both these problems. Golf involved too much political chatter, he hadn't got a garden, he was bad at tennis; then, one day in Broadstairs in the summer of 1965, he saw a notice for a sailing school, thought he would give it a try and, almost overnight, became a dedicated sailor. It has been suggested that there were other reasons for his decision. 'The whole idea that Grocer is interested in sailing was cooked up at a meeting between Geoffrey Tucker [an advertising man who had become publicity director of the Conservative Party] and some worried businessmen,' wrote Auberon Waugh in *Private Eye*. A new image for Heath was badly needed, claimed Waugh. His music had proved unappealing to the masses. A life on the ocean wave – classless, vigorous, adventurous – would do much better. If he made a success of it, it would be better still, but, provided he did not actually drown, the mere fact that he had put to sea would do the trick. Two rich businessmen with links to the yachting world, Graham Dowson and Maurice Laing, were enlisted to provide whatever help was needed. A new Heath was launched.[7]

As is usually the case with *Private Eye* stories, a nugget of truth was buried in a mountain of speculation and innuendo. Heath took to sailing entirely at his own initiative, encouraged in his resolve by his old friend Madron Seligman, but arranging for his own lessons without reference to anyone. The idea that it might enhance his popular image may have occurred to him but can have played little part in his calculations: he accepted, in principle, the need to court public opinion but was never prepared to put himself out very far in what he regarded as an undignified and slightly vulgar quest. But Geoffrey Tucker, for one, did see the use that could be made of this surprising and sometimes dangerous hobby. When, some summers later, it became obvious that Heath intended to devote whatever spare time he had to his yacht *Morning Cloud*, Tucker wrote: 'It is absolutely essential that a plan of campaign should be thought out for this activity as soon as possible. If this is not done a great deal of unfavourable comment would be generated ... Your musical interest has worked beautifully and to your advantage. There is no reason why your boat should not do the same.' When, shortly after he became Prime Minister, Heath asked Tucker what he thought the public reaction would be if he moved on to a second generation of *Morning Cloud*, Tucker replied that he must do what he wanted to do: 'If it relaxes you, if you enjoy it, you'll do better at the other things'. Admittedly, he added cautiously, 'if you wanted to buy a £50,000 as opposed to a £7,000 yacht ...'[8]

It was nearer £7,000 than £50,000, but once Heath had decided that he would not be content to crew in other people's boats but was determined to be skipper of his own, it was clear that it was going to be an expensive business. His investments were doing well; as Leader of the Opposition he earned £4,500 a year as well as his MP's salary of £1,350; in spite of the expense of running Albany he was still living frugally but the £20,000 or so a year which was the cost of running an ocean-going yacht of the size of *Morning Cloud* must have been far beyond him. Though no precise figures exist it seems certain that he was helped substantially along his way by rich supporters, notably the building tycoon, Maurice Laing. It is equally certain that he promised no favours in return. Heath was almost always ready to accept offers of financial or other support (though he seems to have drawn the line at an offer of £50,000 from Charles Forte, to him personally, 'for the one and only purpose of further enhancing your prestige in the eyes of the Party and the country. I am prepared for this purpose *to subscribe even more than the sum mentioned should it be required …* There can be no strings attached to this offer, of course.)[9] But it never occurred to him that, apart from general signs of friendliness, anything could be expected of him. He would have been genuinely shocked, indeed outraged, if he had thought that the support of Laing or anyone else had to be paid for. Gratitude was not one of his more marked characteristics; he tended to think that offers of support, whether political or financial, were no more than his due. If rich admirers were ready to help with the expenses of *Morning Cloud*, then well and good. If they had not done so he would have renounced his racing career; with regret certainly but without hesitation.[10]

Once the plunge was taken, his progress was startlingly rapid. In 1965 he told Madron Seligman that he was going to take up sailing: 'I didn't think he would,' said Seligman, 'but two or three years later, there he was, an expert.' Nicholas Henderson once asked Seligman how it was that Heath, so recently a novice, had outstripped Seligman, an experienced yachtsman. Seligman's explanation was 'that Heath was more dedicated. He also had tremendous physical endurance and courage.' Henderson suggested that Heath liked 'to do something that enables him to triumph over the elements and to prove himself to himself'. Within three years he had bought a Fireball for £250: Seligman tried to talk him out of it but Heath was adamant, 'he was very hurt and said that he was a real sailor now'. His first mentor at the Broadstairs sailing club would have agreed. Heath, he said, was 'a very quick learner. I wouldn't say that he was athletic – he applies his mind more than his body, but that's more important in sailing.' However rough the weather 'he showed no apprehension – he seemed all aglow with it and oblivious to the dangers'. He took part in his first ocean race aboard Maurice Laing's *Clarion of Wight* and, once he had experienced the exultation and excitement of racing a large yacht in high seas, knew that nothing less could satisfy him. In 1969 he bought the first in what was to be a series of ocean-going yachts, called *Morning Cloud*.[11]

At his seventy-fifth birthday party he declared that one of the good things for him about sailing had been that politics were never mentioned, 'he had no idea of the views of his crew members'. He deceived himself; in fact he took it for granted – as it turned out, with justification – that all aboard were broadly speaking sympathetic to his views, and he enjoyed regaling them with anecdotes about political triumphs or disasters: 'We were an audience,' said one of his leading colleagues, Peter Nicholson. Most of his crew joined him en bloc with Anthony Churchill, a publisher and highly accomplished yachtsman, when Heath first set up *Morning Cloud*. They were an experienced and hardened team, all more proficient in their different skills then their new skipper. This caused no problems: Heath never found it difficult to acknowledge that, in any field, there were people who knew more about the subject than he did. He respected his crew's abilities, enjoyed learning from them and relaxed entirely in their company. He loyally supported any of them who needed help in later life – one of his most attractive characteristics, indeed, was his readiness to put himself out to help people who, one way or another, had served him well in the past. He rarely thanked but quite often showed gratitude in a more serviceable way.

Given that Heath was not in the first rank in any of the specialised duties of a yachtsman the layman might wonder what contribution he made to his boat's success. 'He was very analytical and observant,' says Nicholson. 'His post-race analyses were of real value: we lost ten seconds doing such-and-such, he would say, how can we avoid the same thing happening again?' Still more important, he enthused his crew. When he was aboard, says Churchill, 'everyone tried harder and worked better together'. In every field of life Heath was at his best

'HAROLD, YOU'RE CHEATING AGAIN!'

with a small group of like-minded enthusiasts who shared his objectives and were prepared to work hard and loyally in a common cause.
Morning Cloud provided such an environment. For three years Heath
was captain of the British Ocean Racing Team, for two years of the
British Admiral's Cup Team, winning the cup back for Britain in
1971. Still more remarkable, at the very end of 1969, *Morning Cloud*
won the 700-mile Sydney-to-Hobart race, one of the toughest com-
petitions and most coveted prizes in ocean racing. 'Ted is off to
Australia to take part in some Australian sailing races,' Cecil King had
noted sourly a few weeks before. 'I think Ted should be providing
leadership, not playing about in Australia.' Most people thought that
leadership was just what Heath *was* providing – in an unexpected
sphere, perhaps, but in a way which brought a measure of glory to his
country and much credit to himself and his crew. More generous was
Richard Crossman, who admired 'the new enthusiasm, courage and
drive of Ted Heath, who rather gallantly went out to Australia and
won the first prize in the Sydney–Hobart yacht race'. The image of a
rugged, intrepid Heath boldly imposing his will upon the elements

had gradually become established over the previous years; now, Knox Cunningham told Macmillan, 'his sailing victory seems to have done him good in the country and given him a new confidence'.[12]

He needed it. Since he had become Leader of the Opposition he had passed through much choppy water and the occasional gale. All had gone reasonably well at first. Traditionally, the Tory leader, when in opposition, enjoyed more power than his Labour equivalent. He could choose his own party chairman and deputy chairman and appoint as many or as few spokesmen to the front bench as he felt inclined. Heath's first decision was that he would do as little of his work as possible in the rooms in the House of Commons assigned to the Leader of the Opposition: 'drab and depressing', Harold Wilson's close aide Marcia Williams described them; 'the carpet was a down-trodden patch in the centre of the room, with a linoleum surround'. Instead, he set up his headquarters in Albany. The most constant visitor was the head of his office, John MacGregor, a calm, highly efficient and stolid Scot who saw it as his duty not only to impose order on the multifarious responsibilities which his master had to undertake but also to shed a slightly more genial light on the intractable face which Heath habitually presented to the world. The editor of *Punch* sent Heath a copy of that week's edition, saying that he thought it would be of interest. 'Not v. amusing,' noted Heath dourly. 'Mr Heath found it most amusing,' was MacGregor's interpretation of this judgment. Like most of the people who worked closely with Heath, MacGregor found the experience sometimes frustrating, occasionally alarming, but on the whole immensely rewarding. 'I've never had such a stimulating three and a half years,' he told one of Heath's biographers. 'He changed the *scale* of my thinking. He is what I would like to be.'[13]

As foreign policy adviser, Heath plucked Douglas Hurd from the Conservative Research Department. Hurd was a highly intelligent and independent minded would-be MP, who had defected from the Foreign Service and was delighted to find himself so close to the centre of Conservative politics. He was to replace MacGregor in 1968. Altogether there were seven people working in the private office; all except one personal secretary paid for by the party. Quite as important as any of these were the two parliamentary private secretaries: Anthony Kershaw and Jim Prior. They were the links between the Leader of the Opposition and the parliamentary party: a job which, given Heath's disinclination to court the favour of backbenchers or even to remember who they were, was singularly important and frequently frustrating. Prior was selected by Willie Whitelaw because, as a Suffolk farmer, he represented an important section of the Tory party which was almost entirely unknown to the leader. Bluff, down-to-earth and far shrewder than he liked to appear, Prior was to remain extremely close to Heath and one of his most valued advisers. 'Willie says I know nothing about farming or the rural constituencies and your experience at Central Office will help,' Heath told him. 'You've got to help me keep in touch with grass roots feeling and get me into the Smoking Room as much as you can.' This brusque, half-joking style was something to which Prior soon became accustomed: 'At times amounting to rudeness, yet also the shyness of an introvert; and sometimes a reaction of great frustration that he could not always get through to people.'[14]

If he had been free to do all he wished Heath would probably have chopped away some of what he felt to be the dead or dying wood in the Shadow Cabinet which he had inherited from Douglas-Home. With another general election in the offing, however, he felt inhibited from making any significant changes. Whitelaw, whose judgment as Chief Whip Heath valued greatly, urged caution. Heath, he said, should avoid 'drastic action which might create bitterness and disturb unity'. Thorneycroft could be dropped 'but would cause trouble from a back-bench'; Selwyn Lloyd was overdue for retirement 'but the Party are sorry for him'; Hogg (to which name Lord Hailsham had now reverted) didn't do anything but was a popular figure, '*very difficult to drop*'. Whatever happened it was clear that, if he wanted the job, Douglas-Home should be shadow Foreign Secretary. G. E. Christ, the Conservative's liaison officer, wrote to du Cann saying that this 'would be good electorally and excite the press'. Exciting the press did not come high on Heath's list of priorities but he thought Douglas-Home would be the best man for the job as well as the man with the strongest claim. Douglas-Home accepted without demur: it was work he loved and he saw nothing demeaning about serving the man who had so recently been serving him. Whitelaw wanted Edward Boyle to be Chancellor; Heath thought well of Boyle and – since both men were passionately involved with music – found him easy to talk to, but he believed that Iain Macleod was the more formidable figure and that the effectiveness of the Shadow Cabinet would be much reduced if he were not in one of the two or three most important posts. In the end Heath told Selwyn Lloyd, a victim of Macmillan's purge who had been brought back by Douglas-Home, that, though there would be some switching around of portfolios, he had decided to retain the whole front bench – 'a considerable number of changes would be wrong in the sort of emergency situation facing us ... He thought that it would be rather unfair to ask one or two to leave.'[15]

The most pressing problem was whether he should eject du Cann from his chairmanship of the Conservative Party. Heath knew that he and du Cann would never work satisfactorily together but feared the mischief that du Cann might do if forced from his post. Whitelaw or Carrington, the Tory leader in the House of Lords, were the obvious replacements but both had important roles to fill elsewhere. Peter Walker, when consulted, advised that it would be a mistake to change du Cann – 'He was doing well enough with the Party generally' – and Whitelaw too thought it better to leave things as they were. If, Whitelaw later told David Butler, he 'had realised how much they were chalk and cheese he would have pressed Ted to make a change immediately'. As it was, the uneasy relationship dragged on, each man disliking the other and making little effort to disguise the animosity.[16]

Knowing that Wilson was bound to go to the country soon Heath hurled himself into a hectic round of tours around the United Kingdom; a pattern which persisted even when the general election had come and gone and the most urgent pressure had been relieved. 'I had never seen a man drive himself so hard,' wrote Douglas Hurd. 'No Leader of the Opposition had visited so many places or met so many people.' Not all those people were impressed: generally speaking Heath got on well with the real grandees and established a good relationship with the politically conscious editors of provincial papers but he had problems with the retired soldiers and sailors who had become secretaries of golf clubs and the more snobbish elements of the minor gentry. He was ill at ease in Scotland, where he feared people thought that Douglas-Home should still be leader. His public appearances were consistent if sometimes uninspiring: 'EH on and on and on,' wrote Hurd wearily in his diary, 'never superb, always adequate, sometimes good.' Yet on the whole the tours made him far better known and enhanced his reputation. He delivered about 150 speeches a year outside parliament, most of them in the provinces, and however lacklustre Hurd may have found him at the fiftieth time of hearing, in Sheffield, York and many other provincial cities he got a rapturous reception.[17]

His popularity in the party, Hurd observed, tended to be cyclical; rising at the time of each party conference and then dropping away as the effect of the conference wore off. His first conference as leader was at Brighton in October 1965. He broke with precedent by being present for all three days and by speaking at the beginning and at the end. In his second speech he indulged in an unusual display of personal emotion. He spoke of the fervent patriotism he had recently witnessed at the 'Last Night of the Proms' and of the need to provide leadership that would harness this energy to the service of the nation. The speech was hailed as a triumph and certainly when it was delivered made a strong and favourable impression. But the effects soon dwindled. The Labour leaders were on the whole comforted by the record of his first few months as Leader of the Opposition. 'Heath was not as formidable as we had feared,' wrote Benn, while Crossman decided that he was 'dry and too cold' and that his policy would 'be attractive only to young and thrusting businessmen'. For the 'traditional, hierarchical, deferential Right' which was such a significant part of the Tory Party, Maudling would have been far more suitable: 'One can't feel deferential to Heath; one is aware of him as a professional politician – cold, tough, efficient.' He had, Crossman concluded, 'taken the very big decision to drop the socialistic attitude which crept into Tory policy in the last two years of Macmillan's regime. Heath is going to fight much more for free enterprise.' Once again, Crossman got it wrong; but Heath's rhetoric did indeed stress the need to rip away the socialistic controls which were choking the growth of a vibrant free economy. It was to be several years before it became clear that he was at heart the most interventionist of prime ministers and that free enterprise would only be allowed to be free and enterprising if it conformed to what he felt to be the norms of a civilised society.[18]

For the moment, whatever unease there may have been within the Party remained largely unvoiced, if only because unity and a show of confidence had to be preserved until the forthcoming election was over and done with. There were signs, however, that all was not well; the most conspicuous being when Angus Maude, the front-bench spokesman on Colonial Affairs, broke ranks in the *Spectator* to denounce Heath as a dry technocrat who was devoid of all philosophy: the Tory Party, he claimed, 'has completely lost effective political initiative'. For his sins he was banished to the backbenches. Heath never forgave him. As late as 1972, when Boyle suggested Maude as a possible Principal for Swinton College, Michael Fraser replied: 'I fancy I may encounter a little trouble with it in some quarters, as Angus is not everybody's favourite person.' Within the inner conclaves of the party it was clear too that all was not well. At a meeting of the 1922 Committee in December 1965 Heath 'was received with middling applause ... When he ended after questions it was better but not enthusiastic. The Party is divided and uneasy.'[19]

By the time Wilson finally fixed the election date for 31 March 1966 Heath's standing in the polls was lower than Douglas-Home's had been fourteen months before. Party workers and MPs, according to the historians of the election, complained increasingly of Heath's 'coldness, his failure to hold the Party together ... his excessive reliance on a group of youthful advisers, and his apparent inability to communicate with the general public'.[20] Yet though morale was low and Heath's popularity lower still, people were not inclined to blame him for what became ever more obviously an election that was going to be lost. The Conservative programme, based on the paper *Putting Britain Right Ahead* which had been put to the Party Conference in October, placed the same emphasis on the need for competition and the reform of the trade unions as had been the gravamen of so many of Heath's speeches. It was attractive enough but contained nothing sufficiently potent to jolt the floating voters out of their conviction that Labour had not yet been given a fair chance to prove itself and should therefore be re-elected. The only question, in the minds of the more realistic Tories, was how big the Labour majority was going to be. When the results, though bad, were not disastrous, reaction in the Party was more one of resigned acceptance than of recrimination.

Certainly members could not complain about their leader's energy and commitment; he shuttled frenetically around the country in a hired Dakota aircraft and made himself responsible for almost all the broadcasts, on radio and on television, and for the daily press conferences. He persistently demanded a confrontation on television with Harold Wilson but was frustrated by Wilson's insistence that he would only agree to such a debate if the Liberal leader, Jo Grimond, also took part – given the presentational skills of the two men Heath was probably lucky that the opportunity was denied him. Wilson consistently outperformed his rival and, by regularly appearing with his wife in attendance, managed subtly to convey the message that, as a bachelor, Heath was out of touch with the realities of everyday life. Heath's one good quip against Wilson rebounded against him. Wilson, he said, was so addicted to gimmickry that in a month's time he would no doubt be photographed in Number 10 taking tea with a pregnant panda. The image was a pleasing one but the implication – that in a month's time Wilson would still be in Number 10 – was not at all what Heath intended.

Du Cann put much of the blame for the defeat on his leader. Heath, he claimed, had insisted that several of the old hands at Central Office should be pushed into retirement shortly before the election. They then had to be brought back with much damage to the organisation and loss of morale. This, he said, was typical of Heath's attitude towards party workers, whom he considered as his servants. 'The difference between Heath and me in our attitudes to the party was fundamental. It spoilt our working relationship.' Macleod, too, though with none of du Cann's rancour, fell out with Heath over election broadcasts, so much so that Barney Heyhoe, the Research Department official responsible, 'found himself having to act as go-between for the two men'. Yet on the whole Heath's conduct of the campaign improved his standing in the party; even though the final result was that Labour increased its majority to ninety-six, the Conservatives ended the campaign in better spirits than they had started it. 'My congratulations on the magnificent way in which you fought,' wrote Harold Macmillan. 'Each day that the campaign went on you got better and better, and you can at least be satisfied that you have established yourself as a leading personality, the unchallenged head of the Conservative Party, at an age when many people would be quite happy to have just emerged into the leading ranks. This you have done by your determination, courage and imagination.' What most concerned the chief whip Willie Whitelaw was not that the Tories were going to lose the election but that, when they did, their leader might make matters worse by a display of pique. If Heath had to concede defeat, he urged, let it be done 'generously and without any bitterness'. 'I know you would do this,' he went on, somewhat unconvincingly, 'and so feel rather apologetic ... But better safe than sorry.' It would become increasingly clear over the coming years that the generous acceptance of defeat was not one of Heath's most noticeable virtues. In this case, however, he heeded Whitelaw's word and behaved impeccably.[21]

In Bexley, although his majority fell to 2,333, Heath did slightly better than the national swing of 2.7 per cent to Labour. John Boyd-Carpenter, whose perceptions may have been subsequently coloured by the fact that he was dropped from the Shadow Cabinet after the election, recorded that, when he spoke for Heath, the Bexley Tories 'did not seem to have the affectionate enthusiasm for him personally that I have always found in the constituencies of Party Leaders. I feared the worst.' Gerald Nabarro, on the other hand, also spoke for Heath and was 'not surprised to learn that his constituents love him'. Nabarro was probably nearer the truth. When Heath first won Bexley it was one of six highly marginal seats in the area. In the 1966 election Labour won five of them; Heath's majority, though reduced, was still comfortable. The party members were solidly supportive; even the Socialists admitted that he was a conscientious and attentive member. His base was secure.[22]

*   *   *

Heath now felt free to reshape the Shadow Cabinet to his own specifications. He wanted, first and foremost, to reduce both its size and the average age of its members. He told them that his aim was 'to get rid of any feeling of alienation between front and back-benches';[23] no doubt this was a consideration, but the smaller the body, the more he felt at ease and he had always believed that the Shadow Cabinet he had inherited was uncomfortably large. The reconstruction involved removing some of the senior members. Selwyn Lloyd and the Lord Chancellor, Lord Dilhorne, went without demur; Duncan Sandys, John Boyd-Carpenter and Ernest Marples were unhappier. Boyd-Carpenter attributed his removal to jealousy: 'His concern to keep out of the way any colleague who might in any circumstances that he could foresee offer a challenge to him had already made itself apparent.' More probably it arose from the fact that the two men had a different concept of what was meant by opposition. Boyd-Carpenter was an agile and aggressive debater, 'so quick with awkward questions that he was known as "spring-heeled Jack"'. Heath saw the value of such activities but felt that the Shadow Cabinet was a place where future ministers should prepare themselves for the burdens of office. There was no room in it for those whose principal talents were for skirmishes in the House.[24]

Of the major figures in the Shadow Cabinet, Home and Maudling were men on whom Heath knew he could rely. 'There were constant rumours of arguments between Ted and myself,' wrote Maudling. 'They really were not well founded ... Our temperaments were quite different, as were our interests, but there was never, to my recollection, any form of row between us.' Much the same could be said of Macleod; in spite of the mutual irritation when election fever was running high the two men respected each other's strengths and worked well together. Indeed, the new Shadow Cabinet was on the whole a harmonious body, the conspicuous exception being Enoch Powell, whose maverick intelligence, harnessed as it was to an obstinate conviction that everything should be pursued to its logical conclusion, made him, even when things seemed calm, a dangerous and often disconcerting colleague. Edward du Cann claimed that, when Heath and Powell sat round the same table, 'their natural antagonism was electric. I never saw two men dislike each other more, or so obviously.' Heath in fact disliked du Cann far more heartily than he did Powell; he considered Powell 'incurably eccentric' and a potential threat to the unity of the party, but recognised his very considerable qualities and felt that the dangers involved in his removal exceeded those that would be incurred by keeping him where he was.[25]

The new men whom Heath brought in – Geoffrey Rippon, Peter Walker, Anthony Barber – were in social origins nearer to Heath than the men they replaced. Alan Clark wrote in his diary that when he had first tried to become an MP in 1964 the party had still been 'run by the O[ld] E[tonian] mafia'. Heath had been resolved on getting rid of them. 'And who is to blame him? Profumo exposed their essential rottenness. The few who remain – Gilmour, Whitelaw, Carrington – are impossibly defeatist.' If that was in fact Heath's aim, he made a remarkably bad job of it: by 1967 six out of eighteen members of the Shadow Cabinet were Old Etonians and eight out of twenty-four of the other front-benchers. Of the bright young men closest to him, Douglas Hurd, David Howell, Mark Schreiber and William Waldegrave were all Old Etonians. Heath may have found this mildly gratifying, but when it came to political appointments he was entirely meritocratic and indifferent to the social standing of those concerned. The fact that she was a small shopkeeper's daughter was certainly neither here nor there when two years later he appointed Margaret Thatcher to the Shadow Cabinet. Much has been made of Heath's supposed early antipathy to Mrs Thatcher and his hesitation over giving her a taste of power. There seems to be little in it. She was first considered for a slot in the Shadow Cabinet in 1965 but was rejected in favour of Mervyn Pike. 'There will be no doubt about the feeling when she discovers that another woman has been preferred to her,' wrote Whitelaw apprehensively. Instead he proposed that she should understudy Iain Macleod: 'She fancies herself as something of an authority on economic and tax matters.' Heath accepted his advice and was equally happy to agree when, in 1967, Whitelaw suggested that the time was now ripe for her promotion. The matter seemed to him of minor importance; he would have been no less acquiescent if

Whitelaw had pushed for Thatcher instead of Pike two years before. Insofar as he thought about Mrs Thatcher it would have been as somebody who was forceful and effective; mildly irritating and personally unappealing but undoubtedly a potential future minister. He thought well enough of her to commend her strongly to certain key figures in Washington like Walt Rostow and Joe Alsop when she visited the United States early in 1967. 'She is highly intelligent and one of our bright stars,' he assured them.[26]

Mrs Thatcher for her part, when she did accede to the Shadow Cabinet, was rather less complimentary. The meetings, she said, were 'not very stimulating'. Heath was 'a competent chairman' but avoided any discussion which verged on matters of principle. She herself, she remarked, was rarely asked to contribute (to judge by the reports of her colleagues she rose above this problem by contributing without invitation) and was treated as the 'statutory woman' whose role was only to 'explain what "women" were'. Whitelaw painted a very different picture of life in the Shadow Cabinet. Heath, he said, was 'an extraordinarily good Chairman. He wanted ideas from other people and he listened to them ... Basically, Ted's authority rested on the general assumption that he couldn't be got rid of. But also there was the simple fact that in almost any matter even his senior colleagues realised that he knew as much if not more than they about the subject at issue.' Heath certainly did tend to cut short – sometimes brusquely – any discussion which seemed to him to be unprofitably theoretical or verging on the philosophical. To men like Hogg and Powell, who rejoiced in abstract speculation, this seemed evidence of a narrow and stultifying mind. To Whitelaw, indeed to a majority of the Shadow Cabinet, it showed a refreshing disinclination to waste time and a determination to grapple with the practical problems of opposition.[27]

The Shadow Cabinet was not the only institution which Heath wished to see working to full advantage; the party machine, to his mind, also called for drastic overhaul. Here, he felt, the party chairman, Edward du Cann, was the obstacle: 'Instead of shaking up the party machine,' he wrote, 'his only significant changes were in increases in salaries at Conservative Central Office.' Du Cann, however, had no mind to resign and was a skilful operator. Every time his future was in question the newspapers carried stories of rifts within the Party and Heath received a – presumably orchestrated – deluge of letters pleading that du Cann should stay. 'I don't think anyone except yourself has made such a great personal sacrifice to serve the Party,' wrote Ted Leather, one of du Cann's deputy chairmen. 'I just hope and pray that you have the regard, the confidence and the affection in him we all have.' Nabarro believed the real reason Heath wanted to evict the chairman was because du Cann was fiercely opposed to any application to join the Common Market. This may have been an element in Heath's calculations but far more important was the personal hostility between the two men and du Cann's efforts to deny the leader access to the Area Chairmen around the country. 'At the start the fault was Ted's,' judged Michael Fraser, the head of the Conservative Research Department. 'At the end it was du Cann's.' Wherever the blame lay, the situation was obviously damaging to the Party. It was resolved in September 1967, when du Cann grudgingly resigned. He refused to join the Shadow Cabinet – 'I did not like Heath's style of management. He was too dogmatic for my taste and too inflexible in his ways … He was a pragmatist, never an idealist' – but was convinced that he had been promised a job when Heath eventually formed a government. He was replaced as chairman by Anthony Barber. Kershaw would have preferred Jim Prior to be given the job; Barber, he told Heath, was 'wonderfully efficient, respected and liked by everyone' but 'a pale copy of you. There ought to be some contrast between you and the chairman.' Heath felt that there had been more than enough contrast in the past and settled for the pale copy. It worked well enough.[28]

A party chairman who would work to strengthen the leader's position rather than undermine it was going to be badly needed over the next few years. The lull that followed the general election of 1966 did not last long. Sir John Vaughan Morgan, an old-school Tory by no means ill disposed towards Heath, early in 1967 sent his leader a strikingly candid assessment of how he was viewed by the Party. Nobody seriously doubted, he said, that Heath's position was impregnable but:

The most widespread criticism was that you were not sufficiently in command of the front bench or party; that your manner in the House was lacking in the magisterial quality ... It was strongly felt that you did not always back up your colleagues as you should ... The unfortunate result is that sometimes an impression of disunity is necessarily given ... Others thought that, with one or two exceptions, your speeches were seldom memorable and that phraseology tended to be trite ... There is considerable criticism that you do not draw your advice from a wide enough circle; that you need to broaden the base of your support in the Parliamentary Party; that your intimates are too few and unknown; and that your personal staff are remote and not always very competent ... The general mood was of reserved good will but not enthusiasm.[29]

Even the reserved goodwill was missing in large sections of the party. Some of the hostility was based on little more than snobbishness. The Conservatives had picked somebody whom they thought would be a proletarian bruiser capable of taking on Harold Wilson; the bruiser element had proved ineffective, they were left with the proletarian. Du Cann accompanied his leader to a dinner of prominent industrialists. Heath was the only guest wearing a white dinner jacket. 'Our host, a peer and chairman of one of the UK's most successful companies, turned to me and asked "Who's that bloody waiter you've brought with you?" ... As he left, the host said to me "I know you'll do your best to make bricks with the straw you have, and we'll all do our best to help you, but you can't expect us to like the man".' He was treated abominably by certain sections of the Party, thought Sara Morrison; they 'dismissed him as a common little oik'. He should have ignored such an attitude with the contempt it deserved; up to a point he did, but it rankled; against his own better judgment he was sensitive to the slights of those who thought themselves socially superior. In his copy of John Campbell's biography he vigorously marked any reference to his preoccupation with his class, putting a firm 'No' against the suggestion that part of the appeal of the Honourable Artillery Company lay in its social exclusivity. He protested too much; he was more vulnerable than he admitted, even to himself.[30]

'IF YOU CAN KEEP YOUR HEAD WHEN ALL ABOUT YOU...'

The suspicion that he was despised for such ignoble reasons was a factor – small but not insignificant – in his attitude towards the rank-and-file of his party. As Chief Whip he had been notably accessible, always ready to lend a sympathetic ear to a backbencher's doubts and fears. As leader, all changed. Perhaps he suspected that anyone to whom he spoke would be trying to get something out of him; perhaps he felt it was proper to his role to hold himself aloof; perhaps he felt increasing distaste for many of his followers. At all events he made no effort to court, or even be moderately polite to, those on whose support he was dependent. 'I would very much like you to come into the Smoking Room like Winston used to do, and Attlee and Macmillan,' wrote the stalwartly right-wing Cyril Osborne. 'I am sure that half an hour each day, if possible, gossiping with different groups, would pay handsome dividends.' 'I hope to be able to do as you ask,' Heath replied, but 'the pressure is enormous.' The pressure *was* enormous but it was quite as much disinclination to waste valuable time in – as he saw it – making small talk to people whom he did not like or respect. Another problem was that although, in most ways, his memory was phenomenal, names and faces came to him with difficulty. When he cut dead some MP who thought he knew him well, his victim concluded it was wilful rudeness; in fact it was as often as not because he had no idea who was walking by. Heath denied that he was remiss in chatting up backbenchers: 'This unclubbable idea is a myth which has grown up,' he told Peter Hennessy. But he was uneasily aware that the myth contained a fair amount of truth. When Selwyn Lloyd told him that the senior backbenchers were feeling 'a bit out of things', he asked Whitelaw to consider what could be done. 'We could invite them to be members of the business committee,' Heath suggested.[31]

It was not just backbenchers with whom he found it difficult to communicate. The man who at Oxford had been the life-and-soul of every party now seemed ill-at-ease in any gathering except a small group of his close associates. Leo Abse, the Labour MP and amateur psychologist, noted him at a party, 'standing alone, having as he has a rare talent for creating an empty space around himself. His diffidence is notorious.' Humphry Berkeley made the same comment when, at a Council of Europe meeting in Strasbourg, he 'became aware of his cold exterior and of seeing ripples of unease spread among those surrounding him at receptions and meals'. At the best he seemed disinclined to communicate, at the worst offensively remote. Margaret Thatcher accepted that, as a woman, she faced greater problems in getting through to Heath than did her male colleagues yet: 'I felt that, though I had known him for years, there was a sense in which I did not know him at all ... I was not conscious at this time of any hostility, simply of a lack of human warmth.' Richard Marsh, then a junior Labour minister, told Cecil King that Heath had no friends: 'He is impossible to know.' Heath was not impossible to know and he did have friends; but increasingly he was difficult to know, his friends were few, and even the most trusted of them were treated with reserve. David Butler interviewed him in November 1969. 'I have rarely seen anyone so severe, tense and nervous,' he recorded. 'He answered our questions as if they were part of a *viva voce* examination.'[32]

The more traditional elements of the party were also distrustful of the group of young men by whom Heath was surrounded. They were believed to be dangerously radical and too clever by half; disrespectful of the long-established mores of Conservatism. 'I heard criticism of Ted for … allowing himself to be shut off behind a close circle of young men who are his friends,' Knox Cunningham told Macmillan. Mark Schreiber and David Howell would have been flattered to be dignified with the title of 'friends', but Heath enjoyed their icono-clastic zest and took seriously what they said. Their contribution was of value; it only became dangerous when senior colleagues felt that, as a consequence, their own views were not receiving proper atten-tion. Tim Kitson, an Opposition Whip who was to become pps to Heath and one of his closest and most trusted associates, urged caution. 'It is very important that we should kill the myth about the whizzy kids,' he wrote, 'and at the same time foster the impression that you are taking advice from your senior colleagues both inside and outside the "Shadow".' The trouble was that, though Heath listened to what Douglas-Home or Macleod had to say and from time to time might defer to other colleagues in their specialist fields, he had no great respect for the opinions of most of the members of the Shadow Cabinet. He was as likely to pay attention to one of his young advisers as to the individual who was in theory responsible for the making of Tory policy.[33]

'He is a strange person; he is anxious for popularity, and instead of seeking it by courteous manners, by good humour and frank-ness, he is morose and austere.' Mrs Arbuthnot was writing of Robert Peel in the late 1830s, but she could have been describing Heath. Increasingly the Party felt that it was out of touch with its leader. 'In what the Army used to call man-management, the wartime colonel and successful Chief Whip showed himself to be deplorably defective,' wrote Ian Gilmour. The only Tory leader who approached him when it came to apparent indifference to the backbenchers was Winston Churchill and 'what was readily forgiven Churchill in his late seventies was not forgiven Heath'.[34] In the eyes of most Tories the worst failing in a leader was inability to unite the party; with some relish the Labour leaders concluded that this was Heath's most conspicuous weakness. 'He's a splitter,' pronounced Harold Wilson. 'He will split his party, as Gaitskell split the Labour party.' Benn, too, agreed that Heath was 'a basic splitter who insists on getting his own way at the cost of party unity – and is humourless and cannot roll with the punches as Harold can'. When Heath replaced Douglas-Home, Labour had thought the change would be damaging to their prospects; within a year they concluded that it had been positively beneficial. The exultation of Labour was matched by Tory dismay. Norman Collins, the television mogul and Tory activist, told Cecil King that Central Office was in despair while Maudling told Mrs King that a third of the Tory Party in the House of Commons would now prefer Enoch Powell to Heath as leader. In March 1967 Whitelaw told Crossman – according to Crossman at any rate – that he had just had the worst eight weeks of his life. In spite of some good by-election results, Heath was still 'an unsuccessful leader' and the Opposition front bench was divided on a whole range of issues. The nadir of Heath's fortunes perhaps came six months later when Robin Day interviewed him on television. Just before Heath appeared on screen, viewers had seen a bespectacled young Tory voter who was saying 'When we got rid of Sir Alec we said, "God knows we can't have anyone worse than Home". Well, we've got someone worse than Home.' Day then confronted Heath and, with the urbane offensiveness that was his speciality, asked: 'How low does your personal rating from your own supporters have to go before you consider yourself a liability to the party you lead?' Heath did as well as he could. 'Well,' he said, 'popularity isn't everything. In fact, it isn't the most important thing. What matters is doing what you believe to be right ... The question does not arise.'[35]

It had arisen, however, and would not go away. Those who believed in Heath but were dismayed that he could not project himself publicly, and the still greater number who did not believe in Heath but reckoned that they were stuck with him, considered what could be done to improve their leader's image. In October 1966 the Opinion Research Centre produced for Central Office an analysis of Heath's performances in public speeches and on TV. It proved to be a fearsomely harsh indictment. Compared to Harold Wilson, said the report, who was 'generally regarded as being an outstandingly good politician and as also having a good measure of statesmanlike qualities', Heath was 'lacking in the attributes of a statesman and a politician'. He was believed to be honest, 'but he does not give the appearance of being straightforward; this is because he does not seem to be his natural self. His performances often give the impression of being rehearsed, he sounds as though he is reading a prepared script and he appears to be unrelaxed and lacking in confidence ... This impression is exaggerated by lack of emotional feeling in his delivery ... He does not seem at present even to be the true leader of his party.'[36]

Heath took this assessment with commendable calm and made spasmodic efforts to mend his ways. After a television interview he asked his staff to produce a commentary and annotated this with a list of instructions to himself: 'short replies', 'pauses', 'sit back' (in a comfortable position), avoid the unconvincing smile with which he greeted each awkward question. Whitelaw told Knox Cunningham that Heath 'was very worried about his personal popularity in the polls'. To his leader, he said that he should be himself and not give the impression of shifting to take account of the latest criticism; advice that was well intentioned but cannot have been of much use to Heath, who was in such trouble precisely because he *had* been himself and wanted to escape that image.[37]

It was not just a question of public speeches. Jeffrey Archer said that Heath was 'the worst communicator the job has ever seen', while Ian Trethowan – a friend and admirer – deplored his 'curious inability to project his private charm on to a wider stage'. Spasmodic bids were made to improve matters. The American Ambassador, Lewis Douglas, congratulated the Tory grandee Lord Swinton on having arranged for Heath to be photographed with a baby in his arms: 'It is comforting to know that Ted can grin like a Cheshire cat.'[38] In August 1967 Heath was told that his wax model at Madame Tussauds was unworthy of its original. He sent an emissary to inspect the offending dummy and heard that its suit and waistcoat were out of date, the shirt collar was untidy and the tie was badly knotted. His face was marred by a double chin (a feature which was usually only too apparent but which his exertions on *Morning Cloud* had temporarily diminished). The only consolation was that his model was a lot better than 'a villainous Jeremy Thorpe (perhaps based on a spare wax from the Chamber of

Horrors)'. Madame Tussauds were approached to see if things could be improved: a new tie and waistcoat were provided. Nor was the written word forgotten. It was decided that a biography of Heath was needed. Robert Rhodes James was suggested as a possible author, but Michael Wolff, another of Heath's bright young men and his principal speech writer, disliked him. Aidan and Virginia Crawley were both felt likely to be too expensive. Jonathan Aitken and Winston Churchill junior, young men with a name to make, would be cheaper but were deemed to be too inexperienced. Heath was in favour of William Rees-Mogg, but he proved not to be available. Andrew Boyle and Monty Woodhouse were ruled out for the same reason. 'I doubt whether the proposition will be a sufficiently attractive one to any author of repute unless we provide some form of subsidy,' wrote MacGregor gloomily. In the end the lot fell on George Hutchinson, a former chief publicity officer of the Party, who could at least be relied on to eschew scandal or heresy. In the event the book was not nearly as appalling as might have been expected and, for future biographers, has the priceless merit of containing the comments of many contemporaries whose views would otherwise have gone unrecorded.[39]

Geoffrey Tucker, the party's publicity director, felt that the re-shaping of Heath's image could only be achieved through his own efforts. 'No way was he going to be dolled up or be seen cuddling babies,' he said, evidently unaware of the exploits applauded by the American Ambassador. 'He was against anything schmaltzy. I had to work with the grain.'[40] Tucker's conclusion – as far against the grain as it is possible to imagine – was that the leader needed a wife. When an American woman had been bold enough to put this to Heath himself he very sensibly replied that: 'A man who married to become prime minister would be neither a good prime minister nor a good husband.' The intrepid Tufton Beamish, however, took it on himself to ask the pianist Moura Lympany, a frequent companion of Heath's, whether she would accept the charge. 'If he asked I'd consider it a great honour,' she replied, but he didn't ask and, anyway, she was in love with somebody else at the time. Tucker's other inspiration was to persuade the film director Bryan Forbes to make a film covering Heath's visit to the north-east of England. As they toured the slums

'YOU'LL BE SEEING A NEW TED ALRIGHT, WE'VE BEEN FEEDING HIM ON NOTHING BUT RAW MEAT AND WILSON COMMUNIQUES.'

of Newcastle, Heath said meditatively: 'If I lived here I wouldn't vote for Harold Wilson. And I wouldn't vote for myself either.' 'Who would you vote for?' asked Forbes. 'Robespierre!'[41]

The most systematic effort to overhaul Heath's image was made in the first half of 1967 when Tim Rathbone, a bright young advertising man who had been working with Ogilvy & Mather in New York, was enlisted by du Cann to do a public relations job in Central Office. His first recommendation was made within a few weeks. Heath and his entourage, he concluded, represented the liberal, avant-garde wing of the Party. 'There are not, and probably quite rightly so, representatives of clubland or the shire close to the Leader. Therefore the old-fashioned wing of the party must feel divorced from the leadership.' A new pps – perhaps Paul Channon? – was needed to keep the lines open to the right. The premise was obviously sensible but the recommendation seems curiously irrelevant: Jim Prior had been appointed pps two years before with that precise function in mind and, in so far as Heath would let him, was doing an admirable job of keeping the shires in contact with the leadership. Rathbone put in his main report three months later. It took only a short time, he argued, to realise that Heath was 'Highly intelligent. Receptive to new ideas. Conscientious and hardworking. Having a strong conscience.' The problem was to convince people that he was 'Emotionally involved. Completely honest. Highly respected abroad. Tough. Self-reliant. Dedicated to his work,' and not 'Pompous or snobbish. Old-fashioned. Dominated by other people.' What he needed was a full-time public relations consultant who would be involved 'in *all* Mr Heath's activities' and would advise on 'what Mr Heath has to say, how, where and to whom he says it'. His television skills should be taken in hand by a specialist consultant, he should write many more personal letters and keep a bank of 'funny or topical stories'. Trickiest of all, Rathbone concluded that 'the female influence in Mr Heath's life is very faint and, therefore, he is neither seen nor assumed to be caring one fig for female views'. What was needed was a 'politically aware woman' who would have breakfast with him once a week to discuss the woman's angle on current affairs.[42]

Heath, Rathbone admitted, might be uncomfortable with all this. So he would have been, but, though he liked Rathbone and certainly read the report, there was no reason to believe that he took it to heart or made any serious effort to change his ways in the light of its recommendations. Sara Morrison was the only 'politically minded woman' who could conceivably have filled Rathbone's bill, and both she and Heath would have viewed with horror any idea of breakfast meetings artificially crafted to permit discussion of the woman's point of view.[43] Heath was aware of the problem and did make spasmodic, usually ineffectual, efforts to resolve it; more significantly, the Tory Party became inured to their leader's ways and learnt – up to a point – to live with them. The issue was never resolved and was, in the long run, to do Heath irreparable damage, but after the first two years or so of his leadership in Opposition, the worst of the shock wore off. Heath's manner was accepted as a fact of life. He would be judged by his success or failure when it came to an election.

TEN

Problems with the Party

Labour's devaluation of sterling in November 1967 may not have been a decisive turning point but it at least kindled in Tory minds a belief that the worst was over. Heath told the Shadow Cabinet that: 'We must retain our responsible position and not try to make party political capital out of the economic situation,' but his true thoughts, and indeed conduct, were very different. He was particularly incensed by Harold Wilson's ill-judged remark that 'the pound in your pocket' had not been devalued and let himself go on television with a fury which delighted the rank and file but caused some embarrassment to those Shadow ministers – Macleod, Barber and Boyle among them – who privately felt that devaluation was long overdue. When Crossman asked Barber about Heath's speech the new party chairman replied: 'He didn't do it with my advice. He sat down and wrote it in the white heat of anger.' Curiously, on this issue, Heath and Wilson were closer to each other than they were to many of their followers. Wilson hated the idea of devaluation which he saw as being a national humiliation; Heath fully agreed, and when Wilson finally and reluctantly conceded that it was inevitable, the Leader of the Opposition proclaimed that the decision was tantamount to treachery.[1]

Sweeping Conservative gains in the local government elections of May 1968 seemed to confirm that Labour was on the run. 'Magnificent', Heath called them. 'This achievement marks a vital stage in our work in Opposition.' As the party's position strengthened, so Heath's confidence grew. David Astor, editor of the *Observer*, hailed Heath's resurrection:

> I've often wanted to write you a personal letter of sympathy and of admiration [he wrote] when those bastards in your own party have been challenging your persona, your inner workings, almost your soul! and you have carried on undeterred. I now want to congratulate you on what I can only call a spiritual or psychological victory. All my colleagues commented on your psychological growth over two years and the new sense of freedom and strength that you radiated. To have emerged from all that public lecturing apparently unscathed would be a very considerable personal achievement. To have gained in strength through such an ordeal seems to be a real triumph.[2]

The recovery went on. At the party conference in October 1968 Heath made what Whitelaw thought was the best speech of his career: 'Perhaps the prime ministership', he speculated, 'is all that is needed to see him in full command.' A year later Carrington told Cecil King that Heath was doing better both on television and in the House: 'He thinks he may prove to be a great PM even if a thought too dictatorial.' Not everything was running smoothly. There were adverse press reports of a tour of Scotland: 'something about his manner seems to put some people off,' Whitelaw told Swinton. 'Oh dear, oh dear!' But fewer people were being put off and less often. In October 1969, after the debate on the Queen's speech, Wilson, with some irritation, admitted that Heath had produced 'probably the most effective speech he had made as Leader of the Opposition, even if largely unrelated to the world in which we live. But it served its turn and it pleased his troops.' Macmillan assured Heath that the worst was indeed over. 'I know that the last year or two have not been easy for you,' he wrote in May, 'but I feel now that the whole situation has changed. You have the confidence of the Parliamentary party, of the party in the country, and all our supporters generally. It will not take you long to become a truly national figure.'[3]

*   *   *

Quite apart from Heath's merits or demerits, there were plenty of questions on which the party was divided. One was Europe. Ever since he had presided over the abortive negotiations for British entry Heath had been committed to the proposition that Britain should be in Europe and that eventually this object would be achieved. In the election campaign of 1966 Wilson had mocked him for responding too enthusiastically to a hint from a French official that their opposition to British entry might be softening. 'One encouraging gesture from the French government', said Wilson, 'and he rolls on his back like a spaniel' – going on to explain that some of his best friends were spaniels. 'Lies ... revolting, poisonous lies,' stormed Heath, but he in no way modified his position. When Alastair Hetherington, editor of the *Guardian*, told him that entry might involve a lot of British companies being driven out of business, he retorted robustly: 'Yes, and a good thing too!' Their bodies would float down the Channel, he said, and wash up on the shores of Morocco.[4]

He might therefore have been expected to applaud when, in November 1966, Wilson unexpectedly announced that the government was planning to launch a fresh application to join the EEC. 'Duncan Sandys had the sense to welcome it,' wrote Crossman. 'That's what Heath should have done ... instead he tried to nark.' Partly this was the natural indignation of a man who sees his clothes stolen; Europe was *his* cause, it was *he* who should lead the crusade for British entry. Partly he doubted Wilson's motives. He had told Hetherington that any initiative by Wilson would 'be *not* genuine. It would be seen as not genuine on the Continent. It would add to their suspicions towards us.' Wilson, as Heath saw it, reckoned he would win either way. If he got in he could claim that Labour was the pro-Europe party, if he failed he would announce that entry had proved to be incompatible with British interests and that only the unpatriotic Tories could say otherwise. Heath's response was to equivocate. We should argue the case for Europe, he told the Shadow Cabinet, but 'put clearly and frankly what we believed the problems to be'. Opinion among his colleagues seemed to be as divided as ever; the one thing on which everyone agreed was that 'we should at no point seem to be resenting the fact that the Labour government were now making moves towards Europe'.[5]

In the event the matter proved of academic interest only; it quickly became clear that while de Gaulle remained in power there would be no change of heart over British entry. Heath was convinced that it was only by conciliating France that the door to Europe could eventually be opened; the Labour Government supported by the Foreign Office and some leading Tories – Duncan Sandys the most prominent – continued to cling to the hope that France could be isolated and so defeated. *L'affaire Soames*, a piece of bungled diplomacy in which a confidential conversation between de Gaulle and the British Ambassador in Paris, Christopher Soames, about the future of political association in Europe, was leaked to the press by the British Government, put paid to any lingering hopes that the Labour strategy could prove successful. And then the sudden resignation of de Gaulle in April 1969 opened new vistas for Britain. Georges Pompidou, de Gaulle's prime minister whom Heath had known and got on well with since 1962, replaced de Gaulle as president. By nature a cautious man, he took no immediate steps to reverse his predecessor's policies, but it soon became clear that he did not feel bound to follow meekly along the path that de Gaulle had laid down. Nor would his fellow members of the EEC necessarily have let him do so. A few weeks after de Gaulle's retirement, Franz-Josef Strauss, German Finance Minister, told Heath that his successor could not follow the same line: Germany, at any rate, would not 'tolerate such impertinence again'.[6] De Gaulle suspected that his former underling might have ideas of his own and, according to Soames, showed 'rage and resentment'. André Malraux claimed the General felt as if he had been cuckolded by his chauffeur. The doors to Europe were not yet open but the creaking of hinges and fumbling with keys suggested that something might be about to happen.[7]

The possibility revived the latent opposition to Europe that had always been a prominent feature of the Tory Party. The Chief Whip told Heath that there were twenty-nine committed 'antis' in the parliamentary party; twelve who were 'almost anti'; nineteen who were known 'not to be pro' and twenty-one who were 'believed to be cool'. The list included eight Privy Councillors and sixteen former ministers. The figures were pretty accurate, said Whitelaw; if anything they understated the anti-Common Market feeling. It did not need advanced mathematics to work out that a very considerable exercise in persuasion was going to be called for if a united party was to be rallied behind a bid to enter Europe. After Wilson's application was lodged there was angry criticism in the 1922 Committee at the decision to impose a three-line whip on Tory members in support of the Government's policy: fifteen members were in favour of the application but seven were against. Neil Marten, a noted anti-European, told Crossman in September 1969 that Heath had to be careful in his support of entry: 'Heath realises he can't push too far ahead and in speeches this week both he and Maudling have begun to talk about reassessment of the terms. Certainly opposition is growing in the Tory party.' Nabarro was still more vehement. Heath was leading the party to disaster, he claimed. 'Eighty per cent of the country was against it … 100 Conservatives at least wanted to withdraw our application.' Heath himself had no illusions about the state of public opinion; he told the Shadow Cabinet early in 1970 that 'it was heavily against going into Europe'. He took comfort from the fact that a substantial majority was nevertheless in favour of reopening negotiations; in the end, he was convinced, on this as on so many issues, reason would prevail.[8]

Even if Pompidou was better disposed to the idea of British entry than his implacable predecessor, Heath knew that all would not be plain sailing. He had good reason to be cautious. When Pompidou read a report on the views of the Labour minister George Thomson, in November 1969, he wrote indignantly that it was crazy: the British seemed to be imagining that all the existing financial settlements would be up for renegotiation: 'We do not accept that the community's arrangements [*dispositions communautaires*] will cease to have effect the day the English enter.' But though Pompidou had doubts about the credibility of a British application while Wilson was Prime Minister, he had higher hopes of Heath. On nuclear defence, too, he thought that the Tories might prove more flexible. Wilson seemed reluctant to envisage any significant pooling of resources in this field. Heath, on the other hand, had gone a long way towards admitting the desirability of a common nuclear strike force, though he had stressed that it could only be done after consultation with the Americans. Certainly Pompidou was clear that negotiations for British entry would be more likely to succeed if the Tories were in power. But even then there would be many problems. When Heath called on him in Paris in May 1970 the President emphasised the difficulties that would arise with the rest of the world. The creation of this enormous economic superpower would stir up violent opposition in the USA, Japan and Russia; '*il faut être prêt pratiquement à partir en guerre pour la Communauté.*' 'It won't come to that,' said Heath. 'You'll see,' replied Pompidou balefully. 'Anyway,' said Heath, 'if our economic power worries the United States, Latin America or Australia, we must put up with the consequences. If the result was the destruction of the Common Market, our own destruction would follow.'[9]

Heath believed that the British people must be persuaded that membership of the Common Market was in the nation's interest. But should they be consulted directly on the issue? His private conviction was that, if the people voted for a Tory Party which was pledged to negotiate for Britain's entry, then the government could legitimately decide whether or not the terms were acceptable and proceed without further consultation. He kept his own counsel on the question, however. He told the Shadow Cabinet early in 1970 that he felt there was bound to be pressure for a referendum but gave no indication what he himself thought about it; when Hogg commented dryly that those who clamoured for a referendum were usually the very people who complained they could not understand the issues, he let the observation pass without comment.[10] Through the spring of 1970 the issue was much debated but went unresolved. Iain Macleod was the first senior Tory to go public as the supporter of a referendum. Ian Gilmour followed suit, arguing that there were precedents for such a procedure: Balfour in 1910 on tariff reform and Baldwin in 1930 had both envisaged recourse to a referendum. He did not think there was a serious risk that voters, given a chance, would reach the wrong conclusion; whatever the current state of public opinion, it would not be too difficult to win it over when the final terms were known. Charles Morrison wrote to Heath in support of Gilmour.[11] At last Heath made clear his views. 'A bald commitment to a referendum would', he believed, 'virtually make negotiations impossible.' No one would take the British negotiators seriously if it was known that they might subsequently be disavowed by their own electorate.[12] Whether this was the whole story or whether he feared that a referendum, with Labour quite possibly against acceptance and Enoch Powell leading the anti-marketeers in a rampage for rejection, could go disastrously wrong can never be established. Probably he hardly knew himself. At all events, the Shadow Cabinet with some relief shelved the issue without any final decision being reached.

Rhodesia was an issue they could not shelve. Here the split in the party was likely to be even more embarrassing than over Europe. Southern Rhodesia had been stranded when the short-lived Central African Federation had broken up in the 1960s and it had been denied full independence until it accepted terms which would, in the not too distant future, lead to African majority rule. When Ian Smith made his Unilateral Declaration of Independence (UDI) in November 1965, Conservatives and Socialists united in denouncing his behaviour, but when Harold Wilson announced that sanctions would be imposed on the rebellious regime, including a potentially devastating oil embargo, the splits within the Opposition became painfully evident. A small but vociferous minority led by Lord Salisbury rebelled against any attempt to coerce their 'kith and kin' in Southern Rhodesia, who had fought so gallantly with Britain in two world wars. In an attempt to appease them Heath sought to distinguish between 'sanctions automatically arising from UDI' and 'penal sanctions specifically and separately imposed' – i.e., as the Liberal leader, Jo Grimond, unkindly pointed out, any sanction which might possibly work. When he advanced this line in the Shadow Cabinet the Chief Whip said that a lot of Tories in the House would be 'strongly in favour of stringent sanctions'. It quickly became apparent that the pro-Smith lobby in the Tory Party was matched by an equally committed group on the left who refused to condone any rejection of penal sanctions. Lord Alport, a former Minister of State at the Commonwealth Relations Office and High Commissioner to the Central African Federation, wrote to Heath in warning: 'If by any unhappy chance Conservative policy were to be identified in the public eye with the right-wing of the party we would be in a very serious position. I know and sympathise with your difficulties. I would not be too concerned at threats of a split. Their hold on the imagination of the party is very frail – even in the Lords.'

By personal inclination Heath would have sided with Alport and the Liberals but he knew how damaging the consequences of a split might be. In the avalanche of letters on the subject that descended on his office, seven out of eight were in favour of the Smith regime. Sir Frederic Bennett was only one of a galaxy of right-wing luminaries who wrote to say that the influence of the left was 'very, very small ... Of the largest post-bag I have had on any issue for a long time past every single letter without one exception has been favourable to a constructive approach to a Rhodesian settlement and against mounting sanctions.' In an ignoble if understandable effort to hold the Party together Heath decreed that the Conservatives should abstain in the vote on oil sanctions on 21 December 1965. Eighty-one members ignored him: 50 opposing sanctions, 31 supporting them. Nigel Fisher, a front-bench spokesman on Commonwealth affairs, was one of the 31. It was 'a traumatic experience for Heath', he wrote. He was sent for by the leader and told that he must either support the official policy or retreat to the backbenches. 'It seemed to me a perfectly reasonable proposition and shortly afterwards, I think quite rightly, I was dropped.'

Not everyone was so good-natured; there was much bitter acrimony and many grudges were left behind. The man who had the worst time was the Chief Whip, Willie Whitelaw, who wrote Heath eight pages of apology 'while the awful events of the week are still fresh in my mind'. He agonised over the ways in which he could have done a more effective job. 'I want to tell you how much I appreciated your personal kindness to me ... I would have fully understood if you had shown me what must have been in your mind, that perhaps handled differently we might have done better. And yet you merely thanked me. However unjustified at that moment, this meant a great deal to me, as I cannot help becoming emotionally involved.'[13]

From the point of view of discussion within the Party this was as bad as things were going to get. In February 1966 the Shadow Cabinet despatched Selwyn Lloyd to Rhodesia on a fact-finding mission; he found no facts except that sanctions had made the Labour Government unpopular among the whites in Salisbury and that 'the Africans were certainly not behind Mr Smith'. These revelations did not noticeably affect Tory policy: the Shadow Cabinet continued to shilly-shally, on the one hand agreeing that sanctions must be maintained until UDI was rescinded, on the other opposing NIBMAR – No Independence Before Majority African Rule – because it would be unacceptable to the white Rhodesians. Harold Wilson was in no position to criticise Heath for sacrificing principle to preserve party unity but it seemed at times as if the Shadow Cabinet was getting the worst of all worlds; despised by the left and right and leaving the ruck of members in between with a feeling of vague discontent that they were not being given the leadership they required.[14]

The need to keep British armed forces 'East of Suez', particularly in Singapore and the Persian Gulf, was another issue which split the Party; though feelings did not run so high as over Rhodesia and the composition of the competing elements was notably different. Most of the right-wing members wanted Britain to continue to be engaged east of Suez, yet Enoch Powell, an opponent of sanctions against Rhodesia, was to the fore in advocating a British withdrawal. He claimed that Britain could not afford the expensive luxury of keeping armed forces east of Suez and that, anyway, the handful of troops involved served little useful purpose. When the Shadow Cabinet discussed the question in October 1965 most members considered that, in the Gulf at any rate, a continued military presence was essential and would be so for the foreseeable future. Heath, though not taking a strong line, at this stage inclined to Powell's point of view: he shared, in part at least, the Shadow Defence Minister's conviction that post-imperial responsibilities were a sentimental burden that should be shed as soon as possible and was acutely conscious of the financial risks involved in sustaining what could prove to be an unlimited commitment. But he continued to hedge his bets. When there were complaints that Powell's speech at the party conference seemed to herald the abandonment of 'any efforts to contribute to the defence of the Commonwealth', he replied, unconvincingly, that the Tories were not contemplating retreat from east of Suez. But when he was presented with a draft reply to a letter critical of Powell which contained the sentence 'You are right in thinking that Enoch Powell's speech was merely a thought-provoking effort', Heath struck out the words, knowing full well that they were untrue.[15]

It was only when he visited the parts of the world involved and exposed himself to the expostulations of those who felt that they were being abandoned that Heath became fully committed to an East-of-Suez policy. After a visit to Australia in August 1968 he assured Charles Fletcher-Cooke, a former junior minister at the Home Office, that he had made no precise commitments but that the stability of South East Asia was still a vital national interest: 'We are not seeking to revive imperial glories; we are working out a practical response to a real need. We need to operate, not on our own as in the past, but in co-operation with our friends.' The following year in the Persian Gulf he went still further. By this time the Labour Government had set in train the process of disengagement which was to lead to a complete withdrawal of British forces. In Heath's tour of the region, Douglas Hurd remembered: 'He was courteous and patient. He remembered the particular interests, history and idiosyncrasies of each ruler. He set out his own position with the right blend of deference and firmness. He enjoyed the company of these subtle men, and conveyed that enjoyment to them.' But, in the eyes of the Foreign Office at least, he allowed himself to be drawn into indiscretions. British officials urged him not to raise false expectations; he ignored them. In Kuwait, Heath told the Ruler that there would be an election in the spring of 1971. If the Tories won, and 'our friends wanted us to stay' then the new government would do so. The Foreign Office expressed dismay that the Ruler was boasting that 'he had obtained from you an unconditional statement that British forces would remain in the Gulf under a Conservative government'. If, as they hoped, this was not true, would Heath please disabuse the Ruler? There was no need to tell the Foreign Office what he had actually said, suggested Hurd, it would be enough to tell them that he had spoken on the lines of previous public speeches. 'Agreed,' minuted Heath. 'What a guilty conscience they've got.' Possibly his own conscience was not entirely clear, especially when a few days later, he assured the Kuwaiti Ambassador that, if so desired, 'we would work out ways and means of retaining a British presence'.[16]

Apart from the Foreign Office the Shah of Iran was the most overt critic of Heath's pronouncements. He told Patrick Gordon Walker, the former Labour minister, that he strongly disagreed with Heath's view that the withdrawal from the Gulf should be reversed. That, Heath would have retorted, only proved how right he was: domination of the Gulf by Iran, though less harmful than a Communist takeover, was nevertheless contrary to British interests. Enoch Powell, for one, was still unconvinced that the benefits from a British presence could be worth the price. He suggested that, if British troops were to remain in the Gulf, it would probably be necessary to reintroduce conscription. Michael Carver, then GOC of Southern Command and tipped to be the next Chief of the General Staff, agreed that this would probably be the case. 'Why? It didn't under us,' minuted Heath. Against Carver's suggestion that the best way to support the Gulf States would be to send officers to train the local troops, Heath scrawled '! Some v. odd views here'. When the time came to put his words into practice he was to discover that that he was already too late, but in his last years in Opposition he was presenting himself in the uncharacteristic posture of an ardent champion of Britain's post-imperial role.[17]

He followed much the same course when it came to American activities in Vietnam. He felt that America's efforts to disengage could only be sustained if the Communists made similar moves, and strongly defended the bombing of Cambodia. When Professor Birch of Hull University wrote to say that, by taking this line, he was thereby forfeiting the support of the young, Heath replied that he disagreed: 'Young people in this country are above all suspicious of trimming and equivocation in politics, and there is really no substitute for making one's own assessment on the merits of each matter as one sees them and then trying to put that assessment across.' Douglas Hurd suggested gently: 'You and the party are slightly vulnerable to the charge of being more warlike than the Americans,' but Heath had made his own assessment and saw no cause to revise it. 'The man has no political sense,' Cecil King told Tony Benn. 'After all those pictures of the Vietnam war that have just appeared on television, why on earth did he have to stick his neck out and identify himself with the Americans?' Heath would have found King's comment inexcusably vapid: a leader's job was to shape public opinion, not to follow it. He knew he was right; and if the British people could not see that this was the case then they must have the lesson relentlessly rammed home.[18]

Economic decline and the increasing militancy of the trade unions were going to play a more significant part in the approaching election than any issues of defence or foreign policy. Where a large element in his party saw the trade unions as enemies, to be confronted and, if not actually destroyed, then certainly disarmed and rendered impotent, Heath as leader was quite as anxious to work with them as he had been during his brief stint as Minister of Labour. But the unions must be responsible as well as strong; they could not be allowed to operate outside the law. In February 1966 Quintin Hogg wrote a paper for the Shadow Cabinet on the trade unions and the law, in which he advocated an Industrial Relations Court in which a presiding judge would sit with lay members, registration of unions would be compulsory, immunity would be withdrawn from unofficial strikes and there would be sanctions against restrictive practices. This was the very doctrine that Heath had challenged at Swinton College six years before but which he now seemed disposed to accept. The crucial question, unanswered by Hogg or by the Industrial Relations Group under the chairmanship of Robert Carr which took on the task of shaping the Party's policy towards the unions, was how such a law, if it were passed, could possibly be enforced. It was all very well to say that the unions should be placed within a legal framework, but were the mechanisms created by the law appropriate for dealing with the problems that would arise in industrial disputes? The Tory paper *A Fair Deal at Work*, published in 1968, suggested that the new 'National Court' should be able to order a ninety-day 'cooling-off' period and a secret ballot before a strike began. But what happened if the cooling-off period merely generated further heat, if the secret ballot showed a majority for strike action? If the issue was one of pay, an independent body could recommend what it felt to be a fair solution, but what happened if the union rejected it? Should the union be fined? What if it then refused to pay? Could the ultimate sanction of criminal proceedings and imprisonment be invoked? The Donovan Report, commissioned by Wilson in 1965 and finally appearing in 1968, rejected altogether the possibility of legal curbs. Meanwhile industrial strife continued to bedevil the national economy and gravely inconvenience the public.[19]

With commendable courage Harold Wilson and his Employment Secretary, Barbara Castle, introduced their own solution. *In Place of Strife* did not go as far in some important respects as the Tories felt desirable, but it incorporated many of the ideas of *A Fair Deal at Work* and was a great deal better than nothing. If it had been adopted, many of the problems that were to plague Heath's government would never have arisen or would have been far more manageable. Many of the more liberal Conservatives thought that the best course would have been to welcome and support it. This, thought Prior, 'would have done wonders for the country and still left the Labour party seething with discontent. I believe that Ted and Iain Macleod should have spotted our opportunity.' Ian Gilmour felt that the Opposition was hamstrung by their faith in their own planning; they were convinced that they had found the right answer and could not countenance any inferior version. They rejected the Labour project 'in the deluded belief that, once they had gained a mandate from the electorate, the over-mighty unions would not dare to oppose them'. He and Prior were not alone in this view. Even in the 1922 Committee, where union-bashing was more prevalent, opinions on the proper response to *In Place of Strife* were finely balanced. Heath was one of those who felt that the manifest superiority of the Tory solution meant that support for the Labour approach would have been inappropriate. He did not advocate opposing the Labour legislation, but he was instrumental in ensuring that when it came to a vote in March 1969 the Shadow Cabinet opted for abstention. The unions rejected the proposals out of hand, the Home Secretary, James Callaghan, and a large part of the parliamentary Labour Party followed suit, the legislation foundered. In its place the unions volunteered a 'solemn and binding undertaking' to reform their ways. 'Solomon Binding', as the undertaking was mockingly christened, convinced nobody and only added to the picture of a disorganised and demoralised government. Heath had won a battle; it was to be several years before it became evident how much he had thereby contributed to the eventual loss of a war. 'The trouble is', Lord Swinton complained, 'that Ted is not really a politician. He doesn't see the situation as it really is, but as he would like it to be.'[20]

Industrial relations was only one of the fields in which the party had been preparing for government. Heath loved to be busy; he believed in copious planning; as Swinton said, he imagined a future which would roll out smoothly along the lines which he had laid down for it. It is arguable that he planned too much; that the Conservatives when they finally came to office were the prisoners of their own forethought. They took over, an unnamed junior minister remarked, 'more prepared than any before – in Opposition we all studied like billy-o and in the end we were over-prepared'.[21] Heath was particularly preoccupied with the need to reform the machinery of government. A smaller Cabinet, super-ministries, fewer civil servants, was how he saw the future. He would, as he triumphantly told the party conference in 1968, 'purge the body politic of the toxins of waste, extravagance and procrastination'. He would bring in new blood from outside: businessmen, captains of industry, who would inject a badly needed dose of vitality into the clogged and torpid arteries of Whitehall. It sounded admirable in theory; time was to show that institutions run by human beings rarely respond in practice in the way that abstract logic suggests should be the case. Nor was the planning for a reform of the tax system notably more successful; solutions propounded to meet one economic situation can appear curiously irrelevant a few years later when the facts of economic life have changed.

The time which the Conservatives under Heath devoted to preparing for their return to office was not wasted. They were better prepared, had considered more possibilities, resolved more issues, than any administration before or after. But the issues would not stay resolved, the possibilities turned out differently from all reasonable expectations. Heath was celebrated for his habit of taking a long time to make up his mind but sticking firmly to whatever he then concluded. Usually this was a merit; time was to show that sometimes it could prove dangerous.

Unless the individual concerned is a hard-bitten champion of one wing or the other, labels such as left and right rarely fit comfortably on politicians. Heath was generally accounted of the left, but for two or three years he was vilified by many as a fierce reactionary, bent upon confrontation with the unions. Jo Grimond told Alastair Hetherington that Heath was 'Liberal in some aspects ...' He entered a cautious reservation, however, about Heath's attitude to social policies: '... he mentioned welfare and pensions, immigration, law reform and hanging.' On the last count at least he did Heath less than justice. Though as Chief Whip he had found it necessary to try to talk backbenchers into accepting the Government's solution, he was at heart an abolitionist and voted that way on every occasion that a free vote was offered. On other issues he usually inclined as far to the left as he thought was compatible with the unity of the party. Far from being a splitter, as characterised by Wilson, his instinct always was to seek something acceptable to all but the extremists.[22]

On certain issues he was notably more cautious than some of the Young Turks thought necessary. When Wilson wanted to liberalise the Public Records Act by bringing the fifty-year rule down to twenty-five, Heath opposed any change and in the end only grudgingly compromised on thirty. He agreed with Douglas-Home that official historians should not be allowed to see papers in advance of the thirty-year rule: he was particularly concerned about this, he said, because the Munich records would not become available till January 1969. Books using these papers would only come much later: 'This can be important politically in relation to the timing of the next election.' He was determined to put Overseas Development back where he thought it belonged – under the aegis of the Foreign Office. For one who was to become identified with the policy of providing substantial aid to the underdeveloped world, his initial forays into this arena were distinctly cautious. 'What we are proposing', he told Bruce Kenrick of the Centre for International Studies, 'is not a voluntary gift in the tradition of Christian charity, but a transfer by government of funds raised compulsorily by taxes from the whole community.' This could only be justified if that community clearly supported it: 'The individuals and organisations concerned with aid need in my view to spend rather more time persuading their fellow citizens than lobbying political leaders.'[23]

Always his instinct was to restrict the liberty of the individual as little as was possible. Hogg consulted him about some Labour legislation which would have made commercial gaming impossible. Personally he considered gambling 'a totally irrational activity', he told Heath, but he felt this was going too far. 'I am quite illiterate on this subject,' Heath confessed (or perhaps boasted). 'I find it extremely complicated but at the same time fascinating.' He agreed with Hogg: there should be strict controls but if people wanted to gamble they must be allowed to do so. The less Whitehall interfered in the affairs of the nation, the better it would be. 'I've just spent five years going round England and I can't tell you how they all hate central government,' he exploded once in Crossman's hearing. 'Regionalisation is the great thing. We've got to concede this to people if we want to endear ourselves to them.' He was less regionally minded, however, when it was a question of the Scottish people wanting to break up the Union. At Perth in May 1968 he committed the party to support some form of Scottish Assembly – 'it would have been politically suicidal' to do any less, he wrote in his memoirs – but the committee which he then set up under Douglas-Home had as the first of its objectives 'to keep the United Kingdom united'. Privately he thought that the Assembly would be at worst mischievous, at best a waste of time and money. He felt much the same about that shibboleth of the left, the Open University. He told the Shadow Cabinet that it was not cost-effective, was a wasteful misuse of broadcasting time and would put an undesirable strain on local libraries. 'With a wide network of universities covering the country, the Open University was really quite unnecessary.'[24]

*   *   *

One fact of life which meetings of the Shadow Cabinet quickly revealed was that Heath and Enoch Powell were far divided in their approach to politics. Heath was a man of strong convictions but he was still a pragmatist: he sought to establish the facts as they were and then to consider how to find a solution that took account of them. Powell's convictions were quite as strong but he took less account of the existing facts: he decided what should be done and only then began to consider how or whether the facts could be changed to make it possible. Though on almost every issue Quintin Hogg was nearer to Heath than to Powell, he was more like Powell in the way he reached his conclusions: both men relished philosophical discussion and aspired to the ideal rather than the practical compromise. In one discussion of industrial relations in the Shadow Cabinet, Hogg raised some theoretical issues of principle which he felt to be fundamental but which to Heath seemed futile irrelevancies. 'I remember vividly the anger which Ted Heath showed at this interruption,' wrote Powell, '... he always seemed to me a person who had a natural detestation for an idea. If you showed him an idea he would immediately become angry and go red in the face.' One man's idea is another man's waste of time. Whitelaw was much more akin to Heath. He remembered well the meeting to which Powell was referring: 'It started by Quintin going back to what his father did in 1927 ...' Hogg may sometimes have irritated Heath, but in the last resort Heath felt that they were in sympathy with each other. He had no such feeling about Powell. Perhaps in other circumstances they might politely have navigated around each other. In the intimacy of the Shadow Cabinet that proved impossible. Heath confessed to Shirley Williams that he had become so disquieted by Powell's propensity to put on a mad expression and talk nonsense that he had had to change the seating so as to avoid seeing his face.[25]

Immigration and race relations were the issues that most starkly revealed their incompatibility. A substantial element of the parliamentary party and still more of the Tory voters in the country took a line far less liberal than Heath, left to himself, would have preferred. He had to accommodate them and yet not let them dictate policy. It was a delicate balancing act, made all the more difficult by the activities of Enoch Powell. Powell made himself the champion of those sections of the community – Labour quite as much as Tory – which deplored the scale of immigration and believed that it was a threat both to their jobs and to the racial integrity of the nation. Repeatedly he made speeches in which he demanded restrictions on the numbers that could be admitted, particularly that there should be a limit put on the number of Indians from East Africa who enjoyed British citizenship and whom the Conservative government under Douglas-Home had ruled could make a home in Britain if, after independence, their continued existence in Africa became impossible. Heath was not wholly unsympathetic to Powell's views; he had already been making discreet enquiries of the Research Department as to how the threatened influx could be curbed. But demagogic appeals to the electorate which were at variance with official party policy were un-acceptable. 'I am afraid I am getting very fed up with Enoch,' Iain Macleod wrote to Heath. 'This is about the fourth time he has pre-empted a Shadow Cabinet decision and taken a line which is going to be extremely embarrassing.' Heath was fed up with Enoch too, but he was not prepared to ignore the very substantial following that his maverick colleague enjoyed. When Labour introduced legislation to curb immigration from Kenya Heath, though with some doubts and regret, concluded that the official Tory line must be to support it; fifteen Tory MPs, including Iain Macleod, nevertheless voted against the Bill.[26]

Heath was thus in the uncomfortable position of privately sym-pathising with those who opposed the official line that he was putting forward. The same was true when in April 1968 Labour sought to offset their attitude on immigration by introducing a Race Relations Bill designed to outlaw any kind of racial discrimination. Heath tried to hold the Party together by accepting the need in principle for such legislation but opposing the Bill on the grounds that, as drafted, it would not work. Once more he was in trouble with his left wing; one backbencher, Humphry Berkeley, actually leaving the Tory Party in protest. This time Macleod accepted the majority view but Edward Boyle held out for supporting the Labour proposals. The Young Conservatives of the North Western Area passed a motion deploring 'the vacillation displayed by the leadership' and regretting 'that principle has been sacrificed once again for apparent expediency'. In a hurt response Heath argued that the party had behaved with full responsibility in expressing its doubts and reserving its right to revise the legislation when it had seen how it worked in practice. Of course the Young Conservatives could criticise the leadership's conclusions, but 'They do not, however, have the right to attribute to the leading members of the party motives less honourable than their own.'[27]

At least he must have thought that he had done enough to satisfy, or at least contain, the right. He had reckoned without Enoch Powell. Though Powell had appeared to endorse the party line in the Shadow Cabinet, on 20 April 1968, in Birmingham, he made a speech which contained little of substance which he had not said frequently before but which was couched in deliberately emotive terms, in particular in his quotation of the Sybil's prophecy that she would see 'wars, terrible wars, and the Tiber foaming with much blood'. Hogg, Macleod and Boyle were so outraged by what they saw as a wanton incitement to racial prejudice that they declared they could no longer sit in a Shadow Cabinet with Powell. Heath, according to Whitelaw, was angrier still; he summoned an emergency meeting of those members of the Shadow Cabinet most immediately involved and dismissed Powell forthwith. The result was an alarming outburst of popular support for Powell from what Heath professed to believe was a tiny section of the population. It was a conviction he found hard to sustain. Jill Knight, a Conservative MP from Birmingham, told him that Powell had her full support and that everyone she talked to in her constituency felt the same; she hoped, 'most earnestly, that opposition from our own "left-wing" will not cause the party to weaken'. Of the 2,756 letters received in the Leader of the Opposition's office only twelve approved of Powell's dismissal. Eleven constituencies in the south of England went public in their support for Powell. Unkindest cut of all, a poll conducted by the BBC *World at One* programme made Harold Wilson man of the decade and Powell second, in front of President Kennedy, Pope John XXIII and Martin Luther King. Heath was far down the field, beaten even by Ian Smith.[28]

Heath could not fail to be affected by this wave of popular sentiment. The question was how far he could go to accommodate it without alienating his allies on the left, to whom he felt far closer. Whitelaw felt he was in danger of making too many concessions; 'there was a feeling that the party had been going too far right on too many issues'. Heath replied with some irritation that 'the party was bound to shift to the right if the left continued to make trouble for the leadership'. At Walsall, in January 1969, with Enoch Powell in the audience, Heath reaffirmed the right of immigrants to equality of treatment but demanded tough new immigration controls. Commonwealth immigrants were 'aliens' whom a Tory government would only allow in for a specific job in a specific place for a specific time. He must have been unpleasantly conscious of how far he had gone when a member of the audience, to tumultuous applause, said how delighted he was 'that Mr Heath appears to have adopted many of the views expressed by Mr Enoch Powell'. Though his own left wing was dismayed, Labour ministers viewed this new, tougher line with some alarm. 'In my view it is quite a sensible policy,' Crossman wrote in his diary. 'I think it will be very popular indeed. This insistence on doing something about immigration and doing it quickly is a very potent political force which will realign the Tory party and stop the rift.' Violet Bonham-Carter, more orthodox than Crossman in her liberal views, wrote to Quintin Hogg to deplore what she felt to be Heath's '*volte-face* on the racial issue. Every Powellite in the country will acclaim it. I had always admired his integrity and trusted it.' Hogg replied soothingly that he thought she was reading too much into a speech which contained nothing particularly new. He did have doubts, though, and was not alone in doing so: a feeling that the leadership was allowing itself to be carried too far towards the right – particularly in the field of education – was undoubtedly one of the reasons that led Edward Boyle to renounce politics for a new life as Vice Chancellor at Leeds University.[29]

Crossman's fears were justified, however; Heath's new stance on immigration disappointed a few of his friends but did succeed in healing or least patching up some of the worse rifts within the party. Without Powell the Shadow Cabinet was a notably more harmonious body. By the end of 1969, with the polls giving cheerful news and the government discredited by its botched effort to reform the trade unions, Heath looked forward with some confidence to the general election that could not now be far away.

ELEVEN

Victory

The great planning exercise was by now almost complete. Some time earlier, Prior had suggested that Maudling be made chairman of the Policy Committee. 'The broad lines of our policy are now fixed,' he wrote, 'and Reggie would do very little work anyhow ... It would strengthen your position – show leadership through magnanimity etc.' Heath was not interested in showing leadership through magnanimity and had no intention of letting control of policy slip from his hands, even into the relaxed grasp of Reggie Maudling. He kept a close eye on progress and did not hesitate to intervene decisively if he felt things were going awry. When he read the draft report of a group chaired by the right-wing Tory Nicholas Ridley, which urged extensive and immediate privatisation of the nationalised industries, he found it 'alarmingly naïve and even half-baked'. He ridiculed the contention that state industries should be run on strictly commercial lines, with the sole task of maximising their profits. 'How can you,' he asked, 'when they have such a large monopoly element in them?' He was not against denationalisation in principle and did not demur when Macleod in Shadow Cabinet observed that 'it was politically important to denationalise something. The question was what?' But it would take time to create a climate in which the private investor would be ready to take over responsibility from the state. Ridley's approach, he thought, was sloppy and ill-considered. Effectively, the report was killed.[1]

He continued to pay what seemed to some of his colleagues an undue amount of attention to the views of the clever young men by whom he liked to be surrounded. In December 1969 he gave a dinner at which they met the members of the Shadow Cabinet and expounded their long-term plans for the future. Mark Schreiber, with the brisk self-confidence that comes with youth, prepared a brief for him before the event. Only two shadow ministers, he considered – Carrington and Carr – really understood what was going on. Hogg, Macleod, Maudling and Rippon were opposed to such planning because it wasn't 'their style of government'. Barber, Joseph and Mrs Thatcher strongly supported the enterprise but 'do not really understand it'. Mrs Thatcher came in for some special scorn. At a recent meeting with business leaders at Sundridge Park she had spoken with great emphasis about some of the planning problems that had to be faced: 'The devastating naïveté and superficiality of this diagnosis was not lost on the businessmen.' Though Heath encouraged, or at least condoned, such youthful outbursts he was no more disposed to treat his advisers reverentially than they were their elders and possibly betters. When David Howell put in a paper arguing that the party should shun deflation and commit itself to accelerated growth, Heath minuted: 'It is slapstick, ill thought out and will be used against us.'[2]

The merits and demerits of a prices and incomes policy were incessantly debated and as often left unresolved. 'As you know,' wrote Macleod, 'the views of your colleagues range from the belief that an incomes policy in any form is dangerous nonsense, to the belief that it is the vital key to economic policy.' Business people, on the whole, favoured a wage freeze but deplored control of prices; trade unionists were all for control of prices but saw less reason to curb wages. In 1966 Heath was clear that he inclined towards the 'dangerous nonsense' school; 'I believe', he told Maurice Macmillan, 'that the government's decision to impose a statutory freeze on prices and incomes is a step inimical to all that the Conservative party must stand for, and does, in fact, display the great divide between our philosophies.' So far, so clear, but in the Shadow Cabinet, which was every bit as divided as Macleod had indicated, he in the end steered the discussion towards a compromise. It was agreed that the party should approve 'a voluntary wage freeze for a limited period' but should oppose any form of compulsion. This position – a fine example of neither having your cake nor eating it – satisfied nobody but was better than an overt split. By the middle of 1968, by which time wage inflation was alarmingly high, the formula was re-enunciated in a slightly modified form. The Party, the Shadow Cabinet agreed, 'in the long term were against the statutory control of wages and believed in the free operation of collective bargaining,' but only 'provided industrial relations were governed by a new legal framework'. In the short term a majority was in favour of an extension of the Government's powers to delay wage settlements. As the election approached, Heath's personal stance remained equivocal: in principle in favour of free collective bargaining and the working of the market forces without governmental interference; in practice doubtful whether such luxuries could safely be permitted. It was perhaps unsurprising that, when the top brass of the Party met for its final consultative rally at Selsdon Park in February 1970, the paper on prices and incomes was left to the end and somehow never got discussed at all.[3]

On industrial relations the party line was slightly less ambivalent but here too there were misgivings and some dissent. When the Steering Committee of the Shadow Cabinet first considered the planning group's papers on the future of the trade unions, Maudling doubted how far legal sanctions could be made effective, while Macleod pointed out that 'even if collective agreements were made enforceable, employers would often not try to enforce their legal rights'. Heath felt more certain about where he stood in this area than on prices and incomes. The essential thing, he insisted, was that the position of the trade unions in modern society should be defined and regularised. There was to be no question of union-bashing; on the contrary the authority of properly elected and appointed trade union officials should be strengthened, if only to make it easier for them to cope with the unofficial element: 'The trade unions must accept their responsibilities and their position must be established in law.' Throughout the planning period this remained the blueprint for the Policy Group on Industrial Relations and in due course for the legislation which the Tory government introduced when Heath became Prime Minister.[4]

One conspicuous feature of the preparation for government arose from Heath's conviction that Whitehall should be opened up and revivified by the ingestion of high-powered businessmen. It has often been said that Heath was better equipped to be a senior civil servant than a politician. Probably he was too intractable in his opinions and too authoritarian in his cast of mind to have served successfully a minister whom he could neither respect nor dominate. As a minister himself he worked closely and harmoniously with a succession of highly capable civil servants, listening to their opinions with respect though never allowing himself to be overborne by their expertise. But it did not follow from this that he thought Whitehall could not be improved; successful businessmen, if put in the right slot, would bring a new vigour and efficiency to the civil service which could in time transform the whole machinery of government. A high-powered group led by Val Duncan of Rio Tinto Zinc and including Lord Netherthorpe of Fisons, Marcus Sieff of Marks & Spencer and Harold Watkinson of Schweppes was enlisted to consider how best staff could be seconded from industry to government. In principle, this involved no serious problem. The snag, in practice, proved to be that when the time came to lend businessmen to Whitehall on a semi-permanent basis, the businesses responsible were reluctant to sacrifice their brightest prospects and tended to volunteer candidates of the respectable second rank. Sometimes it was even worse. Arnold Weinstock, for many years the controlling genius of GEC, produced a man so inadequate that he had to be returned to his original employer, shortly after which he was sacked. On another occasion Mark Schreiber identified a likely candidate and asked for him to be made available; the result was that he was promptly promoted within his own organisation and Schreiber was told that unfortunately he could not be spared. Recruitment tended to be haphazard: one banker, who did not last long, was selected by Heath on the basis of a casual meeting in the swimming pool of the International Sportsmen's Club. The project was not a complete failure: some outsiders profited from their immersion in officialdom and Whitehall learnt some lessons from its brash invaders. But on the whole the moral to be drawn from the experiment was that the best-laid schemes of mice, men and Leaders of the Opposition rarely worked out as their originator expected.[5]

One thing about this project that concerned Heath was that it might upset senior members of the civil service. In particular he was anxious not to alienate William Armstrong, the head of the Home Civil Service. It was one of Armstrong's duties to keep a line open to the Leader of the Opposition so that, when the government changed, there would be a measure of continuity. The relationship between Heath and Armstrong seems to have been unusually close. In October 1969, after a two-hour meeting in Albany, Armstrong told Heath that 'he would not be able to continue these contacts, but that the channel at private secretary level could remain open if discreetly used'. A few months later Douglas Hurd noted in his diary: 'William Armstrong in and out by the back door.' There was no suggestion of impropriety but Harold Wilson was notoriously prone to detect conspiracies around every corner and Armstrong was anxious not to provide him with food for speculation. In fact, Armstrong had been consulted at an early stage about Heath's plan to 'open up' the civil service to outsiders and had greeted the idea with equanimity if not enthusiasm; so much so that, by June 1969, Hurd could tell Heath that 'the consultants have turned almost full circle on this subject, and no longer see themselves as crusaders against the civil service'.[6]

In September 1969 James Douglas, of the Conservative Research Department, recorded that he and Brendon Sewill had 'a sinister notion, which is to incarcerate the Shadow Cabinet for a weekend when they can really concentrate free from distraction on their policy and strategy for the next election'.[7] This was to be the culmination of the planning process, in which the architects of the new policies would be able to discuss their theories with the people who would have to make them work in practice. Swinton, the Conservative study centre in Yorkshire, would have been the obvious venue if it had not been so far from London. Instead 'Ye Olde Felbridge Hotel' in East Grinstead was put forward. Heath baulked at the idea of anything 'Ye Olde' being associated with what was to be a thoroughly modern conference and the choice fell on Selsdon Park – a neo-Jacobean pile near thrusting, meritocratic Croydon which seemed eminently suitable as a place to plan the sort of future which Heath envisaged. The conference, to be held at the end of January 1970, was to be businesslike and concentrate on policy and strategy, avoiding too many purely social frills. Heath took a keen interest in the agenda, banishing prices and incomes to the latest point in the programme where it could decently be accommodated, and concerned himself with every detail of the arrangements, adjusting the times of the meals and substituting a claret for the proposed Chateauneuf du Pape. 'Ted handled the meeting with his normal ruthless efficiency and was in the chair for fifteen hours,' Michael Fraser recalled. 'There was much fun and hilarity. They got to know much more about each others' personalities … As people don't meet each other in country houses any more, this kind of meeting now has a greater function.'[8]

Selsdon did not and was not intended to herald any dramatic change of policy. 'There never was a Selsdon policy,' Heath told Tony Benn. 'It was invented by Harold Wilson.' Yet the thrust of the planning papers and the tone of much of the discussion supported the idea that the conference had provided, in Carrington's words, 'a fairly assertive restatement of the virtues of capitalism and the benefits of free enterprise … It is simple, and often politically necessary to produce emphatic doctrinal statements when in Opposition.' Norman Tebbit, who was to enter the House of Commons at the forthcoming election, had been hearing what he wanted to hear when he concluded that the Selsdon declaration (as he called it) 'marked the Tory party's first repudiation of the post-war Butskellite consensus', but his reaction was not wholly unjustified.[9] Heath's own contributions were moderate in tone but certainly inclined towards the radical right. On industrial relations, for instance, he said that the balance of power between employer and employee had slipped too far towards the latter. This must be redressed by legislation. But in the last resort the responsibility would always rest with the employers. Strengthen their position but then let them get on with it. They must be told: 'If you don't like wages going up, don't put them up.' ('They will,' put in Mrs Thatcher balefully.)[10] Thatcher also provoked one of

Heath's more left-wing interventions. She was anxious to champion the cause of the privately funded Buckingham University. Heath opposed this, partly it is true on the slightly inconsequential grounds that he remembered Max Beloff, the moving spirit behind the project, as a left-wing socialist at Oxford; more because he believed that any such support would, sooner rather than later, lead to demands for a state subsidy. Not only did he reject the inclusion of a clause in the manifesto supporting the idea of the university, he was reluctant even to let Mrs Thatcher raise the matter at Selsdon. He was cautious about the merits of private schools and universities, saying that he would never 'commit myself to saying whether independent schools are better than state ones or not'. As to the future for Buckingham, he noted tersely: 'Not committing myself to a Royal Charter. Wouldn't trust Max Beloff for a minute. Already got too many universities.'[11]

'The Shadow Cabinet,' wrote Hurd in his diary, 'a basically frivolous body designed to discuss ephemeral House of Commons business, is taken in four long sessions over the whole range of British politics. They are exhausted and enjoy it.' They did not, however, end up with a clear impression that they had moved boldly in any particular direction: 'a judicious muddle', Mrs Thatcher described the manifesto which arose from it. The main reason that Selsdon was popularly believed to have signalled a significant move to the right was that, as Alan Clark put it, 'foolishly and opportunistically, when the press caught on to the existence of the meeting, Heath announced to them (on the advice of Macleod who thought it a vote-winner) that they had been discussing law and order – an issue which had been scarcely touched on'. The press conference was in fact taken by Quintin Hogg, but the decision to stress law and order was indeed a last-minute one, taken in a moment of panic when it became clear that there was nothing very much to say on other issues. Heath certainly approved it. Only a week or so after Selsdon he told the Shadow Cabinet that 'there was great public concern on law and order ... He had himself been saying that organised crime had grown ... We should be prepared to devote a bigger proportion of government expenditure to the police.' The public was left with the delusion that the resolutions reached at Selsdon Park had been far more right-wing and authoritarian than was in fact the case.[12]

Harold Wilson seized gleefully on this. 'I wished its regressive implications to be known and understood more widely,' he wrote. At the annual conference of the London Labour Party he proclaimed the existence of 'Selsdon Man', an uncouth Neanderthal intent on creating 'a system of society for the ruthless and the pushing, the uncaring'. Selsdon Man's message was stark and brutal: 'You're out on your own!' This playful fantasy delighted his party faithful and considerably irritated Heath, but in the long run did the Tories more good than harm. The message the public drew from Selsdon was that the Conservatives were preoccupied by the need to cut taxes and to enforce law and order. They decided that they rather liked it. There was an uneasy feeling abroad that society was on the way towards disintegration; a party that espoused traditional values and promised stern measures to reinforce them was going to command much popular support. Wilson realised the danger. In a Management Committee meeting at Number 10 he referred to the Selsdon Conference as 'a great success'. 'I have seldom heard Harold admit a success to the other side,' Crossman wrote in his diary, 'but he said this had depressed him and that they had pulled off a successful publicity stunt. He was also anxious about the build-up of Heath.' Watching the 'new, confident Heath' on a *Panorama* programme Crossman found him rude and domineering, 'but I suppose from the point of view of proving that he was on top of his form, even this appearance was a good follow-up to the Selsdon Conference'.[13]

But then things started to go wrong for the Conservatives. For no very clear reason, the polls began to move steadily in favour of Labour. A substantial Tory lead after Selsdon was whittled away until, by May, Labour were once more clearly ahead. Brendon Sewill, on 29 April, tried to explain what was happening. More than half the electorate, he told Heath, identified with the Socialists 'because they feel that Labour has a soft heart' but did not necessarily vote that way 'because they feel that Labour has also a soft head. When things are not going wrong they gravitate towards Labour.' Now things were going, if not right, then at least considerably better. The trade figures had moved into surplus, wage inflation had not yet been matched by increased prices, the feeling of prosperity might be spurious but it was potent while it lasted. The best chance that Sewill could see was to 'build up concern about the present situation – recent record price rises, unemployment, strikes, taxation'. It did not seem that this would be enough. A fortnight before Wilson called the general election for 18 June, Knox Cunningham told Macmillan that 'there is a certain amount of defeatist feeling'. Briefly, even Heath seemed to be infected by the mood. He was 'very depressed and dejected', wrote Jim Prior. He made a speech to the Industrial Society in London so disastrously lame that his staff were in despair. Then he rallied. 'He had great reserves of inner strength,' wrote Prior. '… He had fought hard for most things and because he was a loner he was dependent on his own strength and no one else's.'[14]

The manifesto more or less wrote itself after the Selsdon Conference. A year or so before, Heath had told the Shadow Cabinet that there were two things which they should emphasise: trade union reform and government expenditure. Since then, however, other issues had been forced to the fore. 'No one should doubt', wrote Tebbit, 'that at the time of the election in 1970 Ted Heath was committed to the end of that corporate consensus and to the new liberal economics … The 1970 manifesto, with its commitments to the liberation of the economy from the web of government controls, to denationalisation, and its absolute pledge against state control of prices and wages, was music to the ear of radical Conservatives.' Heath, for one, would have denied that he was quite so firmly committed to these propositions. At the time he let the matter ride. In his memoirs he admitted that the firm rejection of 'the philosophy of compulsory wage control' was in fact far removed from the pragmatic policy that he personally favoured. It was to cause him acute embarrassment and, in the end, had to be comprehensively abandoned. For the moment, however, he was stuck with it, forced to fight the election on a platform about which he had serious reservations.[15]

From the moment that the campaign began, almost every serious political commentator took it for granted that Labour would win –

the only speculation was about the size of their majority. Most of the Tory leaders were equally pessimistic: 'I was totally and utterly convinced from the start to the finish that we were going to lose,' confessed Willie Whitelaw. When Keith Joseph said that Macleod would not have agreed, Whitelaw retorted: 'Don't forget that Iain was an incredibly good gambler; he was saying that, but I don't think he really believed it.' The Labour leadership was equally convinced. When the historian Martin Gilbert told Harold Wilson that his vote mattered little since he lived in a safe Conservative seat, Wilson replied: 'There's no such thing as a safe Conservative seat in this election.' Worse still, from Heath's point of view, was the assumption not only that the Conservatives would lose but that the blame for the disaster would rest with the Leader of the Opposition. The press was filled with speculation about who would replace him. Whitelaw was the favourite. Enoch Powell was also often mentioned: so prominently did he figure in the electoral campaign that the Press Association assigned one reporter each to Heath and Wilson, but two to Powell. So much did the threat of Powell alarm the more orthodox Tory leaders that Whitelaw and Maudling arranged to meet at Alec Douglas-Home's house, The Hirsel, immediately after the election so as to consider the succession to the leadership. Carrington told Heath bluntly that he must resign if the Labour majority was more than twenty-five. 'The advice was well-meant', commented Heath, 'but quite unnecessary.'[16] It was not clear whether he meant merely that there was no Labour majority, let alone one of over twenty-five, or that, if there had been, he would have resigned without any prompting. Subsequent history suggests that it was the first.

What Heath himself secretly thought about the Tory prospects is hard to establish. Publicly he maintained a facade of unwavering optimism. At a Party Business Committee, the day after the polls showed Labour with a lead of 7½ per cent, he 'rose briskly from his chair to leave and ... said: "Well, we've been in worse corners than this one before and we've fought our way out before." He made this declaration with a cheerfulness and confidence which provoked a spontaneous cheer.' Whitelaw for one was convinced that the confidence was genuine. 'Ted believed all along that he was going to win,' he told David Butler. 'Naturally a party leader doesn't say he is going to lose, but he can avoid going out of his way to say that he is going to win. On the Monday [before election day] he said to me "After the count, when we have won…" The assurance with which he said it surprised me.' Yet Ian Gilmour was certain that Heath was despondent about the prospects, while Sara Morrison, as likely as anyone to know his mind, remembers that, when she told him that opinion on the ground seemed very different from the picture painted by the polls, he replied gloomily: 'I'm the leader, so that's what they have to tell me.' When the Shadow Cabinet met in his flat in Albany ten days before the election, Peter Rawlinson, the future Attorney General, noted that 'faces were long. Ted was very quiet. Only Iain Macleod exuded confidence. "We shall win," he said. The colleagues looked sceptical.' But though Heath may have been quiet his public display of optimism never wavered. Possibly the truth is that, like Queen Victoria, he was not interested in the possibility of defeat. Whatever the polls or his colleagues might tell him, he *had* to win. The alternative was too horrible to conceive. That was the end of the matter.[17]

He fought a good and sophisticated campaign. Geoffrey Tucker and Brendon Sewill proposed a series of sound bites which Heath was required constantly to reiterate in the same way as Wilson had used 'the thirteen wasted years' and 'a deficit of £800 million' in the previous election. Since inflation was held to be Labour's weakest point, 'the pound in your pocket' was an obvious spectre to invoke. 'Tax rates up by £3,000 million' was another favourite. 'While it was true that the public do not understand statistics expressed in millions,' his advisers explained patronisingly, 'nevertheless this phrase has the advantage of sounding very large, very painful, and what is more, totally putting in the shade the figure of £800 million.' Heath loathed the whole idea of a slick, professional presentation, but he knew that he had a mountain to climb and, for perhaps the only time in his life, let the public relations experts have their way. Tucker's other piece of advice – 'You should rise above the heat of the battle, Mr Wilson will undoubtedly try to niggle you and get you to indulge in a verbal bout of fisticuffs. I suggest you don't do this, and it is done by Mr Macleod and Mr Maudling' – was altogether more palatable, and this too was accepted. Even his appearance was enhanced for the occasion: 'Personally he appeared to great advantage,' wrote Marcia Williams with grudging admiration, 'with his clean and shining silver hair, well-tended and sun-tanned face, immaculate blue suit and tie.' His surroundings were equally well orchestrated: 'On the platform with him were a few people only ... and these had carefully been picked (we thought) for the ability to look attractive.'[18]

He was as fiercely energetic as he had been in the election of 1966. Throughout, it was *his* campaign. Douglas Hurd told the journalist Hugo Young that Heath felt that he was now sufficiently well known around the country to be able to take a less prominent role than had been necessary in 1966: 'He will respond to fewer challenges, not be so constantly in the front line.' This may have been his intention, but when it came to the point he presided over every press conference, made a major speech almost every evening, took an important role in broadcasting and featured in almost three-quarters of the television reports of the Conservative campaign. He refused to be distracted by inessentials and rejected the pleas of those in marginal seats that he should make appearances on their behalf. He would better serve the cause in Gloucester by staying in London, he told Harry Oppenheim. Always, with the odd sound bite thrown in, the message was the same. The nation was in danger of falling asleep: 'As a people we have been flattered and lulled too long by a trivial government. The real problems, the real issues, have been kept from us as if we were children. And meanwhile the world is passing us by ... My message is this. Unless Britain wakes up, Britain will lose the future.' Heath came across as a decent man, considered Mrs Thatcher, '... an honest patriot who cared deeply about his country and wanted to serve it. Though it would not have served him had we lost, he fought a good campaign.'[19]

'No one could describe Ted as a great communicator,' Mrs Thatcher also wrote. In fact his television appearances were notably more polished than anything he had achieved before. He 'came across extremely successfully', judged Whitelaw, adding that in large part this was the achievement of Geoffrey Tucker. Michael Cockerell agreed; Heath benefited from 'the most sophisticated television election campaign ever seen until that time'. One particularly effective sequence showed Heath mixing easily with a friendly crowd. Then came Christopher Chataway's voice-over: 'Hardened newspapermen have been heard to remark that this is a new Ted Heath. It is not a new Ted Heath – it's the old one who has been there all the time. Perhaps he's not an easy man to know but when they know him, people feel that he is a man worth knowing. A man to trust.' Robin Day handled him more roughly on *Panorama* than Wilson had been treated on the same day, but he acquitted himself well. 'If you lose a second time, will you resign the leadership of the party?' demanded Day. 'We are going to win, Mr Day,' replied Heath. 'That is the answer to your question.' (Things could have been worse. On *Election Forum* Day put to the party leaders questions on postcards which had been sent in by voters. One addressed to Heath read: 'Dear Daddy. When you get to Number 10 will you do the decent thing and invite Mummy and me to tea?' Day duly put this question, but only in rehearsal. Heath's 'shoulders shook with silent mirth'.) Heath made one good joke of his own. On several occasions Wilson, when making un-heralded visits around the country, had had eggs thrown at him. The implications were very disturbing, said Heath. Since Wilson's move-ments were not advertised in advance, this must mean that there were 'men and women in this country walking around with eggs in their pockets on the off-chance of seeing the Prime Minister'. A Mr B. G. Williams advised Heath not to try to make electoral play with his achievements on *Morning Cloud*: 'The common touch is vital to all successful leaders ... one glimpse of Bermuda shorts and the sipping of Martinis on Bondi will send thousands to the polls in support of the Labour party.' Heath took the point, Hurd replied, but there was nothing in the least aristocratic or leisurely about life on *Morning Cloud* and 'anyone sipping a Martini aboard would quickly cease to be a member of the crew'.[20]

Enoch Powell, meanwhile, was playing a curiously ambiguous role. No one listening to his speeches could have been left in much doubt about his contempt for Heath in particular and the official Tory opposition in general. He seemed to be intent on distancing himself from the Party, positioning himself, perhaps, for an eventual takeover

LEFT: Edward Heath's father, William, whose character belied his disconcertingly Hitlerian appearance.

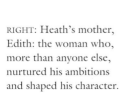

RIGHT: Heath's mother, Edith: the woman who, more than anyone else, nurtured his ambitions and shaped his character.

LEFT: Teddy Heath, aged three. Any dreams of becoming an engine driver were quickly put behind him.

BELOW: Edith Heath with her two sons. John, the younger, is on her right.

ABOVE: The Chatham House 'general election' of 1935. Heath is haranguing an enthusiastic audience, who elected him by a large majority.

RIGHT: Heath looking improbably devout as the Archangel Gabriel in the school nativity play.

BELOW: An Oxford idyll: punting on the Cherwell with a Balliol contemporary, Donovan Martin.

OPPOSITE: The young artillery officer.

ABOVE: A group at Number 10 in 1958. From left to right are the Prime Minister's principal private secretary, Freddie Bishop, Harold Macmillan, John Wyndham, Heath, Philip de Zulueta and Anthony Barber, Macmillan's pps.

LEFT: Feeding the dog at the Aldingtons' house in Kent.

ABOVE: With Madron Seligman,
his oldest and closest friend.

BELOW: With Georg Solti and
Leopold Stokowski in the garden
of Jack and Roslyn Lyons.

ABOVE: With Nikita Khrushchev at a reception in the Speaker's house in London in 1956.

LEFT: Dancing with Tatiana, the wife of his political secretary, Douglas Hurd, at the Party Conference in Blackpool in 1970. Mrs Hurd seems to be enjoying herself rather less than her partner.

bid when they met with electoral disaster. At one point Whitelaw had to talk Heath out of his intention to withdraw Powell's routine letter of support; an action which would have been tantamount to expelling him from the Party. Yet Powell's insistent harping on the theme of immigration, together with his belated, grudging but still emphatic advice that the electors should vote Conservative, undoubtedly decided the votes of many who might otherwise have backed Labour or, more probably, abstained. Powell subsequently claimed that he had won the election for the Tories. That is pitching it too high, but even Heath admitted that Powell had made things a little easier for them.[21]

Yet however well the campaign seemed to be going, the polls obstinately failed to suggest that this was so. On the contrary, they got inexorably worse. On 12 June, with less than a week to go, Heath returned to his hotel in Manchester after what had seemed to him to be a particularly successful meeting to be met with the news that Labour led by eleven points. The bookmakers offered long odds on a Labour victory. 'It is too late to recover lost ground,' announced David Wood in *The Times*. And yet the reports of those canvassing in the field continued to contradict these dire prognostications. Many Tory candidates believed that nationally the cause was lost but continued to feel that, for some unknown reason, their own constituency was insulated from the pervasive fever. Even Barbara Castle felt uneasy. Though Heath was 'making such a pathetic showing personally,' she wrote in her diary, 'I have a haunting feeling there is a silent majority sitting behind its lace curtains, waiting to come out and vote Tory'.[22]

It was. The polls had got it wrong. Things had probably never been as clear-cut as their figures had indicated. Some factors, however, did contribute to a late swing. A set of bad trade figures – artificially bad because they had been distorted by the purchase of four jumbo jets – undermined the Labour claim to have put the balance of payments permanently to rights. The World Cup was lost to Germany: not a calamity that could reasonably be attributed to Labour maladministration yet still contributing to a feeling that perhaps, after all, it was time for a change. Heath was in exceptionally good form in the last few days of the campaign. Yet scarcely anyone believed it was enough. One late poll, published in the *Evening Standard* on election day, put the Conservatives ahead but it was drawn from a tiny base of voters and no one paid much attention. When the polls closed, it was taken for granted by almost everyone that the following day would see Wilson back in Downing Street.

At Bexley, Heath was under the peculiar disadvantage of facing among his opponents a candidate who had changed his name to Edward Heath. The true Heath was told that, while it was legal to change one's surname, there was no way of changing one's Christian name. Legally, therefore, it might have been possible to force this irritating impostor to stand down. The expense of any such action and the unlikelihood of achieving anything before election day convinced Heath that it would be better to suffer silently or, at least, to confine himself to warning voters to be sure that they were marking their papers for the right Edward Heath. Amazingly the false Heath nevertheless gained nearly a thousand votes: some, no doubt, cast out of perversity, but most as a result of carelessly filling in the forms. Fortunately it made little difference to the overall results: Heath still had a majority of 8,058 over the Labour candidate and an overall majority of over 3,000.

By the time the result was announced at Bexley it was clear that the nation had dramatically ignored the conclusions of every poll and every pundit. The first result, a swing of 6 per cent to David Howell at Guildford, might have been a freak, but when the next four or five results all told the same story, even the most sceptical had to accept what was happening. As soon as his own result had been announced, Heath hurried back to London. On the way, Hurd remembered '... the car radio persisted in telling us extraordinary good news ... Extraordinary to me, but not to Mr Heath.' Heath felt pride, elation, immense relief. At Central Office, which he made his first port of call, everyone had been convinced that the Tories would lose badly. The first few results had kindled their hopes, but it was the sight of the media moving all their paraphernalia across the square from Transport House that convinced them that the miracle was really happening. Then a large crowd began to assemble, chanting 'We want Ted!' It was to be several hours before they got him.[23]

The Tories ended up with 46.4 per cent of the vote; their overall

1	**CARTWRIGHT** (John Cameron Cartwright, of 17, Commonwealth Way, Abbey Wood, London, S.E.2., The Labour and Co-operative Party Candidate.)	
2	**CONEY** (Michael Paul Coney, of 87, Broad Lane, London, N.15., Independent Conservative, Anti-Common Market.)	
3	**HARRISON** (Edward Peter Graham Harrison, of 10, Somner Close, Canterbury, Kent, Liberal.)	
4	**HEATH** (EDWARD JAMES ROBERT LAMBERT Heath, of The Regency Hotel and School of English, St. Augustine's Road, Ramsgate, Kent, Conservative and Consult the People Candidate.)	
5	**HEATH** (EDWARD RICHARD GEORGE Heath, of F.2., Albany, Piccadilly, London, W.1., Leader of the Conservative Party.)	

majority in the House of Commons was thirty but they led Labour by forty-three. It was not massive but it was more than enough to run a government with comfort and incredibly much better than had seemed likely a few days before. At the Victory Party in the Savoy ten days later David Butler told Heath that he was still trying to make up his mind whether the Tories had won the election or Labour had lost it. 'You mean to say you don't know that we've won?' crowed Heath. 'Let me tell you, we have won. We did win the election, you know, we did. History is telling what happened. You shouldn't bother yourself with hypothetical questions.' He was immensely pleased with this rejoinder and Butler heard that he had described the exchange to at least three other people at the party before he left.[24]

The fruits of victory flooded in. In the next few days Heath received twenty-one bunches of flowers; three cases, four magnums and two bottles of champagne; four books, including one of carols from William Walton; a couple of letters written by Gladstone; five bottles of cognac; an alabaster lion; a *Sachertorte* from a Viennese admirer; a set of pottery victory bells; three gramophone records; a map of

Ramsgate harbour; the key to the black box which stood beside Beethoven's deathbed ('may it help me unlock some of the problems that lie ahead,' wrote Heath piously in his thank-you letter) and a case of Buchanan's whisky. Some official at Number 10 suggested that this last tribute should be returned. That would be 'heavy-handed', ruled Heath; indeed, since the donor was a director of Buchanan's and Alec Douglas-Home's son-in-law, it would be positively embarrassing.[25] But the best present was the victory itself. By it Heath gained an immense increase in confidence. In a post-mortem on the election result a group of pundits put forward theories as to why their forecasts had been so wrong. 'I think it is a good thing', commented Heath, 'to remind these clever and somewhat verbose people from time to time that *we* had something to do with it!'[26] By 'we', though he would never have said it in so many words, he meant 'I'. It was *his* victory and he knew it. It convinced him, if conviction were needed, not only that he was right, but that the British people would always be ready to listen to him when he explained to them *why* he was right. As John Ramsden has pointed out, Robert Peel had the same illusion in 1841, 'and Heath's gradual repudiation by his party over the next few years was to be not at all unlike Peel's fate in 1846–47'.[27]

'Heath is the hero of the hour,' Cecil King wrote in his diary, 'but how long will he remain so?' He 'does not seem to realise the head-on collision with the trades union movement that lies ahead'. Maudling put it still more concisely. After the election result was clear he was given a lift back from the ITN studios by Peter Rawlinson. 'Now our troubles begin,' he said.[28]

TWELVE

Making a Ministry

Caroline Benn once remarked that all prime ministers were Pedestrians, Fixers or Madmen. Pedestrians were dull but worthy people like Attlee or Douglas-Home. Fixers were political wizards like Harold Wilson. The Madmen were fanatics and visionaries, like Heath or Margaret Thatcher. Mrs Benn's view of Heath would have been widely shared, yet Heath did not see himself as a visionary or driven man. When Michael Cockerell asked him whether he had felt any sense of destiny or history when, for the first time, he entered Number 10 as Prime Minister, he replied: 'No, not really. No. I mean, you've got to get on with the job.' Somewhere, between the sublime and the mundane, was the true Edward Heath.[1]

Certainly he was as well equipped to 'get on with the job' as any recent prime minister. He had never served as Chancellor of the Exchequer or Foreign Secretary, traditionally the two posts which led to Number 10, but he had been Shadow Chancellor at a critical moment and the years he had spent as Lord Privy Seal had given him a wide experience of Foreign Affairs. His long stint as Chief Whip had – or, at least, should have – given him a unique understanding of the Party and how to control it. He was battle-hardened by his years as Leader of the Opposition; he could never hope to match the wit and dexterity of his arch-adversary, Harold Wilson, but he had developed an approach of dogged honesty which often served him well in the House of Commons. Armed with the authority of a prime minister and supported by the resources of Whitehall, he had no doubt that he could hold his own. Not all Tories took as rosy a view. 'Quite frankly,' Robert Jenkins, a former Tory MP, wrote to Enoch Powell, 'if one examines his career, he has no more experience of parliamentary matters than would entitle him to have greater office than a junior minister.' Jenkins believed that the reason Heath was not offering Powell a job in his new cabinet was that he knew he would be so conspicuously outshone.[2] Most Conservative members, however, who had confidently predicted electoral disaster and Heath's subsequent eclipse, were now disposed to welcome him as a miracle-worker who could be relied on to steer the party towards a new and glorious future.

Yet his essential strengths and weaknesses had not been changed by the events of June 1970. John Boyd-Carpenter, a man who thought himself ill-used by Heath, commented that the Prime Minister was like 'one of those Olympic athletes who develop certain qualities of performance to a very high degree at the cost of a complete sacrifice of other qualities which ordinary men possess'. His strengths were obvious, and essential to any would-be successful prime minister: a clear mind, physical and mental stamina, determination, a capacity to listen to other people (even though he often appeared not to be doing so), a memory which matched that of Harold Wilson. Richard Simmonds spoke to him for twenty-five minutes while preparing him for an address he was to make to an audience of Young Conservatives. Heath appeared hardly to pay attention but then proceeded to deliver a speech which, almost word for word, followed Simmonds' briefing. His honesty was patent. Claus Moser, the head of the Government Statistical Service, had been taken on by Harold Wilson and was well known to be a Labour supporter. He had expected Heath to dismiss him but found himself asked to stay on. Shortly before the election he had a problem with Wilson, when the then Prime Minister had pressed him to doctor the trade figures so that the cost of the purchase of four jumbo jets was spread out over a longer period than the rules dictated. Moser had refused and Wilson then concurred. Heath's only general instruction to Moser was that 'we must always behave like knights in shining armour'. And so they did. Moser prepared a set of rules for the proper formulation and presentation of official statistics; Heath accepted them without question and ordered that they should be rigorously imposed.[3] His judgment was sometimes questioned, his manners often deplored, but his integrity was taken for granted by almost everyone. Alex Downer, the Australian High Commissioner, who had initially had doubts, told James Lees-Milne that Heath was: '100 per cent good … Alex said in his quiet voice and gentle manner "He is good in the sight of the Almighty".'[4]

But other attributes of the ideal prime minister were less evident. Heath's sense of proportion could sometimes fail him; he would become obsessed with trivial details which preoccupied him to the detriment of far more important issues. The concomitant of a sense of proportion, a sense of humour, was not lacking but usually found expression in black and aggressive sallies. His technique, Alistair McAlpine, Mrs Thatcher's future treasurer, complained, was to indulge in some mildly offensive comments. If the victim took it as a joke, Heath had meant it seriously; if he took offence, it proved he lacked a sense of humour. When Susan Hampshire featured as the celebrity guest who took the collection at the Broadstairs carol concert, Heath looked at the slip of paper reporting how much money had been raised and pulled a long face. Susan Hampshire was mortified; only a quarter of an hour later did Heath announce that a new record had been set. He himself laughed with immense energy, but even when he was genuinely amused there was a curious air of falsity about the performance. The eyes, somehow, did not seem to be joining in. 'Even when he laughed,' wrote the political journalist Peter Jenkins, 'the shoulders heaving, he had the appearance of a man imitating laughter.' On form, and if so inclined, he could be witty and relaxed in conversation, but if not with those he liked or if disinclined to put himself out, he relapsed into a grumpy silence: 'It varied from one evening to another,' remembered Peter Walker.[5]

Though he was not a vain man, it would have been remarkable if his success had not to some degree gone to his head. He had learned from his mother that he was the centre of the universe; the fact that he was now Prime Minister was merely outward and visible evidence that this was indeed the case. Robert Armstrong once prepared a minute for him in which a view was attributed to the Chancellor of the Exchequer. 'Don't refer to a lesser minister in my minute,' scrawled Heath on the draft. 'He was *probably* joking,' says Armstrong cautiously, but there could too have been a touch of *folie de grandeur*. Even when writing to the Chadds, very old friends to whom he always remained 'Teddy', he habitually used the royal we: 'We are going to Jamaica next week.'[6]

In the eyes of some of his followers he lacked two things which were expected of any Tory leader: a private income and a wife. The first was relatively unimportant. Heath's investments did exceptionally well; and though he could still not have afforded the expense of running *Morning Cloud* without support from wealthy admirers, he ended his term in office richer than he began it.[7] He greatly enjoyed spending money on lavish entertaining in Number 10 or at Chequers, but preferred the money to come from official sources. He begrudged even trivial expenditure. When the aged Marquess of Aberdeen wrote to say that his godfather, W. E. Gladstone, had given him some books and that since then every prime minister had donated a signed volume which was kept in a bookcase presented by Campbell-Bannerman, Heath declared that this was 'a splendid tradition' and presented the Marquess with a copy of Robert Blake's *Disraeli*. The cost, he specified, was to be charged to party funds. When he tried to procure the original of a cartoon by Michael Cummings, he took it for granted that it would be given him or at least offered for a minimal amount. Cummings demanded £30. 'I regret', replied Heath's secretary, 'the cost is somewhat higher than anticipated and we shall therefore have to say no.'[8]

As to the lack of a wife, those preoccupied with the matter had concluded well before the election that there was little hope of coaxing Heath out of his celibate existence and, since he had managed to find his way to Number 10 as a bachelor, the matter now seemed less important. The price was paid not by the Party but by Heath himself. The task of prime minister is anyway bound to be a lonely one: to undertake it without a husband or wife in whom one can confide or let off steam to, in the car going home after some tedious banquet, must make it doubly onerous. Harold Wilson was one of the few people able to appreciate what the pressures must be. He remarked once to John Junor that he found Heath 'cold and uncompassionate' and then added meditatively: 'Do you know, John, he goes home at night to that house all alone and all he has to amuse him is himself.'[9]

While he had been Leader of the Opposition a group of talented subordinates had been preoccupied by his public image and made constant suggestions that might lead to its improvement. Heath had found the whole business distasteful and slightly absurd but went along with it because even he could see that the public perception of his personality and his policies was not all that it might have been. After the election he had neither the time nor the inclination to indulge in such fripperies: the fact that he had found his way to Number 10 proved that the British public had accepted him for what he was, no more was needed. 'It was a return to the idea that advertisers were somehow practising an ill-concealed version of the black arts,' said Barry Day, a collaborator of Geoffrey Tucker, 'that we were manipulators, the hidden persuaders, the Madison Avenue hucksters. If any conventional advertiser stopped advertising when he had a brand leader on the market, his competitors would think he was mad.' Yet that is exactly what Heath did. Occasionally, said his press officer, Donald Maitland, a suggestion would be made about what the Prime Minister should do or say. 'But that would look like image-building,' would be the shocked response, and the subject would be dropped. The group that had been successful in promoting Heath when in Opposition – Michael Fraser, Tucker, Ronald Millar, Barry Day – tried to maintain an informal existence through dinners attended on each occasion by a different cabinet minister. Douglas Hurd, as Heath's political secretary, occasionally came along and reported back to his not particularly interested master. The Prime Minister did not attend a single dinner. What mattered was what he did and said, not how he appeared. When Robin Butler joined the staff, one of his first tasks had been to prepare a speech for the opening of a new wing at Bradford Hospital. Heath read it scornfully. 'Where are the statistics for hospital building?' he demanded. 'I'm the Prime Minister of this country, not the Princess Royal!' The fact that the public had a limited appetite for statistics was immaterial: he was the Prime Minister and he would tell them what they ought to know.[10]

'He was by nature very shy, but forced early into eminent positions, he had formed an artificial manner, haughtily stiff or exuberantly bland.' His enunciation, though clear, was 'marred by provincialisms'.[11] Disraeli was in fact referring to Robert Peel, but it could as well have been Heath. Whether or not he had been 'forced into' eminent positions, the ascent had been vertiginous and the effects, in some ways, dire. Perhaps there had always been two Heaths, speculated Ian Gilmour: 'Gone at any rate was the genial, human and successful Chief Whip and in his place, in public, was a brusque and dour leader of the party.' Crossman, in 1966, had had an unpleasant meeting with him to discuss the organisation of parliamentary committees. 'He has something of Gaitskell's huffiness and much the same cold gleam in his eye'; he was 'thoroughly disobliging … thick and resistant and prickly and difficult'. Whitelaw was in attendance and Crossman saw him 'blanching a bit at his behaviour'. Even Selwyn Lloyd, wondering whether he wanted a job in the next administration, admitted sadly to himself that Heath was 'not a very easy person to work with'.[12]

Nigel Lawson remarked that Mrs Thatcher was unusual among Tory leaders in actually liking the Conservative Party in the country: 'Harold Macmillan had a contempt for the party, Alec Home tolerated it, Ted Heath loathed it.' This is perhaps pitching it too high. The problem was partly geographical: Heath was notably ill at ease in Scotland – except with the Morrisons on Islay – or in those parts of Britain where the traditional Tory squirearchy made him feel out of place, but got on well with the local Tory bigwigs in his own constituency or in the suburban constituencies of Kent and Essex. In general, however, one must accept Robert Blake's verdict that Heath 'did little to hide his disdain for grass roots leaders'. The problem was compounded when Lord Carrington took over as party chairman. To quote Blake again, Carrington's 'patrician manner and dislike of glad-handing party workers' did nothing to mitigate the aloof and slightly disdainful attitude of the Prime Minister.[13] With the party in the country, as in the House of Commons, the electoral victory of 1970 won Heath a temporary surcease from criticism, but the reprieve did not last; by the time things began to go seriously wrong with the Government's policies, the reserves of good will on which a party leader could normally depend were running dangerously low.

Hardly less damaging was Heath's hostility towards the press. By 1970 he took it for granted that every newspaper was against him, every journalist intent on distorting his words or trapping him into indiscretions. Another prime minister might have argued: 'The press does not like me. Therefore I must woo them vigorously.' Heath's reaction was: 'The press does not like me. Therefore I do not like them.' His animosity seemed to have no reference to a newspaper's political leanings. The day before he was due to lunch with the *Financial Times* the paper published a critical article by Joe Rogaly. The managing director, Lord Drogheda, knew nothing about the article before it appeared but Heath took it as a personal affront and cancelled the lunch. The annals of the press abound in instances of notably right-wing journalists treated by the Prime Minister insultingly or at least with scant regard. When Peregrine Worsthorne called at Number 10 a butler came in with a tray of tea. 'You chaps prefer whisky, don't you?' snorted Heath. Worsthorne said he would much prefer tea. Heath poured him a cup but left it on his side of the table, well out of Worsthorne's reach, while sipping his own cup appreciatively. It was probably carelessness rather than a wish to insult, but Worsthorne complained of 'the atmosphere of impatient formality ... no warming up or exchange of civilities or small talk ... no jokes or private confidences, not a trace of the charm or bonhomie with which these rather gaunt occasions are usually enlivened'. Ferdinand Mount fared even worse. When he prefaced a question with the words 'Do you think that Mr Wilson has to some extent ...?', Heath, 'fixing me with a glare that combined loathing with contempt', interrupted, to say: 'I didn't realise this was going to be such a superficial interview.'[14]

None of this helped, but it was only a symptom of a malaise which affected every aspect of Heath's premiership. Cecil King records how a colleague once called on Heath and tried to persuade him to set up a propaganda department responsible for explaining his policies to the world. His job, replied Heath, was to govern, not to explain. 'That remark explains a lot of Ted's mistakes,' commented King. Whether it was arrogance, indifference, caution, a shrinking from contact or a combination of all these factors, Heath as Prime Minister showed himself incapable of sharing with other people the workings of his mind or offering any exposition of what he was doing. Indeed, increasingly, he seemed incapable of maintaining with many of those around him even that minimum level of communication which convenience or common civility required. Ronald Millar described a meeting of the Communications Group at Chequers. As member after member of the Group arrived, even though some of them had come from far away and at considerable inconvenience with no material reward, Heath continued to work intently on his papers. Eventually Douglas Hurd, 'evidently feeling that his lord and master should pay some attention to his guests, goes over and ... gently removes the red boxes ... Whereupon the PM picks up a magazine entitled *Sailing Today* and buries himself behind it.' He meant no offence, Millar concluded. It was 'just the way he is'.[15]

At least the Communications Group eventually had a meeting in which the Prime Minister participated. Conservative backbenchers rarely had such good luck. On the few occasions that he did take the trouble to encourage a promising backbencher the results were excellent. He wrote to congratulate F. W. Harrison on a speech and was told that the recipient was 'thrilled to bits' and 'showing it to all and sundry in the Smoking Room'. 'A few letters like this, where appropriate, would probably be helpful,' Whitelaw hinted hopefully, but somehow they very rarely did seem to be appropriate.[16] Towards the end of 1971 Knox Cunningham reported to Macmillan that the younger members were 'not very happy with Ted Heath. They feel they have no contact with him. He is seldom in the Smoking Room and moves down the lobbies with a few friends, apparently aloof from the rank and file.' When he did get as far as the Smoking Room the results were not always happy. Peter Walker urged him to spend more time chatting up backbenchers. He was gratified to find a few days later that his advice had been heeded; Heath was in conclave with a senior Tory. As he passed them he heard Heath say: 'That was a dreadful speech you made last Wednesday.' A youthful John Nott was picked to move the motion on the Queen's Speech and, as was customary, was given the seat of honour next to the Prime Minister at the eve-of-session dinner. 'It was a terrible experience ... I tried to be pleasant and struggled with a whole gamut of observations – music, sailing, pictures – all to no avail. He did not deign to utter one single word.' Such macabre anecdotes abound. The most celebrated tells of a dinner at which Heath was sitting next to the influential wife of a local dignitary. He ignored her. An anxious aide, provoked beyond endurance, passed him a note reading: 'For God's sake talk to the woman on your right.' Heath considered this, added the words 'I have', and sent the note back. It was not so much black humour, Douglas Hurd considers, as Heath's feeling that, if somebody made a reasonable recommendation, you were bound to respond to it.[17]

A small group of intimates didn't mind, or minded only spasmodically, if Heath had been more than usually ungracious. They even quite enjoyed swapping the latest Ted story, of his impossible rudeness or lack of consideration. Anthony Barber had his fair share of such treatment but, he wrote, he, Whitelaw and Prior 'were all devoted to Ted although he was not the easiest of leaders to "sell". To his friends he was 100 per cent reliable.'[18] But though they knew they could rely on him, there were few indeed who would claim to have known him intimately, or even well. Robert Armstrong, Jim Prior, Tim Kitson, as much as anyone Sara Morrison, did to some extent crack the carapace but even they accepted that at any moment the shell might close again and they would find themselves outsiders.

'I would dearly have liked to be friends,' Enoch Powell somewhat unconvincingly maintained, 'but [a pause] like everyone else, I found it impossible.' Toby Lancaster, a knight of the shires better disposed to Heath than Powell, had the same feeling of remoteness. The difficulty with Ted, he said, was that you never knew him. After a long and significant conversation 'you leave with the impression that he has never been interested in you as a person. A man with wonderful drive and energy, but totally lacking the personal warmth of personality.' Heath accepted that this was commonly cited as a charge against him; he could not understand what people were complaining about. 'I don't feel in the least remote,' he wrote. 'I see a great deal of the colleagues. I have a lot of friends.'[19]

'I do not mean that Mr Heath is a "dictator",' wrote David Watt in the *Financial Times* in June 1972, 'any more than Mr Wilson was, but ... the fact is that the potentialities of the office have already been considerably extended by Mr Heath, and they will almost certainly be expanded still further.' No one else has suggested that Heath was a dictator but the consensus is that, particularly after the death of Iain Macleod, his style of leadership was autocratic. John Biffen, a Euro-sceptic and staunch ally of Enoch Powell, told Woodrow Wyatt that Heath was 'much more domineering than Mrs Thatcher had ever been'. According to Biffen, he packed the Cabinet with yes-men and would accept no disagreement. Certainly he resented, and sometimes treated roughly, anyone whom he felt was wasting time. His disinclination to enter into lengthy debate and limited tolerance for argument were fully apparent from the beginning of his government. Biffen was not the only person to compare Heath to Thatcher. Hurd remarked on their similar styles: 'They are both very definite people, not by instinct very patient with dissent. They are both, by nature, impatient and authoritarian.' Heath, remarked the trade-union leader Vic Feather, 'treats his ministers not as the headmaster treats his staff, but as the headmaster treats his sixth form'.[20] The analogy is not wholly unfair, but as a headmaster Heath was unusually liberal and his sixth form liberated. He did resent, and show his resentment of, long-drawn-out discussions, but this did not mean that he paid no attention to what was said. On the contrary, his favoured style of cabinet government was to listen – sometimes impatiently – to what everyone had to say, often without stating his own point of view, and then to sum up decisively in favour of the course he deemed best. His conclusions were rarely challenged: in part perhaps because members felt nervous about opposing his authority but more because it was usually accepted that he had enunciated the majority view. Even when things were going badly, Heath's Cabinet remained informal and relaxed. 'The Prime Minister was always the dominant figure,' wrote Geoffrey Howe, 'but the Cabinet remained essentially a group of friends as well as colleagues.' Carrington thought that Heath handled his Cabinet well: 'It would be an exaggeration to say that he liked other people's opinions, but he listened and, if convinced, went along with them.'[21]

Even if he was not prepared to devote much time to buttering up his supporters he could have won more loyalty by a judicious distribution of honours. He was known to be against hereditary peerages, partly on the mildly eccentric grounds that if a new peer was created who did not also possess a hereditary fortune he might bring the whole system into disrepute.[22] There was still available, however, a cornucopia of knighthoods and lesser honours with which loyal supporters could be rewarded and rebels bribed into acquiescence. Martin Redmayne, the Chief Whip, in 1969 had urged restraint in handing out such baubles: 'Over the years we created a terrible precedent in this respect.' A twice-yearly distribution of political honours was a mistake; once would be quite enough. 'A lot of sense in this,' Heath commented. Redmayne must have been disconcerted by the zeal with which Heath as prime minister followed his advice. He was himself genuinely indifferent to the lure of honours and found it hard to believe that anyone of any stature would not share his views. When he was drawing up his resignation honours he said to Michael Wolff and Sara Morrison: 'I take it for granted you would both be humiliated by inclusion in this list.' Sara Morrison was genuinely unconcerned; Wolff looked wistful but forbore to argue the point. When Francis Pym took over as Chief Whip he urged Heath to be more generous, particularly when it came to knighthoods for long-serving backbenchers. Heath was unmoved. He created no new baronetcies – a bounty much favoured by previous Tory leaders – and was miserly in his distribution of knighthoods. As for life peers, he nominated only thirty-four, while Labour in the next five years found '144 suitable candidates whom I had, unaccountably, overlooked'.[23] He was, however, capable of responding to an appeal for generosity. Woodrow Wyatt asked him to give Les Cannon, the trade-union leader, a knighthood as he was on the point of dying from cancer and the honour would cheer his last months: 'Ted, whose heart is full of kindness, saw to it at once.'[24] It is doubtful whether this act of

benevolence to a prominent Labour supporter did much to appease
his own passed-over backbenchers. Few if any Tories would have
admitted to having coveted an honour and been disappointed, but
Heath's reluctance to oblige them was one more element in the sim-
mering discontent which grew throughout the party.

For the moment, however, all seemed radiantly hopeful. Heath's
government almost formed itself. The period in Opposition had been
an opportunity to prepare for rule; now those who had been prepared
were ready to perform their designated functions. Of the 46 members
of the Tory front-bench team in the last session of the Labour
Government, 42 got jobs in the new administration. Most of the
portfolios went to those who had shadowed them in Opposition,
though a cut in the size of the Cabinet from 21 to 18 and of ministers
from 88 to 71 meant that a handful of front-bench spokesmen faced
demotion. Maudling would have loved to be Foreign Secretary, but
once Home had indicated that he wanted to go to the Foreign Office
there was no question of any other appointment. Heath had total
confidence in Home's ability and, anyway, thought it only proper that
the former Prime Minister should have whatever post he wanted.
Home for his part was more than content to confine himself to foreign
affairs and to intervene as rarely as possible in other matters. Heath,
in November 1970, invited Home to come with him, Lord Avon,
Macmillan and Wilson to de Gaulle's memorial service in Paris. 'With
all those former prime ministers,' protested Home, 'you won't need
your Foreign Secretary.' 'But you are a former prime minister yourself!' Home laughed: 'Oh, so I am. I'd quite forgotten.' He is one of
the very few politicians who one can believe would have made such a
remark sincerely.[25]

Iain Macleod as inevitably took on the role of Chancellor of the
Exchequer. 'I think economists are the worst things to have in any
government,' Heath told the Chinese foreign minister. 'I never had
any in mine.' Heath's scepticism about Macleod's economic expertise
was more than matched by Macleod's doubts about Heath's political
judgment. The two men existed in an uneasy balance: each respect-
ing the other's abilities; each finding it impossible fully to understand

or sympathise with the other; each realising that only in partnership could they prosper. Macleod knew that he was unacceptable to large sections of the Party. 'Macleod, who you know I don't fancy! has done himself a lot more harm by never coming out pro-white on Rhodesia,' wrote John Morrison to Heath; and Morrison, more perhaps than any other member, spoke with the authentic untamed accents of the traditionalist right wing. Macleod needed the support of Heath, but Heath needed Macleod: his sharp mind, his brilliance in debate; his liberal conscience. If he had lived there would inevitably have been differences between them but it would have been perfectly possible for them to have worked together to the advantage of both men and of the Government.[26]

The relationship between Heath and Macleod would have provided the dynamic for the administration. The third member of the ruling triumvirate, Reginald Maudling, who took over as Home Secretary, was neither forceful nor motivated enough to play a similar role. Maudling's private secretary, Alex Saville, maintained that Heath in Opposition 'was very dependent on Reggie. He asked him for advice and Reggie was often reassuring Ted, saying not to worry about things.' His bedside manner was, indeed, Maudling's speciality but Heath as Prime Minister found increasingly little use for it. Though the title was never officially his, after Macleod's death Maudling was often treated as Deputy Prime Minister and stood in for Heath at the despatch box if the Prime Minister was away. But he was never Heath's chief adviser, let alone rival. Political journalists, wrote Maudling, liked to suggest 'that there were tensions and disputes between Ted Heath and myself. That just was not true ... We never had a row.' The main reason for the lack of rows was that Maudling was too laid-back and too preoccupied by other matters to fight his corner with any vigour.[27]

Heath, concluded Cecil King, had no political antennae 'and he likes to be surrounded in his Cabinet by his friends rather than the ablest members of his party. The result was a very weak Cabinet.' Hugh Fraser, Heath's Balliol contemporary, agreed that the Cabinet consisted of 'people loyal to Heath rather than the most competent available. This is because Heath is very suspicious and has good reason to doubt the loyalty of many serious members of his party.'[28] Both men were speaking of a period when Macleod was already dead. It is hard to see what reservoir of talent there was for Heath to draw on. Should he have brought Soames back from Paris even though he was likely to play a crucial role in the negotiations for British entry into Europe? Should he have resurrected Duncan Sandys, Boyd-Carpenter, du Cann? The Cabinet would not have been notably stronger and might have been less harmonious if he had done so. Enoch Powell was obviously the most capable Conservative left outside, but he was also the most turbulent, the most controversial and the most fiercely anti-European. Heath's exclusion of anti-EEC MPs from his Cabinet has been said to have 'undermined morale within the parliamentary party'. In the *New Statesman* Alan Watkins wrote that he thereby 'deprived himself of any means of communication between the pro and anti marketeers. The latter feel dispossessed.'[29] The latter *were* dispossessed. To have included a token anti-marketeer in a Cabinet committed to seeking entry would merely have ensured much acrimonious debate and eventually, no doubt, a dramatic resignation. What good would that have done?

In fact, Heath's Cabinet was by no means packed with obsequious cronies. Outside the big three, the two most important members of the government were the Defence Secretary, Lord Carrington, and Whitelaw, with a watching brief as Lord President. An unidentified cabinet minister told Margaret Laing, one of Heath's biographers, that Carrington was the only member of the Cabinet with whom Heath had never had a row. This may be so, but it was certainly not because Carrington failed to speak his mind on the relatively few occasions that he disagreed with the Prime Minister. Whitelaw was more emollient than Carrington but he too was no yes-man; in some ways he continued to play the role of Chief Whip: something which called for total loyalty but total honesty as well. The remaining elder statesman, Quintin Hogg, renewed life as Lord Hailsham and Lord Chancellor. He would have preferred to remain in the Commons as Home Secretary but he was happy to fit back into a legal context. In Cabinet he mainly concentrated on his personal role, but he had strong views on a variety of subjects and never hesitated to express them.[30]

Keith Joseph and Margaret Thatcher were the voice of Selsdon, or at least what Selsdon was deemed to signify by the general public. They were – 'whether by chance or calculation', wrote Thatcher – kept well away from the power points responsible for economic policy and instead put in charge of two of the most free-spending departments: Health and Social Security and Education. 'There was such obvious antagonism between Ted and Margaret,' wrote the Attorney General, Peter Rawlinson, 'that anyone could have foretold that if ever opportunity presented itself, the political dagger would be cheerfully slipped out ... They were enemies, naked and unashamed, and they had been from the start.' The start of what? is the obvious question. As MPs they had cooperated amicably in their neighbouring constituencies. If she had really been so mortal an enemy Heath would hardly have appointed her to his Shadow Cabinet. There is no doubt that she irritated him. Geoffrey Howe describes a discussion about the next chairman of the BBC. Howe suggested Andrew Shonfield. '"I think not," said Ted, "he's got much too high an opinion of himself." "But most men *do*," said Margaret. The exchange of glances between Margaret and Ted did not suggest the blossoming of a beautiful friendship.' Howe's absence of a beautiful friendship is more convincing than Rawlinson's fierce vendetta. Heath did not want to be too closely involved with Mrs Thatcher. When she pressed him to spend a weekend at her country house so as to have a long talk about education, Heath told Robert Armstrong: 'I certainly can't spare a weekend. It might be more business-like round the Cabinet table. It would need a couple of hours.' But she was at most a minor irritant, not a serious preoccupation: 'He hardly thought about her,' said Jim Prior. Certainly he never contemplated her as a future threat to his position. She for her part recognised that Heath did not much like her and was suspicious of some of her views: her undersecretary William van Straubenzee, a close ally of Heath's, had, she believed, been sent to the Department of Education to keep an eye on her. If she had a dagger, however, her hand was certainly not yet on the hilt and it is unlikely that it ever entered her head that one day she might deliver a fatal blow.[31]

Certain other ministers – Jim Prior at Agriculture, Tony Barber as

Chancellor of the Duchy of Lancaster to look after the EEC negotiations, Peter Walker at Housing and Local Government – could
indeed be seen as Heath's protégés if not creations. All of them,
however, at that level at any rate, were worth their place. So were the
bulk of the junior ministers. Douglas Hurd found the process for the
appointment of the latter 'astonishingly casual' (a comment which
earned an angry marginal 'no!' from Heath when Campbell quoted it
in his biography). Tim Kitson, who to his great surprise had been
summoned from the Whips' Office to serve at Number 10, agreed
with Hurd. By the time he arrived, a first list of the Government had
been prepared. Glancing at it, he was surprised to see no mention of
Ian Gilmour, van Straubenzee or Robin Chichester-Clark. He asked
why they had been omitted. 'Oh, have we forgotten them?' was the
reply. Inevitably, for every one satisfied appointee, there were two or
three who felt rejected. Peter Emery took exception not so much to
his rejection as to the way he was informed of the decision. The Chief
Whip told him that he was not to feel that 'he had been overlooked'.
'What has happened is that I have been looked at and rejected as
unsuitable in the first seventy odd members of the parliamentary
party necessary to form a Government,' Emery retorted. Obviously a
prime minister must be free to pick his own team 'but it is better to
tell the truth'. The complaint was not unreasonable but it seems
unlikely that Emery would have been better pleased by a blunt asser-
tion that he was not up to the job.[32]

Another of the smaller fry who was subsequently to cause Heath
much grief was Airey Neave. During Heath's time as Leader of the
Opposition Neave had written him a warm letter congratulating him
on his 'splendid leadership' and assuring him of his personal support:
'If there is any particular line on which I can be of help you will no
doubt let me know.' No such line occurred to Heath at the time and
the same proved to be true in 1970. A price would be paid five years
later. No such price was exacted in the case of Charles Morrison, but
much distress was caused. Heath felt warmly towards Morrison, son
of John Morrison of Islay and one of Heath's most loyal supporters.
Morrison had been shadowing the Minister for Sport and confidently
assumed he would be offered the job when the time came. Instead,

Heath not only appointed somebody else but did not even telephone Morrison to excuse his action. 'It was Ted's judgment,' reflected Peter Walker. 'This chap likes me. I am close to him. I don't need to give him a post.' To Heath this seemed a proper rejection of cronyism; to Morrison, though he bore no grudge, it looked more like ingratitude. Charlie Morrison was upset, Whitelaw told Heath. 'I mention this merely because I know that you are going to Islay and should be fore-warned.'[33]

Duncan Sandys was a decidedly more important figure who had expected to be put in charge of the negotiations for entry into Europe and was aggrieved at being excluded. 'I believe that as the months go by he will probably become increasingly more difficult,' warned Whitelaw. As it turned out, however, it was another reject, Edward du Cann, who was in time to make the greater mischief. Du Cann was convinced that he had been promised a job when the time came for Heath to form a government. Heath had no such recollection. Such misunderstandings occasionally occur and there was probably no duplicity on either side. Du Cann, however, was deeply aggrieved – 'he and Ted are apparently temperamentally incompatible,' reflected Cecil King. In due course he would get his revenge.[34]

After kissing hands at the Palace Heath made his way to Number 10, to be met, as ritual decreed, by a welcoming staff lining both sides of the passage that led to the cabinet room. There he settled down with Whitelaw and the Chief Whip, Francis Pym, to plan the new Government. After some time they decided a meal was in order and, finding that there was no food in the house, asked the principal private secretary, Sandy Isserlis, to arrange for something to be sent in. Prior remembers 'warm beer and sandwiches', Hurd 'beer and pork pies', Heath 'coffee and sandwiches' – whatever the menu, Isserlis heralded its arrival by putting his head round the door and shouting 'Grub's up!'. 'This sent Willie into paroxysms of fury,' wrote Heath. '"How can anyone behave like that?" he demanded. "He must be sacked at once".'[35] He *was* sacked at once, though it seems improbable that this was the only or even a prime reason. Isserlis was very much a Wilson man, appointed partly because of his connections in the Labour Party.

William Armstrong, the head of the Home Civil Service, thought a change was necessary and that it would anyway be desirable to have a Treasury man in the slot. His chose his namesake (though no relation) Robert Armstrong, who had the additional advantage of being the son of Sir Thomas Armstrong, a former principal of the Royal Academy of Music, and thus was well equipped to share in the musical life so vastly important to the Prime Minister. It was an inspired appointment: Armstrong was formidably efficient, hardworking, discreet and yet with an engaging sense of humour. Through his father he had known Heath slightly in Oxford days before the war. In the evening of his first day in Number 10, when he was being briefed by Isserlis, the Prime Minister came into the room, looked at him, remarked 'Oh, you're here, are you? It's going to be very hard work, you know,' and disappeared back into the Cabinet Room.[36]

It *was* hard work but immensely rewarding and, thanks to the friendly atmosphere in Number 10, to which both Heath and Armstrong signally contributed, enjoyable as well. He could not have supported the demands of the job, Armstrong believes, if it had not also been enormous fun. He became far more than a private secretary; Heath told Anthony Seldon that he 'became devoted to Armstrong and found him one of the most intelligent, and companionable, officials he encountered in his career'. And yet Armstrong contrived always to preserve the political neutrality required of a civil servant. Robin Butler, who joined the team in 1972, once made a disparaging remark about Harold Wilson. 'Don't let me hear you speak like that again,' said Armstrong sharply. 'You may be working for him in a few weeks.'[37]

The civil service traditionally provides an extremely high-powered team to staff Number 10. Under Armstrong, at various times, served Butler – himself a future head of the Home Civil Service – and Tom Bridges from the Foreign Office, grandson of the poet laureate, son of that quintessential mandarin, Edward Bridges, and a future ambassador in Rome. As press officer Heath chose not, as was usual, a politically sympathetic journalist, but a Foreign Office official who had worked with him during the negotiations for British entry into Europe in 1962 and 1963. Donald Maitland, like Heath, had served in the Second World War, and he believed that Heath felt this created a bond between them which did not exist in the case of the other civil servants. One of the reasons that Heath picked him was probably to emphasise the difference in the running of Number 10 since Wilson's day; certainly Maitland's crisp, straightforward style was very different from that of the intensely political and devious Joe Haines.[38]

Still more marked was the contrast between the political secretary, Douglas Hurd, and his predecessor, Marcia Williams. Before he took to politics Hurd had served in the Foreign Service – 'the perfect diplomat', Heath had considered him – and he found not the slightest difficulty in working harmoniously with his civil service colleagues.[39] Tim Kitson, the parliamentary private secretary, was equally disinclined to stand on his dignity or to pick unnecessary quarrels. As influential as any, though not a formal member of the entourage, was Sara Morrison, wife of the misused Charles and, unlike her husband, promoted by Heath to be vice-chairman of the Conservative Party. Someone once suggested to her that she was cast in the role of substitute wife. 'I think Ted would have been shattered at the idea,' she replied. 'I'm a sort of cock-eyed Mary Poppins, I suppose. I think he looks on me as a somewhat turbulent watch-dog.' In playing that part her barks were sometimes ignored – particularly when her political rather than her personal judgment was in question – but she was often right. When she warned him that unsavoury rumours about Maudling were spreading widely he paid no attention, but later conceded: 'I must remember that all your totally irrational dislikes are not invariably unfounded.'[40]

Caroline Stephens and Penelope Gardner, two girls who worked in Number 10 under Heath and went on to marry eminent politicians, both insist that, even when things were going wrong, it was a particularly happy place to be. In part this was because everyone knew their job and got on with it without backbiting or recriminations, but in large part too it was the doing of the Prime Minister. He failed constantly over the trivialities associated with the good employer – remembering birthdays, enquiring after children or holidays, even thanking for a good piece of work – but he was invariably supportive if there was trouble and remarkably tolerant of any misdemeanour which did not involve disloyalty. In answering a parliamentary question Heath attacked the irresponsible rich and referred to a large sum of money as being the amount 'people of this sort lose in an afternoon at Ascot'. Checking the text for Hansard, Robin Butler thought the words 'of this sort' were dangerous and cut them out. The result was an unholy rumpus and Heath being forced to apologise in the House of Commons. Butler confessed his crime and feared that he would be sacked. Heath merely grunted 'Don't do it again' and left it at that. 'Those who knew him best were loyalest to him,' wrote Peter Carrington. The staff at Number 10 knew him best; they were, to some extent, his family; and though they often grumbled about him, they admired, respected, even loved him.[41]

One loser from Heath's electoral victory was the group of young men – David Howell and Mark Schreiber in particular – with whom he had been so closely associated while in Opposition. It was not that Heath lost interest in reform, but at Number 10 he had neither the time nor the energy to devote to matters remote from the day-to-day issues which beset him. 'The ease and the jokes disappeared very quickly when Ted became Prime Minister,' Howell said. 'He became wooden. I would talk about a problem with him and he would not answer except with a grunt.' The pleas for the reorganisation of Whitehall and the transfer of many powers to non-governmental organisations foundered on the opposition of William Armstrong and Burke Trend, the Secretary of the Cabinet. Even if Heath thought the mandarins wrong, he did not wish unnecessarily to disturb them. He was noticeably less receptive to heretical ideas. Schreiber put forward a scheme for replacing National Service, which had been abolished in 1960, by compulsory social service. Hurd suggested it would be politically hazardous. 'Kill it stone dead at once,' minuted Heath, 'and tell it never to rise again.'[42]

There was still a place, however, for free spirits ready to challenge the establishment and long-established shibboleths. One of the ideas that had been much discussed in Opposition was the need for a body independent of Whitehall which would advise the Prime Minister and other cabinet ministers on long-term strategy. Heath believed that there were important issues which the pressure of time and events prevented being properly considered. He wanted a body, he said, that would 'express the uncomfortable if not think the unthinkable'. He suggested it be called the 'Think Tank', but Burke Trend, who privately deplored the whole idea, insisted that something more portentous was needed. 'The Central Policy Review Staff' (CPRS) therefore became the official title, though it was commonly called by Heath's simpler alternative. After some false starts Victor, Lord Rothschild, scientist, wartime hero, intriguer, Labour sympathiser and head of the British branch of the banking family, was chosen as its first director.[43]

Rothschild duly called on Heath to discuss the project. 'It's funny we have never met,' said Heath. A long pause followed, which the Prime Minister evidently did not intend to break. 'Would not an economist be more appropriate for this work?' suggested Rothschild. 'I did economics at Oxford,' replied Heath, after which another long pause ensued. Desperately, Rothschild reopened the conversation by asking if the Prime Minister could give an example of the kind of subject he would want the group to study. 'The future of Concorde,' suggested Heath. Since Burke Trend and William Armstrong had previously said that Concorde was precisely the sort of subject they would *not* expect the Think Tank to consider, Rothschild found this disconcerting. Unsurprisingly, the suggestion did not survive into the official record, where Heath is made to put forward the development of the seabed as a suitable subject for study. 'Lord Rothschild was inclined to think that in present circumstances this rated a low priority.'[44]

The new body caught the public imagination; sometimes to an alarming extent. A Mr Ronald Poultney wrote to Number 10 to ask: 'Please could you tell me whether or not I am Lord Rothschild and, if by any chance I am, when I can come and see you about it all?' After consulting Heath and Rothschild, Robert Armstrong replied that they thought they had the genuine Lord Rothschild under lock and key. 'However, security in these days is not what it was, and an escape may have taken place.' He enclosed a questionnaire which he believed might settle the matter. The first question was 'When do you think that the price of oil will overtake the price of Chateau Lafite, 1945?' Evidently Mr Poultney found the question too searching: no more was heard of him.[45]

The success of Rothchild's fledgling body somewhat irritated some of Heath's previous advisers. 'In spite of the excellence of the Rothschild staff, they will need rather close political direction from the top,' Schreiber told Hurd. 'I myself find it hard to see a rational pattern behind the programme of work.' It had to be part of the decision-making structure, urged Howell. 'Otherwise no one would pay any attention to it and [it would be used] as the Whitehall dust-bin.' To Burke Trend it seemed that Rothschild enjoyed dangerously easy access to the Prime Minister; Rothschild, on the other hand, felt that Heath was 'sometimes cocooned in his relationship with Trend and Armstrong and that it was not always easy to "break in"'. The Think Tank's finest hours came when its members lectured the assembled Cabinet and pointed out where they were going wrong. Donald Maitland was amused by the ministers' reactions. 'They were quite astounded. Some of them were hearing, it seemed to me for the first time, that there was something called a "strategy" to which they were expected to be a party ... Lord Hailsham, I remember, was very disturbed by what went on.'[46]

But the novelty wore off. 'It was fun to have a maverick at court when one was fresh and keen,' reflected Robin Butler, himself a founder member of the Think Tank, 'but less attractive as one got more tired and jaded.' Even in its heyday it had not been wholly sacrosanct in Heath's eyes. In May 1972 it prepared a paper entitled 'Ten Ways in which the Government could lose the next Election'. 'Pray tell Lord Rothschild', Heath minuted crossly, 'that I have an infinite number of the unpaid who tell me how to lose the next election. I hire people to tell me how to win it; if not they get fired.' Then, in the autumn of 1973, Rothschild made a speech in Wantage suggesting that Britain was on track to become poorer than Portugal or Spain. Unfortunately his outburst coincided with a speech of Heath's in which the Prime Minister was notably bullish about the economy; worse still, Rothschild's speech got more attention in the media. Heath was enraged and publicly rebuked his errant counsellor: Lord Rothschild, he told the House of Commons, 'has undertaken in future to abide by the rules governing public speeches by civil servants'.[47]

Though Heath supported Rothschild when he claimed that the

incident had put no lasting strain on their relationship, it was never glad confident morning again so far as the Think Tank was concerned. When Rothschild submitted a paper entitled 'Strategy 1974', Heath told Robert Armstrong that he had no intention of circulating 'this motley collection of comments on a set of assumptions by no means automatically justifiable, with no value judgements on what is likely and no indication of any real strategy for dealing with any of them'. A few days later, when a paper on the Organisation for Economic Co-operation and Development was being prepared, Armstrong told Rothschild that the Prime Minister hoped it would be 'fully discussed and agreed with the Departments concerned'. Rothschild indignantly replied that he was 'dismayed by the content and autocratic note' of these comments. A Think Tank which merely reflected the views of other departments would be of little if any value. Armstrong backed down to the extent of saying that the Prime Minister only hoped that 'an effort would be made to iron out differences in advance as far as possible', but the truth was that Heath had lost a measure both of interest and of confidence in the enterprise. 'They made a lot of extra work for very busy people,' was Burke Trend's brutal epitaph on the CPRS; it was unfair, but the moral was that any such body was likely soon to run out of steam and, to be of value, would have to be reinvented every decade or so.[48]

A factor in Heath's disillusionment with the Think Tank had been that William Armstrong only tolerated while Trend actively opposed it. When Heath became Prime Minister he was an avowed sceptic about the merits of the civil service, thinking that it shrank from making policy recommendations and was not equipped to take the initiative in technical fields. 'If we are going to be properly serviced in the modern world,' he declared at a seminar at Swinton, 'we have got to have the people to do it and pay them properly.' But when he brought in fresh blood from outside he found that it was, if not contaminated, then at least of inferior quality: it either failed to mix with the existing blood of the civil service or, worse still, was quickly assimilated. Meanwhile he was finding the mandarins of the civil service exceptionally well informed and congenial to work with. Peter

Hennessy quotes an unidentified visitor to Number 10 describing Heath coming down the stairs flanked by William Armstrong and Burke Trend, with Robert Armstrong in attendance. 'There's Ted,' mused the visitor, 'surrounded by the Treasury.' Many noticed that he seemed happier in the company of the permanent secretaries than with his ministerial colleagues. He had already grown close to William Armstrong when in Opposition; now that he was in Number 10 the alliance prospered. Partly this was because he found that Armstrong shared his views on all important subjects, particularly Europe; partly because Armstrong was an uncommonly capable civil servant. 'I could quite see how Ted had come to rely on this man in moments of crisis,' wrote Kenneth Baker. Indeed, the relationship became so close that Armstrong was openly referred to as 'the deputy Prime Minister'. He enjoyed playing politics and found his job as head of the civil service insufficiently absorbing. There was no impropriety about his role in Number 10 but one cabinet minister at least is said to have complained: 'He often went behind my back and we had several rows.' Policy, that minister believed, was too often made in hugger-mugger between the Prime Minister and Armstrong and presented to those responsible for implementing it as a fait accompli.[49]

Burke Trend, mandarin of almost equal refulgence, had neither the time nor the inclination to play such a role. He was the epitome of the correct civil servant, setting out the pros and the cons and leaving it to the minister to make the decision. Heath respected his lucidity and total integrity but was occasionally infuriated by his caution; Trend, for his part, admired Heath's courage and resolution but had doubts about certain aspects of his policies, particularly over Europe. Helen Adeane, wife of the Queen's private secretary, assured Heath that Trend considered him 'the most terrific character – in every single way – that he has ever met. He is really almost besotted about you. I am tremendously delighted that such a dry, correct and *utterly* discreet character should have so collapsed.' That letter was written in August 1972. What provoked such raptures it is hard to say. Certainly in later life Trend was far more measured in his approval. But he *did* appreciate Heath and, like most senior civil servants, found that business was transacted at Number 10 in a way far more satisfactory than they had experienced under Harold Wilson.[50]

Highly though he valued his relationships with Armstrong and other civil servants, Heath knew that the success or failure of his administration depended, above all, on the functioning of his Government. The Cabinet, he decreed, must 'adopt from the outset a new style of administration and a fresh approach to the conduct of public business. They should seek to establish a practice of deliberate and considered working, avoiding precipitate reactions to events and hasty or premature declarations of policy.' He abhorred what seemed to him the leaks and disloyalties that had been rife in Wilson's Cabinet: 'The unity of a Government depended very largely on the relationship of trust and mutual confidence between colleagues; and ministers should be concerned at all times to maintain the standard of discretion which this relationship required.' But though the Cabinet was supreme, it was not well suited for thrashing out complicated issues involving several departments; its agenda should be reserved 'as far as possible, for basic questions of substantive policy and political strategy, and the more detailed consideration of specific issues should be delegated to the appropriate Cabinet Committee'.[51] The more detailed the consideration required, the greater the need for civil servants to take part in the discussions. Heath's preferred policy-making vehicle was a mixture of ministers and civil servants with perhaps expert outsiders drafted in. His ideal subcommittee, some ministers grumbled, consisted of himself and William Armstrong.

It is one of the more curious features of Heath's time at Number 10 that a man who is often seen as dour and joyless should have set out to enjoy the perquisites of office with a vigour and enthusiasm unmatched by any other post-war prime minister. From the moment that he installed his grand piano in Number 10 he made clear his view that this was where he lived and that it should be treated as such. Joan Vickers asked whether a small reception could be held there for the Commonwealth Parliamentary Association. Harold Wilson had agreed to this in the past. Robert Armstrong recommended acceptance. 'I'm sorry,' Heath minuted, 'but I do not propose to use No. 10 as a hotel. Whatever the precedents: it is my home and I shall keep it as such.' He planned to entertain lavishly; but only on what seemed to him properly prime ministerial occasions – rather as the Duke of Omnium would have barred the use of Gatherum Castle for a meeting of the parish council. He immediately put in hand a lavish programme of redecoration and replaced the second-rate portraits of – often equally second-rate – politicians with rather more satisfying examples of British art, including four seriously good Gainsboroughs. In his biography of Heath John Campbell described the new *décor* as being painted with 'strong masculine colours' that reflected both his personal taste and his view of what a modern prime minister's residence should look like. Heath scrawled an indignant 'Nonsense!' in the margin. Barbara Castle, on the other hand, found that 'someone with appalling taste had had it tarted up: white and silver patterned wallpaper, gold *moiré* curtains of distressing vulgarity … It looked like a boudoir.' Heath would no doubt have described that as 'Nonsense!' too. Campbell was nearer the mark. Marcia Williams, who like Barbara Castle would have been happy to think the worst of any alterations, considered them to be 'elegant and co-ordinated', and only questioned the expense.[52]

With entertaining, as with everything else he did, Heath was professional and whole-hearted. He considered the menus, inspected the tables, rearranged the *place-à-table*. He was particularly concerned about the guest list. In Washington, he said, he had been struck by the trouble taken at the White House to find distinguished and appropriate people to meet him. He wanted people whose presence would flatter the guest of honour. For Lee Kuan Yew he demanded 'brilliant, amusing, witty guests who will make an impact on behalf of our "decadent" country'. The first list contained, inter alia, Princess Alexandra and Angus Ogilvy, Anthony and Susan Crosland, Jeremy Thorpe and the bankers Jeremy Morse and Edmund de Rothschild. Heath queried several guests (none of the above) – 'are they bright and amusing?' – and against John Selwyn Gummer wrote 'Doubtful for this one'. 'This list lacks any exciting public characters, which is what Lee likes,' was his concluding comment. Rupert Murdoch was added to supply this need.[53] His trouble was rewarded. After another such dinner, Julius Nyerere wrote to thank him for his hospitality: 'In a completely unobtrusive way I was made to feel welcome and comfortable ... the care with which you selected your guests for dinner ... so that I could meet Dr Walsh as well as Lord and Lady Olivier and others, was evidence of great personal kindness towards me.'[54]

There were too many foreign visitors, complained the diary keeper, Mark Forrester. If valedictory dinners, dinners for backbenchers and musical evenings were excluded then, out of fifty-seven dinners and receptions in 1973, only nine had been for outsiders – university vice chancellors, Nobel Prize winners and the like. 'The PM is often accused of being remote. You and I know that this is not so, but most of the public do not.' Dinners for social workers or comprehensive-school headmasters would 'put him more closely in touch with national life and make this evident to others'. Heath had little enthusiasm for such ideas. He was quite clear who appropriate visitors to Number 10 might be: Nobel Prize winners passed muster; comprehensive-school headmasters did not. The press was another group that he treated with some caution. William Rees-Mogg decided to manifest the independence proper to an editor of *The Times* by going less often to Downing Street; Heath made his resolution easier to keep by inviting him only rarely; the Prime Minister was resolved not 'to seem as obsessed with the media as his predecessor had been'. When he did do his duty by groups for which he had little enthusiasm, the results were not always happy. 'Being a good host is about more than choosing good food and wine,' remarked Prior sagely. 'It's also about enjoying and talking, making people feel happy and at ease. He was never very good at that.'[55]

What he most enjoyed was giving parties for, or in some way distinguishing, people whom he admired, particularly eminent musicians. For the New Year's Honours of 1972 (Heath felt quite differently about honours for people who were not politicians) he suggested L. S. Lowry, William Glock and William Walton. Lowry, he was told, had already refused an OBE, a CBE and a knighthood; Glock had been knighted only the year before. Walton already had an OM and a knighthood. Why not give a seventieth birthday party for Walton, suggested Robert Armstrong. Heath liked the idea, found that his colleague John Peyton was already doing the same and hijacked the affair for Number 10. He asked Benjamin Britten to write a piece for the occasion. 'I am having a very sacred year,' Britten replied, 'closetted [*sic*] with a big new opera. I really dare not say I can write a piece specially for the occasion – nowadays I have a hopelessly one-track mind, besides doing "occasional" work disgracefully badly.' Heath swiftly turned to Arthur Bliss, who was happy to oblige. Herbert Howells composed a Grace, to words provided by Robert Armstrong. Alvar Liddell recited lines from *Façade* (Edith Sitwell's poem which had been put to music by Walton himself); members of the London Symphony Orchestra played Schubert's *Piano Trio in B Flat* which Heath had once heard Walton say was the piece of music he would most have loved to have composed; the Queen Mother came. 'It was a joyous occasion to which he had clearly given much thought,' wrote Peyton. 'A splendid occasion,' agreed Arnold Goodman, though Alvar Liddell was inaudible to many of the guests. Robert Armstrong did most of the work but Heath had paid it much attention and derived immense pleasure from its success.[56]

Chequers, too, Heath refurbished lavishly, though in this case everyone agreed the work was for the better. Years later Woodrow Wyatt told Margaret Thatcher that the hall and dining room were very fine. '"Yes," says Margaret. "Ted Heath was responsible for making it like this." It must be a long time since she paid him a compliment.' Tony Benn thought that the panelling was much the better for having been purged of its dark stain and varnish. It must have cost half a million pounds, he concluded: 'Heath really did spend an enormous amount of money on making his days at Number 10 and Chequers comfortable.' Though he used Chequers often for official entertaining he also invited personal friends and relations. The Aldingtons and the Seligmans were regular guests at Christmas. Nancy-Joan Seligman used to make Heath a stocking. One Christmas Day Heath came down to breakfast looking rather green and asked Mrs Seligman what the sweets in his stocking had been. They were bath essence tablets. 'Serves you right for eating sweets before breakfast,' said Nancy-Joan. On Christmas Eve the carollers came from the local church to sing in the Great Hall. As they sipped mulled claret and ate mince pies after the concert, Heath ask the oldest member of the choir whether this had been done in the past. 'Yes,' said the veteran, 'once under Ramsay MacDonald in 1923. But then, of course, we had to come in by the kitchen, up the stairs and on to the balcony. We weren't allowed to mix downstairs.' Whenever there was an excuse music played a part in the entertainment. On his birthday in 1973 Gina Bachauer played and Georg Solti conducted. As an encore Solti produced what he said was 'a new and important recording'. He had recently recorded *Cosi Fan Tutti* with a strong international cast. At the end of the great sextet each soloist sang 'Happy Birthday, dear Ted' in their own language and then joined in a grand finale in English. Many tense confrontations and critical meetings took place at Chequers; it was a place of work as well as relaxation; but Heath loved it and felt at ease there as nowhere else. Sometimes, late at night during the week, he would be driven down there just for the pleasure of waking up in such congenial surroundings. When he lost office it was Chequers that he missed as much as anything.[37]

———— • • ————

THIRTEEN

The Pains of Office

Only a few weeks after Heath took power the balance of his Government was damagingly, some would say disastrously, disturbed. Iain Macleod was known to be a sick man. He had played a relatively small part in the electoral campaign and his one major speech as Chancellor had been distressingly lacklustre. No one suspected, however, how dangerously ill he was and his death after a heart attack was wholly unexpected. Robert Armstrong remembers Heath telephoning him at about 10.30 p.m. 'He simply said: "Iain's dead," in a totally flat voice. He was clearly knocked sideways by the news.' Kitson agrees: 'He was terribly shaken. He went that night and sat with Eve Macleod for two and a half hours.' Heath was not and could never have been personally very close to Macleod but they had been in partnership throughout the years in Opposition and the Prime Minister knew how desperately he would be missed. 'Politically he was our trumpeter,' said Robert Carr. 'Ted Heath was never a great trumpeter and any party, any government needs a great trumpeter.'[1]

But he had been more than that. His was the liberal voice within the Cabinet. 'With him there,' says Sara Morrison, 'Selsdon Man would have been buried much earlier.' No one could take his place. Ian Gilmour had hoped Quintin Hogg might play the part. 'It is a relief', he wrote, 'to know you will be in a position to scotch Selsdon Man and to keep Toryism on its humane instead of its *laissez-faire* path.' But with his appointment as Lord Chancellor, the now Lord

Hailsham consciously opted out of a major role in the affairs of the Cabinet. Douglas-Home similarly confined himself to his own department. After the introduction of direct rule in March 1972, Whitelaw was preoccupied by the affairs of Northern Ireland. As for the Home Secretary, Heath 'thought him clever but lazy and not too heavily involved in the success of the Government', says Carrington; 'He did not respect Maudling,' says Prior. In his copy of John Campbell's biography Heath scrawled 'Nonsense' against the statement that Macleod had been his only equal, but it is hard to see who else could have been relied on to stand up to him on crucial issues. There were several capable and independent-minded ministers, but in Prior's words, 'Much of the political weight was lost.' 'There was no way that he, or anyone else – however close to Heath – could hope to replace it.'[2] Macleod's biographer believes that his subject would never 'have allowed Heath to become so detached from the Commons, the party and the world beyond Whitehall'. Without Macleod, Heath increasingly turned for advice and support to the civil servants. This, considered Prior, 'added to the resentment already felt by a number of backbenchers that Ted was not paying sufficient attention to the party'.[3]

Certainly Macleod's successor was unlikely to redress the balance. Heath instructed Donald Maitland to tell the press that, to ease Eve Macleod's grief, he did not propose to appoint a new chancellor until after her husband's funeral. This encouraged rather than damped down speculation; an entirely predictable outcome which nevertheless confirmed Heath in his disapproval of the media. Although he must in fact have made up his mind several days earlier, Heath did not reveal his intention until he was in the train returning from Macleod's funeral. The new chancellor was to be Anthony Barber, the man whom Heath had designated as his chief negotiator for British entry into Europe. Within his limitations Barber was a competent administrator, trained in tax law and with Treasury experience. As a counterweight to Heath, however, he was ineffective. He had no illusions about his own inadequacy. Tim Kitson was given the task of extracting him from a dinner at a foreign embassy to hear of his promotion. 'I hope he's not going to ask me to be Chancellor,' Barber remarked apprehensively on arrival at Number 10. He felt that he had been far too long out of touch with Treasury affairs and, after Heath had finished with him, had to be cheered up with a strong whisky. Sara Morrison thought him 'feeble and slimy': according to Cecil King, neither Carrington nor Geoffrey Rippon made any attempt to defend the appointment. But he suited Heath: someone who could be relied on to implement competently the instructions that were handed down to him. The two men were close in a way that Heath would never have been with Macleod. John Junor was having a drink with Barber in Number 11 when he heard a pounding of feet on the stairs and a voice calling out 'Chancellor! Chancellor!' Heath arrived, to be regaled with whisky from a special bottle of Glenlivet evidently reserved for him. What he really wanted, he told Jean Barber, was nuts or biscuits; she rushed into the kitchen in search of them.[4]

Rippon was moved across to take Barber's place: 'a dull man', Carrington judged, 'but an able administrator.' There was, however, another unfortunate appointment in the reshuffle. Anxious to keep the changes to a minimum, Heath replaced Rippon with John Davies, an executive of Shell and former Director-General of the Confederation of British Industry (CBI). Davies had only just joined the House of Commons but Heath was convinced he would bring a vigorous fresh approach to the atrophied corridors of Whitehall. Unfortunately Davies proved to be out of his depth, both in the House and, particularly after his empire had been restructured to form a new Department of Trade and Industry, in his ministry as well. 'His experience seemed to be that of a massive bureaucracy,' considers Michael Heseltine, 'and his lack of political experience reinforced his instinct to control.' Davies was an unequivocal failure – at odds with his aggressively free-market junior ministers, John Eden and Nicholas Ridley, and constantly wrong-footed in the House of Commons. Even Heath, who rarely admitted to a mistake, accepted that it 'was not an inspired appointment'.[5]

It is one of the problems of the political biographer that, for his (or, of course, her) own convenience and for the sake of his readers, he must deal with one subject at a time: Northern Ireland, say, or Britain's entry into Europe. Yet this is not how it happened. Harold

'I SAY SKIPPER, D'YOU THINK DAVIES IS PULLING HIS WEIGHT?'

Wilson's *The Labour Government 1964–1970* is not the most enjoyable of books to read but it is still of enormous value as showing the pressures under which a prime minister is bound to live: crisis following crisis with terrifying rapidity, leaving no time in which to draw breath, let alone for calm reflection. In a single day, not typical, perhaps, but not too remote from reality, Heath might have been woken at 7.30 to the news that Icelandic gunboats were harassing British trawlers outside what the British felt to be national waters. This called for an urgent conversation with the Foreign Secretary, which interrupted his study of the day's telegrams and newspapers and his regular morning meeting with his inner group of advisers. Since the Portuguese Prime Minister was calling at 11 a.m. this disrupted an already packed morning. He barely had time to talk to Joe Gormley of the National Union of Miners, on a covert but potentially highly important visit to Number 10, before it was time to leave for a lunch in the City. He had had to cancel his last lunch with the Stock Exchange two months before, so did not feel he could do so again, but it was infernally inconvenient, because it was the day for Prime Minister's Questions in the House of Commons and he had to be briefed on likely subjects in the car on the way to the lunch and back again. Question Time was quickly followed by a cabinet committee on Northern Ireland in which he was in the chair; again he only had a few minutes in which to digest a formidable brief. He got back to Number 10 in time to dictate a few letters and conduct a long telephone conversation with the British Ambassador in Paris about the likely response of the French President to a new démarche on British entry into Europe. By now it was 6 p.m., and the Minister of Education had been waiting in growing impatience for more than half an hour. And yet there was also a senior member of the Downing Street secretariat at whose leaving party he simply must look in. That left only just time for a shower and to put on a white tie and tails before leaving for a banquet at the Portuguese Embassy. He would have to speak after dinner; he read the draft put up by the Foreign Office in the car on the way, disliked it, and sat in his car a few hundred yards from the Embassy scribbling a few notes, at which he would not even glance when the time came for his speech. The earliest he could politely leave the dinner was 11.30 p.m.; he was back in Number 10 by midnight only to find that the President of the United States had called earlier and was anxiously awaiting a return call to discuss developments in South East Asia. A glance at the latest telegrams and an advance copy of next day's *Times*, ten minutes on the piano and he was in bed by 1.30 a.m. And that was a day in which there was no cabinet meeting, no royal audience, no trips outside central London, no debate requiring his presence in the House of Commons. And so it went on, day after day, week after week, until both mind and body had been so battered by the endless pressure that survival seemed the best that could be hoped for and sage deliberation an unattainable dream.

Various residual problems which had divided the Conservative Party in opposition resurfaced to plague Heath as Prime Minister. Two of the most vexatious related to Southern Africa. The first, and most immediately urgent, concerned the supply of arms to the apartheid regime in South Africa. In 1967 Wilson had bowed to pressure from his left wing and announced that in future no arms would be supplied, even if contracts existed or the material needed was for the maintenance of equipment which had previously been supplied from Britain. The situation was complicated, so far as naval weapons were concerned, by the existence of the Simonstown Agreement, under which Britain and South Africa shared certain responsibilities for the defence of the South Atlantic and Indian Oceans against potential Communist incursions.

The issue was not one about which Heath had thought deeply or felt emotionally committed. His instinctive belief was that boycotts and sanctions would merely reinforce the intransigence of the South African government. When, in May 1970, there had been pressure to cancel the planned South African cricket tour of England, Heath told a correspondent, Mrs Reynolds: 'I believe they are most likely to realise the wrongness and futility of apartheid if they have the widest possible contacts in every field with the outside world.' He told General Gowon, of Nigeria, that he had not always seen things in this light. During the Spanish Civil War and its aftermath he had believed that the Fascist regime should be shunned by the democracies. 'But he had to accept now that this policy had not produced the required results, and that the recent changes in Spain were the consequence of contact with other nations, not isolation from them.' To continue the arms embargo would therefore not merely be legally unjustifiable but politically unwise. Shortly after the election it was announced that sales would be resumed, though only for weapons designed for external defence rather than internal repression.[6]

The predictable consequence was an outburst of indignation from the other African countries, echoed, though less vociferously, by Third World countries of the Commonwealth and, still more mutedly, by Canada. There was 'no indication that any country would go so far as to leave the Commonwealth', Heath told the Cabinet in July 1970, but Britain could expect to come in for some fierce criticism at the Commonwealth meeting in Singapore in the following January. A few days later Douglas-Home announced that Nyerere was threatening to take Tanzania out of the Commonwealth. He and Heath had decided that, while the fundamental policy would not be changed, there would be a statement indicating willingness to listen to what the other prime ministers had to say at Singapore. A disastrous dinner followed at Number 10, at which Kenneth Kaunda of Zambia, who had infuriated Heath by announcing on arrival in London that he had come to appeal to the people over the head of the Government, was berated by the Prime Minister for condemning Britain while himself continuing to trade with South Africa. Next day a Foreign Office official called on Kaunda to pour oil on some exceedingly troubled waters. He found the Zambian Prime Minister 'puffy and despondent'. He had hardly slept all night: 'Never in all his travels', he protested, 'had he received such a reception from the head of a friendly government.' Heath was unmoved, though slightly more disturbed when the following week the Archbishop of Canterbury wrote to tell him that 99 out of the 110 archbishops and bishops gathered at Lambeth had asked him to express disquiet at the arms sale. 'It gives the title of a respectable ally in the free world, to a Government that was suppressing its black majority.' Heath replied at some length, putting forward the familiar arguments about the dangers of isolating and thus strengthening 'those forces which are most determined to preserve the status quo'.[7]

He did not convince the Archbishop and he found his failure painful. He genuinely abhorred apartheid and it distressed him to think that he was seen as associating himself with those who condoned its iniquities. But he never changed his views on the merits of the arms sales. In April 1971 a South African delegation made enquiries about the purchase of two corvettes. Douglas-Home took the line that it would be preferable if the South Africans looked elsewhere. Heath did not agree. In due course the potential order rose to six frigates. Douglas-Home's position remained unchanged and Number 10 complained crossly that the record of the conversation he had had with Heath did not bring out 'the main point made by the Prime Minister, that the South African orders as a whole were substantial and were economically important to us'.[8]

On the other explosive issue in Southern Africa he similarly inclined towards the views of his right wing. He realised that the British

Government could not accept the fait accompli of UDI but longed to be free of an irritating encumbrance and was ready to settle for any settlement with Southern Rhodesia which would have black majority rule as its eventual, even if very distant, goal. He did not think the blacks were ready to govern themselves and viewed with distaste and alarm the activities of those who were in favour of somehow coercing Ian Smith's government into surrender. 'He is a traitor to his country,' he is reputed to have said of Lord Caradon, the formidably liberal representative of the Labour Government in the United Nations. Douglas-Home was notably more hostile than the Prime Minister in his approach to Smith's regime. Heath argued that, if the Rhodesians fielded multiracial teams, at cricket or other games, there was no reason why non-governmental national teams from Britain should not visit the country. There was a lot of racial segregation in Rhodesian schools, said Douglas-Home, and this was getting worse. 'That is not the point,' retorted Heath.[9] In April 1970 Miles Hudson of the Conservative Research Department had put up a paper which assumed that a Conservative Government would make one last effort to reach agreement with Smith. If that failed, the UK should continue to enforce sanctions for, say, nine months; if by that time there had been no progress, the Government should announce that sanctions had failed and should recognise the de facto existence of an independent Rhodesian state. 'This is broadly how my mind works,' wrote Heath. Hudson's paper went even further and envisaged the eventual passage of a bill 'cancelling the colonial status of Rhodesia'. This, commented Heath, 'which really means disengagement and disclaiming any further British responsibility for Rhodesia is also, I hope, being examined'.[10]

In March 1971 Lord Goodman went to Southern Rhodesia to see whether some settlement could be patched up. Heath was shown Goodman's terms of reference, which assumed that, if the rights of the black African majority were to be properly respected, there would need to be a more rapid advance towards racial parity in voting. 'Why?' demanded Heath. 'We have never specified a time ... I don't accept this as a breaking-point.' Against the odds, Goodman returned with an agreement acceptable to Smith and, stretching a point or two, in conformity with the aspirations of the black Africans. When, however, a British judge, Lord Pearce, was sent out to Rhodesia to establish whether the Africans were content with the proposed settlement, he found that they emphatically rejected it. Heath was bitterly disappointed. Only a few months before he had told President Nixon that Goodman and Douglas-Home between them had secured terms far better than the British Government had thought possible. He believed the Africans were bound to accept. Nixon promised to support 'any deal that would work'. 'I am most grateful,' replied Heath. Now it had all come unstuck. Heath was reviled by the Left for trying to sell out the African majority and by the Right for failing to support an honourable fair-minded white administration. To add to his woes, the Foreign Office seemed determined to thwart his preferred policy. Early in 1973 an official spokesman briefed the press to the effect that Britain 'believed in the tightening of sanctions because this would help to bring about a settlement with Southern Rhodesia'. Heath was incensed at what seemed to him a blatant challenge to his personal convictions. 'Once again the FCO is sabotaging Government policy,' he protested. 'The Foreign Secretary should remove the offender at once.' In fact the views of the Prime Minister proved as irrelevant as those of the Foreign Office; once the Pearce Report had been rejected by the Africans every initiative foundered on the intractable opposition of Ian Smith. It was to be another decade before the problem was finally resolved.[11]

It was painfully clear that the issues of Rhodesian independence and South African arms would bulk large on the agenda for the Commonwealth Conference to be held in Singapore in January 1971. Heath was by no means a committed enemy of the Commonwealth; indeed, while Leader of the Opposition, he had gone out of his way to promote the Commonwealth Youth Exchange Council – an activity which could do him no conceivable good electorally and involved him in much time and trouble. But his enthusiasm had bounds. The British Government 'thought the Commonwealth worthwhile', he told Pierre Trudeau on the eve of the Conference, 'even though we probably put in more than we got out of it'. Zambia and Tanzania were the only two countries fundamentally opposed to British policy in Southern Africa: 'However, there were some more who would also disagree with us simply because they did not want to be left behind.' This was humbug, and he told the Canadian prime minister that he did not believe in humbug. Trudeau suggested that 'if some people felt the need for humbug to save their face that was surely not too serious'. Heath did not agree: 'The purpose should be to get people to face reality.'[12]

The issue was envenomed for Heath by his dislike of the Canadian Commonwealth Secretary General, Arnold Smith. Smith's Annual Report was represented in the *Guardian* as being strongly critical of Heath. He telephoned Number 10 to say that he had been misrepresented. Heath commented sourly: 'If Smith writes this stuff he must expect the press to handle it this way. He knows this well and is an enemy of Britain and must be treated as such.' He never changed his view. When Smith finally retired a draft letter was put up for Heath to send to Trudeau which contained some gushing praise for the departing Secretary General. I know this is not your real opinion, advised Bridges, 'but it seems necessary to say something on these lines'. 'Everyone knows my views,' responded Heath, 'and I cannot include para.2.' He was not prepared to condone humbug on the part of the Commonwealth leaders; still less would he indulge in it himself.[13]

When Smith called on the Prime Minister to discuss the forthcoming Conference he stressed that arms to South Africa was an issue that could lead to the break-up of the Commonwealth. This confirmed Heath's fears. He hoped, he said, that the agenda would be as concrete as possible; 'speculative discussion about the future of the Commonwealth ten years ahead would prove unproductive'. If he really believed that the likes of Nyerere, Kaunda and Milton Obote, the prime minister of Uganda, would be content with discussions about trade and aid, he was deluding himself. The reality was worse than he had imagined possible; Heath found himself the target of a torrent of abuse levelled at him by a series of Commonwealth leaders whom he did not believe were either morally or legally justified in their criticism. He did not handle the attacks with patience or good temper; Douglas Hurd, who had considerable sympathy for him and believed that Britain was being unfairly pilloried, nevertheless felt that Heath was too pugnacious, his press conferences were almost insultingly curt.[14] To Heath it seemed that he was being admirably restrained. 'It will be no surprise to you that I found much to disturb me,' he told Nixon. 'I cannot better describe the manner in which the Conference was held than the term "mini United Nations".'[15]

It was not all bad. He had what he told President Nixon was 'a long, useful and most friendly' talk with Indira Gandhi in Delhi on the way to Singapore. Though formally aligned with the critics of British policy in South Africa, Mrs Gandhi had no intention of taking the lead, and on other issues Heath found her intelligent, well informed and comfortingly disinclined to get too deeply involved with Russia. He also found an unexpected ally in Hastings Banda, the president of Malawi. Heath was quite right to sell arms to South Africa, said Banda. What was more: 'There can be no doubt that Mr Heath is a strong Prime Minister. I, for one, like him for it ... What any country wants and expects in a leader is strength of character. And this, Mr Heath has.' He was able, too, to rejoice in the fate that overtook Obote. Obote had been particularly vituperative at Singapore and at one point held an informal press conference at which he assured his listeners: 'Heath is finished, absolutely finished, we have written him off.' A few days later there was a coup in Uganda and it was Obote who was finished. His replacement was a certain Colonel Amin, about whom little was known except that an officer in the Ministry of Defence, who had served in the King's African Rifles, said that he had been the best sergeant in the regiment. By the time Idi Amin arrived in Britain a few months later, an official dossier on him had been compiled. He was 'popular and a natural leader of men but simple and practically illiterate ... Benevolent but tough. Well-disposed to Britain ... God-fearing and deeply religious.' Alec Douglas-Home was rather more perceptive than his officials. 'He's mad,' he told Heath.[16]

Now the Conference was over, Hurd advised Heath, it seemed clear that South Africa and Rhodesia should be considered as two aspects of the same issue. To sell arms to South Africa but to continue sanctions against Rhodesia would generate ill will on every side, so would stopping the arms trade but abandoning sanctions. 'I agree,' minuted Heath, but the conclusion, though logical, was not particularly help-ful.[17] Whatever minor modifications might be possible, Britain was stuck with sanctions and with the arms sales: the most that could be hoped for was that the African leaders might get bored by the issue and think about something else. In the meantime he was resolved that the horrors of Singapore should not be repeated. Towards the end of 1972 discussions began about the agenda for the next Commonwealth Conference, to be held in Ottawa. A 'general chat' of the kind endured in Singapore was a pointless waste of time, Heath told Burke Trend. Two or at the most three days of business-like discussion devoted to specific issues was the most that would be tolerable. 'I have no inten-tion of taking part in anything else.' He would certainly not be there if it happened in August; he had better things to do. He had to eat his words, of course: the Conference lasted eight days and took place in August 1973, but the atmosphere was more congenial than it had been in Singapore. The change was not marked enough wholly to convert Heath, however. When, in September 1973, Jean Monnet pro-posed that there should be regular meetings between the heads of government of the members of the EEC, Patrick Nairne of the Cabinet Office suggested that such meetings might follow the pattern of the 'Commonwealth Conference (Ottawa style)'. 'Not on your life!' Heath commented.[18]

In the meantime, however, another issue had arisen which might well have disturbed the comparative harmony of Ottawa. In spite of his rejection of Powellism, Heath had always been cautious on the question of immigration. He had been one of the majority of Tory MPs who in 1965 had supported Cyril Osborne's private member's bill to impose strict limits on immigration and when he became leader he pressed Maudling to introduce legislation that would abolish the distinction between Commonwealth and foreign would-be immigrants. The Home Secretary, he maintained, should be free to accept or reject any individual case on its merits. Maudling urged him to be less ambitious; the crucial point was that it should be clear the Government intended to limit immigration from the

Commonwealth. In fact the number of heads of families admitted was already down to 1,700 a year and this could hardly be reduced still further. 'With 600,000 unemployed there can surely be *no* justification for admitting *any*,' retorted Heath. He accepted that the British Government could not escape responsibility for the hundreds of thousands of Indians who were living in East Africa but held British passports, yet everything should be done to persuade these potential immigrants to stay where they were. The Kenyan and Ugandan governments, in particular, were making life difficult for their Indian settlers: 'My own view,' wrote Heath, 'is that we should be a good deal tougher with the East African countries over this.'[19]

Kenya at this time seemed to present a bigger threat than Uganda. The 'benevolent' and 'God-fearing' Amin continued to enjoy the favour of Whitehall. In January 1972 he wrote Heath a personal letter asking that Uganda's crushing burden of debt should be rephased. 'Don't let the Treasury bring this regime down as well as Ghana,' warned Heath. Lord Aldington was despatched as the Prime Minister's personal envoy to assess the situation and reported that the President had given him a 'very cordial reception'.[20] But the cordiality waned sharply, on Britain's side at least, when in August of that year Amin abruptly announced that the 57,000 Ugandan Asians who held British passports were sabotaging the economy and would be expelled. Those who were not British citizens could remain, but on sufferance only. The looming threat that the 57,000 might only be a precursor of an avalanche of would-be Asian immigrants from East Africa was very much in the minds of the British Government.

To his credit, Heath made no attempt to escape responsibility for the passport holders. Lord Goodman wrote to congratulate him on his reaction: 'I do not remember an episode of Governmental behaviour as being more clear-cut in relation to morality and principle and less self-seeking in terms of popular appeal.' Praise of this kind and from such a quarter merely reinforced Heath's alarm about the likely response of his own right wing. His main preoccupation was to limit the damage as far as possible. 'It must be made categorically clear to all concerned *et al* that we accept responsibility only for British passport holders ... and we will not accept *a single one of the others.* That is the UN's responsibility. We will *not* budge from that.' Looking ahead, he envisaged an urgent need for legislation that would make clear that citizens of Chinese origin in Hong Kong would enjoy the citizenship of Hong Kong alone and would not have any title to British nationality. In the short term he tried to lighten the burden by persuading Mrs Gandhi that some of the exiles from Uganda should find a new home in India. 'My main concern', he told her, 'has been to avoid the erosion of communal harmony in this country. This is a duty which we owe to the people of this country and particularly to the immigrants who are already settled here.' He got a friendly if not particularly forthcoming response. When Mrs Gandhi visited London in June 1973 he was able to tell the Cabinet that 'relations between India and Britain were better than at any time since independence'.[21]

It was evident, however, that the vast majority of the exiles would end up in Britain. Heath found himself bombarded by protests from MPs whose constituents were in or near revolt. 'The majority of people in this country', wrote John Hall, 'have got to a stage where they no longer care about legal or moral obligations – they just do not want any more immigrants. The letters I have had on this subject are more bitter and, in a sense, more despairing in tone than any I have received on any subject.' 'I have tried swimming against the tide,' wrote Derek Coombs, 'and have firmly come to the conclusion that one is in danger of being engulfed. Reason does not win the day – it only generates more bitterness!'[22] To the atavistic alarm at a proliferation of coloured immigrants was added indignation that citizens of the old Commonwealth were not being given preferential treatment. A Powellite revolt at the annual party conference in 1972 was defeated thanks to the stalwart support of the Young Conservatives, who substituted for a clause demanding further limits on immigration an alternative version praising the Government for its acceptance of the Ugandan refugees. The Young Conservatives, however, were not present in the House of Commons when another Powellite revolt led to the defeat of the Government over new immigration rules which, in the eyes of the rebels, went too far towards favouring workers from the European Community at the expense of the old Commonwealth.

The vote, Heath told Trudeau, followed 'one of the most immoral public campaigns' which he remembered in his public life. The proposed new rules had been on the table for nearly a year and had raised no objection from the Canadian, Australian or New Zealand Governments.[23] Wilson asked whether the Prime Minister proposed to resign in recognition of his defeat; Heath replied that the points which had incurred the displeasure of the Tory members would be re-examined and new legislation in due course laid before the House. In the event the rebels, somewhat aghast at what they had done, were bought off with some relatively minor concessions, but it had been an alarming experience for Heath and reminded him sharply that the right wing of his party was a political force which he would be foolhardy to underestimate.

Idi Amin got the last word when, just before the 1974 election, he wrote to express his sympathy over the economic turmoil Britain was then experiencing. He had set up a Save Britain Charity Fund, and the people of Kizazi district had donated a lorry-load of vegetables and wheat to feed the starving British workers. 'I am now requesting you to send an aircraft to collect this donation urgently before it goes bad.' Bridges suggested that the reply should gratefully acknowledge the funds raised and ask that they should be sent to the UK to assist the Ugandan Asian exiles. The Foreign Office preferred to confine themselves to a polite rejection of the offer. Heath agreed.[24]

FOURTEEN

———— ∘•∘ ————

Europe: The Second Round

There was another piece of unfinished business which to Heath seemed incomparably more important than the parish-pump problems of Southern Africa. Ever since the wounding rebuff of 1963 he had been unwavering in his insistence that, for the sake of Europe's future as well as Britain's, it was essential that Britain should enter the European Community. De Gaulle's resignation in April 1969 had not removed the obstacles to British entry but it had opened the way for their review. By the time of the 1970 election the first steps had already been taken towards renewing the negotiations. Whether a Labour Government would have succeeded must be doubtful. Patrick Reilly, who over many years was closely involved with Britain's relationship with Europe, did not believe that Wilson could have brought it off. He did not have Heath's unyielding determination to succeed. Nor was he well viewed by the French. Pompidou's visit to London in 1966 had been a disaster. Wilson had caused grave offence by failing to turn up at a dinner at the French Embassy on the plea that his backbenchers had demanded an emergency debate on Vietnam;[1] the French prime minister had interpreted this as being a deliberate slight which showed that Britain did not genuinely regard France as a future ally. Even though he might have hesitated to overrule his European partners with the brutality shown by de Gaulle he could have made the progress of the negotiations incomparably more difficult.

The question did not arise. It was for Heath to pick up the gauntlet.

A less ardent Europhile might have decided that the time was not propitious. The polls suggested that de Gaulle's contemptuous rejection of the last British application had sapped whatever enthusiasm there might once have been for a fresh initiative. Two-thirds of the population were said to be opposed to the principle of British entry. Conservative voters were certainly no more enthusiastic than Labour, and a substantial section of the parliamentary party believed that British entry could only be achieved at the cost of betraying the Commonwealth. The Anti-Common Market League was already beginning to foment opposition. Heath, it claimed, was 'a middle-aged bachelor and occasional choirmaster' whose brief experience as a merchant banker no doubt explained his attitude. 'The ranks of the merchant banking fraternity include many ardent "Europeans"; many have but recently come from the Continent.' Heath was not actually accused of being in the pay of the Jews, but the implication was there to be drawn. He was dangerously unsound politically as well, as was proved by his support in the Oxford by-election of 1938 for the 'left-wing Independent candidate Mr A. D. Lindsay' against the official Tory. Even the Labour Party, which had so recently applied for membership, was hedging its bets, hoping to extract electoral advantage from the failure of the negotiations or to complain that whatever terms were finally secured were wholly unacceptable. The gossip in the House, noted Tony Benn, was that the Tories would give up the attempt before it was begun, 'they will see the public doesn't want it and won't run any risk'. But, he went on: 'I wonder if this isn't underestimating Heath's personal passion to get us in.'[2]

It was. It never even occurred to Heath that the application might be shelved: if the public did not see the need for British entry then they must be convinced that they were wrong. And it was he who would convince them. Though Geoffrey Rippon would theoretically be in charge of the negotiations, Heath had no intention of surrendering control nor of leaving it to anyone else to put the case to the electorate. During the first eighteen months of his administration, in spite of the urgent demands of the economy, of the unions, of Northern Ireland, of Southern Africa, it was Europe which above all preoccupied him and about which he cared most deeply. He realised how formidable the problems were going to be. Apart from the Foreign Office and, up to a point, the Treasury, opinion in Whitehall was emphatically against entry. The ministers concerned, with varying degrees of enthusiasm, would no doubt control the excesses of their officials, but the Board of Trade, the Ministry of Agriculture, Fisheries and Food, the Ministry of Employment, would all have to be represented in the negotiations and would see it as their duty to frustrate the Foreign Office's readiness to sacrifice British interests in a mad rush to gain entry. But Heath was as little disposed to leave matters in the hands of the diplomats as of the Home Civil Service. The Foreign Office still believed that the best way to enter Europe would be by isolating France and by encouraging the other five countries of the Community to put pressure on it to abandon its opposition. With de Gaulle gone, they expected France would no longer be prepared to defy its partners. Heath had been had like that once before and did not intend to suffer the experience a second time. Pompidou, he was convinced, was not so totally opposed to British entry as had been his intractable predecessor, but nothing would be more likely to impel him into imposing a fresh veto than the impression that Britain was egging on the other members of the Six to overcome French opposition. The French must be persuaded, not coerced, Heath believed; ultimately that would probably entail a direct confrontation between the President and the British Prime Minister; in the meantime he intended to be fully involved in the preparatory work.

That work, Heath ruled, should be planned and conducted by a 'Europe Unit' in the Cabinet Office, under a 'second permanent secretary' with the relevant departments interlocking through a network of interdepartmental ministerial and official committees. The Foreign Office would, of course, be strongly represented, but they would not be in charge. Geoffrey Rippon, Chancellor of the Duchy of Lancaster, would be responsible and he would work to Heath. So much for the negotiations with the Six. But Heath took still closer control of the separate negotiations which he saw would have to be conducted with the French alone. Here he enjoyed a secret weapon. On holiday in Spain in 1960 he had been making one of his intermittent and usually unavailing efforts to lose weight. This involved following a frugal diet. A Frenchman sitting nearby surprised him by remarking: 'I do not know how you expect to deal with de Gaulle when you eat so little food.' The two became close friends; the Frenchman was Michel Jobert, now Secretary-General to Pompidou at the Elysée.[3] Jobert was a loyal servant of the President but he was also sympathetic to the principle of British entry and convinced that Heath was a 'good European' who should be encouraged and supported. When Pompidou asked him whether Heath was a man to be relied on, Jobert assured him that he was.

A private line was opened up between the Elysée and Number 10 which was to be vastly important over the next twelve months. The Foreign Office deplored this somewhat irregular procedure but could do nothing to prevent it. They tried to stop Douglas Hurd visiting Paris with Robert Armstrong but were overruled. Most of the contacts, however, were between Jobert and Armstrong; together these two conducted negotiations distinct from, sometimes indeed at variance with, the formal discussions that were being conducted in Brussels. The Foreign Office continued to feel disquiet at anything which took place outside the traditional diplomatic channels, but they had to admit that the results were good. At least they were much more aware of what was going on than their opposite numbers in the Quai d'Orsay in Paris. Christopher Soames, who, as a senior Tory politician and the British Ambassador in Paris, had a foot in every camp, once asked Jobert whether he should refer to their conversations when talking to the French Foreign Secretary, Maurice Schumann. 'Schumann does not know, nor should he be told,' replied Jobert. 'If certain officials at the Quai d'Orsay got wind of what was going on they would create difficulties. Secrecy is imperative.' Michael Palliser, Minister at the British Embassy, found it embarrassing when talking to contacts in the Quai to know much more about the thinking of their President than they knew themselves, but all too often such officials were strongly opposed to British entry and it was better that they should be left in the dark. The function of Jobert and Armstrong was to identify and clarify the likely points of disagreement. What they agreed between themselves, of course, did not directly affect the course of the negotiations in Brussels, but it prepared the ground for an eventual resolution of such problems at a higher level.[4]

Though Pompidou held the key to British entry, the other countries of the Community could not be ignored. West Germany, now under the leadership of Willy Brandt, was by far the most significant. When Heath visited Brandt in April 1971 he found that the German Chancellor was an enthusiastic supporter of British entry and ready to do all he could to help. But Brandt also pointed out that 'no one could coerce the French Government, who constituted the main stumbling block'. Any influence the Germans enjoyed in Paris would have to be used with great discretion, too much pressure would drive the French into intransigent opposition. Brandt urged Heath to meet Pompidou face to face, to thrash out the problems. 'What do you think one can achieve by talking to him?' asked Heath. One could hardly expect the President to engage in detailed negotiations. Brandt agreed, 'but in private talks you could say to him what is possible and what is not'.[5] West Germany in an oblique way was in fact already making an important contribution to persuading the French to change their minds. As Germany grew in strength and confidence the French felt that their position as de facto leader in the Community was coming under threat. A possible remedy might be to bring in Britain to act as a counter-balance to German power. 'Those who fear that the economic strength of the Federal Republic could upset the balance within the Community', Brandt had said as early as December 1969, 'should favour enlargement for this very reason.' The argument was reinforced by Brandt's *Ostpolitik*, his efforts to seek some sort of rapprochement with East Germany without giving too much consideration to the feelings of his allies in Western Europe. This caused considerable disquiet in Paris. Pompidou was uneasy about the Ostpolitik, Edouard Balladur, Jobert's eventual successor at the Elysée, told the historian David Marsh. 'Heath was a special sort of Englishman, very pro-European. Pompidou had much more in common with him than with Brandt.'[6]

France's apprehension about Germany was a useful tool for Heath to use in his approach to Pompidou, but it was also a dangerous one which could cut its user. He had to woo the French, but not so ardently that the Germans felt themselves excluded. While the Germans warmly welcomed Anglo-French rapprochement, the British Ambassador in Bonn, Roger Jackling, told Douglas-Home, 'they will be watching for any signs that the French, or we ourselves, are trying to build up an Anglo-French relationship at their expense'. Keeping the triangular relationship in balance was to be a constant preoccupation over the following years. Only a week before Jackling had reminded Whitehall about German susceptibilities, Soames in Paris had reported that Pompidou was offended because a letter from Heath, which he had thought was destined only for him, had also been sent to Brandt. 'It does mean getting away from production-line letters,' commented Heath, 'in which the FCO have been at fault and I have been too busy to redraft. It has been the FCO which has always wanted tit-for-tat – partly because they are terrified Brandt and Pompidou will always compare notes.'[7]

One way of persuading the French that the British had become good Europeans was by espousing international projects which would bind the two countries more closely together. The most conspicuous of these was Concorde. In September 1970 Heath was dismayed to learn that development costs had now risen to £1,000 million. Worse still, BOAC had concluded that they would need a subsidy if they were to operate it. His concern, said Heath, 'was to discover at what point the British Government could, if they so wished, honourably disengage from the Concorde project'. Lord Rothschild was put on the job but came up with no facts that made the project seem economically more viable or politically less embarrassing. His most original contribution was to design a celebratory Concorde tie. 'It is a gay idea, but I am afraid that it will leak and cause more trouble than it is worth,' commented Robert Armstrong. 'I have put it in my bottom tie-drawer where it will be safe,' responded Heath. There it remained. It quickly became clear that disengagement from the enterprise, though perhaps legally possible, would be greeted with extreme resentment by the French. This was not something which, at that time, could be contemplated. By the end of 1971 Heath was recording, with resignation if not enthusiasm, that the Cabinet had concluded 'we should put our full weight behind this project'.[8]

Another, more distant, enterprise was the Channel Tunnel. When Maurice Schumann had put this idea to him, at the beginning of 1970, Heath had been enthusiastic. His only complaint had been that the proposed plan was insufficiently ambitious. 'People wanted to be able to drive in their own cars under the Channel,' he complained, 'and the present scheme did not allow for that.' No practicable scheme was devised that did allow for that but it was still nearly four years before a Channel Tunnel agreement was ready for signature. It was a momentous occasion, declared Pompidou. 'Hitherto, virtually the sole link between the Continent and Britain has been called "Heath". Now we are to have another link.'[9]

Formal negotiations began in Brussels in July 1970. The framework had already been laid down by the previous Labour Government and, for his opening statement, Geoffrey Rippon took over the text prepared for his predecessor, George Thomson. The hope was that this might herald a bipartisan approach to the negotiations; a hope that quickly proved illusory as it appeared that Wilson was intent on extracting as much political advantage as possible from what he felt confident he could present as an abject surrender of British and Commonwealth interests. The problem for Heath was exacerbated by the fact that a substantial element of his own party shared Labour doubts. As in the previous round of talks, the British contribution to the Community budget, the common fisheries policy and New Zealand's exports were the three items most likely to cause controversy – with the French taking a particular interest in the future of sterling as a reserve currency. On New Zealand in particular, Douglas-Home told the Cabinet, Britain was likely 'to face great difficulty in persuading the Community to agree to sufficiently generous terms to satisfy the New Zealand Government and British public opinion'. Only one junior minister, Teddy Taylor, felt pessimistic enough about the issue to resign rather than be a party to the negotiations. It was natural that Taylor should feel bound to make his position clear, Heath complained to the Chief Whip, Francis Pym, but he did seem to be doing so rather more vociferously than was acceptable. Pym was told to point out to Taylor that 'you very much hope that he will not wage the sort of campaign which is going to make it impossible to bring him back into the Government as soon as all this is settled'. Taylor took the hint, did not vote with the Opposition on the critical second reading and in due course rejoined the Government. Others, with less to lose or more passionate convictions, seemed likely to stick to their guns. Early in 1971 the Chief Whip told Heath that 218 Tory members favoured entry, 33 were opposed and 75 in doubt. Of the doubters, 27 were inclined in favour of Europe and 29 against. This last block, which could still be won over, was of vital importance; a 'fierce campaign of conversion' was advocated, including seminars, visits to Paris and Brussels and dinners organised by the Conservative Group for Europe. Even if all these doubters rallied to the cause, however, 10 per cent of the parliamentary party were potentially ready to vote with the Opposition. With a majority over Labour of only 43, it was clear that, even if the negotiations in Brussels went according to plan, the Government's troubles would not be over.[10]

And they were not going to plan. Whatever encouraging murmurs might be coming from the Elysée, the French negotiators in Brussels seemed as reluctant to compromise as ever. On a whole range of issues they continued to insist on terms that they must have known would be unacceptable in London. Even if they intended eventually to relent, Heath feared it might be too late; for protracted and embittered bargaining in Brussels would be bound to foment opposition in Britain. Jean-François Deniau, the European Commissioner for enlargement, warned Heath in January 1971 that there was still strong opposition to British entry within the French Government: 'He reminded the Prime Minister that President de Gaulle's veto in 1963 had been imposed from below; it was not just the General's whim.' Heath himself was by no means sure that he could count on Pompidou. When it was proposed that the French President should be invited to visit London in the spring of 1971, the Foreign Office pointed out that Queen Juliana of the Netherlands would be paying a state visit at much the same time. 'It might be good to have both friend and foe from the Six here close together,' mused Heath. There was no doubt who was cast as the foe.[11]

The time had almost come to take Brandt's advice and confront

Pompidou directly. Peter Moon, the Foreign Office secretary in Number 10 before Tom Bridges took over, told Heath there was some reason to believe that this was what Pompidou wanted. But why he wanted it was another matter. To break the log-jam? To secure more concessions? To reduce pressure on France from other members of the EEC? 'There would seem to be a number of possibilities, not all of which would suit us.' Soames, who through his frequent meetings with Jobert knew as well as any Briton what was going on in the Elysée, also struck a cautious note: if a meeting were to take place, 'success had to be assured beforehand, for failure would be disastrous'.[12] But *could* success be assured beforehand? It would all depend on what Pompidou really thought and how strongly he thought it. Opinions differed. François-Xavier Ortoli, President of the European Commission, told Eric Roussel, Pompidou's biographer, that even as early as 1969 Pompidou had felt that British entry was 'inescapable [*inéluctable*], natural; it was just a question of limiting the risks'. Maurice Druon, shortly to become Minister of Cultural Affairs, was equally certain that Pompidou realised 'that Europe with England would be difficult but that without England it would be impossible'. But the historian Raymond Tournoux remembers that, in April 1971, Pompidou was less decisive: he still believed Britain would enter Europe 'but I won't accept just any terms'.[13]

Soames had reservations. Pompidou, he told the Foreign Office, 'has never been – is not now – enthusiastic about our entry. (Enthusiasm is anyway not part of his make up). He probably does not believe that the present Community will disintegrate if we don't join it. He is not afraid of German pressure ... Pompidou is no European visionary panting for political unification. He is a cautious, hard-bargaining, reticent Auvergnat with limited imagination and no talent for grandeur.' But, Soames concluded, Pompidou accepted that, on balance, 'it is right and necessary that we should come in'. He believed that Pompidou would not see it as his duty implacably to oppose British entry; the question was whether he would see it is as his duty actively to promote it. Soames told Heath that Pompidou was not the sort of man from whom any dramatic initiative could be expected: I have never, he wrote, known the President 'jump a big fence yet'. The door for British entry was ajar, most of those qualified to express an opinion agreed, but it was not fully open. There were booby-traps ahead, and getting through the door was going to call for dexterity, adaptability, patience and, above all, determination. 'Two tailors' dummies would not have done the trick,' wrote Uwe Kitzinger, author of one of the most authoritative histories of the negotiations. 'We didn't want a good meeting,' a participant in the talks told him, 'we needed a very, very good meeting indeed.'[14]

The final confrontation was prepared meticulously; Robert Armstrong and Jobert thrashed out every detail of the potential problems. In the last resort, however, the supporting cast could do nothing; everything would depend on the leading players. Douglas-Home knew what was in the wind but the Cabinet as a whole was told only at the last minute that a summit meeting was in the offing. On 6 May 1971 Heath broke the news to them that he was contemplating a trip to Paris – for the moment 'absolute secrecy' must be maintained; a fortnight later, and it was a fait accompli. 'The Prime Minister said that he believed that M. Pompidou genuinely wished the negotiations to succeed. He had now interested himself personally in the issues involved.' Heath suspected that a potentially serious stumbling block might be Pompidou's determination that French should remain the main working language of the Community. 'He would not be able to give any real reassurance on this subject, but he would propose the development of cultural exchanges between France and the UK and would emphasise that in our schools French was overwhelmingly the most commonly taught second language.'[15]

For two days, 20 and 21 May, Heath and Pompidou met in conclave, with nobody present except the two interpreters. They were never going to become close friends but they quickly decided that they could have confidence in each other and Pompidou concluded that Heath was indeed a good European. In fact he may well have suspected that Heath was a better European than he was himself. Pompidou was above all a Frenchman who put the interests of his own country first and had no intention of letting control over any significant political, military or economic issue become vested in some international body. Heath genuinely believed that the day of the nation state was over and was prepared to derogate to Europe the final word on a wide range of matters of great significance to Britain. This difference of approach was in the future to complicate, though never poison, their relationship; for the moment Heath was content not to explore issues which were not immediately germane to the negotiations.

As expected, the status of sterling proved a controversial issue. Heath was in some doubt as to what Pompidou expected of him. In his official report on the negotiations, Con O'Neill, head of the Foreign Office team concerned with the negotiations, remarked: 'It was never quite clear whether the reserve role of sterling was more objectionable to the French as something which gave us an additional privilege and advantage, or as something which would represent an unacceptable liability and risk.'[16] For Pompidou it was undoubtedly the second but, in either case, it was clear that the French didn't like it and felt it would be an anomaly in a Community enlarged to include Britain. The question was not one about which Heath felt strongly; he was happy to give vague undertakings that the reserve role of sterling would be run down as rapidly as the world's economic position permitted. On the other most controversial issue, Pompidou accepted that the interests of the Commonwealth countries must be respected and implied that the French negotiators in Brussels would be rather less intransigent than they had been in the past.

One question which Heath had expected to bulk large in the talks was nuclear cooperation. Only a week before, Soames had reported that the Minister for Defence, Michel Debré, had applauded Heath's determination to draw nearer to Europe. 'If only the British could disengage from their entanglement with the Americans,' Debré had said, one could envisage 'close co-operation between Britain and France on future nuclear delivery systems'. Could this be the 'open sesame' that would break the deadlock in Brussels? Deniau had said that it would not, telling Heath that Anglo-French nuclear co-operation was not the key to winning over the French and that there would be no point in making any major initiative in this field until the negotiations were completed.[17] Heath, not unreasonably, supposed that the Minister for Defence was more likely to speak for the

French Government on such a subject than a mere Commissioner in Brussels. He knew that he could not commit himself to any precise proposal until he had cleared it with President Nixon, but he came prepared to make hopeful noises suggesting that progress would be possible towards the development of some sort of Anglo/French/ European deterrent. He was surprised to find that Pompidou did not appear particularly interested; certainly not ruling out future cooperation but suggesting that it could be left until after Britain had acceded to the Community. Heath had expected, too, to be pressed on Britain's readiness to join in a common currency as soon as it could be set up. This was something for which he personally felt great enthusiasm, but he knew that it would be unpopular with the electorate and with certain elements of the Government as well. To his relief Pompidou scarcely mentioned the matter – certainly, in no way was it suggested that acceptance of what would one day be the Euro would be a litmus test by which Britain's European credentials would be judged.

Apart from Michael Palliser and Prince Andronikov, who had acted as interpreters, nobody had any idea how the talks had gone – even Douglas Hurd and Michael Wolff were on tenterhooks when Heath and Pompidou came out to face the press conference which had been summoned for the end of the second day. The conference took place in the Salle des Fêtes, the room in which de Gaulle had announced the French veto eight years before. The British officials, on the whole, felt reasonably sure that things had gone well, though quite how well they did not know. The French, who for the most part would have been delighted if Pompidou had played the same role as de Gaulle, looked hopefully for signs of dissension. They were quickly disappointed. 'Many people', Pompidou concluded his statement, 'believed that Great Britain was not and did not wish to become European, and that Britain wanted to enter the Community only so as to destroy it or to divert it from its objectives ... Well, ladies and gentlemen, you see before you tonight two men who are convinced of the contrary.'[18]

For Heath it was one of the most fulfilling moments of his life: as Prime Minister, because he believed he had achieved something which would be of immeasurable advantage to his country and would transform its place in the world over the next decades if not centuries; as an individual, because it was *his* triumph, achieved by *his* determination, persistence and persuasive powers. Patrick Reilly, who had close links with the French officials and had been left with no illusions about the extent of their dismay and surprise, assured Heath: 'I have never had any doubt that the success of that negotiation was due essentially to your handling of Pompidou.'[19] The negotiations in Brussels had, of course, still to be completed. At their final private meeting Pompidou stressed how important it was that the other members of the Community should not think that he and Heath had settled all the outstanding issues without reference to them. But no one doubted that, with the change in the wind from Paris, obstacles which previously had seemed insuperable would turn out to be easily removed. A few of the more intransigent French officials still managed, from time to time, to put a spanner into the works. After one particularly irritating intervention, Soames told Rippon that he was quite sure that this was contrary to the wishes of the President. 'I think it would be worthwhile my trotting down the road [i.e. to the Elysée] to sneak to the Headmaster,' he suggested. 'Sneaking to the Headmaster is a technique to be used sparingly,' commented Robert Armstrong. 'In my view its use should remain under your control because it invokes your relationship with the Headmaster.' 'I agree, keep under my control,' Heath responded. Such interventions were rarely if ever necessary. The French in Brussels could do no more than fight a desultory rearguard action. The scale of Britain's contribution to the common budget was almost the only point on which there was still serious disagreement and even here, once the French had shown that they were willing to be flexible, a compromise was quickly reached. He had been impressed by the warmth of Pompidou's welcome, Heath triumphantly told the Cabinet. He was now satisfied that the President, 'sensing the change of the balance of power both in Europe and in the world as a whole, wished to put an end to the misunderstandings of the last twenty years between Britain and France and to effect a genuine reconciliation between the two countries'.[20]

The battle had been won, it remained to win the war, though against a different enemy. It was clear from the start that the official Labour line was going to be that the terms were unacceptable; vital British interests and the future of the Commonwealth had been thrown away in the interests of securing a settlement. A substantial section of the Tory parliamentary party still shared this view. How many of the hundred or so doubters or hardened Eurosceptics, whom the Chief Whip had identified a few months before, would be prepared to push their opposition to the point of voting against their party when the matter came to the vote? If all or a large majority of them did so, then the vote might be lost. Calculations were made more difficult by the fact that the Opposition, too, was divided. A group of Labour MPs was satisfied that the terms were perfectly acceptable and would have been hailed as a triumphant success if it had been the Labour negotiators who had secured them. They strongly believed that Britain belonged in Europe and were not prepared to jeopardise their country's future for the sake of partisan advantage. The likely composition of these two rebel groups was to keep the Whips on both sides in frenzied uncertainty until the final vote was taken in the House of Commons.

One of the arguments advanced by the Tory rebels was that, regardless of their personal convictions, their constituents felt strongly that Britain was better out of Europe. Their private doubts had thus been reinforced by the demands of the electorate. When the Italian Prime Minister, Emilio Colombo, visited London in June 1971 he expressed surprise at the ignorance about the EEC shown by Members of Parliament and other dignitaries: 'They appeared to apprehend only imperfectly its purposes and methods of work.' In view of this, Heath told the Cabinet, 'the Government would have to make a considerable effort to inform and educate public opinion about the Community if they were to mobilise adequate support for our accession'. He fired the first salvo in early July when he set out to the nation in a radio broadcast the case for British entry. The address had been a distinct success, reported the Opinion Research Centre. He had 'communicated at a very high level' with the voters of all three parties; he had been found easy to understand, the points that had most registered had been positive ones, particularly that Britain must not be left behind. 'In only one respect was the broadcast less than successful – a majority of listeners were suspicious about Mr Heath's sincerity.' Twenty per cent of listeners thought that he was telling the complete truth, 14 per cent 'a lot of truth', 35 per cent 'only some of the truth' and 22 per cent 'very little of the truth'. This did Heath a considerable injustice. No politician can be completely sincere all the time, but Heath got nearer it than most of his rivals. On Europe, he believed passionately in every word that he said. The listeners' verdict reflects on his talents as a broadcaster rather than his real feelings. As such, it must have caused him some disquiet.[21]

Heath's battle for the support, as he saw it for the soul, of his party was launched at the Central Hall, Westminster, a few days after the broadcast. No one accused him of lack of sincerity on this occasion; he spoke with such fervour that the anti-Marketeers described the occasion as the 'Nuremberg Rally'.[22] One idea which he dismissed with especial fury was that the issue should be left to a free vote when it came to the House of Commons. His years as a Whip had left him convinced that party solidarity must be enforced whatever the circumstances; the idea that on an issue of such importance to the party and the nation a decision should be left to the conscience of individual members was to him totally unacceptable. He agreed with Callaghan, he said, that it was up to the Government to get its own people to support its policy and not to rely on the possible aid of Opposition rebels: 'Of course we will have a three-line whip.' Tufton Beamish wrote to tell him that one doubtful Tory MP had said that he hoped there would be a three-line whip because 'it would then be easier for him to justify to his constituents his support for his own Government'. 'I'm sure this is right,' commented Heath. At this stage the Chief Whip fully concurred. 'All my instinct and inclination is utterly opposed to it,' he wrote of the free vote. How could they rely on the Labour rebels to produce enough votes to balance the Tory defectors? But he left the door slightly open: 'It does remain a remote possibility that a free vote *might* yield the best result, but it is much too soon to judge.'[23]

Another possibility that was barely mooted at this point was that, however emphatic the majority in the House, the issue should be put to a popular referendum. The idea had first been aired by a young Tory MP, Philip Goodhart, who, together with Norman St John Stevas, had planned to produce a pamphlet arguing the pros and cons of a referendum on entry into the Community. The project was blocked by the leadership on the grounds that a referendum was contrary to party policy. Goodhart protested: 'If we are not to be saddled with the charge of dragging the country unwillingly into the Market, then there has to be some visible test of public opinion, somewhere, at some time.' Heath does not seem to have intervened personally at this point. His earlier argument, that the knowledge that whatever was decided would be subject to the veto of the British electorate would make the task of the negotiators almost impossible, had to some extent been weakened by the new French position. He made no secret of his conviction, however, that in a parliamentary democracy it would be irresponsible to leave the decision on so critical and complex an issue to the electorate. By sticking to this position he left himself open to charges of bad faith. Into a speech which the Prime Minister made to the British Chamber of Commerce in Paris in May 1970, Douglas Hurd had slipped an assurance that the Community would not be enlarged without 'the full-hearted consent of the peoples and parliaments' of the nations involved. It was a fine rhetorical flourish, but not one to which Hurd gave much thought. Nor did Heath. However, what Heath called the 'ingenuity of the anti-European brigade' later transformed his words into a promise that the people would be given a chance to express an opinion before the deal was finally concluded. It is clear that Heath had not had any such intention when he made the speech; it is equally clear that not much ingenuity was needed to interpret his words in such a way. Indeed, it was the most natural interpretation. The argument that Heath had broken his promise to the electorate was to plague him for many years.[24]

The White Paper published on 7 July 1971, heralding the great debate in the House of Commons, to some seemed equally misleading. It talked of 'a sharing and an enlarging of individual and national sovereignties' and yet argued that, because of the right of veto which each country would retain, there would be no 'erosion of essential national sovereignty'. What seemed 'essential' to the Europhobe might easily be dispensed with by the ardent Europhile; the point was not one which could easily be clarified and certainly not one on which Heath had any inclination to enlarge. His first speech when the debate opened was resolutely low-key and was primarily concerned with emphasising the continuity between the Labour and the Conservative policies towards the EEC.[25] Heath 'quoted copiously from Harold and bored us all', wrote Tony Benn in his diary. 'I dozed off part of the time.' Then Wilson spoke and was equally boring; 'in the circumstances, probably the only way he could tackle the situation'.[26] Heath's first inclination had been to push the question to a vote before the summer recess but the Chief Whip convinced him that this would be unwise, if not suicidal. Public opinion was still emphatically against entry and the Tory rebels, emboldened by this, might well be ready to vote with Labour and defeat the Government. Time was needed to educate the public and to work on the more malleable of the rebels.

Pym's caution was well judged. Organised by the 'Keep Britain Out' campaign, four constituencies held referenda on British entry in August 1971 and all showed substantial majorities for the anti-marketeers. Yet there were signs that the Government's campaign to win over the electorate was having results. In October Philip Goodhart, sticking to his guns despite the discouragement of his leaders, held a referendum in his own constituency, Beckenham. There was a small but clear-cut majority in favour of entry. The Chief Whip grew more optimistic by the day. 'With the constituencies swinging firmly and sharply behind your leadership,' he told Heath in late October, 'all the pressures on Members have been to support the Government. Such a strong and favourable reaction was not expected originally but it has happened.' So far as the Conservative vote was concerned the result would be almost exactly the same, whether there was a three-line whip or a free vote. Victory would turn on the behaviour of the Labour rebels. The Opposition leadership had imposed a three-line whip; if the Tories liberated their members to vote according to their conscience it would make it easier for Roy Jenkins and the other Labour champions of British entry to defy the party line and vote with the Government or, at least, abstain. 'In my minute of 18th August I said that a free vote *might* yield the best result,' advised Pym. 'My conclusion is now that it *will* yield the best result.'[27]

Heath was finally convinced but even then he would not accept the advice of Douglas Hurd and others and announce his volte-face at the Party Conference at Brighton. It was to be very much a last-minute decision but it came soon enough. With the Conservatives free to vote as they thought best, 69 Labour rebels voted with the Government, only 39 Tory rebels voted with the Opposition. The majority for entry was 356 to 244; far better than had seemed possible a few months before. Heath returned in triumph to his flat in Number 10 and played the First Prelude from Book 1 of Bach's *Well Tempered Clavier* on his clavichord. 'It was the right choice for that moment,' he wrote. 'Bach was an early master in the European musical heritage, in which the British share and to which they have contributed so much, and that particular piece of music, at once so serene, so ordered and so profound ... brought us the peace of mind that we needed before plunging into the busy round of celebration.'[28]

On 22 January 1972 Heath flew to Brussels to sign the Treaty of Accession. He invited the leaders of the opposition parties to accompany him. Thorpe, for the Liberals, accepted. Wilson refused: 'You will I think realise that, quite apart from broader issues, the terms of our Motion on the Order Paper would make Labour representation inappropriate.' Any other response would have been unthinkable; Heath's version of it in his memoirs – 'Harold Wilson decided to go to a football match instead' – was characteristically ungracious.[29] As he climbed the marble stairs of the Palais d'Egmont a young woman threw an ink pot at him which splashed its contents over his head and clothes. For a moment he thought that the liquid must be acid. He quickly realised that it was no more than an embarrassing inconvenience, but the incident had given him a nasty shock and a sense of his vulnerability which was renewed when bombers twice made attempts on his life in later years. Physically as well as morally Heath was a brave man, on *Morning Cloud* he remained imperturbable even when conditions were at their worst, but he took his personal security with great seriousness and was to insist on his police guard remaining at full strength long after the Home Office felt any risk was over.

The act of signing was not the end of the story. As Harold Wilson had indicated, the Opposition intended to fight clause by clause the European Communities Bill which now had to be introduced into the House of Commons. The situation seemed particularly precarious since the Labour rebels announced that they had done enough for Europe and that the Government would have to get the legislation through without their help. In the event their bark was worse than their bite, or, more precisely, they barked at the Tory benches but bit the Labour Whips. There was no admitted collusion, but whenever it seemed that the Conservative majority was in peril it always happened that enough Labour members were unavoidably absent. The crucial vote on the second reading came on 17 February. Heath told the Cabinet that morning that he had advised those Tories in the House of Commons who might consider voting against the Bill that it 'had the support of the whole Cabinet and that the Government would therefore regard the issue as one of confidence, on which they could not sustain defeat. The Government must stand or fall together.' Maudling confirmed that this was the view of the whole Cabinet. Sir Henry d'Avigdor Goldsmith wrote to congratulate him on his bold front and reminded him of the words of the prime minister Robert Peel in not entirely dissimilar circumstances: 'While I have the high honour of holding that office, I am determined to hold it by no servile tenure.' Only fifteen Tories ignored his warning but the majority fell to eight. It was enough. Jean Monnet, the father of European unity, was in the House for the occasion. 'It was a great happiness to me that you should be there,' wrote Heath. 'To no one can that decision have meant more than to you.'[30]

Even then it was not all over. It was not until 13 July, by which time there had been 173 hours of debate and 88 divisions, that the third reading passed the House of Commons. Possibly the Cabinet would have forced it through, even if Heath had not been available to lead them. Possibly, in similar circumstances, Pompidou might also have been induced to change his stance. Taking the campaign for Britain's entry into Europe in its entirety, however, it is difficult to believe that it would ever have happened without the persistence, resolution and persuasive powers of Edward Heath. 'I do not believe we would have joined without Ted's determination and resolve,' wrote Anthony Barber. 'By joining the EEC the course of British history was fundamentally changed, and it is no exaggeration to say that this change was brought about primarily through the perseverance of one man.' 'No one other than Ted would have taken Britain into Europe,' wrote Jim Prior. 'In Cabinet, Minister after Minister would set out all the difficulties and recount the insoluble problems. ... But Ted had the sheer determination to find the answers and overcome all the difficulties.'[31] One could cite several other similar statements from those close to the centre of the action, both among those who endorsed his policy and those who thought it disastrous. It does not fall to the lot of many people fundamentally to change the course of British history. By forcing through the abolition of Resale Price Maintenance Heath had transformed the British high street, now he had changed the very pattern of British life. Whatever one's views on European unity, it is impossible not to recognise the grandeur of his achievement.

Whether, to secure these ends, he wilfully misled the British public is a more complex question. Denis Healey thought he had. In the second of the Channel 4 TV programmes *The Last Europeans*, Heath was filmed saying: 'A country's vital interests cannot be overruled.' Oh yes they can, claims Healey: 'If he had laid down the line which he thought it would lead to, he wouldn't have got it through, and he thought it was more important to get it through, even if it was an ignorant and misunderstanding acquiescence rather than support.'[32] There were members of Heath's Cabinet, too, who felt that the Government was glossing over the surrender of independence that would inevitably be involved in British entry into the Community in a way that was misleading if not dishonest. According to the Cabinet minutes an, unidentified, minister protested that one paragraph in particular 'went too far in suggesting that we should never face a choice involving in some sense a sacrifice of national sovereignty'.[33] Drafting changes were made but the thrust of the document remained the same. It was not dishonest but it was disingenuous. Heath did not lie about his intentions but, so far as some of them were concerned, he felt that the less that was said, the better it would be. Any possible surrender of sovereignty was hypothetical and lay in the relatively distant future; why therefore stir up fear and suspicion by discussing it now? Much better stick to emphasising the importance of the national veto and avoid controversy about whether that veto might one day be eroded or even abolished.

Certainly he believed, and never pretended that he did not believe, that there should be far closer political consultation in the Community and that, while a common foreign policy might take time to evolve, this should be the ultimate objective. In a discussion with Jobert shortly before the summit meeting, Robert Armstrong said that Heath did not favour vesting the Commission with the responsibility for organising political consultation – *l'octroi à la Commission d'une compétence dans le domaine de la consultation politique* – though he felt its authority should be enlarged. Similarly he felt that the powers of the European parliament should be increased, even though he accepted that it could never enjoy the position of a true parliament while there was no fully functioning European executive – something which he felt, with some regret, it was premature even to consider. He did not rule out the concept of a directly elected European parliament but felt that this too lay some way in the future.[34] Heath himself said much the same when he spoke a few months later to the new Italian Prime Minister, Giulio Andreotti. Direct elections to the European parliament could wait, he felt, but he 'attached the highest importance to the formation of a European political policy'.[35]

Heath, Robert Armstrong told Jobert, was particularly concerned about the need for a Community summit meeting which would give Europe a new impetus (*'une rélance européenne'*). Such a meeting was held in October 1972. Heath's main objective was to secure the creation of a European Regional Development Fund which might give the more rundown industrial areas of Britain some of the advantages which the Common Agricultural Policy had provided for the French countryside. The French, unsurprisingly, showed little enthusiasm; regional aid, Pompidou argued, was not a proper Community responsibility. On the contrary, retorted Heath, everyone agreed such a policy was essential in the agricultural sphere: 'Otherwise Europe would quickly become a dust bowl under the pressure of low-cost products from elsewhere.' The same was true of industrial areas. Ireland and Holland ardently supported Britain, Western Germany remained silent, nobody backed France. Pompidou must fleetingly have wondered whether he had been wise to allow this turbulent cuckoo into the European nest.[36]

Ireland and Denmark joined at the same time as the United Kingdom. Having so recently and dramatically increased its size, the Community was in no mood to extend still further. The Turkish Prime Minister, however, wrote to Heath in October 1972 to stress that this country was 'inseparable from Europe, as much by its geographical position as by the democratic nature of its political, social and cultural institutions' and that he hoped Turkey would be able to play a full part in the growth of tomorrow's Europe.[37] He would have been disconcerted if he had known that, nearly forty years later, Turkey would still be waiting fretfully in the wings. Heath was in principle not averse to the further extension of the Community but he felt that any growth should be gradual and cautious. Certainly he must have felt that there were several countries better qualified than Turkey to join the European inner circle.

On the whole he felt the summit had gone well. It had been 'a success for all participants', he told Nixon. It had laid down guidelines for the Community's external relationship with the United States. 'As you know,' he continued, with perhaps deliberate ambiguity, 'I regard the latter as a factor of fundamental importance.' There had been some disappointment, he said, about the 'relatively slow progress towards political unity'.[38] This too he regarded as a factor of fundamental importance. Towards the end of 1973 he sent a telegram to all the main British embassies. The Prime Minister, it read, 'believes that political co-operation *à neuf* needs to be fostered and the community needs to develop a positive political personality in international affairs, and that for this purpose more regular and frequent summit meetings are essential ... The direct understanding which Heads of State or Government would gain of each other's minds and problems as a result of such meetings would itself help to develop the habit of political co-operation and the corporate will to agree on further progress towards European union as envisaged by the Paris Summit communiqué.'[39]

Heath was genuinely concerned to maintain a good relationship with Nixon but he had no doubt that the Europeans in general and Pompidou in particular must come first. Pompidou needed delicate handling. In February 1972 he had been due to spend a weekend at Chequers. Problems with the miners meant that Heath thought it necessary to call off the visit at short notice. Pompidou professed not to mind but, when Heath tried to make another date, said that he would not now go to Chequers. Heath must come to him. 'The bourgeois custom in France', Jobert explained to Soames, 'was that if a friend was coming to visit you and you had to cancel him at the last minute, it was for you to visit him the next time.' 'This is extremely tiresome and petty of M. Pompidou,' commented Soames crossly.[40] Heath professed himself ready to go to Paris but feared there would be some delay, whereupon Pompidou relented and said that he would come to Chequers after all. The visit, when it finally took place, was a great success, though here too there was a minor contretemps. Heath met Pompidou off his aircraft wearing sprightly tweeds; Pompidou arrived in a dark grey suit designed for a working day in the City. Nothing was said, but when they got back to Chequers Heath took Pompidou to his room, slipped away to put on a dark suit, and was downstairs in time to greet his guest. The President came down wearing what Michael Palliser remembers as the loudest tweed suit he had ever seen.*

Both men viewed with some suspicion the activities of the European Commission. Pompidou told Heath at Chequers that he thought the Commission was busying itself with matters that were not its concern, behaving as if it were an independent state within the Community. Heath agreed; the Commission, he told the President, 'exists to serve the council and the different states as members of the Community. We don't consider they have any representative role.' He did not exclude, in principle, the possibility that the Commission's powers

---

* Heath, in his memoirs, gives a slightly different version of this anecdote but Palliser is sure that his memory is correct.

should one day be enlarged but in practice he tended to deprecate any act on the part of the Commissioners which seemed likely to have that result. The Commission, he complained to the Cabinet, was 'consistently barging ahead with regulations drawn up to suit themselves, and then coming along, more or less with a take-it-or-leave-it attitude, to present them to us. I really think we must muscle in on this machine now, in a big way, without wasting any more time.' In the short term this could be done through Michael Palliser, now Ambassador to the Community in Brussels, but in the longer term British influence could best be served by ensuring that the right people were sent to serve as Commissioners. Monnet had stressed the critical importance of these appointments. They would, he said, 'touch the heart of all future developments of the Community ... If technicians are to be appointed, however capable, we would thus be emphasising the weakness of the Commission. If they are political men, with recognised authority, and having the experience of how government works, then your appointments will be an example which other governments will follow.'[41] Soames was an obvious choice, and was given responsibility for external relations; for the second vacancy Heath boldly chose George Thomson, who had been principally responsible for European relations in the last Labour Government. It was an excellent appointment: Thomson was notably moderate in his political views and a convinced Europhile; his selection emphasised the bipartisan nature of British policy towards Europe which Heath was still trying to maintain in spite of the hostility of the Labour leadership. Thomson was anxious that Wilson should be told as soon as possible what was in the wind; Heath remarked sourly that, if he *were* informed, he would be bound to leak the news 'and use it for whatever nefarious purpose he can'. Thomson evidently admitted the force of this argument; at any rate, Wilson was told only just before the formal announcement.[42] Thomson was given what was to Heath the key portfolio of Regional Policy.

Another step that Pompidou urged was the setting up of a political secretariat, independent of the Commission and based in Paris. Lord Gladwyn, a former British Ambassador to France and ardent crusader for Europe, felt we should accept the French proposition and that our price should be that the first Secretary General was a prominent Briton. 'Needless to say, our candidate should at least speak excellent French ... There are perhaps not many people in the United Kingdom who would fill this particular bill, but we should just have to produce the appropriate personality.' 'Who, I wonder, does he think this might be?' Douglas Hurd enquired innocently.[43] Sadly, it was not to be – political cooperation was one of the several issues vociferously promoted at the Paris summit but then suffered to languish when more urgent preoccupations took centre stage.

Economic cooperation, culminating in a European Monetary Union (EMU), was prominent among these. The Bank of England had argued that such a Union, allowing Europe to 'stand up to the economic might of the United States and thus command for itself a more powerful voice in world affairs', was in British interests. But the Bank also pointed out that this might imply 'the creation of a European federal state, with a single currency. All the basic instruments of national economic management ... would ultimately be handed over to the central federal authorities.'[44] The word 'federal', which inspired rage in the hearts of the Europhobes and dismay in the minds of the more timorous, held no particular terrors for Heath, but he realised that the country was not yet ready for anything so extreme. As with any other question that involved issues of national sovereignty, he felt that discussion should be kept to a minimum. In 1973 John Davies submitted to Number 10 a draft speech he proposed to make to the Zurich Economic Society, a high-powered group of bankers, industrialists and economists. In it he had included a reference to monetary union, pointing out that such a measure would inevitably mean that the parities of the countries involved would thereby be irrevocably linked. 'Do we really have to spell this out now?' asked Heath. 'Cut!' On the speech as a whole he commented: 'I am never happy about such pieces. They always do more harm than good.' In the end the gnomes of Zurich had to be content with a collection of anodyne clichés.[45]

But though Heath wanted as little as possible to be said in public, inaction was not a possibility. President Nixon had upset the economic apple-cart in August 1971 when a dramatic flight from the dollar led him to suspend convertibility and impose a 10 per cent import surcharge. A few months later Heath proposed to Brandt and Pompidou a plan to realign the exchange rates and reduce the use of national currencies as international reserve assets. He promised total support for Franco-German efforts to stabilise European currencies. In May 1972 Britain joined the 'snake', a system by which every member country limited the fluctuation of its currency against those of the other members to 2½ per cent. The moment was singularly ill chosen; within a few weeks it had been forced out again. By the time Britain at last formally joined the Community on 1 January 1973 the fragility of sterling would have precluded its membership of any monetary union, however loosely constructed. Its new partners viewed Britain's behaviour with disappointment if not disapproval. Pompidou told Brandt that Britain was eager to express opinions on the larger geophysical decisions about Europe's future but left the detailed issues of economic integration to France and Germany. 'It is like a husband who leaves all the questions regarding the apartment, the children's education and the holiday plans to his wife – and only wants to concern himself with whether to open diplomatic relations with China.'[46]

By the time of British accession, therefore, it was clear to Heath both that Britain had not so far been able to make as prominent a contribution to European unity as he would have wished and that political and economic progress had overall proved faltering. This was to be regretted, but neither Rome nor a united Europe were built in a day. It was still an occasion for rejoicing. As early as October 1971 Robert Armstrong had told David Eccles, the Minister for the Arts, that the Prime Minister wanted a Festival of European Art to celebrate British entry 'and that he would strongly deprecate one that went off at half-cock'. Since it was still possible that the negotiations for British entry would themselves go off at half-cock, it took some little time to get things moving. Even then there were setbacks. A plan to borrow the Bayeux Tapestry and show it in Westminster Hall was abandoned when it was pointed out that the butchery of Saxons by Normans was hardly a suitable theme for the occasion. The French refused to lend the *Mona Lisa*, in spite of Heath's personal plea, on the grounds that the British Museum had just refused a loan of the Rosetta Stone for an exhibition in Paris. The Dutch were similarly disobliging over Rembrandt's *The Night Watch*.

A poll towards the end of 1972 showed that 76 per cent of the population were opposed to public money being spent on such a celebration. Heath was undiscomfited; when the day came, he felt sublimely confident, the British people would be delighted by all that was going on. The French offered de la Tour's *Le Tricheur* (also, one might have thought, a slightly sardonic choice for such an event), other countries furnished a Michelangelo, a Rembrandt and a Rubens. Britain decided its contribution to such an exhibition should be a Stubbs. Pictures were only a part of it. 'If there is a suitable football match, it might be a good idea for you to go,' Heath was told. He was unenthusiastic but agreed. Then Eccles designed a tie for the occasion. Could you bear to wear it at the football match? asked Armstrong. 'I doubt it, but I'll try,' promised Heath. It was the music which most concerned him. The Concertgebouw Orchestra visited London for the occasion. There was no need for Heath to be present, Armstrong assured him. 'I have never yet heard the C in the flesh and wd like to go,' Heath minuted.

His own personal contribution was to persuade Herbert von Karajan and the Berlin Philharmonic to squeeze in a visit to London between their many commitments. Karajan agreed to come as a personal favour to the Prime Minister but refused to allow the occasion to be televised. Heath was asked to persuade him but thought that both he and Karajan had already done enough. 'Fanfare for Europe', as it became known, opened on 3 January 1973 with a gala night at Covent Garden which the Queen attended and at which Laurence Olivier, Judi Dench, Tito Gobbi, Elizabeth Schwarzkopf, Geraint Evans and a host of other heroic figures performed. 'My heart was full of joy that night,' wrote Heath. There was not to be much joy for him over the next eighteen months; even the most critical would hardly have grudged him his moment of glory.[47]

FIFTEEN

Ulster

In Heath's eyes at least, Britain's entry into Europe was the most important and pressing of his preoccupations during his first eighteen months in office. 'Important' would perhaps be correct; 'pressing' is another matter. Time and again crises of extreme urgency required the Prime Minister's concentrated, if not exclusive, attention. Of nothing was this more true than Northern Ireland.

The civil rights marches which had begun in 1968 sharply raised the temperature of what had been, over the previous decade, a sullen but largely latent conflict. With Conservative support the Labour Government had sent troops to Northern Ireland; the hope had been that they would quickly restore order and could be withdrawn within a year. Their prime responsibility at first had been to protect the Roman Catholic minority from Unionist bullying and avert a descent into total chaos; in so doing they provoked the resentment of the Unionists and did not earn much in the way of gratitude from the Catholics. The IRA, who took the presence of British troops in Northern Ireland as a wanton provocation, ensured that pacification was impossible; the tally of violence mounted; the luckless British troops found themselves the target for abuse from one side and violence from the other. The Labour Government had, in fact, managed to redress some of the worst of the Catholic grievances; the Protestant Northern Ireland Government at Stormont unenthusiastically accepted the reforms but a breakaway group under Ian Paisley rejected what they saw as the subversion of Protestant rule. In their eyes the British Government was moving, surreptitiously but inexorably, towards the conciliation of the Irish Government in Dublin and eventual union between the two parts of Ireland.

The Conservative victory in 1970 heartened the Unionists. Traditionally their MPs had loyally supported the Tories in the House of Commons. In return they expected to be left in peace to run Northern Ireland as they thought best. James Chichester-Clark, whose brother Robin was a close associate of Heath's, rejoiced in the fact that Westminster's policy would once more be in the hands of patriots who could be expected to defend the interests of the Union. Chichester-Clark was in fact moderate and liberal, accepting that the Catholics in Ulster had had a bad deal and deserved better treatment. If he alone had been responsible for the forming of policy in Belfast an uneasy peace might have endured. But even among his followers there were many who believed that the reforms had already gone too far, whilst the Paisleyites felt that Labour's policies must rapidly be reversed and the Protestant hegemony restored in full.

Chichester-Clark had some reason to fear that Heath might prove to be a disappointment, not merely in the eyes of the right-wing Unionists but even for moderates like himself. Knox Cunningham had spoken to Heath at the end of 1968. Heath, he reported to Macmillan, was a strong supporter of the then Prime Minister of Northern Ireland, Terence O'Neill. 'This has been taken to mean that the Conservatives will put just as much pressure on Ulster as had Wilson and Labour.' Heath had denied that this was his intention, but he had told Knox Cunningham that, if O'Neill lost office and was replaced by someone more extreme, he would denounce the new incumbent. 'I got the impression that he had shut his mind to anything I had to say.' In fact O'Neill was replaced by Chichester-Clark, a man who, though not as vigorous a reformer as his predecessor, still had his heart in the right place – was a dangerous radical, indeed, in the eyes of traditionalists like Knox Cunningham. But he was a compromiser who was reluctant to push things too fast or too far and was well aware of his own precarious position. He wanted London to interfere as little as possible. His brother Robin told Heath that it might have been a good thing for Northern Ireland if Westminster had never set up an independent Stormont Parliament but that for anyone to try to enforce direct rule 'at *this* juncture would be the height of folly'.[1]

Heath, in fact, had no wish to devote much time or thought to Northern Ireland. It was the responsibility of Maudling as Home Secretary, and though Heath doubted whether his colleague could be expected to take any very energetic initiatives, he felt reasonably hopeful that in the long run things would right themselves. He found it almost impossible to credit the ferocity of the irrational hates and fears which had for so long consumed the population of Ulster. Chichester-Clark, he knew, was a reasonable man. Roman Catholics, who had already gained so much, would surely see the advantages they might gain from collaborating with him. The violence of the Paisleyites on one side and the IRA on the other must make it all the more likely that the moderate majority, Roman Catholic as well as Protestant, would wish to negotiate a lasting settlement. Even if such an approach faltered, he told the Ministerial Committee on Northern Ireland, it might be that the entry of the United Kingdom and the Republic of Ireland into the European Community 'would provide the opportunities we sought to modify the divisions in Ireland'. We could hope for a 'quiet spell of ten years', he told Cecil King, after which 'the Common Market would have transformed the situation'. In short, he totally failed to grasp the realities of Ulster politics. Nothing made Heath so angry as an Ulster Unionist, said Enoch Powell: 'That people were prepared to be bombed and shot in order to belong to a particular nation was not only beyond Heath's comprehension, but even made Heath sick.'[2] Nothing, for that matter, made Heath so angry as a member of the IRA. Amend Powell's statement to include extremists on either flank, and it must be admitted that he had a point.

Even at his most sanguine, however, Heath did not imagine that he could afford to wash his hands altogether of the Irish problem. At Burke Trend's urging he took the chairmanship of the cabinet committee on Northern Ireland. Trend saw only too well the problems that lay ahead. In a bleak briefing paper submitted in June 1970 he told Heath that, as things were, the three possibilities in Ulster were spontaneous improvement, 'so unlikely as to be discounted'; the status quo, which would put 'an ultimately intolerable burden on HMG in terms of money and man power'; and 'chaos, involving civil war and Irish intervention'.[3] Some new initiative was essential. Heath dutifully passed on this message to the Cabinet. But it cannot be said that the new measures he envisaged were particularly dramatic. The most striking novelty was that the Home Secretary would shortly visit Ulster. 'The advent of a new Government in the United Kingdom', Heath concluded reassuringly, 'whose commitment to the integrity of Northern Ireland could not be doubted, should calm Protestant apprehensions and contribute to a general reduction of tension and present us with an opportunity of making a fresh start which we should exploit to the full.'[4] Whether Maudling was the man to grasp that opportunity was at the least doubtful. 'What a bloody awful country,' was said to have been his comment in the aircraft on the way home after his first visit.[5]

In spite of Heath's optimistic words, the situation rapidly deteriorated, exacerbated by the arrest of the young firebrand Roman Catholic militant, Bernadette Devlin. 'A new and disquieting feature', the Cabinet was told, 'was the marked decline in the morale of the Royal Ulster Constabulary' (RUC).[6] Chichester-Clark asked for more troops to be sent from Britain; the Cabinet agreed but, as a quid pro quo, insisted that all sectarian marches should be banned until the end of January 1971. A little time had been bought but it had to be used profitably. When urging Heath to devise a new initiative Trend had gloomily added: 'It is almost impossible to see what form a new political approach could in fact take.'[7] Responding to this challenge, Heath decided to open up a new front. In Washington in October 1970 he took advantage of a dinner at the White House at which they were both guests to have a long talk with the Irish Prime Minister, Jack Lynch. Lynch was 'far and away the best Irish Prime Minister we can hope for', the Foreign Office had told Heath; if any kind of a deal was to be done with Ireland it was best negotiated while he was still in power. He won Heath's especial respect by recounting how he had just dismissed the entire board of directors of Radio Telefis Eireann for allowing the head of the Provisional IRA to broadcast in one of its programmes. 'Do you mean that you have just sacked the

Chairman and Governors of your BBC?' asked Heath. 'Yes,' said Lynch. Heath turned to Armstrong, with a gleam in his eye, and said 'Could I do that?' It seemed to Armstrong that this was a notion which should not be allowed to take root in Heath's mind. 'No, Prime Minister,' he replied firmly. 'I'm afraid you couldn't.'

Unfortunately Lynch's position in Ireland was precarious and Heath, to his surprise, was asked to make a statement stressing how much the Irish Prime Minister had done to keep down the temperature on both sides of the border. Would such remarks really be helpful? asked Heath. They would be *most* helpful, Lynch assured him; 'in fact he badly needed them'. Before Heath could oblige, however, Lynch's position in Dublin grew markedly stronger and the propaganda exercise was dropped. For his part, Heath assured Lynch that it was in the best interests of both Ireland and the UK that Chichester-Clark should continue in office: 'He did not accept that the right-wing of the Ulster Unionist Party had effective control.'[8]

In spite of his assurances, the Chichester-Clark brothers were disturbed by this evidence that Heath and his Government were getting close to the enemy across the border. Robin Chichester-Clark wrote to Heath in December to protest at the attitude of 'benevolent neutrality' which was being adopted by the Tory Government, when they should have been concerned to support 'those who are labouring against considerable odds to lift Ulster out of her present political difficulties'. Heath peppered his letter with acerbic marginal comments. Against a complaint that Heath had told Paisley that HMG's relations with the Irish Republic were 'close and friendly', Heath wrote tersely: 'They are.' Against a request that Heath should ask Lynch to do more to stop the drilling of illegal forces on his side of the border, Heath commented: 'He can't stop them, poor man.' A hope that Central Office would provide opportunities for Unionists to speak publicly on Ulster questions earned the response: 'Let them. It's a waste of time.' Chichester-Clark hoped Heath would soon visit Ulster. 'I'd prefer not to get shot by a Unionist,' wrote the Prime Minister (writing to the Home Office, Robert Armstrong interpreted this last remark as 'I judge the Prime Minister's enthusiasm for this is distinctly qualified).'[9]

Three months later, in March 1971, James Chichester-Clark resigned. Before doing so he had a long and agonised telephone conversation with Heath. He was treated with some brutality. Heath dismissed Chichester-Clark's claims that the British Government was not doing enough and challenged him to name a single initiative that he would have taken if the Ulster administration had enjoyed greater independence: 'You're passing the buck when you know that it's quite unjustified to do so.' Chichester-Clark admitted the situation was not entirely rational: 'Well,' retorted Heath, 'I'm perfectly ready to consider irrational solutions if you could tell me what those are.' What he wanted to get across, said Chichester-Clark, was that 'we are not a Sovereign Parliament. This was something that nobody in Northern Ireland would believe.' What *needed* to be got across, concluded Heath, 'is that you are two communities that have got to live together. If you want to do in the IRA you don't do it by a lot of useless gestures.' Heath claimed in his memoirs to have tried hard to persuade Chichester-Clark to stay, even sending Carrington to Belfast to reinforce his arguments. In fact he seems to have considered the Northern Irish Prime Minister was a spent force and to have accepted his departure with equanimity if not relief.[10]

Chichester-Clark's successor was Brian Faulkner. Faulkner was a tougher and more resourceful politician than Chichester-Clark, but a moderate of broadly similar views. If he too failed, the Unionist Party would inevitably fall into the hands of the Paisleyites. The knowledge of this gave him additional bargaining power in Westminster but also made it more likely that he would be replaced not by another local politician, but by a figure of vice-regal authority despatched from London. This Faulkner was resolved if conceivably possible to avoid. 'I agree whole-heartedly with all that you say about the value of our alliance with the Conservative Party,' he told Lord Hailsham. 'We need to make it a closer and more understanding liaison on both sides and I will do anything I can to bring this about.'[11]

He paid his first visit to London as Prime Minister on 1 April 1971. A few days before his arrival Heath had minuted: 'We must take immediate and effective action in Northern Ireland and not allow ourselves to drift into direct rule, nor slide into it through fatalism.'

Faulkner would have said just the same: the problem was that 'immediate and effective' meant something different to the two prime ministers. Their first meeting went well. Faulkner left an interesting account of it. He went to Number 10 with the minister technically responsible for Northern Ireland, Reginald Maudling. Carrington and Douglas-Home were also present.

> Heath dominated his colleagues totally at all meetings I attended during his Premiership. Carrington, who was the least vocal of the triumvirate at meetings, seemed to have a good personal relationship with Heath; one felt that his opinions were made clear privately before and after meetings. Sir Alec was courteous and sociable; he was very much a Unionist, in the traditional sense of favouring the Union. Maudling, relaxed and easy-going, did not fit in too easily with Heath's brusque businesslike style and after some months I began to feel that Maudling was losing influence and being left out of decisions. There seemed to be an element of personal coldness involved ...

Faulkner left with the feeling that Heath was 'an ally who clearly could be relied on in the crises that would inevitably occur'. His aides believed that 'Heath and I, as hard-headed and practical men, would have a special relationship'.[12]

Special or not, this was its high-water mark. Heath wanted fresh initiatives even if, as he had admitted to Chichester-Clark, he had no clear idea what these might be. Faulkner, as political unrest and violence in the province became ever more ferocious, had nothing to offer but a plea for extra troops, better intelligence, stronger security, more arrests. If it had not been for the fact that Heath was pre-occupied by the campaign to get the Common Market legislation through the House of Commons and had determined to let no other controversial issue muddy the already turbulent waters, the con-frontation between the Ulster Government and Westminster would probably have come some months earlier.[13]

Certainly he would have been more ready to challenge Faulkner's insistence that internment without trial was an essential tool if the Ulster Government was to quell the growing disorder. All his liberal instincts led him to recoil from a measure so obviously contrary to the principles of democracy and the rights of the individual. If Faulkner was thwarted, however, it seemed probable that he would resign; the only acceptable alternative would then be direct rule from Westminster. In the end this would probably be inevitable, but the prospect was most unwelcome and the necessary contingency planning was far from complete. If coupled with a ban on political marches it seemed just possible that internment would provide a desperately needed breathing space and that the line could be held until Britain was safely in Europe and a new rulebook would apply. Carrington had argued that internment must be the last fling: 'If this is right,' minuted Robert Armstrong, 'it seems to me that it should be something which you do when you visibly have to, and not before; not as part of a deal for banning marches.'[14] Heath half agreed but took the line of least resistance. On 9 August troops rounded up 337 suspects. All of them were Catholic and suspected of being active members of the IRA.

Lynch, as he was bound to, protested strongly. Faulkner happened to be at Chequers when the Irish Prime Minister's message was received. 'A few unprintable comments were volunteered all round,' he wrote. It does not seem likely that any of them were contributed by Heath – he rarely ventured into the unprintable, and, anyway, was already beginning to suspect that Lynch had a strong case and that the British Government had made a bad mistake. The arrests had been followed by rioting in Belfast and Londonderry, the moderate Catholic Social and Democratic Labour Party (SDLP) in Northern Ireland was as outraged as the Irish Government and there were protests from all round the world. General Ford, the commander of land forces in Northern Ireland, complained that the Unionist Government 'showed absolutely no interest whatever in the internees and their handling'. Nothing was being done to separate the high-risk prisoners from the relatively harmless, or to provide any sort of rehabilitation for those who were only lightly tainted. Worst of all, it became increasingly clear that the wrong people had been arrested. The information provided by the RUC was hopelessly out of date; many of those arrested had been long inactive, some since the 1920s;

most of the present-day IRA leadership had been given ample warning and had slipped away to the Republic. Heath was prepared to swallow the doubtful legality of the exercise, but not its bungling failure. Faulkner was 'not at all in favour', Paisley told Cecil King after one of his few meetings with Heath.[15]

Lynch was bound to protest, but he still believed that something could be done and that Heath was a man with whom it was possible do to it. The two men met in Brussels in January 1972. He was worried about internment, Lynch told Heath, but he wanted to move on. 'It was important to get some movement in the situation. People were saying that Mr Faulkner was dictating the pace of events, while the Prime Minister himself concentrated on Europe. Feelings of fear and frustration were growing.' It was extraordinarily difficult, complained Robert Armstrong, 'to form a clear impression of what Mr Lynch was trying to get at, partly because he had a very heavy cold and partly because his ideas were hazy and far from fully developed'. Heath thought he understood. The IRA, though undefeated, had been given a bloody nose; the Unionists were still frightened; everyone agreed reunification was off the agenda for the moment, 'so perhaps there was room for agreement on some sort of government with minority participation'. Power-sharing was on the agenda.[16]

In the meantime, Heath had paid his first visit to Northern Ireland. For reasons of security he travelled as a junior minister, Geoffrey Johnson Smith. This caused some problems of protocol, when the authorities realised that the formalities suitable for an under secretary had to be revised to accommodate the dignity of a prime minister, but otherwise all went smoothly. Heath was always gratified by demonstrations of military efficiency and the cheerful resourcefulness of the men who were carrying out an extremely disagreeable as well as dangerous task impressed him greatly. 'Strange thing,' he remarked on the flight back, 'we went over to boost their morale in the week before Christmas, and they boosted ours.' His visit was given urgency by the fact that Harold Wilson had the previous month decided that he must visit Faulkner. Heath rang up to warn Faulkner what was about to hit him. He was perfectly happy about it, said Faulkner: 'Are you?' 'Well, obviously not. But that we have to put up with.' Was

Wilson simply trying to upstage Callaghan? asked Faulkner. 'I think he is trying to provide a diversion for his own divisions and upstage everybody.' 'Playing politics with the Northern Ireland situation?' 'Yes, to the utmost,' concluded Heath. The judgment was uncharitable. There was no reason why the Leader of the Opposition should not have real concerns about the situation in Northern Ireland. Nor was Heath unaware that his own visit to Belfast would do something to placate his critics who thought he was unduly conciliatory in his handling of the Irish and of the Ulster Catholics. Heath could never afford to forget that Enoch Powell was on the loose, ready to denounce anything that seemed to savour of betrayal of the Union. 'I don't think anyone can show the right-wing had very much influence on our policies,' he told Margaret Laing proudly. The boast was justified, but if occasional gestures would appease his right wing, he was quite ready to make them.[17]

Wilson followed up his foray to Belfast with a visit to Dublin. This gave rise to a nasty spat between the Prime Minister and the Leader of the Opposition, which showed how the hostility between the two men transcended the conventional sparring that was endemic in their relationship. Before he left, Wilson had told his press secretary, Joe Haines, that he was going to warn Heath that he intended to talk to members of the IRA. When news of the meeting began to leak, Haines was told to telephone Number 10 and let Heath know that, in his speech in the forthcoming debate, Wilson would refer to the meeting and say that the Prime Minister had been warned in advance. Heath's response was to deny absolutely that he had had any warning and to tell Wilson that, if necessary, he would say as much in the House of Commons. Wilson told Haines that he had 'had a word' with Heath at a reception. A casual word at a crowded social gathering is hardly a way to convey confidential information. Neither men emerges with much credit from the episode but, as Haines concluded, 'It was an illuminating illustration of the distrust which for a long time soured the relationship between the two men.'[18]

The bipartisan approach towards Northern Ireland, however, was still uneasily maintained. There was much to strain it over the next few months. In September 1971 it seemed that the relationship between Westminster and the Unionist Government in Belfast was surviving more or less unscathed. 'L T [Little Twister, i.e. Faulkner] seemed satisfied with his Chequers talks', Knox Cunningham told Macmillan. 'Ted was very strong and particularly helpful ... The impression was given that internment would be a continuing process.' Yet at the same time Robert Armstrong and Burke Trend were planning the next step in the constitutional development of Ulster. A Secretary of State responsible for the province was essential. Heath should not take charge himself. 'There are plenty of other things which ought to engage your attention. There is always a risk that something will blow up in Northern Ireland when you ought to be concentrating on something else. There is also a political risk of taking over sole responsibility.' Such an appointment need not necessarily lead to direct rule, but Armstrong admitted that there was a risk that it would be seen as a precursor. Faulkner, of course, had no knowledge of what was being mooted. By the end of the year, he admitted that he was beginning 'to watch with some concern' developments in Westminster but he did not believe that any fundamental changes were being considered. He still felt sure that he could rely on Heath: 'Our relationship', he wrote, 'had continued to be cordial and I believed him to be a man of principle and strong character who would stand by us when the going was rough.' Robin Chichester-Clark considers that he had no grounds for such delusions; he had received many warnings that a radical rethinking of policy was taking place in Westminster. Perhaps he chose to ignore the evidence; at all events his biographer believes that he remained sublimely 'unaware that plans for a takeover were well advanced'.[19]

On 30 January 1972 the paratroops in Londonderry fired on a political march and killed fourteen of the demonstrators. 'Bloody Sunday' did more than any other single event to make direct rule inevitable. Who provoked the incident has not and may never be finally established, but few would dispute that the paratroop reaction was disproportionate in its violence and recklessness. With it perished whatever last hopes Heath might have had that the Unionist Government could stabilise the situation and hold the line until circumstances were more propitious for a lasting settlement. Lynch rang late that night to express his horror. 'It is very bad news,' Heath responded bleakly. He refused to admit that there had been unnecessary violence but at once set up a tribunal under Lord Widgery to establish all the facts. 'I regard is as absolutely essential', he minuted, 'that the Tribunal should sit at the earliest possible moment and conclude its enquiries as speedily as possible.'[20]

Heath, if only because some of the most influential members of his Cabinet opposed it, still baulked at imposing direct rule. If Faulkner could be persuaded to accept that control of law and order should revert to Westminster and that there should be some movement towards power-sharing, then it might still be possible to leave the Unionists theoretically in charge. When, early in March, Faulkner asked Heath to deny the many articles in the press suggesting that direct rule was imminent, Heath assured him that these were 'pure speculation'.[21] So, in a sense, they were, but Heath's reply was still disingenuous. He knew that it was most unlikely that Faulkner would feel able to accept the conditions with which he was going to be confronted, or that his party would allow him to do so even if he wanted. At a meeting in Downing Street in early February Faulkner had already said that if Stormont was denied control of law and order it would no longer be credible as a government. It would be direct rule by another name. Heath suggested that direct rule might in fact strengthen the links between Northern Ireland and the rest of the United Kingdom. On the contrary, retorted Faulkner: 'The Protestant Community would see direct rule as the first step towards a deal between Westminster and Dublin.'[22] (His suspicions would have been even stronger if he had known that at an informal meeting between Heath, Trend, Armstrong and Lord Rothschild it had been felt by everyone that 'the only lasting solution would lie in bringing about the unification of all Ireland'.)[23]

However slim the chance of winning Unionist approval for the move towards power-sharing which he believed essential, Heath still had to go through the motions. On 15 March he spoke to Faulkner on the telephone and asked him to come to London for 'consultations'. When Faulkner suspiciously enquired what was going to be proposed, Heath answered that it was 'really very difficult to put down on a bit of paper'. 'I understand that,' said Faulkner, who clearly understood nothing. He asked Harold Black, the secretary to the Northern Ireland Office, to try to extract some extra information from Burke Trend about the likely agenda but was fobbed off with the answer that the Prime Minister envisaged 'a good going over the ground'. Well, anyway, Black told Trend defiantly, Faulkner would not be able to agree to anything 'beyond what he had proposed in his letters to the PM'. Faulkner quickly discovered that very much more was being asked of him. He assumed, however, that these were proposals put forward for discussion; when he realised that they were, in effect, an ultimatum he was 'shaken and horrified and felt completely betrayed'.[24]

Some of Heath's colleagues were almost equally shaken. 'I really dislike direct rule for Northern Ireland because I do not believe that they are like the Scots or Welsh and doubt if they ever will be,' wrote Douglas-Home. 'The real British interest would, I think, be served best by pushing them towards a United Ireland.' Hailsham was equally opposed, but for rather different reasons. He felt the main objection to direct rule was that it would lead to the loss 'of all cooperation from all the Unionist MPs and some of our own supporters in the House, which might well jeopardise our EEC legislation'. Carrington, too, lined up with those who opposed the Prime Minister. From Heath's point of view it was bad enough to have to overrule some of his most trusted colleagues; it was still worse when the Leader of the Opposition approved his action. Wilson accepted without demur that direct rule was essential: he did not think that the Government should have a lot of difficulty with the Opposition about that, he assured Heath. It is a testimony to Heath's extraordinary authority within his Cabinet that, though qualms were freely expressed, direct rule was 'approved unanimously'.[25] (The word 'unanimously' indicates an absence of sustained opposition rather than positive approval; Heath prided himself on the fact that during his years as Prime Minister he had never found it necessary to have a vote in Cabinet.[26])

The objective, Heath told the Queen, was to achieve a settlement which would be 'acceptable to majority opinion in Northern Ireland and at the same time to a great body of moderate Catholic opinion on both sides of the border'. There would be no change in the status of Northern Ireland as part of the United Kingdom without the consent of the majority of the people, but changes must be made that would give the minority parties 'an active and permanent share in the decisions which shape ... the future of the Province'.[27] In the cauldron of seething hatred that was Ulster it was too much to hope that such benign sentiments would win general acceptance. The Roman Catholics, even the more moderate among them, would take a lot of convincing that a Tory Government in London had any serious intention of improving their lot at the expense of the Protestants who were, traditionally, the Conservatives' most loyal supporters. The Unionists were intensely suspicious of any legislation that seemed likely to threaten their privileged position. Whoever was made responsible for conjuring a settlement out of this unpromising material was going to have his work cut out.

The lot fell on Willie Whitelaw. It was an excellent choice. Patient when he had to be, affable, persistent, blessed with great stamina, with a sharp mind concealed behind a deceptively bland facade, he was as well equipped as anyone to take on the problems of Ulster. He had no illusions about the awfulness of his task. 'Of course, there is Ireland,' he had told David Butler a few weeks before:

> That can't do anything but get worse. It is those utterly impossible Unionists. They won't see reason and I fear it may come to direct rule ... But it has appalling side implications. Still, what can you do? We have absolutely no control over the policy of internment. We don't know who is interned and we cannot get explanations out of Stormont for why they are interned. We are put in a quite impossible position.

As Secretary of State for Northern Ireland his position was a little stronger than Maudling's had been as Home Secretary but he still had to deal with those 'utterly impossible Unionists'. Valiantly, he set about his task. David Hunt, a future Tory minister, visited Ulster in June and reported that already Whitelaw had achieved much. 'There appears to be a great fund of goodwill towards him, except among certain of the Unionist establishment. There are many among the

Catholics who see him as their only opportunity of achieving a peaceful and just society.' Yet even among the Unionists he had won a degree of acceptance; only the most bigoted denied that he was honest and well intentioned and had no wish to ride roughshod over their susceptibilities.[28]

The bigots were soon to be reinforced in their doubts. In mid-June 1972, the editor of the *Guardian*, Alastair Hetherington, recorded that Heath, speaking very much off the record, had told him that 'he didn't entirely rule out a meeting [with the IRA] in some circumstances'. We must take things as they come, Heath had said. Things duly came. A fortnight after Heath spoke to Hetherington the IRA declared a ceasefire and in July Whitelaw met a group of its leaders, including Gerry Adams. The meeting was a farce. The IRA representatives put forward demands which they knew to be unacceptable: the withdrawal of British forces from Northern Ireland, the release of all political prisoners. Possibly their only intention had been to embarrass the British Government; if so, they succeeded in their aim when they leaked news about the meeting to the press. 'Whitelaw's meeting with the IRA has destroyed his credibility,' Knox Cunningham told Macmillan. 'Confidence in him has gone. Some people blame him personally and do not realise that he could not have acted without Heath's approval.' Cunningham was a notorious diehard but Hailsham was almost equally indignant: 'Neither I nor the Cabinet were consulted about the talks with the IRA – in my view a disastrous error.' The fact that the ceasefire almost immediately broke down convinced him even more that he was right: 'This is a military situation and military means must have the priority.'[29]

Military means were obviously indispensable, but Heath sought to invoke the spiritual as well. In August 1971 he had complained about the Pope's failure to condemn the use of violence in Northern Ireland. If it was his purpose to 'invoke divine help in such conditions', then surely he should also 'condemn the devil and all his works'. The Duchess of Westminster was despatched to Rome, not as Heath's emissary but with his recommendation. She found that the Pope had little understanding of the facts of the case; indeed the only man in the Vatican who did was 'a coal black Bishop from Buganda'. The

Pope had seemed reasonably open-minded, however – so much so that Heath decided to make the pilgrimage himself. He visited the Vatican in October 1972 and urged the Pope to condemn violence and encourage those Roman Catholics who were hanging back from constitutional talks to join in the process. The Pope replied that he did already condemn violence and would continue to do so; he did not directly respond on the constitutional talks but made it clear he thought internment was a stumbling block. 'He himself had been brought up to regard Britain above all as the land of liberty. It was internment which for the time being qualified his admiration for world-renowned British justice.' Heath replied that 'he did not disagree. The sooner it could be got rid of the better.' In fact the Pope had been rather more forthcoming than Heath had expected: he condemned violence 'without the usual qualifications' and even discussed the text of his statement in advance with the British Minister to the Holy See.[30]

The Roman Catholics were reluctant to engage in talks, but the Unionists were little more cooperative. Early in 1973 Whitelaw reported to the Cabinet that Protestant armed violence was increasing: 'Although we do not seek a confrontation with the Protestants, we must be prepared to meet one and to demonstrate our determination to sustain law and order.' The Unionist leadership seemed increasingly unable to control its own extremist wing, let alone the Paisleyites and other still more fanatical splinter groups. Heath speculated how far it would be possible to maintain the present relationship between the Tories and the Ulster Unionists; Carrington urged that it should be suspended unless the Unionists put their house in order and, in particular, broke their formal links with the Orange Order.[31]

In Belfast Whitelaw battled on. A plebiscite in Northern Ireland showed that 58 per cent of the electorate actively supported the Union; the great majority of the Roman Catholics abstained. A White Paper was then issued, containing a plan for a new assembly with a power-sharing executive. With some reservations Faulkner agreed to make the best of a bad job and support the new proposals. An election was held in June and made painfully clear how complex and precarious the political balance was in Northern Ireland: Faulkner's

Unionists, with twenty-two seats, were the largest party but the SDLP was only just behind with nineteen and the Paisleyites had almost as many with eighteen. Whitelaw's task was to find some formula for power-sharing which would satisfy all or at least two of these groupings. If the Roman Catholic SDLP was not prepared to cooperate then the whole point of the exercise would have been lost; if the Paisleyites stayed aloof then there would be a very serious danger that they would draw support away from the official Unionists and, sooner rather than later, make the province ungovernable.

So far at least as the SDLP was concerned, Heath believed that the key lay in Dublin. The new Prime Minister of Ireland was Liam Cosgrave; not as affable and easygoing as Lynch but seemingly equally ready to make any settlement work provided it guaranteed a fair deal for the Roman Catholics in Ulster. Cosgrave came to London shortly after his election in March 1973. When he pressed Heath for an assurance that power-sharing would in fact mean what the words suggested, the Prime Minister replied that the British Government would insist that the new executive could not be based 'upon any single party, if that party drew its support and its representatives virtually entirely from one section of a divided community'. Since all the parties laboured under this disadvantage, it would be hard to find a more specific guarantee. Heath did not pretend that all would be plain sailing: 'It was possible that there would be a complete breakdown of normal life in Northern Ireland ... and that there would be extensive industrial action by Protestant workers. But the UK Government were prepared to face up to this situation.' Cosgrave for his part promised to try to get rid of the articles in the Irish Constitution which laid down that Ulster was an integral part of the Irish Republic. He overestimated his powers. When it came to the point his ministers revolted at what they saw as a surrender to the dictates of Westminster. Nobody took the articles very seriously – the Irish Government would probably have been dismayed if it had been required to absorb an economically precarious and largely Protestant Ulster – but their continued existence strengthened the will of those sections of the Unionist Party which feared any appeasement of the Catholics as being a step towards reunification.[32]

Their suspicions were fanned when Heath paid a return visit to Dublin in September. His main purpose was to discuss the creation of a Council of Ireland, in which Ulster and the Republic could discuss issues of common interest. The need for such an organisation was obvious; the possibility that it might be the seed from which would eventually grow a united government was no less apparent to those apprehensive of such a tendency. Cosgrave was interested in Heath's ideas but doubtful what more he could do to help. There was not that much either of them could do, said Heath; it was up to the parties in Northern Ireland. 'At this the Taoiseach's gloom perceptibly lightened. He agreed with the Prime Minister, and said he thought they had got about as far as they could go together.'[33]

Whitelaw still had a lot more to do. Against all the odds he did it. The wave of violence which had followed the IRA's renunciation of their ceasefire seemed, at least temporarily, to have subsided. The confidence of the moderates had to some extent been restored. But the Paisleyites remained as intransigent as ever and the parties which, in principle, were prepared to engage in power-sharing found it impossible to agree on an apportionment of the offices. With endless patience and ingenuity Whitelaw tried formula after formula, cajoling at one moment, threatening to break off negotiations at another. At times he was near despair, then the log-jam yielded and in November 1973 he was able to announce that provisional agreement had been reached. Heath led the Cabinet in congratulating him on a remarkable achievement. It was important, he said, that the significance of Whitelaw's success for Northern Ireland and for the UK should be recognised in the country and in Parliament. 'We should not, however,' he warned, 'give the impression that this is the end of the problem, and in particular we should avoid any suggestion that violence was likely to come to a very early end.'[34]

To set the seal upon this accord, a conference, to be attended by the Irish Government as well as the cooperating parties from Northern Ireland, was summoned to take place at the Civil Service College in Sunningdale at the beginning of December. 'This has now been going on for more than 400 years, so do not be depressed if you do not solve everything by the end of the weekend,' wrote Lord

Hailsham. Faulkner made no attempt to disguise his distaste for the whole proceedings; the one man in the British Government in whom he still had confidence, Willie Whitelaw, had been moved to another job a few weeks earlier, and though he was not prepared to torpedo the proceedings he intended, short of that, to be as difficult as possible. Ian Paisley, a corpulent would-be skeleton at the feast, turned up at Sunningdale and demanded admission. His intention could only be to bluster and condemn; Heath refused him entry to the hall. Things went a little better after the first day, at the end of which the delegates were bundled into buses and swept off to Downing Street for a gala dinner. The Martin Neary Singers sang suitable songs after dinner and drink flowed in abundance. 'By the end of the choral performance,' wrote Faulkner, 'some of those present were becoming more informal than I think Heath had intended. Loud calls of "Give us a song, Paddy" were heard, but Heath skilfully diverted any possible embarrassment by leading us into another room for more coffee and sober conversation.' If rollicking informality on Thursday night meant easier going in the conference next day, Heath would have felt the price well worth paying. One of the SDLP members told him that the only time he had been in Downing Street before had been when he was lying on the pavement outside Number 10 in a protest demonstration. He found this visit a great deal jollier.[35]

The problems still had to be solved. It is a measure of the impossible pressures under which a modern prime minister must labour that, even though he was desperately anxious for the negotiations to succeed and believed that his presence was an important factor, Heath still had to absent himself for a few hours to conduct talks with and preside at a dinner for the Italian Prime Minister, Mariano Rumor. He returned to find that little progress had been made. At 2 a.m. the Irish Prime Minister stormed off to bed. 'It's not because of you or the conference,' he told Heath, 'but my people have become impossible. There's no point in staying up with them.' First thing the following morning, Faulkner announced that he was flying back to Belfast to go to church. His colleagues showed no great enthusiasm for this proposition and Heath left for another meeting with Rumor without knowing what scene of carnage he would find at his return.[36] Instead, things had moved miraculously closer to a settlement. A Council of Ireland with a permanent secretariat was set up. The Irish Government agreed that there would be no change in the status of Northern Ireland unless a majority of its inhabitants desired it. Direct rule would end on 1 January 1974. It had taken four hundred years, as Hailsham had pointed out, but the Irish problem was finally solved.

It stayed finally solved for about two months. Faulkner was quickly deposed and, in the election of February 1974, the pro-Sunningdale Unionists were virtually extinguished. Cosgrave's undertaking on the future of Ulster was challenged in the Irish courts and disallowed. It was back to square one. And yet it was not. The principles that had been thrashed out before and at Sunningdale were not to be forgotten. Sunningdale had shown that an agreement on these lines was possible; when circumstances changed it could be dusted down and tried again. It would be an over-simplification to say that, without Sunningdale, there would have been no Good Friday Agreement, but the link between the two is palpable.

Not everyone praised Heath's role in the negotiations. Heath 'is very arrogant', wrote Cecil King in his diary. 'He has decided what is best for Northern Ireland and is indignant and angry that the Ulstermen are not grateful and acquiescent.'[37] There is a shred of truth in this. Heath was always reluctant to modify his policies so as to accommodate the irrational. But with the benefit of hindsight it is possible to see that he was right and that the Ulstermen were wrong. He had his vision, and he fought for it with courage and pertinacity. Whitelaw was the hero on the field, who bore the brunt of the battle, but without Heath there could have been no Whitelaw and it would have been a different battlefield.

SIXTEEN

Choppy Water

Heath believed himself to be one of the great reforming prime ministers. He was certain that, given another few years in office, he would have transformed the working of government and the structure of society. The boast is not wholly idle, but the word 'modernise' is perhaps more suitable to the cast of his mind than the bold 'reformer'. Apart from the great leap into Europe, his preoccupation was to make things work. He loathed inefficiency or any kind of sloppiness; sometimes it almost seemed as if he would rather be in charge of a smoothly working vehicle proceeding in the wrong direction than a faulty one going the right way. *Private Eye* parodied his style and government as Heathco Ltd, rule by a series of banal injunctions pinned to the office wall. The injunctions were, in fact, seldom banal, but the image conjured up of a strictly businesslike approach, short on humanity and entirely devoid of humour, is uncomfortably apt. Brian Reading, his independent-minded economic guru, perceptively summed up the situation: 'It was as if people had been mowing some grass with an old and rusty lawnmower for years and years and never getting anywhere. And Mr Heath was quite determined that he was going to change all this by looking much further and making fundamental changes. The big problem, of course, was that he had to stop mowing the grass while he was making the changes and the heavens opened, the world situation changed, while he was sharpening the lawnmower. The grass became impossible to mow.'[1]

Heath was no iconoclast but he did not respect tradition for the sake of tradition. If some time-hallowed observance impeded the course of progress, then it must go. When Labour proposed to abolish the ancient ritual by which Black Rod interrupted the proceedings of the House of Commons, Heath said he saw no reason for the Tories to object. An agonised Enoch Powell pleaded that this had been done, certainly since 1306 and probably for two centuries before that. 'This is exactly the sort of thing that does us so much harm,' retorted Heath. 'People simply do not understand that mumbo-jumbo.'[2]

But he wished to destroy because something better could be put in its place; if what was there was working satisfactorily then he was happy to leave it undisturbed. He was a convinced monarchist and would not have contemplated dispensing with court ritual – mumbo-jumbo though it might be. He valued highly his relationship with the Queen. David Butler asked him whether he found his weekly audiences rewarding. 'Oh yes,' he said, 'and besides, the Queen is very interested and has a wide correspondence overseas, particularly on overseas stuff she is very useful, and then there is more to it than that. You can speak with complete confidentiality to her. You can say things that you would not say even to your Number Two.' Rupert Allason, in his as yet unpublished biography of Heath, claims that the Queen's private secretary, Michael Adeane, found it necessary to prepare agendas for the audiences so as to avoid awkward silences, and refers to an exchange of 'terse notes' between Robert Armstrong and Adeane's successor, Martin Charteris, when Number 10 blocked a reference to the current economic crisis which the Queen wanted to include in her Christmas message for 1973. Since the time of Alan Lascelles, at least, every royal private secretary has conferred with the private secretary at Number 10 as to what matters their employers might most usefully discuss (whether their employers stuck to this agenda was another matter). Robert Armstrong can remember no exchange of 'terse notes' with Martin Charteris (a man anyway singularly disinclined to terseness), and says that the Prime Minister considered the Queen's Christmas message to be her own affair about which he did not need to be formally consulted and on which he would never have done more than offer a tentative suggestion if he had been.[3] 'By common repute,' writes Hugo Young, Heath was the only prime minister with whom 'the monarch never succeeded in developing an easy relationship ... a failing which gave Her Majesty something in common with much of the human race.' Heath was no easy conversationalist and it would have been surprising if the Queen had not found her audiences slipped by more easily with the affable, chatty and extraordinarily reverential Harold Wilson. It does not follow that she esteemed Heath any the less. Lady Adeane told Heath that her husband had said: 'He is wonderfully in with the Royals – they are all potty about him.' The evidence she adduced – 'I saw the Queen again yesterday and she said "I had no idea the PM was so good at golf"' – is not totally conclusive, but Heath certainly had an exceptionally warm relationship with the Queen Mother, and even when negotiations over the Civil List involved difficult dealings between Buckingham Palace and Number 10, his relationship with the Queen was never less than harmonious.[4]

The Church was another ancient institution which Heath had no wish to reform. While Prime Minister he recommended forty-five men to the Queen to be diocesan or suffragan bishops and believed that they were better appointments than they would have been if the choice had been left entirely to the Church. Sometimes he overruled the Church's own recommendation. The London vacancy-in-see committee had shortlisted Graham Leonard to be Bishop of London. Heath preferred Gerald Ellison. The committee was displeased but the Archbishop of Canterbury, Michael Ramsey, privately thought that Heath had made the better choice. Though his political views were very different, Ramsey had a high opinion of Heath: 'I felt him to be a man of integrity,' he remarked, 'an impression which I repeatedly got.' When Heath decided to give a dinner for the Roman Catholic bishops, John Hewitt, his adviser on such matters in Number 10, was dismayed. Ramsey, however, thoroughly approved of the proposal and said that he would attend; furthermore he insisted that, on such an occasion, the Cardinal Archbishop should take precedence and sit on the Prime Minister's right. The problem as to who should say Grace was more complex: Heath solved it by doing the job himself. Even when the Church was concerned, however,

Heath's urge to modernise still occasionally prevailed. When a suffragan see under Winchester was established it was proposed to call it Silchester. Heath judged this to be intolerably olde-world; he opted for the less euphonious but more accurate Basingstoke.[5]

His inclination was always to apply his blunt cost-effective approach to questions concerning the arts. He chose the Grosvenor House Antiques Fair in 1971 as the venue for a speech in which he urged the case for allowing works of art to leave the country: 'We have benefited so much in the past from treasures which have come from other lands. It seems to me a somewhat narrow view that in no circumstances should they ever leave our shores.' His audience of dealers no doubt shared this opinion but the public reaction was rather different when it seemed that Lord Harewood's Titian might leave the country. The National Gallery launched an appeal to save it but Heath agreed with the Minister for the Arts, David Eccles, that it would be inappropriate for the Government to contribute. This view would certainly have prevailed if the decision had not been called for at a moment when the Government was on the point of imposing entry charges on museums and galleries. They were already being denounced as vandals, Barber warned Heath; if they were obdurate over the Titian as well the art world would be united in condemning them. Heath could have endured such a fate with resignation if not equanimity, but he was convinced by Barber that the storm of protest would be out of proportion to the saving involved. Reluctantly the Prime Minister agreed that, in the circumstances, there would have to be some special grant. The Chancellor eventually agreed that the Government would match pound for pound whatever was raised by public appeal.[6]

The Titian was saved; free entry to the museums was not. Heath refused to accept that 'there is some over-ruling principle which demands that access to national museums and galleries should be available without any charge'. People who used museums should contribute to their upkeep, just as they did for subsidised drama and music. His only concession was that a proportion of what was raised should be devoted to the arts: a move that seemed reprehensible to the Treasury, who felt that the measure was only part of a campaign to reduce public expenditure and that to allocate the proceeds to some specific cause would be contrary to good practice. When the time came to fix a tariff for admissions Heath was displeased by Eccles's proposal that 10p would be appropriate. This would have brought in some £1m a year. 'This seems a very small amount to raise,' complained Heath. 'How do these charges compare with those abroad?' He supported the Treasury when they pressed for 20p, but eventually agreed to a compromise whereby admission would cost 20p in July and August, the foreign tourist season, and 10p for the rest of the year.[7] When the Minister of Agriculture proposed abolishing the derisory 3d. entry charge for Kew Gardens, Heath commented that 'the real question is whether this fee ought not to be put up to a reasonable sum'. But firm though his convictions were, he held other things still more sacred. It emerged that in certain cases works of art had been left to the nation with a specific requirement that these should be available to visitors free of charge. 'I support charges but dislike over-ruling wills,' minuted Heath.[8]

His personal passions were from time to time indulged. Some papers about the proposed development of the Royal Opera House were sent to Number 10 with the comment that Robert Armstrong might like to glance at them but that they were not 'sufficiently important to bother the PM with'. Armstrong knew better, and passed them up to Heath. 'v.important. Please keep me informed,' was the Prime Minister's instruction.[9] He was unenthusiastic when it came to commemorating himself on canvas, however. In October 1970 the Carlton Club wished to commission a portrait of him and asked him to propose an artist, with the proviso that they were hoping for something 'fairly traditional'. Heath delayed answering for some time, then suggested that Graham Sutherland would be an exciting choice though probably he would be too expensive. Otherwise he suggested Peter Greenham, David Hockney ('a young up-and-coming painter'), Ruskin Spear and Carel Weight. At John Hewitt's suggestion, Anna Zinkeisen was added to the list. Greenham was eventually chosen but it proved hard to fit in sittings and in September 1971 the artist asked if there could be a further delay because 'he thinks you have changed colour over the summer and would prefer to wait until you return to the same shade as you were during his earlier sittings'. 'I prefer my present colour!' wrote Heath, but it was still nearly a year before there was another opportunity to continue work.[10] Things went even worse when it came to commissioning a portrait for the National Portrait Gallery. Here again, Heath specified Sutherland as the ideal painter and, as an alternative, Lucian Freud. Both artists refused the commission; it is said because they feared he would prove too cantankerous a sitter. Various other names were put forward and rejected and in the end Heath remained unpainted. The portrait he himself liked best was an informal study by Derek Hill showing him rugged and windswept, evidently embarking on or returning from some nautical adventure. It is this portrait that is now in the National Portrait Gallery.

The sale of the Harewood Titian was not the only occasion on which Heath recognised that public opinion must be considered. When Keith Joseph proposed to increase prescription charges, Douglas Hurd pointed out that this would 'run counter to our general philosophy of concentrating help on those in greatest need', would give a weapon to the Labour Party and would anyway save very little. 'There is much truth in this,' minuted Heath, and in Cabinet argued that it was important to avoid anything that might smack of 'a callous attempt to undermine the foundations on which the National Health Service was built'. Joseph was told to think again.[11] Nor was it only British susceptibilities that he considered. When the Governor of the Bank of England sent him a specimen of a new £5 note, Heath deprecated the design on the reverse which seemed to show French soldiers in flight before advancing redcoats. It was, he pointed out, 'not quite suited to our new European image' – a case of the Bayeux tapestry in reverse.[12] Sometimes he even invoked the arts of the spin doctor. In December 1970 Hurd had drafted for his signature a memorandum to all cabinet ministers, pointing out that the next few months were going to be difficult politically. The timing and impact of government announcements must be carefully considered:

The guiding principle must be that the best use should be made of every positive piece of news, however small. I should be grateful if all Ministers would consider what positive decisions within their jurisdiction could be taken and announced within this period … When a series of positive decisions are possible they should obviously be spread over a period. Conversely, decisions which are likely to be unpopular should be concentrated on one day.

A private secretary urged that this should not be circulated but used as a speaking brief: 'Documents of this kind nearly always leak.' Nobody questioned, however, whether this manipulation of material was desirable or proper.[13]

In principle Heath was in favour of open government. When William Waldegrave, from the Think Tank, put forward a paper arguing that all facts and analyses used by the Government should be published in full unless there were compelling reasons not to do so, Robert Armstrong suggested that this was 'too extreme and not workable'. 'All this is most interesting. I urge an *early* discussion,' minuted Heath, and insisted that he should take the chair of a group set up to thrash out the matter.[14] Waldegrave's dashing proposals were not put into practice but a junior minister, Geoffrey Johnson Smith, was appointed to watch over all presentational matters. When it came to unauthorised leaks from within the Government, however, Heath took a wholly different view. One of his sharpest criticisms of Wilson's administration had been that it could keep nothing secret. Shortly after taking office he circulated a stern memorandum complaining that there had been premature disclosures of the Government's intentions: 'All Ministers are responsible for enforcing confidentiality on their staffs.'[15] Yet occasionally he strayed himself. When Donald Maitland was told that a senior minister had disclosed to the editor of *The Times* that an important initiative on Northern Ireland was to be announced on the following day, he took it for granted that the Prime Minister would be outraged. So did Robert Armstrong, who drafted a memorandum to send to the private secretaries of the various ministers, asking if it was their master who had been responsible. Discuss first with Burke Trend, instructed Heath: 'I suppose that it ought to be enquired into, but it's a bore.' Enquiries yielded no results and after a fortnight Armstrong suggested that there did not seem to be much point in carrying the matter any further. 'I think this is true: drop it,' agreed Heath. The following day Armstrong wrote again: 'I now learn that the Minister concerned was the Prime Minister ... William [Rees Mogg] must have read more than was intended into what you said ... The question of a leak enquiry falls.' Heath was partly shamefaced, partly amused: it is at least to his credit that he bore Armstrong no grudge for his embarrassment.[16]

When it came to ministerial memoirs he inclined to the liberal view. Public servants, certainly, should be 'under instructions not to publish memoirs', but as to ministers, 'the convention against publication of memoirs shortly after leaving office has now broken down, and I do not see how it could be re-established'. He would have gone even further and relieved the Secretary of the Cabinet of the duty of scrutinising ministerial memoirs in draft, but here the Cabinet felt he was going too far and the procedure was left formally unchanged. As to the literary efforts of ministers while in office, the official doctrine was that these would cause no problem provided that they were 'of a literary, historical, scientific, philosophic or fictional character'. What does 'literary' mean? asked Heath. Does it cover music? Should the word be 'artistic'? On the question of payment for 'non-official' broadcasts, Trend pointed out that any invitation to a minister to broadcast must stem from the fact that he or she was in the Government. 'Not at all,' retorted Heath. 'My sailing and music are *sui generis*.'[17]

In this, as in every other aspect of government, his philosophy always was that individual liberty should be restricted only if it was manifestly damaging to society. When he called on the Pope late in 1972, Paul VI deplored the ravages caused by the permissive society. The British Government should take a more active role in checking these abuses: 'Homosexuality and abortion were aspects of life over which the Government should have some control.' Heath agreed politely, but gave no indication that he planned any new legislation to meet these needs: 'At least in the UK we face a less serious problem as regards drugs than in many other countries, and drugs are the worst aspect of all so far as the permissive society is concerned.' When Peter Walker sponsored a private bill to curb events such as pop concerts which disturbed the neighbourhood at night, the Young

Conservatives protested that it would lose their party the youth vote and, anyway, would not work. I quite agree, wrote Heath: 'It's a monstrous bill.' Adrian Boult urged him to ban smoking in theatres and restaurants; Heath was sympathetic but believed: 'The best way of changing public attitudes to smoking is by education and information, rather than legislation.' He offered a crumb of comfort, however: 'You will be glad to know that, by agreement, no smoking of any kind is permitted at Cabinet meetings.'[18]

His revulsion from unnecessary restrictive legislation did not imply inactivity over environmental issues. One of his first acts as Prime Minister was to tell Julian Amery, at the new Department of the Environment, to put in hand a programme for cleaning public buildings. 'Although we are now doing things to prevent the environment becoming worse,' he asked in June 1971, 'is there not a big scheme we could propose actually to make it better?' The Department listed what was being done. That's fine, said Heath. It should be publicised. He then raised another question 'What about Ralph Nader's criticism of British cars on grounds of pollution as well as safety?' Unsurprisingly, the environmental issues which most affected him personally were the ones which he most vigorously pursued. He was incensed by the delays he endured on his way to Chequers because of roadworks on the Western Avenue. Could these works not be speeded up, he asked; it was not just he who was affected but hundreds of thousands of other commuters. The Department produced the programme for the works and said that it was being rigorously adhered to. 'It is sheer nonsense to say that it takes six months to flatten a roundabout,' Heath protested. 'Any serious group of people could do it in a weekend.' It was all a question of cost, the Department explained. They were under instructions to do the work as cheaply as possible, and speeding up the operation would make it more expensive. 'Social costs as well as financial costs should be taken into account,' grumbled the Prime Minister, before he regretfully subsided.[19]

He was equally ready to be an interventionist when it came to the rights of women. He did not get much support from the woman member of his Cabinet. In July 1970 he asked Mrs Thatcher's advice about how to answer a parliamentary question on the future of the

Women's National Commission and the need for legislation on sexual discrimination. The Commission was expensive and a waste of time, replied the Minister for Education. Her draft answer concluded: 'I have no proposals to make for legislation on the question of discrimination.' Heath felt that this was too negative and substituted: 'In all our policies the Government will bear in mind the needs of women.' He pursued the matter, enquiring into the action taken on the recommendations of the Cripps Committee, 'Fair Shares for the Fair Sex'. 'It is v.important to be able to report progress on this front,' he minuted in September 1970. 'Good. Keep up the pressure,' he commented three months later when told of the recommendations that had been implemented. A little later on he minuted that he hoped officials would 'move quickly to improve the position of the deserted wife'. It was due to his initiative that a Committee on Women's Rights was set up, which produced the proposals for legislation contained in the Consultative Document 'Equal Opportunities for Men and Women'.[20]

Heath regretted the fact that Mrs Thatcher showed so little concern for the less forceful members of her sex, but there is no reason to believe that he thought his Minister of Education was other than a highly competent departmental minister with an irritating tendency to talk too much in Cabinet. She for her part described the first Cabinet meeting in mildly mocking terms. 'Speaking with the same intensity which had suffused his introduction to the manifesto ... he announced his intention of establishing a new style of administration and a fresh approach to the conduct of public business ... There was to be a clean break and a fresh start and new brooms galore.' At the time she was probably rather more impressed. Certainly the Cabinet as a whole was loyal to Heath and, indeed, remained so until the end. At times he treated individual ministers roughly. When Geoffrey Howe, at a ministerial meeting at Chequers, expressed some doubts about the proposed counter-inflationary policy, Heath said contemptuously that he saw no need to waste time on the philosophical maunderings of the 'Minister for keeping down prices'.[21] Peter Walker prepared a paper recommending heavy investment in the steel programme. Heath disliked the proposals. 'I am quite certain that we shall not be foolish enough to accept them,' he told the Cabinet, continuing: 'Secretary of State, I ask you to introduce your paper.' But though he did not welcome opposition, he equally did not resent it. 'He is not a bully by nature,' one cabinet member told Nigel Fisher. He saw it as his role to challenge ministers whose conclusions required defending, so 'it was better to fight your own corner and argue your case if you disagreed with him'. Walker did just that and, after much further debate, 'Ted said in a gruff voice, "Well, I suppose you'd better get on with it," and walked out of the room.' Sometimes ministers were left bruised and affronted, but on the whole members of the Cabinet felt they had had a fair hearing and that, if they had a good case and were prepared to defend it tenaciously, in the end they would prevail.[22]

Any illusions Heath may have had that he would be allowed peacefully to apply his policies were quickly dispelled. Almost before he had moved into Downing Street the dockers came out on strike. 'It is essential that the Government should not give the impression of weakness or hesitancy,' Heath told the Cabinet. On this occasion, as on many others, the hesitancy related only to the degree of weakness that should be shown. The Government assumed emergency powers – the first of five such occasions while Heath was in power. It was a fine, dramatic gesture but only a preamble to their setting up an inquiry to consider the dockers' claims. The inquiry recommended a pay rise which, though less than the dockers had originally demanded, was substantially more than the employers had been prepared to offer. The Government accepted it with alacrity and considerable relief. 'This was not the time or the issue for a bruising struggle,' Heath wrote in his memoirs. But he knew well that the struggle had only been deferred. The reform of industrial relations 'was of the first importance', he pronounced as soon as the strike was over. 'Its preparation and management in Parliament will require an intensive and determined effort.' He had as yet hardly begun to suspect that parliamentary approval would only be the beginning of the story and that a still more intensive and determined effort would be needed to enforce the legislation once it was through.[23]

In rather ostentatious contrast to Harold Wilson, who had started his term in office with a flurry of activity, Heath despatched most of his ministers on their summer holidays and himself spent most of July and August 1970 aboard *Morning Cloud*. His detachment was more assumed than real. When a supporter wrote to protest at the Prime Minister's neglect of his duties, Douglas Hurd replied that Heath on holiday 'had been dealing with a volume of work equivalent, I suppose, to anything that most people deal with in an ordinary working day. Boxes of Government papers have been sent to him nearly every day, and current decisions are regularly referred to him by teleprinter.' But Hurd still felt it necessary to show this exchange to Heath, as an illustration of a 'mood of disillusionment and some impatience for Government action, particularly to curb inflation ... We are in some danger of being forced on the defensive.'[24] Heath had no intention of making any major policy statement himself before the party conference in October, but he accepted the need not only for the Government to be active but for it to be seen to be active. Priority, he was clear, must be given to the economy and the unions. But, as was so often to happen, his efforts to concentrate on what he felt to be most important were frustrated by an unexpected and urgent crisis.

Early in September Arab terrorists set out to hijack four airliners. One attempt failed, the plane landed at Heathrow and the surviving terrorist, Leila Khaled, was arrested. The hijackers added her name to the list of those whom they demanded should be exchanged for the several hundred hostages they now held; for good measure they hijacked another, British, aircraft to add to their tally. The first thing to decide was whether Leila Khaled, who had committed her crime on an Israeli plane outside British airspace, could be tried in a British court. The Attorney General, Peter Rawlinson, decided that she could not. Heath was subsequently accused of having brought pressure on Rawlinson to reach this conclusion. 'The decision whether to prosecute ... was for me, and for me alone,' the Attorney General insisted. Heath 'played no part in the decision. He personally was not consulted.' From that point, however, the Prime Minister took personal charge of the operation. Norman Collins, the broadcaster and author, indeed suggested that his charge was too personal; he made important decisions without even informing, let alone consulting, Alec Douglas-Home. No offence seems to have been taken in the Foreign Office. Heath handled the business with considerable aplomb. The fact that Leila Khaled could not have been tried in Britain was discreetly ignored until the negotiations were over; she was a valuable bargaining counter and as such must appear to be at risk of prosecution. The terrorists' refusal to let any of the Israeli hostages go until a large number of Palestinian prisoners had been released at first seemed a serious stumbling bloc, but ceased to be a problem when it transpired that there were in fact no Israeli hostages. Heath made a personal appeal to Nasser, who seems to have been instrumental in pushing through a deal – Leila Khaled was deported and the hostages were freed. But Heath – with his own right wing at least – earned little credit for his diplomacy. As Enoch Powell and Duncan Sandys saw it, there had been a surrender to terrorism, a criminal caught red-handed had been released to meet the demands of kidnappers. Heath's conduct, wrote Norman Tebbit, had 'cast a doubt over the Government's determination not to compromise vital principles to avoid short-term problems'. Heath could endure with equanimity the abuse of the Powellites but the affair still had damaging consequences for his long-term survival. He was so angered by the zest with which the lobby correspondents reported right-wing denunciations of his cowardice that, in James Margach's words, he 'more or less broke off relations with the political corps'. His estrangement from those journalists who were primarily concerned with reporting his day-to-day activities was in time to do grave damage to his reputation.[25]

It was already clear that the right wing of the Tory Party was suspicious of the Prime Minister and ready to denounce any straying from the path of rectitude. Rhodes Boyson, the member for Brent North, sent him a copy of *Right Turn*, a tract published by the Constitutional Book Club, of which he was a director. 'Another fairly rubbishy book,' wrote Hurd contemptuously. 'There are now at least three publishing houses newly active in this extreme right-wing field, and I imagine they will give a fair amount of trouble.'[26] For the moment, however, they bided their time, approving in principle the rigorous cutting of costs which was the Government's first line of attack in the war to reanimate the economy. Public expenditure must be drastically reduced, ruled Heath: 'This would require a willingness among Ministers to accept reductions in programmes which from a purely Departmental point of view they would be reluctant to make.' But he had in mind more than the mere trimming of budgets, what he demanded was 'a radical review of the services which the Government should provide with the aim of withdrawal from spheres which firms and individuals could more appropriately provide for themselves'. The Ministry of Technology (shortly to be subsumed into the new giant Department of Trade and Industry) was a prime target for retrenchment; the cuts 'would preclude the Government from continuing to provide support for individual private firms which might find themselves in difficulty, however strong the pressures to do so might be'. Many of the projects which the Department had in mind might be desirable, 'but we could not afford everything that was desirable and, in general, it was right to expect industry to stand on its own feet'.[27] Here, indeed, was everything the right wing was hoping for; here Heath expounded the vital principles which, as Tebbit saw it, he would soon compromise to avoid short-term problems. From across the Atlantic Nixon applauded his efforts. 'Bold, gutsy and right,' he called the proposals. 'There is of course a political risk in taking such controversial steps. But the alternative would have been to let Britain continue to slide into a second place position as an economic and political power.'[28]

Heath took an axe, too, to the jungle of committees and advisory bodies which had been allowed to proliferate over the previous decade. At his behest William Armstrong produced a startlingly long list of advisory bodies. 'I hope that you will challenge every activity, using the most rigorous tests that you can devise,' instructed Heath. He was gratified to hear a few months later that 197 bodies, two-thirds of which were the responsibility of the Ministry of Agriculture, had been abolished or proposed for abolition. Encouraged, he began to campaign to reduce the number and size of cabinet committees. Burke Trend commented that every minister always complained about the number of committees he had to attend yet none could suggest committees at which his presence was not essential. He was happy to cooperate in a pruning process, 'but it may not be quite as easy as you make it seem'. When the Prime Minister complained about the immense amount of time needed to get any decision out of Whitehall, Trend cited several examples of rapid and fruitful deliberations but admitted that these were all cases in which Heath personally had intervened and taken charge. This might sometimes be essential, he said, but 'leads to an American model, with the White House separate from the executive department'. It was disconcerting for Heath, one of whose main preoccupations was to distance himself discreetly from the White House, to have to admit that in some ways they did things better in Washington.[29]

Heath formally unveiled the policies of the new Government at the party conference in October. They were as acceptable to his right wing as had been his pronouncements in Cabinet: a reorganisation of the functions of government, cuts in expenditure, the encouragement of businesses and individuals to stand on their own feet, the curbing of inflation by resisting extravagant pay demands. His peroration was a worthy conclusion to what was, in oratorical terms at least, the best speech he delivered as Prime Minister: 'If we are to achieve this task we will have to embark on a change so radical, a revolution so quiet and yet so total, that it will go far beyond the programme for a Parliament to which we are committed and on which we have already embarked; far beyond this decade and way into the 1980s ... We can only hope to begin now what future Conservative Governments will continue and complete. We are laying the foundations, but they are the foundations for a generation.' For several years the party had doubted whether they had chosen wisely in making Heath their leader; even at that moment there were suspicions among the more recalcitrant of his supporters; but on 10 October 1970, in Blackpool, he quickened the pulse of the Conservative Party more effectively than he had done before or was ever to do again.

He also misled them about his true intentions. He meant every word he said but he did not accept the consequences which part of his audience at least believed must flow from his argument. There was a splendid imprecision about his words, which conveyed a message more right-wing, more Selsdonian, than a strict analysis of his text could justify. It was, indeed, his Minister of Technology, John Davies, who spelt out the non-interventionist creed at which the Prime Minister had merely hinted. Davies reserved for the House of Commons a month later the pledge that the Government would not support 'lame ducks' – companies that could not survive without assistance from the state – but in Blackpool he declared with emphasis that they were not in the business of propping up failures. His appointment had suggested to Enoch Powell that a retreat to an interventionist industrial policy might be intended. Possibly the knowledge that he had this reputation led Davies to play the right-wing card with greater energy. 'Perhaps John was trying too hard to prove his credentials, and those of the Government,' suggested Heath.[30] At all events, he gave several hostages to fortune which fortune, as is its way, was in due course to deploy with some brutality.

Having appointed a lightweight as Chancellor, Heath had no intention of standing back and leaving him to run the economy. Terence Higgins, Minister of State at the Treasury, denied that, for the first two or three years at any rate, Heath was 'in prime charge of economic policy'. He took little interest in the tax structure, argued Higgins, and left the preparation of the budgets to Barber. So far as the detailed working of the Treasury was concerned, that was certainly true. He had neither the time nor the knowledge nor the inclination to intervene in such matters. But that is not incompatible with the judgment of Leslie O'Brien, Governor of the Bank of England, that Heath took 'a larger and stronger part in economic affairs than any PM of recent years'. O'Brien, as early as November 1970, told Cecil King that an incomes policy, under some guise, would be essential, 'but Heath is very headstrong and when he has stated his decision tends to press on regardless'. He was right about Heath's readiness to interfere, but overestimated Heath's commitment to market forces as the sole legitimate means of shaping the economy. Heath was far from being a committed monetarist. When the high priest of monetarism, Professor Milton Friedman, called at Number 10 in September 1970, Heath said he did not believe monetary measures alone could solve the problems of growth: 'There were barnacles on the economy, in the form of incompetent and uncompetitive companies, restrictive trade union practices and so on.' Friedman suggested that these could best be removed by competition. Heath was unimpressed. He had found Friedman 'wholly unconvincing', he told Keith Joseph's biographers.[31]

Inflation was the economic problem that most concerned him. A high proportion of the letters from the public which arrived in Number 10 in the six months after the election expressed worry about the rising cost of living and regret that the Government had done so little to combat it. In a way Heath had brought this on himself. In the election campaign he had sanctioned, or at least failed to veto, a press release which had rashly claimed that Conservative policies would 'reduce prices at a stroke'. In context this meant only that, by abolishing or reducing Selective Employment Tax and other such imposts, the Government would reduce the rate by which inflation was growing. No politician, however, can expect to have his sound bites considered in context and when, six months after the election, prices were still rising, his supporters were left with a sense that they had been let down. Heath was caught between the Scylla of creating a sense of panic and the Charybdis of seeming to take things too casually: ministers, he told the Cabinet, 'should seek to convey ... that the country is confronted by a problem of wage inflation which has very serious implications; but that we were not facing an imminent threat of economic disaster'. Even before the end of 1970 he had begun to envisage government interference in the business of the market: 'Without departing from the Government's economic strategy, effective action must now be taken promptly to curb wage inflation.' The Electricity Council, the latest public body to be faced by extravagant wage demands, should be asked to restrict its offer to less than 10 per cent. If it showed signs of faltering, 'the Council might have to be issued with a formal instruction'. To the monetarists in the Cabinet, such an instruction would, by definition, be a departure from the Government's avowed economic strategy. It was the first of many nasty shocks which they were to suffer over the next two or three years.[32]

Barber's mini-budget quickly followed the party conference. He announced cuts totalling £331m for the following year. Ironically, the most controversial of these fell to the minister who had fought most fiercely to preserve her department's budget. Maurice Macmillan, who was managing the operation for the Treasury, insisted that the Open University was a prime target for cancellation. Mrs Thatcher pleaded that it was a critically important part of national education and that it should not only be maintained but expanded. Heath, though still sceptical about the merits of her case, found in her favour, nevertheless urging the minister to consider whether there should be an increase in the fees.[33] As a sop to the Treasury, Thatcher conceded that free milk should no longer be issued to schoolchildren aged between eight and eleven. A howl of outrage followed and the minister was demonised as 'Mrs Thatcher, milk snatcher'. It was unfair but predictable. Heath resisted any temptation he might have felt to let his minister stew in her own milk and defended her valiantly against charges that she was unfeeling or indifferent to the needs of the under-privileged.

One problem for Heath was that, although the unions with their extravagant wage demands seemed to him the greatest threat to economic stability, he found the business world equally irrational and rather more distasteful. Campbell Adamson, the Director General of the Confederation of British Industry (CBI), admitted to feeling that Heath 'loved the trade unionists more than he loved the industrialists. And not only did he consider them by far the more important partner but actually he even seemed at times to be more able to agree with them than with his own kind, as it were.' This overstates the case. It was more that Heath expected the trade unionists to be irrational; he hoped for better things from the industrialists and was correspondingly more disappointed when they failed to perform. Repeatedly he denounced their timidity and their failure to invest in the future. One of his close policy advisers told Martin Holmes that he had attended a large number of dinners at which industrialists met the Prime Minister and 'he always abused them, he never got on with them'. The eminent industrialist Sir Emmanuel Kaye was summoned to Number 10 to advise Heath on the needs of businessmen. Heath quickly interrupted his disquisition. 'That is wrong,' he said. 'What businessmen ought to do is ...'[34]

He was genuinely on the side of business when it came to the removal of unnecessary restrictions. 'I have the impression that all too often we are allowing other policy considerations to over-rule the trade ones,' he wrote. American restrictions on trade with the Communist bloc should be challenged whenever possible: 'British firms should be encouraged urgently to disentangle themselves from these stultifying US controls, by not making use of American products or technology.' When the British firms pointed out that this would always be difficult and often impossible, Heath felt this to be fresh evidence of their unwillingness boldly to tackle the obstacles in their path. But when they did show what seemed to him the true spirit of enterprise, he would support them even against his own ministers. At a dinner at Chequers for 'younger' business men, Neil Wates, from the great building firm, attacked planning controls on the use of land. Peter Walker angrily countered that Wates's assertions contained 'few facts and little reasoned argument'. It was the Department's defence that was 'naïve in the extreme', concluded Heath. 'We all know of dozens of councils hanging on to land they are not using; and land is in short supply over vast areas, prices have shot up and delays are appalling. Why doesn't the Department of the Environment deal with these scandals?'[35]

Though he sometimes despaired of business, he knew that the economic policies of his Government would stand or fall by the attitude of the unions. In retrospect it seems evident that an eventual confrontation between Government and unions was inevitable; but this was not how it seemed to Heath. The fact that, when it did come, it proved so disastrous was largely because there was a fundamental misunderstanding on each side as to what the other really thought and intended. Heath was by disposition conciliatory and eager to pursue a policy which would be acceptable to the unions, yet George Woodcock, by no means one of the more intransigent union leaders, told Alastair Hetherington in November 1970 that he considered the Government 'the most dogmatic since the war ... it is now in a hopelessly entrenched position and it will take a crisis to get it – and also to get the TUC – out of the trenches'. The unions, therefore, started from the assumption that they were fighting for their lives against an embittered enemy and that any flexibility on their part would be treated as a proof of weakness. Heath for his part was equally deluded. He told Cecil King shortly before the 1970 election that the unions 'would accept the mandate for reform the Conservative Government would have after the next election'. 'It just isn't true,' protested King. 'The whole idea of "a mandate" is a politician's idea and has no meaning to the man in the street,' still less to the militant shop stewards. Heath paid no attention. He continued to believe that, while the unions might huff and puff, they would in the long run see reason and accept the verdict of the electorate.[36]

In spite of Woodcock's strictures, Heath personally established a good relationship with most of the union leaders. Vic Feather, Jack Jones and three or four others had been to supper in Albany shortly before the election. 'There is no doubting Ted Heath's sympathy for people, and we quickly established a feeling of camaraderie,' remembered Jones. 'It was a pleasant evening, with Heath talking of his yacht and musical interests ... Vic called out "Play the *Red Flag* for Jack" and the leader of the Tory Party cheerfully played Labour's national anthem. It put the seal on a jolly evening, although I must say that Ted did not play the *Red Flag* very well.' Feather for his part was still more well-disposed towards the Prime Minister. Cecil King quotes him as referring to Heath as 'impossibly stubborn and obstinate', but this, if correctly quoted, must have been uttered in a moment of unusual bad temper; all his other recorded remarks about Heath are uniformly friendly. He was 'a very serious politician,' Feather said on television, 'concerned with the welfare of his party but, overriding that I think, was his concern for the well-being of the country. I don't think he was really a very good Conservative in that sense. He was more of a mind to think nationally.' Norman Tebbit would have heartily endorsed this judgment. Feather, he complained, was 'treated as though he was the ambassador of a powerful foreign state. In contrast the CBI was treated more like a disobedient colony ... I begin to feel that Ted Heath felt no unease – but rather relief – at shedding Conservative principles.'[37]

The trouble was that the genuine goodwill felt by Feather, Jones and certain other union leaders did not translate into acceptance of the Tory Government's plans for union reform. Still less did it extend to the new generation of union leaders – Mick McGahey, Hugh Scanlon – or to the militant shop stewards, who had never been exposed to the delights of an evening at Albany and were convinced that Heath was intent on destroying their standard of living and their power to defend themselves. When the time came to introduce the long-meditated Industrial Relations Bill into the House of Commons, any readiness to give the Tories the benefit of the doubt was quickly dissipated and the union movement lined up with the Labour opposition to fight any reform every inch of the way. Their resistance would have been fortified if they had known that Heath was playing with the idea of changing the law by which families of strikers were entitled to supplementary benefits. Could such payment be treated as loans rather than grants? he asked in the summer of 1970; 'there is clearly a balance to be struck between avoiding hardship and giving an unnecessary subsidy to people involved in disputes', he told a Tory backbencher some time later. In Cabinet he urged measures 'to redress the balance of power between employers and trade unions'. There was a need, he said, 'to increase the financial disincentive to strike action'. Regretfully he concluded that any attempt to recover supplementary benefits would be interpreted as victimisation of the strikers but he never ceased to look for some measure which would make the striker think twice and yet not exacerbate too fiercely the conflict between worker and employer.[38]

He was possessed by a sense of almost frantic urgency in the months before the Industrial Relations Bill was presented to the House. It must be put forward as soon as possible, he told the Cabinet, 'since until the climate of industrial relations could be radically altered, the Government would be perpetually at risk of becoming trapped in the type of sterile confrontation with organised Labour which had frustrated the efforts of their predecessors'. With the benefit of hindsight it is easy to see that the Government would have done better to adopt the legislation which Wilson and Barbara Castle had tried to force through only two years before; it might not have covered so much ground as the Conservative version but it would have put large parts of the Labour leadership in a position where they could not oppose the bill without seeming pitifully two-faced. The

Tories, however, were bewitched by the beauty of their own solution. Heath and Robert Carr, wrote Geoffrey Howe, were satisfied by the new measures 'because of their balance and fairness. Every obligation upon the unions and workers was balanced by an enforceable right or benefit.' Surely even the most purblind union leader must see how fair a deal they were being offered? Heath maintained that the unions were given every chance to consult about the contents of the bill but stood obstinately aloof. It is true that the unions had refused to enter into talks with the Tories while they were still in opposition, but once they were in government the bill was introduced with no preliminary discussion. This failure to consult was disastrous, considered Ian Gilmour, as it united even the most moderate of the unions in obdurate opposition and gave Wilson and Castle a chance to put *In Place of Strife* behind them and join in attacks on the Tory reforms. A former managing director of the Ford Motor Company wrote to plead that there should be full consultation before any bill was put before the House: 'I would earnestly ask you not to rush matters just because this type of legislation was promised.' Heath signed a formal letter of thanks and added in manuscript at the bottom: 'It is one with which I fully agree.' Perhaps he did at the time, but his good intentions were forgotten by the time the issue was discussed in Cabinet.[39]

'In opposition,' wrote Brendon Sewill, 'private talks with trade union leaders had led us to believe that, while the unions would be bound publicly to oppose the introduction of legislation ... once the law was passed it would be accepted.' On another occasion he admitted: 'I never actually discovered when or where those confidential discussions had taken place.' Certainly Heath and Carr must have read more into the talks than in fact was justified; probably, too, the union leaders had underestimated the passion with which the activists in their movement were going to reject the Tory proposals. At the TUC Congress in September 1970, by which time the consultative document had been published, Scanlon denounced the proposals as 'the most serious threat to the liberties of organised labour for well over half a century'. W. L. Kendall, of the Civil and Public Services Association, called on the general council 'to mobilise the entire trade union movement for action'. There was no room here for faint hearts or moderates; if the law was forced through then it must be rendered unworkable. It *was* forced through. In January 1971 the Government decided the debate in the House of Commons was becoming intolerably protracted and introduced a guillotine motion. There were cries of 'Fascist!' and 'Dictator!' Night after night debates went on into the early hours of the morning, and the Tory backbenchers tramped endlessly through the lobbies. It should have been a golden opportunity for the Prime Minister to mingle with them; encouraging, praising, inspiring a spirit of solidarity. Instead he was surrounded always by his entourage of the faithful, speaking to no ordinary private member, remaining aloof and apparently sullen. 'A number of the new young intake appear to dislike him personally,' Knox Cunningham told Macmillan. 'So far he has not got across to them.'[40]

The animosity stirred up in the House of Commons made it all the easier for the more activist union leaders to organise resistance on the shop floor. The bill was the longest piece of legislation laid before Parliament in the post-war period, containing 163 clauses, 8 schedules and 97 amendments.[41] Like most documents which try to foresee and cover every eventuality, it was rich in possibilities for misinterpretation and misuse. Its creation of a National Industrial Relations Court (NIRC), designed with the superficially estimable aim of bringing the trade unions within the orbit of the law, succeeded only in showing how ill designed the courts were to solve industrial disputes. The leaders of organised labour quickly concluded that whatever judges might be appointed to rule in such disputes were not to be trusted.[42] The provision that unions, to secure certain legal protections, would be required to register seemed to Heath a wholly innocuous provision but gave the unions an opportunity to frustrate the working of the Act simply by refusing to register. 'From their narrow short-term point of view,' admitted Carr, 'it was a damnably effective tactic.'[43] By the time the bill had become law the Tory leadership was beginning to realise that it had underestimated the potential opposition; within a few months they saw that they had made a grievously damaging mistake.

The reception that most of the press gave to the new legislation confirmed Heath in his belief that he was being monstrously misused.

It can be taken for granted that every prime minister will be convinced that he is ill treated by the media. Heath, perhaps because he took so little trouble to propitiate them, felt himself peculiarly vulnerable. He told the editor of the *Guardian* that his industrial correspondent should be sacked, so inexcusable had been his treatment of Carr's proposals. 'He admitted that other papers had been almost as bad,' recorded Hetherington. They were 'all obsessed with the unions and didn't take nearly enough notice of the government and industry'. Nor was the BBC much better. Lord Hill, the chairman, noted in his diary that it was clear Heath wanted to get rid of him. The Prime Minister had 'got a deep-seated dislike of the BBC. I gather from his reports of other conversations he has had that he is not very specific. He just makes scornful references.' Heath never took criticism well, even when it was obviously friendly and well intentioned. Coming from people he did not know, working for organisations which he believed to be hostile, his susceptibilities were easily disturbed. He relapsed into a sulky hostility which ensured that his treatment was even worse in future.[44]

In fact, in the first year or so after the election, the Government was generally felt to be doing quite well where industrial relations were concerned. A strike by the dustmen in November 1970 was settled by the local authorities on terms so generous that Heath denounced them as 'patently nonsensical', but when the power-station workers the following month demanded a pay rise of 30 per cent and came out on strike to enforce their claim, the Government was in a stronger position to rally the employers. A state of emergency was declared and power cuts imposed for certain hours of the day. In the long term, in such cases, the infliction of discomfort and inconvenience to the public usually generates demands for a settlement at any price, but the immediate reaction is more likely to be indignation at those who were directly responsible. Feeling themselves unpopular, and displaying a sensitivity to public opinion which their fellow workers in the coalmines were soon to show that they did not share, the power-station workers called off their work-to-rule. Heath was quite as eager not to force matters to a confrontation. He told the Cabinet that, until the Industrial Relations Bill had become law, he doubted whether the Government would be able to 'see through a firm stand on the electricity workers' pay claim'. The compromise, disliked by some members of the Cabinet but accepted by the majority as the only way forward, was to refer the dispute to a court of enquiry.[45] The doubters were won over by a proviso that the court should be required to consider the claim 'with regard to the national interest and to the impact of industrial action on the economy as a whole'. It seems unlikely that this somewhat hazy injunction made much difference to the Wilberforce committee, but their recommendation for a rise of 11 per cent fell within the Government's guidelines – 'one of our few strokes of good fortune during this period', commented Heath. When, early in 1971, the Post Office workers abandoned their claim to a 20 per cent raise and settled for the employers' much lower figure, it began to seem as if the Government would be able to struggle on until the passage of the Industrial Relations Act transformed the industrial landscape and, so Heath and Carr at least believed, restored order and good sense to the scene.[46]

But Heath was not so blindly confident that the Act alone would be enough to cure Britain's ills. He continued to denounce the evils of a prices and incomes policy. The British press were 'convinced that we needed a wages freeze', he complained to Howell. 'Hopeless!' Yet he always kept at the back of his mind the possibility that something of the kind would one day prove essential. At Chequers, on 3 June 1971, he authorised the preparation 'in conditions of great secrecy' of a study of contingency plans 'against the risk of continuing wage and price escalation'. A preliminary report by the civil service mandarins Douglas Allen and Denis Barnes included studies of 'a statutory freeze on pay and prices' as well as other subsidiary measures. In August 1971, in the same month as the Industrial Relations Act received royal assent, Heath authorised further work on this subject 'under the same conditions of great secrecy'.[47] Norman Tebbit may have gone too far when he accused Heath of feeling 'relief' at shedding Conservative principles, but if he had known what was being contemplated at Chequers he would have felt that his comments erred on the side of understatement.

*   *   *

Prices and incomes were not the only field in which the Government seemed ready to stray from the paths of strict Tory rectitude. Lame ducks, Davies had promised, would not be rescued: within a few months the ducks came home to roost. First, and most dramatic, was Rolls-Royce. This company had contracted to supply a new aero-engine to the American firm, Lockheed, at a price which now turned out to be so far below the real cost that Rolls-Royce was threatened with bankruptcy. 'They would need to take hard-headed and, if necessary, hard decisions,' Heath told the Cabinet (cabinet minutes show that Heath extolled the 'hard headed' approach at least three times during the Rolls-Royce imbroglio). The truly hard approach would have been to let Rolls-Royce stew in its own juice, but there were many reasons to make this seem unwise. The company was the standard-bearer for British industry; if it failed it would do untold damage to national prestige. Many defence projects involved Rolls-Royce products; its collapse would certainly be inconvenient and possibly dangerous. The company employed 80,000 people, many of them in areas of high unemployment, and at least as many other jobs would be in peril in firms supplying Rolls-Royce with components.

The Cabinet was nevertheless divided between the purists, who felt national resources 'should not be devoted to doubtfully economic projects', and the hedgers, who argued that the need for the UK to retain a strong aircraft industry made intervention essential. Heath opted for the latter, and prevailed. He appealed successfully to Nixon for help in enabling Lockheed to pay more for their engines than they were contractually committed to do, and led the Government into what was in effect the nationalisation of the greater part of Rolls-Royce.[48] This was *not* the first U-turn, Mrs Thatcher subsequently claimed; it was justified on national grounds and, anyway, proved a success when Rolls-Royce returned to the private sector a few years later. Nevertheless, the volte-face caused disquiet in the party. A back-bencher forwarded to Heath a letter from a constituent complaining that the Government had failed its first major test. 'I am bound to say', the MP went on, 'that I too find an inconsistency between the Government's declared policy and its action in the Rolls-Royce affair.'[49]

For the most part, however, even the most hard or hard-headed right-wingers were prepared to admit that Rolls-Royce was a special case. There was less readiness to make allowances when it came to the Northern Irish shipbuilding firm of Harland and Wolff. In December 1970 Barber put forward proposals for rescuing this concern, which involved an advance of £5m and the renegotiation of existing loans. 'I find this difficult to accept,' minuted Heath. 'A word with the Chancellor, I think.' A desperate hunt for a private purchaser now began. At one time it seemed that the Greek shipping millionaire Aristotle Onassis might come to the rescue, but it was felt that he would exploit the importance of Harland and Wolff to the economy of Ulster so as to extract unreasonable concessions from the Government. 'Do we believe in private enterprise or not?' demanded Heath. It was a reasonable question, but the answer seemed to be that, in this particular case at least, they did not. The Government put up the necessary £5m and a further £10m two years later, by which time Heath had moved so far from his original position that he seems not to have uttered even a mild protest at what was being done.[50]

Harland and Wolff attracted little publicity; the same could not be said of Upper Clyde Shipbuilders (UCS). In mid-1971 this ill-run and under-financed consortium, cobbled together by the previous administration, was on the brink of going into liquidation. The Government was called on to provide £5–6m of extra capital. It was the familiar dilemma, Heath told the Cabinet. To let UCS collapse would create heavy unemployment on Clydeside, an area already in deep depression. On the other hand UCS had 'become the symbol of an ailing enterprise, bedevilled by bad labour relations and poor management, in whose future prospects there could be little confidence'.[51] Predictably, the Cabinet sought and found a compromise: UCS was to be kept alive but the work would be concentrated on two out of the four shipyards. Unfortunately the Government's position had been made more difficult by the leak of a report by Nicholas Ridley, now a junior minister at the Department of Trade and Industry, advocating the complete closure of UCS. Egged on by Tony Benn the suspicious shipworkers staged a sit-in. Faced with the threat of serious civil disorder and the prospect that unemployment might pass the terrifyingly symbolic figure of one million, the Government gave way still further and agreed to keep three of the four yards open. 'It would be necessary', the Cabinet was told, 'to suspend, for the time being, the application of the established policy of accepting that, when concerns ceased to be viable, they should be allowed to go into receivership.'[52]

'It was a small but memorably inglorious episode,' wrote Mrs Thatcher severely. 'I was deeply troubled.' Her trouble did not stop her accepting the policy in Cabinet but those who were bound by no rules of Cabinet solidarity were more outspoken. Heath had already been forced to abandon *Morning Cloud* in mid-race so as to return for a debate on UCS. On that occasion it had been the Government's supposed heartlessness that was in question; the image of the Prime Minister disporting himself on his yacht while tens of thousands of his fellow countrymen were facing the loss of their jobs was deemed unacceptable. 'I must advise you to return,' wrote his press secretary, 'even at much inconvenience, indeed I might almost say especially if it can be done at great and demonstrable inconvenience.' Robert Armstrong agreed: 'If you do not come back for the debate, the fact that you have not done so will be a kind of albatross round your neck in any future contribution you make to the subject of UCS.' Now Heath found himself assailed on the charge of having too much heart; of allowing his concern over unemployment to drive the Government off-course on an important issue of principle. The rescue of UCS, it was pointed out in Cabinet, 'would not be likely to commend itself to the Government's supporters'. That proved to be an understatement: the UCS affair shocked the right wing and left even the moderates disconcerted. It was incomes policy that was to provide the most dramatic U-turn, but the belief that Heath's Government could not be trusted to administer a properly Conservative policy was widespread from early 1972.[53]

The fear of unemployment was by far the most important factor in convincing Heath that intervention in such cases as UCS was on balance justifiable. Indeed, the hectic reflation which marked the second half of his administration was almost entirely inspired by his conviction that every man had the right to work and every government the duty to make that possible. Prior wrote that Heath 'utterly despised and detested the pre-war Conservative Governments who had tolerated between two and three million unemployed'. It was this which divided him most fundamentally from Margaret Thatcher: she had never known the dole queues of the 1930s and viewed unemployment with resignation if not with equanimity, as a regrettable but unavoidable stage in the long march to national prosperity. Heath received every week a 'Special Confidential Count of the Unemployed'; even when he was in Singapore for the Commonwealth Conference his private secretary cabled him the figures. At a meeting to discuss unemployment with the Chancellor, Home Secretary and Lord President, the three ministers all urged the unwisdom of further reflation. Heath turned the argument on its head. It was essential, he argued, to keep down the level of unemployment so that they would not find themselves faced with 'severe pressure for an undesirable degree of general reflation'. Reflate moderately so as to avoid having to reflate extravagantly was the nub of his case; the alternative – not to reflate and thus to incur high unemployment – was unacceptable. When the dread figure of a million unemployed was reached in January 1972 Heath faced a furious Opposition. 'The first dole-queue millionaire since Neville Chamberlain,' sneered Wilson. He made a dignified and effective reply, contending that Britain's membership of the European Community would create the opportunities for growth that would bring down unemployment, but he was still possessed by a sense of failure and a conviction that it was within his power to bring the country back to something very close to full employment.[54]

It was Heath's belief that the British public – the businessmen in particular – had been, as he told Alastair Hetherington, 'worn down by high taxation, strikes, bureaucracy and other disincentives. It had lost its self-confidence.' That self-confidence he saw it as his mission to restore. He told President Nixon that the people were 'punch drunk with taxation'. Only slowly was management realising that 'they must learn henceforward to stand on their own feet'; he had been disappointed by the lack of response to the various economic incentives he had made available. Nixon was sympathetic. When the battle to pass the Industrial Relations Bill was at its fiercest he wrote to say that they could both expect to find the polls running against them. 'I am convinced, however, that people generally have pretty good judgement in the long run – if not in the short run – and that if our policies are right, whether in the foreign or domestic field, they eventually will win public approval.'[55] Heath was buoyed up by the same conviction. 'Set my people free' was his essential creed; provide the opportunities for growth and growth would inevitably follow. When William Armstrong and William Nield put forward various proposals, Heath told Barber 'he was not convinced that they were on a sufficiently large scale'. The Prime Minister feels that a good many industrialists are still doubtful about the prospects for growth, Robert Armstrong told a senior official in the Treasury, 'because they still believe that, if balance of payments difficulties recur, the Government will deflate rather than devalue'. The contrary was true. 'Nothing must be allowed to stand in the way of steady and sustained growth.'[56]

The Chancellor feared that pumping money into the economy before the unbridled wage claims had been curbed would mean not growth but an inflationary increase in the size of pay packets. Barber's budget in the spring of 1971 concentrated on reforming the tax system: reducing SET and eventually replacing it by a valued added tax (VAT) and merging income tax and surtax. Left to himself he would probably have confined himself to such adjustments over the next few years. Heath, however, had no intention of leaving his Chancellor to himself. He was not yet ready to put his foot flat down on the economic accelerator but he was impatient with the slow rate of growth. Huge but distant projects like the Channel Tunnel and Maplin airport were to be encouraged and, so far as was possible, advanced, but they could be of little immediate significance. As for British business as a whole, he was prepared to envisage a degree of intervention, of guidance and encouragement, which would have been anathema to his more doctrinaire free-market colleagues. It was wrong to describe 'less state activity' as a legitimate objective, he told Lord Rothschild. Certainly there were some fields where state intervention should be eliminated, but there were others, for instance the preservation of the environment, where it was essential. 'Nor was it necessarily wrong that the Government should in some degree deviate from the course which they had intended to pursue when they took office, but it was vital that where there was a change of course it should be a conscious one.' Selsdon man would have stirred uneasily in his cave if he had heard such heresies.[57]

There was a time in the summer of 1971 when it seemed that stability in prices and incomes – that prerequisite for sustained and steady growth – might be achieved without governmental intervention. Vic Feather hinted that, if the manufacturers would do something to curb the increase in prices, the unions might be prepared to contemplate a corresponding restraint in wage demands: a prices and incomes policy would be achieved with encouragement from but no direct intervention by the Government. Heath lost no time in putting the proposition to the CBI and in mid-July he was able to tell the Cabinet that they were prepared to 'secure voluntary price restraint by private industry in the hope that this would reduce pay demands and make it possible for the Government to achieve a faster rate of economic growth'. The Cabinet welcomed the initiative and undertook to ensure that the nationalised industries followed the example of their fellow employers in the private sector.[58]

For a moment it seemed that the improbable might be about to happen: the trade unions would agree to cooperate with a Tory Government by curbing wage demands and would thus open the way to a period of stable growth. The TUC General Council came to Downing Street: the meeting was not an entire success and Feather among his colleagues proved to be less amenable than when tête-à-tête with the Prime Minister, but enough common ground was found to make it worth envisaging further meetings. A bunch of relatively modest wage settlements towards the end of the year – with the Local Authority manual workers, the Atomic Energy Authority manual workers, the British Airport Authority – led Heath to tell the Cabinet that 'significant progress was being made in the Government's policy of wage de-escalation'. 'However much one may dislike Heath,' wrote Tony Benn in his diary on 31 December 1971, '– and I personally find him a very unattractive person – he has emerged as a strong and tough Prime Minister ... The economy, after having gone through a difficult eighteen months, is going to pick up and will look good and although unemployment won't drop to acceptable levels and prices won't be held in check, the position won't be too bad from Heath's point of view ... I think after Wilson, who appeared as rather a trickster, the public quite like the feeling of Heath as the strong Prime Minister.'[59]

It proved to be a false dawn. It was the miners who shattered the Conservative dream of wage restraint imposed by the workers themselves. The NUM had not been one of the more truculent unions in recent years but the industry was in decline and the miners felt themselves threatened and left behind in the race for higher wages. For the Government the situation was complicated by the fact that they had no confidence in the National Coal Board (NCB). In October 1970 the then Chairman of the NCB, Alfred Robens, had made an offer to the union substantially above the figure authorised by the Government. 'This is bad,' minuted Heath. 'Ld Robens has let us down.' Early the following year he wrote angrily: 'The NCB is a horror. I hadn't realised how bad it is.' He had hoped that the settlement agreed by Robens, extravagant as it was, would at least satisfy the miners for a year or two: on the contrary, in July 1971 the NUM put in a demand for a rise of 45 per cent. By this time Robens had been replaced as chairman by Sir Derek Ezra. To the Government's dismay Ezra proved even more accommodating than his predecessor. His handling of the negotiations with the NUM, Barber told Heath, 'makes one doubt whether his heart is in negotiating a settlement that would be acceptable to the Government. We shall need strong nerves to come out of this dispute successfully but there is a great deal to play for and I am sure that we should spare no effort to ensure that the NCB keep closely to the Government line.' 'I agree,' wrote Heath.[60]

Nerves were not strong enough. In mid-December the NUM, which had been operating an overtime ban since November, called a national strike for 9 January 1972. Carr told the Cabinet that there was a real risk that the manual workers in the gas and electricity industries would come out in sympathy. 'Plans should be perfected', ruled Heath, 'to take account of the possibility of simultaneous industrial action.'[61] The plans worked, in that there was ample coal stocked at the pitheads to keep the power stations going for several weeks; they proved, however, to be inadequate to cope with the miners' tactic, inspired and organised by a young firebrand, Arthur Scargill, of sending flying pickets around the country to prevent the movement of coal and thus force the power stations to close. Left to himself the moderate president of the NUM, Joe Gormley, would never have resorted to such incendiary methods. Gormley got on well with Heath: 'I found him neither stubborn nor unapproachable ... when I said what I had to say he would listen, and I knew he was listening, whereas Harold Wilson often gave the impression of ... not really listening at all.' But Gormley could not control his militants; effectively the NUM was under the control of men like Scargill and McGahey. The Cabinet met to consider how to counter the threat of the flying pickets. To their dismay they were told by the Attorney General that, for the most part, the picketing had been lawful. Where there had been clear intimidation this was against the law, but 'the activities of the pickets confronted the police with very difficult and sensitive decisions'. Even as he was addressing the Cabinet the Home Secretary was told that the police had given up any attempt to keep open the gates of the Saltley cokeworks in the West Midlands and had withdrawn, leaving the miners' pickets in possession of the field.[62]

This conflict, Heath wrote in his memoirs, 'was the most vivid, direct and terrifying challenge to the rule of law that I could ever remember emerging from within our own country'. The Cabinet had no idea how to meet it. They ruled out any reference to the National Industrial Relations Court, set up under the Industrial Relations Act, on the ground that this would merely alienate moderate members of the NUM. They concluded that the use of troops would seriously exacerbate the situation and might well lead to a complete withdrawal of labour by tanker drivers and a petrol famine. 'The Government now wandering vainly over the battlefield looking for someone to sur-render to – and being massacred all the time,' wrote Hurd in his diary. This vivid phrase incurred Heath's indignation when he read it many years later: 'That's silly!' he snorted. 'Very silly! How can a responsible person produce something like that in his diary? Very silly!'[63] To a less prejudiced eye, Hurd's judgment seems to have summed up the situation very neatly.

Whether Heath admitted it or not, surrender was in the air. After Saltley, wrote Brendon Sewill, 'many of those in positions of influence looked into the abyss and saw only a few days away the possibility of the country being plunged into a state of chaos not so very far removed from that which might prevail after a minor nuclear attack'. No one was more aware of this than Heath. The line of retreat was settled in Cabinet on the day of the defeat at Saltley. The first object-ive, the Cabinet concluded, should be to secure a return to work; 'tac-tical considerations must be subordinated to this purpose'. Strategic considerations, too, it might have added. Any settlement that was acceptable to the miners would leave the Government's pay policy in ruins. The best that they could hope to do was to dissociate themselves as far as possible from the debacle: 'It would accordingly be preferable to proceed by way of a court of inquiry, despite the risk of further delay.'[64]

There was, in fact, remarkably little delay. Lord Wilberforce was once again called in to head the inquiry and presented his report within three days. It was more favourable to the miners than the Government had hoped, giving them a rise of more than 20 per cent, but at least it promised an end to the crisis. And then the end seemed suddenly unattainable. On the day the report was due, the Cabinet considered what could be done if the miners rejected Wilberforce's settlement. Volunteers would have to be drafted in to move coal, Heath himself would probably broadcast to the nation. Ministers were asked to hold themselves in readiness for an emergency meeting. But nobody really felt it possible that things would come to such a pass. Then Gormley called at Number 10. His Executive was not satisfied, he announced; the offer must be improved. Public opinion would not understand this, said Heath. 'If the miners do not go back to work,' said Gormley grimly, 'public opinion will not matter.' The Cabinet convened to discuss this disastrous development. 'Only 14 days more coal ... Abyss,' scribbled Hailsham in his diary. 'Cabinet indecisive, divided ... Carrington made decisive comment. We cannot bin Wilberforce with the ink scarcely dry on the report. I said we should last no more than 6 weeks if we give in.' Heath returned to face the miners' Executive and told them there was no more to give. In fact he conceded a package of minor demands relating to holidays and allowances; it was enough to convince the union that they had won a famous victory and yet let the Government claim that Wilberforce's proposal had not been exceeded. 'Last night ... we absolutely looked into the abyss,' Whitelaw told David Butler. 'We would have had to fight but it would have involved everything – troops, a general election, an enormous embitterment of the situation!' 'It was plain', Butler commented, 'that his relief at getting back from the abyss was far greater than his dismay at the settlement.'[65]

At Cabinet the same day Maudling congratulated the Prime Minister 'for the manner in which, by adhering firmly to the Government's policy, he had succeeded in convincing the Executive of the NUM that they would gain no advantage by continuing to resist the findings of the Wilberforce Court of Inquiry'. The congratulations must have had a hollow ring. The worst, perhaps, had been averted, but the Government had been humiliated and their policy gravely damaged. They could have played it differently, have told the NUM that they would get what the Coal Board offered and no more, have drafted in troops to ensure the flow of coal from the pitheads, have tried to split the miners by cajoling certain pits into a return to work. Mrs Thatcher was to show some twelve years later that there was another way. The union leaders themselves were far from sure that they held a winning hand. It is conceivable that a more aggressive display by the Tories in 1972 might have won the day. But even if he had felt more confident of his ground, Heath would have been profoundly reluctant to resort to extreme measures. Confrontation, he believed, could only embitter the dispute and split the nation. The aspect of the strike which most disturbed him was the supposed political motivation of the strikers. Must we now, he wondered, 'prepare ourselves to face not merely a series of conventional industrial disputes but a political challenge by organised labour to the whole structure of parliamentary democracy'? To avert such a conclusion became the prime consideration of his remaining years in office.[66]

One ray of comfort emerged from the disastrous battle with the unions. Strong elements in the Labour movement were as anxious as Heath to avoid a confrontation which could threaten parliamentary democracy and the stability of the state. Vic Feather called at Number 10 when the miners' strike was coming to a climax and said that the Government should be thinking in terms of an incomes policy which applied to the pubic and private sectors alike. The TUC would be unwilling to cooperate in an incomes policy, retorted Heath. They had never been asked to do so, said Feather. 'They had been asked to accept decisions by the Government. The TUC would always be ready to cooperate, if they were properly consulted and agreed in advance about the basis for cooperation.' Heath saw in these words a foundation on which, with patience and goodwill, a lasting partnership between employers, workers and the Government might one day be erected.[67]

SEVENTEEN

The Approaching Storm

The first few months of 1972 were startlingly stressful for Edward Heath. The miners' strike and the collapse of his policy for wage restraint was only one of the crises that racked his Government. In Northern Ireland the disasters of internment and Bloody Sunday made inevitable the imposition of direct rule; in the House of Commons the entry of Britain into Europe provoked long, exhausting and often acrimonious debates. In all these spheres elements of the Tory Party were fiercely critical of the leadership. The Ulster Unionists and their allies were constantly suspicious that the Government was planning to do a deal with Dublin; the Europhobes raged against a betrayal of national sovereignty; unkindest cut of all, the Conservative Party Trade Union Committee resolved in March 1972 that it was 'both angered and disillusioned by the refusal, even abdication, of the Government to show itself willing to govern during the recent miners' strike'. The handling of the whole issue, they considered, 'showed a serious lack of political judgment which is both dangerous and frightening'. As John Ramsden put it: 'Few heavier brickbats can ever have been thrown at a Tory Government by a national representative body of its supporters.' The 1922 Committee was almost equally restive. Their lack of faith in the Government's policies was made manifest when, towards the end of 1972, it elected as its chairman the man whom Heath had sacked as party chairman and conspicuously failed to employ in his administration, his dedicated enemy Edward du Cann. 'I said to the Committee immediately after the election that you have my full support,' he assured Heath. 'I want you to know that I meant it.' He did not mean it, and the Prime Minister knew he did not mean it.[1]

Heath was undiscomfited. Vic Feather's hints that the trade unions, if properly approached, might be willing to work with the Government so as to achieve sustained growth had fallen on fertile ground. In March 1972 Heath invited the TUC General Council to come to Downing Street for wide-ranging talks; the following week he did the same for the CBI. No commitments were given or indeed asked for during these meetings: Heath treated them as an opportunity to bring home to both camps the extreme gravity of the situation, the imminent risk of runaway inflation, the need for restraint and, above all, the golden opportunities that lay ahead if the Government followed a policy of sustained and vigorous growth. Inevitably the union leaders found it necessary to register protests against the Industrial Relations Act but on the whole the atmosphere was good. Heath was left with the impression that, if the CBI could continue to control prices, the TUC would urge restraint on its members when it came to wages and would cooperate in the removal of those practices which impeded growth.

Growth was the key word. 'The overwhelming view on Fleet Street and in the City at this time', wrote Heath, 'was that we needed an expansionary budget.' He must have been somewhat selective in choosing the voices he listened to: Leslie O'Brien, the Governor of the Bank of England, for one had grave doubts about the wisdom of rapid reflation. But the Prime Minister was in no mood to heed voices urging caution. When unemployment hit one million, said John Nott, 'A diktat came down from Number 10 to the Treasury saying that unemployment should be halved within a year – an absurd and dangerous notion ...' Barber protested at the scope of what was being proposed. He told Martin Holmes that he had even contemplated resignation, but 'thought I ought to soldier on. If the Chancellor of the Exchequer resigns over public expenditure it can have a very bad effect on sterling and is a poor thing for the country.' 'He was a feather-weight,' wrote Woodrow Wyatt contemptuously, 'easily towed along by Ted ... Macleod, with his deft analytical mind and ability to argue forcefully, would never have allowed it.'[2]

Not merely was the Chancellor ignored, the Treasury, to a remarkable extent, was excluded from the formation of economic policy. Douglas Allen, the Permanent Secretary at the Treasury, was dismissed as a congenital pessimist. Instead Heath preferred to listen to William Armstrong. Armstrong, in Allen's view, did not actually egg on the Prime Minister in his urgent quest for growth but he did little or nothing to restrain him. As to Heath's other favoured source of advice, the Think Tank, its role, according to one scornful Treasury official, was confined to 'whooping up public expenditure'. There must always be a temptation for strong prime ministers to shoulder aside departments that they believe to be unduly cautious and conservative. Sometimes such behaviour can be justified. In this case the facts suggest that Heath went too far and too fast. Denis Healey, who was as ready as any minister to impose his will on recalcitrant departments, believes that Heath's policy was a failure, 'partly because he was no more willing to take advice from the Treasury than the Foreign Office.'[3] Whatever the Treasury proposed, Heath wanted more. When the Chancellor suggested various reflationary measures for inclusion in the budget, Heath insisted that 'some further stimulus was justifiable in the circumstances'. An increase in personal allowances was agreed. Regional investment grants were another favoured tool. Heath admitted that these 'would be unwelcome to some sections of Government backbench opinion', in view of the fact that the grants had been withdrawn with some ostentation only a year before.

It was a pity, Heath agreed, that so conspicuous a change in policy was necessary but an appearance of consistency was not the most important consideration. Other ways of achieving the same ends were examined but in the end it was concluded that grants were 'the best and most honest course'.[4] Heath was deluding himself if he supposed that the discontent would be confined to backbenchers. Nicholas Ridley and John Eden, junior ministers under Davies at the DTI, were known to be opposed to any such industrial incentives and had been excluded from participation in the preparatory work. Now they had got wind of what was going on and were, not unnaturally, upset.

Davies asked leave to brief them on the latest proposals. 'Agreed – top secret,' minuted Heath, with some regret. What emerged from this travail, the budget of 21 March, was, John Nott believed, the 'most expansionary since the Second World War'. Its immediate consequence was what was popularly known as the 'Barber boom' – an unfair title for something that Barber had in fact opposed but perhaps deserved in view of the supine acquiescence of the Chancellor in a policy in which he did not believe.[5]

The Industry Act, which in effect was a postscript to the budget, put into practice the measures for ailing industry which Barber had foreshadowed a little earlier. Its object was to stiffen the sinews of British industry so as to equip it to face the competition of life in the EEC: its tools were regional investment grants, a scheme for free depreciation allowing industry to re-equip itself with new plant and machinery, and selective assistance to certain privileged companies whose work was deemed especially valuable to the national economy. Once again, the Treasury was largely excluded from the Act's preparation, though Leo Pliatzky, a Deputy Secretary at the Treasury who was deemed to be more sympathetic than most of his colleagues to expansionism, was drafted in to help William Armstrong work out the policy in detail. It was, said Lord Gowrie, 'the most interventionist piece of legislation passed by Parliament up to that time'. Even the ranks of Tuscany could scarce forbear to cheer; Harold Wilson offered barbed congratulations to Heath on his belated conversion to sound socialist principles. Indeed, even in the ranks of Tuscany there were some who thought it was going too far; it was, considered Edmund Dell, a former Minister of State for Trade, 'the most amazing thing that a Conservative Government has ever done ... It was a Bill so absurd that Tony Benn could approve it.' Unfortunately for Heath, his own supporters were as often as not even more disquieted than Dell. A large section of the party was openly horrified by what seemed to them an arrant betrayal of Tory principles, and while Barber made no attempt to whip up opposition within the Cabinet, at lower levels in the Government there was overt grumbling.[6]

Nobody grumbled more overtly than the right-wing and resolutely non-interventionist Nicholas Ridley. He was called to Number 10.

'Ted was sitting at a desk signing letters to constituents. He did not look up. He did not say good morning. He kept on signing letters until the pile was finished.' Then he told Ridley he wanted his job; he was not making a good enough show of presenting the Government's policy. 'How could anyone make a good case of presenting this Government's policies?' demanded Ridley. 'You have gone back on everything the Tories ever stood for.' Heath offered him a sideways shift to be Minister of the Arts. It was in fact a job that would have suited Ridley very well, but he was so enraged by his offhand reception that he responded: 'I don't want any part of this Government.'[7]

Ridley's eviction was part of a larger reshuffle. Whitelaw's departure to Northern Ireland meant that Carr replaced him as Lord President and Leader of the House, and Maurice Macmillan was promoted to the Cabinet to take over the extremely sensitive portfolio of Employment. There was almost a clean sweep at the DTI, though Davies himself survived long enough to see through the Industry Act. Then he was relegated to be Chancellor of the Duchy of Lancaster, with somewhat nebulous responsibilities for Europe. In his place Heath appointed the energetic and ebullient Peter Walker. Michael Heseltine, another young protégé, joined the DTI with responsibility for aviation. The composition of the Cabinet was little changed but the balance had shifted in favour of Heath's policies. Whatever his arguments in private, Barber remained loyal to the Prime Minister; Joseph and Thatcher, the two ministers who were subsequently to denounce intervention with such fervour, remained discreetly silent.

It was unfortunate for Heath that his dash for growth coincided with an explosive increase in world commodity prices. There was far worse to come, but even by the spring of 1972 it was clear that the cost of imported food was rising rapidly. Higher prices generated larger wage demands. The employers, urged on by the Government, sought to resist all but the most modest applications; industrial unrest, which had enjoyed a brief period of quiescence after the miners' strike, broke out with renewed vigour. By now the Industrial Relations Act was fully operational and the new NIRC was ready to face its first test. It came in March, when the Court ruled that the blacking of container lorries by the Liverpool dockers, fearful at what they thought to be a threat to their jobs, was an unfair practice and must be stopped. The Court won, in that the dockers' union, the TGWU, surrendered in the face of escalating fines and ordered its members to let through the container lorries; in the long term it lost, however, in that the workforce largely ignored its leadership and continued the practice of blacking. Any long-term possibility of the unions working with the NIRC disappeared in a cloud of fractious bitterness.

The atmosphere was already soured, therefore, when in early March 1972 the railway unions demanded a pay increase of more than 16 per cent. 'The successful management of the railwaymen's pay claim would be of cardinal importance to the Government and the country,' Heath told the Cabinet. It was too much to hope that a settlement could be reached within the Government's guideline of 8 per cent but 'on balance it was desirable to secure a negotiated settlement if this were attained at a defensible and reasonable level'. Up to 10 per cent would be acceptable. Arbitration would be certain to produce an unacceptably high settlement; the Government must hold its nerve and allow the Rail Board to continue to negotiate. There followed a dispiriting series of shuffles and withdrawals. Under the Industrial Relations Act the Secretary of State could call for a ballot of union members – a useless proviso, it was agreed, since the majority would undoubtedly opt for industrial action – or for a cooling-off period. The latter would at least buy time in which stocks of coal could be built up at the power stations.[8] The unions reluctantly accepted a fourteen-day cooling-off period but at the end of it no settlement had been reached and the work-to-rule recommenced. The Board could go up to 11 per cent, ruled the Cabinet; if the unions remained obdurate 'the Government might have to be prepared to test their credit with the country by inviting Parliament to pass urgent legislation in order to reduce the industrial power of those who resorted to strike action'. Eleven per cent was in due course also rejected; the Government did not yet feel inclined to test its credit in the way suggested; useless though it might be, the union was instructed to ballot its membership. 'Ask a silly question and you get a silly answer,' commented one Tory backbencher; sure enough, four out of five members supported their leadership and voted for continued industrial action. Recourse was now had to the dreaded arbitration; an award of 12½ per cent was recommended; this too the union rejected and a national go-slow began. The Cabinet now had to decide, Heath told them, whether the Government 'could face a confrontation with the confidence that they would be able to carry it to a conclusion without being forced into ultimate concession of the union's full demand'. Public opinion was the vital factor. Evidently the Government lacked the necessary confidence; it was back to negotiations and an eventual settlement of about 13 per cent. In fact it was not too bad a result, about halfway between the union's demand and the Board's original offer, but in the eyes of the Cabinet, indeed of the public, it was an unequivocal defeat.

As if the Government's problems were not already grave enough, the Home Secretary, Reggie Maudling, was now engulfed in scandal. He had already been tainted by his association with the Real Estate Fund of America. In that case he had escaped involvement in the police enquiries, but now he was damned by his association with John Poulson, an architect who was to be convicted and sentenced to seven years in jail for fraud in the award of building licences. Nobody said – or at least very loudly – that Maudling had himself benefited from Poulson's crimes, but the fact was that he had solicited a donation of £22,000 to the trust fund of a theatre in which he and his wife were interested. While chatting with Heath, John Junor remarked that he thought people would have had better sense than to get involved with a man like Poulson. 'He gave me a brisk nod of agreement. I knew there and then that Reggie was going to get no support from the Prime Minister.' In fact Heath's first reaction had been to question the need for Maudling to resign, given the fact he had ridden out the Real Estate Fund scandal more or less unscathed. The difference between the two cases, Robert Armstrong argued, was the degree of publicity involved. Poulson was resolved not to go down unless he could take a few prominent personalities with him. No Home Secretary could remain in office if police enquiries were in progress that might involve him. Heath had no intention of involving the Government in a major scandal so as to protect a wayward colleague. He told Maudling that he must leave the Home Office, though softening the blow by suggesting a change of job, perhaps a direct swop with Robert Carr. Possibly he put forward the suggestion without any marked enthusiasm; anyway Maudling thought it better to leave the Government. 'Ted Heath acted like a true friend,' wrote Maudling in his memoirs.[9]

Certainly Heath did not behave badly. In Cabinet he dutifully deplored the loss of Maudling's 'wisdom and experience' and suggested that he be sent a message 'of sympathy and good wishes'. A year or so later, however, when the possibility was raised of Maudling coming back, he did not demur when the Attorney General advised against it, saying that he still feared there was a risk 'something may emerge from the forthcoming trials which could implicate Reggie'. Junor had not been far wrong when he had concluded that the Prime Minister was not going to go very far out of his way to protect his errant minister. With Maudling's departure, however, and with Whitelaw in Northern Ireland and Douglas-Home and Hailsham preferring to stick to their own territory, there was less than ever a big gun in the Cabinet ready to challenge the Prime Minister. William Armstrong became increasingly the man to whom Heath would first turn when he wanted an independent view on a major issue.[10]

The Poulson scandal gave fresh impetus to Liberal demands that MPs should register their private interests. The 1922 Committee deplored the idea, even if such a register was voluntary. This was one of the few issues on which Heath agreed with them. His instinct was to defend his privacy at almost any cost, and to this was added his strong resentment at the implication that he might allow conflicting interests to affect his judgments as Prime Minister. If he could help it no busybody would pry into *his* affairs. Regretfully, however, he realised that something must be done to appease public concern and to allow members to protect themselves against unfair imputations. Without investing the business with any urgency, he agreed that some sort of register should be set up. It was to be a long time before it was up and running. By then Heath was out of office and more free to indulge his personal predilections. He urged forcibly that it should be left to individual members to decide whether any particular interest was relevant to matters with which their parliamentary work involved them. The pass was sold, however. It was an issue which was to cause him frequent irritation and provoke much ill-tempered bad behaviour over the next thirty years.[11]

The Industrial Relations Act continued to bedevil the Government's relationship with the unions. In the summer of 1972 the dockers came back into the limelight. A group of dockers on Merseyside had defied the NIRC's ruling and continued to black container lorries. The Court fined the union £55,000; the union appealed, and the Master of the Rolls, Lord Denning, upheld the appeal and ruled that it was the individual dockers and not the union who were responsible. If the fines remained unpaid and the law was to retain any semblance of reality, it was clear that the dockers would have to be prosecuted and, in all probability, imprisoned. 'I remember', recalled Robert Carr, 'we felt we might as well jump off Westminster Bridge that morning.' Tolpuddle would come to Merseyside, a new galaxy of martyrs would adorn the pantheon of the Labour movement. Then, emerging from some dusty recess of the legal system, appeared an obscure *deus ex machina* known as the Official Solicitor. At the instigation of the TGWU, said Government – with the connivance of the Government, said the TGWU – this luminary applied to the Appeal Court to stop the arrests. The Court obliged. The Government breathed again but the respite was a short one. In July another five dockers again defied the NIRC and blocked container lorries trying to cross a picket line in Hackney. They were duly arrested and detained at Pentonville. Feather led a delegation of TUC leaders to Number 10. Though the Minister of Labour, Maurice Macmillan, was present there is no indication in the record that he said a word. Heath, in effect, was acting as his own Minister of Labour, as he had acted as his own Chancellor when the Industries Act was being prepared and his own Foreign Secretary when Britain was negotiating its way into the Common Market. The Government, he assured the TUC, had 'no wish to see men imprisoned for flouting the decisions of the NIRC'. But they could not interfere in the operation of the courts. As to the dockers: 'There could be no doubt of the sources from which they draw their support, which were sources entirely opposed to the interests of the trade union movement.' Feather privately agreed, but argued that the dockers would have obeyed an order from any other court, it was the NIRC that they could not stomach: 'The vast majority of trade unionists regarded it as having a political and penal quality, and rejected it.'[12]

Once again Carr contemplated jumping off Westminster Bridge, once again an outside force came to the rescue. This time it was the law lords, who reversed Denning's judgment and ruled that a union *was* responsible for the conduct of its members. With some relief the NIRC ordered the release of the Pentonville Five, who emerged into a blaze of glory. The strike went on. Jack Jones and Lord Aldington were asked to negotiate a deal which would compensate the dockers for the work which they lost through the use of container lorries. They came up with a solution, only to have it rejected by the dockers. It took another state of emergency and three weeks of damaging strike action before the dockers concluded that they had fully secured their position. For Heath it had been a profoundly dispiriting episode. The NIRC had been made to look ridiculous and the unions were more than ever convinced that it was the tool of the employers and the Government. The Government had shown itself ineffective and Heath's own reputation had been damaged by his association with a policy that was patently proving a disastrous failure. The dock strike had ended in victory for the dockers and a settlement that was manifestly damaging to the nation. Worst of all, and most painfully for Heath, it seemed that the structure of British society was being damaged by the bitter conflicts between the unions and the Government. His apocalyptic gloom was deepened by reports that he received of a dockers' rally outside Transport House. The police had behaved with conspicuous restraint – too conspicuous, Heath felt – when it came to checking some decidedly unruly behaviour. 'The photographs in the press', wrote Heath, 'of the miserable little delegate leaving Transport House with his briefcase, cowering against a wall while being threatened by a docker, does not do credit to anyone, least of all those responsible for maintaining law and order … This can only get us into a worse mess than if effective action had been taken.' And yet the only 'effective action' that could have been taken, which would have pitted police against workers, was the antithesis of everything that Heath believed in and hoped for.[13]

By the middle of 1972 he had begun to suspect that the Industrial Relations Act was not going to provide a structure within which labour relations could be harmoniously developed. There was no question of repealing it. Even if he had not believed that its philosophy was fundamentally sound and would one day win acceptance, he knew that no government could survive the scuttling of its flagship piece of legislation. But something else was needed. That will-o'-the-wisp of which Heath had for so long dreamed – agreement between labour and employees on the way forward in economic matters – now flickered with particular brilliance. Heath was to dedicate the next few months to a gallant if eventually unavailing pursuit of that elusive goal.

He was hardly operating from a position of strength. June had seen a ferocious run on sterling, the bank rate raised to 6 per cent and, eventually, the flotation of sterling with a considerable loss of its value against other currencies. The Government was trailing in the polls, by an average of about 10 per cent in July. The loss of Maudling and the troubles in Northern Ireland added to the malaise. There was rising unease within the Tory Party. Nigel Lawson's acerbic description of the situation as he saw it at this time summed up the view of many members. 'After a reforming start,' he wrote ('reforming' in this context referring to Heath's brief manifestation as Selsdon Man):

> Ted Heath's Government ... proposed and almost implemented the most radical form of socialism ever contemplated by an elected British Government. It offered state control of prices and dividends, and the joint oversight of economic policy by a triplicate body representing the TUC, the CBI and the Government, in return for trade union acquiescence in an incomes policy. We were saved from this abomination by the conservatism and suspicion of the TUC, which perhaps could not believe that their 'class enemy' was prepared to surrender without a fight.

It was with that conservative and suspicious TUC that Heath now set out to do a deal.[14]

It was an operation that he intended to keep very much under his personal control. 'We must pursue our discussions with the TUC so that we can have some "straight" talking,' he told Robert Armstrong. 'No time must be lost ... We must bring our discussions to the point of decision ... I still have a hankering to follow up the hints we had from Jones and Scanlon that they wanted to talk individually to me.' The individual talks never took place and Scanlon was never more than an unenthusiastic participant in the discussions, but Jones warmed to Heath. 'At the outset I thought he represented the hard face of the Tory Party,' Jones wrote in his memoirs, 'but over the years he would reveal a human face of Toryism, at least to the union leaders who met him frequently ... Amazingly, he gained more personal respect from union leaders than they seemed to have for Harold Wilson or even Jim Callaghan.' But it was Feather who pushed hardest and most persistently for discussions that might lead to a genuine consensus. He did not pretend that it was going to be easy to convert his rank and file, let alone the hardline left-wingers. The TUC negotiators, he told Heath, were 'realistic about the economic situation' but they had to 'keep an eye on the shop floors behind them ... It might be that at the end of the day the TUC acquiesced in rather than accepted the final outcome.' The line between acquiescence and acceptance was a fine one, and Heath was more than happy to accept the former if it was on offer. But he too knew what problems lay ahead. 'The only reason trade union leaders should go to 10 Downing Street is with an eviction order,' Mick McGahey had declared, and the voice of McGahey and his like was growing ever more potent in the TUC. If an agreement could be reached between Government, TUC and CBI, Heath asked Feather, would the union leaders be able to deliver the cooperation of their members? '98 per cent of them could,' replied Feather. 'It was only in the docks that nobody could deliver.' They were brave words, but both Heath and Feather must have known that there were many hurdles to cross before this happy denouement could be reached.[15]

The ground was cleared for the tripartite meetings when Heath met the General Council of the TUC early in July 1972. As could have been predicted, the union leaders reiterated their demands that the

Industrial Relations Act should be repealed or at least suspended. The cooling-off period and the ballot had proved counterproductive and the objectionable features of the Act, from the point of view of the unions, far outweighed any benefits they might receive. They knew, of course, that there was no question of Heath accepting this proposition, which they did not make a precondition for beginning talks. Heath countered by emphasising the gravity of the country's economic plight and insisted that the British public considered it the duty of the Government, the TUC and the CBI jointly to find a solution to the problem of inflation. He told the TUC that he would shortly be seeing the leaders of the CBI and speaking to them in the same vein, and he felt reasonably sure that they would be willing to extend their policy of price restraint for another few months. Reporting on the meeting to the Cabinet he said he had grounds for hoping that the TUC and the CBI would soon agree on 'the introduction of some form of independent conciliatory machinery'. This was the first manifestation of what was eventually to become ACAS – the Advisory Conciliation and Arbitration Service. Though Heath did not mention it, indeed perhaps hardly realised, ACAS, if it worked, was going to render superfluous many of the provisions of the Industrial Relations Act.[16]

When he met the CBI the following week he produced much the same arguments but laid more stress on his anxiety to avoid statutory intervention in the fixing of prices and wages. Nevertheless, he insisted – threatened would be an apter word, perhaps – that the Government could not stand by and let galloping inflation ruin the country. If the CBI and the TUC could not reach some accord, then the Government would have to impose its own regulations. The CBI, while not unduly optimistic, were quite prepared to meet the TUC, and by the time Heath reported to the Cabinet the TUC had confirmed that it too would be ready to participate in tripartite talks. The first meeting was fixed for 18 July. At a preparatory discussion Heath stressed once more that restraint on wages and prices imposed from above could lead 'to a renewal of inflationary problems at a later stage'. A voluntary agreement would be well worth purchasing even at the price of some increase in inflation; 'the consequences of failure to secure voluntary agreements would be very serious'.[17]

Over the next three months Heath presided over ten tripartite meetings, lasting a total of fifty-two hours. In the margin of these great set-pieces were innumerable subsidiary meetings to analyse what had gone on in the last plenary session and to prepare for the next one. Feather went privately to Number 10 on at least six occasions: 'These were not negotiating sessions,' wrote his biographer ... 'Feather was trying to guide the Prime Minister's hand to what would be acceptable.'[18] Taken on top of the innumerable other crises which daily assailed the Prime Minister, this additional burden might have proved insupportable. Instead, Heath seemed positively to relish the responsibilities. At the tripartite meetings he was endlessly patient, understanding, resourceful in seeking ways round difficulties. The patent inadequacy of the CBI representatives when it came to fighting their corner meant that ministers sometimes found themselves having to make their points for them, but even the most turbulently left-wing of the union leaders did not claim that Heath was unfair or biased in his presentation of the facts.

The first meeting, which was more concerned with identifying the problems than finding solutions, went reasonably well. Everyone agreed that what was needed was sustained economic growth, an increase in incomes and reduction in the rate of inflation. The atmosphere became less cordial when it came to deciding how these happy circumstances should be brought about. The TUC representatives insisted on firm assurances that prices would be controlled and were doubtful whether this could be achieved except by statutory limitations. On the other hand, when it came to wages, they accepted the principle of restraint but rejected any idea that this should be anything but a voluntary act on the part of each union. The TUC, Heath told the Cabinet, 'now recognised the force of public opinion in favour of an agreement and would not wish to be the cause of a failure'. So far so good, but they also recognised the indignation many of their members would feel if the unions voluntarily accepted limits on their right to bargain for the best terms possible. It became more and more clear that Feather had been right when he had said that the unions might acquiesce in pay restraints imposed by statute but would not be seen as equal partners in the formulation of such a policy. On 3 November

1972 Heath told a disappointed Cabinet that the unions had broken off discussions on the grounds that the proposals put forward by the government at the tripartite meetings 'provided no basis for negotiation'. Nobody, the Cabinet agreed unanimously, 'could have done more than the Prime Minister to seek to reach a reasonable settlement with both sides of industry'. Feather, Jones, indeed a majority of the trade union delegates would probably have agreed with that judgment. However, they would also have concurred with Heath's sombre summing-up: 'The Government faced a troubling prospect ahead, not excluding further periods of industrial unrest.'[19]

Of course it was a disappointment that the talks had broken down, Heath told the ambassador in Washington, Lord Cromer: 'But I do not think that they were wasted because I am sure that all concerned understand each other better and that they will provide the basis for another try later on.' Mutual understanding does not necessarily guarantee a happier relationship, but Heath had also been given a broad hint that, if the Government imposed a prices and incomes policy by law, the unions would protest but not resist. He viewed the prospect with some distaste. As recently as June he had told Alastair Hetherington that he had no intention of imposing a prices and incomes freeze. 'If anyone could show him that it would work, then he might change his mind, but nobody had done so. Why go back to what had failed?' His mind changed slowly and reluctantly. In September a group of his closest advisers prepared a paper putting forward an outline for a prices-and-incomes policy. 'I hope we will not have to resort to this sort of thing, but we may have to,' commented Heath gloomily. Within a few weeks he had accepted that he did have to. At a meeting at Chequers at the end of October he set out the possibilities. The first was that the Government could resort to the previous policy of seeking to challenge each inflationary wage claim as it came along. That had already been shown to be ineffective. Or they could 'operate through macro-economic policy'. That would no doubt be approved by any monetarist members of the party but would 'involve massive deflation, which would be totally inconsistent with the maintenance of growth and the reduction of unemployment'. Or finally they could continue the fight against inflation but with statutory backing. Distasteful though this last approach might be, it was surely the most acceptable of the possibilities? It would at least give the Government something to bargain with when or if negotiations for a voluntary arrangement were resumed.[20]

Put like that, there was obviously no alternative. On 6 November a ninety-day standstill was imposed on pay, prices, rents and dividends. Feather told Heath that, though he could not expect any overt support, all the members of the TUC General Council 'except the nuts' welcomed the measure. He hoped that negotiations could reopen before the freeze ran out and Phase 2 of the anti-inflationary programme was introduced; though perhaps this should be on a bilateral basis since the TUC negotiators found that the presence of representatives of the CBI 'cramped their style'. On the whole the new policy was well received: people recognised the desperate need that something should be done and were disposed to give a chance to any new initiative. But Heath found it hard to justify what was palpably a volte-face. On *Panorama* Robin Day quizzed him mercilessly. Would not the standstill inevitably entail 'a freeze for the little man and an absolute bonanza for the big boys?' 'Absolute nonsense!' retorted Heath angrily. 'It applies right across the board.' Given the fact that he had abandoned all the principles on which he had fought the last general election, continued Day, should he not either get out or call an election to see if he had the support of the people? Heath stoutly maintained that he had the wholehearted support of the electorate; he did the best he could with a shaky brief but, considered Michael Cockerell, 'it was a less than convincing performance'. The recently re-elected President Nixon at least cheered him on from across the Atlantic. 'We're having quite a battle, but I'm sure it's the right thing to have done,' Heath told him. 'How is it being accepted so far?' asked Nixon. 'Well, the unions are being rather silly, but otherwise there's seventy per cent of the country behind it.' 'Seventy per cent?' questioned Nixon in surprise. 'We've just had a poll, yes,' confirmed Heath.[21]

Heath forbore to mention that a section of his own party was being at least as 'silly' as the unions. Powell's outrage was predictable. The Counter Inflation Bill, he claimed, was 'so suddenly assembled and so ill-digested that it took Heath's Cabinet colleagues and Conservative Central Office by surprise ... There is something vertiginous about the spectacle of men solemnly re-committing themselves to a proven absurdity.' Powell's opposition might be dismissed with equanimity, but there was disquiet among many leading Tories who formed part of the Government. 'Margaret Thatcher, Keith Joseph, John Nott and myself', wrote Kenneth Baker, 'suppressed any misgivings in the hope that it would work in the short term.' But the misgivings were there. The philosophy to which they and, up till now, Heath had subscribed was that the economy should be left as free as possible and subject mainly to market forces. 'The Conservatives, in a complete role-reversal, were now advocating one of the most rigid regimes of supervision and control which had ever been proposed.'[22]

Years later Nigel Forman sent Heath a draft chapter for a book he was writing for sixth-formers on modern government. 'You say that I made an "almost personal decision to introduce a statutory incomes policy in 1972",' expostulated Heath. 'This is quite a fallacious statement which has no basis of truth in it at all.' His protest was justified in that the minutes of the various cabinet meetings at which the prices and incomes policy was discussed reveal no significant dissent or even hesitation.[23] These were collective cabinet decisions and theoretically Heath was no more responsible than any other minister. It is impossible, however, that he should not have known that some ministers had reservations. He chose to ignore them. Forman's phrase 'an almost personal decision' was perhaps pitched too high, but it was substantially correct. It is hard to believe that any other member of the Cabinet, if he or she had been Prime Minister, would have had the authority or the will to impose so radical a switch of direction on the Government. Nor did he confine his attention to the broad principles; he took an interest in the detailed application of the new laws which few prime ministers would have thought to be part of their duties. Nothing was deemed too small to merit his attention. When the launderers pleaded that they were a special case and that they should be free to raise their charges, Heath minuted: 'Can they really not be held for ninety days? I find it hard to believe – we must be tough.'[24]

*   *   *

This was not the only issue on which he felt it desirable to be tough; but his problem was that the right wing of his party was convinced that he was feeble and irresolute. In September 1972 the Tory back-bencher Patrick Wall wrote to the Chief Whip to say that he had never known in the House 'such a degree of anger and discontent with what they believe to be the weakness of the Government, who were voted into office to take a firm hand over the question of violence and of strikes'. Pym passed the letter to Heath, saying that it expressed 'in sharp terms what a wide section of the Party is feeling'. Heath peevishly commented: 'I'm sorry that the Chief Whip should believe such arrant nonsense written by an extreme right-winger who has never supported this Government.' But Pym was right; Wall was certainly an extremist but he was voicing a widely held opinion. John Wells wrote to Heath's pps, Timothy Kitson, saying that there was no point in his writing to the Prime Minister 'because he is no doubt completely indifferent to what I think and also unlikely to mend his ways. All I can do is to take as active a part as I can in any moves to get rid of him.'[25]

The Tory backbenchers who opposed the Government's European policy were not necessarily the same as those who deplored the prices and incomes policy and Heath's conciliation of the unions, but they tended to be grouped together on the right. Heath disliked and resented them, but had no wish to exacerbate their hostility. One issue on which he had some sympathy with their views was immigration. He felt strongly that, once in the United Kingdom, immigrants were not to be treated as second-class citizens but he saw no reason why they should necessarily be admitted into a country which was dis-agreeably overcrowded and where unemployment was already high. Towards the end of 1971 he urged that more should be done to per-suade immigrants to return to their homeland: 'We are not prepared to bring pressure to bear upon immigrants to leave this country, but at the same time we should do everything possible to ensure that those who wish to return can do so.' Public opinion, he reiterated in Cabinet a year later, would not tolerate a repetition of the mass immigration of the Ugandan Asians. Pierre Trudeau had told him that it was extremely unlikely that Canada would be able to help out a second time and other countries would probably feel the same. The British people must be assured that the Uganda debacle would never be repeated. It would be sad, put in some unidentified member of the Cabinet, 'if in response to current political pressure the Government adopted harsh measures of which public opinion might subsequently come to be ashamed'. After a summing-up which was beset by a proliferation of 'on the one hand' and 'on the other' Heath concluded merely that 'the Cabinet was now seized of the very serious nature of the problem' and would need to go on discussing it in the future.[26]

While the Government's policy on the economy enraged the right, its housing policy stirred up violent resentment on the left. The Housing Finance Act, originally introduced as a White Paper in July 1971, became law a year later. It in effect abolished all existing house subsidies and rent controls, requiring the local authorities to charge an economic rent, with a provision for rent allowances for those in privately rented homes. For Heath the measure seemed eminently fair and beneficial: the council tenants who could not afford to pay more would be sheltered from the increases; the augmented rents paid by those who *could* afford to pay them would be devoted to the building of new homes or the improvement of old ones; society as a whole would be vastly better off. To those, however, who found themselves expected to pay increased rents, in some cases sharply increased rents, the Act seemed a monstrous imposition. The Labour leaders privately saw little wrong with the principle – Crossman told Peter Walker that the bill was more socialistic than anything he would have dared put forward – but were delighted to fan the flames of public indignation. It was, proclaimed Crosland in the House of Commons, 'the most reactionary and divisive measure that is likely to be introduced in the lifetime of this Parliament'. Some local authorities refused to levy the new charges; in Derbyshire eleven councillors in Clay Cross carried their opposition so far that they were personally fined for their obduracy. Even when the councils gave way, the tenants often continued to fight; up to 100,000 local authority tenants refused to pay and the rancorous backlash could still be felt years after the bill became law.[27]

1972 had been a singularly testing year. The culminating blow fell when the Liberals in a by-election in early December captured what should have been an impregnable Tory fortress at Sutton and Cheam. But things could have been worse. The Government was certainly unpopular but there did not seem to be any reason to believe that the nation felt any more enthusiastic about the Socialists. Labour still enjoyed a substantial lead in the polls but the gap had been narrowing over the previous few months. Heath's assurance to Nixon that the prices and incomes policy was popular in the country was borne out by the figures in various polls. The trade unions had grumbled but seemed content to leave it at that, and there was no indication that any serious confrontation was in the offing. Economic growth was strong, unemployment was once more well down below the fateful million. Heath was battered and perhaps bloody, but he had good reason to be unbowed. It did not seem unreasonable to hope that the year ahead would prove less testing; it was even conceivable that the Government's policies might work out. Safely ensconced in Europe, with prices and incomes temporarily under control and the unions apparently disposed to cooperate, it seemed at least possible that Britain might finally enjoy the social and economic renaissance of which the Prime Minister had dreamed.

EIGHTEEN

Foreign Affairs

Heath, wrote Henry Kissinger, was 'the only British leader I encountered who not only failed to cultivate the special relationship with the United States but actively sought to downgrade it ... All of this made for an unprecedented period in Anglo-American relations.' Nigel Lawson went even further, calling Heath 'obsessively pro-European and almost equally anti-American'. Heath denied the charge, adding an angry 'No' in the margin of John Campbell's biography where it was suggested that he was trying deliberately to cool the relationship with Washington. When Anthony Royle passed on to him a letter from a constituent complaining about Heath's animosity towards the United States, he replied: 'You need have no hesitation in quashing as firmly as you like any accusation that I am anti-American. I have always believed that part of the point of developing the unity of Europe is that a united Europe will then be able better to co-operate with the USA for the benefit of the whole free world.'[1]

Certainly it was no fault of President Nixon's if the special relationship languished. So delighted was he by Heath's electoral victory that he called Kissinger, who happened to be in Mexico, several times on an open line to tell his Secretary of State how pleased he was. A few days later he told Heath that a special emissary, Bill Rogers, was coming over to see him and Alec Douglas-Home. Nixon referred to the 'uniquely harmonious' relationship between the UK and the USA: 'From what you and your colleagues have said, I know that we will carry on this tradition.' Early in October 1970 he dropped off for lunch at Chequers. He was only able to stay for a few hours – Heath looked with some dismay at the wad of briefs the Foreign Office had prepared and minuted: 'Thank you. I didn't realise he was staying at Chequers for 2 days.' This was relayed back to the Foreign Office as: 'The Prime Minister has indicated that he feels the list of briefs is somewhat formidable given the length of the visit.' In fact, he made even less use of them than he had expected. A few days before Nixon was due to arrive Robert Armstrong announced that he had 'a fairly weighty spanner to throw into the works'. The Queen had decided that it would be discourteous if she did not fly down from Balmoral to meet the President on his first visit to Britain. This left even less time for serious discussion.[2]

Nevertheless, or perhaps because of this, the visit went swimmingly. Heath later told the Queen that he believed Nixon 'was genuinely anxious to have a close relationship', he had stressed that he felt the special relationship to be 'essentially a matter of personal relations, and these words seemed to be a indication of his wish to put fresh life and meaning into the concept'. John Freeman, the British Ambassador in Washington, told Robert Armstrong that Nixon had found the Prime Minister 'very fit, alert and on top of his job'. On the Middle East, Kissinger – 'who does not lightly share the intellectual limelight with others' – had told Freeman that Heath's analysis was 'the most original and cogent he himself had yet heard from any quarter'. The President clearly wished to establish a close relationship with the new Government, Heath told the Cabinet. He had emphasised that 'he hoped that each country would be able to discuss its policies with the other with complete freedom and frankness'.[3]

So far, so good; but Heath was by no means sure that he wanted to establish a close relationship with the American Government. It was unlikely that he and Nixon would ever have forged any genuinely close personal relationship. As Kissinger pointed out, the two men had too much in common 'for these two quintessential loners to establish a personal tie ... Less suspicious than Nixon, Heath was not any more trusting. Charm would alternate with aloofness, and the change in his moods could be perilously unpredictable. After talking with Heath, Nixon felt somehow rejected and came to consider the Prime Minister's attitude towards him was verging on condescension.' It was typical of the relationship that once, after dinner in the White House, Nixon pointed to a grand piano and suggested that he and the Prime Minister might play a duet. Heath shrugged his shoulders, said nothing and walked on. And yet he scarcely suspected that on this or any other occasion he had given offence. Ray Seitz, an American diplomat who served three times in London, ending up as ambassador, once asked Heath which British prime minister and American president had had the best relationship. '"Heath and Nixon," he replied. I almost choked on my asparagus.' In spite of their promising start and Nixon's good will, concludes Seitz, 'the personal relationship ended up in mutual contempt and, once they left office, the old lions were barely civil to each other'.[4]

There is no suggestion in the correspondence and transcripts of telephone conversations that the relationship came to such a pass but Heath believed, and let others see that he believed, that the European connection was for him all-important and that, if a close personal link with the American President was going to impair that connection, then it must be eschewed. Up to a point, it was going to be possible to preserve both relationships. Heath told the Belgian Prime Minister that Britain had 'good relations and certain operational links' with the United States, 'and we valued them. He himself believed that this British relationship would be useful to the Community.' But Europe came first, and the Americans must adapt themselves to this reality. Neither Nixon nor Kissinger understood how Europe works, he told the German Chancellor, Willy Brandt. 'At times they said it was difficult to deal with Europe because it did not speak with one voice, but when Europe did get together and speak with one voice, the Americans complained that they were being presented with a confrontation or *fait accompli*.'[5]

This allegation, that Washington did not understand how Europe worked, constantly recurred, particularly where Kissinger was involved. Kissinger, Heath complained to Pompidou, insisted on considering Europe as a regional grouping – '*un ensemble régional*'; this, he told the Cabinet, 'showed a serious lack of understanding of the whole nature of the Community'. Burke Trend reported a conversation with Kissinger in which the Secretary of State asked whether Britain's entry into the Community would affect Heath's dealings with the President. Trend said he saw no reason why it should, provided the Americans 'made the mental adjustment which is required by the fact that we are now a member of the EEC'. Kissinger, Trend reported, 'received this with obvious pleasure'.[6]

His pleasure was misplaced. Heath, partly to reinforce his European credentials, partly from personal inclination, was determined that Britain should not only not be pushed around by the Americans but should make it clear to everybody else that it was *not* being pushed around. Over the Middle East he complained that Kissinger seemed to feel that Europe should fall into step behind the United States, 'but he could not expect Europe to follow tamely because Europe simply would not do it'. When it came to the recognition of an independent Bangladesh, Heath said that it was reasonable to seek the views of the American Government but 'we were under no obligation to them in the matter'.[7] Kissinger, for his part, had a knack of irritating Heath by conduct which, at other times, might have been harmless, but which in the early 1970s was calculated to cause offence. In October 1973 he came briefly to London and summoned the German and Italian Foreign Ministers to call on him. 'It seemed an odd thing to do,' grumbled Heath. Kissinger's prime offence, however, was announcing that 1973 was to be the 'Year of Europe'. Heath reacted furiously, complaining that he might as well stand between the lions in Trafalgar Square and proclaim that Europe was embarking on a year to save America. Kissinger insists that his suggestion had been entirely innocent, intended to mark the fact that there would be a new relationship between Europe and the United States. He realises now that he handled it rather tactlessly but thought he had discussed it sufficiently with various European leaders and had their general support. He was certainly justified in thinking that, if Heath had not been in a mood to take offence, the initiative would have caused no such uproar.[8]

The animosity between the two came to a head in November 1973 when Heath chose a dinner for American correspondents as an occasion for making some strikingly frank criticisms of American foreign policy in general and Kissinger in particular: 'Apparently, Dr Kissinger did not like having a Dane speaking for Europe. Well, he would have to get used to it!' His remarks, no doubt picturesquely embellished, were quickly passed back to Washington, whereupon an indignant Secretary of State cancelled appointments he had made to see Heath and Alec Douglas-Home in London a few days later. Douglas-Home, not for the first time, found himself pouring oil on water which his Prime Minister had troubled; he succeeded up to a point but Lord Cromer reported a few days later that Kissinger was still 'very sore'. Press stories 'about the alleged bad relations between myself and Dr Kissinger were wholly without foundation,' Heath maintained unconvincingly, '... my own relationship with Dr Kissinger was then and remains now warm'. 'Heated' might have been a better word. In March 1975 Kissinger said with relief that relations with the UK were 'a great deal better than they had been not so long ago'. He would hardly have expected to say as much of Harold Wilson's administration a few years before. And yet, though relations with the United States were impaired, they were never severely strained. 'Nobody ever said that the special relationship precluded disagreements,' said Kissinger; what it did mean was that 'we had a degree of confidence in British leaders that we did not have in leaders of any other country'.[9]

Heath would have been gratified by the compliment but not particularly impressed by the reference to the special relationship. Kissinger maintained that Heath had thrown away this asset without gaining anything in return. 'What is the asset?' demanded Heath. 'What it does is to estrange us from our European colleagues because they're insulted by the idea that they are inferior.' What was in it for the UK, he repeatedly demanded. We were constantly being asked by the Americans for facilities in our remaining island dependencies, he complained to Alec Douglas-Home. 'Could you let me know what we get in return for this? I may be wrong, but so far this seems to me to be very much a one-way movement.' He *was* wrong, Douglas-Home replied. Britain benefited enormously from the 'massive American military, technological and intelligence machine'. Heath subsided, but no other post-war Prime Minister would have questioned the balance of advantage in the relationship between Britain and the United States.[10]

If only because he knew more about the value of the American connection and was more sensitive to the feelings of the Commonwealth, Douglas-Home was less Eurocentric than the Prime Minister. But there was no serious divergence of views. When Nixon, 'in particularly warm terms', wrote to invite Heath to Washington directly after the 1970 election, it was Douglas-Home who recommended that Heath should accept in principle but suggest no specific time; 'too early a date would be open to misunderstanding in Europe'. Cromer, Heath's personal choice as Ambassador – 'a very old friend of mine, in whom I have great trust', Heath told Nixon – was probably the man who most regretted the change of course. There was, he told Heath in November 1971, a feeling in Washington that 'a long-trusted partner, always staunch albeit irritating on occasion, is leaving the old firm for a new firm at a time which happens to coincide with some shakiness in confidence in the old firm'. It is perhaps not entirely a coincidence that two months later Heath told Douglas-Home he was not sure how long he wanted Cromer to stay in Washington: 'He has not really clicked there, and he and she are both obviously unhappy.'[11]

The loss of confidence in the old firm to which Cromer referred had been provoked by a monetary crisis earlier that year. Heath had seen it coming in June. 'An enlarged EEC', he told Cromer, 'simply would not stand for a situation in which the Americans took the line that the United States could run a balance of payments deficit and sustain the existing exchange rate of the dollar against gold indefinitely.' The Americans, unsurprisingly, saw things differently, and in August 1971, without consultation or even warning, imposed a 10 per cent import surcharge and suspended the convertibility of the dollar. Indignantly, Heath denounced behaviour which seemed to him irresponsible and inconsiderate; the Americans, he told Pompidou, had 'destroyed the then existing pattern of exchange rates, created new barriers to trade ... and undermined the foundation of the systems of international trade and payments established in 1946'. The crisis was eased when Nixon removed the import surcharge and a realignment of currencies was cobbled together by the Smithsonian Agreement at the end of 1971, but Heath was confirmed in his belief that Europe must be able to survive and thrive independently of the United States. What would happen, he asked Pompidou, 'if some post-Nixon President threatened to withdraw from the nuclear defence of Europe unless its monetary and commercial conditions were accepted?' It was the vision of a divided Europe as a perpetual poor relation, condemned to dance to the tune played by its richer kinsman across the Atlantic, that made Heath, more than any other British politician, an enthusiast for European monetary union. True union was still a distant goal, but in May 1972 Britain, though not yet a member of the EEC, joined 'the snake', the system by which the members of the Six locked their individual currencies into a mechanism which limited fluctuations against each other. The move proved sadly premature; the strong balance of payments surplus achieved in 1971 melted away in 1972 and after only two months in the snake Britain had to make a humiliating and expensive withdrawal. Unpleasant though it was, this fiasco did not shake Heath's confidence that complete monetary union in Europe was possible in the not too distant future, that Britain must be part of it and that, until it had been achieved, the imbalance between the two sides of the Atlantic would never be corrected.[12]

By the time Heath met Nixon in Bermuda at the end of 1971 the worst of the financial squall had blown out. The atmosphere was cordial but not intimate. Heath reported that he had been struck by 'the extent to which the formulation of the broad lines of policy ... is confined to the President and his immediate advisers in the White House'. The Indo-Pakistan war, which led to the creation of an independent Bangladesh, had only recently occurred. The British were determined not to become involved in a war between two Commonwealth countries; the Americans took the side of the Pakistanis. They feared that India had committed itself to the Soviet bloc and railed against the ingratitude which the Indians had shown towards the United States in spite of the aid that had been lavished on them. Heath countered that gratitude was an uncommon phenomena in international relationships and it was naïve to expect it from the Indians. No one knew better than the British how difficult the Indians could be; 'but India was a democracy and would not (we believed) wish to allow herself to fall completely under the dominance of the Soviet Union'. Nixon appeared satisfied; Kissinger was less so and chalked up another minus score in the deteriorating Anglo-American relationship.[13]

In the American view Heath was determined to have his cake and eat it too. He ostentatiously refused to foster the special relationship which might have given Britain privileged access to information about American intentions, yet protested acrimoniously if, as with the import surcharge or the Indo-Pakistan war, the United States went ahead to defend what it saw as its vital interests without warning Britain of its plans. A striking example, in which both parties were convinced that they were in the right, occurred in October 1973 in the context of the Arab–Israeli Yom Kippur war. The Americans, alarmed by a build-up of the Soviet fleet in the Eastern Mediterranean and increased Russian support for the Egyptian air force, put their troops across the world on red alert. This action, provocative in the eyes of the Russians, brought the world dangerously closer to a confrontation which might have had calamitous results for Western Europe. Heath demanded an immediate report. Why had he not been consulted or, at least, warned in advance? The American justification for its behaviour seemed to him patently inadequate:

We had known for many days the scale of the Soviet fleet; and, in fact, after the cease-fire the Soviet air supply dropped drastically whereas the American air supply went on at full strength ... Personally, I fail to see how any initiative, threatened or real, by the Soviet leadership required such a world-wide nuclear alert ... We have to face the fact that the American action has done immense harm, both in this country and world-wide. We must not underestimate the impact on the rest of the world; an American President ... apparently prepared to go to such lengths at a moment's notice without consultation with his allies, bound to be directly involved in the consequences, and without any justification in the military situation at the time.

The Americans found this attitude incomprehensible. Their action had been as much in the interest of their allies as themselves: Kissinger told Cromer that the President was 'extremely pained at your Prime Minister's refusal to endorse the alert'. To the French Ambassador he was even blunter, telling him that the Europeans had behaved 'not as friends but as hostile powers'. A situation in which Kissinger tells the Russian Ambassador: 'We are holding off the British ... We don't want to talk with them till we hear from you' suggests that Anglo-American relations were indeed in a parlous state. In his discussions with his European allies Heath made it clear where his loyalties lay but did his best to limit the damage. 'Our American friends are in a difficult mood at present,' he told Brandt. We 'must be patient with the Americans, who obviously think that America's partners are being too European'.[14]

It was the Middle East which provoked the most serious falling out between the United States and Europe. Heath's view of the area was very much that of the Foreign Office; he thought that his tour of the Gulf had given him a special understanding of the Arab mind and he believed that, in the Arab–Israeli conflict, the Arabs had been as much sinned against as sinning. He would have rejected with horror any suggestion that Israel as a nation should be destroyed, but he did not consider that to be a serious possibility and he felt that the Israelis, by their intransigence and indifference to Arab sufferings, were making a permanent settlement impossible. When Golda Meir passed through London he insisted that he must entertain her: 'After all, we look after the Arabs when they are here and we should do the same for members of the Israeli Government, and especially the Israeli Prime Minister.' But when he and Douglas-Home met Mrs Meir, the discussions were 'pretty rough'. Mrs Meir said that she had been shocked by the British Government's recent pronouncements on Israel's possible future frontiers. Heath gave no ground, but he told Gromyko the following month that there was much sympathy for Israel in Britain because it was, as Britain had been in 1940, 'a small country surrounded by hostile people'. Gromyko retorted that Israel had already colonised the United States, and the United Kingdom must be careful that the same thing did not happen to it. Privately, Heath thought that Gromyko had a point. He told President Tito when they met at Chequers at the end of 1971 that 'although it was widely believed that the United States could control the Israelis, in fact it was Israel that exploited their relationship, especially for arms supply'.[15]

Although not remotely anti-Semitic, Heath was sensitive to any suggestion that Jewish interests were ganging up to influence his judgment or change British policy. In September 1972 plans were being finalised for a 'Day of Soviet Music' in London, to be organised by Victor Hochhauser and featuring such Russian artists as Shostakovich and Oistrakh. Heath mistakenly believed that the Zionists were bringing pressure on Hochhauser to call off the festival. 'It is shameful that Hochhauser, who has made so much money out of the Soviet exchanges, should capitulate in this way,' Heath commented. 'HMG will have nothing whatever to do with it. If the Jews don't like the concerts they need not go.' As tension rose in the Middle East in 1973 he continued to believe that it was in large part the fault of the Israelis. When the Board of Deputies of British Jews called on him to protest that the British Government was taking the Arab side, he denied that this was so but said he felt 'that the Government of Israel could do more to promote negotiations and reach a settlement ... If no move was made, he was sure that Israel would lose public sympathy.'[16]

The British attitude towards Israel caused Kissinger especial offence, but for Nixon Heath's rejection of the special relationship seemed a more general and, indeed, personal affront. In July 1973 Nixon issued a pained remonstrance, expressing his dismay about 'the situation in which we seem to find ourselves'. He had thought that he and Heath were agreed that the Atlantic relationship should be revitalised, in the interests of both Europe and the United States. Yet every attempt at multilateral consultation had been rebuffed and the United States was accused of exploiting the 'private bilateral contacts' which the British Government had previously sought to foster. Heath seems to have been disconcerted and even distressed by Nixon's *cri de coeur*. He was shocked, he replied, that Nixon imagined 'that Europe had developed what you describe as an attitude of almost adversary bargaining toward the United States'. His first preoccupation had been to put the relationship between Europe and the United States on a basis of equal and friendly partnership. 'I regard the relationship between us as being as close and intimate as ever. There is in my mind no incompatibility between that bilateral relationship and the multilateral relations between Europe and the United States.'[17]

Possibly Nixon accepted these protestations, certainly Kissinger did not. 'The special relationship is collapsing,' he told Cromer. British entry into the European Community should have raised Europe to the level of Britain. Instead 'it had reduced Britain to the level of Europe'. The French were now being allowed to dominate European thinking on the Atlantic relationship and were seeking to build up Europe on an anti-American basis. This could not happen, he concluded, 'without the tacit help of the United Kingdom'. It is perhaps indicative of the way international diplomacy was conducted, even by men as blunt as Heath and Kissinger, that when Kissinger lunched at Number 10 some three weeks later, such fundamental issues were never aired. In his thank-you letter Kissinger wrote: 'The generous hospitality at your luncheon created an atmosphere conducive to the frank and constructive exchange of views between friends and allies. As often in the past, our countries are called now to common action towards important mutual goals.' 'Pompous ass!' Heath scrawled in the margin.[18]

Not all the entries were on the debit side. Heath resolutely refused to criticise American action in Vietnam, telling the Swedish Prime Minister that he could not accept that the policy was 'wrong and immoral' and that they must agree to differ. To Senator Percy he said that he thought the American policy of 'Vietnamisation and at the same time giving the North Vietnamese an occasional bloody nose' was the right course to follow. Nixon was particularly grateful that Britain had not condemned the American bombing of North Vietnam, which, he told Heath early in 1973, had 'in fact brought the war in Vietnam to an end'. If Heath was sceptical about this somewhat sanguine forecast he forbore to say so. There were already more than enough points of disagreement.[19]

When the Yom Kippur war broke out in October 1973 the Syrian and Egyptian armies took the Israelis by surprise and for a few days seemed to be winning. The United States unequivocally supported the Israelis; Europe tried to remain disengaged and Britain refused to allow American planes to use bases in Cyprus as a staging post on their way to carry supplies to Israel. Cromer called on Kissinger the day after the war began. 'And whose side are you on?' asked the Secretary of State. Cromer said he found this most offensive and urged the United States to avoid any overt intervention. 'This led to Kissinger retorting gloomily that did I expect him to sit by and do nothing while the Egyptians drove the Israelis into the sea.' Cromer said that this was a preposterous scenario. He denied that the Americans had been forbidden the use of British bases – 'the Americans never asked us for such rights' – and argued that Cyprus was irrelevant since 'all American aircraft could get as far as Cyprus, this was so close to Israel that they could easily complete the voyage'.[20]

If the Americans did not ask for the use of British bases, it can only have been because they knew that the request would be refused. At a staff meeting in the State Department Kissinger angrily burst out: 'The Europeans behaved like jackals. Their behaviour was a total disgrace. They gave us no support when we needed it ... And when this is over, as it will be in a few days, it is absolutely imperative for us to assess just where we are going in our relationship with the European allies.' Heath for his part told Cecil King that the Americans were doing nothing to restrain the Israelis and that they handled the situation in 'the worst possible way'. Not everyone in the Cabinet was happy about Britain's failure to condemn the Arabs or to allow the Americans the use of British bases. Mrs Thatcher was one of the recalcitrant ministers who suspected that the policy was based more on the fear that the Arabs might otherwise cut off supplies of oil than on the merits of the case. She argued the point in Cabinet but got nowhere. Douglas-Home, she wrote, defended his case courteously; Heath displayed 'a rigid determination to control an issue which – as he saw it – would determine the success or failure of our whole economic strategy. Finally he told us bluntly that he was having a note circulated laying down the public line ministers were expected to take.'[21]

The most controversial decision taken by the British Government was the refusal to supply the Israelis, not merely with new weapons but with ammunition and spare parts for weapons which the UK had sold them in the past. Heath claimed that this was part of an even-handed approach to the problem: the embargo on arms supplies affected the Arabs as much as the Israelis. That was true, but it was the Israelis who were by far the worse affected. David Owen was appalled by the refusal to supply shells for the Centurion tanks which the Israelis had bought over the previous few years. 'I considered it … the most cynical act of British foreign policy since Suez. It showed not just the Arab influence within the Foreign Office but a total lack of principle in standing by one's commitments from two politicians [Heath and Douglas-Home] whom I had hitherto respected.' Mrs Thatcher was not the only minister to share Owen's view. The British attitude, Hailsham told Douglas-Home, was 'ignoble and immoral'. If you sell weapons, he maintained, 'you implicitly undertake to pro-vide spare parts and ammunition … If you are not prepared to do this you should not sell the weapons … It is not, as you put it, a question of emotion, except in the sense that all questions of fair dealing cause emotion among honourable men.' Heath himself seems not to have had an entirely clear conscience. Roslyn Lyons, wife of the business-man Sir Jack Lyons and hostess at many musical parties which Heath attended, taxed him with treating the Israelis unfairly. He more or less explicitly apologised and put the blame on the French. He had found it difficult to take seriously the threat posed by the Egyptian army, he told Lady Lyons: 'The only warlike Egyptians I have ever heard of were in *Aida*.'[22]

However ready he might be to play down the special relationship, there was no possibility of extricating Britain from the embrace of the United States when it came to nuclear weapons. The so-called 'inde-pendent deterrent' relied on American expertise and the supply of vital components, and there could be no question of pooling resources with Europe without the blessing of Washington. Heath, however, cherished the vision of a joint Anglo-French deterrent, held on behalf of Europe. He tried this out on Nixon at Camp David in December

1970 and was agreeably surprised by the President's positive response. If such collaboration would help to bring France back into NATO then, Nixon said, 'it would have American support'. Kissinger was much less enthusiastic about the proposition and told Burke Trend afterwards that the President would run into severe squalls, both among the military and with public opinion, if he pushed on too energetically with the idea. There followed a curious period of shadow diplomacy, with nobody sure how far he could commit his country, or, indeed, to what he would be committing it. Early in 1972 Trend summarised Nixon's position as being: '(1) If you want to talk to the French, get on with it but don't tell anybody,' and '(2) I don't mind your talking to Pompidou. But don't let it go any further; and don't let any hint of this subject surface until the Presidential Election [due later that year] is over.'[23]

When Heath finally did speak to Pompidou, the exchange was conducted by covert winks and nudges. 'We shall naturally have to continue to keep the US informed,' wrote Carrington. 'Only to the President through me,' minuted Heath in response, 'in *no* circum stances *any* channel, however unofficial, from MOD.' Ten years later he said that he had 'proposed to President Pompidou that the British and French forces be co-ordinated. But Mr Pompidou had been unable to accept this.' That gives a misleadingly forthright account of what seems to have been a most elliptical discussion. 'If anyone in Parliament asks me whether we discussed nuclear questions I shall reply that we did not,' Heath told Pompidou. 'I assume you'll take the same line.' In fact there seems to have been a somewhat vague agree-ment that there should be an exchange of information about the next generation of nuclear weapons, with little being done to follow it up. The main reason for this seems to have been the extreme reluctance of the French to become embroiled in any sort of tripartite arrange-ments over nuclear weapons involving the United States. A year later Pompidou told Heath that he accepted the importance of Europe's relationship with America but 'he would not take part in any discus-sions with the United States on European defence'. Furthermore, he pointed out, this was not an issue affecting only Britain and France: Helmut Schmidt had already said that the creation of an Anglo-

French nuclear force would drive Germany into neutralism. The only firm conclusion which the two men reached was that 'their discussion and any follow-up talks should be Top Secret'.[24]

If Heath made any serious attempt to overcome French susceptibilities, it is not recorded; probably by then he had accepted that this was an issue which was best transferred to a back-burner and left to simmer for a decade or two. Certainly the future of Britain's own nuclear deterrent could not be allowed to linger in the same twilight world. At the end of 1972 Heath, Douglas-Home, Barber and Carrington met to discuss whether the Polaris submarine-borne missile should be abandoned, improved or replaced. An independent British strategic nuclear capacity was deemed to be essential and improving Polaris seemed the most sensible way of setting about it. It must have been galling for Heath to go cap-in-hand to the Americans but in January 1973 in Washington he asked Nixon whether the experts could begin to explore the possibility of attaching a British warhead to a Poseidon missile. Nixon replied that he, personally, would be in favour of letting the British have Poseidon but he foresaw problems with Congress.[25] Issues of this kind are seldom if ever settled quickly. Given the relationship between the two governments when the Yom Kippur war ended, it was perhaps fortunate that nothing had been decided by the time Heath lost power. From the point of view of Anglo-American relations, it is difficult not to feel that Heath's replacement by Wilson in February 1974 gave an opportunity for a fresh start that can rarely have been more badly needed.

The accepted picture of the administration of British foreign policy during Heath's government was that the Prime Minister took personal control of Britain's relationship with Europe and, in so far as the two were interrelated, with the United States, and that Douglas-Home was otherwise left to conduct foreign affairs as he thought best. That is more or less correct. Heath had complete confidence in Douglas-Home's abilities, respected him as a man and was grateful to him for the grace with which he had handled the transformation from Prime Minister to Foreign Secretary. But he took a keen personal interest in foreign affairs and cherished his relationships with certain foreign dignitaries in which Douglas-Home played a subsidiary role. Brandt was the foreign statesman with whom he felt the greatest rapport. He began with some reservations. Brandt's policy of improving relations with East Germany and the signature of a German–Soviet treaty caused him some qualms. 'Close relationships between Germany and the Soviet Union had seldom been to our advantage in the past,' he warned the Cabinet. It was important to ensure that Brandt's Ostpolitik was not weakening Germany's links with the West. But he was soon satisfied that Brandt was to be relied on and shared with him a vision of Europe quite different from the cautious and nationalist-oriented philosophy of the French. It was because he had confidence in the German Chancellor that in March 1973, with the world's currency markets in disarray and a flood of unwanted dollars swamping Europe, he made a dramatic proposal that could have changed the structure of the Continent's financial system. A British initiative, wrote Brandt, 'brought us very close to a point from which the breakthrough to monetary union might have succeeded'. Left to themselves Heath and Brandt would have embarked on a joint flotation, a pooling of the reserves of Britain and Germany, which, if all had gone well, might have led to the same thing being true of the whole Community. 'It turned out', concluded Brandt sadly, 'that the ifs and buts of the experts weighed heavier in the balance than the political will of the British.'[26]

Heath made his démarche at a state dinner at the Schloss Gymnich, some twenty miles north-west of Bonn, the solemnity of the occasion being marred only by the fact that it was the festival of Weiberfestnacht, when the women of the Rhineland had the playful habit of cutting the end off any tie that a man was rash enough to wear. Most of the German high officials therefore wore polo neck sweaters. Heath made a speech which appeared to be unscripted and which certainly had been prepared without consultation with the Treasury, in which he referred to Churchill's offer of union with France in 1940. In the present financial crisis, he suggested, the time might have come for a similar initiative in the financial sphere. The effect of his speech was electrifying and in the excitement of the moment euphoric pledges were made on every side. But then the officials discussed the issue late into the night. 'Is any EEC member ready for this in political terms?' asked Derek Mitchell, of the Treasury. 'Do we have the Community institutions to support the massive transfer of sovereignty that is implied?' German officials were equally ready to pour cold water on their leader's exuberance. Next day in conclave with Brandt, Heath reiterated Britain's interest in joint floating and its hope of quickly rejoining the currency bloc but stressed that 'reserves would have to be available for use for the support of any currency without payment of interest and without fixed payment arrangements'.[27] Brandt did not demur, but the sceptics were at work. Heath, when the Cabinet assembled at Chequers, did not feel able to say more than that Britain would rejoin the float only if the right terms could be negotiated, and that this 'would not be easy'. On such an issue as this the Treasury could not be ignored and Barber, urged on by his officials, offered unusually stout resistance. 'The longer we have to stay out the more damage we shall do to our wider interests,' Heath insisted. 'I do not think the Treasury and the Bank of England are sufficiently aware of these wider implications. I quite see that they do not wish to see a repetition of the events from 1964 to 1967. But we did not join the Community in order to behave like little Englanders.' There were too many little Englanders – and little Germans and little Frenchmen – to allow of any visionary adventure. Whether or not Heath and Brandt, given their heads, would have compounded Europe's economic problems or found a solution to them will never be known. The forces of prudence and inertia frustrated their enterprise and both men were out of power long before any serious progress had been made.[28]

One way in which Heath and Brandt were particularly close was in their understanding of and sympathy for the problems of the developing world. Heath, however, was not above using aid as a tool to strengthen the British economy. Early in 1971 he argued strongly for a realignment of aid so that it was channelled to those countries which produced the raw materials on which Britain depended and whose stability was therefore of particular importance. He called for a paper which would set out the priorities in terms of national interest. When it appeared, he dismissed it contemptuously: 'I want action, not cotton wool!' The next attempt was read first by Lord Rothschild, who described it as: 'Good, worthy, painstaking, informative, cautious, realistic – and deadly. Needless to say, it recommends further studies which God only knows how long it will take to complete.' 'I require action,' reiterated Heath.[29]

He never got it; or not in so far as any serious realignment of British aid was concerned. Nor would he have thought it worth the price if it had involved serious deprivation for countries that did not happen to enjoy substantial quantities of essential raw materials. His profoundest feelings on this subject were well expounded in the comments that he made on a report on the Debt Burden of Developing Countries, a document which he felt to be unduly dismissive of the problems faced by the developing world:

> What perturbs me more than anything about this report is its apparent failure to comprehend in any way the real problems of the developing world; and without such comprehension our policies will more often than not end in failure if not disaster.
>
> The great majority of the 1,200 million people of the developing world are living in appalling conditions of poverty, hunger, disease and social squalor. Yet every day of their lives their leaders are able to tell them ... that the people of the developed world ... are rapidly improving their standard of living so that the gap between the developed and the undeveloped world becomes ever wider. Who can blame them for demanding a growth rate of at least 6 per cent? Who can blame them for overthrowing any Government apparently content just to go along with much less? Who can blame them for repudiating the debts they owe to the wealthy? Who can blame them if they become politically frustrated with constant lectures from Western treasurers on restraint and protracted, indeed interminable, meetings about debt renegotiations, all of which seem to leave them worse off than they were before?
>
> These are the real problems of the developing world. It is for these that Britain in the European Community and the United States must find an answer. The United States, confronted with its own disorders

and its present mood of withdrawal from active participation in the world scene, is unlikely to play much of a part. It is up to us.[30]

This is Heath at his best: clear-headed, compassionate, committed. It is true he was propounding a problem rather than suggesting a solution, but like few other people at the time, he was aware of the problem, he saw the situation more clearly than the majority of his colleagues. It was this awareness that, seven years or so later, was to bring him together again with Willy Brandt when a commission was set up under the auspices of the World Bank to consider the whole problem of development issues, aid programmes and the plight of the Third World.

The other area in foreign affairs in which Heath, with rather less justification, felt that he enjoyed some expertise was the Gulf and the general question of a British military presence east of Suez. Here defence issues and the needs of the national economy overlapped with foreign policy and the Prime Minister had good reason to take a prominent role. When Heath had toured the Gulf states in 1969 he had been told on every side that it would be a disaster if Britain withdrew its troops. The Ruler of Kuwait had refused to believe that this could seriously be British policy. Why, in that case, he asked, was expensive construction work still going on at the base at Sharjah? Heath did his best to explain that it was normal for a British Government to lavish money on works which they were about to abandon – it would be unwise to read into such activity any indication that a change of policy by the Labour administration was on the cards. The Ruler was not entirely convinced. Even the Shah of Iran, who looked forward to profiting from the power vacuum which withdrawal would create, told Heath that he found that the British policy represented 'an incomprehensible loss of will-power'. Further east Heath was equally disturbed by Labour plans to withdraw British forces and abandon the great base at Singapore. The suggestion that troops could be sent out at short notice if need arose he dismissed as preposterous: 'They would arrive too late, ill-equipped and not acclimatised.' In the Godkin lectures, delivered at Harvard in 1968, he maintained: 'Britain has existing commitments which have to be discharged and in my Party we believe we must discharge them ... The most expensive way of saving money is to pull troops out of a place before there are local forces able to provide protection against attack from outside and a local political structure which can resist subversion from within.'[31]

When he came to power he tried to put his doctrines into practice. When the FCO proposed sending a letter to various Commonwealth leaders saying that the Cabinet was considering how to retain 'a small military presence in Malaysia/Singapore', the Prime Minister struck out the word 'small': 'I don't want any of them saying we are going back on our word. We are not.'[32] But to hold by his word proved harder than he had expected. The retreat from Singapore was already far advanced and to reverse it would have been unacceptably expensive. Nor did the Prime Minister of Singapore, Lee Kuan Yew, seem disposed to facilitate the process. The New Zealand Minister of Defence complained that Lee was flirting with the Russians and was saying that the presence of British, Australian or New Zealand ground forces would serve little purpose. Heath added that Lee was reinforcing this message by demanding a high rent for the real estate occupied by the Commonwealth contingent.[33] If the people whom the Commonwealth forces were supposed to be defending did not want to be defended, how could an expensive military presence be justified? In the Gulf, where the various Arab rulers had already made alternative plans for their own defence, the FCO, the Ministry of Defence and, above all, the Treasury deplored any suggestion that the withdrawal should be reversed, or even checked. Heath in the end had to accept that a British military presence east of Suez was unsustainable. In spite of his autocratic reputation he was, on almost every issue, ready to back down if a majority of the Cabinet was against him and was prepared resolutely to maintain its position. This was such a case.

Not that Heath was by instinct an interventionist in the Middle East. In September 1970 the Archbishop of Canterbury urged him to send troops to Jordan to help the King quell the ever more active Palestinian rebels; otherwise, he feared, there would be some 'spectacular move' on the part of the Israelis. King Hussein would find such an enterprise 'far from welcome', replied the Prime Minister.[34]

Ten days later the Syrians invaded Jordan. Hussein appealed for the 'moral and diplomatic support' of the British and Americans, backed, if necessary, by a threat of military action. He also asked Britain to urge Israel to launch an air strike against Syrian forces. The Cabinet quickly decided that this last task would be best left to the Americans. What should be said, though, if the Americans decided to intervene and asked for British support? It was, in a way, a dress rehearsal for the Yom Kippur War. There was general agreement that 'our limited resources and the damage to our interests in the Arab world' were conclusive arguments against any British involvement, either alone or with the United States. Even offering the American facilities in the UK or in Cyprus 'would gravely damage our standing with the Arabs'. British prosperity depended on Arab oil and in 1970 as in 1973 Heath was not disposed to countenance any policy which would put the national economy in danger.[35]

Heath enjoyed the business of entertaining foreign potentates and would take endless trouble over the arrangements. When the Portuguese Prime Minister, Professor Caetano, visited the UK in 1973, Heath refused to give a dinner for him in Hampton Court on the grounds that it was 'rather seedy for a formal state occasion'. He countered with Greenwich approached by river. This idea was adopted. A poem about the sea, thought to be by the Portuguese poet Camões, was shown to Heath and Tom Bridges suggested that it be translated and set to music. Heath asked the Poet Laureate to handle the poetic side; Betjeman said he could not translate from the Portuguese but would happily versify a free translation. The Master of the Queen's Musick was enlisted to set it to music. It turned out that the poem was not by Camões and Betjeman's translation was hardly a distinguished addition to the canon of English poetry, but at least Professor Caetano cannot have been left thinking that no trouble had been taken over his entertainment.[36]

Heath made more use than most prime ministers of Chequers as a place for entertainment; he found the beauty, the dignity and yet the informality of the surroundings worked wonders in putting even the most truculent of visitors into an amenable frame of mind. Its charms were severely tested when Dom Mintoff, Prime Minister of Malta, stayed there in September 1971. Mintoff was a turbulent and talented Rhodes Scholar, whose period at Oxford had signally failed to inspire any wish to preserve a close relationship with Britain if it would serve Maltese interests better to abandon it. He came to power with a mandate to demand vastly increased financial aid in exchange for the continued use of Valetta as a naval base. Heath responded robustly to his ultimatum: 'I do not recall', he wrote to Mintoff, 'having received such peremptory messages from another Head of Government; and I should be doing less than justice to the feeling which they have provoked within my Government if I did not make it clear to you that we regard it as impossible to do business on this basis.' Eventually he suggested that the matter would best be discussed face to face. Mintoff prevaricated but after some blustering and a last-minute decision, arrived at Chequers. For a long evening and during the following morning Heath and Carrington listened patiently to Mintoff's ranting and explained why the British could not meet all his conditions. Carrington left after lunch: 'I went home feeling that the Prime Minister had done a remarkable job,' he wrote; and Heath felt able to reassure the Cabinet that Mintoff was ready in principle to accept the propositions put forward by Britain and NATO: 'In general, our relations with the new Maltese Government now seem to be developing on a more stable and realistic basis.'[37]

Events took a curious twist after Carrington's departure. Mintoff's aristocratic English wife was estranged and living in England. According to Heath's memoirs the Prime Minister, without telling Mintoff, invited her to Chequers, installed her in the White Parlour, and then conducted Mintoff there, saying that there was 'somebody there whom he would be very glad to see'. Carrington, however, maintains that Heath telephoned him in a panic to report that Mrs Mintoff had arrived without warning; Mintoff, Heath claimed, had asked his wife 'to meet him here. Here! To talk things over, over tea, with me!' Heath's version, Carrington says today, must be nonsense; he 'didn't even know that Mrs Mintoff existed'. Certainly Heath's account seems unconvincing. Why he should have claimed to have played Cupid in this haphazard and dangerous way is hard to understand; perhaps he thought it made a better story and had told it so often that by the time he came to write his memoirs he believed it to be true. Things did indeed go rather better with Malta after the Chequers visit, although dealing with Mintoff was never going to be easy. Heath told Emilio Colombo, the Italian Prime Minister, that Britain would be very happy to hand over its facilities in Malta to Italy and would even contribute to their upkeep. 'Signor Colombo, smiling broadly, said that he recognised the selflessness and generosity of Mr Heath's offer.'[38]

Christopher Hill and Christopher Lord, in their admirable essay on the foreign policy of the Heath Government, have pointed out the similarities between the cases of Malta and of Iceland. In each case a small country with a left-wing government and pressing economic problems sought to overturn existing international agreements so as to improve their lot. In each case NATO facilities were threatened. In each case Britain was the principal victim. In August 1971 Iceland arbitrarily extended its fishing limit to fifty miles and began to harass British trawlers that defied the ban. 'As a sailor myself,' wrote Heath, 'I was certainly not prepared to see seamen victimised in this way.' Even if he had been less stalwart, the extremely vociferous members of the Conservative Party Fisheries Committee would have insisted that a strong line be taken. Heath asked how the British could retaliate and, when told what damage a ban on Icelandic fish imports would inflict, announced: 'It is essential that it should be forcibly emphasised to the Icelandic Government that we have many cards in our hand and we will not hesitate to play them.' The Foreign Office pointed out that regrettably few of the cards were trumps and that it was by no means certain that the rest of Europe would join Britain in a ban on Icelandic fish. Douglas-Home said that, if the cod war of a few years before was resumed, we would get no support from the United States or our other NATO allies. The final result might well be a humiliating withdrawal. Iceland threatened to declare war: a faintly comical contingency but one that nevertheless would have had embarrassing repercussions. A negotiated interim arrangement was the best that could be hoped for.[39]

Regretfully, Heath accepted the inevitable. The Royal Navy was withdrawn from the disputed areas and the Icelandic Government was told that Britain was ready to compromise. Heath spoke to the Icelandic Prime Minister on the telephone. 'Of course I have to save my face as you have had to do,' Johannesson told him, but he agreed to come to London. There could be no question of a cosy stay at Chequers. The talks took place in Downing Street with Heath conducting the negotiations and displaying his habitual mastery of the issues involved. The arrangements arrived at involved British fishermen in some loss but were better than had at one time seemed likely. They anyway lasted only a few years, after which the cod war was resumed.[40]

Because France had been the key to British entry into the Community and without French cooperation the sort of Europe which Heath envisaged would never be a possibility, it was with President Pompidou that the Prime Minister was most anxious to maintain close and friendly relations. This did not always prove easy. The French, in British eyes at least, showed an irritating tendency to refuse to respect their undertakings in one field unless concessions were made to them in another. 'We should not be unduly influenced by the attitude of the French Government,' Heath told the Cabinet, 'which was their customary position for purposes of tactical negotiation ... We must be prepared to defend our own interests as vigorously as the French Government defended theirs.' Brave words, but in fact he was usually anxious to find sops with which to propitiate the French. The continuation of work on Concorde was one. The Channel Tunnel was slightly different, in that although there were doubts in the Cabinet about its viability, Heath himself, like Pompidou, vested it with an almost mystical significance. Pompidou told Heath that he saw the tunnel as 'the umbilical cord between Britain and Europe' (a curious metaphor given the fate that normally attends umbilical cords); Heath replied that 'we had to demonstrate that the continent was no longer isolated'. By now he had reluctantly accepted that his dream of being able to drive his own car to France and back was technically impossible, but the symbolic importance of the link was no less great and he pushed it forward as urgently as possible.[41]

One point on which he and Pompidou differed, though not radically, was over the attitude the Community should take towards Spain. Heath's memories of the Spanish Civil War were still lively; he detested the Franco regime. When Alec Douglas-Home, in an off-the-record press conference in Madrid, said that he did not think Britain would oppose Spain's eventual entry into the Community, Heath remarked tartly that this was 'not helpful. Spain must be a fully democratic country before it can be admitted to the EEC – we must stand by that.'[42] But Heath and Douglas-Home were as one on the problem of Gibraltar. Heath told López Bravo, the Spanish Foreign Minister, that there could be no question of Britain telling the Gibraltarians what to do; they must first be persuaded that any change would be to their advantage. 'Many people in Britain felt very strongly on this issue and any British Government which ignored this feeling would fall.' The same, he remarked with some prescience, was true of the Falkland Islands.[43]

'I have always loved travelling,' Heath wrote in his memoirs, 'finding out for myself at first hand what is going on.'[44] He might have added that, like most people, he preferred to travel in some comfort and with somebody else paying. Over the next thirty years he was to cover the world repeatedly; as Prime Minister his opportunities were inevitably more circumscribed but he still managed to venture abroad more often than any of his immediate predecessors and successors thought practicable. One country he missed out on was Russia. In April 1971 he had suggested the possibility of a visit. Douglas-Home was discouraging, arguing that it would be premature to go to Moscow while four-power talks on Berlin were still in progress.[45] Heath concurred, and any change of heart was precluded when, a few months later, MI5 urged that the army of intelligence officers which the Russians kept in London, masquerading as trade officials, cultural representatives or under similar guises, should be drastically reduced. 'Throw the lot out!' was Heath's robust response; according, at least, to the slightly unreliable MI5 functionary Peter Wright. This was more than the Foreign Office, or even MI5, thought wise, but it was still decided to expel 105 agents, a formidable total which, predictably, caused outrage in Moscow. George Walden, usually a stern critic of Heath, felt that in this case he was 'superb: resolute and clear-minded'. Others felt that he had overreacted. It was very much his personal ruling, with cautious approval from Douglas-Home. The Cabinet would understand, Heath assured its members, 'why it had not been possible to discuss the decision' with them in advance. Whether they did or didn't – and one or two didn't – the second part of his remark was incontestable: 'Public opinion in this country has in general shown a ready understanding of the Government's action.' Walden's view was widely shared: Heath was hailed as a brave and resolute defender of British interests.[46]

'Agreed', Heath had written at the bottom of Douglas-Home's note suggesting that a visit to Russia be deferred. 'I hope I get to Peking before the President.'[47] He did not. There had not been full diplomatic relations with China since the Revolution of 1949 and Chiang Kai-shek's retreat to Taiwan. Heath saw no reason why this blinkered refusal to accept reality should continue any longer and Douglas-Home had been quietly negotiating a settlement. Then, almost without warning, it was announced that the United States was recognising China and that Nixon would shortly be visiting Peking. Four weeks later Heath received a personal message from the President explaining the reasons for this decision: 'It is difficult to avoid the impression', observed the Foreign Office, 'that the letter is a rather belated attempt to make up for the shortness of the notice we received.'[48] Heath was aggrieved, but resolved that, even if he could not beat Nixon to China, he would follow closely on his heels. China, he felt, was culturally and historically fascinating as well as being an export market of immense potential. Douglas-Home blazed the trail, shortly after the American President had paid his visit, and plans were made for Heath to follow at the beginning of 1974. It was not to be; he was Leader of the Opposition before he paid his first visit to a country that was to play a signally important part in the rest of his life. He did, however, gain the consolation prize of being the first British prime minister to visit Japan. Unlike China, to which he felt curiously drawn both politically and culturally, he viewed Japan purely as a trading partner. But in that role it was of first importance – effectively, as he said in Cabinet, 'at the centre of international and monetary affairs'. There were signs that the Japanese Government was beginning to adopt more reasonable trading policies. An 'urgent and careful study' of the ways of overcoming obstacles to exports to Japan must be put in hand: 'The rewards could be very important indeed.'[49]

In June 1972 Tony Benn stood in for Harold Wilson at a dinner at Number 10 for a Senegali delegation. After dinner, remembered Benn, Heath made 'a mad, impassioned speech about Europe and Africa and how, now the imperial period was over, Europe was united and it would work with Africa to be an influence in the world. It was nineteenth century imperialism reborn in his mind through status within the Common Market.'[50] The comments were unfair – Heath had not the slightest wish to revive imperialism in Africa in another guise – but Benn correctly identified the food for Heath's passion. He was genuinely concerned about the plight of the developing world, he regretted the inability of Britain in its present state to do much about it, and he was convinced that, as part of Europe, not only would the country be reborn but it would inspire a united Europe to play in the world the role that had been the lot of Britain in its heyday. This was his dream and he worked heroically to make it a reality. No one considering the state of Europe today could claim that it corresponds with his ambitions, but there was a nobility about his vision and in 1974 it did not seem wholly impracticable. If the generation of European leaders that followed had shared his dream, even if he himself had remained in power for a few more years, it is not impossible that the European Union could have developed on very different lines.

NINETEEN

Hurricane

The mood of modest optimism in which Heath had ended 1972
survived for the first few months of the following year. The problems
of Northern Ireland seemed closer to a permanent solution than they
had done for many years. Rhodesia was quiescent. There were no
important new crises on the industrial front. The economy was, at
least temporarily, in remission. The polls suggested that the electorate
was reasonably well satisfied with the Government's performance.
Even the more ferocious elements of opposition in the Conservative
Party were comparatively temperate. But not all was set fair. For one
thing, the Chancellor of the Exchequer was growing restive. On the
last day of the old year he wrote to Heath to say that he had run out
of new ideas, was tired, wanted to see more of his family and would
like to get out of politics – as soon as possible, but at all events before
the next election. The reasons he gave were perfectly valid but it does
seem, too, that he had had enough of being pushed around and finding all the major decisions taken out of his hands. John Nott, Barber's
Minister of State, claims that Heath 'held the Treasury in complete
contempt. More and more he came to rely on the advice of William
Armstrong ... and on the political and moral support of Carrington
and Whitelaw ... Barber could make no headway. I often saw Tony
depressed after his meetings at Number 10.' He agreed to stay on for
another year but his relationship with the Prime Minister did not
improve. When he was in Nairobi in the autumn of 1973 the Cabinet,

without consulting him, pushed through various economic measures to bolster the prices and incomes policy. Nott believes that Barber telephoned Heath and 'said that it was intolerable that such measures should be considered in his absence'. The worm, if indeed it had turned, soon turned back again; Barber soldiered on; but even if the crisis which provoked the 1974 election had not quickly followed, it seems unlikely that he would have remained as Chancellor for much longer.[1]

More immediately threatening, the formal posture of the unions remained hostile, even if individual union potentates could prove reasonable. In mid-February Heath met the TUC General Council and found that it supported the gas workers in their industrial action and wanted the Government to spend an extra £600m a year on food subsidies, rent limitation and such measures. 'There seems little prospect of any constructive discussion on economic and industrial affairs with the TUC in the near future,' Heath told the Cabinet. A week later things seemed still darker. There were indications that public support for the Government was being eroded. The Cabinet, said the Prime Minister gloomily, 'must be prepared to face a difficult period of industrial unrest'. One ray of comfort seemed to be that the TUC was growing perceptibly less hostile to the idea of Europe. A few months later Tom Jackson of the Post Officer Workers' Union told Heath that he thought it just possible that, at its forthcoming meeting, the TUC might decide to cooperate more fully with its European equivalents. The key vote would be that of the miners, and Jackson urged Heath to have a private word with the miners' leader, Joe Gormley, on the subject. Maurice Macmillan strongly discouraged the idea; word of the approach would be bound to leak out and could do untold damage and anyway 'one cannot be certain that he would not make a real mess of it – as he has done before'. As for Heath's idea that he might ask Jean Monnet to enlist the European union leaders in the cause, Macmillan was equally doubtful; the fact that 'even so distinguished a European had sought to put pressure on the NUM would be very damaging and could be disastrous'. Gormley, in fact, needed no persuasion; he spoke in favour of TUC participation in European institutions, but the resolution was still defeated.[2]

But though the trade unions maintained their formal opposition to the prices and incomes policy, in private some welcomed and most accepted it. The Prime Minister announced the details of Stage Two at a press conference in January 1973; some thought that the task might more appropriately have been given to the Chancellor but it was Heath's policy and he had no intention of letting anybody else accept the credit or shoulder the blame. Pay increases were limited to £1 plus 4 per cent, with an annual limit of £250; the highest earners, therefore, would be little better off, the low-paid could proportionately do much better. A Price Commission was set up to monitor proposed price increases and veto any that appeared excessive. To the Tory right wing such micro-management of the economy was anathema, but to most people, including many Labour voters, it seemed fair and, in the circumstances, necessary. The white paper had, on the whole, been well received, Heath told the Cabinet, but 'there was a widespread belief that Stage Three would be even more stringent than Stage Two whereas ... the Government's intention was that there should be a progressive move away from the present standstill'. Whatever his private views about the need to retain some sort of incomes control, he was intent to protect his right flank by insisting that the measures were temporary and forced on the Government by exceptional circumstances. There was a growing impression, he said, that the control over prices and incomes was to become permanent: 'It would be important to take every opportunity to correct this.'[3]

Over the next few months Britain's economic future was framed by the Prime Minister in consultation with William Armstrong and certain union leaders, with a minimal contribution being made by other ministers. The pattern was set as early as the end of January, when Heath met Frank Chapple of the Electricians' Union at William Armstrong's house. Chapple took a conspicuously moderate line and warned that the extremists in the union movement 'would concentrate their main efforts on the miners, since the miners still commanded a special sympathy which workers in Fords, for example, could not'. He did not think that the mass of the miners would want a strike.[4] In March Feather and Sidney Greene of the NUR lunched at Number 10: they said that their chief concern was over the likely behaviour of Jack Jones and Scanlon; each separately was reasonable enough but each felt an obligation to be more conspicuously militant than the other.[5] The preoccupation of the union leaders with their public image and the discrepancy between what they were prepared to say to him in private and what they professed when with their rank and file were a constant irritant to Heath. Feather told William Armstrong that he knew Scanlon was 'extremely willing, indeed keen, to meet the Prime Minister privately but that he was extremely worried as to how to ensure that the meeting remained secret. He felt himself to be in a particularly vulnerable position vis-à-vis his own union.'[6] A dinner held in special secrecy was attended by Heath, Jack Jones and William Armstrong in Lord Aldington's house in April. Jones said that the TUC feared the Government intended to limit wages by statute on a permanent basis. That was a complete misunderstanding, said Heath, the statutory limits would not be retained a day longer than was essential, though the Government would continue to seek voluntary agreements with both employers and unions. Jones considered this 'an important declaration of the Government's long-term intention'. He inveighed against inefficient management. Heath said that he 'strongly agreed with Mr Jones's strictures on the general quality of management in Britain at the present time'.[7]

Nothing was published about these meetings and very little said in Cabinet. It was personal diplomacy conducted in the most stringent confidentiality. Inevitably, however, Heath's colleagues knew something of the discussions and felt some disquiet at their exclusion. Sometimes, too, reports in the press gave hints of what was going on. In early May one of his private secretaries, Christopher Roberts, suggested that, in view of 'today's revelations', he might wish to consider saying something to his colleagues about 'your private talks with the TUC and your reasons for keeping these discussions secret'. Heath did not pay much attention to this suggestion but at least he took Barber with him when, in May, he went to a dinner with the CBI. These were the people who should have been the stoutest allies of a Tory leader. Heath had tested them severely in the past, losing few opportunities to lecture and berate them, but at this dinner he was comparatively restrained, contenting himself with telling his audience that 'there were some signs of a new spirit on the trade union side'. He urged those present to establish a new climate in industrial relations 'by the development of new means of associating work people with management decisions and keeping them fully informed about the activities, progress and problems of the business in which they worked'. Lord Melchett, the radically minded chairman of the British Steel Corporation, was enthusiastic, but the general reaction to the Prime Minister's plea was suspicious distaste.[8]

Even the most sceptical of employers, however, had to admit that in the spring of 1973 things could have been a great deal worse. With 'three million workers having now received pay increases deferred during the pay standstills and a further 1½ million having accepted subsequent increases based on the Stage Two pay policy', Heath told the Cabinet on 5 April, it was clear that 'the Government's pay policy was increasingly becoming accepted'. A week later the Cabinet learnt that the prospects seemed good for a settlement within the policy by the rail unions and the water industry, while the shop stewards at Fords 'appeared to be having difficulty in maintaining the confrontation with the employers in the face of decreasing support from the workers'. When the top six of the union leaders came to Number 10 in mid-April – once again with the ubiquitous William Armstrong in attendance but no other minister present – it was generally agreed that the Government had achieved the objectives of Stage 2. Feather said that he wanted to avoid talking in terms of victories and defeats but Scanlon said bluntly that he 'did not wish to make any bones about it: the Government had won and he had not expected it to do so'. He did not suggest, however, that Stage Three would go smoothly. A report prepared by the well-informed French Embassy in London concluded that the unions had conceded victory to Heath but only temporarily: 'The final success of the plan is possible but it is not yet guaranteed'.[9]

In all this the chief victim – apart from the leaders of the CBI, who felt themselves cold-shouldered, and those members of the Cabinet who resented their exclusion from the negotiations – was Sir John Donaldson's NIRC. Its work was being undermined by the misrepresentations of the unions, complained Donaldson, and the Government made no attempt to support it: 'Are ministers not interested in the fate of the Act and the Court or do they not understand the situation which exists?' Heath sympathised, and agreed that the Lord Chancellor should discuss with various colleagues what could be done, but in fact he felt that this was no time to remind people about the activities of the Court. The Chief Whip stressed that a debate on the subject 'would involve the risk of giving a platform to those opposing the work of the Court'; and that was the last thing Heath wanted. Better to let the Court moulder and decide what if anything should be done about it when Stage Three had been implemented and something approaching normality restored.[10]

A 'relaxed and amiable' Tom Jackson came to Chequers in August on yet another of those visits by union leaders organised by Heath without any participation by other ministers. The last thing the unions had wanted had been a confrontation over Stages One and Two, Jackson said, but he also warned that during Stage Three things would be different unless the Government could show that it was really doing something more about prices.[11] Price inflation was, for Heath, a problem second only in urgency to unemployment. In 1973 the average rate was 9.2 per cent and it was rising rapidly. He viewed its progress with alarm and some embarrassment. Early that year Rothschild produced a report in which he somewhat brutally remarked that any state suffering an inflation rate of more than 15 per cent qualified as a banana republic. If widely disseminated, Robert Armstrong pointed out, this could cause some dismay. The Prime Minister 'would (with some regret) prefer you to find a phrase which will probably be less vivid, but will also be less open to misunderstanding'. But whatever the terminology, Heath privately thought that Rothschild was right and that Jackson, the most amenable of union leaders, was if anything being over-cautious when he predicted trouble if prices continued to rise. When a group representing the retail trade came to Number 10 early in 1973 Heath commented: 'We shall have to impress on them that all our emphasis is going to be placed on stable prices ... The price increases envisaged in the proposals put before the tripartite talks are now no longer tenable.' In Cabinet a few months later he said that increases in the price of food were especially damaging. 'The closest control over price increases was essential if there was to be any hope of securing the TUC's agreement to a realistic pay and prices policy in Stage Three.' The problem was that, with commodity prices soaring around the world, nothing was going to stop the cost of food in British shops increasing. The retailers could reasonably complain that they were being asked not to cut their profits but to sell at a loss – and that way lay certain bankruptcy. Warning signals were being posted when Joe Gormley told Heath in mid-July that, while he personally understood the reasons for the cost increases, 'this did not convince the miners at the pithead; their view was that rising prices were a matter for the Government and the Government should be doing something about it'.[12]

Heath was reluctant to curb the economy which he had stimulated so enthusiastically but by mid-1973 even he had to concede that the dash for growth had become an ill-disciplined stampede. The money supply had swollen by nearly three-quarters, the banks had vastly increased their lendings, growth was running at 10 per cent, nearly double the declared target. Edward du Cann, in his extremely hostile assessment of Heath's Government, claimed that the growth figure was spurious: 'Nothing real grew; there was no sudden increase in our productive capacity, only a violent rise in property prices that was not founded on a rise in real values.' The comment was unfair; the fact that exports continued to grow showed that something of value was being created. But clearly things could not continue at this hectic pace. 'It was time to ease gently off the accelerator,' Heath put it in his memoirs; it was past the time for slamming on the brakes, his critics would have said. 'If action is not taken to control the growth in public expenditure … the whole structure will be at risk,' he told the Cabinet; a turn of phrase which sounds more like sharp braking then an easing of acceleration. It was important, he added hopefully, 'that this should be seen as a controlled response to changing circumstances rather than as a precipitate reaction to impending crisis'. Barber then announced that savings of £500m would be immediately put in hand, cuts which, if not precipitate, certainly had a flavour of crisis about them.[13] It was characteristic of Heath that he did not admit to members of his party who were concerned about the way things were going that such measures were being planned. Geoffrey Howe recalls that the Party Finance Committee called on the Prime Minister to express its qualms. Instead of saying that the Government was already working on the problem, Heath replied: 'Oh, ye of little faith. Don't you know we have embarked on a programme of expansion?' This, wrote Howe, 'fortified an impression of him being fairly cavalier in relation to the reaction of the party'.[14]

'The defence of the Pound appears less important to Mr Heath than the reconstruction and relaunch [*relance*] of the economy,' the Quai d'Orsay told Pompidou in mild wonder, in their briefing for a visit by the Prime Minister in late May.[15] Heath was indeed aware that strong economic growth, though essential for the welfare of the nation, could also damage the fabric of society. Late in 1973 David Howell wrote an article for *Crossbow*, the journal of liberal conservatism, in which he argued that it was the function of the Conservative Party to conserve all that was best in British life: 'Keep the Britain we know. Keep the grass green and the air clean.' Heath, Hurd cautiously commented, 'would ... put a rather higher emphasis on economic expansion, but I do not think he would actually dissent from anything you write'. He too wanted to keep the grass green and the air clean, and he also believed that the arts should figure prominently in the national growth. In July 1973 David Eccles put forward an ambitious programme which included a new site for the National Theatre, an extension to Covent Garden, opera houses in Edinburgh and Cardiff, concerts halls in Poole and Birmingham and the new British Library. 'If these were put in hand now your Government would never be forgotten by all who care about art,' claimed Eccles. 'This is certainly right,' concluded Heath.[16]

Although the economy and the unions were Heath's main preoccupations, in 1973 other even more irritating distractions from time to time arose. In May Lord Lambton was photographed in bed with a prostitute, Norma Levy, and featured prominently in the *News of the World*. To add to his problems, a quantity of cannabis was found by the police in his flat. He duly resigned. The loss of an under-secretary for whom Heath anyway had little respect would not have cost him much sleep, but a few weeks later it was rumoured that Lord

Jellicoe, Lord Privy Seal and Leader of the Party in the Lords, was involved with the same prostitute and that incriminating photographs were about to be published in Germany's weekly news magazine *Der Stern*. The story was in fact an absurd mistake, based on a confusion between Lord Jellicoe and a public house of the same name. When summoned to Number 10, Jellicoe denied that he had ever met Norma Levy, let alone slept with her. Next morning, however, he returned to say that, though his story had been true, he had in fact used call girls, summoned to his flat and hired through the Mayfair Escort Agency. Heath agonised, debated with Douglas-Home, Carrington, Whitelaw and the Chief Whip, and concluded that, after the Lambton affair, the Government could not handle another scandal. He broke it to Jellicoe that he felt he should resign. The affair was handled with great discretion and Heath, who liked and admired Jellicoe, behaved with sympathy and understanding. There were no hard feelings.

> Now that I have caught my breath [wrote Jellicoe a few days later] I feel that I must write to thank you for the kindness and consideration which you have always shown me both professionally, as it were, and privately – and not least last week. In a situation of horrible embarrassment and difficulty you extended to me a degree of courtesy and human understanding which I shall never forget. Thank you for all that you did to take so much of the sting out of the most bitter moments of my life.[17]

Heath might have felt more disposed to take a risk by retaining Jellicoe if scandal had not recently involved another senior member of the Tory Party. Lonrho was an Anglo-African trading group, which had sailed exceedingly close to the wind when it had deposited $100,000 tax free in its chairman's account in the Cayman Islands. The chairman in question was Churchill's son-in-law and former Minister of Defence, Duncan Sandys. Heath chose a dinner of the Scottish Conservative and Unionist Association – an occasion usually doomed to hear the most bland and platitudinous of speeches – to denounce the Lonrho affair as 'the unacceptable face of capitalism'.

It was a telling phrase which Douglas Hurd had originally suggested but had assumed would end up, with almost all the other sound bites he had proposed over the years, on the cutting-room floor. Heath liked it, however, and used it again in the House of Commons. In Perth, for good measure, he followed it up with a ferocious attack on British industry for being cowardly and inefficient and on the Conservative Party, particularly in Scotland, for being smug, upper and middle class and spending its time debating self-congratulatory resolutions. His little claque of advisers – Michael Wolff, Hurd, Kitson and Sara Morrison – had urged him to take advantage of the occasion to speak strongly but had not dared to hope that he would go so far. Sara Morrison, Wolff told his wife, 'leapt from her chair as if she had had (for the first time) a you-know-what but everyone else felt they had had a slap across the face and were still tingling from it 24 hours later'. Wolff and the others followed Heath to his hotel room and sat talking till 12.45, 'discussing how to implement all these fine ideas into reorganising the Tory party in *England now*'. As so often happens with fine ideas discussed in the small hours of the morning, they were overtaken by the rush of events and little was done to implement them; but the occasion was still a memorable one.[18]

Heath's hard feelings towards big business, if not particularly British industry, were fomented by the behaviour of the giant Swiss chemicals company, Roche. In April 1973 the Monopolies Commission concluded that Roche were overcharging grossly for their tranquillisers, Librium and Valium. An Order was made, reducing prices to the level proposed by the Commission. Roche appealed and, three months later, announced that they proposed to defy the Order and restore the original prices. This is disgraceful, commented Heath. 'Is there nothing we can do legally to stop them?' The answer seemed to be 'not much', but the Government had fallen before the affair could be concluded. The episode confirmed Heath in his suspicion that manufacturers were not merely inefficient and unenterprising but likely to be unscrupulous as well. The only difference between the Swiss and the British was that the former were slightly more efficient and less scrupulous. Both were to be deplored. In April 1973 the Cabinet Secretary designate, John Hunt, remarked sadly: 'our industry has yet to show convincing signs of its readiness to take advantage of the commercial opportunities of membership [of the EEC]'. 'True,' minuted Heath.[19]

The Party, which he had attacked so vigorously at the dinner in Perth, was, for the moment, relatively placid. As the prices and incomes policy seemed to be working then, for a time at least, they would go along with it. But there was unease beneath the surface and sometimes overtly as well. In mid-July the Chief Whip told Heath that, in the 1922 Committee, those ill-disposed to the Prime Minister were decrying the policy as already a failure and one bound to get worse. 'Most of the party, of course, desperately hope for success … The vacuum of which members are becoming increasingly conscious is the absence of any philosophical or intellectual foundation for our present interventionism. Is it permanent, if so what is our attitude to private enterprise? If not, how do we get back to where we want to be?' Heath sidelined the last few sentences. No, it was not permanent, that was clear enough. But exactly where he wanted to be instead and how he proposed to get there was more difficult to answer. Stage Three, he hoped, would point the way. In the meantime, he accepted that elements of the party were implacably opposed to him and his policies. In September a Eurosceptic backbencher, David Mudd, wrote to warn him that he had been invited to join a luncheon party of some twenty Tories, including one or two junior ministers, 'to initiate moves for a change of leadership'. The coup was to begin during the party conference at Blackpool and would include organising 'a shorter-than-usual display of appreciation'. 'I will not be party to disloyalty to you personally,' concluded Mudd. Heath knew that, provided things continued to go reasonably well, he could afford to ignore such rumblings. But if the prices and incomes policy ran into difficulties, then he was going to be in serious trouble himself.[20]

Stage Three was formally unveiled on 8 October 1973 Heath had warned the Cabinet some weeks before that this was likely to coincide with a steep and sustained rise in prices, due largely to higher import costs: 'There is now a risk that the pay increase permitted in Stage Two would be completely eroded before the beginning of Stage

Three.' Selective subsidies on food imports might help provide an answer but Heath pinned his hopes on threshold agreements which would tie wage increases to the retail price index. 'On current predictions,' he declared hopefully, 'this would entail a once-only increase in October 1973.' Current predictions, as they so often do, proved disastrously awry; the oil crisis, which was now just around the corner, was to upset every statistic and drastically affect the balance of power between Government and the unions. For the moment, however, Stage Three, with its ingenious but labyrinthine mosaic of regulations, was grudgingly agreed by most people to be fair and, with luck, workable. The unions protested but more from force of habit than conviction. What came after Stage Three expired – Stage Four? The free-for-all resumed? Some sort of voluntary agreement? – was cogitated by many but little discussed in public.[21]

At his side, when the Prime Minister presented Stage Three to the public, was William Armstrong. Highly intelligent, articulate, ambitious and politically aware; Armstrong was in many ways a most valuable element in Heath's entourage. But his judgment was unsound, he excited Heath when he should have calmed him, alarmed him when he should have reassured him. He saw things in the starkest black and white; the miners, for instance, he identified as dangerous revolutionaries. Heath never wholly accepted this extreme view, but the constant objurgations of Armstrong over the next few months were to make any settlement with the NUM even more difficult to obtain. He was 'a bad influence', Jim Prior subsequently concluded – though he had not fully realised it at the time. Willie Whitelaw told John Campbell that when he returned from Northern Ireland he found that the 'Armstrong syndrome' was a reality; Heath was hopelessly enmeshed in the minutiae of his prices and incomes policy and had lost touch with political reality. It is possible to make too much of this. Robert Armstrong considered that Heath relied on his namesake, William, 'when considering how to proceed on incomes policy, but I do not think otherwise'. Ian Gilmour denied that there was widespread worry in the party at William Armstrong's excessive influence. At the least, however, he was seen by certain ministers as an obstacle in the way of their achieving any serious rapport or even interchange

of ideas with the Prime Minister. The intimate and secretive relationship which Heath and Armstrong cultivated with the union leaders
was well intentioned and, on the whole, beneficial but it caused an
irritated disquiet among people with whom it was essential for Heath
to retain the closest and most confidential contact and who had
reason to feel that they were being excluded from their proper field
of responsibility.[22]

Never was this more manifest than in the meeting between the
miners' leader, Joe Gormley, and Heath and William Armstrong in
the garden of Number 10 on 16 July 1973. A fortnight earlier the
NUM conference had called for a pay increase of 35 per cent; a claim
which, if accepted, would have made nonsense of the Government's
pay policy. The object of Gormley's visit, said Armstrong, was to help
the Government 'find out the miners' mood in private' and to establish whether there was any way by which their demands could be met
within the structure of the prices and incomes policy. Gormley was
almost as anxious as the Prime Minister to find a solution. He suggested that a wage increase was not the only way to satisfy the miners;
an 'increase in payments for unsocial working hours' would have the
same effect and would leave the pay code technically inviolate. 'As far
as I was concerned, I had given them the biggest possible hint as to
how they could find a way round the problem,' Gormley wrote in his
memoirs. 'And I was convinced that they had both taken the hint,
because they turned to each other and said: "We never thought of
that!"' Nothing was said to the Cabinet about the meeting, but a
provision allowing for special rewards for working unsocial hours was
built into Stage Three and ministers were told that this should offer
enough flexibility to avoid direct confrontation with the NUM.
Unfortunately Gormley was promising more than he could deliver.
The NUM was increasingly dominated by a militant group which had
no intention of making things easy for the Government. Worse still,
Gormley had thought that he was securing preferential terms for his
union. When he found that everyone would be able to benefit by the
concession, it lost its charm. 'I must say that I wasn't best pleased,' he
wrote. 'I had gone there to try to solve our problem, not to give them
help in running the country as a whole.'[23]

Things moved inexorably towards disaster. Early in October the Coal Board offered the miners a rise of 13 per cent, including an element for unsocial hours. Somewhat ineptly, they had opened negotiations by pledging the maximum which the Government was prepared to endorse and had thus left themselves no room for manoeuvre. Derek Ezra was much criticised for adopting such unsubtle tactics. Almost certainly it made no difference; the miners were in no mind to accept any pay deal that would be acceptable to the Government, be it never so skilfully presented. In early November an overtime ban was threatened. The Cabinet muttered nervously about the need to avoid another confrontation and there were reminders that the popular press had recently shown some sympathy for the miners' cause. Heath undertook to brief the editors of the *Daily Mirror* and the *Sun*; a risky undertaking since, though he was capable of being uncommonly persuasive, he was equally liable to hector the unfortunate journalists and drive them into still more intransigent opposition. Fortunately he was in the former mood when he met the NUM Executive some three weeks later. The atmosphere, he told the Cabinet, had been 'relatively good ... there were signs that the arguments advanced ... had made a genuine impact on at least the more moderate members of the Executive'. At this point Heath seems still to have believed that the miners could be induced to settle on reasonable terms and that, if it did come to a confrontation, the Government would be able to stick to its guns and, this time, win. Cecil King attended a music party at Chequers as the crisis was brewing up. Heath, he noted in his diary, 'looks well and confident. He clearly enjoys being PM. Any idea that he is a deeply worried man putting a brave face on it is quite untrue.'[24]

An important change in the Prime Minister's entourage occurred in October when Burke Trend retired as Secretary of the Cabinet to be replaced by John Hunt. Hunt was more of a Europhile than his predecessor and so more acceptable to Heath, but no more than Trend did he make any attempt to rival William Armstrong's personal relationship with the Prime Minister. According to Rupert Allason, Hunt felt that he was boarding a sinking ship; he recalled 'a smell of death hanging over the Government with very tired ministers not

RIGHT: On the golf course. 'I had no idea the Prime Minister was so good at golf,' the Queen is said to have remarked.

BELOW: With the Queen and President and Mrs Nixon at Chequers in 1970.

ABOVE: Visiting the troops in Ulster at the end of 1971.
'Strange thing,' he remarked during the flight home.
'We went over to boost their morale in the week before
Christmas, and they boosted ours.'

BELOW: Signing the Treaty of Accession in Brussels
on 24 January 1972, flanked by Alec Douglas-Home
and Geoffrey Rippon. 'The proudest moment of my
life,' Heath described it.

ABOVE: Greeting Henry Kissinger on his arrival at Number 10. The joviality did not last long once they were inside.

BELOW: The grand piano being manoeuvred carefully into Number 10.

LEFT: Heath has his first encounter with a panda.

BELOW: One of Heath's many meetings with Deng Xiaoping in Beijing.

ABOVE: Book signing sessions saw Heath at his most genial and also most successful.

BELOW: On the rostrum. A rehearsal with the London Symphony Orchestra.

ABOVE: The entourage in the early years of the Long Sulk. From left to right: Richard Simmonds, Roger Martin, Peter Luff, Charles de Lisle, Lindsay Martin, Heath, Michael Young, Sara Morrison, Rosemary Wolff and Ian Gilmour.

BELOW: At the gate of Arundells with Robert Armstrong.

THIS PAGE: Resplendent as a Knight of the Garter.

ABOVE: At his final birthday party on 9 July 2005.
Just over a week later he was dead.

making the best decisions'. Be that as it may, he joined enthusiastically in a new crusade to streamline the processes of government. At the end of November he recommended the abolition of 53 out of a grand total of 166 ministerial and official committees. Heath eagerly approved the enterprise and, when Hunt reported a few weeks later that the task had been almost completed, minuted in some disappointment: 'I thought 53 was only a beginning. Can we not abolish a lot more?' The question was rhetorical, Robert Armstrong told colleagues, and did not require a precise answer. Nevertheless, early in the new year, Hunt reported that they had abolished two more and were searching for fresh victims. The Prime Minister 'is glad to know that you will remain on the warpath', Robert Armstrong told him, 'and hopes that you will find yourself able to add to your collection of scalps. There ought to be some sort of capitation award – the opposite to a productivity bonus.' Nor was it only Hunt that Heath pursued in his quest for slim and efficient government. A few months earlier he had seen a letter from Lord Windlesham, Jellicoe's successor as Lord Privy Seal, about the expense of hiring typists and secretaries. The quantity of paper circulated in the civil service must be reduced drastically, Heath proclaimed. 'All Departments must immediately cut their paper to suit their secretaries.' Heath enjoyed an almost Churchillian propensity to pursue minor issues at a time when, by all the rules, he should have been exclusively preoccupied by the major crises.[25]

Few crises can have been more major than that which currently threatened to overwhelm him. The miners' go-slow, with the threat of an eventual all-out strike, had been faced by the Government with comparative equanimity. They were better placed to stand a siege than in 1972, coal supplies at the power stations were much larger, public opinion – though on this there were differing opinions – seemed to be more sympathetic to the Government's point of view. Having surrendered abjectly after the first battle with the miners, ministers were convinced that the second could and must be won. It was oil which upset their plans. OPEC, the cartel of the oil-producing countries, had already increased the price of oil twice early in 1973, by 6 per cent each time. Now the Yom Kippur War led first to a damaging decrease in the amount of oil supplied to Western Europe and then to a crippling rise of 70 per cent in its cost. By early December Rothschild was reporting that the 'intersection point' had now been reached; coal was definitely cheaper than oil and would remain so even if the miners' pay demands were met. 'v.interesting' was Heath's non-committal comment.[26] The Government's strategy had been that, in the event of a protracted strike, it would be possible to replace coal by an increased use of oil. Now the oil might well not be there and, even if it was, would be economically less advantageous. The bargaining position of the miners had been immeasurably strengthened.

Whatever room for manoeuvre the Government might have had was limited by the economic crisis. The worldwide recession, provoked particularly by the action of the OPEC countries, was causing havoc in British industry. Even though exports had risen strongly, the Treasury was forecasting a balance-of-payments deficit in 1974 of £3 billion. The economy was likely to contract by 4.5 per cent. Public spending had to be fiercely curbed and, in an emergency budget in mid-December, Barber announced a surcharge on those liable to pay surtax, restrictions on credit and hire purchase and capital gains tax on major land developments. With the nation in deflationary mode, the arguments against conceding a lavish pay increase to the miners seemed still more pressing. 'A settlement in manifest breach of Stage Three', advised Hurd and Waldegrave, 'would not be possible for this Government, because it would destroy its authority and break the morale of the Conservative party.' Heath accepted the argument and prepared for trench warfare. On 13 December he told a startled House of Commons that, in the New Year, industry would be put on to a three-day week. That evening he went on television to explain to the nation what was happening. The broadcast was not a success; he was lacklustre and unsympathetic. When taxed with his failure to put himself and his case to the nation, Heath responded: 'I don't think a miners' strike is the time to come on television and ooze charm, do you?' But he did worse than fail to ooze charm, he failed to carry conviction. 'His face grey with fatigue and his eyes like slits, the Prime Minister had never looked worse on television,' wrote Michael Cockerell. 'Ted Heath seemed to match his anagram: the death.' He appealed for national unity, but gave no convincing explanation of whom the nation was to unite against or why it should chose to rally behind his Government. Worst of all, he sought to convey an atmosphere of imminent and drastic crisis, yet at the same time gave the impression that everything was under control and that there was no need for anyone to worry. The public was left with a suspicion that the Prime Minister was scare-mongering, and inflicting on it the inconvenience and financial loss involved in the three-day week when there was really no need for so extreme a course.[27]

By this time Whitelaw had been brought back from Northern Ireland to take over what was at that moment the most critically important of posts, that of Minister of Employment. The move was a mistake. For one thing, though Whitelaw had done extremely well to persuade the Unionists and the SDLP to sit down at a table together and talk more or less amicably about their differences, the job was still only half done and his experience and negotiating skills would have been of great value at the Sunningdale Conference. For another he was tired, battered and, by his own emollient standards, exceptionally tetchy. Some believe that he thought his recall was in part at least due to Heath's jealousy at his success in Northern Ireland and the Prime Minister's determination that nobody except himself should take centre stage at Sunningdale. If he had harboured such suspicions they would have been unjustified, and it anyway does not seem that he felt any serious resentment. There were strong arguments for him to run the Sunningdale Conference, he told Hugo Young, 'but other strong ones for Ted to do it and make it his triumph'. Yet he was certainly in a mood to criticise and complain. He told Selwyn Lloyd that, when he got back from Ulster, he was 'enraged to find Heath was a total dictator of Cabinet policy'. The Industrial Relations Act had been a disaster; as to the Prime Minister, he 'could not realise he was not liked'. Those who knew Whitelaw well say that this was uncharacteristic and no more than a fleeting mood. 'It must have been Willie, thoroughly worn out by what he had endured in Northern Ireland,' says Lord Carrington. 'I remember that he was quite unlike himself for some time afterwards.' Both Carrington and Peter Walker agree that it was absurd to characterise Heath as 'a dictator' in the Cabinet: 'It would be an exaggeration to say that he liked other people's opinions,' says Walker, 'but he listened and, if convinced, went along with them.' The fact that Whitelaw, however fleetingly, thought otherwise shows vividly how strained the atmosphere had been and how difficult Heath was finding it to handle a Cabinet which, though still united, was profoundly disturbed about its future prospects.[28]

Certainly, Whitelaw felt that he was never given a clear brief, nor even allowed to play the hand as he thought best. 'When I got into the job, Ted was already in command,' he told Young. 'He knew the detail of the price code down to the last comma, and I could never understand it for a single moment ... this gave me a weak position ... I could not be a completely effective influence on him.' Shortly after he took over he found that he had not been invited to one of Heath's meetings with William Armstrong and some union leader. He rang up to ask what had been decided and why he had not been included. Robert Armstrong was politely evasive. Whitelaw then appealed to Heath: 'Tell me what you want to do with this department. Do you want me to settle, or do you want war?' He received, he remembered years later, 'no reply of any clarity'. He told Selwyn Lloyd that he thought it would have still have been possible to settle with the miners for £3 a week on top of the existing offer, but probably by the time he took over it was too late, the opposition armies were heavily entrenched and meaningful negotiations were impossible. Jack Jones still pinned his hopes on him. Whitelaw, he told Hetherington, 'was the one man in the Government from whom one might expect conciliatory policies in the industrial field ... Heath was a man of principle with strong views but he had not enough knowledge of industry to deal with the situation.' But anyone who hoped that Whitelaw would pull some miraculous rabbit from his hat was in for a disappointment. In Cabinet he reported gloomily that a pithead ballot would probably show support for a continued overtime ban. His only advice was that the Government should spin it out, so that the crisis came not in February – when the Government had had to give in during the previous miners' strike – but in March 'when other factors would begin to work in the Government's favour'.[29]

A glimmer of hope became visible when Gormley raised with Heath the possibility that a special payment might be made for the time miners had to spend waiting at the pithead or washing after they had emerged from their stint underground. Unwisely, he told Wilson what he was proposing, and the Leader of the Opposition wrote to Heath to support the idea. Heath replied that his preliminary view was that this would cost too much; Wilson promptly published the correspondence and thus put paid to any possibility that the Government would pursue the idea. Gormley was indignant at what he saw as the wilful sabotage of his peace-making formula: 'I will never forgive Harold Wilson for it,' he wrote in his memoirs. In fact it seems unlikely that a bathing-time allowance could have produced enough to satisfy the miners unless it was blatantly at variance with the Government's pay policy. Nor was Wilson's conduct as nefarious as Gormley suggests; at the same time he wrote a separate, confidential letter to Heath, telling him that his soundings of coalfield opinion had left him with the strong impression that the traditionally moderate miners' leaders were as militant as the usual activists: 'I believe this is a serious matter,' he told the Prime Minister. Heath's reply was coolly non-committal; he would have done better to heed Wilson's warning.[30]

When the TUC leaders came to Number 10 on 19 December there was much bad-tempered criticism of the Government's imposition of a three-day week without any prior consultation. The crisis over oil, it was argued, reinforced the case for flexibility. If the Government was prepared to pay over the odds for oil, asked Sidney Greene, why should it not do the same for coal? But it should have been clear to Heath that, whatever the attitude of the miners, the union leaders as a whole were not spoiling for a fight. The meeting coincided with a public opinion poll which showed a swing back towards the Conservatives. It was alarmingly evident to the moderate unionists that many voters believed the union movement in general and the NUM in particular to be dominated by Communist or near-Communist extremists whose objective was as much to destroy the Government as to secure better pay. They were anxious to do nothing that would fortify this impression. Their sympathy for the miners, at any rate for the more intransigent members, was strictly limited. They were almost as eager as the Government to secure a settlement.

Heath knew this to be true and yet simultaneously suspected that the union movement was out of control, dominated by extremists who might not be in a majority when the TUC came to Downing Street but who still wielded the real power behind the scenes. He pressed MI 5 to target the unions, so as to secure advance warning about their plans to disrupt the economy and to detect the links which he believed existed between Moscow and certain elements of their leadership. Burke Trend deplored Heath's 'propensity to want action and to supply it himself if it was not forthcoming from his Ministers'. He tried to deter the Prime Minister by reminding him of Wilson's ill-judged denunciation of the seamen's union leaders as 'a tightly knit group of politically motivated men', only to find that, in Christopher Andrew's words, 'this was almost the only one of his predecessor's actions of which Heath wholeheartedly approved'. Heath did not press the point in the face of MI 5's reluctance to take action which they considered to be outside their proper field of operation, but his views remained unchanged. He told a Common Market summit in Copenhagen that the reds were behind the current strife in British industry. He felt that the British people increasingly shared his views. He was, as ever, anxious to avoid taking any step that might irrevocably divide the nation, but he believed that responsible opinion was behind him and, provided that he remained resolute, would not waiver in its support.[31]

It was in part his sense of his own rectitude and his belief that the country was moving behind him that led him to reject the TUC's final effort at conciliation. On 9 January 1974 the TUC proposed that the miners should be treated as a special case; they undertook that whatever settlement was needed would not be treated as a precedent by other unions when they came to negotiate their own pay claims. The proposition was sprung on Barber at a meeting of the National Economic Development Council (NEDC). Some reports suggest that he rejected the offer out of hand or after a hurried telephone call to Heath. His initial response was certainly discouraging but the question was in fact fully discussed in Cabinet the next day. According to Lord Aldington, Heath was disposed to distrust the offer because it had been put forward not privately but in a public meeting. That showed that it was not a serious suggestion but an empty gesture put forward for reasons of propaganda. That may have been an element in his thinking but in Cabinet a majority concluded that 'any settlement with the miners beyond the terms of the Stage Three Pay Code would demonstrate once and for all that the Government could never withstand the monopoly powers of unions: and that would not only put an end to all possibility of a rational economic policy, but would strike at the heart of democratic government'. A minority of ministers argued that, as there was no means of putting pressure on the miners and increasing unemployment would make the Government unpopular, it would be best to secure a settlement on any terms. The Cabinet minutes do not reveal which line the Prime Minister favoured but it would be astonishing if he had not supported the majority view.[32]

The unions did not immediately give up hope of a settlement. At a meeting a week later, when Heath pointed out that their self-denying ordinance would not stop individual unions claiming exemption from Stage Three on different grounds, they accepted that this was the case but undertook that, if such a claim were made, they would bring no pressure on the Government to accept it. As for the miners, they agreed that they could not be given carte blanche and promised only to back them if they put forward 'a reasonable claim'. What was 'a reasonable claim', asked Heath, and could they guarantee that other unions would not defy the ruling of the TUC? They didn't know, and they couldn't, was the gist of their reply. It was a question of trust and so far as Heath was concerned the trust was lacking. Len Murray, the new general secretary of the TUC, told Hugo Young that Heath's insistence on a 100 per cent guarantee showed that he did not understand real life. The unions could never promise that one of their members would not break ranks and insist on parity with the miners; what they could do was guarantee that such action would be exceptional and would be vigorously discouraged. What the Government had rejected was not just a formula; it was an attitude of mind. 'The TUC opened the door and the Government slammed it shut,' wrote

Frank Chapple, one of the most moderate of the union leaders. 'The Prime Minister was wrong in every way, politically, industrially, tactically, even morally. Ted Heath's pigheadedness and his refusal to pick up the TUC olive branch ... was his biggest error.' Today many of the prominent Conservatives of the epoch, though expressing it rather differently, would agree with Chapple. If the Government had accepted the unions' offer, a settlement with the miners could quickly have been reached. The unions would then have been forced to try to honour their promise. If they had failed, Heath would have been in a far stronger position to go to the country and fight an election on a platform of the Government, the law and the nation against the unions.[33]

That he would have to go to the country without seeing out his full term of office was becoming increasingly obvious, though Heath himself was one of the most reluctant to accept it. The Government was divided. Carrington, who had now taken over as Secretary of State for Energy in a new department carved, to Peter Walker's indignation, out of the old DTI, was the most bullish of the ministers, calling for an election from early in December. Whitelaw, if only because an election would imperil the fragile settlement in Northern Ireland, was strongly for postponement. The Party as a whole was undecided. Even as late as 10 January 1974, only four out of the twenty backbench MPs who spoke at the 1922 Committee were unequivocally in favour of an immediate dissolution. But the tide was turning; every week more Tory MPs rallied to the camp of those who wanted an early election. Why Heath was so slow to accept their arguments is hard to establish. Andrew Taylor, historian of the NUM, believes that he still clung to the belief that he could talk the miners into acceptance of a compromise: 'This is a remarkable testimony to Heath's self-confidence; a self-confidence bordering on delusion.'[34] Certainly his conviction that in the end reason must prevail was still a factor in his thinking. But, much more, he was uncertain whether he would win. To call an election when it is not essential is always a risky tactic. Would the voters agree it *was* necessary? Would the Government be able to keep the focus on the central issue of the miners' strike? When he dined with the Whips in early January to discuss the possibilities he found that opinion was equally divided, and their hesitation fortified his natural caution. Public speculation was by now rife, and the dithering had unfortunate consequences for the Party. They had considered holding an election, it was said, but had run away from the possibility because they thought that they would lose. There was just enough truth in the contention to leave the Tory leadership thoroughly discomposed.

The Pay Board's report on relativities – opening the way for a more generous treatment of unions which, for one reason or another, had slipped behind in terms of the rewards gained by other groups of workers – seemed briefly to offer an escape route for the Government. It was published on 24 January. Three days earlier, by which time everyone knew what was coming, Len Murray had met the Prime Minister. 'They had given Heath many nods and winks across the table,' he told Alastair Hetherington. 'He had not seemed to want to take up any of their nods and winks, and when they eventually said to him was there anything they could say which would enable him to give extra money to the miners before the end of Stage Three, there had been no response.' Heath denies that he was given any reason to believe that the unions would cooperate in an attempt to give the miners a significant advantage over any other group of workers, but Whitelaw later reproached himself for not having grasped the opportunity: 'I had never really thought of it. It was short-sighted of me.' In the frenzied atmosphere of January 1974 it is easy to see that any overture from the TUC would have been treated with suspicion, but in retrospect it seems obvious that the Government would have done better at least to try to settle with the miners on the basis of the Pay Board's report. The battle would no doubt only have been deferred but it could then have been fought at a better time and on more promising terrain. Another window of opportunity was briefly open but then slammed shut. On 24 January the NUM decided to hold a ballot on an all-out strike; on 4 February more than 80 per cent of the miners voted to support the policy of their union. The strike was to begin four days later.[35]

Meanwhile one of the main protagonists had been abruptly removed from the scene. William Armstrong had been visibly overwrought as the crisis deepened. His namesake, Robert, first became seriously alarmed when the head of the Home Civil Service arrived at Number 10 when the Prime Minister was away, asked to be taken to a room where they could not be overheard, lay on the floor and ranted about the Communist menace and the imminent collapse of society. Next day he summoned a meeting of Permanent Under Secretaries, locked the door and continued to air his apocalyptic forebodings. Douglas Allen escaped on the plea of a call of nature and went to consult Robert Armstrong. They agreed that Lady Armstrong should be telephoned and warned that her husband was unwell. He was being sent home and should see a doctor. He did so, and disappeared on sick leave. He never returned to office. The collapse of his most trusted adviser must have been an unpleasant shock, if not wholly a surprise, for Heath; it also, incidentally, withdrew from the scene one of the voices raised most persistently against an election. The miners must first be 'smashed', Armstrong had argued; only then would it be safe to appeal to the nation.[36] At the end of November Hugh Cudlipp had told William Armstrong that 'if the country chose to have a snap election on the issue of who governed the country, the *Daily Mirror* would oppose this and describe it as a "bogus election"'. Delighted to have his views reinforced by one of the most influential shapers of public opinion, Armstrong hastened to tell the Prime Minister, who passed it on to all his senior ministers. At that time Armstrong's view was shared by the majority of the Cabinet; the shifting of opinion in favour of an election was a painful and, some would say, disastrously protracted business.

Heath himself was one of the last to be convinced. Margaret Thatcher somewhat uncharitably complained to Kenneth Baker that 'Ted was dithering, probably because he did not relish the prospect of losing both of his official homes'. No Prime Minister in his senses is going to call an election without considering the possibility that his party might lose but Heath had by now overcome his fears and was confident that public opinion was moving behind the Government. Indeed, it seems that he was as much concerned by the possibility that the Conservatives might win a landslide victory as that they might be defeated. Michael Wolff told a journalist that the Prime Minister feared such a result 'would sweep away the moderation which post-war Tories went into politics to defend. It would be a triumph for the extremists.' Tim Kitson took the same view. Heath, he said, believed that a very large Tory majority would be damaging to the country's prospects. He also feared that an election would be fought on a platform of 'union bashing'; an issue that might in the short term be advantageous but would make more difficult the eventual settlement with the unions which he was convinced was both desirable and attainable.[37]

Within the Cabinet, Whitelaw was the most reluctant to go to the country. 'I had been brought back from Ireland for the specific purpose of seeking a solution to the miners' dispute,' he wrote in his memoirs. 'I was bound to dislike a confrontation.' He was supported by Lord Hailsham, who thought that the Government would be condemned for abandoning its post in a moment of crisis, and, as important as anyone, by the Chief Whip, Humphrey Atkins, who told Heath that he didn't think the British people would understand it if he called an election. Carrington was chief among those pressing for an election: he saw the force of Heath's argument that the country must be convinced everything possible had been done to reach a settlement but felt that 'we were hanging on too long'. Prior, equally a champion of a quick election, had one of his few rows with Heath on the subject. He told the Prime Minister on 17 January that Labour was rejoicing at the failure of the Government to go to the country in early February. 'It's all your bloody fault,' said Heath. 'If you hadn't allowed Central Office to steam this thing up, we would never have got into this position.' 'If you had told us definitely that you were against an election, it wouldn't have been steamed up,' retorted Prior.[38]

Heath did not tell them because he was not definitely for one thing or the other. All accounts agree that he was unusually indecisive. Nigel Lawson was at a meeting of the Steering Committee which debated the issue. Heath was 'an odd chairman', Lawson remembered. 'He didn't take a strong line, he didn't stop people who waffled on, he just sat and listened ... It was a very strange manner of proceeding.' Carrington was the only vigorous champion of a particular course of action. 'The others were strangely silent because Ted Heath was so silent. They didn't know what he was going to say and so they didn't like to expose themselves.' It was Heath's practice to listen to what people had to say and then to pronounce his inflexible decision. This time he listened but failed to decide. Towards the end of December John Nott, convinced that a golden opportunity was being lost, bearded Heath in the lobby and asked if he could have a word with him. Heath replied brusquely: 'If you want to resign, put it in writing!' Nott looked so disconcerted that Heath realised he had gone too far and invited Nott to his room. Nott duly explained why he thought an immediate election was essential. 'He did not react or speak. I would not have expected him to do so.' Others expected, or at least hoped, for more. They did not get it. Mrs Thatcher was 'surprised and frustrated' by his attitude. 'He seemed out of touch with reality. He was still more interested in the future of Stage Three and in the oil crisis than he was in the pressing question of the survival of the Government ... There was a strange lack of urgency.' Finally Heath did invite small groups of ministers to come to his office to discuss the issue. Thatcher and John Davies urged quick action. 'Ted said very little. He seemed to have asked us in for form's sake, rather than anything else.'[39]

That meeting took place in mid-January, at which point an announcement had to be made if an election was to be held on 7 February. The champions of an early vote made feverish attempts to convert their leader. At Chequers on 12 January the Communications Group, the technicians who would organise the presentation of the Party's case, unanimously called for an immediate election. Heath 'does not commit himself but listens carefully and the feeling is that he agrees', Ronald Millar remembered. If he did, the agreement was short-lived; the meeting was on Saturday; by Monday he was proposing further negotiations with the unions. On 16 January Carrington, Prior and the other champions of an early election worked energetically on the Prime Minister and thought that they had finally won. They left Downing Street in the evening, leaving Kitson on guard with instructions to shield his master against any malign influences. They reckoned without Whitelaw, who arrived unexpectedly, took Heath out for a meal and swung him back to the cause of inaction. The deadline passed and there had been no announcement. It was not until the all-out strike had been called that Heath accepted the inevitable and on 4 February 1974 asked the Palace for a dissolution. By then the first date possible for an election was 28 February.[40]

In a volume of memoirs Lord Hailsham pointed out that responsibility for the timing of the election 'cannot be attributed, as it often has been, to Ted Heath'. He consulted his colleagues and his choice was 'the result of a collective decision'. Heath was gratified. 'I am glad that you have put yourself frankly on the record that we were all involved in the decision to have a general election in February 1974 ...' he wrote. 'None of my other colleagues have [sic] had the courage to say so.' Technically it is true that this was a collective decision for which the Cabinet as a whole must take responsibility. In reality it was Heath's and Heath's alone. Early in February he had told Michael Fraser that he was being pressed to go for an early election but still had grave doubts. Fraser himself was against an election and told Heath that he was the Prime Minister, that he must not let himself be pushed around and that he should go to the country only when he thought the time was ripe. After the election Heath told Fraser that this advice had been decisive. 'You altered the course of history,' he said – hardly a compliment, given the result of the election. The recollection comes from Fraser. It seems unlikely that the Prime Minister needed to be reminded of his prerogative, though certainly the advice of so experienced and hardened a campaigner would have been listened to. But whatever the influence of Fraser and of Whitelaw, of Carrington and of Prior, in the last resort only Heath could decide.[41]

It is accepted wisdom that this decision was disastrous. Nobody can prove that if Heath had gone to the country a fortnight or, better still, a month earlier, the Tories would have won the election. This is, however, the belief of the Labour leadership, supported by the evidence of the polls. Things went wrong during the campaign which would not have happened if it had taken place a few weeks earlier, the popular mood changed, a golden opportunity was lost. It was Heath's mistake. It cost him his tenure of 10 Downing Street; in the not-so-distant future it was to cost him the leadership of the party.

TWENTY

Defeat on Points

Even more than had been the case in 1966 or 1970, Heath took
personal charge of the 1974 electoral campaign. To his previous
domination of press, television and the hustings he added a series of
apparently spontaneous yet usually well-organised walk-abouts. He
acquitted himself well. In the months before the election his staff had
been seriously concerned about his health and his morale; he seemed
tired and lacklustre. But once the election was called, all was changed;
Heath was infused with a new vigour and came dramatically to life.
Butler and Kavanagh, the historians of the election, pay tribute to his
performance: he was no great orator, they say, 'but his zest and conviction transcended his flat phrases and humourless, admonitory
manner ... There is no doubt that Mr Heath performed well. He was
much more relaxed than in 1970; he spoke eloquently without notes
and displayed great versatility and grasp of detail.' Some Labour
leaders were equally appreciative. Tony Benn compared his performance favourably with that of his own leader – Wilson, he wrote in his
diary, is 'really fooling about on the fringes, seen at press conferences
and ticket-only meetings; whereas Heath is on the streets in walk-
abouts, giving a sort of de Gaulle impression'.[1]

But though his performance was impressive, it was not necessarily
in the best interests of the party. Sara Morrison was not the only
person to feel that Heath's dominance of the campaign – hogging the
limelight, as some of his colleagues less charitably saw it – detracted

from the status of the other ministers. At press conferences, she felt, Heath should have done more to project the idea that he was *primus inter pares*, a member of a team, 'he ought more often to have shrugged his shoulders, said "I don't know", and passed the question on to someone else'.[2] But this was not his way; he *did* know and had no intention of pretending otherwise. The belief was subliminally fostered that this was a one-man band and that the other ministers were not up to much. Worse still, the fact that Heath was seen to personify the Tory Party reminded many voters that this was not a persona for which they greatly cared. Whatever they might think about his policies or his achievements as Prime Minister, the voters had reservations about him as a human being. This should, perhaps, not be a decisive, or even an important, element in an electoral campaign; but if somebody projects himself with such vigour it is inevitable that his personality will prove to be a significant factor. It was so with Heath.

He had, fairly or unfairly, gained the reputation of being withdrawn, suspicious and, too often, rebarbative. His attitude towards the various books written about him provides a good illustration of how he contributed to this impression. Three biographies or quasi-biographies appeared while he was in office: the official biography by George Hutchinson – competent, insipid and inevitably hagiographic; a more informal study by Margaret Laing – neither profound nor searching but fair and generally sympathetic; and Andrew Roth's waspish but entertaining and well-informed *Heath and the Heathmen*. Heath refused to admit that Laing and Roth had any business to write about him or that there could be any merit in their books. When Lady Dalkeith asked him to sign a copy of Margaret Laing's book so that she could auction it in a charity bazaar, Tim Kitson replied apologetically: 'I am afraid this is not a very popular edition and he is not signing copies of it – or of Andrew Roth's.' It was more embarrassing still when Walter Hallstein, first President of the European Commission, contributed a preface to a German translation of *Heath and the Heathmen* and sent a copy to Heath. 'Although you do not like the Roth book,' Tom Bridges minuted, 'the Hallstein introduction contains some appreciative reminiscences about you … I expect therefore that you will wish to thank him.' This not unreasonable expectation seems to have been confounded; there is no evidence that Heath even acknowledged receipt of the offending biography.[3]

Whatever public gesture he made, Heath had a knack of getting it slightly wrong. He contributed to a cookery book in which three hundred people were asked to name their favourite dishes. As his choice he nominated lobster thermidor with two wine sauces. Wilson opted for Cornish pasties with brown sauce. Hurd was dismayed: 'How did this happen? A very bad choice.' 'I can see no real harm,' replied Heath loftily, but the *Daily Mirror* rejoiced in the contrasting tastes of the two leaders. 'The Party is still in distress about Lobster Thermidor, which had lousy reception in the tabloids and on radio, in comparison with Wilson's pasty,' remonstrated Hurd. 'C'd we please make sure that future recipes are modest?' When it comes to popular appeal, classical music was as remote from everyday life as lobster thermidor. Heath was perceived as a highbrow, far removed from the interests of the vast majority of voters. He did nothing to dispel the impression; indeed, almost went out of his way to foster it. Ian Trethowan tried several times to convince him that BBC radio had a duty to serve a wider public than the minority who listened to the Third Programme. Heath remained unconvinced: 'Why do you want all that pop?' was his response.[4]

His refusal to play to the crowd or indulge in any of the populist gimmicks traditionally employed by electioneering politicians was in many ways admirable but was not a good way to win votes. He was determined to distance himself from Harold Wilson and as a result sometimes came over as aloof and out of touch. He did indeed show what was for him unusual fervour in the 1974 electoral campaign, but he still eschewed purple passages or sentimental appeals. Douglas Hurd went with him to Worcestershire where he was to speak in a by-election a few weeks before the election proper was called. 'Any other politician', wrote Hurd, 'would have seized and used the emotion hanging in the air. The country was tense, a struggle had begun on which our future seemed to rest ... He could have whipped them up against the miners. He could have sent them excited and enthusiastic into the streets. It did not occur to him to do so. What mattered was that they should understand the complexities of the issue, the objective facts and figures.' '*C'est magnifique*,' Maréchal Bosquet might have remarked, but it was not the best way to win elections.[5]

So was Heath on the whole an asset or a liability for the Tory Party in the election? Michael Fraser, as well placed as anyone to make a balanced assessment, had no doubts. 'What had mattered most in the election and gone best for the Conservatives,' he told David Butler, 'was the extraordinary performance of Ted, and his success in getting across in a way that he never had before.' Michael Wolff was equally struck by 'his eloquence and sense of conviction at the press conferences and elsewhere'. Normally Heath was a slow starter, not very alert in the early morning and reluctant to do much before eleven or twelve. During this campaign, however, at the unusually early hour of 7.30 a.m. he was 'brimming with ideas and plans for the day, and even prepared to sketch out notes for his speeches'. Nearer to the grass roots, however, where the Prime Minister was a remote and somewhat forbidding figure, there was less enthusiasm. Humphrey Atkins, who had taken over as Chief Whip when Pym replaced Whitelaw in Northern Ireland, was concerned about Heath's failure to connect with his backbenchers. He brought the officers and executive of the 1922 Committee to dinner at Number 10 in what was intended to be a grand rapprochement. It proved to be calamitous. 'He was in a grumpy mood throughout,' remembered du Cann. 'I had hoped that good reports of our meeting would have spread through the Parliamentary Party and redounded to his credit: in the event the opposite happened. Once again as so often, I saw Heath lose the goodwill of Party workers.'

Du Cann was hardly impartial. When he wrote that almost every Tory candidate met with the refrain 'I have nothing against the Conservative Party but I do not like Mr Heath', he was putting the case as blackly as he could. David Simpson, the Conservative agent in Burton-on-Trent, for one, claimed to have encountered no anti-Heath feeling. But even he noted that, in the agents' offices, 'there were pictures of virtually every Conservative leader in the past fifty years except Edward Heath'. Nor did Heath figure prominently in the election addresses. A post-election Gallup poll found that a large majority of Labour and Liberal voters considered that Wilson and Thorpe had been assets to their parties. When the same question was put about Heath, the voters were clearly divided. On the whole it seems reasonable to conclude that the Tory Party would have fared even worse in February 1974 if it had not been for the performance of Heath, but this was not the view of many Conservatives. Their opinion was to count heavily against the leader in the months to come. What is clear is that the prominence which Heath assumed during the campaign ensured that he would be held responsible if things went wrong.[6]

And things did go wrong. At the onset of the campaign it was taken for granted by almost everyone that the Conservatives would win, and win handsomely. In a time of emergency, it was believed, the country would be bound to rally behind the established authority: patriotism would blend with self-interest to produce a swing away from anarchy to security and stability. Sara Morrison was one of the few in Central Office who felt doubts. They seemed 'to be caught up in their own propaganda', she told David Butler. 'They felt their case was so blindingly strong that they could not conceive a rational elector voting any other way.' Nor was it only the Tory establishment who felt so confident. Tony Benn in mid-February was convinced that there would be a Tory landslide and that he would lose his seat. 'Now, at midnight,' he wrote in his diary, 'having watched a lot of television and seen Heath doing a brilliant party political broadcast and Harold floundering away about the price of petrol, I am going to bed tired, exhausted and rather depressed.'[7]

A series of Tory setbacks, some predictable, some not, soon restored his morale. Enoch Powell's onslaught was inevitable, though its fury exceeded Heath's worst fears. In a letter to his constituency chairman, designed for publication, he denounced the election as 'an act of gross irresponsibility', and claimed that it was 'essentially fraudulent, for the object of those who have called it is to secure the electorate's approval for a position which the Government itself knows to be untenable, in order to make it easier to abandon that position subsequently'. He advised voters to support Labour. His impact on the election was certainly significant, perhaps decisive. 'I put him in and I took him out,' he would announce triumphantly in later years. That was perhaps vainglorious, but it is significant that the national swing to Labour was 1 per cent, while in the East Midlands, Powell's heartland, it was 3.9 per cent.[8]

A setback in Northern Ireland was equally inevitable but, once again, sharper than expected. The Paisleyites, raging against the Sunningdale agreement and the betrayal of what they saw as Ulster's interests, swept Faulkner's Unionists into oblivion. Instead of a group of docile followers, Heath was in future to be confronted by eleven embittered enemies prepared to defeat his Government irrespective of who might benefit by its downfall. A swing to the Liberals could also be expected but the Tories had assumed that this would be at least as much at the expense of Labour as of themselves. Across the board this may have been the case but the accidents of constituency boundaries meant that more marginal seats held by Tories were lost to the Liberals than was the case with Labour.

Such problems had to some extent been built into the Tory calculations. What they had not allowed for was a series of mischances which disrupted their campaign. Shortly after Powell launched his bombshell the trade figures for January showed the largest deficit which had ever been recorded. The figures could largely be blamed on the increase in the price of oil, but they still left the electorate with the impression that a Government which prided itself on its sound management of the economy was falling down on the job. Two days later this feeling was reinforced when Campbell Adamson, the Director General of the CBI, in an unguarded moment proclaimed that the Industrial Relations Act had been a disaster and that it should not be revised but totally repealed. If this was the view even of businessmen, how could the Government defend its policy? It was extraordinary enough that Adamson felt the way he did, wrote Heath; to broadcast his views at such a moment was unforgivable.[9]

Worse still was a leaked announcement by the Pay Board that the National Coal Board had been basing all its calculations on erroneous figures; the implication being that the dispute could easily have been settled without coming anywhere near an all-out strike. In fact it was the Pay Board that was in error but by the time this had been established the damage was done. Heath, taken by surprise, handled the business badly. 'We are cruelly savaged by the Pay Board putting out entirely new figures for miners, more favourable to their case,' Douglas Hurd wrote in his diary. 'Ted simply retires in a cloud of stubborn and unconvincing negatives.'[10]

Public relations in general were handled far less professionally than in the previous election. The team which had then operated so successfully had largely been disbanded. 'Heath enjoyed being a Prime Minister and a statesman more than he enjoyed being a party man and a television personality,' wrote Geoffrey Tucker, and 'public relations in all its aspects took a back seat. When he called a snap election in February 1974 we were all unprepared.' Unprepared, and to some extent demoralised: Barry Day, another key member of the team, complained that they had been kept out of Downing Street because Heath believed that 'the business of government had nothing to do with the business of elections'. By the time electoral issues were once again top of the agenda it was too late. They were 'called "the outside help" and there was not the same total dedication there had been in 1970'. Heath for his part handled the press with notable insensitivity. Anthony Bevins, political correspondent of the *Sun*, annoyed Heath at press conferences by asking questions which Bevins felt to be penetrating and challenging but the Prime Minister found offensive. Heath tried to exclude Bevins from the group of journalists who accompanied him on his election tours; the *Sun* stuck by its correspondent; the *Sun* won.

Such peevish gestures suggest that Heath was not as confident as he appeared. If doubts existed it does not seem that they were strongly held: the possibility of defeat hardly entered his mind. But he still felt impelled to grasp at anything which he thought might improve his chances. Dr Kissinger passed through London a few days before the election and asked whether he could say anything to the press that might help the Conservative cause. Heath urged him to avoid anything that might seem like intervention in the campaign but, his aide was told, if he were asked about the relationship between the two governments, or between Kissinger and the Prime Minister, it might be helpful if he were to emphasise the 'continuing closeness of relations ... and play down any suggestions of personal resentment or ill-feeling. He could perhaps recall that he has met and been entertained by the Prime Minister on each of his visits here.'[11]

But there were underlying weaknesses in the Tory campaign more significant than any of these factors. The election had been called on a single issue but, as the Conservative Research Department had warned a few months before, 'however much a Government ... may wish to fight an election on one issue there is no guarantee that the electorate or significant parts of it will not decide to vote about something else, with possibly disturbing results'. And the issue itself was a hazardous one. 'Who governs Britain?' was the question put to the electorate. 'You, and not the miners' was the hoped-for response. But were they not equally likely to reply: 'Well, *you're* clearly not managing to do so, so we'd better try someone else ...'? And even if the need to confront the miners at the polls was accepted, the nagging question remained whether an election would in fact settle anything. What happened if the Tories won the election and the miners continued their strike? The collapse of the economy? Civil war? The Tories dismissed such a possibility with unconvincing conviction: the electorate was less sure. So, perhaps, was Heath. What will you do if you win the election and the strike is still on in August, asked Woodrow Wyatt. 'Go to Cannes,' replied the Prime Minister.[12]

Douglas Hurd monitored the fluctuations in public opinion. In mid-January a substantial majority of the electorate supported the Government's refusal to give way to the miners' demands. A week later the mood had shifted: 57 per cent favoured accepting the miners' demands, only 38 per cent were against it. A particularly turbulent tirade by McGahey led to a move back in favour of defiance but by 4 February the mood had changed once again – 52 per cent favoured a settlement on the miners' terms, 46 per cent opposed it. 'The beginnings of a slow slide, as foreseen,' commented Hurd gloomily.[13]

But though there were some forebodings the only real question still seemed to be the size of the Tory majority. All the polls pointed that way, the margins of victory varying between 2 and 5 per cent. Translated into seats, that would have put the Tories ahead by forty or fifty, perhaps more if, as in the previous election, the polls had underestimated Tory support. Even before he set out for Bexley, however, the first exit polls were suggesting that things were going to be a great deal closer. The early results showed the Liberals gaining heavily at the expense of both parties. Heath himself, with changed constituency boundaries, increased his majority to nearly 10,000, but by the time he left Bexley to return to Downing Street it was clear the final tallies were going to be desperately close. Even if he could cling on to power, there was no possibility of his obtaining the strong majority he had hoped would overawe the miners. Richard Simmonds was in the car with Heath as they drove through Bexley. They stopped at a phone box so that Heath could call Carrington to get the latest news of the exit polls. He got back into the car, visibly discomposed but saying nothing. Simmonds asked what was happening. Heath grunted. When they arrived at the count they found that the announcement had been delayed. Simmonds offered Heath a Polo mint, the Prime Minister ate the entire packet in twenty minutes. He did not get back to Downing Street till 4 a.m. Penelope Gardner was one of the staff still waiting up when he came in, tired and obviously dejected. 'Are you all right?' he asked. 'Thank you for all you've done,' and he trudged upstairs without waiting for a reply. They were left feeling that there was nothing they could say or do to help.[14]

As the final results began to come in it seemed possible that Heath might still lead the largest party, but though the Tories had nearly a quarter of a million votes more than Labour, Labour won 301 seats to the Conservatives' 297. The Liberals gained only three seats, to fourteen, but secured 19 per cent of the national vote. Whoever was going to be the next Prime Minister would be leading a minority Government, dependent on the sufferance if not the support of the minor parties. Normal practice would have been for Heath to tender his resignation to the Queen and advise her to send for Harold Wilson as leader of the largest party in the House of Commons. Heath saw things differently. He called a Cabinet meeting and asked them to consider whether 'in a situation where the two main parties were so close, where the Conservative Party had obtained the majority of the total votes cast and where nearly six million votes has also been cast for the Liberal Party, the nation would expect him to attempt the formation of a right–centre coalition before handing over power to the Labour Party'. It was a question expecting an answer 'yes', and it duly got it. One member stressed that 'it would clearly be wrong for the Conservative Party to hang on to power at the expense of its principles', but only three ministers, two of whom were identified by Lord Hailsham as Keith Joseph and Margaret Thatcher, felt it would be improper to try to reach an accommodation with the Liberals. 'An immense majority of the electorate,' wrote Hailsham in his diary, 'voted for parties committed to the EEC and a statutory incomes policy, and I am sure these are essential in the national interest. There can be nothing wrong – and in my view everything right – in seeking an arrangement to give effect to these two considerations.'[15]

Such an arrangement, everyone agreed, if it was to have any chance of lasting, would have to take the form of a coalition, with the Liberals being offered certainly one senior post in the Cabinet, plus a couple of Ministers of State and Parliamentary Under Secretaries. Carrington and Gilmour believed that the Liberals would be ready, if not eager, to join a coalition; Heath himself, though he had reservations about some Liberal members, was sure that any ideological divide could be surmounted. Indeed, he felt closer to most Liberals and even to some moderate members of the Labour Party than he did to his own right-wingers. At a conference at Königswinter William Waldegrave re-members Heath looking across the room at Shirley Williams and remarking musingly: 'That is the sort of person we ought to be working with.' (Mrs Williams would have been surprised by this obser-vation. She remembered sitting next to him at dinner and his failure to respond to any gambit she made. She asked the man on her other side whether Heath ever spoke to women. 'He doesn't speak to many people at all,' was the reply.)[16]

The question was what sort of quid pro quo the Liberals would demand in return for their cooperation. It seemed certain they would want a Tory commitment to proportional representation. The most that would be possible, the Cabinet agreed, would be a Speaker's Conference on electoral reform, with a promise that the Conservatives would enter it with open minds. Nothing more extreme would stand a chance of being accepted by the House of Commons: the Labour and Ulster Unionists would vote solidly against it and the Conservative Chief Whip reckoned that there might be as many as fifty Conservative rebels who would join the Opposition on such an issue. Heath was authorised to put the proposition, without commitment, to the Liberal leadership. 'I think they will turn it down,' concluded Hailsham. 'A number of intransigents do not wish to do business with us on *any* terms. Of the remainder who are more sensible, Frank Byers is against.'[17]

The possibility of trying to include the Ulster Unionists in such a coalition seems barely to have been discussed: they would be unreliable, Heath told the Cabinet, and no one contradicted him. Cecil King claims that Ian Paisley telephoned him to say that he did not want a Labour Government and would undertake to support the Conservatives 'on condition there was a fresh election to the Assembly'. King passed on the message to Heath (why Paisley should have adopted this oblique approach rather than speaking directly to Heath or Pym is obscure) but the Prime Minister did not respond. Harry West, the chairman of the Ulster Unionists, was more direct. He approached Pym and asked for an urgent meeting with him or, preferably, the Prime Minister, to discuss 'mutual co-operation'. There would be great dangers in a meeting with West or Paisley, the Secretary of State for Northern Ireland advised. This overture, too, was rebuffed. In Cabinet two days later it was agreed that there was no possibility of a deal with the Ulster Unionists 'who would seek to undermine the Sunningdale Agreement'. It was the Liberals or nothing.[18]

Heath felt reasonably sure that the Liberal leader, Jeremy Thorpe, would personally be well disposed to the idea of joining a predominantly Tory government. There were problems, however. Thorpe was embroiled in a complex of lurid scandals which at this stage were no more than the subject of gossip whispered between those in the know but which were likely soon to burst into the public sphere. Even though it would have been advantageous to the Conservatives to have damaged the Liberal cause, Heath, said William Waldegrave, had firmly vetoed 'any use at all in the election campaign of the many scandalous stories that were circulating'. In this attitude he was entirely consistent: he loathed tittle-tattle and would never have used it against even the most personally disliked of political opponents. But he was well acquainted with the background and realised the risks involved in dealing with a man who might bring discredit on any government with which he was associated. The most alarming possibility was that Thorpe might hold out for the office of Home Secretary, an appointment that would have been totally inappropriate for a man who was likely to find himself involved in murky criminal proceedings. Robert Armstrong says that the possibility was discussed and dismissed: Heath would have been prepared to offer Thorpe an important job – perhaps Industry – but not one of the great offices of state.[19]

Reporting to the Cabinet after their meeting, Heath said that Thorpe had agreed that the two parties felt alike on Europe and incomes policy. The following day he had telephoned to say that 'things were moving in a hopeful direction'. There were, however, two problems. One was the leadership of the Government. Certain elements of the Liberal Party would find it very difficult to accept Heath as leader. On this issue 'he felt he could handle his party', but he wanted to know the official Tory position. The second was electoral reform, 'on which the Liberals would expect specific and urgent action'. Even then, the Liberals would probably not wish to do more than offer general support, on the understanding that they would hope to be able to enter into a coalition after a few months. The general feeling in Cabinet was that Thorpe was offering too little and asking too much. Under no circumstances would the Tories agree to a change of leadership and no firm commitment could be made about electoral reform beyond a promise to consider the issue urgently.[20]

In his memoirs Heath suggests that Thorpe was 'very keen to enter a coalition'. Thorpe dismisses this as 'an extraordinary claim'. He was personally opposed to the idea of a coalition but felt that 'if the Prime Minister of the day requested a meeting, one had an obligation to go'. He had stressed that his party would have 'grave reservations' about Heath leading a coalition Government and made no comment when told that the Cabinet were 'adamant that they wished to continue to serve under his leadership'.[21] The difference is more one of emphasis than substance. Thorpe was definitely attracted by the idea of a post in Cabinet and he told Nigel Fisher that, though he was not very close to Heath, he considered him 'by far the most able man we had' and one under whom he would be happy to serve. Personally, he might even have been prepared to make concessions on proportional representation, but on this issue his party left him no room for manoeuvre. They would not even consider joining a coalition unless the Tories would pledge themselves to support electoral reform. This Heath could not promise even if he had wanted to. The negotiations foundered. 'I am sorry, this is obviously hell – a nightmare on stilts for you,' were Thorpe's final words. It was no understatement. Until the last moment Heath believed that it might be possible to cobble together some arrangement that would keep him in power. He desperately wanted to do so. He believed that things were at last going right, that if he could only surmount the present crisis the way would be relatively clear towards the reformed and re-invented Britain that was his aim. To let Wilson back into Downing Street would be to reverse all that he had achieved and doom his country to another period of stagnant deterioration. Personal ambition and his reluctance to surrender the delights of office were certainly factors in Heath's manoeuvring, but so also was a patriotic conviction that, for the sake of Britain's future, it was essential that he should remain in power.[22]

From Friday morning, by which time the final election results were clear, until the afternoon of Monday 4 March, when he went to Buckingham Palace to resign, the uncertainty continued. Heath was much criticised for not accepting the inevitable more rapidly and more gracefully. 'The prolonged horse-trading was making us look ridiculous,' Margaret Thatcher wrote in her memoirs. 'She certainly did not say that at the time,' retorted Heath.[23] In fact it was clear that she and Joseph disliked the idea of negotiating with the Liberals, but they did not maintain their opposition in the face of the majority. The Cabinet as a whole supported Heath's approach. As with the date of the election, however, the decisive voice was the Prime Minister's. If he had taken a different line and insisted that he should resign at once, the Cabinet would equally have acquiesced. Carrington and Gilmour would have argued the case for an approach to the Liberals but they would not have stood out against the Prime Minister, any more than Joseph and Thatcher stood out when Heath's voice went the other way.

The Party as a whole was uneasy. No less could have been expected of the hardened opponents of the Prime Minister. Norman Tebbit was surprised that Heath did not resign at once, 'and as it became plain that he was seeking Liberal support for a coalition government my surprise turned to real anger'. John Nott was 'appalled that we did not immediately surrender office'. When Heath asked all ministers to be available for consultation over the weekend, Nott wrote: 'I refused to return to London. I had had enough of my own government and had no intention of remaining as a minister.' But others, better disposed towards Heath, were no more enthusiastic about his manoeuvrings. Kenneth Clarke had to ring round those members for whom, as a Whip, he was responsible, to tell them of Heath's approach to Thorpe. None of them approved. The member for Rutland, an archetypal knight of the shires, told Clarke: 'Just tell that man to stop messing about. We have lost an election, we cannot form a government, we have just been defeated and we must go with dignity.' Clarke admitted to Heath that he felt much the same.[24] The negotiations for a coalition left the country at large with the feeling that Heath was a bad loser. The *Spectator* expressed the view with particular venom: 'Mr Edward Heath's monomania was never more clearly seen than in the days after the general election when, a ludicrous and broken figure, he clung with grubby fingers to the crumbling precipice of his power. The spectacle was ludicrous; it was pathetic; it was contemptible. And Mr Heath, having been over the weekend a squalid nuisance, remains as Leader of the Tory Party just that.'[25] It was unfair, it was even grotesquely unfair, but it was not unrepresentative of the popular view. Like some inverted Thane of Cawdor, nothing in Heath's premiership so ill became him like the leaving of it. It left a sour memory in the minds of many Tories which was to serve him badly in the uneasy times that lay ahead.

Thorpe floated the idea of a grand coalition of all the parties and Woodrow Wyatt urged Heath to approach Wilson on this basis. A coalition of this kind might last six or nine months; then, when the economic crisis was over, there could be another election. 'If Labour refuses they will look very bad,' urged Wyatt. 'If they accept, there will then be joint responsibility for necessary measures ... Either way you would look very good.' Heath dismissed such ideas out of hand. Wilson would never be allowed by his left wing to join such a coalition, he told Thorpe, and Wilson himself 'would wish at all costs to avoid the role and fate of Ramsay Macdonald'. He dutifully reported the overtures to Cabinet but gave no impression that he took them seriously. Such 'grand alliances' cannot be made artificially, Hailsham noted in his diary. 'They are born of an identity of view concerning what needs to be done.'[26]

The Cabinet met for the last time before the final breach with the Liberals had been formally acknowledged but by this time everyone knew that the attempt had failed. 'Ted did not thank his colleagues – nor did they thank him!' recorded Cecil King. More convincingly Heath recollects that 'I took the opportunity of thanking my Cabinet colleagues for the support they had given me over the three-and-three-quarter years that we had been in Government together. Lord Hailsham spoke in similar terms on behalf of the Cabinet.'[27] There was at least one more intervention. A minister spoke in warm, almost impassioned terms about the privilege it had been to serve in a Cabinet so harmonious and so united. Given the story of the Conservative Party over the next twelve months, there is some irony in the fact that the speaker was the Minister for Education, Margaret Thatcher. 'You fought a gallant fight against great odds,' Richard Nixon telegraphed consolingly from Washington. 'I look forward to seeing you in the future as the Leader of what I know will truly be Her Majesty's loyal Opposition.'[28]

And so it was off to the Palace and farewell to the plumed troop and the big wars. As he got into his car to return to Downing Street, his security officer said goodbye. 'Where on earth are you going?' asked Heath. 'Sir,' was the reply. 'You are no longer Prime Minister and therefore no longer entitled to special protection.'[29]

TWENTY-ONE

The Uneasy Truce

Not merely had Othello's occupation gone, but he had lost his house as well. Saying goodbye to Chequers was probably the single thing that caused Heath the greatest distress after the loss of the election, but a more immediate problem was where he was going to sleep while he was in London. The lease of his flat in Albany had come up for renewal shortly before the election; Heath let it lapse for fear that the press would find out if he did otherwise and would announce that he was insuring himself against defeat. The lease had been taken over by a French couple who turned a deaf ear when Heath suggested that they might make way for him. 'So much for European unity!' he wrote in his memoirs, though there seems no reason why the new occupants should have inconvenienced themselves to accommodate his needs. His pps, Tim Kitson, gallantly came to the rescue, offered Heath the use of his flat near Vauxhall Bridge and himself crowded in with another Tory backbencher. It was supposed that this arrangement would last for a couple of weeks; in fact Kitson was deprived of his flat for four months while Heath searched for a more permanent home. Once Heath asked how much rent he should pay. 'Nothing,' said Kitson, and added jokingly, 'Leave me something in your will.' The offer was accepted, but when the will was read more than thirty years later there was no mention of Kitson, or indeed, several others who might have been expected to be beneficiaries. Heath was not unappreciative, however. When Kitson's watch broke, he produced

443

a tray full of watches which he had accumulated on his travels and encouraged his benefactor to pick and keep one of the most expensive.[1]

The Duke of Westminster extricated both Heath and Kitson from their predicament. He was an ardent Europhile who believed that Heath deserved well of the nation and he put his views into practice by offering the ex-prime minister a house in Wilton Street, in plushest Belgravia. The rent was a mere £1,250 a year, less than a tenth of its market value. The house, with three floors and a basement flat for a housekeeper, large enough to entertain yet not intimidatingly grand, suited Heath admirably. He moved in in July 1974 and retained it until ill-health and his inability to manage the stairs forced him to give up spending much time in London.

Every prime minister, when ejected from office, must feel deprived of the smooth machine that manages the complications of daily life and makes it possible to operate at full efficiency. Heath was spared one privation. Some years before, in what Marcia Williams described as 'a magnanimous and imaginative gesture', he had decreed that the Leader of the Opposition should be allocated a car and driver. Cynics might protest that this was done merely so that he would benefit by the same arrangement if he found himself once more Leader of the Opposition. This would be unfair. For one thing, Heath genuinely had not supposed that he would ever occupy such a position; he took it for granted that he would serve as prime minister for a decade or so and then retire in glory, handing over a healthy and prosperous country to his successor. For another, he knew that if such a contingency did arise, Conservative Central Office would provide him with a car. It was still satisfactory, however, to enjoy the luxury as of right. A deposed prime minister cherishes every vestige of consequence which will remind him and the world of what he once was. Heath disliked Wilson but he respected his office and felt that it must be suitably maintained. (It was not the only thing for which Wilson had cause to thank Heath: when he returned to Downing Street he found that the greater part of the Christmas card list had been reclassified as 'official' and was thus paid for by the Exchequer. It saved him some £2,000 a year.)[2]

Heath needed every scrap of consolation he could gather. His defeat had had a dramatic effect on his morale and his self-confidence. Cecil Parkinson had been at the 1922 Committee meeting at which Heath announced the election: 'He was hugely impressive and had about him an air of greatness.' Four weeks later in the same forum: 'He seemed almost physically diminished and, instead of being impressed by him, one just felt very sorry for this desolate and lonely figure.' Lord Barnetson, a press magnate who saw a lot of Heath, told Cecil King that he seemed to be suffering from 'severe shell shock. It took him weeks to recover.' Weeks, or even months: early in August Chris Patten was saying that the real trouble was that 'the leader had never got back on to form, he had been muddled and groping, he certainly hadn't the detailed ascendancy he used to have'. Douglas Hurd confirmed that the Shadow Cabinet had had some very unsuccessful meetings. 'The colleagues had been accustomed to a slightly firmer lead from Ted when he was Prime Minister and they didn't adjust to the new situation. They talked around and around things while Ted sat silent at the centre.'[3]

Some felt that he was a sick man. In the months before the election Hurd had been seriously alarmed at the Prime Minister's 'tired and lack-lustre' state. He revived dramatically for the campaign but seemed then to slip back into a morass of inert depression. It was 'terrifying' to see how difficult he found it to stay awake, remembers Sara Morrison, but though she repeatedly questioned Heath's doctor, Brian Warren, she found that he refused to take the matter seriously. John Campbell has suggested that he was already suffering from the thyroid deficiency which was only diagnosed in 1975 but which contributed greatly to the 'uncharacteristic indecisiveness, lethargy, even paralysis of will' which was increasingly evident during his second period as Leader of the Opposition.[4]

Heath himself denied this. His friends told him he looked tired, he recalled, but 'I remained sound in mind and limb throughout and, despite everything, actually felt very healthy and robust'. It is notoriously difficult to prove a negative but most of those who were close to Heath consider that he showed no loss of powers before the election and was only marginally affected during 1974. In September of that year, Michael Fraser told David Butler that Heath was a 'remarkably physically durable person. He knew of no person who could compete with Ted in this sphere in the 50–60 age group.' Caroline Stephens and Penelope Gardner, who worked closely with him, saw no symptoms of illness during his years at Number 10. Jim Prior and Robert Armstrong are equally convinced that Campbell's thesis is misguided. They witnessed no signs of indecision or slowing up. Douglas Hurd, though at one point concerned about Heath's health, saw no evidence of his drowsiness until 1975, after which it became increasingly apparent. Doctors who treated Heath in later years believe that, though Dr Warren may not have been the most astute of diagnosticians, it would have been impossible for him to miss the symptoms of thyroid deficiency if they had been present to any serious extent. The most likely though tentative conclusion seems to be that, if the condition did exist while he was still Prime Minister, it had no significant effect on his performance and that it was only towards the end of 1974 that it became a serious handicap.[5]

'He seldom came out from his closet; and when he appeared in the public rooms, he stood among the crowd of courtiers and ladies, stern and abstracted, making no jest and smiling at none. His freezing look, his silence, the dry and concise answers which he uttered when he could keep silence no longer, disgusted noblemen and gentlemen who had been accustomed to be slapped on their back by their royal master.'[6]

Macaulay was writing about King William III, but it could as well have been Edward Heath. His reluctance, inability perhaps, to ingratiate himself with those whom he did not esteem, even sometimes with those whom he *did* esteem, had been more marked ever since he had become Leader of the Opposition. Now, when of all times some slapping on the back was necessary, it seems never to have entered his head that he should do so. 'Ted's great weakness', wrote Maudling, 'was that he gave the impression to the Members of the House that he did not care for them; that he regarded them merely as troops who were there to support him, and that he was the officer in command. He was seldom seen in the Smoking Room, he never fraternised with the rank-and-file.' Even those whom he knew well and trusted could be rebuffed. Carrington became so concerned about Heath's loss of touch with the rank and file of the Party that he persuaded the leader to have a conversation with the critical but loyal backbencher, Harmar Nicholls. 'The meeting was a complete flop. Ted took no interest in what Nicholls had to say and had recourse to polite questions about his family.'

At least on this occasion the questions were polite. Sometimes he was gratuitously rude. Julian Critchley was dining in the House of Commons with Jim Prior and two or three other Conservative members. Heath walked by and stopped to talk to Prior. 'By no word, glance or gesture did he acknowledge the existence of the rest of us. As he left, Jim said to us despairingly "What on earth can I do with him?"' And yet he knew that backbenchers and Tory supporters outside Westminster had views, sometimes sensible views, and that he could not afford totally to ignore them. In August 1974 Kevin McNamara asked him to support a bill that would make hare-coursing illegal. Personally he was against hare-coursing, Heath replied 'but many members of the Party are not. In my view this is very dangerous from the election point of view.' Given that McNamara was a Labour MP, his reply was strikingly candid. It showed both that he thought McNamara was worth listening to and that he was aware of the force of opinion among Tory voters and the need to take account of it. He would have taken similar account of the views of Critchley and his friends if they had raised a point of political importance. It was only when it came to personalities or trivial chit-chat that he was not prepared to make a minimal effort to be conciliatory or even civil. Denis Healey once asked Anthony Powell whether he had based the uncouth yet formidable Widmerpool on Heath. Powell claimed he had never even thought of it and dismissed the idea, but when the Tory Monday Club invited him to address them at dinner on 'Heath as Widmerpool', he began to wonder whether the resemblance was more marked than he had supposed.[7]

Even if he were the most popular of men, any Tory leader who loses an election must expect speculation about his chances of remaining in office. According to the *Daily Telegraph*, immediately after the defeat of February 1974 a number of backbenchers went to see du Cann, as chairman of the 1922 Committee, to demand an election for leadership. Du Cann would personally have relished Heath's immediate dismissal; unless, of course, he shared the views of the unnamed but malevolent Tory backbencher who told Norman Fowler that he wanted the leader to remain at the helm for a while yet: 'Heath has not suffered enough, he observed chillingly.' But du Cann knew that it would be premature to mount a challenge. For one thing, Wilson might at any moment decide that ruling with a minority government had become impossible and ask for a dissolution. To fight another election with Heath still leader might seem unpromising, but to fight it with a divided party and an unproven replacement at its head could only be disastrous. For another, no prominent Tory was prepared to mount a challenge. With Maudling in disrepute if not disgrace and Douglas-Home and Hailsham non-starters, the only plausible replacement was William Whitelaw. Whitelaw was not quite the bluff and remote cavalier which he professed to be. He was certainly ambitious and ready to fill Heath's shoes if they were pressed upon him. Julian Critchley recorded that 'Willie – the heir apparent? – was telling his friends ("in total confidence") that Ted was not behaving like a gentleman. He should have resigned.' But though Whitelaw may have harboured such thoughts and may even have confided them to his intimates, he was too sensible to voice them publicly. The party must stick with Heath at least until after the next election; if that too were lost it might be time to reconsider the position, but for the moment unity was all-important.[8]

But this did not mean that Heath's position was a strong one: paradoxically, it was impregnable but weak. For many people he remained leader on sufferance. When he appeared before the 1922 Committee only one member, Maxwell-Hyslop, questioned whether he should remain in office and his reception was generally warm. But, like Parkinson, the backbenchers 'felt very sorry for this desolate and lonely figure'. Theirs was a vote of confidence, but a singularly unconfident one. Sara Morrison told David Butler that Heath had been helped by the extremely boring and tactless way 'that Hyslop had raised the issue of the succession'. Heath would definitely survive until the next election – probably in October – but 'he would survive in the wrong way: the Conservatives would talk about it and do nothing'. The Tory powers, sneered Cecil King, had decided that 'it would be unkind to deprive Ted of the leadership now. The leadership is evidently thought of in personal and "club" terms, not in connection with winning the forthcoming election.' King got it wrong. The Tories kept Heath as leader because otherwise they thought they stood no chance of winning the forthcoming election. But he was right in supposing that the enthusiasm was muted and that no solid base of loyal support existed on which Heath could confidently depend.[9]

A leader who has just lost an election that he had been expected to win is not in a strong position radically to reform his team. One important change was forced on Heath. Barber finally proved that his wish to retire as Chancellor of the Exchequer was no idle pretence and Heath found himself forced to seek a successor. Keith Joseph was probably best qualified and certainly considered the post should be his, but Heath had viewed with disquiet Joseph's increasingly strident criticism of the prices and incomes policy and his avowal of the monetarist theories advocated by such right-wing gurus as Alfred Sherman and Alan Walters. Instead he played safe by installing the Home Secretary, Robert Carr, a sensible and honourable man but no more likely than Barber to challenge his leader's views on economic matters. Carr was 'even more committed to the interventionist approach that had got us into so much trouble', wrote Mrs Thatcher reproachfully. His appointment proved that Heath had 'set his face against any policy rethinking that would imply that his Government's economic and industrial policy had been seriously flawed'. Prior, another equally dependable loyalist, took over at the Home Office while Geoffrey Howe was promoted to replace Joseph in charge of Social Services. John Biffen, one of the most articulate and energetic of the critics on the right, complained that Heath must have been paying too much attention to the scriptures, 'since he had decided to make the team in his own image'. Certainly Heath made no particular effort to promote those who were wont to contest his views, but the most spirited of the young rebels – Nicholas Ridley, Jock

Bruce-Gardyne, Tebbit, Biffen himself – had no obvious claims to ministerial office, while the big guns of the past – du Cann, Soames, Maude, Thorneycroft – were either otherwise engaged or did not seem suitable.[10]

Mrs Thatcher was not a full member of the 'Steering Committee', the inner Shadow Cabinet which met from time to time to discuss questions of party strategy. Neither she nor Keith Joseph attended the first meetings; later they were usually in attendance but their listing in a second-eleven team with other minor dignitaries suggests that they were there by invitation rather than by right.[11] Thatcher, given her status in the party, would have been unsurprised by this; Joseph had more reason to be aggrieved. In the course of 1974 the ideological differences between Heath and Joseph became both more marked and more public. Having been denied the Treasury, Joseph refused any formal office but asked that he should be empowered to study Britain's long-term economic strategy and the measures that were necessary to improve it. To aid him in this task he set up the Centre for Policy Studies (CPS), an organisation that was to be distinct from the Conservative Research Department. Heath accepted the existence of this institution with no great enthusiasm on the understanding that it was to 'examine how the market system worked in the various countries of the world'. This seemed innocuous enough, and Heath is said to have remarked that it would do Joseph, and his designated vice-president, Margaret Thatcher, no harm to gain 'practical knowledge of the real business world'. He should have been warned by the fact that the running of the Centre was entrusted to Alfred Sherman, high priest of the free market, who preached his detestation of state intervention with all the fervour to be expected from a lapsed Communist. As his representative in the Centre Heath put in Adam Ridley from the Think Tank. From the start Ridley was alarmed by the course that the CPS was following. At its opening, he reported to Heath, there had been no members of the Shadow Cabinet beyond Joseph and Thatcher, no representative of Central Office or of the Research Department: 'The list is the brainchild of one person alone – Alfred Sherman – but it is symptomatic of something.' Suspicions darkened when it became clear that the CPS was competing for funds with

Central Office. Oliver Poole, a former Tory chairman now in charge at Lazards, reported to Whitelaw that Joseph was addressing personal appeals to prominent City figures, soliciting donations. The tradition was that the merchant banks only contributed to Party funds at election time; Whitelaw spoke sternly to Joseph and no more letters of the kind were sent.[12]

Meetings of the Shadow Cabinet became increasingly acrimonious as the differences between Heath and his critics became more apparent. The fault lay predominantly with Heath. Joseph was obstinate and opinionated but not a man to pick a quarrel; Heath found disagreement hard to stomach, particularly when it was reiterated and, to his mind, irrational. Heseltine sat next to Joseph at Shadow Cabinet meetings and was dismayed by the leader's growing truculence: 'My first doubts as to Ted's ability to hold the party together', he wrote, 'stemmed from the brusqueness and brutality he displayed in the conflicts between the two of them.'[13] In fact, Heath was not always unconciliatory. In a speech at Elgin he stressed that 'a firm and consistent control over the money supply' was an important weapon in the war against inflation, and admitted that 'on that score we may have lessons to learn from our past experience. We will not be too proud to learn them.' But this was no more than a half-hearted attempt to paper over a rapidly widening crack.

In July Joseph wrote at length to Heath to plead with him to abandon all ideas of a freeze on prices and incomes. Such a freeze could not last long and was bound to fuel a demand for early and higher pay claims: 'True, it is effective for a few months but, as you told us, it has to be unwound and that involves either a flood ... or a wretched series of income stages.' 'This is the usual nonsense,' Heath scribbled on the letter. He told Waldegrave to acknowledge Joseph's letter and thank him for it but, by an oversight, this was not done. Three weeks later Waldegrave asked if he should now acknowledge. 'Ignore it,' instructed Heath. At one Shadow Cabinet meeting, Joseph was so emphatic in his dismissal of a prices and incomes policy that Heath protested: 'Your analysis of the Government's record has left me heart-broken.' This cry of dismay was recorded by Kenneth Baker, who was so surprised by his Leader's uncharacteristic expression, that he at once wrote it down. Though some members of the Shadow Cabinet felt that Joseph was being roughly used, they were almost unanimous in their rejection of his thesis. Only Mrs Thatcher regularly supported him, and she with reservations. At a meeting in June 'it was generally agreed that the country was heading for an explosive wages free-for-all and that – even if a Conservative Government were to make approaches for a voluntary policy – it would be necessary to reserve the right to take the appropriate statutory powers'.[14]

Early in September Joseph turned an open secret into open warfare. He announced that he proposed to make a speech in Preston in which he would distance himself conclusively from what was still the Conservative economic policy. Howe and Thatcher, as being the two members of the Shadow Cabinet most sympathetic to Joseph's views and yet still formally loyal to the official doctrine, were despatched to persuade him to tone down his speech. Joseph agreed to make a few cosmetic changes but the main thrust of his speech remained unaltered: unemployment was a lesser evil than inflation; the false Keynesian gods must be abandoned and a return made to true Conservatism. More significant still, considered Howe, was the long-term impact of this 'brief, unplanned conclave. Consciously or unconsciously, it seemed somehow to consolidate a nascent sense of partnership between the three of us.' The speech was an unequivocal challenge to Heath's leadership. Some people felt that it would be followed by Joseph's dismissal from the Shadow Cabinet, but though Heath would have had the support of most of his colleagues, with a general election obviously imminent he felt that it was better to tolerate a measure of disunion rather than to provoke an open split.[15]

It would have been relatively easy for the Tories to have engineered the defeat of the Government at any moment between the two 1974 elections. The first opportunity would obviously have been at the end of the debate on the Queen's Speech when the new House of Commons met for the first time. Heath hinted that they might be prepared to force a decisive vote. Wilson promptly retorted that this would be at the Tories' peril; he would at once ask for a dissolution and a new election. In theory the Queen could have refused the request and given the Tories another chance to cobble together some kind of coalition government. In practice she would almost certainly have felt bound to grant the dissolution. 'I do not think we stand to win if Wilson resigns,' warned Hailsham. 'I also think that there is danger to the Monarchy if a dissolution were refused.' Heath needed no such admonition. As he wrote ruefully in his memoirs: 'People understandably resent having their lives disrupted by elections, and tend to look unfavourably on parties which cause such contests to take place.' He had paid the price for this once already; now he knew that the electorate would be likely to feel that Labour had not been given a fair chance and would return them with a working majority. Heath 'hastened to withdraw his threat,' wrote Wilson triumphantly, 'and even said that his remarks had been misinterpreted'. This was not how Heath remembered it: the Labour Party, he maintained, had gone back on their threat to abandon Stage Three of the prices and incomes policy and so made it unnecessary for the Opposition to defeat them on the issue. Wilson's version of events is nearer the mark. A sizeable section of the Tory Party – probably as many as forty strong – said that they would not support any attempt to defeat the Government on an issue in which they felt their own leadership was fundamentally misguided. If Heath had pushed matters to a vote he would have exposed the rift among his followers and been made to look ridiculous.[16]

The Conservatives were therefore condemned to a policy of opposition which could never be sustained to a point where it might become effective. In the immediate future, Heath told the Steering Committee, 'opposition should be concentrated in the form of speeches', rather than in amendments or divisions. This would upset the parliamentary party, he recognised, but the mood of the country was clearly 'Give them a chance' and it would be folly to ignore it. 'Willing to wound, and yet afraid to strike' is an ignoble posture, yet it was forced on the Tories at this time. Heath was quite right in thinking that it would upset the backbenchers. Angus Maude forwarded to Heath a letter he had received from a constituent denouncing 'the utter spinelessness' of the Opposition: 'I am afraid it does represent a fairly widespread feeling at the Party grass-roots.' 'Ask him if he would like to have a General Election at a time which would give Wilson a larger majority,' Heath replied crossly. Robin Maxwell-Hyslop was still more vehement. He protested against 'the farce of protecting the Government against defeat ... by arranging for enough Conservative Members not to vote ... This play-acting is devastating to the morale of the Party in the constituencies but, alas, typical of what passes for leadership in our Party today.' He continued to write indignantly in this vein until finally Heath retorted that he did not intend to respond to 'your gratuitously offensive letters'.[17]

'I am sure that you, Willie and Alec should be making sombre, magisterial speeches, in measured tones, recalling the country to a sense of destiny, service, self-respect and even self-sacrifice,' Hailsham urged Heath in June. 'William Waldegrave also tells me I should be maintaining a high moral tone,' Heath replied. 'Perhaps there is an All Souls conspiracy.' The trouble was that the rank-and-file of the Tory Party did not want 'sombre, magisterial speeches'; they wanted savage in-fighting with blood on the floor, preferably Wilson's blood. Heath's control over his backbenchers had been tenuous ever since his electoral defeat; now every day of muted opposition weakened it still further. 'The lack of leadership and communication has produced something of a crisis of confidence,' admitted Pym. 'I have indicated my anxieties about the way the Party is being run to Tim [Kitson] and to Willie, but nothing more than that. I know from what others have said that I am not alone in this view.' Coming from a former Chief Whip, that is a formidable indictment. Even Peter Carrington mused that, though there was no real threat to Heath and no possible replacement was available, his position was not a happy one. 'The trouble about Ted was that, although he was admired, nobody in the Party really liked him. The trouble with the Conservative Party was that they put too much of a premium on being nice at coffee mornings.'[18]

Heath was neither good at coffee mornings nor disposed to indulge in rancorous opposition. Still less would he take part in the bandying of personal abuse. Before the February election, he had refused to make any reference to the gossip surrounding Jeremy Thorpe; now he discountenanced any use of the various shadowy scandals which involved the Prime Minister, the newly ennobled Marcia Falkender, the purchase of gravel pits and a heady broth of unsubstantiated and largely groundless rumours. At a lunch party in May 1974 Chapman Pincher, journalist and polemicist who specialised in the political underworld, proclaimed that Heath was now changing tactics and had sanctioned a press campaign making use of all such allegations. William Waldegrave, Pincher maintained, had told him: 'It's all systems go now.' Martin Gilbert, who was present at the same lunch party, demanded evidence that such was indeed Heath's new policy and, when none was forthcoming, appealed to Heath himself. 'There was no substance at all in the remarks you attribute to Chapman Pincher,' Heath assured him. 'Neither directly nor indirectly have I given any green light to a campaign of attack on the Prime Minister on any of the grounds you mention.' Waldegrave was equally emphatic: his name, he said, had been taken in vain: 'At no time did I give Mr Pincher any reason to believe that the Leader of the Opposition or his office were anxious to launch a campaign of attack against the Prime Minister on these sorts of grounds.' The denials are totally convincing: Heath was always scrupulous in his refusal to handle dirt. But his squeamishness did not gain him much popularity in the party. Some at least of his followers felt that the use of any weapons was justified against an enemy whom they deemed devious and evil. Heath's failure to lead the attack was, in their eyes, as reprehensible as the muted nature of his opposition in the House of Commons.[19]

It was no affection for Harold Wilson that led Heath to eschew such slanderous attacks. 'Not since Gladstone and Disraeli', wrote Butler and Kavanagh, 'has there been so protracted and personalised a duel across the floor of the House.' Heath's feud with Margaret Thatcher has obscured the fact that, for most of Heath's active political life, Wilson was the real enemy. The two men, so similar in age, background and attainments, were mutually antipathetic: the Artful Dodger against Mr Gradgrind. Each despised the other; Wilson merely disliked Heath, Heath hated Wilson. To the humiliation of having been defeated by a man whom he considered morally and politically his inferior was added indignation at Wilson's superior skills in the House of Commons. Heath, even when in office and enjoying all the advantages from which an incumbent prime minister must benefit, had never completely got the measure of Wilson, but he had held his own. Now that he was back in the less favoured role of Leader of the Opposition he found that his adversary's ingenuity and wit, backed by the formidable machinery of government, were once again too much for him. Wilson, in fact, was not the man he had been; already he was playing a less prominent role and preparing himself for retirement. But in the cockpit of the House of Commons he was still able to command the field: constantly Heath knew that he himself was right, knew that he had the better arguments, knew that Wilson was being evasive or dishonest, but could not land a decisive blow. Pierre Trudeau, when he had been narrowly defeated in an election in which he had campaigned in a notably high-minded style, declared that he was henceforth going 'to take the politics out of politics and give the people anything they want'; Heath used to quote this remark, said his friends, with 'a mixture of puritanical disapproval and wistfulness'. The wistfulness was real, but the disapproval predominated.[20]

Two months after the election Heath escaped from Westminster on a visit that was radically to affect his future life. As early as 1966 he had told a reporter that he was anxious to visit China 'because I haven't been there and that's the place where there's most to be found out. There's something very exciting being near the beginning of a great power.' He had told Peter Walker when Walker took over at Trade and Industry that he wanted him to go to China and stay there as long as possible because it was 'the country of the future'. 'I want you to go out to China and make some agreements with them,' he said. 'I don't mind whether they are on trade, on science, on the environment, or indeed anything, but I do want us to establish a very strong relationship.' He particularly admired its achievements in the field of higher education. His plans to visit China himself had been forestalled by the election but, as Leader of the Opposition, he revived the idea. Douglas Hurd, who while in the Foreign Service had served in Peking, as Beijing was then called, was uncertain. He feared that the Chinese strict adherence to protocol 'might create a visit well below the level which Ted and the British media would think acceptable'. Heath was prepared to take the risk and was proved right.

The Chinese were genuinely appreciative of the fact that he had been eager to visit them long before Nixon had made his dramatic venture. Politically, they saw nothing to choose between Heath and Wilson: indeed Mao Tse-tung told Kissinger that he preferred dealing with Conservative Western leaders 'because they were more suspicious of the Soviet Union. I like rightists. People say that Prime Minister Heath is also to the right. I am comparatively happy when these people on the right come into power.' Most of all, they respected Heath as a champion of a united Europe and were anxious to foster the concept of Europe and China as a counter-force against Russia. Heath's welcome, the Belgian Ambassador told him on the authority of his Chinese counterpart, had been 'inspired by admiration for your courageous and realistic European policy'.[21]

Shortly before Heath left, Wilson wrote to wish him a safe journey and to reassure him that he did not intend to ask for a dissolution while the Leader of the Opposition was abroad. It was a friendly gesture, but Wilson was nevertheless irritated by the fact that Heath had stolen a march on him and undertaken a journey likely to earn him much, and favourable, publicity. He complained angrily to Martin Gilbert that Heath was 'letting himself be used by China, as part of China's campaign against Russia'. Heath would have rejected the word 'used' but have accepted the rest of the charge with equanimity. The wider the rift between Russia and China the better, he felt, it would be for the West and the more likely it would be that China would evolve towards liberalism if not democracy.[22]

Any fears that Heath may have nurtured about his reception were allayed when he arrived in Peking in May 1974 to be greeted by several thousand young people dancing and waving flags. The welcome was tumultuous but not impressive enough to satisfy Chairman Mao. Why was there no military guard of honour? he asked Chou En-lai. We thought it would upset Mr Wilson, was the hesitant reply. 'Upset Mr Wilson?' exclaimed Mao. 'When he leaves Peking Mr Heath will have a full guard of honour.' Until the meeting took place it was by no means certain that Heath would be granted an interview by the Chairman. In the hope that it would transpire, William Waldegrave had been told to find a suitable present. Mao was said to be a fervent admirer of Charles Darwin, so Waldegrave took the matter up with the Darwin/Keynes family. He failed to persuade them to part with a presentation copy of *Das Kapital* inscribed from Marx to Darwin and clearly unread, but secured a photograph of Darwin by Mrs Cameron signed by its subject with the statement that it was the photograph of himself which he liked best. To this was added, at the cost of £40, a first edition of *The Descent of Man*. When finally he was summoned to the Forbidden City Heath caused some surprise by asking if he could bring his staff along to be presented to the Chairman. 'It was much appreciated that you asked that the rest of us should meet Mao,' wrote Waldegrave. 'No one seems to remember a similar occurrence here – which I take as an indication that most political leaders pay less attention to their staff than you do.' Heath responded to his reception with warm and unquestioning enthusiasm. Hurd found that his most important function was trying to persuade his leader that all was not necessarily as rosy as it appeared on the surface; a task which he found it necessary to reverse when he escorted Mrs Thatcher to China a few years later.[23]

Heath found Mao in valedictory mood: 'I am sick all over my body,' he began. 'I am sick too,' chipped in Chou. The conversation turned to the need to increase trade, encourage the development of Hong Kong with a view to a smooth handover in 1997 and make common cause against the Russian threat, after which Mao slipped back into musing on mortality. 'I have an intimation from God,' he said. 'He has asked me to visit him.' Heath said politely that he hoped the invitation would not be accepted for some time. 'I have not yet replied,' said Mao, laughing uproariously. Heath was determined to enjoy everything: even a concert in which he had hoped to hear Chinese classical music but instead was regaled by a choir singing such ditties as 'Taiwan Must be Liberated' and a male chorus singing 'We are a Militia Squad of Chinese People'. The Ambassador advised that a return dinner should be given in the Great Hall of the People. It would cost about £1,000, 'payable by the Conservative Party. Is that all right?' Heath was never slow to spend Government or party funds on a good cause. It *was* all right. In his speech at the banquet he devoted most of his energies to extolling the success of Europe, which was 'welcomed by everyone', particularly 'the countries of the Commonwealth, who see in Britain's membership a guarantee that the policies of the Community will take their interests into account'. When talking to the vice premier Deng Xiaoping that afternoon Heath had complained that 'for a strange variety of reasons some members of the present Government did want Britain to leave the Community. Some thought that they would never be able to have socialism in Britain in the form they wanted so long as Britain was a member.' In the Great Hall of the People he expressed the hope that it would 'not be long before Britain too is once again in a position to play an active part ... The day when we recapture the impetus of our advance towards European unity may not be too far distant.'[24]

So it was back to London, to attempt to bring that day a little closer. The organisation of the Conservative Party, both in the country at large and in Central Office, had grown sadly rusty before and during the years of Government. Sara Morrison, from her vantage point as vice-chairman of the party, never missed a chance to point out the antiquated social attitudes and vapid amateurism of many of the local Tory bigwigs. The deputy party chairman, Michael Fraser, was a figure of lofty eminence whom it was difficult to attack directly; indeed Heath still had considerable respect for his abilities and would not have wished to dislodge him. Sara Morrison convinced him, however, that new blood and a firm hand were urgently needed in Central Office. Heath found them in his political adviser and speech-writer Michael Wolff, who was appointed Director-General in May 1974. The choice was a sound one – Wolff was not given much time but he was still able to overhaul the machinery and introduce much-needed reforms. Heath, however, made the change with characteristic gracelessness. Fraser was left with a feeling that he was being bypassed if not supplanted and the senior officials felt that Wolff was a brash intruder, inexperienced and 'not one of us'. To the party in the country it seemed yet another example of Heath's determination to turn Central Office into his personal fief. Hugh Fraser went on record as saying that the result was the 'total domination of the party by one man'. To appear in public as a harsh authoritarian while in practice failing to impose any real authority is to get the worst of both worlds. This was Heath's fate. If he had been given another year or two it is possible that a revived and rejuvenated Conservative Party formed in his own image might have emerged. As it was, the organisation of the party was not much improved and doubts about his leadership grew ever more pronounced.[25] Electoral prospects could have been improved if Heath had persuaded the Ulster Unionists to rejoin the Party but, with some clumsiness, he offered to restore the Whip only to seven out of the eleven members, pointedly excluding Ian Paisley and three other militants. It is unlikely that the Paisleyites would have accepted the Whip if it had been offered them and even the more moderate elements of the Party would have made awkward allies. But an attempt to form a united front for a limited period might have paid dividends and Heath's tactics turned potential allies, however unreliable, into embittered foes.[26]

Wilson's determination to renegotiate the terms under which Britain had joined the Common Market did little to ease Heath's relationship with his party. His position was an awkward one. He maintained that the renegotiation was unnecessary, that it could easily harm Britain's position in Europe and could not hope to yield more than a few trivial concessions; on the other hand he hoped that the negotiations would go well and that the Labour Party would therefore feel able to support Britain's continued membership of the EEC. He thereby offended two distinct though overlapping sections of the Party: those who were against the idea of Europe and hoped the renegotiations would fail, and those who thought that Heath was too mealy-mouthed in opposition and should denounce the whole charade. When the Prime Minister told the House of Commons that negotiations were going well and that agreement was coming nearer, Heath, in Wilson's words, 'warmly blessed it, indeed with generosity'. Warm blessings and generosity were not at all what the more recalcitrant Tories felt was called for. Heath did make some friends. Michael Manley, the Prime Minister of Jamaica, reported that he had had successful talks with the Labour Government. 'It is quite clear that the ready and sympathetic grasp of our problems which you showed earlier this year has profoundly influenced the climate with which I have had to deal on this occasion. For that I, and indeed the Caribbean, are much in your debt.' But even if the rank-and-file of the Tory Party had been aware of Mr Manley's enthusiasm for their leader, they would have been singularly unimpressed. For every member who sympathised with Heath's attitude there was at least one other who thought that this was yet another occasion on which he was disastrously out of touch with the party and the country.[27]

One slightly unexpected field in which he sought to create a populist image for himself was women's rights. In July Waldegrave approached Central Office to say that the leader was very anxious to do something to outflank Roy Jenkins on this issue: 'He minutes that there are some things left, particularly in the field of taxation and social services.' Sara Morrison, herself a woman's right incarnate, was put in charge of the operation but it foundered under Heath's successor, who had managed perfectly well herself without special treatment and had no particular interest in giving special treatment to other women. Although not many women who had endured his company at dinner parties would agree, Heath was no misogynist, but he certainly had no particular enthusiasm for increasing the number of women in high places. What he was, however, was a champion of anyone whom he felt was being misused by society. His pps, Kenneth Baker, wrote that he had 'grown fond of Ted ... He was passionately concerned to ensure that his policies were fair and just.' If women were being unfairly treated, this must be put right. If the policy happened to be a vote-winner, then well and good, but it was not a wish to gain female votes that dictated his behaviour.[28]

As if he did not have more than enough to preoccupy him already, tragedy struck in early September. Since his successes in the Admiral's Cup in the second *Morning Cloud* Heath had continued to devote what to some of his followers seemed an inordinate amount of time to ocean racing. By 1974 *Morning Cloud* was in its third edition, though still crewed by some of the same people as had sailed with Heath for a decade or more. The summer of 1974 had brought fresh successes during Cowes Week and later in the 'Round the Goodwins Race' at Ramsgate. Heath then went ashore to attend some celebration in Antwerp, leaving *Morning Cloud* to sail back with a passage crew from Burnham to Cowes. Aboard was Christopher Chadd, Heath's godson and son of his friend and former commanding officer, George Chadd. Unexpectedly, the boat found itself in a Force 9 gale. It was in no real difficulties until a freak wave knocked it over. The boat righted itself but two members of the crew were washed into the sea. One was recovered, the other, Nigel Cumming, disappeared. While they were searching for him *Morning Cloud* was struck by a second wave and again overturned. This time Christopher Chadd was swept overboard. By now the boat was leaking badly and the five surviving crew members took to the life raft. After eight extremely dangerous and unpleasant hours they were washed ashore near Brighton. The bodies of the two missing men were found some days later. The loss of *Morning Cloud* would have been a great blow to Heath, but the death of the two men turned misfortune into tragedy. The fact that one of them, a relatively inexperienced sailor, had been his godson gave the tragedy especial poignancy. Heath rushed to Brighton to see the survivors, then broke the news to the Chadds. In no way was it anybody's fault, certainly not Heath's, but he still felt that in some way it had been his responsibility. He was distraught, remembers Margaret Chadd; though she had known him well for many years she had never suspected that he could feel so much.[29]

Politically too the storm was gathering force. It had seemed almost certain for several months that Wilson would call a general election some time in the autumn. Heath, in public, remained resolutely optimistic: the country had been guilty of a shocking aberration, now that it had had time to regain its senses it would surely vote back the only government that could restore the nation's prosperity. It seems unlikely that privately he believed this to be true; if he did he was almost the only prominent figure in the Opposition to do so. Every pollster and every pundit was convinced that the electorate would decide that the Labour Government had done well enough in impossible circumstances to deserve a proper chance. The only question was the size of its majority.

A few of Heath's closest associates, notably Sara Morrison and Ian Gilmour, believed that there was one last card for the Conservatives to play that might prove to be the ace of trumps. The economic plight of the country was so disastrous and the problems of forming a strong government apparently so remote, that the time had come to raise again the possibility of a coalition, incorporating certainly the Liberals, conceivably even a few of the more *bien-pensant* socialists. Nigel Lawson had put the point to Heath as early as mid-March. 'If we are now to come out openly today in favour of a National Government (of all three parties) this would be no gimmick or even *volte face*,' he told Heath; 'on the contrary, given the present parliamentary situation, it is the only line that is consistent with our manifesto and campaign theme of the overriding need for strong government.' (Looking back today, Lawson says that the concept of national unity was nonsense. Heath, he believes, felt the same – at first at least. 'He was never receptive to new ideas.')[30] A fortnight after Lawson put forward this proposal, the Steering Committee discussed the possibility of a fresh approach to the Liberals. Most people were cautiously in favour, though accepting that all the obstacles that had existed in February were still as strong a couple of months later. Heath showed that Lawson's view of him was correct when he observed that there was 'a real danger of creating a Conservative minority government through giving away seats to the Liberals. In his view, the only cooperation that would interest Mr Thorpe would be ways of obtaining more seats for the Liberals.'[31]

Ian Gilmour, the most senior of the would-be coalitionists, believed that Heath did no more than make 'polite noises' when the idea was put to him. Carr and Carrington, however, were more hopeful. For a brief period it seemed a real possibility, but 'the professionals at Central Office were strongly opposed to the idea and effectively killed it'. It was not only the professionals who deplored the concept of coalition. Du Cann told a Central Office meeting that MPs on the 1922 Committee were anxious lest 'we might do a deal with the Liberals', while the Luton branch of the Monday Club resolved to disown the Leader of the Opposition: 'After innumerable about-turns in office it appears that he is now prepared to compromise his party even further by entering into unholy alliances in order to continue to hold power.'[32]

Still the idea did not die. At a meeting of the Shadow Cabinet it was agreed that 'the country was currently going through one of its coalition moods.' This could not be ignored. Once again Heath emphasised that there was no more reason to believe that the Liberals in July would be any more amenable than they had been in February. But he still refused to rule out the idea altogether. 'The deep interest in a national government is still there, I believe,' Douglas Hurd told William Waldegrave in late August. 'This is still the best way for EH to disarm criticism of himself and win us the election if it comes.'[33] When the election did come Heath's inner circle of young advisers continued to urge him to play the national party card. One night, on an election tour in Manchester, Waldegrave was eloquently holding forth on the need for an immediate démarche. A somnolent Heath suddenly opened his eyes, looked at Sara Morrison's bare feet and said disapprovingly: 'Have you no bedroom slippers, Sara?' 'May I suggest', said Waldegrave tartly, 'that Sara's slippers are not really relevant to this discussion.' Suitably chastened, the leader paid more attention to Waldegrave's arguments and next day discussed the matter on the telephone with Lords Aldington and Carrington. But it never got further than discussion. The possibility of coalition, thought Chris Patten, was one of the essential issues which most needed action, but 'they just talk and talk and talk about that'.[34]

One of the reasons Heath was content to talk and talk rather than to take resolute action was that the possibility of coalition was linked with his own political future. In the first round of negotiations Thorpe had made it clear that it would be much easier for the Liberals to enter a coalition government if its leader was someone other than Heath – Whitelaw seemed to be the most obviously acceptable candidate. Now some of Heath's closest advisers urged him to make a virtue of necessity and volunteer to stand down if it would help the formation of a government. It could well be, it was suggested, that the very fact that he was prepared to sacrifice his position would so impress potential allies that it would turn out to be unnecessary for him to do so. Carrington, Prior and Aldington, as well as such trusties as Kitson and Sara Morrison, all advocated such a course: Whitelaw, presumably because he so obviously might be the beneficiary, refused to endorse it. Heath would probably have refused to contemplate resignation even if Whitelaw had urged it. He remained convinced that he was the only man fit to lead the Party and found it to be his duty as well as his wish to remain in office. When Prior, some time in the summer, put it to him that he should make the supreme sacrifice his only response was a brusque '*Et tu*, Jim?'

When the possibility was raised at a press conference on 7 October he said firmly that 'I am the Leader of the Conservative Party'; and that he would only be inviting other people to join if he were at the head of a majority government. This attitude effectively eliminated any benefit that might have accrued from an adroit promotion of the concept of 'national unity' – 'a coalition of all the talents' was the phrase that Heath somewhat reluctantly accepted. Michael Fraser said that even if Heath had been prepared to endorse the concept whole-heartedly, it would have made little difference; for any Liberal who might have been seduced, a Conservative would have been de-moralised by what would seem an admission of weakness. An element within the Shadow Cabinet was equally sceptical: Joseph and Thatcher were conspicuously silent when the question of coalition was dis-cussed. But the idea was not absurd or wildly far-fetched. Bernard Donoghue, from his vantage point in Number 10, believed that if the Tory idea of a government of national unity had been capped by an offer from Heath to stand down, then it could have presented a serious threat to Labour's prospects: 'The idea of Ted's renunciation did worry the Wilson camp.'[35]

Wilson finally announced on 18 September that the election would be held three weeks later on 10 October. It quickly became apparent that Heath proposed to handle his campaign in a style very different from that of previous elections. His major public speeches, never conspicuously rabble-rousing, were now muted, even diffident; he allowed other ministers to play a prominent role at press conferences; he forbore from violent attacks on Labour. When questioned about his new style he replied blandly: 'I am adopting the technique you have so often urged upon me of quiet, reasonable conversation.' The public response to this subfusc approach was unenthusiastic; the ritual cheers with which the faithful were wont to greet any sally from their leader were slow to come and sometimes absent altogether. But Wilson was conjuring up little more excitement. The electorate was jaded; it had already had one election in 1974; no new issues or new personalities seemed to have emerged; what was there to get excited about? On the whole, Sara Morrison told David Butler, the first week of the campaign had been a success: 'It had made Ted happy. He had been able by his sustained low-key approach to show that he really was a new man ... There had been only fifty per cent of the red carpet treatment in recent elections ... Overall, Ted's performance had been impressive.'[36]

Overall, the Party did not agree. The fact that Heath was believed to be, if not a liability, then at least a doubtful asset was indicated by the number of references to him in the electoral addresses of the various candidates. In February he had featured in a – not very impressive – 33 per cent; in October the figure was only 11 per cent (the corresponding total for Harold Wilson was 5 per cent, so too much significance should not be attached to this statistic). Gallup found that only 27 per cent of voters approved of Heath; the lowest tally since 1967. His new, emollient style did not seem to be doing much to improve matters. Jack Galloway, a Conservative West Midlands agent, complained that Heath was not only no communicator himself but was jealous of and sought to distance those who could do better than him in this respect. Angus Maude was a really effective communicator but Heath had 'sulked and left him out of everything. Ted might, indeed, have done for the party as well as himself.' The first four or five days of the campaign had gone well, thought Ian Gilmour, 'but Ted threw away opportunities – he acted a bit like a dazed man'. His unpopularity with the electorate became ever more marked, considered du Cann: 'My colleagues returned to Westminster with the clear conviction that with a different leader we might have garnered many more votes, perhaps even won the election.' 'I personally think that this was nonsense,' he added unconvincingly.[37]

In the hope of bolstering his new image, Heath submitted to various cosmetic changes. A gap in his lower set of teeth 'which sometimes gave him a snarling appearance on television' was plugged with a false tooth. He was coaxed into wearing rope-soled sandals and venturing out in shirt sleeves. He was presented, said David Wickes, a film director who helped organise his election tours, as 'a rather jovial, overweight and always tanned grocer with 32 tombstone teeth and a big laugh'. But it didn't work. He still came over as stiff and stilted. Perhaps it would have been better, mused Sara Morrison, if he had been allowed to follow his instincts: 'I know they don't like me. Why should I pretend to be a nice guy? It won't achieve anything.'[38]

The new sugar-coated Heath presented to the electorate was not evident in the Shadow Cabinet. 'Ted laid down the law,' remembered Mrs Thatcher. He insisted that: 'We must speak to the manifesto and nothing else, and any amplification of policies must be made only after discussions.' No one, she added dryly, 'had the slightest doubt about the target for these remarks'. Though neither she nor Keith Joseph had any wish to rock the boat at so critical a moment, they were by now notably disaffected. Thatcher, in particular, was put out by Heath's talk of a government of national unity. 'He had somehow convinced himself', she wrote, 'that he represented the "consensus". This accorded with neither his record nor his temperament.' She must even at times have wondered whether Enoch Powell would not have been a more congenial associate. Powell remained as obdurate as ever in opposition to Heath's leadership. Tom Stuttaford, the Tory candidate for the Isle of Ely, asked Powell to speak for him; his constituency contained many Powellites, he said, and 'I would not have been adopted if I had been a "Heathman"'. Powell did not relent. To support any Conservative candidate, he replied, would mean advising the electorate 'to return a Heath government and to endorse those policies on inflation and on Europe which I consistently spoke and voted against in the last parliament'.[39]

An unexpected ally, however, was the multimillionaire maverick James Goldsmith. He flew back to England from a holiday in Italy to help in the build-up to the campaign. The Tory advertising was deplorable and their constituency organisation badly needed reform, he reported: views with which Michael Wolff and Sara Morrison heartily concurred. Even if he had been disposed to put himself out, however, Goldsmith would have been too late to make any serious impression. As it was, his enthusiasm for the Tories was muted by his dislike of Heath's European policies. His leading obsession at the time was proportional representation and he would have been prepared to devote far more money and time to the cause if Heath had pledged himself to join with the Liberals in promoting electoral reform. Several times he raised the issue with Heath, only to have him change the subject and avoid any firm commitment. This indicates how anxious Heath must have been to propitiate a potentially valuable ally. He knew that, whatever his personal feelings might be, he would find it extremely difficult to impose proportional representation on his party. In any other circumstances he would not have hesitated to make this absolutely clear to Goldsmith. He hated being evasive and must have felt the less of himself for being so on this occasion. Only the imminence of election day can have induced him to be, if not dishonest, then at least less than frank.[40]

It would have taken a regiment of Goldsmiths to check Labour's progress. It was not so much that the Conservative campaign went badly as that nothing happened to disturb the nation's conviction that Labour deserved a proper chance. There was no dramatic swing but the two-million drop in the total vote affected Conservative and Liberal seats more seriously than Labour. In public Heath remained resolutely cheerful. When David Frost asked him whether he thought he could survive as leader if he lost the election he replied that the question did not arise; whatever the polls might be saying, the reports from the candidates on the ground made it clear that there was a groundswell of opinion in favour of the Tories. It had been so in 1970, it would be so again in October 1974. What the polls did say was that Labour enjoyed a lead of 14.5 per cent. Those nearest to Heath have little doubt that he was expecting defeat if not disaster. At Bexley for the declaration of the poll, he listened to the results from the first few constituencies to declare. They were unexpectedly promising. Heath caught the eye of William Waldegrave's companion, Victoria Roths-child, and shrugged, as if to say: 'We know this is all nonsense.'[41] And so it proved to be. There was no landslide, but it was a decisive defeat for the Tories. From leading Labour by some 200,000 in the popular vote, they now trailed by nearly a million. Labour only enjoyed an overall majority of three, but they had 42 more seats in the House of Commons than the Conservatives and the composition of the minor parties meant that they could expect a reasonably secure few years in office. At Bexley, Heath's own majority fell by more than 2,000. Whatever the mitigating circumstances, however much worse it might have been, the fact was that Heath had lost two general elections in a row and three general elections out of four. The Conservative Party was not traditionally generous to losers; there was no reason to think that it would make an exception on this occasion.

TWENTY-TWO

Defeat by Knockout

The Tories, wrote Barbara Castle a few days after the election, 'are in real travail over the leadership'. She had told her husband that she was sure Heath would still be leader when the next election came in four years or so. 'He's incredulous and has bet me two to one, but my hunch is strong.'[1]

Most people would have offered her still more generous odds. Almost everyone in a position to form a considered opinion took it for granted that Heath would quickly be replaced as leader; perhaps within a few weeks, probably within a few months, certainly well before the next election. There was one conspicuous exception: Edward Heath himself. At the first meeting of the Shadow Cabinet after the election he told his colleagues that he thought the Opposition had fought 'quite a good containment exercise'. So, indeed, they had, but to some at least of those present he seemed complacent and woefully indifferent to the question of whether his continued leadership was what the party needed. 'Everyone except Ted', wrote Mrs Thatcher, 'knew that the main political problem was the fact that he was still leader. But he thought we should now concentrate on Scotland, on how to improve our appeal to the young and how to increase our support among working-class voters.'[2]

He was in fact well aware of disaffection in the party. The little band of intimates whom he knew to be on his side was almost unanimous in urging him to stand down. Prior, Kitson, Sara Morrison, Wolff, all argued that there was nothing to be gained by hanging on; at the very least, said Hurd, the issue of the leadership should be confronted and resolved. The Party, he wrote, 'will not become a serious opposition until the question is settled. We shall spend far too much time scurrying and backbiting among ourselves, and this will be the only part of our activities which the media will notice ... There is at the moment a swing back in favour of yourself caused by personal sympathy – and by bafflement as to a successor, but ... in the judgment of all MPs to whom I have spoken – and in my own – this swing back is not likely to be enough.' Kenneth Baker was still more emphatic. The morning after the election he went round to Wilton Street at 11.00 a.m. to find Heath still in his dressing gown. 'You had better resign now as leader if you don't want to be hurt,' he advised. 'There are many people in the party who are out to destroy you – the malicious, the malcontents, the sacked, the ignored and overlooked, are all blaming you ... Central Office is deeply divided and the old guard are openly attacking you.' Most outspoken of all was Sara Morrison. If he were genuinely working-class, she exploded, he'd understand the advantages of 'gentlemanly' behaviour, if only as a way of serving his own best interests. As it was, he was stuck behind a carapace of bottomlessly middle-class self-righteousness, incapable of seeing himself in the round, let alone imagining how he must appear to others. Heath endured this outburst with commendable calm, but it did not noticeably affect his conduct.[3]

A few of Heath's counsellors were more optimistic about his prospects, but even they were equivocal. Lord Aldington urged Heath to stay where he was and fight it out, but he subsequently admitted that he believed the leader was resolved to do this in any case and saw no reason to try to push him into a course of action entirely contrary to his nature. 'Ted is too truculent and too aggressive to give in,' he told Baker.[4] Michael Fraser was another voice raised cautiously in favour of intransigence. He forwarded to Heath a letter from Robert Rhodes James, hoping strongly that the leader would soldier on, and added: 'It may be that no "antis" bother to get in touch with me, but it is a fact that I have received no "anti" statements whatsoever direct.' Yet to David Butler a few months later he admitted that it would have been better both for Heath and for the party if he had retired directly after the election: 'But that just wasn't in character ... Ted always thought slowly about his own affairs and he wasn't a quitter.'[5]

Francis Pym was one of those who felt that Heath could and should stay on but that, if he was to do so, he should at once present himself before the 1922 Committee so as to justify his action and offer himself for re-election. It was a tactic which, in the short term at least, might have worked. Heath's greatest asset in the weeks after the election was the absence of an obvious substitute. Whitelaw would have been most people's choice but, whatever his private views about the situation, he had no intention of mounting a public challenge to his leader. Powell was anathema to the great majority of the party. Joseph was a possibility, but many members who wanted to get rid of Heath had little enthusiasm for this alternative, either on grounds of policy or of personality. He was 'too lacking in warmth and too like Heath to be acceptable', judged Jeremy Thorpe; 'the only dull Jew I know', had been Harold Macmillan's sour comment. Thorpe's own money was on Christopher Soames because, he thought, the Tories would be 'comfortable with a more old-fashioned upper class leader'. Subsequent history does not suggest that he was right; anyway, Soames had a well-paid and important job with the European Commission and would have taken much persuasion before returning to the choppier waters of domestic politics. Harold Wilson, whose fervent wish it was that Heath should remain leader of the Conservative Party in perpetuity, thought that it was a condemnation of Heath's record that the Shadow Cabinet was so bereft of leadership material. 'He had six heirs apparent in his Cabinet, Ted had none,' Hetherington recorded him as saying. It was a reasonable criticism, but if it was a failing it worked now to Heath's advantage.[6]

If Heath had taken Pym's advice and offered himself for reelection, he might have got away with it. It would have had to be done quickly, however. 'Every day that passes without an initiative from him is another nail in his coffin,' wrote Hurd in his diary. But, as Michael Fraser had noted, such precipitate action would not have been in character. Heath told Hurd that resignation would be 'the least attractive of the options'; to have offered his resignation in the hope that the offer would not be accepted would have been slightly less distasteful but risky and, in Heath's view, unnecessary. Prior was another who urged him to submit himself as soon as possible to a leadership election. Heath said that he did not intend to do so because he was determined to fight the right wing. 'I told him that if he refused to go he would probably end up giving them exactly what they wanted … My impression was that Ted by then was only hearing the advice he wished to hear.'[7]

Heath had no conception of the dislike which he inspired in the rank-and-file of the party. The question at Westminster, wrote Geoffrey Howe, was not 'Should Heath go' but when:

> Members just back from three weeks 'on the doorstep' all echoed the same tale. It was Heath's personality above all that had turned the electorate away from us. Hatred – yes, that was the word used – for 'that man' was no less than it later became for 'that woman'. He was regarded as stubborn and insensitive: the verdict was all too simple and less than just, but that was the perception. He was thus seen by his parliamentary colleagues as a loser. It was inconceivable that they would let him lead them into a third campaign.

If Howe is right, then there was probably nothing Heath could have done in the few months after the election of October 1974 to improve his image. Certainly he made not the slightest effort to do so. Until the campaign for the leadership was actually under way, he remained as unapproachable and as abrasive as ever. Michael Heseltine had been an ardent devotee but that did not stop Heath telling him that he was too ambitious and interested only in himself. Heseltine complained to Michael Wolff. Join the club, responded Wolff: Heath treated everyone like that, it was a sign that he took them seriously. But he was 'only human', protested Heseltine, and bound to react adversely to such harsh treatment. Heseltine had reason to feel loyalty to Heath: most of those who were ignored or insulted by him had no such obligation. Many backbenchers still felt a grudging respect for Heath; few indeed would have claimed to feel affection.[8]

*　　　*　　　*

There was even less scope for Heath to reshape the Shadow Cabinet than there had been after the February election but he did make one significant and, from his own point of view, unfortunate change. After a few months in charge of the Environment Mrs Thatcher was moved to the Treasury team. Her position was junior to that of the Shadow Chancellor, Robert Carr, but she was to enjoy a high degree of independence and was given the brief to lead the attack on Labour's Finance Bill. It was the opportunity which Heath himself had been given in the final stages of Alec Douglas-Home's period as leader. The newspapers were filled with speculative stories about her future with suggestions that she would soon be in command of the Treasury herself. Carr was put out. 'I find it difficult to believe that Margaret did not have a chance to kill them, had she wished to do so,' he told Heath. 'This seems to bode ill for a partnership between us. It is, I am afraid, clear that the economic right-wing in the party will try to drive a wedge between us, to my disadvantage.' If he was to remain as Chancellor, he went on, 'my position must be reaffirmed beyond challenge and the second Treasury spokesman must be clearly seen as the Number Two'. If Mrs Thatcher would not accept this then either somebody more amenable must be found to fill the role or Carr himself would go. Heath, presumably, made some soothing reply: things, anyway, moved too rapidly for the potential conflict to be resolved.[9]

Thatcher took her chance with the same energy and authority as Heath had shown a decade before. For the first time she was taken seriously as somebody who had the potential, eventually if not immediately, to become herself the leader. Nigel Lawson described the decision as bizarre: 'Splitting the position of Shadow Chancellor in two, giving the job of the front legs of the pantomime horse to Robert Carr and that of the back legs to Margaret Thatcher.' Unfortunately for Heath, and indeed Carr, it turned out that it was Thatcher who occupied the front legs, uttering the neighs and attracting the most attention. Alan Clark has suggested that Heath intended not so much to promote Thatcher as to destroy her. He thought that she did not understand economics and that, when the time came to attack Labour's budget, she 'would be seen as inadequate, and in the fullness of time, could justifiably be relegated to a "women's" portfolio and then, after a decorous interval, be sacked'. This makes Heath out to be more devious and more prescient than he really was. There is no reason to think that at this time he saw Thatcher as a potential rival; he did not like her but he respected both her ability and her pugnacity. He gave her the task for the same reason as he had been given the task himself in 1964; that she was the best equipped of those available to lead a vigorous and sustained attack on Labour's economic policies. If he had been told that he was thereby opening the way for the rival who would replace him, he would have been incredulous.[10]

Another change that Heath sought to make was to introduce du Cann into the Shadow Cabinet. His intention, presumably, was to propitiate a formidable enemy – uncharacteristic conduct for a man who rarely sought to propitiate anyone, least of all someone whom he disliked and despised. He gained nothing. Du Cann rejected the offer – 'undermining my attempt to unify the party' in Heath's view. Du Cann saw it differently. By the time the offer was made it had already been decided that there should be a ballot for the leadership. Whether 'he genuinely felt that I had something to contribute or whether he sought to neutralise me, I have no idea,' wrote du Cann, but as Chairman of the 1922 Committee 'I was the umpire in the contest to come.'[11] It seemed at the time that he might be a contender as well as an umpire. At a meeting of dissidents in the House of Commons in mid-November, Nigel Fisher, in the chair, said that all sections of the Party were concerned about the leadership. 'He felt all would agree that Ted could not continue – and the only alternative was du Cann ... He has charm and personality. Financial flair. Is friendly and warm and has a charming wife.' It was believed that he could be induced to stand, but he would have to commit himself and stop shilly-shallying within the next few days. Ian Gilmour, who thought du Cann hopelessly unsuitable as leader, nevertheless believed he would probably have won on the first ballot if he had chosen to compete. In the event he pulled out of the race. The reason he gave was that his 'charming wife' did not fancy the thought of being married to the leader of the Conservative Party. Others consider that he realised he had too many inveterate enemies within the Party to stand a chance. Gilmour wrote cryptically that 'he decided not to run for reasons which had little to do with his incapacity for the job'; presumably a reference to financial problems. At all events, long before the Party got close to making its decision it was clear that du Cann would not be on the list of those opposing Heath in the first round.[12]

That a substantial element of the Party was resolved that *somebody* should do so had been clear since the election. Heath's approval rating fell in the polls to a derisory 27 per cent. Even a would-be loyalist like Patrick Jenkin, whose career had been made by Heath, agreed with his constituency chairman that 'I just do not think we can go into another general election with him as our leader.' An editorial in *Crossbow*, a journal which had traditionally been written by and for the Heathite wing of the Party, complained that this 'trouble-shooting managerial style has placed such great strains on the loyalty of the party that it can never be enthusiastically reunited while he remains at its head'. But it was not just a question of personalities. A strong element within the Party had been ideologically estranged by his interventionist policies and his European ideas. They would have rejected Heath even if he had been the most affable and electorally seductive of men. Eighty-five per cent of the members of the '92 Group' and the Monday Club fell into this group of principled opponents. Conversely, most members of the left-wing Bow Group and of PEST (Political, Economic and Social Toryism) were going to back Heath in spite of their reservations about his electoral appeal. The opposition to Heath, as Chris Patten put it, was 'much more a peasants' revolt than a religious war', but the element of a religious war was still there. Doctrinal reasons were enough to set the right wing solidly against him. A proportion of those of the centre and left who were not natural supporters had turned against him on grounds of personality. The combination of these two elements was to prove disastrous.[13]

The executive of the 1922 Committee met to discuss the future of the Party shortly after the election. Du Cann claims that he went out of his way to ensure that supporters of Heath had a fair hearing but that there were few of them to be found. Everyone agreed that there must be a leadership contest; most felt that Heath should immediately stand down. Du Cann hastened to Heath's office to break the news. 'Don't they realise what they are doing to our party?' demanded Heath. Anyway, he pointed out, the executive had to be re-elected whenever there was a new parliament; the members of the present executive spoke for nobody except themselves. Despite this, du Cann called them to a further meeting at his offices in Milk Street. Heath was warned of this by William Waldegrave and instructed his press officer, Maurice Trowbridge, to make sure that the newspapers were alerted. Trowbridge did his job nobly and coined the phrase 'The Milk Street Mafia', thus stamping the executive members in the popular mind as a bunch of furtive malcontents plotting the overthrow of their leader. But though this was entertaining enough it made no real difference. At a full meeting of the 1922 Committee Maudling and a handful of others defended Heath but the mood was overwhelmingly hostile.

> I was no longer a supporter of Ted Heath [wrote Julian Critchley]. Some of my reasons were less creditable than others. I was piqued by the dinner party snub and disappointed that my talents, such as they were, had not been recognised ... I was weary of having to defend him in private to my constituents, the less charitable of whom made frequent allusions to his sexuality. 'Why hasn't he a wife,' was the complaint of the stupid and ill-disposed. The voters of Aldershot evidently much preferred dull wives to no wives at all.

By the next meeting the mood had, if anything, hardened still further. Kenneth Baker reported that half a dozen or so members were for Heath's immediate resignation; all felt that there must be an election in the near future. This *must* be within the next twelve months, concluded Baker.[14]

Heath decided that he must confront the 1922 Committee himself. At a meeting in his room in the House of Commons a few days before, it was agreed that the alternatives were to put Heath's leadership to a vote of confidence or to hold an election. Jim Prior disliked both possibilities but felt that the situation would otherwise become untenable. The danger in the vote-of-confidence approach, it was felt, was that it would 'concentrate the anti-Ted vote'. Whitelaw feared that if there were an election du Cann might win. Both Carrington and Hailsham agreed that they could not work with du Cann. Joseph, it was generally felt, would not be so impossible.[15]

Armed with this counsel Heath advanced into the lions' den. He handled the meeting more adeptly than his friends had feared was likely. He was 'dignified, even courageous', recorded Critchley. He reminded those present that most of his predecessors had been similarly unpopular at one time or another. He felt that the rules for appointing a leader should be revised but said that he was perfectly ready to stand for re-election once this had been done. Stand again he would, though: there was no hint of resignation. 'Ted's speech was quite humble in parts,' wrote Critchley, 'and he went on to say that he would be calling more widely upon backbenchers for occasional front-bench performances. He was applauded, somewhat coolly, for all of seven seconds.'[16]

His supporters urged him to rally backbench support by vigorous attacks on the Labour Government. 'The party will fall apart unless opposition constant and robust,' wrote Hailsham in his diary. 'It is probable Govt policy will make this easy.'[17] But it was not always as easy as all that. In April 1974 Heath had urged members to vote with the Government on Northern Ireland so as to show that the Opposition still supported the Sunningdale agreement. Carr warned 'that the Opposition was in danger of getting themselves into a posture of only voting with the Government and never against it'.[18] Ireland, Heath pleaded, was a special case. But, however special, it contributed to the general malaise and the feeling that not enough was being done to oppose the Government. In November, Ian Gilmour urged Heath not to speak in the Northern Ireland debate. 'He was, I believe, thinking of your own position,' advised Whitelaw. 'He thinks that we can have nothing except generalities to say on the positive side but that the kind of generalities which you would want to put forward will not be helpful to your relations with the Parliamentary Party. I think there is a force in this argument.'[19] On this occasion Heath listened to his friends and remained discreetly silent, but he did not find it easy to trim his sails to accommodate his critics on the right. The Conservative College at Swinton seemed to him to have become a hotbed for all that he disliked most about his party. Early in December a backbencher, Peter Hordern, wrote a pamphlet on inflation under the imprimatur of the College. Heath thought it nonsensical. 'Another right-wing production from Swinton,' he scribbled angrily. 'The quicker it is closed the better.' The lease was to run out in 1977 and Whitelaw felt that this would be the moment to put an end to the College. By then the leadership of the party was to have very different views of what constituted nonsense.[20]

Alec Douglas-Home was put in charge of revising the system by which party leaders were elected. The changes were subtle but significant. To win in the first round the leading candidate would in future have to secure both an absolute majority and at least 15 per cent more votes than the runner-up, the percentage being based on the total of those entitled to vote. Previously the 15 per cent provision had applied only to those who had actually voted. The result was that, by abstaining, a member could make it more difficult for the person securing most votes to win on the first round. This was generally perceived as making things more difficult for Heath who, since Whitelaw and most of his other colleagues in the Shadow Cabinet had announced that they did not intend to put themselves forward in the first round, was expected to have a relatively easy run.

Another new rule was that, if a challenger came forward when the party was in Opposition, the leader should be subject to re-election at the beginning of every parliamentary year. In the short term it seemed that this would work to Heath's advantage. If he was re-elected but failed to retain the confidence of a majority of members it would be possible for the party to eject him after twelve months. The need to depose him now was therefore less urgent. On the whole, however, Heath was the loser by the changes. They were promptly dubbed 'Alec's revenge', though the change from votes cast to eligible voters had in fact been made as the result of a suggestion by Peter Carrington, who feared that otherwise the winner might not necessarily command the support of more than 50 per cent of potential voters. Heath, in the *Daily Telegraph*, denied that he felt any rancour towards Douglas-Home or anybody else responsible for the changes, but he admitted in his memoirs that they filled him with 'great misgivings' and Selwyn Lloyd noted in his diary that Heath was 'furious with the new rules'. Certainly Douglas-Home had not been actuated by any malign intent, but not all those involved in recommending the changes were so disinterested. James Douglas, an official from the Conservative Research Department who played a major part in the work, later admitted that 'the new arrangements were deliberately framed to unseat the leader'.[21]

The one thing on which everyone except Heath himself was agreed was that the election must come quickly. John Cordle was only one of scores of Tory members who registered their views on this with Central Office: the matter, he urged, was 'of *great* urgency if the Conservative Party is to remain united'. Heath, however, saw no need to hurry. 'Your supporters among the younger members have become definitely dispirited in the last ten days by the absence of any initiative from you on the leadership,' Douglas Hurd told him in mid-January 1975. 'They would be v.dismayed if you gave the impression that you regarded talk about the leadership as confined to right-wingers and malcontents! I'm sure you're aware of this. It can be remedied tomorrow.' It was remedied a few days later. On 23 January Heath announced that he proposed to stand for re-election as leader under the new rules laid down by Douglas-Home and that the ballot would take place a fortnight later on 4 February.[22]

In fact the campaign was effectively already in full swing. Once it was clear that Heath proposed to stand, the only question was whom his opponents would find as their champion. 'I was totally loyal to Ted Heath,' maintained Whitelaw. 'I firmly believed that it would be in the best interests of the party that he should remain leader.' His real feelings were, perhaps, a little more equivocal. At the end of 1974 he speculated with Selwyn Lloyd about what might happen if Wilson asked the Opposition to join in a government of national unity. Heath would certainly refuse, at which point Whitelaw said that he would break ranks and take with him more than half the Shadow Cabinet. Only Joseph, Thatcher, Walker and Hailsham, he thought, would refuse to contemplate such a move. He told Lloyd that he had asked

Heath whether, if the party insisted on a change of leader and chose him as the replacement, Heath would be prepared to serve under him. 'No,' Heath had said. 'It wouldn't work.' For his part, Whitelaw would be ready, though reluctantly, to serve under Margaret Thatcher, but in no circumstances under du Cann. If it came to a second round, with Heath still in the running, he gave Lloyd the impression that he had not yet made up his mind whether or not he would stand.[23]

If the same conversation had taken place two months before it would have been Keith Joseph, not Margaret Thatcher, under whom he would have contemplated serving. By early October Joseph was telling all and sundry that he was ready to stand against the leader: 'You have my authority to tell that to anyone who asks,' he told Nick Ridley. Thatcher was ready to accept his primacy. 'I had virtually become Keith's informal campaign manager,' she wrote in her memoirs. But though he had many admirers, Joseph was never completely convincing as a candidate. He was Jewish – a factor which at that time seemed more significant that it was to prove when Michael Howard became leader twenty-eight years later – he was uninspiring, worst of all he was unsound. 'The mad monk', Heath's hatchet men called him: useful enough as a minister but not to be trusted with supreme power. If he had been the aspirant facing Heath in the leadership election he might well have lost. Heath enjoyed no such good fortune, however. Shortly after he had told Ridley that he proposed to stand, Joseph made a speech in the Powellite Midlands in which he suggested that the lower classes were breeding faster than they should and that ways should be found to discourage them. In Mrs Thatcher's eyes he had done no more than show 'lack of judgment, i.e. willingness to think for himself', and in truth there was nothing very dreadful in what he said but the speech played into the hands of his enemies who claimed to detect overtones of Hitlerian eugenics and denounced the speaker as a dangerous fanatic. If Joseph had persisted he might still have remained as Heath's main challenger but he was a man of strikingly thin skin, he saw that he had blundered, and he withdrew with some relief from a conflict to which he had not been looking forward. When Airey Neave, resolved to be prominent in any movement to supplant Heath, tried to persuade Joseph to resume the battle, the request was not only firmly refused but Joseph declared that, as a member of the Shadow Cabinet, he would feel it his duty to tell Heath of Neave's approach. 'He'll kill us! He'll kill us!' Neave told his co-conspirators apprehensively.[24]

With Joseph retired hurt, Margaret Thatcher decided that she must take on the mantle of challenger. She did not believe that she was likely to succeed but she thought that she would make a respectable showing and felt it important that criticisms of Heath's policies and style of government should be voiced and voiced emphatically. At the end of November, having taken soundings of her friends and concluded that she had enough support to make her enterprise worthwhile, she went to tell Heath of her decision. According to one report he grunted, 'You'll lose' and turned his back on her. By her own account, 'He looked at me coldly, turned his back, shrugged his shoulders and said: "If you must".' Heath himself denies that he did more than thank her politely for the warning. This is not the only occasion on which confrontations between Heath and Thatcher were remembered differently by the two protagonists. They were alone and no other record exists. On this occasion, however, Mrs Thatcher's version sounds the more convincing.[25]

She was not alone in rating her chances low. Barbara Castle, who as a good feminist would have rejoiced at Thatcher's success, and, anyway, stood to win the bet with her husband, concluded that, though she would give Heath a good run for his money, she had very little chance of gaining the leadership: 'You can't find two Tories to agree on an alternative to him.' The fact that she was a woman was felt by many to be a crippling disadvantage, some considered her inexperience disqualified her, others that her personality was little more attractive than that of the present incumbent: 'Ted with tits,' Soames described her. Until the moment nominations closed, some members were still looking around for a better candidate. Nigel Fisher told Hailsham that he could not vote with enthusiasm for Heath or Thatcher – or, indeed, for Whitelaw. Would not Hailsham stand? Hailsham replied that he would have no support in either the party or the Shadow Cabinet. Regretfully, Fisher accepted the decision: 'But the party is deeply worried and I think it inevitable that there will be a large number of abstentions on the first ballot – and very little enthusiasm for any other candidate.' As it turned out, there was another candidate. Heath's Balliol contemporary, Hugh Fraser, decided that he should stand. Nobody, including, it would seem, Fraser himself, really understood how he reached this conclusion. He won only sixteen votes, gained probably at the expense of Heath, though some of them may have come from people who disliked Heath but could not bear the thought of voting for a woman.[26]

Loyalty was Heath's trump card. He took it for granted that everyone whom he had promoted to any kind of office would vote for him. His confidence was not always justified. He was deeply put out when the Chief Whip, Humphrey Atkins, told him that he felt the Whips should be strictly neutral in the election. 'I appointed you all,' he told Atkins, with clear implication that their support was due to him and him alone. Atkins, a covert Thatcherite, managed to remain largely above the conflict, but the Deputy Chief Whip, Bernard Wetherill, attended Heath each day with the latest voting estimates.[27]

Heath's previous campaign for the leadership had been conducted with skill and energy by Peter Walker. Heath would have liked him to take on the same task in 1975 but Walker felt that a backbencher would do the job better. Heath then entrusted the task to his two pps's, Kitson and Baker. Kitson rejected the responsibility, on the grounds that he was known as Heath's man and everyone would therefore tell him what Heath wanted to hear, not the truth. In the event Baker did most of the work, Kitson helped out, and Walker exercised a vague supervisory role. The results were not happy. Baker and Kitson, wrote John Ramsden, 'managed to be both complacent and over-aggressive at the same time, mainly because they could not believe that their master might be unseated by such an inexperienced woman candidate'. Nigel Lawson remembers that he was pressed far more energetically to vote for Heath than he was by the backers of Mrs Thatcher. Du Cann was struck by the stridency of the attacks on Thatcher as an individual. When they had thought he was a likely candidate he himself had been the principal target. Then the onslaught switched to Keith Joseph. 'Then the dirty tricks brigade concentrated on Margaret and their attacks were fierce.'[28]

Heath's campaign was not wholly negative. Hurd and Waldegrave urged him to open a new chapter in his relationship with the party, to put the emphasis on 'greater openness and conciliatory discourse'. They were encouraged by his readiness to agree, 'until he remarked at the end of their conversation that, of course, he did all this already'. He did concede that something must be done to woo the back-benchers whom he had neglected or insulted over the previous few years. Baker and other trusties gave a series of dinners and Heath himself was the host at lunches at Bucks, at which the loyalists were supposed to be rewarded and the doubtful courted by a demon-stration of their leader's charms. 'These certainly proved to be helpful,' wrote Heath in his memoirs. Nobody else saw their value. Kenneth Clarke attended one dinner. It was 'a complete fiasco. Ted wouldn't really address a word to anyone much, certainly not backbenchers of whom he had never heard. I did join in, trying to steer the con-versation so that he would talk to Ivan Lawrence, and he wouldn't. It just summed up what was wrong with him. Completely hopeless!' Before the dinner Lawrence had told Clarke that he had never spoken to his leader; after the dinner he confirmed that the situation remained unchanged. Those summoned to *à deux* meetings with Heath in the House of Commons did at least exchange words with him but the experience proved to be neither enjoyable nor instructive: 'It was rather like being summoned to the Headmaster's study,' said Baker, 'one knew one was there for a purpose, it was rather un-comfortable, and the sooner it was over the better.' Heath was still formidably good at expounding policy to sympathetic groups; he could still, if in a good mood, relax and communicate freely with his intimates; but he seemed to have lost whatever capacity he had once enjoyed to establish a one-to-one relationship with those whom he neither knew well nor saw any reason to respect. After one par-ticularly grisly dinner a potential supporter concluded his letter of thanks to Baker with the words: 'Perhaps it would be better if you just let us get on with it, without actually producing the leader.'[29]

At first the Thatcher campaign seemed little more professional. She was better than Heath when it came to buttering-up potential sup-porters but she did not seem to rate her own prospects particularly high and gave the impression that she was standing to make a point rather than in serious contention for the leadership. Everything changed when, on 6 January, Airey Neave took over the management of her campaign. Neave was more an enemy of Heath than a partisan of Thatcher. From the time of the October 1974 election, he had been resolved that Heath must go, and go quickly. First he had made overtures to Whitelaw but got nowhere. Then he approached du Cann, but found that he too was a non-starter. Keith Joseph seemed more promising but the Birmingham speech put an end to his campaign before it had really started. Only then did Neave put his formidable powers as an organiser and an intriguer at the disposal of Mrs Thatcher. His technique was skilful and subtly varied. He concentrated on the many backbenchers who felt, or could be induced to feel, that their talents had not been properly recognised. 'Margaret wondered why you hadn't got a job,' he would say. 'Did you have some reason for refusing one?' No commitment was made, but a feeling was left behind that, if there were a change of leadership, a wrong would soon be rectified. To Cecil Parkinson and many others he took a still more oblique approach. 'Ted is bound to win,' he would say. It was important, though, that he shouldn't win too easily and feel emboldened to divide the Party still further by banishing Thatcher and any similarly minded people from the Shadow Cabinet. If Parkinson did not feel that he could vote for Thatcher then, in the best interests both of Heath and of the Party as a whole, it would be wisest to abstain. To those whom he knew, given a chance, would support Whitelaw rather than Heath, he took a similar line; only if enough members abstained or, better still, supported Thatcher would there be any possibility of a second round in which Whitelaw might be induced to stand. To Douglas Hurd, whose loyalties obviously lay with the leader, he pleaded the need for mitigating Heath's dangerous though well-justified over-confidence: 'I see now', says Hurd ruefully, 'that it was part of his tactic of underplaying her prospects.'[30]

Shortly before Christmas an incident occurred which gave a temporary fillip to Heath's campaign. He had been at Broadstairs conducting the annual carol concert and was only five minutes from his home in Wilton Street when the IRA threw a two-pound bomb against the house. Nobody was hurt, although considerable damage was done to the property. 'The bastards! Almost makes me sorry we voted against the rope,' was Julian Amery's characteristic comment. If he had left Broadstairs a few minutes earlier Heath would have been in some danger. The event gained him considerable sympathy, and respect for his courage the following day when he set off intrepidly on a visit to Northern Ireland, but it seems unlikely that it affected a single vote when the election took place. In the country at large the impression was longer-lasting. It was again and again shown to be the case that the Tories outside Westminster – partly perhaps because they had seen less of him at close quarters – felt far more warmly towards their leader than did the members of the House of Commons. A Harris Poll on 3 February showed that 70 per cent of Conservative voters would have supported Heath in the leadership election. Belatedly, the campaign managers began to suspect that such a discrepancy existed and sought to redress it. A few days before election day an advertisement appeared at the bottom of page 2 of *The Times*. 'Ted Heath is still the Tories best bet,' it proclaimed. 'If you agree, say so now, send a telegram to your MP, c/o House of Commons … ask him to VOTE HEATH in next week's ballot.' If this sort of appeal had been launched two or three weeks earlier, a gale of public opinion might have been whipped up. Coming when it did, it was interpreted as showing a lack of confidence in the Heath camp and probably did more harm than good.[31]

The Heath camp did, in fact, feel remarkably confident at the dawn of polling day. Forty-eight hours earlier the Whips had told Heath that they believed he had 89 firm votes against only 43 for Thatcher. There were still many question marks but, if the tide was moving at all, it seemed to be in favour of the existing leader. The Whips' final list showed Heath on 128, Thatcher on 106 and Fraser with a derisory 6. William Shelton, who was doing the same job for the Thatcher camp, was closer to the mark; he calculated that there would be something near a tie, with each candidate receiving approximately 120 votes.

Heath waited tranquilly in his office for the news to be brought him. Vernon Bogdanor, a leading constitutional historian, has pointed out that the first ballot was never intended to be decisive: 'It is a vote not to choose a new leader, but to consider whether the existing Leader retains the party confidence.'[32] Heath, however, believed that in this case it would be decisive, that even if he did not win by the necessary margin to secure total victory he would go into the next round with such a convincing majority that his position would be virtually impregnable. Instead, an aghast Kitson hurried in, blurting out: 'I am sorry, Ted, but it's all up.' Thatcher had gained 130 votes to Heath's 119; Fraser had picked up 16. 'I am more sorry than I can possibly say,' wrote the Deputy Chief Whip. 'I'm afraid our figures were wrong and this despite the fact that we were able to check them against Shelton's list. I cannot believe that we were *deliberately* misled and I apologise for the fact that we failed to prepare you for what happened. I hope, despite it all, that you will remain with us. We desperately need your wisdom and experience in the days ahead.' Probably they *had* been deliberately misled; more than two dozen Tory MPs are said to have assured both camps that they could be certain of their vote. The number of abstentions, too, was substantially higher than expected. John Nott and Norman Tebbit tried to persuade Michael Heseltine, who was known to be a Whitelaw man, that unless he voted for Thatcher there would be no second round and thus no chance to support his favoured candidate. They could not push him that far but, nevertheless, Heseltine abstained. Whitelaw, of course, cast his vote for Heath, but William Waldegrave suspects he advised some of his followers to vote for Mrs Thatcher or at least to abstain.[33]

'The Party's taken leave of its senses. This is a black day,' said a horrified Maudling. Heath was more restrained. 'It has all gone wrong' were his first words. He realised at once that there could be no recovery from such a disaster and settled down to drafting his letter of resignation. But though outwardly dignified, inwardly he was enraged and aghast. When Hugh Fraser came into the leader's room to say how sorry he was about the result, Heath ignored him. He believed that he had been cheated. 'I do not think it was conducted in the way of colleagues,' he said of the election. In 1965 they had not carried on

> in great television and radio campaigns, and press campaigns behind the scenes. You can say I was simple and taken unawares, but I am afraid I had standards. I think the other thing which upset me was to find that after the elections there were celebrations with champagne. Now I really don't think that's a relationship between colleagues. It's something Reggie Maudling, Enoch Powell and I would never have dreamt of for a moment. It's an indication of the different attitudes right from the beginning.

This was a refrain that, with variations, was to be heard constantly over the next twenty years.[34]

'Even now I am not quite sure how it all happened,' Mrs Thatcher told Bernard Wetherill. 'Had I been asked four or five months ago if it *could* happen, I should have said "No". Perhaps after all there is a destiny which shapes our ends.' Heath's complaint was that the destiny had been unscrupulously manipulated. By talent, experience and achievement it was he who was the rightful leader of the Tory Party. One day, he believed, he would recapture that position. 'They have gone mad,' Carrington told him from Australia. 'But that is little consolation for you, and those of us who felt and feel that you are the right man for the job ... Don't forget that there are very many people like myself who have over the years admired your courage and capacity, and been proud to serve you and hope to do so again.' It is doubtful whether Carrington had any real belief that this hope was likely to be fulfilled. Heath was convinced that it would come about. It was to be a decade at least before he finally accepted that his hope was in vain.[35]

TWENTY-THREE

Adjusting to a New Life

'I intend to remain in the House of Commons to look after the interests of my constituents,' Heath announced the day after his eviction. 'I have no intention of going to the House of Lords or of taking up a European appointment ... I shall do all I can to serve the interests of my country and my Party by concentrating on the great issues facing Britain at home and overseas.'[1]

It was a message that must have caused a chill of apprehension among those who hoped he would retreat gracefully into semi-retirement in the Lords or, better still, accept some post in Brussels. All too evidently he had no plans to go gentle into that good night. His pain was to some extent mitigated by the wave of valedictory tributes which now washed around him, though it is unlikely that du Cann's thanks, on behalf of the 1922 Committee, 'for all that you have achieved for our Party during the time that you were its Leader', did much to improve his mood. He would have preferred Chris Patten's patently heartfelt words: 'You stand for the sort of Conservatism which we believe in. You are the reason for some of us being in – or staying in – politics.' One of the most generous of the testimonials came from Harold Wilson, as committed an enemy of Heath as was du Cann and yet at this moment seeming to feel real warmth and sympathy towards his humiliated rival. He spoke eloquently in tribute in the House of Commons. Lord Aldington, Heath's closest political ally, wrote to thank him for his gesture: 'The words you used and the thoughts behind them were – and will remain – splendid.' At the time Heath, too, seemed genuinely moved; his letter of thanks to Wilson was expressed with appreciation and even affection. It was sadly typical of him that, in later years, he felt unable to admit that the Prime Minister's words meant anything to him: 'Typical politician's nonsense,' he would snort. 'Neither of us meant a word of it.'[2]

When the second round of voting was held Heath did not stand himself and refused to commit himself publicly to any candidate. Several of those who had refrained from opposing him in the first ballot now came forward, including Whitelaw, Prior, John Peyton and Geoffrey Howe. Of these, Whitelaw was the one who seemed most likely to run the Government in a style acceptable to his predecessor. Heath had told him that he would not be prepared to serve under him, but when it came to the point he would probably have accepted some suitable offer. To his dismay, however, the momentum which Mrs Thatcher had built up in the first round made her unstoppable: she gained nearly twice as many votes as Whitelaw, considerably more than half the total votes. The Tory Party had found a new leader and one who, in Heath's eyes, in terms of economic and social principles, political experience, temperament and – not least – sex, was supremely ill qualified to succeed him.

The following day, Mrs Thatcher called at Wilton Street. According to Heath he had the previous day received through Tim Kitson a message that the new leader wanted to offer him a job in the Shadow Cabinet and would like to pay him a visit to discuss the matter. He replied that, for the time being at any rate, he did not wish to join the Shadow Cabinet, and assumed that that would be the end of the matter. He was therefore disconcerted when she nevertheless turned up at his house. He received her politely, refused to comment when she asked for his advice about how to handle the press, and thanked her for coming when she rose to leave some five minutes later. 'At no time during the meeting did she invite me to become a member of the Shadow Cabinet or to play any part on her front bench.' After leaving Heath's room, Mrs Thatcher asked Kitson if she could spend another ten minutes or so in the house so as not to lead the representatives of the press on the pavement outside the house (assembled,

Heath assumed, at the behest of Thatcher) into thinking that the meeting had been a disaster. Thatcher, on the other hand, claims that, though she was frankly relieved to find that Heath did not want to serve in the Shadow Cabinet, she went to Wilton Street in full readiness to grant him any post he wanted. When she was ushered into his room: 'He did not get up, and I sat down without waiting to be asked.' She offered him an unspecified job in the Shadow Cabinet. He refused. She then asked him whether he would lead the Conservative campaign in the projected referendum on Europe. He again refused. Since there was nothing more to say, she then left his room but spent a few minutes chatting to Kitson so as to fill in time before leaving the house. When the Thatcher camp later leaked an account of what they claimed had passed during the visit, Heath angrily denied the 'monstrous allegations made about a lack of courtesy shown in my own home ... I must state categorically that there was no discourtesy of any kind at any time.' As to the important issue – the offer of a job in the Shadow Cabinet – it seems likely that there was a genuine misunderstanding. Thatcher thought that she was renewing the offer which had been made informally the day before; Heath assumed that the issue had already been settled and did not recognise her new initiative, which he would anyway have rejected. As to the question of courtesy, it was, perhaps, in the eye of the beholder. Kitson remembers Heath piling up books on two out of the three chairs in his study so as to make it impossible for his visitor to sit down (presumably she removed the books herself). He refrained from accompanying her to the door so as not to be seen side by side with her when she finally left the house. It is always easier to be a gracious winner than a gracious loser and Heath was not notably successful in either role. It seems likely that, for Mrs Thatcher, the visit to Wilton Street was primarily a public relations exercise designed to show magnanimity and to make it clear that, if there had to be a rift, it was not of her making. If so, it was successful. Heath gave the impression, as he had done after the February 1974 election, that he was a bad loser.[3]

'They are absolutely mad to get rid of me,' Heath angrily told the chairman of the Parliamentary Labour Party. 'Absolutely mad!' 'I'm in reserve,' he went on. His brooding presence in the background was one of the factors that inhibited Mrs Thatcher from making any major changes to the Shadow Cabinet. Heath wrote in his memoirs that he had been 'shocked' to hear that Robert Carr and two or three minor shadow ministers had been dropped, but nearly all the more important figures whom he had thought of as his supporters – Whitelaw, Carrington, Prior, Hailsham – remained in place. He would have been grateful if they had resigned in protest against his removal but still retained enough grasp of political reality to accept that this was not a practical possibility. His successor was less cautious when it came to reshaping the machinery of the party. Whitelaw was replaced as chairman by Peter Thorneycroft, one of the elder statesmen whom Heath had conspicuously failed to employ. Sara Morrison, the vice-chairman, withdrew, getting her resignation in, she believes, only just before what would undoubtedly have been her dismissal. Ian Gilmour was replaced by Angus Maude as chairman of the Research Department. Finally, Heath's recently appointed nominee as director-general, Michael Wolff, was sacked out of hand. Wolff was so much Heath's man that Thatcher can hardly be blamed for getting rid of him but it was still a mistake. Michael Fraser thought Wolff was an asset to the party – 'he had done a lot of things quite well and had sensible ideas about what should be done' – his abrupt eviction smacked of vengefulness. On the whole Mrs Thatcher handled the transfer of power with some grace; Wolff's dismissal was one of the few blemishes on her performance.[4]

By the time he heard of it Heath had retired from the political scene to lick his wounds unobserved. In mid-February his secretary wrote to say that he would not after all be able to attend a much-heralded concert by the Israel Philharmonic Orchestra, featuring Zubin Mehta and Artur Rubinstein, because: 'He left for Spain yesterday, and is not expected to return to London until mid-March.'[5] Only under the greatest pressure would he have cancelled such an engagement, but after the humiliation of his defeat his most urgent wish was to be well away from Westminster. Once again Kitson came to the rescue, arranging for him to stay at a friend's villa in the south of Spain. A series of sympathisers visited him during his exile: Kitson himself, Wolff, Geoffrey Tucker. None of them would have wanted to fan the flames of his resentment, but this was what they achieved; indeed, so rancorous was his mood that he became ever more obsessed by the folly, the malignancy, the ingratitude of those who had supplanted him. He returned to England in mid-March, seeing enemies everywhere and detecting conspiracy in the most innocent of actions. The *Spectator* reprinted an article which he had written in the 1940s criticising a plan to admit state schoolboys to public schools on scholarships. The inequality of education must be eliminated, he argued, not kept alive by turning the state schoolboy into 'a pawn to be used if and when necessary for the continued existence of the public school system'. Such views were obviously far removed from the current policy of the Conservative Party and indeed from Heath's own opinions. The *Spectator* not unreasonably thought the evolution of Heath's views a matter of some interest: Heath regarded its resurrection of his youthful excesses as part of a vicious campaign to embarrass him. Patrick Cosgrave, the political commentator at the *Spectator* and an ardent supporter of Mrs Thatcher, was the victim of Heath's blackest bile. When he saw Cosgrave at a party given to honour a retiring official from Central Office he snapped angrily: 'What on earth are *you* doing here? Spying again, I suppose!' His mood did not offer much encouragement to those who sought to reconcile him to the new regime. 'Teddy seems to be standing up to the blows reasonably well, though I still don't think he knows [what] hit him and why,' Madron Seligman told Roy Jenkins. 'I expect a mellowed Mark 2 version will emerge from the ordeal.' It seems unlikely that somebody who knew Heath as well as Seligman did can have nourished that illusion for long. Few people could have been less mellow than the Heath who resumed life in the political world which opened before him in the spring of 1975.[6]

Fortunately for his peace of mind he had an urgent and important task to do. He had refused to take formal charge of the campaign over the referendum, but it was still a matter of prime importance to him. On almost any other issue Heath might have sulked Achilles-like in his tent, but when Britain's place in Europe was in question he felt bound to join the battle and to do so wholeheartedly. Wilson's

decision in January 1975 to put to a national referendum the renegotiated terms for Britain's membership of the Common Market
had been taken against his own better judgment to placate his left
wing. It led to the eventual resignation of the pro-European Roy
Jenkins and several other ministers of similar persuasion. Heath and
Thatcher were at one in opposing the proposal on constitutional
grounds: the British people had elected a government to rule the
country on its behalf; what sort of sense did it make to select one issue
and decide that on this the Government was unfit to decide? Heath's
first inclination was to boycott the whole process, but he soon
concluded that the stakes were too high. If the British public were to
reject Europe in a referendum it might be impossible ever to reverse
the decision. The only practical course was to ensure that Britain
made the right decision and to secure a vote of confidence in its continued membership of the Community. William Waldegrave questioned the wisdom of this conclusion. 'If the campaign were to be lost,'
he suggested, 'the best position for us to have been in would have been
to have taken no part in the referendum campaign and to have argued
consistently throughout that it was irrelevant and unconstitutional.'
Heath saw the force of the argument but saw also the overwhelming
case for participation. 'It is difficult to envisage us all sitting on the
sidelines,' he concluded. 'It wouldn't be understood anywhere.'[7]

Once he had decided to participate, he never doubted that he
would play a prominent part. When he got back from the south of
Spain he was in a gloomy mood. He dined in Nuffield College a few
days after his return and was 'very pessimistic about the referendum',
noted David Butler. 'He obviously was projecting his general dis-
comfiture with life on to the issue he was most involved with.' His
pessimism had rather more substance than Butler's comment suggests. It was still uncertain how vigorously Harold Wilson would lead
the majority of his ministers in supporting acceptance of the renegotiated terms, nor was it clear whether Mrs Thatcher would show
any great enthusiasm for the cause. If, as seemed most probable,
Wilson did prove himself a wholehearted advocate of acceptance,
might this not repel some Conservatives who would otherwise have
rallied to Europe? Someone at the dinner unkindly suggested that his

own championship of the European cause might have the same effect. 'Not half as much as Maggie Thatcher,' he retorted: a reflection which, though up to a point consoling, did not offer much cheer so far as the referendum was concerned.[8]

His fears were soon allayed. Wilson handled the matter with considerable skill. He recognised that this was not an issue on which he could hope to see his Cabinet present a united front and allowed each minister to adopt his or her own position; he himself playing the role of a patriotic Briton who had secured an improvement in the entry terms so considerable that he was now convinced it was in the best interests of the nation to participate. Some Tories, particularly those with Europe most at heart, may have been irritated by his attitude, but none can have been induced to change his position as a result. As for Margaret Thatcher, she made it clear that she was unequivocally in favour of continued British membership but that she had no wish to play a prominent role in bringing it about. The more Heath could be persuaded to take the lead, the happier she would be. The disadvantage of this, as she claimed subsequently to have discovered, was that Heath's appetite for power was whetted and that 'the forces inside and outside the Conservative Party which were determined to get rid of me would seek to use the all-party coalition campaigning for a "Yes" vote as the nucleus of a movement for a coalition of the "centre"'. There were certainly forces – or at least one force – within the Conservative Party that were determined to get rid of Thatcher but it does not seem any alliance forged in the battle for Europe was relevant in such a quest. Heath, however, was certainly allowed, indeed encouraged, to claim any prominence he wished in the campaign. Thatcher had 'rather late in the day, realised that there is to be a referendum campaign', reported Hurd in early March. The Conservative Group for Europe was to hold a grand dinner in the St Ermin's Hotel on 16 April designed 'to stir the Party, which is still lethargic on the matter'. Thatcher had agreed to speak but wanted Heath to take the chair. 'It is a lot to ask. But those of your friends who are most closely involved in planning the campaign hope that you may agree. It would make a most impressive occasion.'[9]

It did. Mrs Thatcher not merely praised Heath to the skies but adopted a tone of ostentatious modesty: 'It is naturally with some temerity that the pupil speaks before the master, because you know more about it than the rest of us.' He listened approvingly: this was perhaps the nearest to a true reconciliation that the old and the new leaders of the Conservative Party would ever achieve. He did indeed 'know more about it' than anybody else in any party. He was content to serve as Vice President of Britain in Europe under the titular leadership of Roy Jenkins but he knew that in the eyes of the world he bulked larger on the scene. A Harris Poll taken in the first week of April 1975 showed that 94 per cent of those asked knew who he was; 42 per cent 'respected and liked' him, a figure which left him in a tie with Harold Wilson; 78 per cent knew that he was a partisan of British membership – a figure almost exactly double that achieved by Jenkins. Jenkins himself paid tribute to his contribution. Heath, he wrote, waged an extremely effective campaign, 'and my respect for him, already considerable at the beginning, went steadily up as it progressed'. But even here a note of equivocation could be detected. And yet, Jenkins reflected, he was 'always a difficult morsel to swallow. He never tried to be awkward but there was a certain inherent awkwardness about his character and indeed his physique. He stood resolutely there, as impervious to the waves and as reliable in his beam as a great lighthouse, but sometimes blocking the way. But he was never negligible.'[10]

Great lighthouse or not, he could not afford totally to ignore the prevailing wind. He laid as little emphasis on the surrender of sovereignty involved in Britain's membership of Europe as had been the case in the debates at the time of Britain's entry in 1972. This was undoubtedly a deliberate policy but he was always sensitive to accusations that he had sought wilfully to mislead the country on the issue. When he was writing his memoirs one of his aides produced for him a Britain in Europe advertisement prepared for the referendum campaign which read: 'Forty million people died in two European wars this century. Better lose a little national sovereignty than a son or daughter.' This met the point, the aide suggested, that the pro-Europeans had avoided the issue of sovereignty in their campaign. 'Excellent discovery!' minuted Heath approvingly, and instructed that it should be reproduced in his book.* It did, indeed, make his point but there were few similar instances. His most resounding contribution on the subject came in the debate in the House of Commons in April 1975 when he claimed that sovereignty was not 'something to be hoarded, sterile and barren' but something 'for us as custodians to use in the interests of our own country. The question we have to decide, therefore, in carrying through this great political purpose ... for the peace and freedom of Europe and of our own country, is how we are entitled to use that measure of sovereignty which is required.' His answer on this occasion was bravely unequivocal. For the most part, however, while the champions of British withdrawal made copious references to the surrender of precious national independence involved in membership of Europe, the pro-Europeans preferred to suggest that any such possible sacrifice lay many years ahead and could easily be opposed when the time arose.[11]

Another subject on which Heath had to tread with some delicacy was the renegotiation of the terms of British entry which Wilson made the basis of his support for continued membership. Privately Heath believed that the whole business had been a ridiculous charade which had produced almost nothing of significance. Whenever he referred to renegotiation the words 'so-called' were appended, or were implicit in the ghostly quotation marks that seemed to float around the offending concept. Yet there were many people who took renegotiation seriously and made it their reason, or at least their excuse, for changing their position on British membership. Heath had no wish to contradict their argument. His solution was rarely to refer to the negotiations which had been taking place over the previous few months: if he had to deal with them he did not so much belittle the negotiators' achievement as stress the immeasurably more important principles which provided the true basis for British membership.

Jenkins had every reason to praise Heath's achievements in the referendum campaign. Freed from the shackles of leadership, preaching a cause in which he passionately believed, rejoicing in an opportunity to reclaim the limelight from which he had been

---

* In fact it did not appear but the same point was made forcibly in other ways.

unceremoniously ousted: Heath not merely made a striking mark in the country but greatly enjoyed the process. 'The one man who had done really well so far was Ted Heath,' observed Chris Patten in early May. He attributed Heath's success partly to Stephen Sherbourne, who was writing his speeches and working in his office: 'Sherbourne was terribly good as a speech writer and Heath's office was miraculously efficient compared to any other office on the political scene at that moment.' Sherbourne confirms that he was responsible for drafting most of Heath's speeches and articles, many of which appeared virtually unaltered. Without Sherbourne Heath's performance would have been notably less effective, without Heath the pro-European campaign would have been deprived of its biggest gun. Given the fact that the leaders of all the main parties were unanimous in their support for British membership it seems unlikely that the referendum would have been lost if Heath had not participated; equally, it is hard to believe that the emphatic victory of the 'Yes' lobby would have been achieved if Heath's energy and inspiration had been lacking.[12]

His finest hour came in a debate in his old training ground, the Oxford Union. The fact that the proceedings were carried on national television ensured that they were witnessed by an audience vastly larger than anything he had dreamt of during his days at Balliol. Heath was supported by Jeremy Thorpe, another former President of the Union, and opposed by Barbara Castle and Peter Shore, two able debaters but neither entirely at ease in the somewhat idiosyncratic surroundings in which they were now embroiled. Castle began to suspect that she had agreed to an unfortunate venue when Heath walked into the chamber. 'The catcalls of delight were uncontained. It was a near pandemonium of enthusiasm and I suddenly realised what we were up against. Heath was the hero of the hour as he had never been as Prime Minister.' When the time for the speeches came, wrote Castle, 'the most remarkable phenomenon of the evening was Heath. The audience was all his, and he responded to it with a genuineness which was the most impressive thing I have ever seen from him. He stood there, speaking simply, strongly and without a note. They gave him a standing ovation at the end, and he deserved it.' The only reason for the referendum, Heath maintained, was that neither

Castle nor Shore was prepared to accept the decision of parliament. But his main theme was the horror of two world wars and the desperate need to avoid a third by helping to create a Europe so united that any conflict between its members would become impossible. 'Those who oppose the motion want to remain with the past organisation of the nation state which has brought about two world wars and mass genocide in Europe.' It was a message which resonated with its immediate audience and with a far wider audience outside. James Lees-Milne, hitherto no admirer of Heath, watched the debate on television. Heath, he wrote in his diary, 'spoke like a true statesman in the best tradition. I call it a truly great speech, in which he called upon us to honour our word and our great history and pull ourselves together. Oh yes, it was a great speech … Heath was in deadly earnest, unemotional and controlled. He delivered no backhand blows, and indulged in no side jibes. He showed himself to be a big man. So.'[13]

The vote on the motion in the Union was overwhelmingly in favour of Europe, but complete though the victory was it was hardly more remarkable than the national result, in which more than two-thirds of the voters were in favour of Britain's membership. Richard Simmonds was driving back to London with Heath on the evening of the day on which the results of the referendum were announced. He suggested that they should pass by the statue of Winston Churchill in Parliament Square, where a vigil was being held. 'No,' said Heath. 'I would be recognised'; but then he relented and paid a brief visit to the monument. On the eve of the referendum he saw Mrs Thatcher on television, cavorting in the same place in a sweater emblazoned with the flags of all the European nations. 'What does she think she looks like?' he demanded, with mingled scorn and satisfaction.[14]

The European cause was to remain central to Heath's political life until the day he died. He had told Mrs Thatcher, however, that he did not want any sort of job in Brussels, and to that course he adhered. Whether he would have held to the same position if he had been offered the presidency of the Commission must be uncertain. In January 1976 Giscard d'Estaing and Helmut Schmidt told Wilson that they would accept a British nominee for the presidency, that they did not favour Soames, but that either Heath or Jenkins would be most welcome. For Wilson this offered an enticing chance to get Jenkins safely out of the way in Brussels where he could make no mischief; he saw no similar advantage in exiling Heath, indeed he was pleased to have him in London plaguing Mrs Thatcher. It does not seem that he even mentioned the possibility to Heath. Two years later it was decided to appoint 'Three Wise Men' to look at the future of European institutions. Once again Heath was an obvious candidate to fill the British seat; this time it was Callaghan who failed to offer him the chance – presumably because he felt that he would be too partisan in the European cause. Instead he came up with the decidedly minor figure of Edmund Dell. Heath lost little by his exclusion. The idea of the '*Trois Sages*' had been conceived by the French in the hope that they would recommend a radical restructuring of the Commission's powers; they failed to do so; the French lost interest and the exercise fizzled out without producing anything of importance.[15]

Anyone who had hoped that Heath's triumphant success over the referendum would lead to a reconciliation between the new and the old leaders was quickly disappointed. In the House of Commons on 9 June Mrs Thatcher went out of her way to make warm comments about Heath's contribution to the campaign; Heath not merely failed to respond in kind but sat in stony silence without acknowledging even by a smile or nod the tributes paid to him. 'It seemed an ungracious reaction, which was noticed by everyone and caused much unfavourable comment,' wrote Nigel Fisher. It was worse than ungracious, it was gratuitously offensive. Implicitly if not explicitly he henceforth missed no chance to distance himself from the Shadow Cabinet; to underline how right he had been and still was, how every deviation from the policies he had followed as prime minister was likely to prove disastrous to his party and the country. In the debate on prices and incomes in early July, the general view, according to Mrs Castle, was that Mrs Thatcher had made a weak and ineffective speech. Heath's speech, however, was 'the best he has ever made ... it made Margaret look like a tinny amateur and speculation began to circulate as to whether she could survive'. Thatcher's recollection of the debate was unsurprisingly different. She admitted that her speech had not gone well and that the Opposition's decision to abstain on the Government's bill was difficult to defend on anything except grounds of expediency but 'Ted bailed me out by regretting that we were not supporting the Government and then refusing to back our critical amendment'. Both Castle and Thatcher had a point. Heath's speech was more forceful, more logical and more principled but it offended against the sacred Tory principle that the party must unite against the common enemy. Heath was seen by many as behaving disloyally; whether he was right or wrong was a secondary consideration, the fact that he was breaking ranks and giving comfort to the Government was what stuck in the minds of the Tory rank and file. Whitelaw told Alastair Hetherington that he hoped Heath would quit politics altogether. His performance from the back benches was putting a tremendous strain on the party. 'If Heath got up and agreed with the front bench, that would be taken as no more than a routine endorsement of what Thatcher and Joseph were planning. If he showed even a modest differing of line, it would immediately be taken as rebellious and petty ... as soon as Heath began to seem critical of Thatcher on a consistent basis he would be ostracised by the majority of Conservative members and would find his position untenable.' His obstinacy and resolution were such that he never did find it untenable, but even in the summer of 1975 it was clear that there were troubles ahead, both for the Tory Party and for its former leader.[16]

The party conference at Blackpool in October 1975 provided a forum in which any potential storm could have been whipped up or miraculously stilled. Kenneth Baker urged Heath to stay away. He insisted he must go, but compromised by deciding not to speak: 'It is important', he wrote, 'for a new leader to establish his or her own authority at a conference.' Despite this resolution he could not resist making a somewhat dramatic entry and taking his seat in the front row to loud cheers. Mrs Thatcher reacted well, joined in the applause and shook hands with Heath as they left the platform. Encouraged by this, Whitelaw decided that the time had come to bury the hatchet for once and for all. Heath, he explained to Mrs Thatcher, for reasons of pride would be loath to visit his leader in her suite on the second floor but would be happy to receive her in his humbler but still suitably grandiose rooms two floors above. Thatcher was happy to agree to this. An hour and a half passed, and Thatcher decided time was pressing. 'I rang Willie and asked what was happening. I was told that Ted had had second thoughts. The hatchet would evidently remain unburied.' It was not the only party conference that was to be the scene of an aborted reconciliation. In 1977 Waldegrave and Patten thought that they had worked out an arrangement by which, if Thatcher would say something polite about Heath in her leader's speech, he would reciprocate with an approving smile or even by making some obliging remark about her to the media. She did her bit by praising his political courage. 'That was the "quid". We awaited the "quo". There was no "quo". Despite Waldegrave's best efforts Ted sat impassive ... no smile, no acknowledgment, no response.' At Brighton there was at least no open rebuff of this kind, but behind the scenes Heath made no secret of his discontent. 'This was the first occasion', wrote Baker, 'on which Ted established the alternative Court of malcontents whom he entertained during Party Conference time. His friends in the media loved it because he was quite open about accusing the group around Margaret of "going for me".' As for Mrs Thatcher, Heath described her as 'a traitor'. 'All these phrases were immediately and lovingly reported and actually did Ted no good at all.'[17]

Some people who genuinely esteemed both parties never lost the hope that they could be brought together. Lord Hailsham, in July 1975, tried to make Mrs Thatcher's flesh creep with speculation that Harold Wilson, faced by a split in his own party, might invite Heath and Grimond to join the Government:

My present estimate is that such a Government might be popular and might well command the support, e.g. of *The Times* and Lord Shawcross ... I am sure you wd be wise if at all possible (wh. I fear it may not be) to heal the breach with Ted Heath as soon as may be. I do not myself believe there is an ideological difference between you. On the other hand, in politics, personal difficulties can be as troublesome, and as lasting, as ideological differences.

In her reply, Mrs Thatcher admitted that the prospect of a national Government with a socialist majority was an alarming one. 'On your other point – about healing the breach – I do try, but it takes two.' He would not dream of suggesting that the fault for the present impasse lay with her, protested Hailsham. 'But obviously, so long as you and he are at arms' length, there is the possibility of a permanent split in the party which wd, at any rate for the time being, destroy us in the country.' He now switched his fire to Heath. He would be very sorry, he said, if it was felt that his continued presence in the Shadow Cabinet was 'an act of disloyalty to our friendship or ingratitude for the many kindnesses I have received from you'. He refrained from urging a reconciliation with Mrs Thatcher – no doubt calculating that this would be better raised face to face – but warned against the perils of a so-called national Government based on a socialist majority. 'They would not abandon the more damaging items in their programme, and any Conservatives who joined it would therefore become their captives.' Heath knew that it was supremely unlikely that Wilson would contemplate inviting him to join the Government; nor would he have accepted if such an offer had been made. The only circumstances in which he might have been tempted to join a national Government would have been if Labour had become ardent champions of the European Community while the Tories wanted to leave it. Since this was not and was never likely to be the case, he found Hailsham's forebodings slightly ridiculous. He assured Hailsham, though probably not with complete wholeheartedness, that he entirely understood why he was still in the Shadow Cabinet and that there was 'nothing I should like more than for us to have a talk about our present predicament'. There the matter was allowed to rest.[18]

Hailsham, however, never wholly despaired of being able to contrive a rapprochement. Some time later he approached Tim Kitson and asked him whether he thought the time was yet ripe. Kitson advocated delay: 'An awful lot of our colleagues are of the opinion that, until the new policies of the party are agreed by the Shadow Cabinet, it would be extremely difficult for Margaret to work with Ted.' The flaw about this argument was that a reconciliation would be even more difficult to achieve once the new policies *had* been agreed. Heath disliked the present policies of the Thatcher Shadow Cabinet and felt it almost certain that he would dislike them more and more as the remaining Heathite economic and social principles were extirpated and a brave new world of monetarism and confrontation took their place. Peter Carrington had him to stay for a weekend in January 1976. He was 'in cracking form, being rude to everybody', Carrington told Hailsham. He said that he had told Heath that 'he ought to have gone around during the past few months being a good loser, kissing Margaret on every possible opportunity and saying what a splendid woman she was'. Heath was baffled by this proposition. He looked at his host in amazement 'Why on earth? I do not think she is very good. I am much better and I ought to be there still.'[19]

But though he was disinclined to come back into the fold, he seemed equally uninterested in the possibility of forming his own group in opposition. A small but potentially significant body of dissidents existed, who had either been dismissed by Mrs Thatcher, felt that such a fate was imminent or saw no prospects of promotion while she was in power. They looked to Heath to provide some leadership. We hoped 'he would at least have a drink now and then,' one former Minister lamented, but 'this had not happened and Mr Heath has withdrawn completely'. He rarely attended backbench committees and, when he did, sat inconspicuously near the door and made no effort to control or even influence the proceedings. 'It fitted in with his behaviour as leader towards the party,' remarked one Tory member. The Tory Reform Group, a coalition of various elements from the left of the Party united in their wish to preserve Disraelian Tory principles, might have been expected to provide a sympathetic base from which Heath could have sought to exercise influence. Certainly he looked benevolently on its activities, but he showed no wish to take the lead or even figure in its deliberations. From time to time he would ask Heseltine for information about the new leadership's attitude towards Europe but he never suggested that they should embark on any common initiative.

For some this reticence seemed disappointing; other were relieved. Kenneth Clarke was a member of the Amesbury Group, composed of junior members of the Shadow Cabinet who felt vaguely ill at ease

with certain aspects of their leader's policies. 'I didn't believe in the King across the water,' he told his biographers. 'I didn't think Heath would ever come back. The main aim of the Amesbury Group was not to be Heathites in exile: it was to keep us in touch with mainstream politics.' David Howell told David Butler that Heath could not make up his mind whether to 'go off and be Mr Europe', pull out of politics altogether or rejoin the team. 'He hung around, to the embarrassment of many of his friends, in his odd sulking position. He was really very isolated though he still had a bit of a coterie around him.'

Butler asked of whom the coterie was composed: Baker and Kitson were the only names forthcoming.[20]

He appeared less often in the House of Commons. Unlike Harold Wilson, whose record of voting improved dramatically when he ceased to be prime minister, Heath on the back benches had the worst record of any member. In 1975–6 he managed to vote in a little over a third of the divisions; in 1976–7 this fell to a pitiful 19.6 per cent.[21] Partly this was because he was disinclined to put himself out to record an extra vote for Mrs Thatcher; more importantly he had other things to do. For the first time in many years he had to consider seriously how to earn a living. As leader of the Party and prime minister he had been well looked after; his only extravagance had been *Morning Cloud*, the cost of which had largely been borne by others, and the logistical back-up required for his political work had been provided for him. Now this was lost. He enjoyed a prime minister's pension of £10,000 and his investments had been handled shrewdly but this could not have begun to cover the cost of the entourage by which he liked to be surrounded, to organise his life, write his speeches and brief him on current topics. The most urgent need was for funds to staff and equip his office. These were provided by a consortium of rich businessmen, organised by Lord Aldington, and benefiting from – for the first years at least – a generous contribution by James Goldsmith. Stephen Sherbourne, who continued as head of Heath's office after he ceased to be leader, was never quite certain from where his salary was coming, though Aldington seemed more nearly responsible than anyone else and Kitson played a large part in organising the day-to-day expenses. Wilf Weeks, who in due course replaced Sherbourne, found that he was expected to accompany Heath on most of his extensive travels but had largely to look after himself when it came to meeting the cost of such excursions. This rarely proved difficult; the businesses which bore the cost of Heath's travels were usually ready to find the extra money needed to provide him with the support he deemed necessary. Pre-eminent among these, from the beginning of 1978 when he joined its advisory board, was the giant international firm of accountants and consultants, Arthur Andersen. Andersen's had more than two hundred offices around the world and they considered that it redounded to their credit and kept the staff of the various offices on their toes to have a former British prime minister visit them and report back to head office on what he found. For the most part the lustre of his presence was all that was expected from him but from time to time more practical help was requested. He was able to appeal directly to the Ruler of Dubai when Arthur Andersen were deprived of some lucrative business to which they had been accustomed. The appeal did not go unheard; indeed Heath boasted that, as a result of his intercession, they had got all their old business back and more besides. For more than twenty years Arthur Andersen gave him a generous retainer and paid for his first-class travel and accommodation, plus the expenses of an assistant, to nearly three-quarters of his destinations. Heath thought he gave good value for the money; Andersen evidently agreed, there were no complaints on either side.[22]

Heath remained secretive about his money matters. He refused to cooperate with the Registrar of Interests by identifying the under-writing syndicates to which he belonged at Lloyd's and was equally reluctant to divulge details about the various lavish presents which from time to time the potentates he visited bestowed on him. The system by which retired presidents and prime ministers can earn grotesquely large sums of money by lecturing or making after-dinner speeches had not yet fully evolved, but even in the 1970s Heath was earning good money by such activities. Weeks found that one of his duties as head of Heath's office was negotiating such arrangements: he became adept, he said, at 'thinking of a figure and then doubling it'. As with Arthur Andersen, Heath gave value for money: he was witty, eloquent and incisive and gave his audience the feeling that they were being admitted into a private world where only the most privi-leged could expect to penetrate. A problem from the point of view of Weeks and subsequent private secretaries was that, highly though his would-be hosts valued his services, Heath valued them more highly still; he never admitted to surprise at the scale of his remuneration and frequently complained that with a little extra pressure still bigger fees could have been extracted.

*　　*　　*

One source of income he denied himself. Before he had been a year out of office Harold Wilson had completed a massive volume covering his first period as prime minister. On his way to de Gaulle's funeral in November 1970 he told Heath no less than three times that he 'intended to hold nothing back'. He was to be well rewarded for his indiscretion; the book rights had been sold for £30,000 while the *Sunday Times* paid a prodigious £260,000 for the serial.[23] There was no reason why Heath should not earn at least as much; especially if he was prepared to write freely about the circumstances of his replacement by Mrs Thatcher. He had no objection in principle to doing so: on the contrary he rather looked forward to putting his own side of the case and washing a certain amount of other people's dirty linen in public. But he did not think the time was ripe. Harold Wilson might see fit to offer the public what he clearly did not believe was the final instalment of his life story, but, when he wrote *The Labour Government 1964–1970*, he was still very much in command of his party. He was the man who would return to Downing Street if he won the next election. Heath had no such certitude; to most people it seemed unlikely that he would even be in the Government, let alone in Number 10. Heath himself did not accept this. He was sure that, somehow, the party would return to its senses and restore its rightful leader. Already Mrs Thatcher was floundering, her inadequacies becoming every day more apparent. Within a few months, years anyway, he would be on top again. How was he to write a book which would end in this gigantic uncertainty? Would it not suggest that his career was over? Much better wait until the matter was resolved.

But because he was not going to write that book, it did not follow that he would write *no* book. It was Sir Charles Forte, the owner, and Lord Longford, the chairman, of the publishers Sidgwick & Jackson, who persuaded him that it would be both enjoyable and profitable to write a book to be called, simply, *Sailing*; mainly, of course, based on his personal experiences but broadening out, whenever he felt inclined, into general observations about the nature of yachting and yachtsmen. Heath took to the idea with alacrity, dictated the book – a brisk 40,000 words – over the summer, added a handsome selection of photographs, most of which featured the narrator in a variety of nautical poses, and had it ready in good time for Christmas 1975. The book, essentially the story of the various *Morning Clouds*, was as breezy as its subject: Heath was no stylist and abhorred the purple passage, but given a story to tell with which he felt personally involved he could tell it lucidly and with vigour. The reviewers liked it. William Golding, author among other novels of *Lord of the Flies*, praised his prose for its 'remarkable clarity and simplicity. It is a professional job. Mr Heath has enjoyed his racing and I have enjoyed reading about it.' Nicholas Monsarrat, whose *The Cruel Sea* had established him in the front rank of nautical bestsellers, wrote that the book exhibited the same 'maritime virus infection' as he had endured himself from the age of eight. He rejoiced at the book's success, he said, which 'having done those sums which are so absorbing to all true men of letters, I calculate will certainly take care of *Morning Cloud V*'.[24]

The reviewers' praise delighted Heath, but so too did Monsarrat's calculations. The book was commercially a phenomenal success. Heath set new records for the author's signing session, reaching his peak on a spitefully snowy and slushy Monday at John Smith's bookshop in Glasgow. The weather was so foul that Heath feared the day would be a disaster; by the time he signed the first copy the queue wound three times round the shop and down the pavement outside, turning the corner into the next street. By one o'clock the thousand copies available had all been signed, a further 400 were then sold in advance to people still waiting in the queue. The strongest sales at a signing at John Smith's till then had been recorded by Alistair Cooke, who had sold 750 copies of his book *America*; Heath, as he proudly recorded in his memoirs, had almost doubled that figure. The success was repeated at forty-six other venues; by the end of the year more than 100,000 copies were in circulation, 90,000 sold.

No publisher would have been willing to leave so triumphant a debut without a sequel. A book which did for his music what *Sailing* had done for his life on *Morning Cloud* might easily match its predecessor in sales and popular esteem. Stephen Sherbourne urged caution. Publishers, he pointed out, always tried to squeeze all they could get out of an author 'even if this is not always in the interests of the author himself'. A second book was unlikely to produce the same impact as *Sailing*, the signing sessions would not attract the same crowds, it would be, if not a flop, then at least much less of a success.

> Perhaps I can put the whole argument more bluntly. There are a hell of a lot of people who want you to continue to make a real political impact in Britain. If they see you dashing around the country a second time almost within a year on a great sales campaign they will begin to have doubts about the seriousness of your political commitment ... Either the press begin to treat you as a kind of 'show biz' character, always popping up in the gossip columns, or they continue to treat you as somebody with a serious contribution to make to British politics.

'I agree with what you say,' wrote Heath. Probably he did agree at that moment, but when the scent of battle stirred him, all such inhibitions were forgotten. *Music: A Joy for Life* was launched in the Big Room of the Grosvenor House Hotel, with Heath conducting the London Symphony Orchestra in Haydn's cello concerto and Schubert's fifth symphony. There were twenty-four shop signings and a celebratory hundredth signing session at Grosvenor House, when Lord Longford presented Heath with a gold Cartier pen. He received even more letters than had been inspired by *Sailing*, many of them thanking him for introducing the writer to a new world. He was remarkably conscientious in his replies. A Mr Midgley of Torquay received a long letter encouraging him to take up the violin even though he was forty-one, advising him how to find a teacher and suggesting the best recordings of Mahler's symphonies. Sales did not quite match those for *Sailing* but they ran to a very satisfactory 60,000. Publication was at much the same time as that of Harold Wilson's *The Governance of Britain*. Heath was told that Wilson had been to the printers to sign 5,000 copies. 'v.optimistic,' he commented with some satisfaction.[25]

The critics had been kindly about *Sailing, Music* attracted less attention but generally got a friendly press, but when the following year Heath produced *Travels: People and Places in My Life*, their patience ran out. Heath is 'no stranger to platitude and longitude', judged the *Observer*; in the *Sunday Times* Paul Theroux headed his review 'Round the world in 80 clichés'. It was, indeed, a trivial book; bland observations and flaccid anecdotes cobbled together into an unappetising whole. Possibly in recognition of its weaknesses, the publishers excelled themselves when it came to the promotion. Sidgwick & Jackson hired a special train which was launched with a press conference in Paddington before its departure and conducted a week's tour with signings in car parks and on platforms. Not since Gladstone's Midlothian tour, wrote Kenneth Rose, has the progress of a politician by train 'provoked such ribaldry. Yet it has been a melancholy spectacle. Mr Gladstone's progress delivered him in triumph to Downing Street; Edward Heath's merely swelled his bank balance at the expense of his reputation.' Ribaldry or not, the tour was a striking success, collecting huge crowds and all the publicity Sidgwick & Jackson could have hoped for. Sales exceeded 40,000; a further steep drop from the peaks achieved by its predecessors but still an eminently satisfactory performance. 'We look on you, as I need hardly tell you, as our most valuable author,' Frank Longford assured him, 'and like to feel that your success and ours go forward together.' Like most valuable authors Heath was not averse to taking a sharp bite at the hand that fed him. A would-be reader in Oldham complained that he had been unable to buy a copy of *Travels* in the town's leading bookshop. 'Mr Heath asked me to tell you that he feels it is disgraceful that the public cannot buy his books and that Sidgwicks are not trying to sell them,' wrote a secretary. 'Perhaps a consignment of books ought to be dispatched forthwith to Oldham!'[26]

There is no evidence to suggest that Sherbourne and Kenneth Rose were right in thinking that the publicity generated by these book tours militated against Heath's reputation as a serious statesman. Possibly if he had been on the brink of returning to power some damage would have been done. But Heath's main problem now was how to remain prominently in the public eye. Authorship was a respectable occupation, and though the razzmatazz generated by the publishers might seem vulgar to the more squeamish, in the public's mind it associated him with a meritorious enterprise and deserved success. The vision of a benign Heath communicating with his admirers as they milled around him seeking his autograph on copies of his books was a welcome corrective to the severe and withdrawn figure which had become the accepted image over the last seven or eight years. By the time he finished the first lap of his literary career (which included *Carols: The Joy of Christmas*, an inflated pamphlet described by the *New Statesman* as 'a naked piece of book-production' with a 'tritely egocentric preface'), Heath was both a much richer and a more popular man.

He continued to practise what he preached. He spent as much time as ever on his sailing, though the glory days of the late 1960s and early 1970s were never repeated. *Morning Cloud IV*, perhaps because it was launched too late to allow its crew to become fully habituated to its ways, was not selected for the Admiral's Cup in 1975. 1976 was no more successful, but *Morning Cloud V* seemed to recapture some of its predecessors' magic qualities and Heath was again captain of the British Admiral's Cup ocean racing team in 1979. The disastrous Fastnet Race in August of that year, in which fewer than half the boats finished and fifteen lives were lost, cost Heath a badly damaged leg and very nearly brought to an end his yachting career and, indeed, his life. He and *Morning Cloud* survived, however, and were still counted among the more formidable contenders in the world of ocean racing when Heath, aged seventy, finally retired in 1986. 'I never had any doubt that my sailing was beneficial, both for my physical health and for my sanity,' he concluded in his memoirs. 'I would not have missed it for the world.'[27] This introverted and lonely man found in his life aboard *Morning Cloud* a companionship and an unstrained sense of partnership with others of similar tastes and aspirations which he could never hope to experience in a Cabinet or Shadow Cabinet. Heath was not a man to whom human relationships came easily; without his yachting he might have found them impossible.

As his yachting life waned, his musical career gained new prominence. Professional musicians were never going to admit that he was one of them, nor would he have claimed any such distinction. If he had not been a former prime minister, his appeal to the giants in the world of music would have been far less potent. Nevertheless, conductors of the renown of André Previn, Georg Solti or Herbert von Karajan do not entrust their orchestras to an amateur unless they are confident that he will not merely not make a fool of himself but that he will acquit himself with honour. Heath comfortably attained this standard. First he was allowed to conduct individual pieces with the London Symphony Orchestra – Elgar's 'Cockaigne' overture or the overture to Wagner's *Meistersinger*. Then in 1976 Solti invited him to conduct an entire programme with the Chicago Symphony Orchestra: the *Meistersinger* overture again, Elgar's *Enigma Variations* and Beethoven's eighth symphony. By 1978 he had conducted in ten countries, including the United States, China and Russia. His association with the European Community Youth Orchestra, of which he was the first president and guest conductor, was even more rewarding. Music, he believed, was the common language of Europe; by encouraging the youth of Europe to play together he was both cementing the unity of the Community and offering the cream of the continent's youthful talent a chance to hone its skills in an international forum. His finest hour came in Dublin in 1978, seven years after the introduction of internment in Ulster. Lorin Maazel, who was supposed to conduct the orchestra on this occasion, was injured at the last moment, and Heath stepped in, arriving on the podium to the astonishment of the audience. The programme began with the Irish national anthem. 'I suspected', wrote Heath, 'that this was the first – and surely the last – occasion on which a former British prime minister has conducted this particular work.'[28]

It would be extravagant to pretend that such diversions could compensate for the crushing disappointment of his political defeat. Nevertheless his yachting and his music, the success of the referendum campaign and his triumphant progresses as an author, meant that the two years after February 1975 were more rewarding than he could have felt possible when the blow fell. He suffered one extra loss, however. On 11 October 1976 his father, in typically ebullient form, celebrated his eighty-eighth birthday with his family and friends. Four days later he was dead. Heath at best was irritated by, at worst actively disliked, his stepmother but he had never ceased to visit his father regularly and, though he had little in common with him, he enjoyed his company and was grateful to him for much support and encouragement over many years. William Heath had remained robustly cheerful to the end. On his eightieth birthday he had been asked whether there was anything about his life which he deeply regretted. 'Yes,' he replied, 'that the permissive society did not begin fifty years earlier!' One can hardly imagine Edward Heath making any such response, but he appreciated it in his father and in part at least envied the vitality and the undiscriminating clubbability which had made life so much easier for William Heath than it had been for his son. He still from time to time saw his brother but the two had never been close and grew ever further apart. His brother's children he barely knew. The death of William Heath closed a chapter in Ted Heath's life, the most important part of which had ended a quarter of a century before when his mother had died. Now he was even more alone.

TWENTY-FOUR

The Long Sulk

Heath was engaged in one of his innumerable signing sessions for *Sailing* in March 1976 when an excited Kitson telephoned to report that Harold Wilson had resigned. To Heath the news was incomprehensible; that a man of his own age, apparently in good health and still on top of his job, should voluntarily relinquish power was a stark reversal of all that seemed reasonable or proper. There is no reason to believe that he subscribed to any of the more exotic conspiracy theories which were advanced to explain Wilson's retirement, but his astonishment was made very clear to the journalists who besieged him as he left the signing, clamouring for his reaction to the news. His astonishment was suppressed when he spoke in the House of Commons: he 'rose above party prejudice,' wrote Bernard Donoghue, 'and with his natural sense of a historical moment paid a superbly phrased tribute to Wilson'. Margaret Thatcher, on the other hand, 'got the tone wrong, was graceless and point-scoring, and missed the mood of the House'. Heath praised Wilson for his political skills, his resourcefulness and his persuasive powers and congratulated him on joining and doubling the membership of that most exclusive club, former prime ministers still in the House of Commons. It was almost the last charitable remark he was to make about his old adversary. In his memoirs he was coolly dismissive: Wilson was 'a great political survivor, a fine politician if, perhaps, never truly a great statesman'. In conversation he was less temperate. Wilson was a cheat, a liar, a charlatan; he should never have been entrusted with high office. Only his genuine affection and respect for Wilson's widow, Mary, stayed Heath from giving wider expression to his feelings.[1]

Wilson's disappearance from the scene was bound, in the not very long run, to exacerbate the split within the Tory Party. Wilson's successor, James Callaghan, was a man whom it was very easy to distrust but difficult to hate. Heath, in fact, rather liked him. While Wilson had been there, Heath and Thatcher had been united on one thing at least, their detestation of a common enemy. With Wilson gone, Heath found that he was increasingly likely to see merits in the Labour point of view. He never forgot that he was a Tory and that fundamentally his loyalties lay with the Conservative cause; but he was ever more likely to conclude that true Tory principles were being ignored and to find the leading enemy on the Conservative front bench.

The uneasy truce between Heath and the Tory leadership grew ever more precarious through 1976. Devolution was one of the issues which first revealed its frailty. Heath had always been in favour of a high degree of devolution for Scotland and Wales, with directly elected assemblies which could raise revenue and be responsible for all matters which affected only their areas of the United Kingdom. When the Labour Government introduced legislation designed to bring this about, Heath accepted it in principle, though unhappy about certain elements, which he believed might make the scheme unworkable and much less attractive to the Scots and Welsh. At first this also seemed to be the attitude of the Tory front bench, but by the time of the Second Reading in December 1976 their position had hardened and they resolved to vote against the bill. This, to Heath, seemed to be a wilful rejection of the principle of devolution, something to which he was not prepared to subscribe. I do not think, he told the House of Commons, that 'anybody would expect me to vote against the Government's Bill. People know my history. I may be inflexible and very obstinate. On the other hand it may be that I sustain my beliefs ... I believe that the best way of maintaining this Union is to have devolution.'[2]

Whatever the Shadow Cabinet may privately have expected him to do, they publicly proclaimed their position when they imposed a three-line whip on the vote on the Second Reading. Heath held back from the ultimate act of rebellion by voting with the Labour Government but, for the first time in his life, abstained on a three-line whip. He had heard of a poacher turning gamekeeper, said the former Suez rebel, John Biggs-Davison, but this was the first time he had seen a gamekeeper turned poacher. Twenty-seven other Conservatives joined Heath in abstaining, five voted with Labour. 'What matters now is to get the present bill right, or as near right as we can,' Heath told Lord Hailsham. 'In this you will no doubt have better opportunities of working together for good than will be permitted us in the Commons. The decision to have a three line whip ... was a disaster. Will they ever learn?' When the maverick Labour MP George Cunningham introduced an amendment ruling that 40 per cent of the Scottish electorate must support devolution, not the proposed 33⅓ per cent, the Tory front bench refused to adopt any firm position; many Conservatives voted for the amendment, Heath and three others voted against it. It was a clear statement, if such a statement were still needed, that on any matter of importance he intended to consult his conscience and vote according to his convictions. If the front bench did not like it, then they would have to lump it.[3]

His increasingly ardent determination to go his own way and to distance himself conspicuously from Mrs Thatcher began seriously to perturb those of his friends who were still loyal to the Tory leadership. At the end of July 1976 his biographer and admirer George Hutchinson wrote him an open letter published in *The Times* claiming that he was damaging both himself and the Tory Party. 'You are already estranged from a number of old friends ... You are in danger of losing the goodwill and respect of the party. Nobody is asking you ... to join the Shadow Cabinet, but simply to speak up for its leader and her chosen colleagues, most of whom were your own.' Other, even more faithful voices joined in the same refrain. Sara Morrison invited Douglas Hurd to her house in Wiltshire where Heath was staying the night. The Conservative Party, they told Heath, was about to issue a policy document which would be broadly compatible with his views. This would give him a splendid chance 'to confound his enemies and come aboard again'. He should endorse it as soon as it appeared. 'The advice was better received than I expected,' remembered Hurd. 'But we were soon bogged down in arguments about the loyalty or lack of it of the party's present leaders. Over several hours Ted and I drank a bottle of claret each and, not for the first time in such encounters, I went to bed thinking we had made real progress.' But by the time he got down the following morning Heath had already left; 'our quarry had in the end eluded us'.[4]

They had perhaps made more of an impression than they realised at the time. At the party conference that autumn Heath not only attended but made a major speech. The next Conservative Government, he said, would have to take tough and difficult decisions: 'I have complete confidence that they will be taken by Margaret Thatcher and her colleagues on the platform.' It was not, perhaps, the most rousing of endorsements but it was good enough. Mrs Thatcher was the first to rise and applaud him at the end of the speech; the following speaker got tumultuous applause when he expressed his hope that Heath would soon be back in the Shadow Cabinet. For a dizzy moment it seemed that he might after all be returning to the fold. By-elections had reduced the overall Labour lead to a single seat, a general election must be imminent, if the Tories returned to power pledged to the moderate economic courses that Mrs Thatcher appeared at that moment to be espousing then surely Heath would put his loyalty to the Party and the country before his pride and agree to serve in the new Government? Even at that moment such hopes were probably illusory; as it was, a deal with the Liberals extended Labour's grasp on power, Thatcher's control over her party became more firm and, in Heath's eyes at least, the Opposition began a move towards the right in a way which ruled out any likelihood of his participation. Nor was it Heath alone who detected such a trend. According to Lord Hailsham's diary, in March 1977 Carrington told him that he was 'disturbed at the way the party is being run. We are giving the impression of an extreme right-wing party.' Two people, he said, were particularly to blame: Thatcher herself and Keith Joseph. 'I said I had warned again and again but had been ignored.' The two men agreed that no change of leadership was for the moment possible, though Hailsham argued that Whitelaw, Pym, Prior or even Heath himself would do better than the present incumbent. 'We both agreed Margaret [was] an extremely nice person, but I said that I had never had much confidence in her judgment and my fears had been realised.' Carrington and Hailsham were at the moderate centre of Mrs Thatcher's Shadow Cabinet; the disquiet they felt was inconsiderable compared with the growing dismay of Prior, Pym, Gilmour and the other remaining Heathites.[5]

The 1977 party conference failed to demonstrate any improvement in the relationship between Heath and Thatcher: on the contrary, Heath was conspicuously disobliging, refused to respond to the tentative overtures made by Thatcher or her followers and was vociferously critical of the Shadow Cabinet's policies in the private and not-so-private discussions that took place outside the main forum. Over the next twelve months matters grew steadily worse. The Labour Government had set a guideline for pay rises of 5 per cent. Heath thought this sensible and acceptable to the British people: he publicly affirmed his approval. Mrs Thatcher denounced the concept: she did not explicitly commit the Party to a return to free collective bargaining but it seemed clear that this was the main thrust of her policy. Heath took even less trouble to disguise his hostility on this as on other issues. When immigration was debated in the Commons early in 1978, Mrs Thatcher was given a torrid time by the Labour benches. Dennis Skinner shouted across the floor: 'She's having a rough afternoon, isn't she, Ted?' The normally impassive Heath responded with 'a grin and a huge, meaningful wink'.[6]

The party conference of 1978 did not so much bring a rift into the open, for it was embarrassingly evident already, as formalise it. Heath had been provoked by an appearance on television by Mrs Thatcher a few days before in which she had been contemptuously dismissive of any sort of legislated prices and incomes policy. In what Geoffrey Howe described as a 'powerful if graceless speech', Heath came close to denouncing Thatcher for irresponsibility. His audience, knowing that an election could not be very far away, took exception to what seemed a dangerously divisive initiative and gave him only tepid applause. Howe, who followed him, made what he claimed to have intended as a 'carefully balanced compromise' between the two points of view; to most people it seemed a rousing affirmation of the Thatcher–Joseph line. It was received with a standing ovation. As if this was not irritating enough for Heath, his speech did not feature in the television coverage of the conference while Howe's was reported prominently. His riposte was to appear on the *News at Ten* programme that evening, admitting openly that his views were radically different from those of Mrs Thatcher and arguing that free collective bargaining could only lead to damaging inflation. David Butler arrived at the conference that evening to find that Heath's speech and the subsequent television appearance were the talk of the day. Butler, with Robin Day and Hugo Young, met Heath for a drink at midnight. 'I made a hash of today's speech,' Heath told them. 'I should have said "Our leader says this. Jim Prior says 5 per cent. Please, where do we stand?"' But that, noted Butler, was more or less what he had said. He 'emphasised both the contradiction in Conservative policy and his own isolation (for neither Jim nor Margaret can have been pleased) ... It was said that he would not have souped things up on TV after his speech if Margaret had stood up to give him a standing ovation. As it was, the Tories were almost all very angry with him, underlining their neuroticism about unity.' Chris Patten told Butler that Heath's performance in the second half of 1978 had made life difficult for the moderates: 'Without realising it, he had undermined his own ideological position and that of his supporters in the party.' By the time discussion moved to the conference, Heath was 'very eager for a fight, always suspecting slights ... Margaret, of course, was surrounded by a group of malcontents who fed her suspicions of Ted ... and these had probably captured her ear before and during the Party Conference.'[7]

Mrs Thatcher, in her memoirs, blamed Heath for creating this open split within the party at a critical moment. Until then informal talks had been going on about possible cooperation between the present and the former leader during the general election: 'Ted's intervention had blown all that out of the window.' At a certain level discussions had always been kept open between the increasingly uneasy Heathites and the more moderate supporters of Mrs Thatcher, but Heath himself gave little thought to cooperation and made his feelings ever more evident. He paid a price for his intransigence. When the Tories failed to win the Berwick and East Lothian by-election in late October 1978, some Tory MPs blamed Heath's performance at the conference for the setback. 'I went on ITN,' wrote Thatcher, 'and – with perhaps an excess of charity – exonerated him.' The charity was applied with marked economy and did not save Heath from much angry abuse within the party. To the outward eye he seemed to treat such hostility with insouciance, almost to rejoice in it. According to Wilf Weeks, who worked closely with him over this period, he was in fact badly shaken by the experience; under the veneer of bravado he was acutely sensitive to criticism. In his own mind he was not being disloyal, or even provocative. He told Edward Boyle that he could not see these complex and critical issues as being suitable for 'adversary politics ... There is no doubt at all that the great majority of the public would like to see some common approach to a solution to these problems, but I am afraid the more ardent of our supporters would like us to oppose everything within range.'

The evidence suggests that he indeed reflected the nation's views more faithfully than did the Tory faithful who reviled him. A National Opinion Poll showed that 71 per cent of those consulted were impressed by reports of his speech at the conference, against 56 per cent who favoured Thatcher's closing speech. Fifty-five per cent thought Heath would make a better prime minister than Mrs Thatcher, only 33 per cent felt the opposite. To be applauded by the nation yet isolated within one's own party is a position which may give a politician some moral satisfaction but offers little prospect of a return to power. Even if things had continued to go well for Labour it seems impossible that Heath could ever have regained the leadership. As it was, the dramatic catastrophes that overtook the Labour cause during Callaghan's 'Winter of Discontent' opened the way to a Conservative victory and Heath's continued exile.[8]

However exacting the demands of authorship or domestic politics, Heath continued to see himself above all as an international statesman. There were few parts of the world about which he was not ready to express a view – usually well informed – and few problems to whose solution he did not feel he could contribute. When the son-in-law of Garfield Todd, the liberal Rhodesian, appealed to him to help secure his father-in-law's release from a jail in Salisbury, Heath at once wrote to Ian Smith, urging him to let Todd go; to do so would, he suggested, 'make a considerable impact on many of us here who want to see the restoration of good relations between our peoples'. The response was a brush-off from Smith's office; if only, it said, England and other countries would stop trying to bring Southern Rhodesia to its knees, there would be no such problems. 'Typically stupid,' minuted Heath, 'and from a private secretary!' It is characteristic of Heath that he was almost as much put out by the fact that Smith had not bothered to answer Heath's message in a personal letter as by the tenor of his reply.

It was, of course, above all with Europe that he was linked in the public mind: he rejoiced in the association and believed that he had a unique role to play. In the autumn of 1975 George Weidenfeld had suggested that he might write a book about Britain and Europe. He consulted Douglas Hurd, who thought the project was worthwhile but that, if Heath concentrated too obviously on one element of his time as prime minister, it might be taken as an admission that none of the other achievements really mattered. Heath took the point. He did not wish just to be known as 'Mr Europe'. As a subject for a book it was indefinitely postponed.[9]

China was second only to Europe in his priorities. After his first visit he had returned with two pandas and a greatly enhanced opinion of the Chinese Government and its prospects for the future. Eighteen months later in the autumn of 1975 he went back, to find that the fact that he was no longer even Leader of the Opposition made no difference to the warmth of his reception. He was received by Deng Xiaoping, who told him apologetically that, for reasons of health, Chou En-lai would be unable to see him and that it had also not been possible to make arrangements for him to visit Mao Tse-tung. The British Ambassador commiserated with Heath on his failure to see either of these veterans, but Heath had noted the different formulae used by Chou and Mao and did not abandon hope that the Chairman might nevertheless receive him. Sure enough, at short notice Heath was summoned to call on Mao. He had by now concluded that effective power had largely moved from Mao and Chou to the Vice-Premier Deng, but he still regarded Mao as one of the giants of the age who shared with Churchill, Adenauer and Tito 'the ability to go to the heart of the matter, to sort out the great matters from the small, to see their policies through to the end'. Mao did not disappoint him on this occasion; he was obviously ill and old but as affable as ever. He treated Heath with all the respect due to a major international figure. Within a year both he and Chou En-lai were dead and Deng had finally overcome the Gang of Four, including Mao's widow, and was installed in power. When he next saw Heath he told him how he had been plotted against, removed from office and humiliated, but had nevertheless won through. 'Ah,' Heath responded wryly, 'the Vice-Premier gives us all cause for hope.'[10]

The years that passed after Heath's fall from power seemed to make no difference to the Chinese: he continued to be received with honour and treated as a figure of influence and power as well as wisdom. 'Mr Heath is a good friend of China,' the Minister of Culture told Miloska Nott, 'and we remain loyal to our friends – we do not change old suits for new ones.' Heath remained equally loyal to China and found it hard to admit that anything in that country was less than perfect, or at least that anything wrong was not rapidly being put right. Mrs Nott told him that she and her husband had just spent two weeks in China and had been horrified by the lack of individual freedom. 'They have an aim,' Heath replied. 'I respect them. They know where they are going.'[11]

Apart from feeding his sense of his own importance Heath secured substantial benefits from the Chinese connection. His easy access to the top levels of Chinese bureaucracy and the seriousness with which his views were considered meant that he was uniquely well equipped to promote the interest of any international firm seeking to do business in China. Such enterprises met his expenses on a lavish scale and often remunerated him in other ways. A giant shipping and transport company like COSCO, anxious to benefit from the rapidly growing Chinese economy, were happy on several occasions to bear all his internal costs in China and, when his memoirs were finally published, put up £5,000 to pay for the launch party ('*No* publicity for this,' enjoined Heath anxiously). Jardine Fleming were recommended strongly to Premier Zhu Rongji by Heath, together with the Commercial General Union: 'Two particularly fine British companies who are currently hoping to receive licences [to trade in financial services]. I would be very grateful if you and your colleagues could look favourably upon them.'[12] Heath's private secretary, much of whose life was spent establishing who was going to pay for Heath's expensive progresses, thought that Jardine Fleming were insufficiently grateful for Heath's championship of their interests. Its chairman said that his company could not afford to pay for a suite at the Mandarin Hotel in Hong Kong and offered only a standard room. 'If that is their attitude to EH, who has done so much to help them in China, there is no point in staying at the Mandarin,' wrote the secretary indignantly. He settled for an 'extremely nice harbour view suite' at another hotel. Jardine Fleming were suitably chastened by the snub. The deputy chairman, reported the private secretary, 'has arranged a very special boat for EH on the Sunday and a lavish lunch on board'.[13] Usually the Chinese Government met any cost for internal travel within China if COSCO did not foot the bill; Heath had some difficulty in persuading the Chinese Ambassador that, since Hong Kong was part of China, their responsibilities began there and not when he arrived in Beijing. The Chinese seem to have thought none the less of Heath because he so vigorously promoted the interests of British firms. Only once did they show mild disquiet: when they decreed that only one British insurance company could operate in Beijing. Heath recommended one; the Chinese worried lest it might not be the choice of the British Government: 'Can't you agree with the Ambassador?' asked the minister responsible.[14]

In the years after he fell from power Heath travelled enormously, to China in particular, frequently to the United States and Western Europe, more occasionally to at least another dozen countries. His writing, his music and his sailing made great demands on his time and energies. Even though his attendance record in the House of Commons was poor, he still regarded his political activities as the central feature of his life. Yet throughout 1975 and 1976, indeed until the 1980s, he was a sick man. Even though he still spent many energetic hours at sea he was noticeably overweight. In Paris in 1978 Nicholas Henderson was struck by his fatness; to which he seemed indifferent. Indeed, he made something of a joke of it. When thanking Lady Aldington for Christmas presents which included some blue pants, he remarked that they were 'both practical and pleasant, but to be perfectly honest I was a little hurt that they should be labelled "extra very large"'. When taken to one of Paris's better restaurants he protested that he never ate lunch, then devoured a hearty meal. He gobbled sweets and chocolates whenever offered them. Overeating in itself was of little significance, but when coupled with his increasing tendency to fall asleep at inappropriate moments suggested that something might be seriously wrong. The worst moment had been when he was sitting next to the Queen at a dinner at Number 10. After finishing with the dignitary on her right she turned to Heath, only to find that his eyes were closed and he was snoring peacefully. By 1975 he would often drop off in the middle of a conversation and resume it a few moments later with no apparent awareness that there had been any interruption. Sara Morrison continued to urge Dr Warren to take some action, but found that he still pooh-poohed any suggestion that there was something seriously wrong. Then Kitson mentioned to the Aldingtons that he had just left Heath shivering in three layers of jersey crouched over an electric fire. Lord Aldington had long been worried about Heath's condition; now he took charge and called in an eminent diagnostician. Within twenty-four hours an underactive thyroid had been detected. The condition was seriously debilitating, but not difficult to treat. Once convinced that he was ill, Heath on the whole proved a conscientious patient. He never wholly cured his tendency to sleep at inappropriate moments – perhaps because he sometimes neglected to take his medicine – and suffered something of a setback in the spring of 1981, but he was to enjoy another twenty years of on the whole excellent health before he went into a decline in extreme old age.[15]

After the open clash at the 1978 party conference there was never any serious doubt in Mrs Thatcher's mind that there would be no room for Heath when eventually she formed a government. Early in 1979 she was interviewed in the *Observer* and said that there were two ways of putting together a Cabinet: 'One way is to have in it people who represent all the different viewpoints within the party. The other way is to have in it only the people who want to go in the direction in which every instinct tells me we have to go – clearly, steadily, firmly, with resolution … As Prime Minister, I couldn't waste time having any internal arguments. It must be a conviction Government.' Several members of the Shadow Cabinet must have wondered where this left them. Heath could have been in little doubt. His relationship with the party had grown increasingly stormy. Shortly after the 1978 conference he had received a letter from Paddy Ridsdale, the wife of a prominent Tory MP (and said to have been the model for James Bond's Miss Moneypenny). Like most Conservatives, she said, she worked very hard and willingly for the party without getting anything in return. 'You have taken everything and have given nothing in return. You cannot say that you are thinking of the country. Anyone who helps the return of a Socialist Government is certainly not thinking of the country.' Heath replied that he did not usually bother to answer letters of personal abuse,

> but I must take exception to your extraordinary statement that I have taken everything and given nothing in return. For thirty years I have made great personal sacrifices because I believed in our party – sacrifices that may not be apparent to people in your position. As I still believe in our party I shall continue to speak out for what I consider to be right. But I must add that you should not expect me to heed the advice of those who have carried out a vicious campaign against me personally … Stanley Baldwin knew what it was all about: it's a pity that a later generation doesn't.[16]

The two sides became ever more deeply entrenched: the party activists convinced that Heath was guilty of gross disloyalty, Heath equally clear that he was the victim of a monstrous campaign of denigration, organised by people very close to Mrs Thatcher. Peter Thorneycroft, the party chairman, repeatedly passed on to Heath resolutions passed by various regional associations criticising the attitude of the former prime minister. 'I should tell you as a friend', he wrote on one occasion, 'that the number of complaints of this type coming to me appears to me growing in recent months.' The Galloway Conservative Association was advised by Thorneycroft to write direct to Heath – 'This will add weight to your views' – while to the Ealing North Association Thorneycroft admitted: 'I share the concern of your Association, and Mr Heath has been made aware of the criticisms which have arisen.' To Heath such resolutions were further evidence of the conspiracy against him. He counterattacked when Patrick Cosgrave wrote a biography of Margaret Thatcher and George Gardiner reviewed it in the *Conservative Monthly News*. Gardiner criticised Heath's refusal to accept any of Thatcher's olive branches and accused him of planning to create and lead a Government of National Unity: 'How tragic it would be if he were to become entrenched as a kind of permanent centrist.' How disgraceful it was, Heath protested to Thorneycroft, that 'so partisan and untrue' an article should appear in an official Tory publication. 'How can you as Party Chairman expect to achieve unity within the Party when such unjustifiable attacks are allowed?'[17]

Nevertheless, when Callaghan finally called a general election for May 1979, it still seemed possible to some that the breach between Heath and the Tory leadership might yet be healed. Heath worked closely with Central Office, toured the country assiduously and was generally agreed to have been one of the more effective elements in the Tory campaign. He performed so well, indeed, that when things seemed to be moving in favour of Labour, Thorneycroft suggested that he be entrusted with the next party political broadcast. Mrs Thatcher exploded indignantly: 'Scared rabbits! They're running scared, that's what's the matter with them! The very idea! How dare they?' More temperately in her memoirs, she explained her view that 'to invite him to deliver a Party Political for us was tantamount to accepting defeat for the kind of policies I was advancing'. Probably Heath never knew of this exchange; if he had he would hardly have dared hope that he might be offered not just a job in the Cabinet but the post of Foreign Secretary. Yet he seems to have believed that that might be the case. Nor was it totally impossible. Long before Heath had done such good work in the election, Carrington had told Roy Jenkins that he thought that, if the Tories won, there was a 60–70 per cent chance that he, Carrington, would be at the Foreign Office: 'He doesn't totally exclude the Heath possibility but thinks it unlikely.' To Heath at least, by May 1979 the possibility seemed not merely likely but eminently proper. 'If I'd been offered Foreign Secretary,' he told the political commentator, Adam Boulton, 'which is the normal thing – I did with Alec Home – I'd have taken it.' In the small hours of the morning after the election Heath rang Mrs Thatcher to congratulate her. She chose not to take the call herself but asked her secretary, Caroline Stephens, to thank him. It was hardly encouraging but next day William Waldegrave was sent round to the new Prime Minister, carrying a letter in which Heath assured her that he put himself entirely at her disposal. At that moment, Waldegrave believes, Heath, without being wholly confident, still thought he would probably find himself back in the Cabinet in the post that, short of being Prime Minister, he most coveted.[18]

If Thatcher ever contemplated such a move she must quickly have dismissed it. To have a former prime minister in one's Cabinet, said Lord Rosebery, was 'a fleeting and dangerous luxury'. Douglas-Home, miraculously free from resentment, happy to confine himself to his own concerns, agreeing with Heath on all significant matters, had been the exception that proved the rule. Heath, in a Thatcher Cabinet, would have been a perpetual source of trouble. He would not have wanted to sit there as a member of the team, she told John Junor. All the time he would have been trying to take over. 'I have to tell you this, John. When I look at him and he looks at me, I don't feel that it is a man looking at a woman. More like a woman looking at another woman.' Quite why Mrs Thatcher *had* to tell Junor this is unclear, but the comment reveals the antipathy between the two which was more apparent on the side of Heath but was to be found lavishly in both parties.[19]

Heath spent that weekend with the Morrisons in Wiltshire. He arrived late on Friday night and stumped off to bed, saying merely: 'An egg 3¾ minutes at 8.10.' Heralded by a telephone call, a courier from Downing Street arrived even before the egg, bearing a letter to Heath from the new Prime Minister. Sara Morrison took it up to him in bed. He tried to make her leave the room while he read it but she refused to go, so Heath read it aloud. 'I have thought long and deeply about the post of Foreign Secretary,' wrote Mrs Thatcher, 'and have decided to offer it to Peter Carrington who – as I am sure you will agree – will do the job superbly.' The letter was signed coolly 'Margaret Thatcher', a detail that annoyed Heath almost as much as the message itself. A few hours later a further letter arrived from Carrington, filled with proper sentiments about his sense of awe at taking on the job and the value he would attach to Heath's counsel. 'I have always objected to your references to "Lord Creepington",' said Heath grumpily to Sara Morrison, 'but I must admit the evidence is beginning to add up!' Later that day they went to look at yet another house in the neighbourhood which Heath was thinking of buying. On the way back Heath asked if they could stop at a pub so that he could hear who Mrs Thatcher had appointed to Cabinet. Why did he not use the car radio? Sara Morrison asked him. 'Because I don't want the driver to see my face,' he replied.[20]

'Ted out. A pity,' Hailsham noted laconically in his diary. Others were more emotional. A Mrs Walker wrote to Lord Thorneycroft to express her 'utter disgust' at Heath's exclusion from the Cabinet. Thorneycroft replied emolliently that nobody doubted Heath's abilities or the contribution he had made during the election. 'Nevertheless, the number of posts available for an ex-Prime Minister is clearly limited and the claims of the new generation of Ministers ... simply cannot be ignored.' There were, he added, 'more ways of being of service to a country or a party than by filling a particular post in the Cabinet.[21] One of those ways was about to be suggested to Heath. Ten days after the election Mrs Thatcher wrote to him to offer him the post of British Ambassador in Washington. 'Who ever heard of a former Prime Minister running an Embassy,' snorted Heath indignantly. It was, indeed, an odd appointment to offer a man who had devoted much of his energies while in office to distancing Britain from the United States. Heath viewed it as a transparent attempt to get him safely out of the way; an offer which was intended to protect Mrs

Thatcher against the charge that she had totally cold-shouldered her predecessor. Certainly there was no real expectation that it would be accepted. A few days later Carrington offered the job to Heath's Balliol contemporary, Nicholas Henderson: 'Nicko,' he wrote, 'you should know that the offer was made first to you know who. It was a Num question.' ('Num' in Latin was traditionally the prefix to a question expecting the answer 'No'.) If Thatcher had hoped to appease an enemy, she failed signally. Roy Jenkins met Heath a few days later and found him in 'a very grumpy mood, partly because he had had snarl-up with Mrs Thatcher over her incredibly foolishly sending him a written offer of the Washington Embassy. A delicate sounding might have been one thing, a formal written offer was ludicrous.' Heath, Jenkins noted, 'showed every sign of wanting to pursue this with understandable vigour'.[22]

Not many people shared Mrs Walker's view that Heath's exclusion from the Cabinet was an outrage, and many of those who were prepared to be sympathetic were put off by his obvious rancour. Some of his closer associates began to distance themselves from someone who bore the stigma of being not merely a loser but a bad loser. Peter Walker, noted Roy Jenkins in his diary, 'disavowed Ted Heath, saying he had never been a close friend of his, though perhaps he ought to go and see him because he thought he was in a very poor condition and had taken to eating chocolate biscuits from morning until night, which was a very bad sign'. Heath was prepared to condone if not to applaud those of his former colleagues who took jobs in the new Cabinet, but he found it hard to forgive his younger protégés who one by one found employment under Thatcher. A moment of pique could have been excused but his ability to nurse grudges almost indefinitely became ever more apparent over the years that followed. He never forgave William Waldegrave for taking a job in the Government and hardly spoke to him; then one day in the lobby observed sardonically: 'You're not doing very well, are you?' 'I'm very angry with you,' he told Caroline Stephens, when she began to work for Mrs Thatcher in the House of Commons: she would have liked to think that he was joking but his manner made it all too clear that he was not. He would move to one side to avoid having to acknowledge the presence of

Nigel Lawson; for years he spoke hardly a word to Douglas Hurd. The main loser by this was himself: Waldegrave and Hurd admired Heath and genuinely wished him well; they would have welcomed a chance to keep in touch; but life moved on, they had careers to pursue, it was Heath who was left to feel abandoned. Tim Kitson, who had no serious political ambitions, decided to stick with his former master. If, one day, Heath managed a comeback, well and good; if, as Kitson privately thought was much more likely, he continued to languish in the wilderness, then at least Kitson could congratulate himself on his loyalty. One of the few figures from the past who remained in close touch with Heath in spite of working for the new Prime Minister was Robert Armstrong. Even Heath could hardly reproach a serving civil servant for continuing to do what he was paid for. Mrs Thatcher was equally accepting of the situation. At one point Armstrong felt bound to tell her that he had become a close friend of Heath while he had been serving him at Number 10 and was continuing to see him. 'I would think much the worse of you if you did not,' was the Prime Minister's admirable response.[23]

The period after Mrs Thatcher formed her first administration was the unhappiest of Heath's professional life and, since Heath's profession was his life, the blackest he was ever to experience. He had still not finally exorcised the dream that one day, by some twist of fate, he would return to power. Once, at Chequers, Mrs Thatcher took her guests on a tour of the house. They came to the Long Gallery, where every previous prime minister had installed his coat of arms on a stained-glass window. Every prime minister except one: Mrs Thatcher pointed out the omission. 'A tragedy. He thinks he'll be back, you see.'[24] So at first he did, but every month that passed made it more certain that he was irrevocably sidelined. There was still much to occupy him, many hours of pleasure lay ahead, but in a sense the game was over. He was almost sixty-four years old but there was more than a quarter of a century of life ahead of him. It remained to find a way to pass that time as agreeably and profitably as possible.

TWENTY-FIVE

Phased Retreat

'Why do people hate me so much?' Heath wistfully asked Peter Carrington as they stood side by side in a lavatory after the first 1974 election. The truthful answer would have been that he took remarkably little trouble to make them do anything else. A dinner at The Other Club illustrates his social manner. Someone in Woodrow Wyatt's hearing told Heath that Callaghan had resigned from the club because Wyatt had become a member. 'How sensible of him!' Heath commented. Robin Day then asked Wyatt why he didn't sit next to Heath. Wyatt turned to Heath. 'Because you wouldn't like me to sit next to you, would you?' he asked. 'No, I wouldn't,' agreed Heath. His celebrated grumpiness was in part affectation but it did not endear him to its victims. He never stopped to consider their reaction. Claus Moser invited him to the Royal Box at Covent Garden for what turned out to be a rather undistinguished performance of *Così fan tutte*. It was a tradition that when a prime minister or similar grandee was in the Box, he or she would go down on to the stage after the final curtain to meet the cast and conductor. The house manager duly invited Heath to do the honours. Heath refused: 'I would not be able to congratulate them.' The thought that good manners might require a measure of dissimulation and that he would be embarrassing his host and hurting the feelings of the cast did not enter into his mind. He had not enjoyed the production and saw no reason why he should pretend otherwise.[1]

Surrounded by innumerable acquaintances and with a number of people who could reasonably consider themselves his friends, Heath was still a lonely man. He always reacted indignantly to any such suggestion. When the journalist, Terry Coleman, remarked that he was said to have very few friends, he responded angrily that it was a myth: 'I can't bother about myths. Friends are part of one's private life. I've said again and again that the real problem is to have sufficient time to think.' It was absurd to say he had no friends, he told Nanette Newman on television.[2] He deluded himself. His closest friends – Sara Morrison, Madron Seligman, Toby Aldington – were all in the world of politics themselves; his musical or yachting friends, though they might believe otherwise, were peripheral, confined to one small, if important, sector of his life. With nobody was he intimate: intimacy and Ted Heath were indeed almost incompatible. His closest friend was his piano. When tired, depressed, anxious, it was in his piano that he found relief. What sort of music would he listen to if depressed? he was asked on television. He wouldn't listen to music, he would play it, Heath replied. Once, after a particularly stressful evening, he played the piano to Sara Morrison. 'Aren't you going to talk to me?' she demanded crossly. 'I *am* talking to you,' he retorted. Through music he could, indeed, achieve a sort of intimacy. But its effects were neither profound nor long-lasting. Late one night in Luxembourg, when Heath showed no signs of wishing to go to bed, his host, the then Ambassador, Patrick Wright, suggested that they might play two-piano duets. Heath agreed.

I have never seen a personality change so quickly or completely [Wright recalled]. After his rather taciturn behaviour earlier in the evening, he became lively and enthusiastic, virtually shouting instructions to me to play faster, slower, more loudly or softer … it must have been well after two o'clock when we finally retired for the night. Next morning, at breakfast, it was as though this had never happened; indeed, he gave the impression that he could hardly remember who I was!

One compartment in his life had opened, another closed; communication between the two was rarely possible.[3]

Outside music, he did not have the cultural resources to expand

towards new horizons. He studied newspapers with some thorough-
ness but his reading of books, unless directly connected with a job in
hand, was confined mainly to political biography and memoirs. He
rarely read fiction or poetry (and never, as he asserted with some
pride, the novels of Jeffrey Archer). He had once thought of taking
up painting but decided that it would cut too deeply into the time he
needed for his music. He enjoyed looking at other people's work and
had a good eye for quality in the more traditional fields, but painting
was not a significant feature of his life. David Butler once encountered
him by himself in the National Gallery and he claimed quite often to
drop in there, but he rarely attended exhibitions and, as he grew older,
ventured less and less beyond his own collection. His cultural life was
richer than that of most politicians, but where most of his former
colleagues had spouses and children to occupy them, Heath was
thrust back on himself. He would not have had it otherwise, but it left
a gap in his life which it was to become ever harder to fill.

He was not wholly a misogynist, but when he met a woman for the
first time his expectation was that she would not be worth talking to.
The Queen Mother once suggested to Woodrow Wyatt that he should
give a dinner party in his house which would include both her and
Heath. 'She's very fond of him,' Wyatt noted in his diary. 'She said,
"Of course, he doesn't like women".'[4] He would have made an exception of Queen Elizabeth, but as a generalisation her comment was well
founded. He liked to have a roster of unattached women who would
accompany him to concerts and operas. Michael Wolff's widow,
Rosemary, was one of them. So, though she was more likely to be a
performer than a companion, was the pianist Moura Lympany. Heath
greatly admired Lympany's playing. When Malcolm Williamson
recommended her for a DBE, he supported the proposal enthusiastically: not only was she a superb pianist but: 'She is more generous
than any other musician I know in the giving of her time and energy
for those causes she espouses.' But after that it was the story of Kay
Raven over again. 'Dearest Ted,' began a letter from Lympany, inviting him to two concerts and a birthday party. 'Dear Moura,' began
the typewritten reply, refusing all the invitations. 'I think she chased
him,' said Nancy-Joan Seligman. 'She was too obvious.' Lympany

once admitted to Denis Healey that she would have liked to have married Heath but he backed off; when the papers began to hint at a romance he recoiled still more obviously.

There was not even a suspicion of romance when it came to June Osborn: 'He had never so much as held her hand,' she told James Lees-Milne, 'far less breathed a word of love.' Nevertheless he had grown accustomed to her being available when he wanted an intelligent and musically well-informed companion at Glyndebourne or Covent Garden. Had he been a cosy companion? asked Lees-Milne. 'No, for he shuns all conversation, all intimacy. He is terrified of talk which is not about national or international issues.' He treated her with characteristic offhandedness. Once she drove him back from Glyndebourne. He spoke not a word until they were a few hundred yards from their destination, when he began to bark out a series of directions: 'Left here. Stop there.' He then stumped off into the night without a word of thanks. Yet he was, by his own lights, fond of Mrs Osborn and valued her company. He would unhesitatingly have put himself out to help her if she had been in any sort of difficulty. When she married the eminent lawyer, Jeremy Hutchinson, he treated her thereafter with marked coolness; he had never contemplated marrying her himself but when she settled for someone else he felt let down. At dinner with the Hutchinsons, Lees-Milne noticed that Heath ignored his hostess and the woman on his right but talked across the table to Yehudi Menuhin. 'He has no social graces whatever,' wrote Lees-Milne. 'For this I like him. He is not faintly interested in women, and probably not in men either.'[5]

One of his preoccupations was to find a permanent home. Wilton Street served well as a London base but he hankered for something out of the city, more spacious, where he could display his rapidly growing tally of possessions and entertain on a grander scale than was at present possible. With the death of his brother in 1982 his links with Broadstairs, which had been growing more tenuous over the years, finally snapped. The Isle of Wight seemed an obvious alternative, but as sailing began to play a smaller part in his life the disadvantages of exile with five miles of water separating him from potential visitors became more apparent. He made use of his loyal friends – Sara Morrison and Tim Kitson in particular – to scour the country in search of a suitable house, but though they visited many properties on his behalf all seemed to have fatal flaws. Then his pps, the MP for Salisbury, rang to say that a house in the Cathedral Close had come available for a long lease. Heath visited it the following day and was instantly convinced that this was where he wished to spend the rest of his life.

Arundells is a medieval house substantially rebuilt in the late seventeenth century. A Victorian ballroom had been tacked on at the back but was removed when the Dean and Chapter let out the house in the 1960s. Its handsome Queen Anne facade is set well back from the narrow road that skirts the Close and the 1.6 acres of garden include splendid lawns running down to the river Avon. The lease was for an initial twenty-one years at £500 a year, after which there was an option to renew at a price to be mutually agreed. The price of the lease was originally set at £250,000, though Heath seems to have paid less for it. It was expensive but it was worth it and Heath knew that it could and must be managed. Its crowning glory was the spectacular prospect of the Cathedral from the front windows. Roy Jenkins spent the night there and was duly impressed. 'Ted, it must be one of the ten finest views in Britain,' he said at breakfast the following day. 'Oh, really, which do you think are the other nine?' Heath retorted.

No one disputed the splendour of its situation or the handsomeness of its facade, but some were more critical of the interior. 'Very disappointing,' James Lees-Milne found it. 'From a dreary flagged hall a long straight passage leads past a drawing room on the left to the sitting room … in which we wait. Ceiling spotlights focus on nothing worth looking at. Several tiers of watercolours of yachts on green seas.' Possibly Lees-Milne was prejudiced by the fact that Heath knew nothing of his guests and treated them in a decidedly offhand manner. He described his host disparagingly as an 'enormous behind, bulging over baggy trousers. Quite short he is, up to my shoulder. Appearance suggests a beer barrel aboard deck poised on two inadequate supports.'[6]

The watercolours of yachts, pleasant enough in themselves, were only a minor part of a distinguished collection. In 1997, before Wilton Street was disposed of and the furniture and pictures in the main brought down to Salisbury, the contents of the two houses were valued for insurance purposes at £1.16 million. Of this more than half was accounted for by painting and prints. The most valuable were the two oils by Winston Churchill; one, a landscape of the South of France, with the curious distinction of having been signed twice – once when originally painted and once some years later when Churchill failed to notice that it already bore his signature and added a second for good measure. Together these were valued at £140,000. They had both been gifts, as had the two Sargents (£85,000) and a Sickert. The paintings by John Piper, including two of Arundells, had for the most part been bought but at advantageous prices. As much as any of the paintings he cherished the original working sketch of the concluding bars of *Der Rosenkavalier*. Strauss had autographed this and given it to Margot Asquith; it had been presented to Heath when he was prime minister.

The collection was that of a man who had natural good taste but did not enjoy spending money unnecessarily. This was particularly marked in the assembly of Oriental ceramics. All the finest pieces – a pair of Qianlong Chinese globular bottles (valued at £30,000), a Tang horse (£14,000) and a Qianlong blue-and-white vase (£12,000) – had been given him by foreign governments or grateful clients. Without asking directly for coveted items (except once when he persuaded Arthur Andersen to let him have a desk in their Edinburgh office which had belonged to Lloyd George) he was delighted to receive gifts, preferring to describe them as 'presentations'. The phrase became something of a joke: Richard Burn, his private secretary, told Heath that he had found one or two good bits of Chinese porcelain 'but can't think of anyone to make the presentation'. Some gifts were more mundane. Sir David Alliance, the immensely rich creator of Coats Viyella, sent him a case of Dom Perignon champagne for Christmas. He got his money's worth. A few months later he was anxious to secure a visa for an Iranian whose wife was due to have a Caesarean section in London. The Consul in Tehran rejected the application. Alliance appealed to Heath, who in turn approached Douglas Hurd, by then Foreign Secretary. Hurd said that the Consul's ruling must be upheld but relented when Heath pointed out that there were strong humanitarian reasons for making an exception. Another case of Dom Perignon arrived at Arundells the following Christmas.[7]

Heath knew where he was with the paintings; when it came to the ceramics he was content to depend on the advice of experts. He brought a young Chinese to call on Michael Butler, who had a notable collection of blue-and-white, sat unexpectedly silent as Butler expatiated on his pieces, and at the end said in some surprise: 'I never knew there was so much to say about porcelain.' He was most put out when Butler pointed out that a piece of blue-and-white presented to him by the Chinese Government was a modern copy.[8] Of higher quality was a group of early nineteenth-century bone ship models valued at £76,000. As well as all this was a mass of memorabilia including four silver models of the various *Morning Clouds* and a host of framed and signed photographs featuring Heath and the Queen, Heath and Churchill, Heath and Macmillan, and Heath with a host of other dignitaries deemed worthy to grace his grand piano or other suitable surfaces. The overall effect was by no means as undistinguished as Lees-Milne suggested but it was perhaps too tidy, too correct, very much the house of a bachelor who prided himself on his possessions and felt ill at ease if anything was out of place.

He took equal pride in his garden and liked to think that he made an important contribution to its planning. When Stuart Craven, who was to play an ever more important role in the life of Arundells until Heath's death and, indeed, thereafter, took over as head gardener, Heath sought to impress him by airing his knowledge of Latin names. Craven found that he had a gardening encyclopaedia in his room and would swot up the details before venturing an opinion. At one point he threatened to adopt a more hands-on approach but, perhaps fortunately, fell off a ladder when pruning a magnolia and never offered to help again. Even in extreme old age he would love to walk down the lawn as far as the river: he could not tell one bird from another – on one occasion failing even to recognise a magpie – and took little interest in the local fauna but he grew fond of an Egyptian goose, known as Pharaoh, which had taken up residence on the bank.

Pharaoh was enough of a rarity, and behaved with sufficient eccentricity, to become something of a talking-point in the neighbourhood. In Heath's eyes, thought Craven, it conferred distinction on the house and thus was classed with the Churchill paintings or the models of *Morning Cloud* as a valued possession. Not everyone admired the choice of flowers. Sara Morrison took exception to the red geraniums which were a prominent feature of the gardens. 'What's wrong with them?' demanded Heath. 'They're as bad as gnomes!' 'Elitist snobbery,' snorted Heath dismissively. When Craven asked him whether he would like the geraniums changed, he ruled that they should stay. 'It seems to annoy some people,' he observed with satisfaction.

Increasingly Heath became attached to Arundells, often being driven down from London late at night so that he could wake up in the Close rather than Wilton Street. His routine when there was almost invariable. He watched television often but usually only for news and current affairs, occasionally cricket or tennis. He took a surprising interest in American football and infuriated Sara Morrison by not taking her to the Cup Final, which he knew she would have adored, but instead trying to persuade her to accompany him to the United States for the Super Bowl – a fate which she would have thought little, if at all, better than death. He listened only occasionally to music on his extremely sophisticated and expensive system; he played the piano himself a lot for the first decade or so at Arundells but increasingly gave up thereafter.

For food he favoured traditional French cooking, was unenthusiastic about Italian, and deplored Indian and Chinese – at least as served in Salisbury. After 1990 or so he never ate a cooked breakfast, never drank milk and ate little bread. He preferred fish to meat, finding it easier to digest. He fancied himself as an authority on wine but his housekeeper, who was genuinely expert, maintained that he was guided only by the label and would not have been able to tell claret from burgundy in a blind tasting. He rarely smoked, and then only cigars. He loved to entertain and was a generous host: lunch for ten or twelve on Sunday being his favourite occasion. He enjoyed mixing up celebrities of different species: Princess Margaret and Dame Maggie Smith, Sir Alec Guinness and the Archbishop of Canterbury, a stray ambassador and Michael Palin. The *place à table* was rigidly formal, the conversation often general and orchestrated by the host. Nicholas Henderson found the atmosphere at such lunches 'painfully tight. Even as host he could not bring himself to say more than a few words to the women on either side.' It depended, perhaps, on the woman: Sally Sampson, wife of the writer Anthony, was a particularly favoured guest who rarely found conversation dragged. On the other hand, when a bold but neglected neighbour at dinner asked him crossly: 'Well, are you going to talk to me?' Heath is said to have reflected for a moment and then answered 'No'. The possibility that he might abruptly fall asleep was still a threat. Sara Morrison and Mary Lou de Zulueta were lunching at Arundells on Derby Day and were particularly anxious to watch the race. 'I think that could be arranged,' promised Heath, but as the time grew nearer and a large Stilton was put on the table in front of him, he merely stared glumly at it. Impatiently, Sara Morrison snapped: 'Are you going to do anything with that Stilton or just look at it?' Heath sprang into action and dismissed them to the television, joining them a few minutes before the race. By the time the horses came under starter's orders he was fast asleep.

He was both a considerate and a notably unobservant employer. When his housekeeper at Arundells was being asked to do too much and was near breaking point, it took strong remonstrances from Sara Morrison and Minta Aldington to persuade him to do anything about it. His housekeeper in London once asked him whether she was doing all he required of her. 'I don't know,' Heath replied unhelpfully. But when he became aware that somebody who worked for him was in need he was generous and considerate. When the Salisbury housekeeper fell ill he insisted on paying all the expenses. Stuart Craven's marriage broke up and Heath took a keen interest in the proceedings. He strongly urged Craven not to take her back: 'If she's gone you can never trust her again.'[9]

Arundells cost Heath £10–12,000 a year to run; something which for the first ten or fifteen years after his loss of office was easily within his resources. He was indignant when an article by John Junor in the *Mail on Sunday* in 1996 described him as fabulously rich. 'How did

Sir Ted become loaded?' asked Junor. Could it perhaps be 'through having pursued a policy throughout his life of seldom if ever putting his hand in his pocket?' 'What a filthy insinuation to suggest that I have lived by begging, borrowing or stealing from other people,' expostulated Heath. He had lived frugally, had paid for his house and possessions by 'continuous hard work, by saving and by avoiding every kind of extravagance', he had written three bestselling books and was well paid for his lectures. He was indeed: in the 1980s and 1990s he earned on average more than £100,000 a year from lecturing: $15,000 from the University Club in Milwaukee, $20,000 from the Ford European Advisory Council, $25,000 from the Mastercard International Conference in Beijing. He made no bones about the fact that he expected to be rewarded and rewarded handsomely for his contributions. In 1983 the Economic Club in Detroit asked him to address them but said there would be no fee. 'I see no reason', Heath replied indignantly, 'why I should speak to a large gathering of tycoons who all proclaim themselves to be entrepreneurs and doubt-less as a result earn large incomes – and I see no reason why they should come to benefit from any experience I may have had or know-ledge I may have accumulated without payment of any kind.'

If the money was right he was not too concerned about the nature of his audience. A Canadian newspaper claimed that Heath had given three addresses at meetings of the World Peace Organisation, a front for the Unification Church, the Moonies. Fees paid by this body averaged between £35,000 and £50,000. Heath retorted that Al Haig and Gorbachev had spoken in the same forum, that he had never met the Revd Mr Moon and was not a member of the movement and that he had simply told his audience about the international situation as he saw it. He refused to discuss the scale of his fees. When to such earnings is added such items as the 30,000 Hong Kong dollars paid in August 1997 as the latest quarterly payment from COSCO it becomes clear that Heath was, if not fabulously rich as John Junor maintained, at least very well off. He found it hard to admit or even to believe that this was so. Like many people who have once been seriously poor, he could not accept that his prosperity was here to stay; at any moment the crock of gold might disappear or turn to lead. He was obsessed by the need to accumulate, to build up a cushion of financial security which would guarantee a comfortable and dignified old age.[10]

In the mid-1990s he had need to encroach upon his accumulated wealth. Legislation had recently been passed which permitted holders of long leases to convert their leases into freeholds. If the property was above a certain value, however, the owner, when the lease was drawn up, had the right to insert a clause which removed the tenant's right to buy out the landlord. Arundells was comfortably above that level, but by an oversight the estate agent who handled the matter for the Dean and Chapter omitted to include an exceptive clause. Heath's solicitors spotted this and advised their client that, if he wanted, he could acquire the freehold. The value was put at £700,000. The Dean, Hugh Dickinson, tried to persuade Heath that the house was a valuable part of the patrimony of the Cathedral. If he insisted on exercising his legal rights and acquiring the freehold, the decent thing would be to return it to the Dean and Chapter after his death. 'Unsurprisingly,' writes Dickinson, 'he didn't see it that way and I got a dusty answer.' News of the affair got into the papers and Heath was much criticised. 'I haven't at any point had any contact whatever with the press about the purchase of Arundells,' Dickinson told him. 'The implication of my photo alongside yours in the *Express* feature is quite false.' Nevertheless, the fact that the Bishop, Dean and Chapter felt that they had been hardly used became well known and most of those living in or around the Close took their side. Even such a habitual supporter of Heath as Jim Prior considered that his behaviour had been deplorable: 'He was in honour bound to let Arundells return to the Church of England after his death.' The dispute was exacerbated by Heath's habit of gloating over the way in which he had put one over the Dean and Chapter and bought the freehold of Arundells against their wishes.[11]

There was never any question of Heath being ostracised within the Close. The Bishop and Dean continued to visit him and their intercourse was superficially affable. Nevertheless, there was a certain coolness about the relationship. This was sad, because Heath loved the Cathedral and contributed energetically to the campaign to save the spire. He was offended when girls were admitted to the choir – 'We don't want bloody women,' he told the Dean – but he took an enthusiastic interest in the music and was a frequent attender at the services. The Close was a tightly knit society. Heath would never wholly have integrated with it; it was not his way to do so; but his social life would have been easier and he would have felt less lonely if the affair of the freehold had not added a touch of poison to the atmosphere.

The money for the freehold was raised by a mortgage. Heath disliked being in debt and his wish to pay off the loan was one of the factors that made him finally address himself to the long outstanding matter of his memoirs. The path to their publication was protracted and at times somewhat murky. In 1984 he had signed a contract with Weidenfeld & Nicolson for 'a lively, forthright, anecdotal and colourful book of reminiscences as well as analysis'. He would, he promised, 'spill every uncensored detail'. Gratified by this prospect the *Sunday Times* took on the serial rights. Michael Trend, son of Heath's former Cabinet Secretary, was enlisted to do the donkey work. The book would, it was promised, be ready in the near future. A year later Andrew Neil, editor of the *Sunday Times*, froze his offer: there was no evidence that real progress was being made and 'since with every day the Heath years recede into the distance, this contract becomes less valuable to me'. Weidenfeld, who had paid Heath a substantial advance, though out of money provided by the *Sunday Times*, soldiered on. In 1988, when things at last seemed to be moving, the *Sunday Times* reinstated its offer. Six months later George Weidenfeld was writing pleadingly to Heath, urging him to give 'the writing of your memoirs the kind of concentration and priority it requires ... This is not just a hectoring letter on the part of a deeply frustrated publisher, it is a genuine *cri de coeur* ... Your voice should be heard and your views be authoritatively documented in the shortest possible time.'

When in doubt as to how to respond to a letter Heath's usual tactic was to ignore it. Weidenfeld got no reply to his appeal, nor to his rather more reproachful letter six months later in which he accused Heath of agreeing with another publisher to write a book on Europe without even offering it to Weidenfeld & Nicolson: 'May I ask you to have the friendliness and courtesy to tell me quite candidly whether you are still working on the memoirs and, if so, when you intend to complete the manuscript?' Another six months passed and Weidenfeld tried the ploy of asking whether Heath would be prepared to collaborate on an authorised biography which would '... be largely under your control ... Please, Ted, for the sake of our long acquaintance and, dare I say, friendship, send me a letter by return.' The return passed but no letter came.[12]

Meanwhile an important but unauthorised biography appeared. Heath had refused to cooperate but had given John Campbell the impression that he would not seek to deter other people from doing so. To du Cann he suggested that he should treat Campbell 'like any other journalist. I am not assisting Dr Campbell with his book as I am myself involved in writing my memoirs but I have no objection to anyone else seeing him.' To his closest allies he was more outspoken. He had only met Campbell once, he told Robert Armstrong, 'when we discovered he was following us canvassing in Bexley and eavesdropping on the doorstep. Personally, I did not form a very good impression of him ... May I suggest that it would be appropriate for you to decline Dr Campbell's request.' Campbell's biography appeared in 1993, a fair and balanced account which, though inevitably limited by the fact that he had seen none of Heath's or the official papers, provided a remarkably full and authoritative account of Heath's career. Heath, unsurprisingly, did not find it to his taste. His line, when asked what he thought of it, was to say that he had not had the time to read it. To Robin Day he unwisely added that, even if he had time, he could not afford £20. Day at once volunteered to lend Heath his copy. 'You're trying to lead me astray,' said Heath. 'I don't think I could do that,' Day retorted. Heath's protestations would have been more convincing if he had not heavily annotated the first 350 pages of his copy of Campbell's book, marking with particular emphasis any suggestion that he was preoccupied by his social standing.[13]

'I'd hate that to be the final record,' Heath told Sara Morrison. It was as much a wish to put the record straight, to correct the errors of interpretation of which he believed Campbell to be guilty, as a need for money, which led him at last to throw himself more energetically into the task of writing his memoirs. Another factor was the appearance on the scene of the literary agent, Michael Sissons. Sissons surveyed the backlog of correspondence with some dismay. 'What is missing', he wrote to Heath in August 1994, 'is any sign of a real determination or impetus on your part to tackle the project within a finite time scale.' Satisfied that Heath really did now intend to address the task, he concluded that the partnership with Weidenfeld had been irredeemably soured; indeed, that the fact that Heath was unable to work with his publishers was one of the main factors inhibiting any progress on the book. The best thing to do was to cancel the contract, repay the advance and look for a new publisher. All went relatively smoothly, Hodder & Stoughton took over the project, and by the end of 1994, three research assistants were 'working intensively on different sections of the book'. He still lacked 'a main assistant', Heath told Sissons. Martin Gilbert was summoned to lunch to advise on who could perform this task and soon realised that he was being cast for the role himself. He regretfully refused. In the event Michael McManus, Heath's private secretary, did most of the research, while Robert Armstrong gallantly volunteered to mastermind the whole operation.[14]

The first draft was disseminated widely. The response was unenthusiastic. Mark Garnett, another of the younger men who had done preliminary work on the book, said that the bits of text he had seen were 'as dry (if not worse) than they were when I stopped working on them'. He had hoped that Heath would produce a book which 'it would be difficult for the right to attack. I'm afraid that, as a result of my failure, the project seems to have lapsed into a mechanical exercise in making money for Sir Edward whatever the critical consequences.' Sara Morrison, the recipient of this wail, responded sympathetically: 'Oh dear, it's sad and difficult – but time will pass. One day someone will write a book that is about the real and whole Ted. He couldn't reveal or allow that in his lifetime.' Her own complaint was about the lavish use of 'I'. 'I am fearful this will set in motion all the critics who will berate for smugness, self-regarding complacency or something of the kind.' A phrase that particularly offended her was: 'When I won the 1970 General Election ...' At her suggestion this was changed to 'When the Conservatives ...' Tom Bridges took similar exception to the reference to 'my Government'. It was not Heath's Government, he pointed out to McManus, 'it's the Queen's Government'.[15]

In April 1998 Tony Benn asked Heath when his memoirs were coming out. In September, he was told, but 'they're very expensive'. That's because of the quality of the book, said Benn, and possibly 'because they don't think there'll be a huge sale. So he laughed and his shoulders shook, as they do.'[16] Heath's intention had been to call his book *The Last Laugh*: 'This title might have conveyed something of my true view of the world – a little sardonic at times, perhaps, but never, I hope, jaundiced.' In the end he was persuaded that this would be unwise; it was the reviewers who were going to have the last laugh and to offer them an opening of this kind would be tempting fate. He was called on to provide a list of Americans who were both prominent and well disposed. He suggested David Rockefeller; Kay Graham, proprietor of the *Washington Post*; his old Balliol friend, the ambassador Phil Kaiser. What about Kissinger? he was asked. 'He won't like my bits about him.' Sure enough, he didn't. Having tarried so long over the writing, Heath was reluctant to let it go and, until the final proofs were wrenched from him, indulged in frenzied last-minute tinkering. 'The quantity of amendments you have produced is unprecedented (about fifteen times greater than any other author in my two decades of editing),' complained the publisher. 'I understand the desire to get the book right, but the elastic has now snapped.' McManus proposed that the launch party should be held in the Cabinet War Rooms – 'a very atmospheric venue', he suggested. Atmospheric perhaps, but the wrong atmosphere, Heath considered: 'I don't want myself or the book to be associated with war. Drop it.'[17] In the end the party was held in the publishers' offices. When the time came for him to speak Heath announced, in a loud and portentous voice: 'At last we can say: "the sulk is over".' It wasn't, of course.

Given the number of cooks intent on spoiling the broth and the fact that Heath himself was a dry, even ungainly writer, *The Course of My Life* is remarkably readable and even, at points, revealing. The critics did not fail to point out its flaws. 'His prose style tends to the aldermanic and his jokes to the ponderous,' wrote Ian McIntyre in *The Times*; 'The author's famous arrogance and his lack of generosity towards those whose contribution he judges inferior are writ large here to the point of self-caricature,' wrote Matthew Parris in the *Sunday Telegraph*; 'You learn little of what made him the way he is,' was Michael Cockerell's complaint in the *Observer*. All these were fair comments. But Parris also said that bits were 'really quite fun. Other parts are little short of moving. The whole is well-written and the style personal. Those who feared this book would be "ghosted" should set their fears at rest. Though breaks in the prose style suggest that Sir Edward has relied on assistance with certain sections, the work retains a distinct and individual flavour.' This is the strength of the book. It is written with a personal voice – not necessarily melodious or particularly comfortable to listen to, but strong, clear, and appropriate to the material. The most unexpected praise came from one of his fiercest critics, Alan Clark. In the *Daily Telegraph* Clark opened with a denunciation of Heath's record as leader – his destruction of the Ulster Unionists, mishandling of the economy and the unions, bungling of elections – but then continued: 'I was surprised at how absorbing and sympathetic I found his autobiography. It is written without obvious rancour. There is neither whinging nor self-advertisement ... I now find myself filled with respect and (if it were not impertinent to say so) affection for Ted.' 'Freedom from rancour' is perhaps over-generous but it is indeed impossible to read *The Course of My Life* without enhanced respect for the author and a better understanding of the forces that impelled him.[18]

The publication of his memoirs was not accompanied by the sort of razzmatazz that Sidgwick & Jackson had indulged in for his earlier books. Partly this was because of the nature of the book; partly – as Benn had suggested – because expectations of sales were not particularly high; most of all because of Heath's own inclinations. Heath was over eighty by the time his autobiography came out, and, though still fit for his age, was overweight and reluctant to indulge in anything too stressful. Over the previous years he had cut down heavily on his interviews and appearances on television or radio programmes. He was still a prominent figure, however, and from time to time re-appeared in the public eye. At the end of 1988 Madron Seligman's daughter, Olivia, who was producer for the series, had asked him to do the Christmas edition of *Desert Island Discs*. Heath had evidently forgotten that twelve years before he had agreed with Stephen Sherbourne that the formula was sketchy and unsatisfactory and the programme not worth appearing on. On this occasion it was the BBC who proved reluctant, telling Miss Seligman that Heath had already appeared on the programme and was thus ineligible. Researches were made and it was discovered that Ted Heath had indeed featured: it was, however, the eponymous bandleader who had reigned supreme in the 1950s and 1960s. The way was clear for Heath to choose his own eight records.

His selection was eclectic and comfortably free of any attempt to impress his audience. He chose the slow movement from Dvorak's *New World Symphony*; his own recordings of Elgar's 'Cockaigne' overture and the carol 'Hark! The Herald Angels Sing'; Topol singing 'If I were a Rich Man' from *Fiddler on the Roof* – an odd choice, he admitted, but one which conveyed 'the sadness of people who aren't in their own homes and find very little possibility of ever getting to what they really regard as home'. He chose that particular song, he said, because he knew that he was never going to be worried by the problem of what to do if he were a rich man himself – the trio from the last act of *Der Rosenkavalier*; Vaughan Williams's *Sea Symphony* and Schubert's Piano Trio in B Flat. As his book he asked for a complete set of Hansard going back to the eighteenth century but was denied it and made do with 'a comprehensive volume of the works of the impressionist painters'. His choice of luxury, fishing tackle, was similarly rejected but, after some hesitation, suntan lotion was permitted.

The record he picked as the one he would retain if all others had to be sacrificed was the 'Prisoners' Chorus' from *Fidelio*. *Fidelio*, he claimed, was the greatest of operas, and above all others extolled the glories of freedom, 'and this is really what I've always looked for in my political life'. To some extent he may have identified with Florestan, languishing as he was, if not in a dungeon, then in political exile, while wicked Pizarro/Thatcher triumphed over him. The Don Fernando who rescued him was to materialise in the slightly improbable guise of Geoffrey Howe. Heath's tragedy was that he had no Leonora, that with the downfall of Pizarro/Thatcher he emerged into the light of liberty but had no one with whom to share his joy. As the gloriously triumphant 'Hail to the Day!' acclaimed the return of freedom, Heath was left to trudge back alone to Arundells and shut the door behind him in a house that was comfortable, elegant, luxurious even, but sadly empty.[19]

TWENTY-SIX

Filling in Time

Heath's main preoccupation in the twenty or so years or so that followed his fall from power was to convince himself that he was doing something of importance. Even when he had accepted that there was no way by which he could hope to find a way back into the Cabinet, let alone Number 10, he sought to remain in the public eye and to be seen to be performing a role of national, better still international, significance. To put it more positively: he knew that he still had much to offer and was anxious not to waste his talents.

The needs of the developing world, providing as they did a cause which Heath genuinely had at heart, and which offered the opportunity of almost limitless travel, seemed particularly suitable. Heath had been active in this world since the first United Nations Conference on Trade and Development (UNCTAD) in 1964 in Geneva, when he had represented the British Government. Since then he had consistently argued the case for greater aid for the underdeveloped world and for generous policies over trade and tariffs. When the president of the World Bank, Robert McNamara, decided in 1977 to set up a high-powered independent commission to consider development issues and invited the former German Chancellor, Willy Brandt, to act as its chairman, it was likely that Heath would be one of the first people to be asked to serve. The other British name suggested had been that of Alec Douglas-Home: Brandt told Roy Jenkins that he thought Heath was more appropriate for the role. From the developed world came also Olof Palme, former prime minister of Sweden; Kay Graham; and Peter Peterson, an immensely rich American businessman and briefly Nixon's Secretary of Commerce. Most active from the developing countries was Sonny Ramphal, Secretary-General of the Commonwealth, but there were also the Kuwaiti Foreign Minister and an Indian, Algerian and Colombian who were prominent in their countries' administrations. The terms of reference were as imposing as the membership. Its Report was to aim at 'the reconstruction of the world economy'. The North had unused resources, the South insatiable demand; unless these two could be reconciled the South could never prosper and the world must inevitably drift into recession.[1] The money for the study was mainly put up by the Dutch. 'Mrs Thatcher's government contributed nothing,' Heath wrote in his memoirs, a comment that seems a little ungracious given that in April 1978 Judith Hart, Labour Minister for Overseas Development, had told him that her ministry had promised £150,000 for the work of the Commission.[2]

The Commission met ten times in nine different countries. By the time their final meeting was held at Leeds Castle in Kent, Mrs Thatcher had become prime minister and Carrington foreign secretary. Heath wanted the Government to grant the delegates VIP status. A letter was drafted for him making this request. The original draft went on to say that he would have asked the British Government to meet the full cost of the meeting, as every other Government had done. However, he had refrained from doing so since: 'I did not wish the Commission to receive a rebuff from HMG. The total cost of the meeting is therefore being covered by the Swiss and Netherlands Governments.' Presumably Heath realised that this sentence would be calculated to annoy Carrington and thus make it more likely that his request for VIP status would be refused. He struck it out. It represented his real views, however. 'Please keep this excellent first draft,' he minuted.[3]

The Commission's report, North-South: A Progress for Survival, was completed early in 1980. Sonny Ramphal and Heath largely took over from an ailing Brandt and were responsible for presenting a draft at Leeds Castle and steering it through the sometimes turbulent debate that followed. It was, claimed Heath with some vainglory, 'the clearest analysis of the problems of the North and South, together with the most constructive and detailed series of proposals for dealing with them, that has ever been published'. Oliver Wright, the British Ambassador in Bonn, reported that Brandt had praised Heath's performance to the skies and said that without his efforts 'the necessary compromises would probably not have been found'. Heath did not return the compliment. He makes it clear in his memoirs that, as a chairman, he considered Brandt to have been a disaster: ill-organised, histrionic and with no clear vision of where he would like the Commission to go, let alone by what route it should proceed. Nevertheless, the report was well received by the experts and, thanks largely to Heath's efforts, attracted a lot of attention in the UK. It was published by Pan and by the end of March had sold more than 30,000 copies with a reprint imminent. In the bestseller lists for April 1980 it lay tenth among the paperbacks, just ahead of Egon Ronay's *Good Pub Guide*.[4]

In the long term the Brandt Report undoubtedly helped awaken consciousness of the plight of the developing world and a realisation that something must be done. In the short term it achieved little. Donald Maitland summed up the attitude of the British Government as 'Benevolence without enthusiasm'. 'Is there a better example of tactful bureaucratese?' asked Stephen Sherbourne. 'Agreed,' minuted Heath. So far as President Reagan was concerned there was not even benevolence. At a conference in Mexico in October 1981 to debate the issues Reagan stressed that the Third World countries must learn to stand on their own feet; the West should help them to become self-supporting but not offer financial support. 'In other words,' he told President Nyerere, 'I will help you buy the fishing rod, but after that the rest lies with you. You must fish in your own pond to support yourselves.' 'But what happens if you haven't got a pond with any fish?' retorted Nyerere. Heath styled the conference 'a terrible disappointment' and accused the western leaders, by implication Thatcher as much as Reagan, of a 'lack of imagination and willpower'. He himself continued to press for greater aid for the developing world and a better understanding of its problems. He made little progress within his own party; indeed the fact that he was advocating such a course may even have dimmed whatever limited enthusiasm for the project there might have been, but at least Labour seemed more ready to listen. In July 1981, in the House of Commons, Stanley Clinton Davis wound up the debate for the Opposition with a tribute to Heath for 'his dedication ... in making a unique and remarkable contribution to international thinking. It is an inspiring example.'[5]

Heath was wholly sincere in his support for the developing world and did not delude himself that it was a cause likely to win him much support from the British electorate. He was not driven by self-interest. All the same, he did relish being at the centre of the stage, especially since his presence there was likely to cause irritation to Mrs Thatcher. In October 1990 another opportunity arose to claim the limelight and annoy the Prime Minister, but this time in a cause which he felt would be generally more popular. In August of that year Saddam Hussein's Iraq invaded and annexed the oil-rich emirate of Kuwait; an area which the Iraqis claimed had long been part of their proper patrimony. The United Nations, under American leadership, began laboriously to build up a force in the Gulf capable of evicting the Iraqis and restoring Kuwait to independence. Heath, with some reservations, accepted the need to prepare for war but insisted that first every diplomatic avenue should be explored. In a television interview with Brian Walden he argued that a major war was unnecessary; the Arabs could perfectly well sort the matter out for themselves. Comparisons which were being made between Saddam Hussein and Hitler were wide of the mark. The West should make generous concessions to Iraq so as to render a withdrawal from Kuwait more palatable. He took this line in part because Mrs Thatcher was being notably belligerent and it was a pleasure to gainsay her: much more, however, he believed that the Kuwaiti regime was corrupt and decadent, that the Iraqi case was not wholly without merit and that a settlement could be reached which would not imperil the stability of the Middle East and involve the almost certain destruction of the Kuwaiti oilfields. When Tony Benn urged him to join with Brandt, Pierre Trudeau, J. K. Galbraith, Rajiv Gandhi and others in an appeal for peace, he did not rule out the possibility and suggested that Robert McNamara might also be a signatory. He felt that American opinion was changing and that, in the House of Commons, a lot of Tory back-benchers were beginning to have doubts about the Government's hard line.[6]

Faced with the threat of war, Saddam rounded up a large number of foreign nationals living in Iraq or Kuwait, including more than a thousand Britons, and dispersed them around the country as hostages in what was termed a 'human shield'. Some of these prisoners were in poor health. Heath's stance had earned him some criticism as an appeaser of an aggressive dictator but he had more generally become recognised as an independent-minded moderate who had refrained from actually endorsing Saddam's regime but was likely to be viewed by it as more sympathetic than the ultra-belligerent Thatcherites. He had the potential to be a useful go-between and soon he began to receive letters from relatives of the internees, asking him to intercede with Saddam on their behalf. What happened then varies according to whose account is considered more reliable. Heath's version is that he forwarded such letters to the Foreign Office but took no further action. Then the Government decided that it would be a good idea for some eminent but unofficial Briton to visit Baghdad so as to see if the release of, at least, the most frail hostages could be arranged. Callaghan, David Owen and Heath were all considered as possible emissaries; it was concluded that Heath would be the most suitable and William Waldegrave, now Minister of State at the Foreign Office, telephoned him to ask if he would be willing to take on the mission. The Government would pay the bills and make arrangements for Heath's security. Heath at once accepted and began to make the necessary plans. However, in New York, the Foreign Secretary, who was now Douglas Hurd, told Mrs Thatcher what was planned. She exploded indignantly and two days later an embarrassed Waldegrave had to break it to Heath that the visit was now off. He could go under his own steam if he so wished, but the Government would neither pick up the bill nor guarantee his security. Heath said that he had already spoken to some of the relations of the hostages and felt himself committed. 'To say that Douglas Hurd had given in to Mrs Thatcher's

anger would be no justification in the eyes of relatives concerned about their loved ones.'[7]

The recollections of Hurd and Waldegrave are significantly different. The idea that Heath should go to Baghdad originated with the brother-in-law of one of the detainees, a Mr Wilbraham. Hurd doubted whether the visit would accomplish anything and, in a conversation recorded at the time, pointed out the risk that it might be exploited for propaganda purposes by the Iraqis. He said, however, that 'there was a humanitarian case for a visit' and that, if Heath undertook it, 'he would not be criticised by us'. The Prime Minister was unenthusiastic about the project but made no attempt to block it. 'Ted was, I think, plain wrong about the origin of the visit,' Hurd recollected, 'and read more encouragement into our conversation than was intended.' People hear what they want to hear and remember what they want to remember. Hurd's statement that he 'not very valiantly, neither encouraged nor discouraged' is convincing; it is equally understandable that Heath should have supposed the Foreign Office to be more wholeheartedly behind his venture than was in fact the case. At all events, Heath decided the visit must go ahead however insubstantial the governmental support, and with the head of his private office, Robert Vaudry, and his Salisbury doctor, Jeffrey Easton, he set off for the Middle East on 19 October 1990. Richard Branson paid the cost of the fares and provided a properly equipped aircraft for the return journey with what it was hoped would be a full load of the sicker hostages. (A few years later Heath was able to return the favour when he appealed to the Chinese authorities to grant Virgin Airways overflying rights.)[8]

Dr Easton, in his diary describing the visit, records that he asked the Foreign Office official responsible whether he thought the expedition would be safe. 'Provided you stick close to Heath it should be all right' was the not entirely reassuring answer. In fact on arrival Heath was whisked away by the British Ambassador and soon moved on to see the Foreign Minister, Tariq Aziz. To Tariq and, the following day, to Saddam, Heath stressed that if the Iraqis did not leave Kuwait, war would be inevitable. He found Saddam obsessed by the role the Americans were playing in the Middle East but not in the least resembling the half-crazed mini-Hitler portrayed in the West. 'He is not mad in the least,' he told the *Independent*. 'He's a very astute person, a clever person ... he made a misjudgement about Kuwait, and I'm sure he recognises now that it was a misjudgement.' It was two hours before Heath was able to raise the question of the hostages but when he did so he found that Saddam was disposed to release all those for whom he specifically asked. He left the meeting exhausted but was revived by a heavy lunch. 'Taste my food,' he ordered his doctor. 'I am not sure if he was serious,' commented Easton. That afternoon he went out to visit British nurses detained in the hospital: 'Heath very charming and sympathetic,' noted Easton. The return journey to London at the head of his flock of hostages was something of a triumph, with champagne provided by Branson flowing in abundance. Easton thanked Heath for affording him this unique experience; he had, he said, learned much about the workings of dictatorships. 'Heath thought(?) I was talking about the British Government.'[9]

Heath was offended by the fact that the Foreign Office sent only its most junior Under Secretary of State to greet him and the returning hostages. He had better reason to feel aggrieved when Mrs Thatcher was decidedly grudging when the affair of the hostages was discussed in the House of Commons. She did not even mention Heath's role until Neil Kinnock, no doubt intending to annoy, asked her to join him in 'unreserved praise for the humanitarian efforts of Edward Heath'. She had already done so, replied Thatcher (though nobody could remember when). 'We welcome the return of the hostages whose release was secured by Mr Heath. We regret very much that there are still over 1,400 there.' Douglas Hurd called on Heath at Wilton Street: an act intended as a courtesy but interpreted by Heath as being further evidence that the Foreign Office wished to dissociate itself from his exploits. 'Call on Ted who is grumpy,' was Hurd's diary entry. On the whole the episode benefited Heath's reputation: he received more than a thousand letters of support against less then fifty which criticised him for appeasing dictators. It did him less good within the Conservative Party. Paul Bryan, a protégé of Heath's who could generally be counted among his supporters, acquitted him – with some equivocation – of having undertaken the mission primarily to irritate Mrs Thatcher, but added: 'After he came back he was endlessly on television, full of scorn for the Allied leaders in their incredibly difficult position ... Perhaps a wife would have prevented the hardening of his nature.'[10]

This was not the end of his involvement with Iraq. In December 1993 he paid a further visit to try to secure the release of three Britons who had been arrested on trumped-up charges of espionage and were being held in the hope that their plight would induce the British Government to unfreeze blocked Iraqi assets. He proved to be pushing at an open door. Saddam's first words were: 'Of course, I know why you're here, and you may take them home.' In a long conversation with Tariq Aziz, Heath agreed that the fault for the present imbroglio lay with the West and far in the past: 'The imposition of unnatural borders on conflicts settled by force does not work.' In response Tariq Aziz vouchsafed that he thought Iran's very public campaign against Salman Rushdie was 'silly; it is far easier just to eliminate someone quietly in private'. Once more Heath returned in triumph with his trophies. On this occasion, he recorded with relish, 'in contrast to the autumn of 1990', he received a letter from the Prime Minister, now John Major, 'who generously described my trip as courageous – and right'.[11]

Tony Benn, who, as the years went by, found that he had more in common with his old adversary, went up to Heath in the House of Commons and told him that they agreed not only about Iraq but about the bombing of Serbia. 'He laughed in a sort of friendly way and I said, "You know, the old men have got it right; these young people are making a mess of everything!" And he laughed quite hard.' Heath was indeed strongly opposed to any intervention by Britain or by NATO in the former Yugoslavia. 'The media', he told the historian Asa Briggs, 'have created the "something must be done" syndrome. It is very dangerous and difficult to counter. I am afraid the Government and its more avid supporters get deeper and deeper into "the basics" mess. If only they could realise the harm which it is doing then they might be able to swing over to a forward look. But they do not appear to be so minded.' The fiercely pro-Serb foreign correspondent of the *Observer*, Nora Beloff, saw him as a potential ally and bombarded him with material supporting her case. 'I thoroughly agree with your position,' wrote Heath, 'and I am grateful to you for continuing to keep me briefed on the situation,' but he found her emotional approach unappealing and had no intention of enlisting under her banner. Could she come to talk with him in Salisbury, she asked: 'I love professional excuses for enjoying dream gardens.' He would be away for the next few weeks, he countered. 'Perhaps we can talk on the telephone on my return.' Yet he continued to agree with most of her opinions. He was reluctant to blame any individual, he told Beloff in November 1996, but: 'I share your view that Western policy has been driven too much by ideological and domestic political considerations, and not enough by a realistic consideration of the situation on the ground.'[12]

Part of his hostility to western policy in Yugoslavia arose from his conviction that the strings were being pulled in Washington and that, almost by definition, anything the Americans might wish to do was likely to be wrong-headed and contrary to the true demands of peace and international security. His reluctance to blame an individual for what he saw as the mess in Bosnia and Serbia did not extend to Iraq. In May 1991 he strongly opposed the presentation of the European Prize for Elder Statesmen to President Bush. When asked why, he answered: 'I believe he unnecessarily went to war in the Middle East without allowing a proper time for sanctions to produce the desired result. His motives were revealed when directly after the conclusion of the war he declared that by winning the Gulf War he had wiped out the stain on the United States of losing the Vietnam War.' The destruction of the oil wells in Kuwait and the continuing massacres of Palestinians in that country could, he felt, be laid at Bush's charge. 'For these reasons I do not consider President Bush to be of the world stature worthy of the distinction which one of your prizes would confer on it.'[13] Discussing the risks of political assassination Tony Benn remarked that, while Spencer Perceval was the only British prime minister to have been murdered, it had happened frequently to American presidents. 'Not frequently enough so far as the present one is concerned,' said Heath grimly.[14]

When prime minister, Heath could legitimately claim that he was pro-European but in no way anti-American. In the years of semi-retirement this defence became less convincing. When Walter Annenberg was American Ambassador in London, Heath had once 'disinvited' him from a dinner at Number 10 on the grounds that he would not mix happily with one of the other guests. Annenberg accepted the rebuff with apparent grace but did not forget it. Some ten years later, when Annenberg was in London, he was due to meet Heath at dinner with the current Ambassador, Charles Price. 'Your continuing campaign against President Reagan and the United States makes it embarrassing for me for you to be present at Ambassador Price's residence in the evening of 14 June,' wrote Annenberg with some relish. 'I trust you will be understanding.' Heath did not attend the dinner but felt he understood only too well. Price subsequently apologised for what he said had been a misunderstanding. 'I accepted his apology, and the matter is therefore closed,' Heath told Annenberg. But Annenberg had a point. Heath did go out of his way to criticise American policy and to condemn those who were responsible for it. When American aircraft in 1986 bombed Libya he chose to announce on American television that, if he had been prime minister, he would have refused flying rights. The attack had been illegal and it would strengthen Gaddafi rather than weaken him.

When asked whether he did not think that Britain had a duty to support the Americans, who were defending Europe by their military presence, Heath retorted that the defence of Europe against Communism was as much in America's interests as in Europe's. There was no reason why Europe should follow the US blindly in other spheres. The point of view was a perfectly sensible one and would probably have been shared by most thinking Britons, but for a former prime minister gratuitously to advance it on American television was stirring up trouble that must have caused tremors of dismay in Whitehall.[15]

Anti-American or not, his championship of a united Europe remained the most impelling of his concerns. In March 1983 a small group of the former members of Jean Monnet's Action Committee met in Brussels to consider the future of the EEC. The committee had been suspended after Monnet's death, but it was now felt that it should reconvene. Apart from Heath, the group included Emilio Colombo, Helmut Schmidt, Joop van Uyl, Leo Tindemans and the President of the European Commission, Jacques Delors. All of these were ardent Europeans but Heath, though he felt entirely at one with them, was painfully aware that he did not speak with the authority of his Government; indeed that, in the eyes of his fellow members, the Government now in power in London was conspicuously out of sympathy with European aspirations. A year later, when the group met again, Schmidt pointed out that Europe was not at the centre of the thinking of the French Socialist Party. Heath said that, if the Socialist Party was difficult or negative, 'we ought to go ahead with those who *were* positive'. You could not ignore the French Socialists, argued Schmidt; Franco-German agreement would be vital to any progress. 'This was particularly true in view of the negative attitude which the United Kingdom was likely to continue to take. No British Prime Minister after Mr Heath had been genuinely committed to Europe. The differences between Wilson, Callaghan and Thatcher had been only of style. At root, Mrs Thatcher only wanted her money back.'[16]

This was so obviously true that Heath did not even try to deny it. As Thatcher rampaged in Brussels and threatened to withhold the

British contribution to the budget if satisfaction was not given her on the share for which the UK was responsible, he became ever more alarmed. After an inconclusive debate in the House of Commons, in which it seemed to him that the Prime Minister was refusing to address herself to his concerns, he issued a solemn remonstrance.

> I could not support [he told Mrs Thatcher], indeed I would strongly oppose any sort of illegality by HM Government affecting the European Community – just as I have always opposed illegality at home. Moreover, as the Chief Whip will confirm, this is also the position of many senior members of the party in the House of Commons as well as that of many backbenchers who did not make their views heard this afternoon. I hope that the Cabinet will appreciate this in any discussions it may have on these matters.

They were brave words, but they did not reflect reality. Only a handful of Tories, whether senior members or backbenchers, shared Heath's views on Europe; a majority felt Mrs Thatcher was right in her strident championship of British interests. When in 1988 she dismissed the extremely pro-European Lord Cockfield from his post as one of the two British commissioners in Brussels, Heath denounced it on *Newsnight* as 'sheer spite', 'a disgrace', 'a public scandal', but in the Party hardly a tremor was to be detected. He was booed when he pleaded the European cause at the party conference in Brighton in September 1988 and dismissed by Jonathan Aitken as 'a peddler of dreams for Broadstairs-*les-deux-Eglises*'.[17]

It was at Bruges in September 1988 that Mrs Thatcher made the speech which ensured that the gulf between her and Heath would be as much ideological as personal. She was responding to Jacques Delors' somewhat ill-advised boast that within six years a European government would be making 80 per cent of the laws relating to economic management and social policy. 'We have not', she proclaimed, 'successfully rolled back the frontiers of the state in Britain, only to see them reimposed at a European level, with a European super-state exercising a new dominance from Brussels.' 'Hostile and ill-informed,' Heath described her speech. His outrage was redoubled when the

Secretary of the Bruges Group – a lobby group dedicated to resisting any further European integration – sent him a copy of a paper arguing the case against European Monetary Union. 'Who is this man?' demanded Heath. 'Where does his money come from? What counter-action are we taking?' But 'this man', however offensive his activities might appear, was to Heath no more than a puppet under the control of 'that woman'. In the last two years of Mrs Thatcher's rule, all the rancour and resentment which he had felt against the enemy who had supplanted him, all his disapproval of what he saw as her destructively divisive social policies, were subsumed into a high tide of indignation that she should be seeking to shatter for ever his noblest achievement, Britain as a central player in an ever more united Europe.[18]

When John Major replaced Thatcher at the end of 1990, Heath welcomed him as the man who would restore the Conservative Party to its true principles, particularly over Europe. 'I am proud to support John Major,' he asserted. 'What this country needs is for John Major to continue to show his commitment to a united Europe.' Up to a point he did; in spite of the objurgations of the Eurosceptics, Britain did its best to struggle along within the Exchange Rate Mechanism (ERM) of the European Monetary System. But it was an operation conducted at the wrong time and with the wrong tools. Within two years the experiment had failed disastrously, Britain was forced out of the ERM and Major's Europeanism, never held with the fervour of a true devotee, became ever more threadbare. Have you been disappointed by John Major's performance as prime minister, Robin Day asked Heath in February 1994. He had been disappointed by Major's behaviour over Europe, Heath replied: 'I don't think he should try to appease the Eurosceptics.' By the end of the following year it had become clear to him that the demise of Thatcherism had not scotched or even seriously weakened the forces of anti-Europeanism within the Conservative Party: 'We simply cannot afford', he told Julian Critchley, 'to be the political prisoners of a disloyal and outmoded minority who fail to understand that times have changed.' But was it a minority? The Conservative Party went into the 1997 general election with its attitude towards Europe at best equivocal, hesitant to challenge too overtly James Goldsmith's Referendum Party which was outflanking the Tories on the right with a heady brew of prejudice and patriotism.

> You are right to say that we are once again in danger of being left behind as the rest of Europe moves on [he told Vernon Bogdanor]. Of course, there are many others who also recognise this, but too many of them have been intimidated into silence either by the increasingly vituperative anti-European tenor of our newspapers or by their desire to put loyalty to their political parties ahead of their principles during the run-up to a difficult General Election. I myself shall certainly continue to put the case for the United Kingdom taking the lead in the European Union, and I shall go on encouraging others to do the same. If the voices of sanity are stilled by intimidation, we might lose this argument by default, and the country could suffer the most appalling consequences as a result.[19]

Heath fought the election as a loyal Conservative, but his heart was hardly in it. 'The Conservative Party in the 1980s', he wrote in his memoirs, 'lost sight of the balance between rights and responsibilities.' Though Major's intentions had been good he had failed to put his party back on to the right path. Labour's victory under Tony Blair in 1997 meant that 'people are, once again, concerned with ideas of justice and security'. On Europe, too, he felt that he was closer to Blair's Labour than to his own party. 'I suppose Blair is 100 per cent with you on the European question?' Benn had asked him some time before. '"Absolutely," said Ted, as if Blair was one of his children, and I think that is the position.' But Blair had as much need as Major to take account of the doubters in his own party and Labour was no more united than the Conservatives in its view on European unity. Inevitably Heath was going to be disappointed. 'I am right, aren't I,' asked Benn after Labour's first year in office, 'in saying that Blair has thrown away the leadership of Europe?' 'Yes,' agreed Heath sadly. The reason for Heath being so pro-European, Benn considered, was 'that he hates being bossed around by America'. That was never more than part of the story, and a relatively small part at that, but in his old age Heath's belief that Europe must unite in order to provide a counter-force to the new transatlantic imperialism bulked far larger in his mind than it would have done when he first negotiated British entry.[20]

It was the belief that they were sounder on Europe than any other party that led Heath briefly to contemplate the possibility that he might join the Social Democrat Party (SDP), a splinter group of Labour moderates led by Roy Jenkins. In April 1980 Ian Gilmour advised Jenkins to try to include Heath in his new party: 'You and Ted would be a formidable combination.' Jenkins followed up the suggestion to the point of inviting Heath to his country home for a tête-à-tête lunch. 'He showed a certain but not a vast interest in what I might or might not be doing in British politics,' recorded Jenkins. 'We agreed to keep in touch.' That was as far as it went. Probably Jenkins had doubts as to how easily Heath would fit into what was otherwise a relatively homogeneous band; Heath for his part claimed that the idea of jumping ship 'never for one moment appealed to me personally'. As much as anything, it would have meant that he had abandoned the Conservative Party to the Thatcherites; yet he continued to believe that, even if it might not be under his leadership, he would one day help restore it to the paths of righteousness. He retained a benevolent interest in the SDP. In March 1982 he went to the Hillhead constituency in Glasgow, where Jenkins was standing. Heath was in theory speaking in support of the Tory candidate and secured him the largest audience he was to achieve during the whole campaign. When he spoke, however, Jenkins recorded that he 'delivered a slashing attack on Mrs Thatcher's whole policy … made some amiable remarks about me at a press conference, and departed. It was a mystifying performance.' Heath felt no mystification: he admitted to Sara Morrison that his intention had been to promote the cause of Jenkins.[21]

Heath and Jenkins found themselves in competition in another forum when the death of Harold Macmillan at the end of 1986 caused a vacancy in the Chancellorship at Oxford. As a former prime minister from a major college with a distinguished Oxford history, Heath thought that he was the most appropriate candidate from the right to oppose Roy Jenkins as champion of the left. He was disconcerted when he discovered that the historian Robert Blake, Provost of Queen's, was also standing. Blake seems to have been urged to put himself forward by Conservative Oxonians who resented Heath's treatment of Mrs Thatcher. Why he agreed to compete is harder to understand; he must have known that he would split the right-wing vote and thus ease Jenkins's passage. Probably he reckoned that he had a better chance than Heath of defeating Jenkins and that the job was one which he would like to do and which he would do well. On the first of these points, at least, it turned out that he was correct.

Heath made a slow start to his campaign, though Sir John Templeton, the multi-millionaire founder of Templeton College, contributed handsomely to his expenses. His first list of sponsors came entirely from Balliol. Jenkins, too, was a Balliol man and it was traditionally a left-wing college, but by a curious quirk Heath was considered to be the candidate of the left while Jenkins was loathed by the orthodox socialists for being a renegade to the party. There was also a group which believed that to vote for Heath would be the surest way of annoying Mrs Thatcher. In this they were partly right – privately, she would rather have seen Blake installed as Chancellor – but she had no intention of being seen to oppose Heath's candidature. Whitelaw and Douglas-Home, Woodrow Wyatt learnt, 'have got together and decided to support Ted because otherwise he will say there was another Conservative plot inspired by Margaret to do him down'. The Chief Whip told the vice chairman of the Candidates' Association: 'You will appreciate that it would not be right for me to prefer one Conservative candidate to another. It may be considered that Ted Heath has a much better chance of defeating Jenkins than does Robert Blake, in which case it is clearly in the Party's interest for Ted to receive the widest support.' Nigel Lawson for one was left in no doubt that he should vote for Heath.[22]

Once he realised that he had got a serious contest on his hands Heath gave more attention to the business of whipping up support. A second list of sponsors was prepared, designed to show the eclectic nature of his appeal. Hailsham and Whitelaw, Barber, Peyton and Waldegrave for the politicians, Patrick Nairne and Burke Trend for the civil servants, Lord Goodman for the floating voters, all lent their names to the cause. Heath wrote to Stephen Sherbourne to solicit his vote. Sherbourne replied that he had no vote to cast as he had never got round to taking his MA. 'That's no problem,' said Heath, and within a few hours the necessary application forms were on Sherbourne's desk. Even du Cann was canvassed on Heath's behalf and assured Richard Burn he was doing all he could to whip up support. Balliol was known to be divided in favour of Heath by 49 votes to 36.*

By the time Heath arrived in Oxford on the day of the election and took up his station in the Master's rooms at Balliol he felt reasonably confident that the victory was his. It was February 1974 over again. A flood of MAs, with wholly unpredictable intentions, arrived in Oxford from all directions. Only when they had voted did it become clear how strong the animosity against Heath, whipped up by what was seen as his churlish and disloyal treatment of Mrs Thatcher, had grown around the country. Anthony Kenny, Master of Balliol, had posted his son in the Clarendon Building with instructions that he was to report the instant the result was known. He arrived, out of breath, to announce that Jenkins was the winner. Heath had come second. He did not take the news too badly, recorded Kenny. 'I think he had seen it coming.' Those close to him believe that he had not expected anything of the sort but that he took some consolation from the fact that he had out-voted Blake and that, if the right-wing votes had been added together, he would have won. Before he got into the car to leave Oxford he had been given the painful truth. Jenkins had gained 3,249 votes, Blake was second with 2,674, Heath trailed with 2,348. 'What! I did worse than Blake!' he exclaimed. In the car he relapsed into a morose silence and spoke hardly a word to Burn during the journey back to Salisbury.[23]

It was more than a year before he was able to patch up his damaged self-esteem by a visit to China. There, at least, he was treated with proper deference. He continued to repay Chinese attentions by loyally

---

* The undergraduate body was perhaps more radical. Kenny recalls only one undergraduate being sent down, except for academic reasons, during his time at Balliol. His crime was to write 'Fuck Heath!' on the window of the Senior Common Room one night when the then Prime Minister was dining there.

defending their cause on almost every occasion. When Ludovic Kennedy in 1999 remarked that what the Dalai Lama had told him when he had seen him after his escape from China was very different to Heath's own account of events, Heath replied that the Dalai Lama's 'memories and mental processes had developed quite remarkably since he had signed the agreement with Mao Tse-tung – admittedly as a very young man – and his suggestion that Tibet should have become a member of the United Nations showed how far he was from reality'. To the Chinese Deputy Foreign Minister, Heath explained that people in the West tended to forget that there had been for more than forty years 'an agreement between Mao and the Dalai Lama providing a sound basis for the relationship between Tibet and the People's Republic'.[24]

The fact that the mainland territories, on which Hong Kong was dependent, were due to revert to China in 1997 meant that the future of the colony became an increasingly urgent issue in the preceding twenty years. As early as 1983 Heath had found himself employed as an intermediary. Deng Xiaoping asserted bluntly that the Chinese Government intended to assert its sovereignty over the whole of Hong Kong. All the existing treaties would be abrogated. The British must withdraw completely as a colonial power. But once that had been conceded there was room for arrangements that would mean that, socially and economically, Hong Kong would be left largely inviolate. 'Four words are enough to encapsulate Deng's insight,' Heath told the British Government, '"One country, two systems".' Serious negotiations to bring this about must be launched at once; otherwise China would settle matters for itself as it thought best. Why Deng should have chosen to convey this message to Mrs Thatcher through a man whom he knew she particularly disliked, rather than by way of the British Ambassador in Beijing or the Foreign Office, is hard to understand. Possibly he thought it would be taken more seriously if it came through such a channel: the Chinese could never entirely accept that Heath had ceased to wield effective power. Certainly Heath felt no embarrassment in passing on the message. On American television a few years later he said that the transfer of power was inevitable and that it would work because wherever the Chinese were given an opportunity they made a success of it. They realised that Hong Kong was vital to the economy of China and were flexible enough to respects its traditions. The inhabitants of Hong Kong would adapt without too much difficulty to Chinese suzerainty: after all, the Chinese inhabitants of Singapore did not find it necessary to march in the streets denouncing Lee Kuan Yew as a tyrant.[25]

The Tiananmen Square massacre of June 1989, when Chinese soldiers shot dead between two and three thousand demonstrators in the centre of Beijing, caused Heath intense embarrassment. His first, unguarded reaction was to claim that the Chinese Government had the right to take police action on its own territory and to suggest that the incident was, in essentials, no different from Bloody Sunday. As the enormity of what had happened became more apparent Richard Burn persuaded him, without much difficulty, that this line was indefensible. He had never condoned what had taken place, he maintained in the House of Commons: 'How could those in authority in Beijing have allowed this massacre to happen?' He did not hesitate to tell the Chinese Prime Minister, Li Peng, about the 'concern' which the massacre had caused in the West: 'Beijing can say that that was an internal affair but the world today is a smaller place and everything has an effect.' Shortly after the massacre, he argued in the House of Commons that the only way to restore confidence in Hong Kong was to speed up the process of democratisation. But second thoughts gave way to third. Problems in China, he began to remind people, were on a scale that demanded different treatment from what would have been appropriate in the West. Things had obviously gone too far, but … As for democratisation, within a year of the massacre he said in the House of Commons that he did not see 'that the situation in Hong Kong could be dealt with by saying that democratisation must be extended'. He maintained resolutely that Hong Kong would prosper after 1997 'because I believe it will be good for China to do so'.

Increasingly he became irritated when people reverted to the massacre as being a reason for treating the Chinese Government with suspicion or hostility. On *Newsnight* in February 1997 Heath remarked how much he had admired Deng Xiaoping, who had died the day before. 'He killed rather a lot of people in Tiananmen Square, didn't he?' said the interviewer. 'Well, of course, this is just like the British,' protested Heath. 'It is the only thing which you can bring up, and we are the only country that does still bring it up. There was a crisis in Tiananmen Square after a month in which the civil authorities had been defied and they took action about it. Very well, we can criticise it in exactly the same way as people criticise Bloody Sunday in Northern Ireland, but that isn't by any means the whole story, and why can't we also look at the rest of his achievements?' One press report transferred the words 'very well' from the beginning of one sentence to the end of the previous one, thus implying that Heath was suggesting that the police operation had been very well carried out. This was, of course, unfair, but even without such amendment, Heath's remarks suggest an alarming readiness to condone the activities of a brutally repressive regime. It seems not to have occurred to him that this would disturb even moderately liberal opinion; or, if it did occur to him, he dismissed the reflection as of small importance. He had what he considered a sensible point to make the possibility that by putting it in the way he did he would hurt or offend many people who would otherwise have been reasonably well disposed towards his argument was not worth consideration.[26]

Even when he admitted the full extent of the horrors of Tiananmen Square he saw no reason why it should, or indeed could, affect the agreement on the future of Hong Kong which had been reached between the British and Chinese Governments at the end of 1984. When Chris Patten was appointed Governor by John Major in July 1992 to run the colony through the last few years before the transfer of power, Heath saw no reason for alarm. Patten had once been something of a protégé of Heath's; he had prospered under Thatcher but had never ceased to belong to the liberal fringe of the Party with which Heath felt most at ease. When he tried to put those liberal principles into practice in Hong Kong, however, by pushing the colony down the road towards full democracy in a way that could not easily be reversed after the transfer of power, Heath took fright. In other circumstances he would probably have applauded Patten's actions; in Hong Kong in the 1990s he deplored anything which seemed calculated to annoy the Chinese Government and make the takeover more difficult. In particular he was critical of Patten's reform of the Legislative Council. This meant that the Council due to be elected in 1995, and thus still in power when the Communists took over two years later, would no longer be the choice of a privileged minority – a group unlikely to favour any policies calculated to upset the new rulers – but of the far less predictable electorate at large.

The Chinese Government reacted angrily to what they saw as an unwarranted attempt to change the rules after a deal had been done. Heath fully sympathised. When Alaistair Goodlad, the Conservative Chief Whip, wrote to *The Times* to justify the Governor's action Heath scrawled an angry commentary in the margin. Against the statement that the Chinese Government had been 'consulted', he wrote: 'This was *not* consultation. It was briefing. Patten refused to consult.' On the claim that it would have been impossible to hold secret talks with the Chinese without first letting Hong Kong know what was being discussed, Heath observed: 'Rubbish. This infuriated the Chinese.' As to the suggestion that such behaviour would have created 'a climate of uncertainty and instability', Heath retorted that: 'This is what Hong Kong has now got as a result of Patten.' He stayed with the Governor on several occasions between 1992 and 1997 and, according to Patten, caused considerable embarrassment by criticising British policy to all and sundry. He never forgave Patten. 'The bad relations over Hong Kong were quite unnecessary,' Heath told the Chinese Foreign Minister a year after the transfer of power. 'Governor Patten has just published a book which explains why he made so many mistakes and, of course, he received a much worse result in the end than had he just carried out the agreement.' His determination to see the Chinese point of view fused with his increasing dislike of all things American. A few days before writing the letter quoted above, Heath saw the president of the Chinese People's Institute of Foreign Affairs and told him that Tony Blair ought to stop supporting President Clinton. 'People in the UK do not like the British Prime Minister sucking up to the US President. International relations should be conducted on a sound footing, but not if it causes embarrassment on either side.'[27]

* * *

From time to time after 1979 Heath became involved in the affairs of Europe, China or the Middle East, but domestic politics remained his primary concern and, for a decade at least, the bane of his existence. During this period he not merely refused to cooperate in any way with Thatcher's Government, he set out on almost every occasion to revile and condemn their activities. His friends pleaded with him to be more flexible, to at least admit the possibility of harmonious co-operation. He thought they were wrong and told them so.

In the summer of 1997, shortly after the disastrous Fastnet Race, Sara Morrison was staying with the Gilmours in Italy. Together they prepared a letter to Heath, which does not appear in the archive at Arundells but a draft of which survives.

> I sense you should give some thought to various alternative 'game plans' in the autumn [Morrison wrote]. It might be worth envisaging the various possibilities of the middle term future ... and having an overall position ready for situations as they become evident. The risk of 'boat-rocking' and similar accusations are far greater, and distortion and muddle more damaging, if there is no theoretical compass. I am sure you have all this in mind ... Obviously flexibility is vital, we can't foresee which way opinion and needs will go in detail, but it seems silly to be more '*ad hoc*' than absolutely inevitable. The future 'thinker' might also consider which issues (domestic) you might adopt as particular themes for speeches.
>
> Sorry! – bossy, boring and largely obvious points – but if you are around – which you are – and occupying a large space on the political map in the public mind – to some extent it is no longer practical to plan in accordance with relatively immediate issues.[28]

The proposition, that Heath should work out a long-term strategy and not merely snipe opportunistically at targets as they offered themselves, was perfectly reasonable but took no account of the fact that, in his own eyes, he was working to a perfectly coherent strategy already. The governmental boat was proceeding in the wrong direction at a vertiginously dangerous speed; it was his duty as well as his pleasure, if not to torpedo it, then to rock it as energetically as could be managed. The problem for him was that even those most sympathetic to him did not see his behaviour as being part of a principled campaign but as a series of vengeful assaults directed above all at Margaret Thatcher. 'We on the liberal wing didn't have a leader,' said the Tory MP Cyril Townsend sadly. 'Ted was carrying out a vendetta.' Heath did little to correct the impression; indeed he constantly enhanced it. When Mark Schreiber doubted the wisdom of his expedition to Iraq, arguing that Saddam was an evil man, Heath retorted: 'It all depends what you mean by evil. *She*, after all, is an evil woman.' Stephen Sherbourne wrote to him in 1987 to report that he was leaving Number 10. 'So pleased to know you are rejoining the human race,' replied Heath. He would have claimed that such remarks were jokes, not to be taken literally. They were black jokes, however, and revealed the genuine bile beneath. He was fond of quoting Churchill's maxim: 'In victory magnanimity: in defeat defiance.' His defiance, though, smacked too often of spitefulness and ill temper.[29]

This made it all the easier for Mrs Thatcher to be magnanimous. When Heath, in October 1981, delivered what she described in her memoirs as 'a vitriolic speech in Manchester attacking my policies', she felt strong enough to ignore it and leave it to her supporters to rally to the defence. Du Cann duly obliged, characterising Heath as a splitter and saying that the Tory Party had no room for 'Teddy Bears'. At the same party conference Geoffrey Howe attacked Heath for abandoning the principles which he had championed when he became prime minister: then he had argued that the need to check inflation was all important; now he seemed to think unemployment was the only significant peril. Every time Heath made a fresh attack on the Prime Minister, another former supporter despaired and rallied to his critics. After a particularly fierce diatribe on *Newsnight*, Robert Key, the MP for Salisbury, wrote to tell him that he had been under great pressure from the media to comment. 'Until today I have not done so. Like so many of your friends, I am really *very* sorry that you have found it necessary to be quite so harsh in your condemnations.' 'Ignore,' wrote an unrepentant Heath in the margin.[30]

The Falklands crisis in 1982 put him in an awkward position. Perhaps fortunately for him, he was in China when the Argentinians occupied the islands and so avoided saying anything that could later have embarrassed him. His instincts were for conciliation. If he had been in charge there would undoubtedly have been greater efforts to involve other nations and to arrive at a negotiated solution. On the other hand, he supported the assembling of the Task Force and rejoiced at its success. He said as little as he could on the subject, though this did not save him from abuse from the extreme right of the Party for his supposed defeatism and striving for appeasement. He thought that Carrington's resignation was unnecessary: 'If there was a failure of responsibility, it was a failure of collective responsibility.' He sent an informal message to Mrs Thatcher to the effect that he was at her disposal if he could help in any way. Possibly he still nourished a glimmer of hope that he might be called back to the Foreign Office. Given the state of his relationship with the Prime Minister it was clear to everybody else that no such invitation would be forthcoming. Francis Pym was duly appointed Foreign Secretary and the feud went on.[31]

Though he could hardly have admitted it, even to himself, the worst feature of the Falklands War was that Margaret Thatcher emerged as Boadicca, the 'warrior queen' who heroically led her forces against Britain's enemies. Before the war it had seemed odds on that the Conservatives would lose the next election; once the war was won she could do no wrong. She resisted the temptation to call a snap election to cash in on her victory but when she went to the country in 1983 the only question was how large the Tory majority would be. Heath suppressed his animosity during the campaign and campaigned loyally, if with limited energy, for the Conservatives. It did not save him from one jibe from the Prime Minister. Pym, somewhat rashly, had said that he hoped there would not be a Tory landslide since 'there were considerable dangers in large majorities'. Mrs Thatcher said that she wholly disagreed. Pym was showing 'an ex-Chief Whip's natural caution. There is a club of ex-Chief Whips. They are very unusual people.' This emphatic confirmation of Thatcher's grasp on power finally convinced Heath that for him there could never be a return to office.[32]

Although Heath continued to be a lone voice, at variance with the majority of his party, as the years went by there were an increasing number of issues on which he found that he had significant support. When Mrs Thatcher abolished the Greater London Council in 1984, Heath opposed what he described as a 'spiteful measure, carried through to prevent it competing with the Whitehall government'. It was, he claimed in the House of Commons, something close to 'the greatest gerrymandering in the last 150 years'. Nineteen Tories joined him in voting against the measure. Most of them were senior figures who would not be standing at the next election, but there was evidence that the triumphalism induced by the Falklands War was wearing off and that more and more Tory backbenchers were questioning the policies of the Government. Sensing that the mood was shifting, Heath held on tenaciously to his position within the Party. He, he insisted, represented the true spirit of conservatism. At the end of 1984 the Chairman of the Federation of Conservative Students wrote to suggest that Heath was no longer welcome as the organisation's Life Patron. He was out of touch with the present Government's philosophy, particularly on unemployment. 'The present generation of Conservatives are mindful of the traditional Tory acceptance of the fact that Government can no more dictate the level of unemployment than it can legislate for good weather.' 'You commit a gross calumny when you equate your own policies with traditional conservatism,' retorted Heath. 'To me they seem to be indistinguishable from the nineteenth century Liberal tradition of unfettered *laissez-faire* and extreme libertarianism.' As to the suggestion that he was not wanted as Patron: 'I wish to make it clear that I have no intention of resigning … I shall continue to be available to you and your officers, and individual Associations, for any help or assistance you may require.'[33]

He found even more promising ground on which to attack when, after the 1987 election, the Government introduced the community charge, the 'poll tax', a measure which abolished the traditional rates in favour of a fixed tax per adult resident. Although account was to be taken of a person's ability to pay, the net result would have been a shifting of the tax burden from the rich to the poor. 'That is not a radical proposal,' Heath thundered. 'It is a reactionary, regressive proposal.' Probably no single measure did more to discredit Margaret

Thatcher and to prepare the way for her political demise. The following year he made one of his most effective onslaughts on the Government when he attacked Nigel Lawson's budget for its exclusive dependence on interest rates as a means of controlling the economy. 'In golfing terms,' Heath told the House of Commons, 'the Chancellor could be described as a one-club man, and the club is interest rates ... But, if one wishes to take on Sandy Lyle and the rest of the world, one needs a complete bag of clubs.' The accusation that he was a 'one-club golfer' stuck, Lawson admitted ruefully: 'It was an excellent example of how a good phrase can transfigure a bad point.'[34]

It was Europe rather than the poll tax or the economy which was the immediate cause of Mrs Thatcher's downfall but more than any of these was the general feeling that she had been there too long, was out of touch, failed to take any account of the views of her ministers, let alone the backbenchers. For Heath it was a moment of exquisite gratification but not one to which, in the short term, he had made any personal contribution. He sat in total impassivity as Geoffrey Howe, late in 1990, delivered a resignation speech which ruthlessly attacked Thatcher's policy towards Europe and style of government and made inevitable a challenge to her leadership. Neither at the time nor afterwards did he say a word to Howe about the speech. His only contribution was to take aside the Chief Whip, Tim Renton, and remind him that, if there were a leadership contest, it was his duty to be 'strictly and visibly impartial' (advice not wholly compatible with his indignation when Humphrey Atkins was similarly neutral at the time of the leadership contest in 1975).[35]

He made no attempt to conceal his jubilation when, in the first ballot, Thatcher failed to secure the majority which would have meant that she was automatically re-elected leader. As Heath had done some fifteen years before, she resigned rather than face a second round. Was it true, Michael Cockerell asked Heath, that when he heard the news of Thatcher's resignation he had telephoned his office and said: 'Rejoice! Rejoice!' No, replied Heath after some deliberation, 'I said it three times: Rejoice! Rejoice! Rejoice!' Woodrow Wyatt remarked how cheerful he was looking. 'He chortled and said, "Yes, of course

to have her defeated makes me feel very good".' It was a 'second spring time for Ted,' wrote Ronald Millar. 'What was for so long the face of acrimony and high dudgeon had acquired the benevolence of *A Christmas Carol*.' The fact that she too had been defeated led to some slight reduction in Heath's resentment of his supplanter. The two had always been capable of sustaining a facade of courtesy when they met, now there were moments verging on affability. But there was no question of a real rapprochement. Heath continued to speak of her with contempt and hostility; if a note of pity was now sometimes added it was tinged with *schadenfreude*. In May 1993 Rosemary Wolff sent him a leaf torn from a pamphlet about agricultural machinery. It advertised a gadget described as a 'De-Thatcher Scarifier'. 'I am particularly attracted by the fact that it is "noise control approved",' wrote Mrs Wolff. Would Heath like it for Christmas? Heath replied that he feared the Dean and Chapter would look askance at 'such an offensive piece of machinery'.[36]

Heseltine, Hurd and John Major fought out the next round to replace Mrs Thatcher. Three 'able and moderate men', Heath described them: he never admitted how he had voted, though the Heseltine camp had him down as a supporter. He was equally well satisfied with John Major. In time he was to be disappointed by what he felt to be Major's inadequate championship of Britain in Europe but he no longer felt an urge to express himself on every controversial issue. With Mrs Thatcher's departure he resigned himself to being what he very patently was, an elder statesman. In 1975 he had refused an honour on the grounds that he was still active in politics and would do nothing that suggested he was permanently on the shelf. When in 1992 he was appointed a Knight of the Garter, he felt no such inhibition. Peregrine Worsthorne in the *Sunday Telegraph* referred to Lord Melbourne's celebrated comment on the Garter and said 'there certainly was no damned merit about Heath ... not only was he a rotten Prime Minister but also a most disgraceful man'. His 'unchivalrous conduct' towards Mrs Thatcher 'is a case book study of boorishness unequalled in the annals of British public life'. Considering the abuse which he had borne with equanimity over the last decades, Heath was surprisingly put out by this tirade; his political secretary, Robert Vaudry, tried to find a leading Tory statesman who would write a rejoinder to Worsthorne's article and Heath took some persuading that he would do better to ignore it. Everything else about the honour delighted him; he felt that it was a worthy crown to his long parliamentary career. He was not yet ready to close that career by retiring from the House of Commons but from the moment that he donned the robes of a Knight of the Garter and joined the ranks of the, mainly ancient, worthies who shuffled each year from the Upper Ward of Windsor Castle to St George's Chapel, he considered that he was now above the political fray.[37]

TWENTY-SEVEN

Declining Years

Heath's last twelve or thirteen years were marked by a gradual withdrawal from public life. In the eyes of some, particularly the Tory would-be MPs who hoped to inherit his seat at Bexley, the withdrawal was a great deal too gradual. He clung on pertinaciously in the House of Commons: partly because he craved the distinction of being the Father of the House – a somewhat illusory honour which carried no duties and no privileges except for a supervisory role when a new Speaker was elected; still more because it helped to fill his days. With his yachting life now closed to him, and even his musical life more and more confined to listening, he was, for the first time in his life, faced with the threat of being under-employed. At the age of 77, as he was when he was returned with an increased majority in the general election of 1992, under-employment was something which most people might have contemplated with equanimity, but Heath had been intensely busy all his life and did not know what to do if he stopped. In June 1992 a magazine featured a photograph of an unknown couple captioned: 'The Rt Hon Edward Heath, former Prime Minister of England, and Mrs Heath.' Jim Callaghan tore it out and sent it to Heath. The accompanying letter commiserated with Heath on an operation which he had just undergone and went on: 'I expect it was caused by the double life you have been leading. But you can't keep it secret for ever!' Heath enjoyed the joke but may at the same time have regretted the fact that he *had* no double life: he had only one life, lived intensely and to the full but leaving a fearsome void around it.[1]

The operation had been for cancer. A malignant tumour on the colon had been detected in the spring of 1992. It had been caught early and posed no urgent threat; indeed it proved possible to defer the operation so as to allow him to attend his first Garter ceremony, but for a man of his age it was still a serious undertaking. The doctors told him that there was no reason why it should recur but every cancer victim must be aware that the threat will never wholly disappear. And this was only part of it. Heath had been notably healthy for most of his life; he faced illness with resignation but it was still disruptive and unpleasant. His limbs were swollen, he moved with increasing difficulty, he was quickly out of breath. There was merry banter about his condition in the Whips' office. 'What do you make of Ted's ankles?' asked one Whip. 'They've swollen terribly.' 'It's fluid retention,' said another Whip knowingly. 'Not a good sign.' 'They look like elephant's feet.' 'They *are* elephant's feet. Ted never forgets.' In fact, increasingly, he *did* forget – not forget an enemy, perhaps, but forget the armoury of details and statistics which had made him so formidable in debate. He and Harold Wilson had both benefited from phenomenal memories. Wilson had realised that his was slipping away, could not bear to appear at a disadvantage where formerly he had reigned triumphant, and withdrew from the battlefield. Heath rejected any such solution. His case was less desperate than Wilson's – he was far from suffering from any form of senile dementia – but even if he had been more infirm in body and mind than in fact he was he would not have seen any urgent need to retire. If only because his enemies, and indeed many of his friends, thought that it was time for him to move on, he was resolved to stay. It was his life, and he felt that there was still an important contribution which only he could make.[2]

By the time John Major led the Conservative Party to crushing defeat in the election of 1997 and opened the way for the brave new world of Tony Blair, Heath had lost hope in him as a champion of Britain in Europe. It was a turbulent and embittered campaign, with Heath finding himself singled out as the pet hate of James Goldsmith's rabidly Europhobic˜ Referendum Party. Boundary changes were anyway going to make his constituency far less secure; in the circumstances, given the national swing to Labour and the spirited campaign for the Referendum Party waged in Bexley by his former economic adviser, Brian Reading, Heath did remarkably well to keep his majority above 3,500. Major's defeat made his loss of the leadership inevitable; the two main contenders for the succession were the former Chancellor of the Exchequer, Kenneth Clarke, and the 36-year-old William Hague. Clarke was the most ardent Europhile remaining in the Government, Hague a noted Eurosceptic. For this reason alone Heath would have backed Clarke; when Hague won the day, Heath wrote in dismay to the defeated candidate: 'I was so sorry when the Parliamentary party chose to ignore common sense, as well as the views of business leaders, party workers and the general public. This flies in the face of all political logic, and truly leaves the party with a mountain to climb.' 'We will stay in opposition for a generation', replied Clarke, 'if William Hague insists that he wants to turn the party into a nationalist party.' That, Heath feared, was just what the new leader did intend. He wrote hopefully to Hague to wish him well in his task of uniting the party: 'As you know, we shall need to develop policies as quickly as possible to make us once again the dominant party in the political main stream. That is the only way in which we shall return to government.' Even as he wrote, however, he knew that Hague's policies would never come near his own. 1997 was the last time at which Heath believed his voice might still be heeded in the higher reaches of the Tory Party; the final death of this illusion did not silence him but more and more he felt himself a voice crying in the wilderness without even the ravens to offer him a hearing.[3]

The publication of his memoirs in 1998 coincided with, and perhaps partly inspired, a move in his constituency to urge him to retire. 'Well, he will be 85 at the next election and he'd like to stay,' wrote Benn in his diary. 'He doesn't want to be in the Lords with Thatcher. But the pressure to go builds up and I don't want that to happen to me.' A few weeks later Benn met Heath in the Lobby and put the question to him directly: 'Oh, Ted, are you standing for Parliament in the next election?' 'Why do you ask?' replied Heath. 'I've got to make my mind up and, as we were elected the same year, I couldn't bear the thought that you were here and I wasn't, or I was there and you weren't.' Heath 'shook with laughter and said "I haven't made up my mind. I'll let you know."' He did at least play with the idea of joining the now Baroness Thatcher in the upper house. It was Benn again who at the end of 2000 bemoaned the fact that, under Blair, the House of Commons counted for nothing, the Prime Minister never turned up, the media had taken over everything. Heath, he suggested, should be made a peer by resolution of the House of Commons, as was traditionally done with the Speaker. 'Oh, I don't know about that,' replied Heath, but Benn thought that he had not rejected the idea out of hand. He did not hesitate for long. To become a new boy in a strange environment, at an age when the faculties were dwindling and energy running out, would have been irrational, even grotesque. Lady Thatcher or no Lady Thatcher, the House of Lords was no place for him.[4]

One demanding and time-consuming occupation was preparing to give evidence to the Savill Inquiry into the events of Bloody Sunday. This involved reading and digesting a huge volume of paper and preparing for what was likely to be a hostile as well as rigorous cross-examination. The effort paid off: Heath successfully rebuffed any suggestion that he or any other politician had issued secret instructions that led to the carnage in Londonderry. He would rather have been spared the ordeal if it had been possible but it gave him something to do and Robert Armstrong believed that it actually helped to prolong his life.

Heath rejoiced in anniversaries. Every birthday was celebrated with a garden party at Arundells; in February 1990 480 people gathered at the Savoy to commemorate his fortieth year as an MP – each guest contributing £40 of which a quarter was spent on a splendid silver bowl to join the trophies in Salisbury. Mrs Thatcher attended and they exchanged a few private words. She was there again ten years later when the Speaker, Betty Boothroyd, gave a party to celebrate Heath's fifty years in the House of Commons. Tony Benn remarked how nice it had been of her to come. 'Oh well, you know,' answered Thatcher. 'As you get older you get mellow.' 'It was very interesting,' Benn observed about the gathering. 'It was like going to Madame Tussaud's, with the waxworks being able to speak. I should think the average age was well over seventy.' Heath himself did not seem to be noticeably mellower. Peter Carrington saw him sitting alone on a sofa at the Speaker's party and told him how kind it had been of Betty Boothroyd to give the party. 'She's wearing the same dress as last night,' Heath grumbled. 'Last night' had been a vast dinner at Claridges, similarly in honour of Heath's half-century as a Member. The pace of inflation was marked by the fact that tickets had gone up since 1990 from £40 to £100; Heath then sold the story to *Hello!* magazine. Sara Morrison remonstrated with him: her snobbery, he retorted, was far worse than the realism he displayed by accepting that *Hello!* was dependent on the doings of people like him for its survival.[5]

Even though he had told Benn he had not made up his mind, it does not seem likely that Heath had any serious intention of standing again in 2001. The physical strain involved became greater, the rewards less obvious. He still hesitated finally to commit himself but a year at least before the election the officers in his constituency knew that they should be looking for a new candidate. For some years he had been finding it increasingly difficult to get up the stairs at Wilton Street. For a while he retained the house as an office and kept on his Spanish housekeeper, but once he had committed himself to leaving the House of Commons the use he made of it became so limited that the expense seemed unjustified. A London base was unnecessary: he preferred to wake up in Salisbury however late he had been in London the night before and would sleep peacefully in the back of his government car, waking briefly on arrival at Arundells but soon being asleep again. Life was comfortable, tranquil, restricted, a little dull. Once he had given up his seat he lost interest in Bexley; partly because his replacement was hardly to his taste. The choice was between a Eurosceptic and a woman; Heath found the first the less distasteful and thus contributed to the selection of Derek Conway, a former chief executive of the Cats' Protection League, who was to land himself in considerable trouble a few years later when it was discovered that he had been paying his son a substantial salary out of official funds for research work that seemed to yield remarkably little information likely to be of use to an active politician. Heath had been a conscientious constituency member and even when he was prime minister had devoted a fair part of his energies to cultivating his supporters. Another gap was left in the responsibilities demanding his attention.

Asked on television in 2000 what was the worst thing about growing old, Heath replied: 'One finds one's friends slipping away and you gradually find yourself getting into an era where the others seem a long way away.' He continued to deny that he was lonely – 'It's not really loneliness, because I'm doing so many things with so many other people' – but outside the tiny circle of his household he in fact did things with other people with increasing rarity. He was sensitive to the possibility that he might be poor company. When Sara Morrison suggested that they go out to dinner, he said wistfully: 'You must trade me in for a new model. It's not fun for you any more.' His most regular companions were James Elder, his political secretary, and Stuart Craven, who had started as head gardener but had gradually become general factotum and almost minder. Neither of them in fact resented the demands that he made on them but the fact that there was a professional relationship between them meant that he felt less inhibited in expecting their companionship. Where no such relationship existed he was increasingly less confident. Of his oldest friends, Lord Aldington died at the end of 2000. Madron Seligman survived another eighteen months, but though he was always close to Heath and, when he was in hospital, Heath rang every day to enquire about his progress, they met relatively rarely. When Seligman died, noted Dr Easton, Heath showed no emotion. The fact that he showed no emotion does not prove that he did not feel it, but as he had told the television interviewer, he had entered an era where 'the others seem a long way away'.[6]

Except for a few cherished close relationships he seemed almost consciously to be distancing himself from anything but the most formal and superficial intercourse. The daughter of his old friend Teddy Denman wrote to protest that she had always used to receive Christmas cards addressed to 'Amanda and Nick' and signed 'Uncle Teddy'. The most recent cards had been addressed to Mr and Mrs Wood and were signed 'Edward Heath'. 'Have we got on to some other list for correspondence?' she asked. They had: the secretary added an apologetic 'Eek!' at the foot of the letter and the Woods at once received a placatory message. It was, indeed, no more than a secretarial slip. But Heath had not noticed it or, if he had, had not felt it worthwhile to correct it.[7] He had never taken much trouble over the cultivation of friendships; now the effort seemed less than ever worthwhile. Apart from Sara Morrison, Robert Armstrong was almost the only figure from the outside world to appear regularly in Heath's private life. Armstrong accepted, to a remarkable extent, the burden of keeping his friend afloat, making sure that his affairs ran smoothly, interpreting him to a forgetful and inattentive nation. But Armstrong had many time-consuming duties; no longer Secretary of the Cabinet but prominent if not pre-eminent among the great and the good who made the country work. With the best will in the world he could not devote to Heath's affairs as much attention as Heath felt they deserved.

More and more days were spent alone at Arundells; even if he had a visitor it left much of the day to fill in. Almost every evening he would set out with his driver and security officer to some pub in the area of Salisbury; sometimes to dine, sometimes just for an after-dinner drink. He never visited pubs in the city itself but preferred to drive for twenty minutes or half an hour into the neighbouring countryside. He had a roster of pubs which he visited regularly, where he was known and welcomed, where the landlord had a bottle of one of his favourite malt whiskies ready for him. Sometimes he got into conversation with another visitor, more often he sat in silence which, without being morose, gave little feeling of conviviality. Occasionally he would meet a friend. Michael Wade of Trafalgar Park found him once in front of a pint of beer in the King's Head in Redlynch. Heath looked slightly taken aback. 'Ah, the great estate owner has come to join us!' he exclaimed.[8] Each year he would give a party for the landlords and landladies whose premises he patronised; they were slightly strained occasions but his guests immensely valued the good intentions that lay behind the invitation. Life set into an undemanding pattern: there seemed no reason why, allowing for a gradual degeneration in his health, it should ever change.

*   *   *

In August 2003 he went on what had become an annual pilgrimage to Salzburg. He was due to return on the 15th but a day or two before the date of his departure the hotel where he was staying became seriously concerned about his health and transferred him to a local hospital. The symptoms had been those of a violent stomach upset; only when he got to the Landesklinik was it discovered that he had suffered two pulmonary embolisms – clots on the lung, in laymen's language: the first while he was still in Salisbury; the second, more serious, a few days before. The hospital saw no reason for surgery and felt the condition could best be treated by drugs. James Elder flew out to be with him and it was judged that Heath's condition was stable enough to allow him to return to London by air ambulance. He did so on 26 August and was installed in the King Edward VII Hospital – 'Sister Agnes' – in Beaumont Street.

It was clear from the start that he would never walk again – a few faltering paces were the most that could be hoped for. His brain was unaffected. There was no reason why he should not linger on; equally, he was acutely vulnerable and the balance of possibilities seemed to be that he would not last more than a year, or two at the most. From Sister Agnes he went to a convalescent home in Buckinghamshire. This proved a disaster. He was bored and discontented. Most of the other residents were elderly ladies. Supper was served at 6 p.m.; Heath insisted on going out to dinner every night at, usually expensive, restaurants in the neighbourhood. He complained that his bed was uncomfortable and slept in an armchair. He moved to a hotel in Jersey that had been recommended to him. In theory it had closed for the winter but for him they kept a floor open. It was a great improvement on Buckinghamshire but not many people came to see him, he read with difficulty, once again he was bored. He longed to return to Arundells, where he could re-establish something close to a normal routine. He got his way, and was back in Salisbury in time for Christmas.

By this time a chair-lift had been installed so as to give him access to his bedroom. Heath had at first strongly opposed the idea, mainly on the grounds of expense, partly because he felt humiliated by the need to be propelled around his own house by so undignified a device. Regretfully he accepted that it was essential. At first he insisted that, if anyone visited the house, the chair-lift should be out of sight, behind the first corner on the staircase. Later he became used, even attached, to it and, like Babar first encountering an elevator in New York, made quite unnecessary journeys up and down for the pleasure of the motion. Two nurses had arrived a few days before him: one for the days, one for the nights. Heath had originally asked for male carers but, when told this was impossible, accepted women with good grace. Kay Davidson, from New Zealand, was the night nurse for the first ten weeks or so. She found her patient polite and considerate; the only problem was his formidable weight which made him a difficult proposition when it came to helping him from bed to chair or from chair to lavatory.

Even though he had been forced to give up drinking alcohol, the tradition of visiting pubs in the neighbourhood of Salisbury was at once revived, and she was expected to accompany him. The apparition of a former prime minister who drank only water, accompanied by a nurse and policeman who, being on duty, drank only fruit juice, must have been a little unsatisfactory for the landlords, but Heath was a celebrity and the fact that he was known regularly to visit a certain pub was an attraction to those who liked to share space with the great. Kay Davidson found that, while Heath would almost never initiate a conversation, he was delighted if people spoke to him and asked his views on current matters. If people asked her whether that was really Ted Heath at the table over there, she would suggest that they come over to talk to him; the success of an evening for her was measured by the number of meetings she had been able to engineer.[9]

When they got home after one of these outings Heath would sit up late, sometimes until the early hours of the morning, watching the news programmes on television. He never played the piano and rarely listened to music. He read newspapers assiduously and usually had a book beside him, though often it remained unopened. More and more time would be spent in reverie, only half awake, aware of what was going on around him but not particularly concerned about it. One of his few regular expeditions was to the Cathedral, where his wheelchair was always installed in a position of honour at the front. He insisted on being taken there by car, even though it would have been quicker and less trouble for everyone concerned to have wheeled his chair the two hundred or so yards across the Close. Such a procedure, he felt, like the use of the chair-lift, would turn him into a helpless bundle, even a figure of fun. He was resolved that his dignity should be maintained.

It was as much the threat to his dignity as to his independence that led to his indignation when he thought people were trying to take over his life and to push him into a course of action which did not appeal to him. Even before his illness he had been growing resentful of any kind of interference; over the last eighteen months of his life he became almost paranoid in his suspicions. Robert Armstrong was the first to incur his resentment when in April 2003 he wrote to say how relieved he was that Heath was investigating the possibility of having a chair-lift installed. But this would not be enough. There ought to be someone permanently on hand 'to help you look after yourself'. The present staff – effectively just the housekeeper and Stuart Craven – could not cope and might 'feel unable to carry on. And the police cannot be expected to undertake that sort of support on a continuing basis.' It would be important to find somebody whom Heath liked but 'whoever it was would not need to be with you the whole time'. It was true that this would involve considerable extra expense, but: 'I truly do not think that you can afford not to make some arrangement on these lines, because the consequences of not doing so could be much worse.' 'This has been a difficult letter to write,' Armstrong concluded. 'If it has been difficult to receive, you must attribute it to my caring that you should be as comfortable, as content and as well looked after as possible.'[10]

It *was* a difficult letter to receive and Heath dealt with it, as was his wont, by pushing it to the back of his mind and deferring any decision to a later date. His pulmonary embolism in Salzburg settled the matter: if he was to return to Arundells the full-time attendance of trained nurses would be essential. Now it was Sara Morrison who came into the firing line. She wrote him a letter which he interpreted as proposing that he should leave Arundells and move into a nursing home. In fact she had never intended this as being more than a temporary measure but Heath was in no mood to make allowances. She wanted 'to get rid of me', he told Richard Burn, 'to put me in a home. She thinks she can take everything over.' Burn suggested that he discuss the matter with Robert Armstrong. 'He's in on the whole thing!' Heath retorted. It did not take too much persuasion to convince him that Armstrong was not a participant in what he described, only half jokingly, as 'the big plot', but though they spoke frequently on the telephone, it was to be almost a year before Sara Morrison was fully restored to favour. For a man as solitary as Heath, the loss of the woman whose company he so much relished was a serious deprivation. By the time she came fully back his life was already slipping away.[11]

There was not much left to be done to put his affairs in order. When he and Jim Callaghan were attending John Smith's funeral, Tony Benn asked what they were going to do with their papers. Callaghan said that he had got fifty-three boxes of papers and that they were going to the London School of Economics. 'I have got 115 tons of papers,' said Heath proudly, 'and they are going to Balliol.'[12] Massive though his archive was – he used to boast that he had thrown nothing away since the age of fourteen – it weighed, of course, nothing approaching 115 tons. Nor was it going to Balliol. Heath had conceived a dream, based loosely on the presidential libraries which were established after the retirement of each President of the United States, by which Arundells after his death would become both a shrine at which his memory would be kept finely burnished and a place of study in which scholars could pore over the documents he had accumulated. Even though money was tight over the last years of his life he had refused to take out a mortgage on Arundells in case it complicated his plans for the house's future. As Robert Armstrong, who was eventually to find himself responsible for executing Heath's will, knew only too well, however, there were other far more significant problems. For one thing there was nowhere at Arundells where the papers could properly be stored and catalogued, no facilities for servicing and supervising the scholars who might consult them, not even a room in which those scholars might sit. For another, to run such a library, not to mention to open Arundells to the public, would be an expensive business. Yet the most substantial element of

Heath's £5.4 million estate was the house itself and its contents. The only way by which the money could possibly be found to run Arundells after Heath's death was by finding someone who would buy the archive – thus, of course, destroying an integral part of Heath's vision. Armstrong and others tried to persuade Heath that his plans were impracticable if not actively undesirable. He would have none of it. Something would turn up. His one concession to reason was to accept that, if his Trustees could not carry out his wishes, then they would be free to dispose of his estate and apply the money raised on whatever educational or musical purposes they thought he would have felt appropriate.

He did not wish the time for that decision to be long postponed. More than thirty years before, he had seen and amended a letter signed by Douglas Hurd to a lady who had enquired about Heath's views on euthanasia. He is personally opposed to it, said Hurd. 'Voluntary euthanasia necessarily includes the collaboration of a doctor or other suitable person, and he is of the opinion that no circumstances can be envisaged in which it would be right to impose that responsibility on any individual.'[13] But though he had no wish to saddle any other person with the responsibility for taking his life, he saw no reason why he should seek to protract it indefinitely himself if he found it burdensome. He told Jeffrey Easton that, while he was determined to celebrate his eighty-ninth birthday, he had no wish to live to the age of ninety. His eighty-ninth birthday party would be his farewell to the world; after that, let things take their own course – he would do nothing to prevent them.

Stuart Craven pleaded that he would find the strain of a large party intolerable; surely it would be better to have a few old friends with whom he could talk in tranquillity. Heath would have none of it. His last birthday would be celebrated with all the traditional trimmings, a marquee would be set up on the lawn, all the habitués would be welcome. By the time 9 July 2005 arrived he was spending most of his days in bed, for much of the time barely conscious. It took him a long time to get dressed and most of the guests had been there for about an hour by the time that he was wheeled in by Stuart Craven. His friends rose and clapped, then one by one were led up to pay their respects. None of them can have doubted that this would be the last time that they would see him. He could barely speak but he appeared to know well who each person was and smiled broadly as they spoke to him. Then, after forty minutes, with his head slumped forward on his chest, he was wheeled away.

He had said his last goodbye. Two days later he slipped into a coma. On the evening of 17 July, just over a week after his farewell party, Edward Heath died.

His funeral was held in Salisbury Cathedral. The coffin was drawn on an old funeral hand-cart from the front door of Arundells to the West Door of the Cathedral. 1,600 people were there, with more than 500 standing outside the Cathedral. John Major attended, so did Lady Thatcher, looking 'pale and frail' alongside Michael Howard, the Leader of the Opposition. Tony Blair could not be there as he was lunching with the French Prime Minister, but Geoff Hoon, Leader of the House of Commons, represented him. Robert Armstrong read the traditional 'Let us now praise famous men' from Ecclesiasticus and Richard Burn the splendid verses from Corinthians 15 – 'O death, where is they sting? O grave, where is thy victory?' The Bishop, who gave the address, remarked that Heath was 'a shy person, who did not have much time for smooth words and social pleasantries'. It was generally felt that this was a delicate compromise between honesty and unconvincing discretion. The 'last post' was sounded by Lance Corporal Woollams of the Honourable Artillery Company. Heath's body was cremated and the ashes buried in the South Crossing of the Cathedral.

Perhaps I may be forgiven a final personal note. All biographers must from time to time ask themselves what their subjects would think of their book. I have little doubt that Heath would have found much of mine unappetising. I can imagine him angrily scoring 'Nonsense!' in the margin here, 'Rubbish!' there; 'How?' in one place, 'Why?' in another. I hope he would nevertheless have felt that the study was a sympathetic one. From the time that I first did odd jobs for him in the Foreign Office when he was Minister of State I respected and admired his courage, his integrity, his determination. He was clear-headed and resolute; he knew what he wanted and was determined to get it, but though exigent he was never unreasonable. He recognised the limitations of the individual as well as of the system and was prepared to take account of them. He was the sort of minister every young official is proud and pleased to serve.

Even at that early stage I could see that, if there was a way of making things difficult for himself, Heath would surely find it. With the years that propensity grew ever more alarming. Ernest Bevin, when someone remarked that Herbert Morrison was his own worst enemy, is supposed to have retorted: 'Not while I'm alive, he ain't.' No one, not Harold Wilson, not Margaret Thatcher, would have said that of Heath. Again and again, when by a small capacity to conciliate, to take into account the feelings of others, to see himself as others saw him, he could have made immeasurably smoother the path before him, he blundered into a course that was calculated to create the highest measure of opposition, lost battles which he should have won or won them at a price that made the victory hardly worth having. He was a great man, but his blemishes, though by far less considerable, were quite as conspicuous as his virtues, and it is too often by his blemishes that he is remembered.

His memorial service in Westminster Abbey was even more star-studded than his funeral. The Duke of Edinburgh was there, the Duke of Kent was there, this time Tony Blair made it, the Archbishop of Canterbury was there, the Cardinal Archbishop was there. 'I'm glad I went,' Tony Benn wrote in his diary, 'because I was fond of Ted and he had integrity.'[14] Coming from a man who for most of his life had been Heath's bitter political opponent, it was no bad epitaph.

NOTES

CHAPTER 1: *The Child and the Boy*

1 *Family History. Journal of the Institute of Heraldic and Genealogical Studies.* 'The Ancestry of Mr Edward Heath', by C.R. Humphrey-Smith and Michael G. Heenen, Vol. 4 (19), pp.3–12 and 'Further Notes on Mr Heath's Ancestry', Vol.4 (20–21), p.114.

2 George Hutchinson, *Edward Heath* (London, 1970) p.2.

3 Heath to Iain Macleod, 14 September 1962, Heath papers 1 1/7.

4 Edward Heath, *The Course of My Life* (London, 1998) p.3.

5 Conversations with Nancy-Joan Seligman, Lady de Zulueta and Margaret Chadd.

6 John Campbell, *Edward Heath* (London, 1993) p.18. Heath's annotated copy is currently at his house in Salisbury.

7 Margaret Laing, *Edward Heath: Prime Minister* (London, 1972) pp.14–15.

8 Campbell, *Heath*, p.7.

9 Keith Hunt in Michael Cockerell's film, *A Very Singular Man* (1998); Heath, *Course of My Life*, pp.3–4; Heath papers 1 1/1.

10 Laing, *Heath*, pp.13 and 15.

11 John Junor, *Listening for a Midnight Tram* (London, 1990), p.191; conversations with Nancy-Joan Seligman, Lady de Zulueta and Margaret Chadd.

12 Marian Evans, *Ted Heath: A Family Portrait* (London, 1970), p.18; Laing, *Heath*, pp.18 and 23.

13 Edward Heath, *Music: A Joy for Life* (London, 1976), pp.10 and 7; Evans, *Ted Heath*, p.13.

14 Testimonial of 11/1/34, Heath papers, 1 1/2; September 1970, Heath papers, 3 4/9.

15 Hutchinson, *Heath*, p.10; Bryan Forbes's film, *Sir Edward Heath: A Life Beyond Politics*; Heath, *Course of My Life*, p.67.

16 Laing, *Heath*, p.33.

17 This and subsequent extracts from reports are drawn from the admirably maintained archives of Chatham House.

18 Cockerell, *A Very Singular Man*.
19 Laing, *Heath*, p.34.
20 Reg Thain in Cockerell's film *A Very Singular Man*; Heath, *Course of My Life*, pp.17–18.
21 Edward Heath, *Travels* (London, 1973), p.9.
22 Heath, *Music*, p.12.
23 Arnold Goodman, *Tell Them I'm On My Way* (London, 1993), p.37; Hutchinson, *Heath*, pp.12–13.
24 Ken Evans to Heath, 23/3/35, Heath papers 1 1/3.
25 Hutchinson, *Heath*, p.18; Morris to Norman, 6/6/34, Heath papers 1 1/2; Norman to Morris, 8/6/34, Chatham House archives.
26 Morris to Heath, Jan 1935, Heath papers 1 2/1.
27 Chatham House archives.
28 Heath papers, 1 1/3.

CHAPTER 2: *Balliol*

1 Heath, *Course of My Life*, p.24.
2 Balliol College archives.
3 Heath to Norman, 28/11/35, Chatham House archives.
4 Andrew Roth, *Heath and the Heathmen* (London, 1972) p.29.
5 Cockerell, *A Very Singular Man*; Evans, *Ted Heath*, p.63.
6 Terry Coleman, *Guardian*, 9/6/70.
7 Heath to Norman, undated, Chatham House archives; letter to author from David Willcocks of 9/6/08; Hutchinson, *Heath*, p.19.
8 Hutchinson, *Heath*, p.19; Laing, *Heath*, p.48; conversation with Lord Healey; Hutchinson, *Heath*, p.35; conversation with Sir Nicholas Henderson.
9 'Freddy' to Heath, 10/8/39, Heath papers, 1 1/3.
10 Conversation with Sir Nicholas Henderson; A. C. Tickner to Heath, Heath papers, 1 1/3.
11 Nigel Nicolson, *Long Life* (London, 1997), pp.65–6; Denis Healey, *The Time of My Life* (London, 1989), p.33; conversation with Lord Healey; David Walter, *The Oxford Union* (London, 1984), p.164.
12 Ken Evans to Heath, 26/8/35, Heath papers 1 1/3; Roth, *Heath and the Heathmen*, p.26.
13 Kay Raven's letters to Heath are in the Heath papers but uncatalogued.
14 Heath, *Course of My Life*, pp.29 and 44–5; Hutchinson, *Heath*, p.25.
15 Ian Harvey, *To Fall Like Lucifer* (London, 1971), p.49; Heath, *Course of My Life*, p.38.
16 Ken Evans to Heath, 15/4/36, Heath papers 1 1/3; Campbell, *Heath*, p.20; *Isis*, 25/1/39; Hutchinson, *Heath*, p.27; Terry Coleman, *Movers and Shakers* (London, 1987), p.122.
17 *Isis*, 19/2/36 and 11/3/36.
18 November 1938, Heath papers 1 1/4.
19 Tickner to Heath, 8/5/37, Heath papers 1 1/3.
20 Heath, *Course of My Life*, pp.58–9; Liddell Hart to Heath, 24/1/63, Heath papers 1 1/6.

21 John Barnes and David Nicholson (eds), *The Empire at Bay: The Leo Amery Diaries 1929–1945* (London, 1988); *Isis* 8/3/39.
22 Walter, *Oxford Union*, pp.110–11.
23 January 1940, Heath papers 1 1/15.
24 *Christian Values* (London, 1996). Contribution by Heath on 'Christian Values in Politics'.
25 Heath, *Course of My Life*, p.55 and *Travels*, p.39.
26 *Course of My Life*, p.53; Jack Jones, *Union Man* (London, 1986), pp.69–70; letter to author from Mick Jones of 18/03/09.
27 Campbell, *Heath*, p.334; Heath to Winckler, 6/9/47, Heath papers 1 2/4.
28 Heath, *Course of My Life*, p.44 and *Travels*, p.39.
29 Roy Jenkins, *Life at the Centre* (London, 1991), p.30; Heath, *Travels*, p.49; Heath to Winckler, 6/9/47, Heath papers 1 2/1.
30 Copy of letter from Seligman to his parents, Heath papers 1 1/5.
31 Hutchinson, *Heath*, p.35; testimonial by Lindsay, 14/10/39, Heath papers 1 1/2; 'CR' to Heath, 28/7/39, Heath papers 1 1/3.
32 Balliol College archives.
33 Philip Ziegler, *Harold Wilson* (London, 1993), p.21.

CHAPTER 3: *War*

1 Heath, *Course of My Life*, p.68.
2 Armstrong to Heath, 26/8/89, Heath papers 1 4/13.
3 Jack Weston to Heath, 29/12/37, Heath papers 1 1/3.
4 Heath papers 1 1/5; Tickner to Heath, 31/8/39, Heath papers 1 1/13.
5 'Alan' to Heath, 31/8/39, Heath papers 1 1/3.
6 Report on tour, Heath papers 1 1/5.
7 1/12/39, Heath papers 4, uncatalogued.
8 Diary, January 1940, Heath papers 1 1/15.
9 Heath papers 1 1/6.
10 Diary, March 1940, Heath papers 1 1/15.
11 *The Man who went to the Country* (TVS, 1985).
12 Heath papers 1 1/6.
13 Laing, *Heath*, p.73; Hutchinson, *Heath*, pp.41 and 43.
14 19/7/42 and 27/8/44, Heath papers, uncatalogued.
15 Bligh to Heath, 2/4/40, Heath papers 1 1/3.
16 5/4/45, Heath papers, uncatalogued.
17 Heath, *Course of My Life*, p.93.
18 Campbell, *Heath*, p.43.
19 Heath papers 1 1/6; Heath to Winckler, 6/9/47, Heath papers 1 2/4.
20 Heath, *Course of My Life*, p.103; Rupert Allason, 'Ted Heath', ts pages 41–2; Sir Bill Jeffrey to Lord Armstrong, 24/12/09.
21 Roth, *Heath and the Heathmen*, p.51; Heath, *Course of My Life*, p.102.
22 Heath, *Course of My Life*, p.101.
23 Roth, *Heath and the Heathmen*, p.55.
24 Heath, *Course of my Life*, p.106.

CHAPTER 4: *In Waiting for Westminister*

1 Diary, Jan 1940, Heath papers 1 1/15.
2 Evans, *Heath: A Family Portrait*, pp.15–29.
3 Heath, *Course of My Life*, p.109.
4 Heath papers 1 2/1.
5 Hutchinson, *Heath*, p.47; Allason, *Ted Heath*, ts p.47.
6 Hutchinson, *Heath*, pp.50–51; Heath, *Course of My Life*, p.113.
7 Masefield to Heath, 29/4/92, Heath papers 1 1/6.
8 Hutchinson, *Heath*, pp.50–51.
9 Humphry Berkeley, *Crossing the Floor* (London, 1972), p.102; Heath, *Course of My Life*, p.117.
10 Hutchinson, *Heath*, pp.54–5; Roth, *Heath and the Heathmen*, p.60.
11 Heath to Winckler, 1/12/47, Heath papers 1 2/1.
12 *The Man Who Went to the Country*.
13 17/11/47, Heath papers 1 2/1.
14 Heath to J. B. Cartland, 10/1/48, Heath papers 1 2/1; 'Joe' to Heath, 5/6/48, Heath papers 1 2/1.
15 Bernard Palmer, *Gadfly for God* (London, 1991), p.198.
16 Roth, *Heath and the Heathmen*, p.62; Nicholas Bagnall, *A Little Overmatter* (Lewes, 2002), pp.6–7.
17 Palmer, *Gadfly for God*, pp.198–9; 'Joe' to Heath, 30/7/48, Heath papers 1 2/1; Heath to J. B. Cartland, 3/8/48, Heath papers 1 2/1.
18 William Heath to Heath, 20/3/49, Heath papers 1 2/1; Hutchinson, *Heath*, p.64.
19 Heath, *Course of My Life*, p.126.
20 'Frank' to Heath, 8/7/48, Heath papers 1 2/1.
21 Jenkins to Heath, 2/5/48, Heath papers 1 2/1; Heath to Winckler, 1/12/47, Heath papers 1 2/1.
22 *The Journals of Woodrow Wyatt*, ed. Sarah Curtis, vol. 2, Pan edition (London, 2000), p.243.
23 Heath, *Course of My Life*, pp.126, 136 and 138.

CHAPTER 5: *The Young Member*

1 Heath, *Course of My Life*, p.140.
2 Ian Trethowan, *Split Screen* (London, 1984), pp.51 and 57.
3 Hutchinson, *Heath*, p.71.
4 Conversation with Kenneth Clarke.
5 Roth, *Heath and the Heathmen*, p.79; Beaverbrook to Martin, 9/8/62, Heath papers 1 1/5.
6 Heath, *Course of My Life*, p.148.
7 House of Commons, 26 June 1960.
8 Eden to Heath, 26/6/50, Heath papers 1 2/1; Heath, *Course of My Life*, p.145.
9 Peter Walker, *The Ascent of Britain* (London, 1977), p.62.
10 Heath to Marc Glendening, 15/12/84, Heath papers 1 6/1.
11 *Contemporary Record*, vol.9, No.1 (London, 1995), p.193; Edward Heath, *Parliament and People* (Conservative Political Centre, London, 1960), p.26.

12 Heath, *Course of My Life*, p.140.

13 Laing, *Heath*, p.93; Roth, *Heath and the Heathmen*, p.93.

14 Ian Gilmour, *Whatever Happened to the Tories?* (London, 1997), p.48; Timothy Raison, *Tories and the Welfare State* (London, 1990), p.26.

15 Conversation with John Selwyn Gummer.

16 Macleod to Heath, 5/1/51, Heath papers 1 2/1.

17 Anthony Seldon, *Churchill's Indian Summer* (London, 1981), p.527; Tim Renton, *Chief Whip* (London, 2004), p.279.

18 7/12/68, Heath papers 1 2/7.

19 Laing, *Heath*, p.107.

20 Allason, 'Ted Heath', ts p.58.

21 Evans, *Heath*, p.90; Laing, *Heath*, p.107.

22 7/12/68, Heath papers 1 2/7; *A Very Singular Man*; Evans, *Heath*, pp.89–90; John Peyton, *Without Benefit of Laundry* (London, 1997), p.102.

23 Robert Babcock to Douglas, undated, Heath papers 1 2/5; Heath, *Course of My Life*, p.152.

24 Heath to Martin Verden, 8/8/51, Heath papers 1 2/1.

25 *A Very Singular Man*.

26 Margaret Roberts to Heath, 16/10/51, Heath papers 1 1/7; Heath, *Course of My Life*, p.153.

27 Kay Raven to Heath, 17/10/51 and 10/9/50, Heath papers, uncatalogued.

28 Laing, *Heath*, p.100; Evans, *Heath*, p.104.

29 *A Very Singular Man*.

30 *New Statesman*, 23/4/07; conversation with Brian Coleman.

31 Heath, *Course of My Life*, p.154.

32 Renton, *Chief Whip*, p.280.

33 Heath, *Course of My Life*, p.151; 7/12/68, Heath papers 1 2/7.

34 Heath, *Course of My Life*, p.158; Nicolson, *Long Life*, p.147.

35 Conversations with Lady Soames and Lady Aldington.

36 Heath, *Course of My Life*, p.165.

37 Hutchinson, *Heath*, pp.82–3.

CHAPTER 6: *Chief Whip*

1 21/12/55, 21/12/55 and 29/12/55, Heath papers 1 2/13.

2 Moore to Heath, 25/12/55, Heath papers 1 2/13; Geoffrey Fisher to Heath, 24/12/55, Heath papers 1 2/13.

3 Harold Macmillan, *Pointing the Way* (London, 1972), p.29; Hutchinson, *Heath*, p.87; Heath, *Course of My Life*, p.172.

4 Renton, *Chief Whip*, p.89.

5 Jock Bruce-Gardyne and Nigel Lawson, *The Power Game* (London, 1976), p.42; Laing, *Heath*, p.113.

6 Gerald Nabarro, *NAB 1* (Oxford, 1969), p.56; Tony Benn, *Years of Hope* (London, 1994), p.243.

7 Woodrow Wyatt, *Confessions of an Optimist* (London, 1985), pp.260 and 340; Jim Prior, *A Balance of Power* (London, 1986), p.39.

8 18/7/57, Heath papers 2/8.

9 Heath papers 1 2/9; Hailsham to Heath, 26/6/59, Conservative Party Archives (CPA) CCO, 26/6/59.

10 Hutchinson, *Heath*, p.83; Clark to Heath, 20/5/58, William Clark, Mss 153.

11 Laing, *Heath*, p.119; Price to Heath, 13/11/57, Heath papers 1 2/9.

12 Anstruther-Gray to Heath, 24/4/58, Heath papers 1 2/13.

13 Conversations with Lady de Zulueta and Kenneth Clarke.

14 Heath to Oliver Poole, 10/1/56, Heath papers 1 2/9.

15 Heath to Macmillan, 6/1/59, Heath papers, uncatalogued; Norman Fowler, *Ministers Decide* (London, 1991), p.13; Allason, 'Ted Heath', ts p.295.

16 Heath to Oliver Poole, 29/7/58 and 10/9/58, Heath papers 1 2/9.

17 Heath to Macmillan, 13/11/58, Heath papers 1 2/13.

18 Laing, *Heath*, p.113; Berkeley, *Crossing the Floor*, p.103.

19 Crookshank to Heath, undated but probably 1957, Heath papers 1 2/4.

20 Heath to Churchill, 25/8/54, Heath papers, uncatalogued.

21 Anthony Courtney, *Sailor in a Russian Frame* (London, 1968), pp.150–51; Allason, 'Ted Heath', ts pp.77–80.

22 Edward du Cann, *Two Lives* (Malvern 1995), p.194; Peter Walker, *Staying Power* (London, 1991), p.20.

23 Campbell, *Heath*, p.102; Heath, *Course of My Life*, p.164; Heath papers, undated 1 2/7.

24 Campbell, *Heath*, p.297; Lord Butler, *The Art of the Possible* (London, 1971), p.198; Anthony Eden, *Full Circle* (London, 1960), p.349.

25 Heath to Eden, 3/2/56, Heath papers 1 1/5; Robert J. Jackson, *Rebels and Whigs* (London, 1968), p.139.

26 Jackson, *Rebels and Whigs*, p.139; Roth, *Heath and the Heathmen*, pp.100–101.

27 Heath papers 1 2/9; Roth, *Heath and the Heathmen*, p.103.

28 *The Macmillan Diaries, The Cabinet Years*, ed. Peter Catterell (London, 2005), pp.590 and 601; William Clark, *From Three Worlds* (London, 1986), p.173.

29 Heath, *Course of My Life*, p.169; NA PREM 11/1152; cf. *Whitehall and the Suez Crisis*, ed. Saul Kelly and Anthony Gorst (London, 2000), pp.69–70.

30 Laing, *Heath*, p.116; Shackleton to Heath 2/11/56, Heath papers 1 3/22.

31 Andrew Denham and Mark Garnett, *Keith Joseph* (Chesham, 2001), p.73; Roth, *Heath and the Heathmen*, p.98; Jackson, *Rebels and Whigs*, pp.284–5; Nicolson, *Long Life*, p.165.

32 William Clark to Heath, undated, Heath papers 2/9.

33 Roth, *Heath and the Heathmen*, p.107; Jackson, *Rebels and Whigs*, p.150.

34 Turner to Heath, 6/12/56 and Heath to Turner, 7/12/56, Heath papers 1 2/14.

35 9/11/57, MS Macmillan Dep. c432 f43; Heath to Poole, 30/1/57, CPA CCO 20/1/5, *Harold Nicolson, Letters and Diaries*, ed. Nigel Nicolson (London, 1968), p.366.

36 Nicolson, *Long Life*, pp.199–200.

37 Lord Kilmuir, *Political Adventure* (London, 1964), pp.281 and 314; Stuart to Heath, 21/1/57, Heath papers 1 2/9.

38 Heath, *Course of My Life*, pp.177–8.

39 Hornsby to Heath, 17/12/56, Heath papers 1 2/14; *Punch*, 7/8/57.

40 Bancroft to Heath, 16/1/57, Heath papers 1 2/9; Heath, *Course of My Life*, p.179.

41 Heath, *Course of My Life*, pp.182 and 250; Conversation with Lord Baker; Alistair Horne, *Macmillan, Vol II 1957–1986* (London, 1989), p.10.

42 Heath, *Course of My Life*, p.181; Macmillan, *The Cabinet Years*, p.615; Roth, *Heath and the Heathmen*, p.118.

43 Roth, *Heath and the Heathmen*, p.124; Heath papers 13/3/56, 4/7/55, 13/11/58, uncatalogued.

44 John Ramsden, *The Winds of Change, Macmillan to Heath 1957–1975* (London, 1996), pp.68–9.

45 Robert Shepherd, *Iain Macleod* (London, 1994), p.147; Ramsden, *Winds of Change*, p.37; Gilmour, *Whatever Happened to the Tories*, p.145.

46 Heath to Lennox-Boyd, 13/2/58, Whips' Notes; Heath papers, uncatalogued.

47 Whips' Notes, Heath papers, uncatalogued.

48 Harold Macmillan, *Riding the Storm* (London, 1971), p.373; Campbell, *Heath*, p.98.

49 Richard Davenport-Hines, *The Macmillans* (London, 1992), p.283; Heath, *Course of My Life*, p.191.

50 Thatcher to Heath, 15/10/59, Heath papers 1 3/22.

CHAPTER 7: *Europe: The First Round*

1 Macmillan, *Pointing the Way*, p.19; Heath to Macmillan, 18/11/59, Heath papers 1 2/16.

2 Macmillan to Heath, 23/12/59, Heath to Macmillan, 23/12/59 and 15/1/60, Heath papers 1 2/16.

3 Hutchinson, *Heath*, p.89; Norma Major, *Chequers* (London, 1987), pp.216–17.

4 NA CM cc 4/60, 2/2/60; cc 8(60), 12/2/60.

5 Heath to Macmillan, 10/2/60, Heath papers 1 1/7.

6 NA CM cc 33/60, 26/5/60 and cc 46(60), 26/7/60.

7 Eric Wigham, *Strikes and the Government 1893–1981* (London, 2nd edition, 1982), p.125; 13/5/60, Heath papers 1 1/7.

8 Stuart to Heath, 22/6/60, Heath papers 1 1/7; Feather to Heath, 28/7/60, Heath papers 1 1/7.

9 Lewis Baston, *Reggie: The Life of Reginald Maudling* (Stroud, 2004), pp.321–2.

10 Roth, *Heath and the Heathmen*, p.150; 24/7/60, cit. Nabarro, NAB 1, p.56.

11 NA CM cc 3(61) of 31/1/61.

12 Edward Heath, *Old World, New Horizons* (Harvard, 1970), p.26; NA FO371.158173; Keith Middlemas, *Power, Competition and the State*, vol II. *Threats to the Post-war Settlement in Britain 1961–74* (London, 1990), p.34; Heath to Kilmuir, 30/11/60, Kilmuir to Heath, 14/12/60, Heath papers 4 1/6.

13 Chatham House papers, 23/10/61, RIIA 8/2781.

14 Heath, *Course of My Life*, p.207; NA cc 9(61) of 21/2/61.

15 NA cc 29(61) of 30/5/61.

16 NA 371, 158177, 15/6/61.

17 NA 371, 158176, 14/5/61.

18 Dixon to Reilly, 12/5/61 LNA 371, 158176; Harold Macmillan, *At The End of the Day* (London, 1973), p.118; Richard Lamb, *The Macmillan Years* (London, 1995), p.147; Heath, *Course of My Life*, p.211.

19 Norman Brook to Heath, 15/8/61, Heath papers 4 1/6; Lamb, *Macmillan Years*, p.162.

20 Eric Roll, *Crowded Hours* (London, 1985), pp.113–14; Donald Maitland, *Diverse Times, Sundry Places* (Brighton 1996), p.113; Conversation with Sir Donald Maitland.

21 Jean Monnet, *Mémoires* (Paris, 1976), p.535; 4/9/61, Monnet papers cit. Mark Deavin, unpublished PhD thesis, 'Macmillan's Hidden Agenda', p.588.

22 NA cc 53(61) of 5/10/61 and cc 56(61) of 17/10/61; 23/10/61, RIIA 8/2781.

23 NA FCO 371 164778; Heath, *Course of My Life*, p.219.

24 Nora Beloff, *The General Says No* (London, 1963), p.114; Lamb to Heath, 8/9/94, Heath papers 1 1/4.

25 Minute of 21/1/62, Heath papers 4 1/6; George Ball, *The Discipline of Power* (London, 1968), p.81.

26 Maitland, *Diverse Times*, p.115; 13/11/61, 9/3/62, 23/7/62, Heath papers 4 1/5.

27 R. A. Butler papers, RABF 9614 16/5/62.

28 22/6/61, Heath papers 4 1/4; Philip Goodhart, *The 1922* (London, 1973), p.184.

29 Robert Rhodes James, *Ambitions and Realities* (London, 1972), p.107.

30 27/11/61, Heath papers 4 1/4.

31 Macmillan, *At The End of the Day*, p.131; Horne, *Macmillan,* vol II, p.355; NA cc 57(62); Heath papers 1 1/7.

32 NA cc 44(62), 5/7/62; Piers Dixon, *Double Diploma* (London, 1968), p.289.

33 *Sunday Times*, 30/10/62; NA cc 73(62), 6/12/62; NA cc 3(63), 10/1/63.

34 10/3/62, FO371, 171149.

35 26/12/62, Horne, *Macmillan,* vol II, p.444; Heath, *Course of My Life*, p.227.

36 Macmillan, *Pointing the Way*, p.118; Conversation with Sir Michael Butler.

37 Heath, *Course of My Life,* p.228; NA cc (63)5. 22/1/63; Roll to Anthony Seddon, 16/1/98, Heath papers 4 3/23.

38 Ball, *Discipline of Power*, p.82; Codel 98 and 100 of 28/1/63 and 29/1/63. Soames papers; Heath papers 4 1/6.

39 Laing, *Heath*, p.143; Christopher Soames, first draft of unpublished autobiography.

40 NA cc (63)8, 29/1/63.

41 Shuckburgh to Heath, 4/2/63, Heath papers 4 1/6; Lamb, *Macmillan Years*, p.203.

42 Hutchinson, *Heath*, p.120.

43 D. R. Thorpe, *Alec Douglas-Home* (London, 1996), p.283.

44 *The Times*, 11/10/63 cit. Randolph Churchill, *The Fight for the Tory Leadership* (London, 1964), p.111.

45 Telegram No. 5130 of 19/6/63, Dept of State Papers, JFK Presidential Library.

46 Laing, *Heath*, p.157; Thorpe, *Douglas Home*, p.293; Heath to Hailsham, July 1990, Heath papers 4 6/13.

47 Prior, *Balance of Power*, p.33.

CHAPTER 8: *Minister*

1 Laing, *Heath*, pp.162–3; Campbell, *Heath*, p.167.

2 Laing, *Heath*, pp.162–3.

3 2/9/65, Heath papers 1 1/12.

4 19/12/70, Heath papers 3 4/9.

5 Conversation with Lord Kingsland.

6 TVS, *The Man Who Went to the Country*.

7 Evans, *Heath*, pp.85 and 123.

8 Conversations with Nancy-Joan Seligman and Lady Aldington.

9 Heath, *Course of My Life*, p.256; conversation with Sir Timothy Kitson.

10 Conversations with Lady Cromer and Sir Nicholas Henderson.

11 20/3/67, Adeane Papers.

12 *The Cecil King Diary 1965–1970* (London, 1972), p.204.

13 Hugo Young, *One of Us* (London, 1991), p.84; Heath, *Course of My Life*, p.257.

14 NA CM (12/64) 18/2/64; Heath interview with David Butler, 4/4/65; Ronald Butt, *The Power of Parliament* (London, 1967), p.259.

15 Baston, *Maudling*, pp.218–19.

16 22/2/50, Heath papers 2 2/2.

17 Laing, *Heath*, p.159.

18 Conversation with Christopher Roberts.

19 Heath, *Course of My Life*, p.259.

20 NA CM 3(64), 14/1/64.

21 Mark Garnett and Ian Aitken, *Splendid! Splendid! The Authorised Biography of Willie Whitelaw* (London, 2002), p.61; Renton, *Chief Whip*, pp.303–4.

22 Goodhart, *The 1922*, pp.196–7; Channon to Butler, 24/1/64, RAB. H, 96/77; Thorpe, *Douglas-Home*, p.355.

23 NA CM 19(64), 17/3/64; Douglas-Home to Heath, 7/4/64, Heath papers 1 1/7; Campbell, *Heath*, p.155; James Margach, *The Abuse of Power* (London, 1978), p.132; Heath, *Course of My Life*, p.263.

24 Hutchinson, *Heath*, p.128; Rhodes James, *Ambitions and Realities*, p.109; Butt, *Power of Parliament*, p.266; Du Cann, *Two Lives*, pp.88–9; Kershaw to Heath, undated, Heath papers 1 1/12.

25 Boyle in 'Edward Heath – His Own Man', BBC, 6/2/75; Bruce-Gardyne and Lawson, *Power Game*, p.272; Privately made film of birthday party, Heath papers.

26 Gilmour, *Whatever Happened to the Tories?*, pp.206–7; D. E. Butler and Anthony King, *The British General Election of 1964* (London, 1965), p.23; Peter Hennessy, *The Prime Minister* (London, 2000), p.281; John Boyd-Carpenter, *Way of Life* (London, 1980), p.186.

27 *Sunday Express*, 19/1/64; Heath, *Course of My Life*, p.267.

28 Hutchinson, *Heath*, p.131; Blakenham to Heath, early October 1964, CCO 20/1/13; Michael Cockerell, *Live From Number Ten* (London, 1988), p.119; Gilmour, *Whatever Happened to the Tories?*, p.212; Butler and King, *Election of 1964*, p.172.

29 Heath, *Course of My Life*, p.266; Heath to Blakenham, 5/2/64, CCO 20/1/12.

30 7/2/65, 10/5/65, 1/7/65, MS Macmillan Dep, Sir Knox Cunningham's Reports; Conversations with Lords Marlesford and Walker; Baston, *Maudling*, p.255; Richard Crossman, *The Diaries of a Cabinet Minister*, vol 1: *1964–1966* (London, 1975), p.208.

31 Walker, *Ascent of Britain*, p.58; Robert Shepherd, *Enoch Powell* (London, 1996), p.284.

32 John Ramsden, *The Making of Conservative Party Policy* (London, 1980), p.236.

33 Brendon Sewill, 'Policy Making for Heath', in *Preparing for Government: The Conservative Research Department 1929–2009*, ed. Alistair Cooke (London, 2009).

34 *Daily Mail*, 26/5/65; *Contemporary Record*, vol 3: No.3, 1990, p.37.

35 Kershaw to Heath, 9/11/64, Heath papers 1 1/2; *Daily Telegraph*, 7/2/65.

36 Berkeley, *Crossing the Floor*, p.105; Du Cann, *Two Lives*, p.99.

37 Many such letters survive among the Heath papers, e.g. Heath to Mr S. Bailey, 2/7/65, Heath papers 1 2/22.

38 Nigel Fisher, *The Tory Leaders* (London, 1977), p.120; Garnett and Aitken, *Whitelaw*, p.66.

39 Hutchinson, *Heath*, p.144; Rhodes James, *Ambitions and Realities*, p.110.

40 Selwyn Lloyd diary, 22/7/65, SELO 4/42; Garnett and Aitken, *Whitelaw*, p.68; Selwyn Lloyd diary, 23/7/65, SELO 4/42.

41 King, *Diary 1965–70*, p.24; King to Heath, 12/3/65, Heath papers 1 1/7; Selwyn Lloyd diary, 25 and 27/7/65, SELO 4/42; Macmillan diary, 27/7/65, MS Macmillan Dep.d.53; Shepherd, *Macleod*, p.56; Du Cann, *Two Lives*, p.101; Morrison Halcrow, *Keith Joseph* (London, 1989), p.36.

42 Walker, *Staying Power*, p.42; Conversation with Lord Walker; King, *Diary 1965–70*, p.24; conversation with Lord Lawson; Baston, *Maudling*, p.256.

43 26/7/65, MS Macmillan Dep, c443.

44 William Whitelaw, *The Whitelaw Memoirs* (London, 1989), p.55; Julian Critchley, *A Bag of Boiled Sweets* (London, 1984), p.114; Crossman, *Diaries of a Cabinet Minister*, vol 1, pp.292–3.

45 MS Macmillan Dep, c443; Walker, *Ascent of Britain*, p.58.

CHAPTER 9: *Leader of the Opposition*

1 *The Man Who Went to the Country*, TVS, 1985; David Butler interview, 27/3/69; John Cole, *As It Seemed To Me* (London, 1995), p.80; David Frost interview, 1/10/75.

2 Phillip Whitehead, *The Writing on the Wall* (London, 1985), p.30; King, *Diary 1965–1970*, p.37; Harold Wilson, *The Labour Government 1964–1970* (London, 1971), p.128; James Griffiths, *Pages from Memory* (London, 1969), pp.186–7.

3 Roth, *Heath and the Heathmen*, p.187.

4 Tony Benn, *Out of the Wilderness, Diaries 1963–67* (London, Arrow edition, 1988), p.208 (cf Crossman. *Diaries*, vol 3, p.706); Howe to Heath, 29/7/65, Heath papers 1 6/6.

5 Hutchinson, *Heath*, p.183; Shepherd, *Macleod*, p.424; Ian Trethowan, *Split Screen* (London, 1984), p141; 1/5/68, MS Macmillan Dep. c446.

6 Alexander to Barber, 8/6/68, CCO 20/8/12; Albert Alexander and Alan Watkins, *The Making of the Prime Minister, 1970* (London, 1970), p.52; 12/2/70 and 14/4/70, Mss Macmillan Dep. c448.

7 *Private Eye*, 'HP Sauce' Column, 11/9/70.

8 Tucker to Heath, 8/4/71, Heath papers, 3 2/24; Butler interview with Tucker, 16/7/70.

9 Forte to Heath, 22/10/69, Heath papers 1 1/12.

10 For all aspects of Heath's yachting life I am most grateful for the expert advice of Robin Aisher, Anthony Churchill and Peter Nicholson.

11 Nicholas Henderson, *Mandarin: The Diaries of an Ambassador* (London, 1994), pp.40–41; Laing, *Heath*, pp.206–7.

12 King, *Diary 1965–1970*, p.300; Crossman, *Diaries,* vol. 3, p.788; 26/1/70, MS Macmillan Dep. c448.

13 R. M. Punnett, *Front Bench Opposition* (London, 1973), p.96; Marcia Falkender, *Downing Street in Perspective* (London, 1983), pp.27–8; 15/11/65, Heath papers 1 6/6; Laing, *Heath*, p.214.

14 Prior, *Balance of Power*, p.39.

15 Whitelaw to Heath, 30/7/65, Heath papers 2 4/12; Christ to du Cann, 23/7/65, CPA CCO, 20/8/8; Selwyn Lloyd diary, 4/8/65, SELO 4/42.

16 Walker, *Staying Power*, p.45; Whitelaw interview with Butler, 8/10/70.

17 Douglas Hurd, *An End to Promises* (London, 1979), p.12; Douglas Hurd, *Memoirs* (London, 2003), p.174; conversations with Lord Hurd; Ramsden, *Winds of Change*, pp.245–50.

18 Benn, *Out of the Wilderness*, p.337; Crossman, *Diaries,* vol 1, pp.351–2.

19 *Spectator*, 14/1/66; Ramsden, *Winds of Change*, p.255; Knox Cunningham report, MS Macmillan Dep. c443.

20 D. E. Butler and Alan King, *The British General Election of 1966* (London, 1966), p.72.

21 Du Cann, *Two Lives*, p.119; Shepherd, *Macleod*, p.420; Macmillan to Heath, 4/4/66, Heath papers 1 1/12; Whitelaw to Heath, 29/3/66, Heath papers 1 1/12.

22 Boyd-Carpenter, *Way of Life*, p.195; Nabarro, *NAB I*, p.57.

23 20/4/66, Heath papers 2 4/10.

24 Boyd-Carpenter, *Way of Life*, p.197; Andrew Alexander and Alan Watkins, *The Making of the Prime Minister, 1970* (London, 1970), pp.99–100; Stuart Ball and Anthony Seldon, *The Heath Government, 1970–74* (Harlow, 1996), p.23.

25 Reginald Maudling, *Memoirs* (London, 1978), p.142; Du Cann, *Two Lives*, p.127; Heath, *Course of My Life*, p.290.

26 Alan Clark, *Diaries* (London, 1993, Phoenix edition, 1994), p.154; Whitelaw to Heath, 19/4/66, Heath papers 2 4/12; Heath to Rostow, 14/4/67, Heath papers 1 6/8.

27 Margaret Thatcher, *The Path to Power* (London, 1995), pp.143–4; Whitelaw interview with David Butler, 8/10/70.

28 Heath, *Course of My Life*, p.290; Leather to Heath, 27/2/67, Heath papers 1 1/12; Nabarro, *NAB I*, p.66; Fraser interview with David Butler, 25/6/70; Du Cann, *Two Lives*, p.126; Kershaw to Heath, undated, Heath papers 1 1/12.

29 Vaughan Morgan to Heath, 1/2/67, Heath papers 1 1/12.

30 Du Cann, *Two Lives*, p.114; conversation with Sara Morrison.

31 Osborne to Heath, 15/7/68, Heath papers 1 6/9; Hennessy, *Prime Minister*, p.348; Heath to Whitelaw, 18/2/68, Heath papers, 2 4/12.

32 Leo Abse, *Wotan, My Enemy* (London, 1994), p.229; Berkeley, *Crossing the Floor*, p.104; Thatcher, *Path to Power*, p.135; King, *Diary 1965–1970*, pp.324–5; Heath interview with David Butler, 27/11/69.

33 18/12/69, MS Macmillan Dep. c447; Kitson to Heath, 22/2/66, Heath papers 1 1/12.

34 cit. Douglas Hurd, *Robert Peel* (London, 2007), p.131; Gilmour, *Whatever Happened to the Tories*, p.226.

35 Fisher, *Tory Leaders*, p.127; Benn, *Out of the Wilderness*, p.337; King, *Diary 1965–1970*, pp.247 and 192; Richard Crossman, *The Diaries of a Cabinet Minister,* vol 2: *1966–68* (London, 1976), p.284; *Panorama*, 16/10/67; Robin Day, *Grand Inquisitor* (London, 1989), pp.233–4.

36 Copy in Heath papers 1 2/22.

37 20/1/67, MS Macmillan Dep. c445.

38 Philip Norton, *Conservative Dissidents* (London, 1978), p.229; Trethowan, *Split Screen*, p.57; Douglas to Swinton, 15/8/68, Swinton papers, SWIN I 7/15.

39 Heath papers 1 1/15 and 1 1/9.

40 Cockerell, *Live from Number Ten*, p.146.

41 Roth, *Heath and the Heathmen*, p.9; Cockerell, *A Very Singular Man*; Cockerell, *Live From Number Ten*, pp.148–9.

42 Reports of 21/6/67 and 15/5/67, CPA CCO 20/8/10.

43 Conversations with Lord Prior and Sara Morrison.

CHAPTER 10: *Problems with the Party*

1 11/2/67, Heath papers 2 4/10; Crossman, *Diaries,* vol 2. p.583.

2 Heath to Alderman Arthur Jones, 14/5/68, Heath papers 1 6/9; Astor to Heath, 23/5/68, Heath papers 1 1/12.

3 King, *Diary, 1965–1970*, pp.213 and 291; Whitelaw to Swinton, 11/9/68, SWIN 7/17; Wilson, *Labour Government 1964–1970*, pp.721–2; Macmillan to Heath, 5/5/69, Heath papers 1 1/3.

4 Wilson, *Labour Government 1964–1970*, pp.217–18; 29/6/65, HETH 10.

5 Crossman, *Diaries,* vol 2, p.118; 1/2/66, HETH 12; 14/11/66, Heath papers 2 4/10.

6 20/5/69, Heath papers 2 4/3.

7 Christopher Soames, draft of unpublished autobiography, chapter 8, Soames papers.

8 Whitelaw to Heath, 22/7/69, Heath papers 2 4/12; Cunningham to Macmillan, 3/5/67, MS Macmillan Dep. c445; Crossman, *Diaries,* vol 3, p.642; Nabarro interview with David Butler, 1/12/69; 23/2/70, Heath papers 2 4/11.

9 Eric Roussel, *Georges Pompidou* (Paris, 1994), pp.389–90.

10 23/10/70, Heath papers 2 4/11.

11 Gilmour to Heath, 19/5/70 and Morrison to Heath, 20/5/70, Heath papers 4 2/13; Shepherd, *Macleod*, p.514.

12 Heath to Morrison, 20/5/70, Heath papers 4 2/13.

13 Wilson, *Labour Government 1964–1970*, p.179; Alport to Heath, 25/10/65, Heath papers 1 1/12; Bennett to Heath, 22/11/65, Heath papers 1 6/6; Fisher, *The Tory Leaders*, p.131; Whitelaw to Heath, 23/12/65, Heath papers 1 1/12.

14 Lloyd to Heath, 21/2/66, Heath papers 2 4/10; Heath to Michael Alison, 24/10/68, Heath papers 1 6/9.

15 27/10/65, Heath papers 1 2/20; Shepherd, *Enoch Powell*, p.305; Heath to Brian Harrison, 25/10/65, Heath papers 1 6/6.

16 Heath to Fletcher-Cooke, 30/8/68, Heath papers 1 6/9; Hurd, *Memoirs*,

pp.177–8; NA FCO, 8/979; 21/4/69, Heath papers 2 4/5.

17 Patrick Gordon-Walker, *Political Diaries: 1932–1971* (London, 1991), p.324; Heath papers 2 4/1.

18 Heath to Birch, 8/5/70, Heath papers 2 4/5; Hurd to Heath, 4/4/65, Heath papers 2 4/5; Tony Benn, *Office Without Power: Diaries, 1968–72* (London, 1989), p.30.

19 Geoffrey Lewis, *Lord Hailsham* (London, 1997), pp.242–3.

20 Prior, *Balance of Power*, p.48; Gilmour, *Whatever Happened to the Tories*, p.240; Ramsden, *The Winds of Change*, p.286; Roth, *Heath and the Heathmen*, p.ix.

21 Martin Holmes, *The Failure of the Heath Government* (London, 1997), p.5.

22 28/7/65 HETH 10.

23 Peter Hennessy, *Cabinet* (London, 1986), p.284; Heath to Douglas-Home, 15/8/67, Heath papers 2 4/4; Heath to Bruce Kenrick, 20/1/70, Heath papers 2 4/4.

24 Hogg to Heath, 9/9/66; Heath to Hogg, 30/9/66, Heath papers 2 6/8; Crossman, *Diaries,* vol 2, p.536; Heath, *Course of My Life,* pp.295–6; 11/12/68, Heath papers 2 4/10.

25 *Contemporary Record,* vol 3, no. 3, 1990, p.37; conversation with Richard Simmonds.

26 Heath to Conservative Research Department, 11/10/67, Heath papers, uncatalogued; Macleod to Heath, 12/2/68, Heath papers 1 1/15.

27 24/7/68 and 2/8/68, Heath papers 2 4/10.

28 Garnett and Aitken, *Whitelaw*, pp.78–9; Knight to Heath, 21/4/68, Heath papers 1 6/9; Ramsden, *Winds of Change*, pp.294–7.

29 Garnett and Aitken, *Whitelaw*, pp.78–9; Shepherd, *Powell*, p.378; Crossman, *Diaries,* vol 3, p.340; Violet Bonham-Carter to Hogg, 27/1/69 and Hogg to Bonham-Carter, 29/1/69, HLSM.

CHAPTER 11: *Victory*

1 Prior to Heath, 12/9/68, Heath papers 2 4/10; Denham and Garnett, *Keith Joseph*, p.167.

2 Schreiber to Heath, 2/12/69, Heath papers 2 4/19; Heath to Howell, 9/10/67, Heath papers 2 4/10.

3 Macleod to Heath, 7/2/68, Heath papers 1 6/9; Heath to Macmillan, 2/8/66, Heath papers 1 6/8; 7/3/68, Heath papers 2 4/10.

4 14/9/65, Heath papers 2 4/10.

5 Conversation with Lord Marlesford.

6 Memo by Hurd, 16/10/69, Heath papers 4 4/19; Lord Hurd's unpublished diary, 7/6/70; Hurd to Heath, 26/6/69, Heath papers 2 4/19.

7 Ramsden, *Making of Conservative Party Policy*, p.275.

8 Fraser interview with David Butler, 3/2/70.

9 Tony Benn, *Conflicts of Interest: Diaries 1977–1980* (London, 1990), p.505; Lord Carrington, *Reflect on Things Past* (London, 1988), p.255; Norman Tebbitt, *Upwardly Mobile* (London, 1989), p.120.

10 Transcript of Selsdon proceedings, Ramsden, *Making of Conservative Party Policy*, p.258.

11 John Campbell, *Margaret Thatcher*, vol 1 (London, 2000), p.203; Denham and

Garnett, *Keith Joseph*, p.186; Raison, *Tories and the Welfare State*, p.68; CCO 500/56/1.

12 Hurd, *Memoirs*, p.183; Thatcher, *The Path to Power*, p.160; Alan Clark, *The Tories* (London, 1998), p.339; 9/2/70, Heath papers 2 4/11.

13 Wilson, *Labour Government 1964–1970*, pp.757 and 759; Opinion Research Centre Report of 2/270, Heath papers 2 4/11.

14 Sewill to Heath, 29/4/70, CCO/20/8/15; Cunningham to Macmillan, 6/5/70, MS Macmillan Dep c448; Prior, *A Balance of Power*, p.56.

15 2/12/68, Heath papers 2 4/10; Tebbit, *Upwardly Mobile*, p.94; Heath, *Course of My Life*, p.303.

16 Whitelaw, *Contemporary Record*. vol 3, no. 3, 1990, p.38; conversation with Sir Martin Gilbert; Shepherd, *Powell*, p.392; Thorpe, *Douglas-Home*, p.402; Heath, *Course of My Life*, p307.

17 Alexander and Watkins, *The Making of the Prime Minister*, p.166; Whitelaw interview with David Butler, 29/7/70; conversations with Lord Gilmour and Sara Morrison; Peter Rawlinson, *A Price Too High* (London, 1989), p.141.

18 Tucker and Sewill to Heath, 30/4/70, Heath papers, 2 4/10; Tucker to Heath, 23/5/70, Heath papers 2 6/8; Falkender, *Downing Street in Perspective*, p.51.

19 Hugo Young, *The Hugo Young Papers*, ed. Ion Trewin (London, 2008), p.5; Heath to Oppenheim, 27/5/70, Heath papers 2 4/27; Rhodes James, *Ambitions and Realities*, p.257; Thatcher, *Path to Power*, p.162.

20 Whitelaw, *Memoirs*, pp.69-70; Cockerell, *Live from Number Ten*, pp.156 and 166; Day, *Grand Inquisitor*, pp.232–4; Heath, *Course of My Life*, p.305; Hurd to Williams, 5/5/70, Heath papers 2 6/1.

21 Garnett and Aitken, *Whitelaw*, p.84; Shepherd, *Powell*, p.403.

22 *The Times*, 15/6/70; Barbara Castle, *The Castle Diaries, 1964–1976* (London, 1990), p.408.

23 Hurd, *End to Promises*, p.26; conversation with Dame Joan Varley.

24 Conversation with David Butler.

25 Heath papers 2 6/8.

26 11/12/70, Heath papers 3 2/3.

27 Ramsden, *Winds of Change*, p.317.

28 King, *Diary 1965–1970*, p.334; Ramsden, *Winds of Change*, p.317.

CHAPTER 12: *Making a Ministry*

1 Day, *Grand Inquisitor*, p.235; Cockerell, *Live from Number Ten*, p.340.

2 Jenkins to Powell, 21/11/73, POLL 1/1/20A.

3 Boyd-Carpenter, *Way of Life*, p.193; conversations with Richard Simmonds and Lord Moser.

4 James Lees-Milne, *Ancient as the Hills* (London, 1997), p.161.

5 Alistair McAlpine, *Once a Jolly Bagman* (London, 1997), p.190; Laing, *Heath*, p.204; Peter Jenkins, *Mrs Thatcher's Revolution* (London, 1987), p.60; Walker, *Staying Power*, p.130.

6 Conversations with Lord Armstrong and Mrs Chadd.

7 Jim Slater, *Return to Go* (London, 1997), p.153.

8 7/7/70 and 24/11/72, Heath papers 3 2/24.

9 Junor, *Listening for a Midnight Tram*, pp.148–9.

10 Cockerell, *Live from Number Ten*, p.170; Ronald Millar, *A View from the Wings* (London, 1993), pp.218–19; conversations with Sir Donald Maitland and Lord Butler.

11 Benjamin Disraeli, *Lord George Bentinck* (London, 1851), p.311.

12 Gilmour, *Whatever Happened to the Tories?*, p.220; Crossman, *Diaries*, vol 2. p.74; 3/1/68, SELO, 4/53.

13 Nigel Lawson, *The View from No.11* (London, 1992), p.14; Blake, *Conservative Party*, p.376.

14 Margach, *Abuse of Power*, p.159; Peregrine Worsthorne, *Tricks of Memory* (London, 1993), p.238; Ferdinand Mount, *Cold Cream* (London, 2008), p.232.

15 *The Cecil King Diary, 1970–1974* (London, 1975), p.327; Millar, *View from the Wings*, p.220.

16 Whitelaw to Heath, 28/2/68, Heath papers 1 6/9.

17 17/11/71, MS Macmillan Dep. c448; Walker, *Staying Power*, p.120; John Nott, *Here Today, Gone Tomorrow* (London, 2000), p.145; Conversation with Lord Hurd.

18 Anthony Barber, *Taking the Tide* (Norwich, 1966), p.75.

19 Shepherd, *Powell*, p.464; Margach, *Abuse of Power*, p.163; *Evening Standard*, 25/5/72, Heath interview with Charles Wintour and Robert Carvel; Edward Heath, *My Style of Government, Evening Standard*, 1/6/72.

20 *The Journals of Woodrow Wyatt*, vol 1 (London, 1998), p.72; Hennessy, *Prime Minister*, p.342; King, *Diary, 1970–1974*, p.273.

21 Geoffrey Howe, *Conflict of Loyalty* (London, 1994), p.72; letter from Lord Carrington to author, 17/4/08.

22 Junor, *Midnight Tram*, pp.183–4.

23 Redmayne to Heath, 10/4/69, Heath papers 1 1/13; conversation with Sara Morrison; Norton, *Conservative Dissidents*, p.237, Heath, *Course of My Life*, p.324.

24 Wyatt, *Confessions of an Optimist*, p.260.

25 Heath, *Course of My Life*, p.468.

26 16/9/98, Heath papers 4 4/6; Morrison to Heath, 9/12/65, Heath papers 1 1/12.

27 Baston, *Maudling*, p.270; Maudling, *Memoirs*, p.189.

28 King, *Diary 1970–1974*, pp.9 and 56.

29 *New Statesmen*, 26/2/71, cit. Philip Norton and Arthur Aughey, *Conservatives and Conservatism* (London, 1981), p.253.

30 Laing, *Heath*, p.227; Rawlinson, *A Price Too High*, p.248.

31 Thatcher, *Path to Power*, p.200; Rawlinson, *A Price Too High*, p.248; Howe, *Conflict of Loyalty*, p.72; 13/10/70, NACM 864; conversation with Lord Prior; Campbell, *Thatcher*, vol 1, p.219.

32 Coleman, *Movers and Shakers*, pp.12–13; Campbell, *Heath*, p.299; conversation with Sir Timothy Kitson; Emery to Heath, 25/6/70, Heath papers 3 1/6.

33 Neave to Heath, 5/4/66, Heath papers 1 6/8; Walker, *Staying Power*, pp.118–19; Whitelaw to Heath, 4/8/70, Heath papers Misc. Box 5.

34 Whitelaw to Heath, 4/8/70, Heath papers Misc. Box 5; King, *Diary 1970–1974*, p.111.

35 Heath, *Course of My Life*, p.309; Hurd, *End of Promises*, p.31; Garnett and Aitken, *Whitelaw*, p.86.

36 Conversation with Lord Armstrong.
37 Ball and Seldon, *Heath Government*, p.62; conversations with Lords Armstrong, Butler and Bridges.
38 Conversation with Sir Donald Maitland.
39 Heath, *Course of My Life*, p.274.
40 Cockerell, *Live from Number Ten*, p.212; conversation with Sara Morrison.
41 Conversations with Lady (Caroline) Ryder, Penelope Gummer and Lord Butler; Carrington, *Reflect on Things Past*, p.252.
42 Renton, *Chief Whip*, p.294; conversations with Lords Howell and Marlesford; 23/1/73, Heath papers 3 2/18.
43 Heath, *Course of My Life*, p.315; Tessa Blackstone and William Plowden, *Inside the Think Tank* (London, 1988), pp.25–6.
44 Lord Rothschild, *Random Variables* (London, 1984); 28/1/71, NA PREM 15.406.
45 19/11/73, Heath papers 3 4/9.
46 17/3/71, NA PREM 15.406; Howell papers 31/12/70; Blackstone and Plowden, *Inside the Think Tank*, p.54; *Contemporary Record*, vol 9. no.1, 1995, p.210.
47 Conversation with Lord Butler; 8/5/72, Heath papers 3 2/18; Rose, *Elusive Rothschild* (London, 2003), p.190.
48 25/3/73, NA PREM 2101; 28 and 29/11/73 NA PREM 2232; Rose, *Elusive Rothschild*, p.194.
49 Ball and Seldon, *Heath Government*, p.78; Hennessy, *Cabinet*, p.74; Kenneth Baker, *The Turbulent Years* (London, 1993), p.35; Holmes, *Heath Government*, p.131.
50 Ball and Seldon, *Heath Government*, pp.64–5; Hennessy, *Cabinet*, p.20; Helen Adeane to Heath, 6/8/72, Heath papers 1 1/9.
51 23/6/70, NA CM 1(70).
52 22/12/73,Heath papers 3 1/7; Campbell, *Heath*, p.292; *Castle Diaries 1964–1976*, p.428; Falkender, *Downing Street in Perspective*, pp.104–5.
53 16/2/71, NA CM 500; 1/10/71, NA CM 655.
54 13/10/70, NA CM 151.
55 23/1/74, CPA CCO, 20/8/16; John Grigg, *The History of The Times*, vol VI (London, 1993), p.157; Prior, *A Balance of Power*, p.101.
56 20/9/71, Heath papers Misc. Box 5; Heath to Britten, 1/12/71, Heath papers, uncatalogued; Peyton, *Without Benefit of Laundry*, pp.136–7; Goodman, *Tell Them I'm On My Way*, p.314.
57 *The Journals of Woodrow Wyatt*, vol 1, *1985–88* (London, 1988), p.62; Tony Benn, *Against the Tide, Diaries 1973–1976* (London, 1990), p.265; conversation with Nancy-Joan Seligman; Norma Major, *Chequers*, p.238.

CHAPTER 13: *The Pains of Office*

1 Conversations with Lord Armstrong and Sir Timothy Kitson; Ramsden, *Winds of Change*, p.321.
2 Conversation with Sara Morrison; Gilmour to Hogg, 21/6/70, HLSM 2/7/60; conversations with Lords Carrington and Prior; Campbell, *Heath*, p.203; Prior, *A Balance of Power*, p.77.

3 Shepherd, *Macleod*, pp.538–40; Prior, *A Balance of Power*, p.77.

4 Maitland, *Diverse Times*, p.178; conversations with Sir Timothy Kitson and Sara Morrison; King, *Diary 1970–1974*, pp.27 and 35; Junor, *Midnight Tram*, p.183.

5 King, *Diaries 1970–1974*, p.35; conversation with Lord Heseltine; Heath, *Course of My Life*, p.321.

6 Heath to Mrs Reynolds, 4/5/70, Heath papers 2 4/5; Heath to Gowon, 13/6/73, NA PREM 15.1803.

7 NA CM 5(70) of 16/7/70 and 6(70) of 20/7/70; NA PREM 15.221.

8 23/10/70, NA CM 668; 11/11/70, Heath papers 3 2/20; 29/4/71 NA PREM 15.1215.

9 Berkeley, *Crossing the Floor*, pp.106–7; 4/8/72, NA PREM 15.1876.

10 23/4/70 and 25/4/70, Heath papers, uncatalogued.

11 25/3/71, NA PREM 15.621; telephone conversation with Nixon, 25/11/71, NA PREM 15.570; 6/2/73, NA PREM 15.1876.

12 Conversation with Dr David Dilks; 11/1/71, NA PREM 15.449.

13 NA CM 1970.667; 1/2/74, NA PREM 15.2026.

14 8/9/70, NA PREM 15.275; Hurd, *End to Promises*, p.55.

15 1/2/71, NA PREM 15.280.

16 Heath to Nixon, 1/2/71, NA PREM 15.280; Jan 1971, Heath papers 3 2/20; Heath, *Course of My Life*, pp.482–3; July 1971, NA CM 707.

17 23/1/71, Heath papers 3 2/20.

18 30/10/72, NA CM 780; 26/9/73, NA PREM 15.1527.

19 24/6/70 to 3/8/70, NA PREM 15.444.

20 18/1/72 and 5/4/72, NA PREM 15.1257.

21 Goodman to Heath, 1/9/72, NA PREM 15.1259; 14/9/72, NA PREM 15.1259; Heath to Gandhi, 24/1/73, NA PREM 15.1641; 25/6/73, NA PREM 15.1641.

22 Hall to Heath, 12/9/72 and Coombs to Heath, 22/9/72, Heath papers 3 1/16.

23 31/12/72, NA CM 765.

24 21/1/74, NA PREM 15.2230.

CHAPTER 14: *Europe: The Second Round*

1 Reilly to Heath, 15/1/99, Heath papers 4 3/23.

2 Uwe Kitzinger, *Diplomacy and Persuasion* (London, 1973), p.233; Benn, *Office Without Power*, p.305.

3 Heath, *Course of My Life*, p.365.

4 Conversations with Lord Hurd, Lord Armstrong and Sir Michael Palliser; Soames, first draft of an autobiography, chapter 9, Soames papers.

5 8/4/71, NA CM 20(71); NA PREM 15.880.

6 David Marsh, 'Blood, Gold and the Euro', unpublished, ts pp.5 and 8.

7 Jackling to Home, 22/12/71, NA FCO 330/271; 13/12/71, NA PREM 15.899.

8 15/9/70, 29/11/71, 6/12/71, NA PREM 15.736.

9 23/1/70, Heath papers, uncatalogued; 16/11/73, NA PREM 15.1841.

10 6/5/71, CM 24(71); Heath to Pym, 18/8/71, NA PREM 15.549; 1/2/71, Heath papers 4 2/13.

11 3/1/71, NA PREM 15.364.

12 Moon to Heath, 18/3/71, NA PREM 15.369; Soames autobiography, ts chapter 9.

13 Roussel, *Pompidou*, pp.20, 448–9 and 438.

14 21/4/71, NA PREM 15.371; 29/3/71, NA PREM 15.370; Kitzinger, *Diplomacy and Persuasion*, p.118.

15 6/5/71, NA CM 24(71); 18/5/71, NA CM 26(71).

16 Marsh, 'Blood, Gold and the Euro', p.14.

17 Soames to Home, 7/5/71, NA PREM 15.372; 3/1/71, NA CM 299.

18 Heath, *Course of My Life*, p.372.

19 Reilly to Heath, 15/1/99, Heath papers 4 3/23.

20 Soames to Rippon, 12/7/71, NA PREM 15.357; 24/5/71, NA CM 27(71).

21 30/6/71, NA CM 35(71); Opinion Research Centre report, Heath papers 3 2/3.

22 Kitzinger, *Diplomacy and Persuasion*, p.176.

23 David Butler interview, 5/3/71; Beamish to Heath, 10/8/71, Heath papers 3 1/16; Pym to Heath, 18/8/71, NA PREM 15.574.

24 Goodhart to Pym, 18/12/70, CPA CCO 20/32/4; Heath, *Course of My Life*, p.362; conversation with Lord Hurd.

25 John W Young's thoughtful essay in Ball and Seldon, *The Heath Government*, pp.259–84, provides a most reliable summary of the whole operation.

26 Benn, *Office Without Power*, p.360.

27 Pym to Heath, 28/10/71, NA PREM 15.574.

28 Heath, *Course of My Life*, p.381.

29 Wilson to Heath, 17/1/72, NA PREM 15.880; Heath, *Course of My Life*, p.381.

30 17/2/72, NA CM 7(72); D'Avigdor Goldsmith to Heath, 16/2/72, Heath papers 4 2/13; Heath to Monnet, 17/2/72, cit. Deavin, unpublished PhD thesis, p.700.

31 Barber, *Taking the Tide*, p.77; Prior, *A Balance of Power*, p.85.

32 *The Last Europeans*, 26/11/95; conversation with Lord Healey.

33 1/7/71, NA CM 36(71).

34 Jobert's record of meeting with Armstrong, 27/1/72, Heath papers 4 2/13.

35 2/10/72, NA PREM 15.1047.

36 20/10/72, NA PREM 15.895.

37 17/10/72, NA PREM 15.895.

38 Heath to Nixon, 30/10/72, NA PREM 15.895.

39 3/11/73, NA PREM 15.1385.

40 NA PREM 15.904.

41 Roussel, *Pompidou*, p.500; 21/11/71, NA PREM 15.351; Monnet to Heath, 13/3/72, Heath papers, uncatalogued.

42 22/9/72, NA PREM 15.2007.

43 Hurd to Heath, 11/4/72, Heath papers 4 2/13.

44 Marsh, 'Blood, Gold and the Euro', ts p.12.

45 NA PREM 15.1777.

46 Marsh, 'Blood, Gold and the Euro', ts pp.23–4.

47 NA PREM 15.1489; Heath papers 4 2/10; Heath, *Course of My Life*, p.394.

CHAPTER 15: *Ulster*

1 9/12/68, Mss Macmillan Dep. Sir Knox Cunningham's Reports; Chichester-Clark to Heath, 11/9/69, copy in Hailsham papers 2/26/5; conversation with Sir Robin Chichester-Clark.

2 Heath papers 3 2/14; King, *Diary 1970–1974*, p.129; Shepherd, *Powell*, p.116.

3 21/6/70, NA PREM 15.100.

4 23/6/70, NA CM 1 (70) 4.

5 J. J. Lee, *Ireland 1912–1985* (Cambridge, 1989), p.434.

6 29/6/70, NA CM 3 (70).

7 21/6/70, NA PREM 15.100.

8 NA PREM 15.474; Heath to Lynch, 21/10/70, Heath papers 3 2/14.

9 1/12/70, NA PREM 15.474.

10 19/3/71, NA PREM 15.474; Heath, *Course of My Life*, p.426.

11 28/3/71, HLSM 1/1/2, Sec 6.

12 26/3/71, NA PREM 15.474; Brian Faulkner, *Memoirs of a Statesman* (London, 1978), pp.91–3.

13 Michael Carver, *Out of Step* (London, 1989), p.404.

14 4/8/71, Heath papers 3 2/14

15 Faulkner, *Memoirs*, p.127; Heath's note of conversation with General Ford, 4/1/72, NA PREM 15.1000; King, *Diary 1970–1974*, p.185.

16 23/1/72, NA PREM 15.881.

17 Maitland, *Diverse Times*, p.183; 15/3/72, NA PREM 15.1004; Laing, *Heath*, p.223.

18 Joe Haines, *The Politics of Power* (London, 1977), p.129.

19 1/9/71, Mss Macmillan Dep, Sir Knox Cunningham's Reports; Armstrong to Heath, 24/9/71, NA PREM 15.487; Faulkner, *Memoirs*, p.132; conversation with Sir Robin Chichester-Clark; David Bleakley, *Faulkner* (London, 1974), p.105.

20 NA PREM 15.1001 and 2136.

21 Faulkner, *Memoirs*, p.149.

22 4/12/72, NA PREM 1034.

23 19/4/71, NACM 611.

24 15/3/72, NA PREM 15.1004; Faulkner, *Memoirs*, p.152.

25 Douglas-Home to Heath, 13/3/72, Heath papers 3 2/14; Hailsham diary, 7/3/72, HLSM; Maudling, *Memoirs*, p.190; Heath, *Course of My Life*, p.436; Wilson to Heath, 16/2/72, NA PREM 15.1002.

26 *The Listener*, 22/4/76.

27 Heath to the Queen, 9/3/72, NA PREM 15.1004.

28 David Butler interview, 19/2/72; Hunt to Heath, 21/6/72, CPA CCO 20/40/1.

29 Interview of 14/6/72, HETH 19; Mss Macmillan Dep, Knox Cunningham's Reports; 21/7/72, HL SM 1/1/5, Sec 7.

30 31/8/71 and 16/9/71, NA PREM 15.1017; 4/10/72, NA PREM 15.1047; 6/10/72, NA CM 44(72).

31 8/2/73, NA CM 5(73); Carrington to Heath, 5/1/73, CPA CCO 20/40/1.

32 8/3/73, NA PREM 15.1703; Heath, *Course of My Life*, pp.441–2.

33 13/9/73, NA CM 40(73) and 2/10/73, NA CM 43(73); 17/9/73, NA PREM 15.1704.

34 22/11/73, NA CM 57(73).

35 Heath, *Course of My Life*, p.443; Faulkner, *Memoirs*, p.232.

36 Heath, *Course of My Life*, p.444.

37 King, *Diary 1970–1974*, p.309.

CHAPTER 16: *Choppy Water*

1 'Edward Heath – His Own Man', BBC, 6/2/75.
2 Whitehead, *Writing on the Wall*, pp.32–3.
3 Interview with Butler, 5/3/71; Allason, *Ted Heath*, ts pp.192–3; conversation with Lord Armstrong.
4 Young, *One of Us*, p.490; Lady Adeane to Heath, 16/9/71, Heath papers 3 4/8.
5 Heath, *Course of My Life*, p.314; Bernard Palmer, *High and Mitred* (London, 1992), pp.271–4.
6 3/3/71, NA CM 741.
7 1/12/70 and 25/3/71, NA PREM 15.1407.
8 15/7/70, NA PREM 15.1407; 29/9/73, NA PREM 15.1408.
9 April 1971, NA PREM 15.1617.
10 Heath papers 3 1/1 and 1/9.
11 Hurd to Heath, 11/5/71, Heath papers 3 2/14; 29/4/71, NA CM 23(71).
12 9/6/71, NA PREM 15.324.
13 7/12/70, NA CM 99.
14 NA PREM 15.1682.
15 28/7/70, NA CM 9(70).
16 NA PREM 15.1191; conversation with Lord Armstrong.
17 NA PREM 15.427; NA PREM 15.1320.
18 NA PREM 15.1407; Heath papers 3 2/16; Heath to Boult, 15/11/71 and 14/10/71, Adrian Boult Mss Add 72631.167.
19 Heath, *Travels*, p.10; NA PREM 15.436; NA PREM 15.704.
20 NA PREM 15.1614.
21 Thatcher, *Path to Power*, pp.194–5; Howe, *Conflict of Loyalty*, p.76.
22 Walker, *Staying Power*, p.110; Fisher, *Tory Leaders*, p.141.
23 20/7/70, NA CM 6(70); Heath, *Course of My Life*, p.321; 30/7/70, NA CM 10(70).
24 Hurd to John Burnham, 27/8/70, and to Heath, 28/8/70, Heath papers 3 1/1.
25 Rawlinson, *A Price Too High*, p.158; King, *Diary 1970–1974*, p.46; Tebbit, *Upwardly Mobile*, p.100; Margach, *Abuse of Power*, p.161.
26 Hurd to Heath, 25/9/70, Heath papers 3 1/1.
27 23/7/70, NA CM 8(70); 14/9/70, NA CM 16(70); 28/9/70, NA CM 23(70).
28 Nixon to Heath, 18/11/70, NA CM 156.
29 NA CM 939; 28/1/72, NA CM 940.
30 Shepherd, *Powell*, p.408; Heath, *Course of My Life*, p.330.
31 *Contemporary Record,* vol 9, no. 1, 1995, p.201; King, *Diary 1970–1974*, p.51; 18/9/70, NA PREM 15.42; Denham and Garnett, *Joseph*, p.245n.
32 13/11/70, NA CM 37(70); 17/11/70, NA CM 38(70).
33 30/7/70 NA CM 11(70).
34 Whitehead, *Writing on the Wall*, p.84; Holmes, *Failure of the Heath Government*, p.51; conversation with Sir Martin Gilbert.
35 27/8/71 and 31/5/71, NA CM 900; 3/1/72, NA PREM 15.1195.
36 12/10/70, HETH 18; King, *Diary 1965–1970*, p.263.
37 Jack Jones, *Union Man* (London, 1986), p.215; King, *Diary 1970–1974*, p.94; 'Edward Heath – His Own Man', BBC, 6/2/75; Tebbit, *Upwardly Mobile*, p.110.
38 28/9/70 and 9/8/72, Heath papers 3 2/14; 3/11/70, NA CM 35(70).

39 20/7/70, NA CM 6(70); Howe, *Conflict of Loyalty*, p.49; Heath, *Course of My Life*, p.334; Gilmour, *Whatever Happened to the Tories*, p.256; 20/8/70, Heath papers 3 1/1.

40 Brendon Sewill, *British Economic Policy 1970–1974* (London, 1975), p.33; *Contemporary Record*, vol 2, no. 1, 1988, p.38; Patrick Bell, *The Labour Party in Opposition* (London, 2004), p.57; 2/2/71, Mss Macmillan Dep, 448.

41 Robert Taylor, *The Trade Union Question in British Politics* (Oxford, 1993), p.190.

42 J. A. G. Griffiths, *The Politics of the Judiciary* (London, Fontana 3rd edition, 1985), pp.68–70.

43 Whitehead, *Writing on the Wall*, p.93.

44 Hetherington interview, 12/10/70, HETH 18; Lord Hill, *Behind the Scenes* (London, 1974), p.230.

45 14/11/70, NA CM 314 and 20/11/70, NA CM 45(70).

46 12/12/70 and 14/12/70, NA CM 46(70) and 47(70); Heath, *Course of My Life*, p.336.

47 Howell papers, 31/12/70, 5/8/71, NA CM 819.

48 15/10/70, NA CM 30(70); 19/10/70, NA CM 31(70).

49 Thatcher, *Path to Power*, p.206; Geraint Morgan to Heath, 20/11/70, Heath papers 3 1/1.

50 24/5/71, NA PREM 15.1643.

51 14/6/71, NA CM 31(71).

52 4/11/71, NA CM 53(71).

53 Thatcher, *Path to Power*, p.213; 30/7/71, NA CM 604; 24/12/72, NA CM 10(72).

54 Prior, *Balance of Power*, p.74; 3/5/71, NA CM 528; H of C 24/1/72.

55 30/6/71, HETH 18; 17/12/70, NA CM 161 and 1/3/71, NA CM 280.

56 10/1/72, NA CM 818; Armstrong to Bealey, 25/2/72, NA CM 818.

57 2/7/71, Heath papers 3 2/18.

58 Heath, *Course of My Life*, p.345; 15/7/71, CM 38(71).

59 2/12/71, NA CM 61(71); Benn, *Office Without Power*, p.392.

60 NA PREM 15.984.

61 14/12/71, NA CM 63(71).

62 Joe Gormley, *Battered Cherub* (London, 1982), p.124; 10/2/72, NA CM (72)6; Andrew Taylor, *The NUM and British Politics*, vol 2, 1969–1995 (Aldershot, 2005), p.65.

63 Heath, *Course of My Life*, p.351; 18/2/72, NA CM (72)11; 21/1/72, NA CM (72)3; Hurd, *End to Promises*, p.103; Cockerell, *A Very Singular Man*.

64 Sewill, *British Economic Policy*, p.33; 10/2/72, NA CM 6(72).

65 17/2/72, NA CM 7(72); NA PREM 15.986; Butler interview, 19/2/72.

66 19/2/72, NA CM 8 (72); Robert Taylor, *The Fifth Estate* (London, 1978), p.265; NA PREM 15.819.

67 15/2/72, NA PREM 15.985.

CHAPTER 17: *The Approaching Storm*

1 Ramsden, *Winds of Change*, p.354; du Cann to Heath, 17/11/72, Heath papers 3 1/16.

2 Heath, *Course of My Life*, p.398; Nott, *Here Today*, p.147; Holmes, *Failure of the Heath Government*, p.129; Wyatt, *Confessions of an Optimist*, pp.339–40.

3 Conversation with Lord Croham; Blackstone and Plowden, *Inside the Think Tank*, p.64; Healey, *Time of My Life*, p.354.

4 Record of meetings between Heath and Barber, 5/3/72 and 8/3/72, NA CM 813.

5 Heath to Robert Armstrong, 13/3/72, NA CM 818; Nott, *Here Today*, p.147.

6 Holmes, *Failure of the Heath Government*, p.49; *Contemporary Record*, vol 9, no. 1, 1995, p.199.

7 Nicholas Ridley, *My Style of Government* (London, 1991), p.4; Junor, *Listening for a Midnight Tram*, pp.193–4.

8 2/3/72 and 6/3/72, NA CM 11 and 12(72); Jock Bruce-Gardyne, *Whatever Happened to the Quiet Revolution?* (London, 1974), p.85

9 Junor, *Listening for a Midnight Tram*, p.183; 19/7/72, NA PREM 15.1914; Baston, *Maudling*, p.426; Maudling, *Memoirs*, p.193.

10 20/7/72, NA CM 37(72); 26/10/73, NA PREM 15.1914.

11 13/7/72, NA CM 36(72); 14/6/73, NA CM 31(73).

12 Whitehead, *Writing on the* Wall, p.78; 24/7/72, NA PREM 15.975.

13 22/8/72, NA PREM 15.977.

14 Lawson, *The View from No.11*, p.7.

15 Heath to Armstrong, 26/5/72, NA CM 969; Jones, *Union Man*, pp.261–2; 8/10/72, NA CM 820; *The Times*, 6/7/72; 28/6/72, NA CM 969.

16 6/7/72, NA CM 34(72).

17 10/7/7, NA CM 969; 13/7/72, NA CM 36(72); 13/7/72, NA CM 819.

18 Eric Silver, *Victor Feather TUC* (London, 1973), p.210.

19 NA CM 45, 46, 47 and 49(72).

20 Heath to Cromer, 13/11/72, Cromer papers; 14/6/72, HETH 19; 25/9/72, Heath papers 3 2/17; 28/10/72, NA CM 820.

21 13/11/72, NA CM 822; Cockerell, *Live from Number Ten*, p.187; 8/11/72, NA PREM 15.1269.

22 *The Times*, 9/10/71; Baker, *Turbulent Years*, p.36.

23 Heath to Forman, undated, Heath papers 4 6/12; See, in particular, NA CM 1, 2 and 3 (1973).

24 11/11/72, NA CM 822.

25 16/9/72 and 20/9/72, Heath papers 3 1/17; Wells to Kitson, 30/12/72, Heath papers 3 1/17.

26 7/11/71, NA CM 956; 9/11/72, NA CM (51)72.

27 Heath, *Course of My Life*, p.454; Campbell, *Heath*, p.378; Bell, *Labour Party in Opposition*, p.61.

CHAPTER 18: *Foreign Affairs*

1 Henry Kissinger, *Years of Renewal* (London, 1999), p.603; Lawson, *The View From No.11*, p.529; Campbell, *Heath*, p.342; Royle to Heath, 4/9/74, Heath papers 3 6/25.

2 Kissinger, *Years of Renewal*, p.602; Nixon to Heath, 7/7/70, NA CM 211; NA PREM 15.714.

3 NA PREM 15.714; 5/10/70, NA CM 26(70).

4 Kissinger, *Years of Renewal*, p.602; Raymond Seitz, *Over Here* (London, 1998), pp.310 and 316–17.

5 NA PREM 15.753; 6/10/73, Heath papers 4 2/13.

6 Roussel, *Pompidou*, pp.548–9; NA PREM 15.1555; 16/1/73, NA PREM 15.1976.

7 NA PREM 15.1989; 11/1/72, NA CM 1(72).

8 NA PREM 15.1564; Heath, *Course of My Life*, p.493; conversation with Dr Kissinger.

9 NA PREM 15.1989; Heath to Major General Hutson, 29/7/74, Heath papers 3 6/25; 7/3/75, HETH 22; Peter Hennessy and Caroline Anstey, 'Money Bags and Brains, The Anglo-American "Special Relationship" since 1945', Strathclyde Analysis Paper no.1, 1990.

10 Hennessy and Anstey, 'The Special Relationship'; Heath to Home, 8/9/70, Home to Heath, 18/9/70, NA PREM 15.718.

11 3/7/70, NA CM 161; Heath to Nixon, June 1967, NA CM 211; Cromer to Heath, 5/11/71, NA PREM 15.310; Heath to Douglas-Home, 28/1/72, NA PREM 15.2077.

12 Heath to Cromer, 18/6/71, NA PREM 15.1265; Heath to Pompidou, 24/11/71, NA PREM 15.326; Roussel, *Pompidou*, p.505.

13 7/1/72, NA PREM 1268.

14 28/10/73, NA PREM 15.1382; 31/10/73, NSA Documents 90; 26/10/73, State Dept Cable to US Embassy, Paris 211737; 12/11/73, NA PREM 15.1565; Alistair Horne, *Kissinger's Year, 1973* (London, 2009), p.245.

15 4/11/70, NA PREM 15.105; 28/10/70, NA CM 194; 8/11/71, NA PREM 15.2001.

16 NA PREM 15.2220; 19/3/73, NA PREM 15.1853.

17 Nixon to Heath, 26/7/73, Heath to Nixon, 30/7/73, NA PREM 15.1981.

18 24/11/73, NA PREM 15.2232; Kissinger to Heath, 26/12/73, NA PREM 15.2232.

19 13/9/72 and 23/11/70, NA PREM 15.1281; 8/2/73, NA CM 5(73).

20 Memo by Cromer, undated, Cromer papers.

21 23/10/73, NSA Documents, 63; King, *Diary 1970–1974*, p.315; Thatcher, *Path to Power*, p.230.

22 David Owen, *Time to Declare* (London, Penguin edition, 1992), p.209; 14 and 15/10/73, Hailsham papers 2/7/61; conversation with Lady Lyons.

23 Heath. *Course of My Life*. p.488; Trend to Heath. 17/2/72, NA PREM 15.787.

24 Carrington to Heath, 11/4/72, NA PREM 15.177; Heath to Monnet Action Committee, 15/3/84, Heath papers 4 2/21; Roussel, *Pompidou*, p.507; 24/5/73, CM 30(73); Roussel, *Pompidou*, pp.653–6.

25 14/11/72, NA PREM 15.1359.

26 3/9/70, CM 12(70); Willy Brandt, *My Life in Politics* (London, 1992), p.424.

27 Henderson, *Mandarin*, p.56; 1/3/73, NA PREM 15.1576.

28 3/3/73 and 12/3/73, NA PREM 15, 1459.

29 NA PREM 15.1115.

30 10/4/72, Heath papers 3 2/18.

31 NA CM 122; 9/7/70, NA PREM 15.36; Heath, *Old World, New Horizons*, p.69.

32 26/6/70, NA PREM 15.36.

33 14/4/71, NA CM 236.

34 Armstrong to Fisher, 14/9/70, NA CM 126; 21/9/79, NA CM 20(70).

35 21/9/70, NA CM 20(70).

36 NA PREM 15.1826.

37 Heath to Mintoff, 7/7/71, NA PREM 15.521; Carrington, *Reflect on Things Past*, pp.244–5; 26/1/71, NA CM 4(71).

38 Heath, *Course of My Life*, p.499; Carrington, *Reflect on things Past*, pp.244–5; conversation with Lord Carrington; 23/1/72, NA PREM 15.381.

39 Ball and Seldon, *Heath Government*, p.298; Heath, *Course of My Life*, p.490; NA PREM 15.955.

40 NA PREM 15.1637.

41 19/7/73, NA CM 38(73); 2/5/73, NA PREM 15.1554.

42 Press conference of 27/11/72, NA PREM 15.1580.

43 Heath to López Bravo, 8/5/73, NA PREM 15.1580.

44 Heath. *Course of My Life*, p.601.

45 26/4/71, NA PREM 15.1148.

46 Peter Wright, *Spycatcher* (London, 1987), p.344; George Walden, *Lucky George* (London, 1999), p.147; 29/9/71, NA CM 48(71).

47 26/4/71, NA PREM 15.1148.

48 11/8/71, NA PREM 15.1988.

49 21/9/72, NA CM 42(72).

50 Benn, *Office Without Power*, p.437.

CHAPTER 19: *Hurricane*

1 Barber to Heath, 31/12/72, Heath papers 1 1/12; Nott, *Here Today, Gone Tomorrow*, pp.153–7 and p.161.

2 15/2/73, NA CM 7(73) and 20/2/73, NA CM 8(73); NA PREM 15.1951.

3 23/1/73, NA CM 3(73) and 27/2/73, NA CM 11(73).

4 26/1/73, NA PREM 15.1664.

5 28/3/73, NA PREM 15.1672.

6 24/7/73, NA PREM 15.1674.

7 2/4/73, NA PREM 15.1672.

8 2/5/73, NA PREM 15.1672; conversation with Christopher Roberts.

9 5/4/73, NA CM 22(73) and 12/4/73, NA CM 23(73); 19/4/73, NA PREM 15.1672; May 1973, Heath papers 4 2/13.

10 NA PREM 15.1654.

11 20/8/73, NA PREM 15.1951.

12 Armstrong to Rothschild, 27/2/73, NA PREM 15.1409; 3/1/73, NA CM 823; 10/5/73, NA CM 26(73); 16/7/73, NA PREM 15.1680.

13 du Cann, *Two Lives*, pp.131–7; Heath, *Course of My Life*, p.417; 14/5/73, NA CM 27(73).

14 *Contemporary Record*, vol 9, no. 1, 1995, p.214.

15 May 1973, Heath papers 4 2/13.

16 Hurd to Howell, Heath papers, 3 1/16; 16/7/73, NA PREM 15.2101.

17 Jellicoe to Heath, 2/6/73, NA PREM 15.1904; conversations with Lord Armstrong and the late Lord Jellicoe.

18 Michael to Rosemary Wolff, 15/5/73, Sara Morrison papers; conversations with Lord Hurd and Sara Morrison.

19 23/6/73, NA PREM 15.1858; 12/4/73, NA PREM 15.1529.

20 Pym to Heath, 16/7/63, Heath papers 3 1/16; Mudd to Heath, 25/9/73, Heath papers 3 1/17.

21 17/7/73, NA CM 37(73)

22 Conversation with Lord Prior; Campbell, *Heath*, p.492; *Contemporary Record* vol 9, no. 1, 1995, p.209; conversation with Lord Gilmour.

23 Holmes, *Failure of the Heath Government*, p.102; Gormley, *Battered Cherub*, p.125.

24 1/11/73, NA CM 52(73) and 29/11/73, NA CM 58(73); King, *Diary 1970–1974*, p.315.

25 Allason, 'Ted Heath', ts p.268; NA PREM 15.2014 and 2023.

26 12/12/73, NA PREM 15.2126.

27 Hurd, *End to Promises*, pp.117–18; *British Politics since 1945*, ed. Simon James and Virginia Preston (Basingstoke, 2001), p.123; Cockerell, *Live from Number Ten*, p.194.

28 Norton and Aughey, *Conservatives and Conservatism*, pp.170–71; *Hugo Young Papers*, p.67; 27/3/75, SELO 4/65; conversations with Lords Carrington and Walker.

29 *Hugo Young Papers*, p.68; Garnett and Aitken, *Whitelaw*, p.172; 27/3/75, SELO 4/65; 8/1/74, HETH 21; 12/12/73, NA CM 61(73).

30 Gormley, *Battered Cherub*, p.135; Andrew Taylor, *The NUM and British Politics*, vol 2: 1969–1995 (Aldershot, 2005), p.92; Ziegler, *Wilson*, p.398.

31 19/12/73, NA PREM 15.1844; Taylor, *The Fifth Estate*, p.82; Christopher Andrew, *The Defence of the Realm* (London, 2009), pp.587–90.

32 Holmes, *Failure of Heath Government*, p.110; 10/1/74, NA CM 2(74).

33 17/1/74, NA CM 3(74); Ball and Seldon, *Heath Government*, p.186; *Hugo Young Papers*, pp.31–32; conversations, inter alia, with Lords Armstrong, Gilmour and Prior.

34 Taylor, *NUM and British Politics*, vol 2, p.97.

35 29/1/74, HETH 21; Heath, *Course of My Life*, pp.510–11; Stephen Fry and Hugo Young, *The Fall of Heath* (London, 1976), p.29.

36 Conversations with Lords Armstrong and Croham.

37 Baker, *Turbulent Years*, p.39; Ramsden, *Winds of Change*, p.373; conversation with Sir Timothy Kitson; conversations with Lords Hurd and Waldegrave.

38 Whitelaw, *Memoirs*, p.132; Geoffrey Lewis, *Lord Hailsham* (London, 1997), p.323; Francis Pym, *The Politics of Consent* (London, 1984), p.4; Carrington, *Reflect on Things Past*, p.265; Prior, *A Balance of Power*, p.74.

39 Lawson interview with David Butler, 18/4/74; Nott, *Here Today, Gone Tomorrow*, pp.162–3; Thatcher, *Path to Power*, p.233.

40 Millar, *View from the Wings*, p.221; Garnett and Aitken, *Whitelaw*, p.178; conversations with Lords Carrington and Prior and Sir Timothy Kitson.

41 Lord Hailsham, *The Door Wherein I Went* (London, 1975), p.298 and *A Sparrow's Flight* (London, 1990), p.387; Heath to Hailsham, 4/11/75, HLSM 1/1/10 Part 7; conversation with D. R. Thorpe.

CHAPTER 20: *Defeat on Points*

1 David Butler and Dennis Kavanagh, *The British General Election of February, 1974* (London, 1974), pp.81–3; Benn, *Against the Tide*, p.106.

2 Conversation with Sara Morrison.

3 Kitson to Lady Dalkeith, 1/11/72, Heath papers 3 1/1; Bridges to Heath, Jan 1974, Heath papers 3 4/9.

4 *Daily Mirror*, 5/4/73 and minutes on Heath papers 3 1/1; Trethowan, *Split Screen*, p.128.

5 Butler and Kavanagh, *The British General Election of February, 1974*, p.118; Hurd, *Memoirs*, p.218.

6 David Butler interviews with Fraser, 21/2/74 and Wolff, 11/3/74; du Cann, *Two Lives*, pp.197–8 and David Butler interview, 20/2/74; Butler and Kavanagh, *The British General Election of February, 1974*, p.269n.

7 David Butler interview, 26/2/74; Benn, *Against the Tide*, p.106.

8 Butler and Kavanagh, *The British General Election of February, 1974*, p.66; Shepherd, *Powell*, p.449.

9 Heath, *Course of My Life*, p.516.

10 Mark Stuart, *Douglas Hurd* (Edinburgh, 1998), p.85.

11 Ball and Seldon, *Heath Government*, p.369; Cockerell, *Live from Number Ten*, p.198; Margach, *Abuse of Power*, p.169; NA PREM 15.2232.

12 Ball and Seldon, *Heath Government*, p.355; Wyatt, *Confessions of an Optimist*, p.341.

13 Heath papers 3 2/3.

14 Conversations with Richard Simmonds and Penelope Gummer.

15 1/3/74, NA CM 9(74); Hailsham diary, 2-3/3/74, HLSM.

16 Conversation with Lord Waldegrave; Benn, *Against the Tide*, p.579.

17 1/3/74, NA CM 9(74); Hailsham diary, 2-3/3/74, HLSM.

18 1/3/74, NA CM 9(74); King, *Diary 1970–1974*, pp.348–9; 2/3/74, NA PREM 15.2069; 4/3/74, NA CM 10(74).

19 Waldegrave to Daniel Korn, 24/4/96, Heath papers 4 6/18; conversations with Sara Morrison and Lords Waldegrave and Armstrong.

20 4/7/74, NA CM 10(74).

21 Heath, *Course of My Life*, pp. 518–19; Jeremy Thorpe, *In My Own Time* (London, 1999), pp.114–17.

22 NA PREM 15.2069.

23 Thatcher, *Path to Power*, p.239; Heath, *Course of My Life*, p.519.

24 Tebbit, *Upwardly Mobile*, p.134; Nott, *Here Today, Gone Tomorrow*, p.163; Andy McSmith, *Kenneth Clarke* (London, 1994), p.50; conversation with Kenneth Clarke.

25 *Spectator*, 9/3/74.

26 2/3/74, NA PREM 15.2069; Wyatt to Heath, 3/374, NA PREM 15.2069; Hailsham diary, 4/3/74, HLSM.

27 King, *Diary 1970–1974*, p.352; Heath, *Course of My Life*, p.519.

28 Ramsden, *Winds of Change*, p.359; Nixon to Heath, 4/3/74, Heath papers 3 2/20.

29 Heath, *Course of My Life*, p.520.

CHAPTER 21: *The Uneasy Truce*

1 Heath, *Course of My Life*, p.520; conversation with Sir Timothy Kitson.

2 Falkender, *Downing Street in Perspective*, pp.29 and 21.

3 Cecil Parkinson, *Right at the Centre* (London, 1992), p.48; King, *Diary 1970–1974*, p.364; Patten and Hurd interviews with David Butler, 8/8/74.

4 Hurd interview with David Butler, 18/3/74; conversations with Wilf Weeks and Sara Morrison; Campbell, *Heath*, p.576.

5 Heath, *Course of My Life*, p.511; Fraser interview with David Butler, 18/9/74; conversations with Caroline Ryder, Penelope Gummer and Lord Prior.

6 Lord Macaulay, *History of England* (Albany edition, London, 1898), vol 3, p.341.

7 Maudling, *Memoirs*, p.207; King, *Diary 1970–1974*, p.361; Critchley, *A Bag of Boiled Sweets* (London, 1984), p.141; Heath to McNamara 10/8/74, CPA CCO 20/8/18; Anthony Powell, *Journals 1982–1986* (London, 1995), p.37.

8 Fowler, *Ministers Decide*, p.7; Critchley, *A Bag of Boiled Sweets*, p.140.

9 David Butler interview, 14/3/74; King, *Diary 1970–1974*, p.352.

10 Thatcher, *Path to Power*, pp.241–2; *Daily Telegraph*, 10/11/74.

11 Heath papers 3 4/23.

12 Halcrow, *Keith Joseph*, p.65; Ridley to Heath, 22/10/74, Heath papers 3 4/23.

13 Heseltine, *Life in the Jungle* (London, 2000), p.157.

14 Denham and Garnett, *Keith Joseph*, p.259; Joseph to Heath, 31/7/74, Heath papers 3 6/25; Baker, *Turbulent Years*, p.41 and conversation with Lord Baker; 21/6/74, Heath papers 3 4/23.

15 Howe, *Conflict of Loyalty*, p.168.

16 Harold Wilson, *Final Term* (London, 1979), pp.15–16; 15/3/74 HLSM 1/19 Sect 3; Heath, *Course of My Life*, p.522.

17 25/3/74, Heath papers 3 4/23; Maude to Heath, 25/5/74, Heath papers 1 1/15; Maxwell Hyslop to Heath, 9/5/74, Heath papers 3 6/25.

18 Hailsham to Heath, 15/6/74, Heath papers 3 6/25; Pym to Heath, 11/6/74, Heath papers 3 1/9; Carrington interview with David Butler, 21/9/74.

19 Austen Morgan, *Harold Wilson* (London, 1992), pp.445–6; Martin Gilbert papers; conversation with Sir Martin Gilbert.

20 David Butler and Dennis Kavanagh, *The British General Election of October 1974* (London, 1975), pp.13 and 35.

21 *Evening News*, 18/11/66; conversation with Lord Walker; Hurd, *Memoirs*, p.127; Kissinger, *Years of Renewal*, p.146; 21/6/74, Heath papers 3 2/20.

22 Wilson to Heath, 22/5/74, Heath papers 1 1/15; conversation with Sir Martin Gilbert.

23 Heath, *Course of My Life*, pp.629–31; Waldegrave to Heath, 25/5/74, Heath papers 3 3/8; conversations with Lords Hurd and Waldegrave.

24 Heath papers 3 3/8.

25 Conversations with Sara Morrison and Dame Joan Varley; Behrens, *Conservative Party from Heath to Thatcher*, pp.32–3.

26 Ramsden, *Winds of Change*, p.388.

27 Wilson, *Final Term*, p.97; Manley to Heath, 9/4/74, Heath papers 3/2/20.

28 Waldegrave to Loudon, 30/7/74, CPA CCO 20/8/18; Baker, *The Turbulent Years*, p.45.

29 Conversation with Margaret Chadd.

30 Lawson to Heath, 14/3/74, Heath papers 1 1/9; conversation with Lord Lawson.

31 1/4/74, Heath papers 3 4/23.

32 Gilmour, *Whatever Happened to the Tories?*, p.294; Ramsden, *Winds of Change*, p.386.

33 3/7/74, Heath papers, 3 4/23; Hurd to Waldegrave, 21/8/74, Heath papers 4 6/12.

34 Sara Morrison interview with Butler, 12/11/74; conversations with Sara Morrison and Lord Waldegrave; Patten interview with Butler, 8/8/74.

35 Patten interview with Butler, 24/10/74; Kitson interview with Butler, 28/11/74; Butler and Kavanagh, *British General Election of October 1974*, p.125; conversations with Lords Baker, Patten, Prior and Waldegrave; Michael Fraser interview with Butler, 15/11/74; Kenneth Baker interview with Butler, 24/3/75; Donoghue interview with Butler, 23/10/74.

36 Butler and Kavanagh, *British General Election of October 1974*, pp.106–7; Morrison interview with Butler, 12/11/74.

37 Butler and Kavanagh, *British General Election of October 1974*, pp.237 and 266; Galloway interview with Butler, 1/10/74; Gilmour interview with Butler, 13/10/74; Du Cann, *Two Lives*, p.198.

38 Cockerell, *Live from Number Ten*, pp.210–12; Morrison interview with Butler, 30/9/74.

39 Thatcher, *Path to Power*, pp.257–9; Powell to Stuttaford, 28/8/74, POLL 1/1/22C.

40 Geoffrey Wansell, *Sir James Goldsmith* (London, 1982), p.111.

41 Conversation with Lord Waldegrave.

CHAPTER 22: *Defeat by Knockout*

1 Castle, *Diaries 1964–1976*, p.509.

2 Thatcher, *Path to Power*, p.263.

3 Hurd to Heath, 16/10/74, Heath papers 1 1/9; Baker, *Turbulent Years*, pp.43–4; conversation with Sara Morrison.

4 Baker, *Turbulent Years*, p.43.

5 Fraser to Heath, 25/10/74, Heath papers 3 4/23; Fraser interview with David Butler, 14/3/75.

6 Pym, *Politics of Consent*, p.4; Thorpe interview with Hetherington, 8/5/74, HETH 21; Hailsham Diary, 12/11/74, HLSM 1/1/9; Wilson interview with Hetherington, 22/1/75, HETH 22.

7 Conversation with Lord Hurd; Prior, *Balance of Power*, p.98.

8 Howe, *Conflict of Loyalty*, p.89; Michael Crick, *Michael Heseltine* (London, 1997), pp.179–80; conversation with Lord Heseltine.

9 Carr to Heath, 3/11/74, Heath papers 1 1/15.

10 Lawson, *View from No. 11*, p.13; Clark, *The Tories*, p.385.

11 Heath, *Course of My Life*, p.529; Du Cann, *Two Lives*, p.204.

12 13/11/74, record of meeting in Bernard Wetherill's papers, WEA/PP W8; Gilmour, *Whatever Happened to the Tories?*, p.296.

13 Ramsden, *Winds of Change*, pp.434–6; Philip Cowley and Matthew Bailey,

'Peasants Uprising or Religious War?' *British Journal of Political Studies*, vol 30, part 4, Cambridge, 2000, p.599.

14 Du Cann, *Two Lives*, pp.200–202; conversation with Lord Waldegrave; Critchley, *A Bag of Boiled Sweets*, p.141; Baker to Heath, 7/11/74, Heath papers 1 1/15.

15 Hailsham Diary, 12/11/74, HLSM 1/1/9.

16 Critchley, *A Bag of Boiled Sweets*, p.143.

17 22/10/74, HLSM 1/1/9 5cc 7.

18 Shadow Cabinet, 4/4/74, Heath papers 3 4/23.

19 Whitelaw to Heath, 27/11/74, Heath papers 3 2/16.

20 6/12/74 and 17/12/74, Heath papers 3 4/23.

21 CPA CCO, 20/39/7; *Daily Telegraph*, 3/2/75; Selwyn Lloyd diary, 16/12/74, SELO 4/63; Garnett and Aitken, *Whitelaw*, p.206.

22 CPA CCO, 20/39/8; Hurd to Heath, 19/1/75, Heath papers 1 1/15.

23 Whitelaw, *Memoirs*, pp.141–2; Selwyn Lloyd diary, 16/12/74, SELO 4/65.

24 Denham and Garnett, *Joseph*, p.265; Thatcher, *Path to Power*, p.261; John Ranelagh, *Thatcher's People* (London, 1991), p.136.

25 Whitehead, *Writing on the Wall*, p.327; Thatcher, *Path to Power*, p.267; Cockerell, *A Very Singular Man*; Heath, *Course of My Life*, p.530.

26 Castle, *Diaries 1964–1976*, p.552; Ranelagh, *Thatcher's People*, p.71; Fisher to Hailsham, 20 and 21/1/75, HLSM 1/1/9, Sec 10.

27 Renton, *Chief Whip*, p.89; Walker, *Staying Power*, p.128.

28 Fisher, *Tory Leaders*, p.126; Walker, *Staying Power*, p.128; conversations with Lord Walker, Sir Timothy Kitson and Lord Baker; Ramsden, *Winds of Change*, p.447; conversation with Lord Lawson; Du Cann, *Two Lives*, p.207.

29 Hurd, *Memoirs*, p.231; Heath, *Course of My Life*, p.531; McSmith, *Clarke*, p.57; conversation with Kenneth Clarke; Baker, *Turbulent Years*, p.44; Ramsden, *Winds of Change*, p.447.

30 Parkinson, *Right at the Centre*, p.128; Hurd, *Memoirs*, p.230; conversation with Lord Hurd.

31 Heath, *Course of My Life*, p.532; *Daily Express*, 3/12/75; John Grigg, *The History of the Times*, vol VI, p.324.

32 Vernon Bogdanor, *Politics and the Constitution* (Aldershot, 1997), p.64.

33 Wetherill to Heath, 4/12/75, WEA/PP W8; Behrens, *Conservative Party from Heath to Thatcher*, p.40; Tebbit, *Upwardly Mobile*, p.141; Heseltine, *Life in the Jungle*, p.161; conversation with Lord Waldegrave.

34 Baker, *Turbulent Years*, p.44; conversations with Lord Waldegrave and Caroline Ryder; Cockerell, *Live from Number Ten*, p.218.

35 4/2/75, WEA/PP W8; Carrington to Heath, 5/2/74, Heath papers 1 1/5.

CHAPTER 23: *Adjusting to a New Life*

1 Heath, *Course of My Life*, p.535.

2 Du Cann to Heath, 14/2/75, Patten to Heath, 12/2/75, Heath papers 1 1/15; Ziegler, *Wilson*, p.455; conversation with Sir Edward Heath.

3 Heath, *Course of My Life*, pp.536–7; Thatcher, *Path to Power*, pp.282–3; Campbell, *Heath*, p.689; conversation with Sir Timothy Kitson.

4 Benn, *Against the Tide*, p.319; Heath, *Course of My Life*, p.537; conversation with Sara Morrison; Fraser interview with Butler, 14/3/75.

5 19/2/75, RPS MS 367, *f*172.

6 Margach, *Abuse of Power*, p.170; Seligman to Jenkins, 12/3/75, Jenkins papers (I am indebted to John Campbell for letting me see this letter).

7 David Butler and Uwe Kitzinger, *The 1975 Referendum* (London, 1976); see, in particular, pp.11 and 64; Waldegrave to Heath, 28/10/74, Heath papers 4 2/17.

8 David Butler record of discussion, 21/3/75.

9 Thatcher, *Path to Power*, pp.530–31; Hurd to Heath, 7/3/75, Heath papers 4 2/16.

10 Campbell, *Heath*, p.683; Philip Goodhart, *Full Hearted Consent* (London, 1976), p.152; Jenkins, *Life at the Centre*, p.416.

11 2/6/88, Heath papers 4 3/23; House of Commons, 9/4/75.

12 Patten interview with Butler, 6/5/75; conversations with Lord Patten and Sir Stephen Sherbourne.

13 Castle, *Diaries 1964–1976*, pp.605–6; David Walter, *The Oxford Union* (London, 1984), p.193; James Lees-Milne, *Through Wood and Dale* (London, 1998), p.35.

14 Conversation with Richard Simmonds.

15 Roy Jenkins, *European Diary 1977–1981* (London, 1989) pp.3 and 349; conversation with Sir Crispin Tickell.

16 Fisher, *Tory Leaders*, p.184; Castle, *Diaries 1964–1976*, p.637; Thatcher, *Path to Power*, p.304; 9/4/75, HETH 22.

17 Baker, *Turbulent Years*, p.45; Thatcher, *Path to Power*, p.307; conversations with Lords Patten and Waldegrave; Millar, *View from the Wings*, p.243.

18 Hailsham to Thatcher, 21/7/75, Thatcher to Hailsham, 27/7/75, Hailsham to Thatcher, 29/7/75, Hailsham to Heath, 29/7/75, Heath to Hailsham, 3/8/75, HLSM 1/1/10 Part 4.

19 Kitson to Hailsham, 8/7/76; Hailsham Diary, 20/1/76, HLSM 1/1/10 Part 9.

20 Behrens, *Conservative Party from Heath to Thatcher*, p.108; Martin Holmes, *The First Thatcher Government 1979–1983* (Brighton, 1985), p.78; Norton and Aughey, *Conservatives and Conservatism*, p.236; conversation with Lord Heseltine; McSmith, *Clarke*, p.71; Howell interview with Butler, 8/10/75.

21 Heath papers 7 6/1.

22 Conversations with Sir Stephen Sherbourne, Wilf Weeks and Richard Batey.

23 Ziegler, *Wilson*, p.360.

24 *Guardian*, 27/11/75; *Daily Telegraph*, 11/1/76.

25 Sherbourne to Heath, 20/5/76 and 18/6/76, Heath papers 4 3/1; Heath to Midgley, 25/5/77, Heath papers 4 3/1; Heath to Armstrong, 7/10/76, Heath papers 4 3/3.

26 *Observer*, *Sunday Times* and *Sunday Telegraph*, 18/12/77; Longford to Heath, 8/8/77, Heath papers 4 3/1; 16/6/78, Heath papers 4 3/1.

27 Heath, *Course of My Life*, p.674.

28 Heath, *Course of My Life*, pp.539–62.

CHAPTER 24: *The Long Sulk*

1 Bernard Donoghue, *The Heat of the Kitchen* (London, 2003), p.184; Wilson, *Final Term*, p.235; Heath, *Course of My Life*, p.357.

2 House of Commons, 2/12/76.

3 Behrens, *The Conservative Party from Heath to Thatcher*, p.108; Heath to Hailsham, 3/1/77, HLSM 2/7/63; Bogdanor, *Politics and the Constitution*, p.229.

4 *The Times*, 31/7/76; Hurd, *Memoirs*, p.247.

5 Heath, *Course of My Life*, p.553; Hailsham Diary, 29/3/77, HLSM.

6 Behrens, *Conservative Party from Heath to Thatcher*, p.105.

7 Howe, *Conflict of Loyalty*, pp.103–4; notes by Butler on Conservative Party conference; Patten interviews with Butler, 22/7/78 and 19/12/78.

8 Thatcher, *Path to Power*, pp.415–16; conversation with Wilf Weeks; Heath to Boyle, 18/11/78, Heath papers 4 6/12; Campbell, *Heath*, p.713.

9 Heath to Smith, 24/1/76, Heath papers 4 4/1; Hurd to Heath, 21/9/75, Heath papers 4 1/2.

10 Heath, *Course of My Life*, pp.640–41.

11 Nott, *Here Today, Gone Tomorrow*, p.128.

12 7/7/98, Heath papers 4 3/23; Heath to Rongji, 6/9/99, Heath papers 4 4/1.

13 Correspondence between Anthony Stadden and Richard Burn, August–September 1998, Heath papers 4 4/6.

14 Conversations with Lords Howe and Hurd, Sir Michael Palliser and Richard Burn.

15 Henderson, *Mandarin*, p.149; conversations with Sir Nicholas Henderson, Sara Morrison and Lady Aldington.

16 Heath, *Course of My Life*, pp.571–2; Mrs Ridsdale to Heath, 30/10/78, Heath to Mrs Ridsdale, 1/1/79, Heath papers 4 6/12.

17 CPA CCO, 20/1/32; Heath to Thorneycroft, 25/4/78, Heath papers 4 6/12.

18 Campbell, *Thatcher*, vol 1, p.440; Thatcher, *Path to Power*, p.456; 'Sunday with Adam Boulton', 7/7/96; conversations with Lady Ryder and Lord Waldegrave.

19 cit. Thorpe, *Douglas-Home*, p.404; Junor, *Listening for a Midnight Tram*, p.231.

20 Conversation with Sara Morrison; Heath, *Course of My Life*, p.574.

21 Hailsham Diary, 5/5/79, HLSM; Thorneycroft to Mrs D. Walker, 17/5/79, CPA CCO 20/1/32.

22 Conversation with Sir Timothy Kitson; Henderson, *Mandarin*, p.366; Jenkins, *European Diary*, p.449.

23 Jenkins, *European Diary*, p.535; conversations with Lord Waldegrave, Lady Ryder, Lord Lawson, Lord Hurd and Lord Armstrong.

24 Norma Major, *Chequers*, pp.252–3.

CHAPTER 25: *Phased Retreat*

1 Conversations with Lord Carrington and Lord Moser; Wyatt. *Journals*, vol II, p.481.

2 Coleman, *Movers and Shakers*, p.122; *Sir Edward Heath: A Life Beyond Politics*. Produced and directed by Bryan Forbes, 2000.

3 Conversation with Sara Morrison; letter from Lord Wright, 13/12/08.

4 Wyatt, *Journals* vol I, p.309.

5 22/11/83, Heath papers 4 6/1; Lympany to Heath, 11/9/71, Heath papers 3 3/1; conversations with Nancy-Joan Seligman and Lord Healey; James Lees-Milne, *A Mingled Measure* (London, 1994), p.178; conversation with Sir Nicholas Henderson; Lees-Milne, *Ancient as the Hills*, p.171.

6 James Lees-Milne, *The Milk of Paradise* (London, 2005), pp.198–9.

7 Burn to Heath, 5/8/94 and Hurd to Heath, May 1995, Heath papers 4 6/16.

8 Conversation with Sir Michael Butler.

9 I am indebted to many people for their recollections of life at Arundells, particularly Stuart Craven, Sara Morrison, Lord Armstrong, Sir Nicholas Henderson, Sally Sampson, Lady de Zulueta, Hugh Dickinson, Lady Aldington, Nancy-Joan Seligman and Richard Burn. See also Heath, *Course of My Life*, pp.680–83.

10 Heath papers, 1 Misc and Heath to H. Walker, 25/7/83; Heath papers 4 6/16 and 6/18; conversation with Richard Burn.

11 Letter from the Very Rev H. G. Dickinson, 7/11/07; Dickinson to Heath, 9/7/96, Heath papers 4 6/17; conversations with Lord Prior and the Very Rev H. G. Dickinson.

12 Heath papers 1 1/17.

13 Heath to du Cann, 28/10/87 and to Armstrong, 27/1/88, Heath papers 1 1/15; Heath interview with Robin Day, 11/2/94.

14 Conversations with Sara Morrison and Michael Sissons; Sissons to Heath, 23/8/94, Heath papers 1 1/17; conversation with Martin Gilbert.

15 Garnett to Morrison, 28/2/98 and Morrison to Garnett, 4/3/98, Morrison papers; Morrison to McManus, 6/1/98 and Bridges to McManus, 23/1/98, Heath papers 4 3/23.

16 Tony Benn, *Free at Last!* (London, 2002), p.476.

17 Draft foreword for paperback edition, Heath papers 4 3/23; conversation with Henry Kissinger; Peter James to McManus, 1/4/98, Heath papers 4 3/23; McManus to Heath, 7/7/98, Heath papers 4 3/23.

18 *The Times*, 8/10/98; *Sunday Telegraph*, 11/10/98; *Observer*, 4/10/98; *Daily Telegraph*, 3/10/98.

19 Heath papers 4 6/6.

CHAPTER 26: *Filling in Time*

1 Jenkins, *European Diary*, p.103; *The Brandt Report – Restoring the Health of the World Economy*, Royal Society of Medicine, Stevens Lecture, 1981.

2 Heath, *Course of My Life*, p.607; Hart to Heath, 26/4/78, Heath papers 4 4/13.

3 Heath to Carrington, November 1979, Heath papers 4 4/13.

4 Heath, *Course of My Life*, p.610; Wright to Heath, 18/12/79, Heath papers 4 4/13; Heath, *Course of My Life*, pp.608–9.

5 Sherbourne to Heath, 8/8/80, Heath papers 4 4/14; Heath, *Course of My Life*, pp.611–13; Campbell, *Heath*, p.721; House of Commons 24/7/81.

6 Tony Benn, *The End of an Era* (London, 1992), p.603.

7 Heath, *Course of My Life*, p.654.

8 Conversations with Lords Hurd and Waldegrave; letter from Lord Hurd of 12/3/08; Branson to Heath, 5/7/94, Heath papers 4 6/16.

9 Dr Easton's diary, Heath papers 4 4/24; conversation with Dr Jeffrey Easton.

10 House of Commons, 25/10/90; conversation with Lord Hurd; Sir Paul Bryan, *Wool, War and Westminster* (London, 1993), p.231.

11 Easton diary, Heath papers 4 4/24; Heath, *Course of My Life*, p.667.

12 Benn, *Free at Last!* p.217; Heath to Briggs, 15/1/94, Heath papers 4 6/14; Beloff–Heath correspondence, Heath papers 4 6/24.

13 May 1991, Heath papers 4 6/6.

14 Tony Benn, *More Time for Politics* (London, 2007), p.51.

15 Annenberg–Heath correspondence, Heath papers 1 1/15; 'Meet the Press', 20/4/86.

16 Heath papers, 4 2/19 and 2/21.

17 Heath to Thatcher, 21/3/84, Heath papers 4 2/61; Campbell, *Heath*, p.765.

18 Heath, *Course of My Life*, p.706; 4/11/89, Heath papers 4 5/15.

19 Campbell, *Heath*, p.799; Heath interview with Robin Day, 11/2/94; Heath to Critchley, 14/12/95, Heath papers 4 6/17; Heath to Bogdanor, 21/1/97, Heath papers 4 5/15.

20 Heath, *Course of My Life*, pp.598–9; Benn, *Free at Last!* pp.248–9 and p.466.

21 Jenkins, *European Diary*, p.587; Heath, *Course of My Life*, p.577; Jenkins, *Life at the Centre*, p.554; conversation with Sara Morrison.

22 Heath to Templeton, Heath papers 4 5/15; Wyatt, *Journals*, Vol 1, p.308; circular letter from Chief Whip, 9/3/87, copy in Heath papers 4 5/15; conversations with Sir Anthony Kenny and Lord Lawson.

23 Conversations with Sir Stephen Sherbourne, Richard Burn and Sir Anthony Kenny.

24 Heath to Kennedy, 11/11/98, Heath papers 4 6/17; Heath to Deputy Foreign Minister, 7/9/99, Heath papers 4 4/1.

25 Howe, *Conflict of Loyalty*, pp.362–3; Heath, *Course of My Life*, p.645; conversation with Peter Batey; interview by John Kane on *Visions* programme, February 1989.

26 Allason, 'Ted Heath' ts, pp.324–5; conversation with Richard Burn; House of Commons, 13/7/89 and 19/4/90; Heath to Li Peng, undated, Heath papers 4 4/1; *Newsnight*, 19/2/97.

27 *The Times*, 11/12/92, Heath papers 4 4/1; conversation with Lord Patten; Heath to Tang Jiaxuan, 16/9/98, Heath papers 4 4/6; record of meeting with Mai Zhaorong, 14/9/98, Heath papers 4 4/6.

28 Sara Morrison papers.

29 Martin Holmes, *The First Thatcher Government* (Brighton, 1985), p.75; conversations with Lord Marlesford and Sir Stephen Sherbourne.

30 Margaret Thatcher, *The Downing Street Years* (London, 1993), p.167; Campbell, *Thatcher*, vol 2, p.123; Key to Heath, 26/7/88, Heath papers 1 1/15.

31 Heath, *Course of My Life*, p.580.

32 Michael Cockerell, Peter Hennessey and David Walker, *Sources Close to the Prime Minister* (London, 1984), p.226; conversation with Peter Batey.

33 Heath, *Course of My Life*, p.587; House of Commons, 11/4/84; Marc Glendening to Heath, 28/11/84, Heath to Glendening, 15/12/84, Heath papers 7 6/1.

34 House of Commons, 2/7/87 and 29/11/88; Lawson, *The View from No. 11*, p.847.
35 Conversation with Lord Howe; Renton, *Chief Whip*, pp.88–9.
36 Cockerell, *Observer*, 4/10/98; Wyatt, *Journals*, vol II, p.482; Millar, *A View from the Wings*, p.373; Wolff to Heath, 1/5/93, Heath papers 4 6/15.
37 Heath, *Course of My Life*, p.594; Crick, *Heseltine*, p.354; *Sunday Telegraph*, 3/5/92; CPA, CCO, 20/1/54.

CHAPTER 27: *Declining Years*

1 Callaghan to Heath, 23/6/92, Heath papers 4 6/14.
2 Gyles Brandreth, *Breaking the Code* (London, 1999), p.358; conversation with Dr Easton.
3 Heath to Clarke, 23/6/97, Clarke to Heath, 3/7/97, Heath to Hague, June 1997, Heath papers 4 6/17.
4 Benn, *Free at Last!*, pp.504, 524 and 646.
5 Benn, *Free at Last!*, p.589; conversations with Lord Carrington and Sara Morrison.
6 Bryan Forbes, 'Sir Edward Heath, A Life Beyond Politics'; conversations with Sara Morrison and Dr Easton.
7 9/7/97, Heath papers 4 6/18.
8 Conversation with Michael Wade.
9 Conversations with Kay Davidson and Stuart Craven.
10 Armstrong to Heath, 6/4/03, Heath papers, uncatalogued.
11 Conversations with Sara Morrison, Richard Burn and Lord Armstrong.
12 Benn, *Free at Last!*, p.242.
13 Hurd to Catherine O'Brien, 9/11/70, Heath papers 3 2/14.
14 Benn, *More Time for Politics*, p.277.

SOURCES AND BIBLIOGRAPHY

Manuscript Sources

Sir Edward Heath's own archive is at the time of writing still to be found at Arundells, his house in Salisbury. The papers are roughly catalogued on principles partly chronological and partly thematic, but many, including some of the most important, have escaped categorisation and are to be found in separate boxes. The catalogue numbers given in my reference notes will, anyway, be irrelevant once the papers have been deposited in their final home. I have sought to give sufficient information about each document to make it possible for future researchers to track it down without too much difficulty.

The next most important source of information about Heath's career is undoubtedly the National Archives at Kew. The two sections which provide the richest material are the Prime Ministerial series (NA PREM 15) and the Cabinet minutes and supporting papers (NA CM); among the other papers the Foreign Office and Board of Trade papers are particularly relevant. The Conservative Party Archives deposited in the Bodleian (CPA CCO) also provide much invaluable information, particularly for the period when Heath was Leader of the Opposition.

Other manuscript collections on which I have drawn, in some cases to a considerable extent, are those of Lord Adeane (The Hon. Edward Adeane); Sir Adrian Boult (British Library); Lord Butler (Trinity College, Cambridge); Colonel and Mrs Chadd (Mrs Margaret Chadd); the William Clark Mss (Bodleian); the 3rd Earl of Cromer (Countess of Cromer); Sir Martin Gilbert (Martin Gilbert papers); Lord Hailsham (Churchill Archives Centre); Sir Roy Harrod (British Library); Lord Howell (Howell papers); Harold Macmillan, Lord Stockton (Bodleian) and, in particular, the reports to Macmillan by Sir

Knox Cunningham (Bodleian); Selwyn Lloyd (Churchill Archives Centre); Lord Monckton of Brenchley (Bodleian); Sara Morrison (The Hon. Mrs Sara Morrison); Enoch Powell (Churchill Archives Centre); Lord Soames (Churchill Archives Centre and certain papers, including a draft section of an autobiography, still in the possession of Lady Soames); Lord Swinton (Churchill Archives Centre); Bernard Weatherill (Templeman Library, University of Kent). The Balliol College Archives and the Chatham House Archives (Ramsgate) are most valuable for the periods of Heath's life which they cover. A limited number of papers from the National Security Archive in Washington are also available, though the process of declassification means that this material is limited.

The Heath archive contains tapes and recordings of many broadcasts on the radio and on television. I have found of particular value the recordings of interviews with Sir Robin Day, Sir David Frost and Jeremy Paxman. Films of particular interest were *A Very Singular Man* (Michael Cockerell, Blakeway Productions, 1998); *Sir Edward Heath: A Life Beyond Politics* (Bryan Forbes, 2000); *The Man Who Went to the Country* (TVS, 1985) and *Edward Heath – His Own Man* (BBC, 1975).

Records of interviews conducted by Alastair Hetherington (London School of Economics) contain much of interest. By far the richest source of material of this kind, however, is the treasure-house of interviews with Professor David Butler to be found in Nuffield College, Oxford.

I am fortunate in having been privileged to see the hitherto unpublished thesis by Dr Mark Deavin, 'Macmillan's Hidden Agenda', as well as two books which, at the time of writing, are similarly unpublished, Rupert Allason's 'Ted Heath' and David Marsh's 'Blood, Gold and the Euro'.

Books, Pamphlets or Contributions to Other Publications by Edward Heath (in Chronological Order)

One Nation – A Tory Approach to Social Problems (London, 1950)

Parliament and People (Conservative Political Centre, London, 1960)

Old World, New Horizons: Britain, the Common Market and the Atlantic Alliance (Godkin Lecture, Oxford, 1970)

'My Style of Government' (interview with Charles Wintour and Robert Carvel for the *Evening Standard*, London, 1–2 June 1972)

Sailing (London, 1975)

Music: A Joy for Life (London, 1976)

Our Community (Conservative Political Centre, London, 1977)

Travels (London, 1977)

Carols: The Joy of Christmas (London, 1977)

North–South: A Programme for Survival (Noel Buxton Lecture, Colchester, 1980)

The Brandt Report – Restoring the Health of the World Economy (Stevens Lecture, Royal Society of Medicine, London, 1981)

An Atlantic Approach to North–South Relations (David Bruce Memorial Lecture, University of Keele, 1982)

The State of Britain to Come (London, 1986)

Politics and Consensus in Modern Britain (London, 1988)

European Unity over the Next Ten Years (Lothian Foundation, London, 1988)

'Christian Values in Politics' (Contribution to *Christian Values,* ed. Edward Stourton and Frances Gumley, London, 1996)

The Course of My Life (London, 1998)

Books Entirely or Primarily About Edward Heath or his Government

Alexander, Andrew, and Watkins, Alan, *The Making of the Prime Minister: 1970* (London, 1970)

Ball, Stuart, and Seldon, Anthony, *The Heath Government, 1970–74* (Harlow, 1996)

Campbell, John, *Edward Heath* (London, 1993)

Evans, Marian, *Ted Heath: A Family Portrait* (London, 1970)

Fry, Stephen, and Young, Hugo, *The Fall of Heath* (London, 1976)

Holmes, Martin, *The Failure of the Heath Government* (London, 1997)

Hurd, Douglas, *An End to Promises* (London, 1979)

Hutchinson, George, *Edward Heath* (London, 1970)

Laing, Margaret, *Edward Heath: Prime Minister* (London, 1972)

MacShane, Denis, *Heath* (London, 2006)

Roth, Andrew, *Heath and the Heathmen* (London, 1972)

Other Relevant Books

Abse, Leo, *Wotan, My Enemy* (London, 1994)

Andrew, Christopher, *The Defence of the Realm* (London, 2009)

Bagnall, Nicholas, *A Little Overmatter* (Lewes, 2002)

Baker, Kenneth, *The Turbulent Years* (London, 1993)

Ball, George, *The Discipline of Power* (London, 1968)

Barber, Anthony, *Taking the Tide* (Norwich, 1966)

Baston, Lewis, *Reggie: The Life of Reginald Maudling* (Stroud, 2004)

Behrens, Robert, *The Conservative Party from Heath to Thatcher* (Farnborough, 1980)

Bell, Patrick, *The Labour Party in Opposition* (London, 2004)

Beloff, Nora, *The General Says No* (London, 1963)

Benn, Tony, *Out of the Wilderness: Diaries 1963–67* (London, 1988)

Benn, Tony, *Office Without Power: Diaries 1968–72* (London, 1989)

Benn, Tony, *Against the Tide: Diaries 1973–76* (London, 1990)

Benn, Tony, *Conflicts of Interest: Diaries 1977–80* (London, 1990)

Benn, Tony, *The End of an Era: Diaries 1980–90* (London, 1992)

Benn, Tony, *Years of Hope: Diaries 1940–1962* (London, 1994)

Benn, Tony, *Free at Last! Diaries 1991–2001* (London, 2002)

Benn, Tony, *More Time for Politics: Diaries 2001–2007* (London, 2007)

Berkeley, Humphry, *Crossing the Floor* (London, 1972)

Blackstone, Tessa, and Plowden, William, *Inside the Think Tank* (London, 1988)

Blake, Robert, *The Conservative Party from Peel to Thatcher* (London, 1985)

Bleakley, David, *Faulkner* (London, 1974)

Bogdanor, Vernon, *Politics and the Constitution* (Aldershot, 1997)

Boyd-Carpenter, John, *Way of Life* (London, 1980)

Brandreth, Gyles, *Breaking the Code* (London, 1999)

Brandreth, Gyles, *Brief Encounter* (London, 2001)

Brandt, Willy, *My Life in Politics* (London, 1992)

British Politics Since 1945, ed. Simon James and Virginia Preston (Basingstoke, 2001)

Brittan, Samuel, *Left or Right: The Bogus Dilemma* (London, 1968)

Bruce-Gardyne, Jock, *Whatever Happened to the Quiet Revolution?* (London, 1974)

Bruce-Gardyne, Jock, and Lawson, Nigel, *The Power Game* (London, 1976)

Bryan, Sir Paul, *Wool, War and Westminster* (London, 1993)

Butler, David, and King, Anthony, *The British General Election of 1964* (London, 1965)

Butler, David, and King, Anthony, *The British General Election of 1966* (London, 1966)

Butler, David, and Pinto-Duschinsky, Michael, *The British General Election of 1970* (London, 1971)

Butler, David, and Kavanagh, Dennis, *The British General Election of February 1974* (London, 1974)

Butler, David, and Kavanagh, Dennis, *The British General Election of October 1974* (London, 1975)

Butler, David and Kitzinger, Uwe, *The 1975 Referendum* (London, 1976)

Butler, Lord, *The Art of the Possible* (London, 1971)

Butt, Ronald, *The Power of Parliament* (London, 1967)

Campbell, John, *Margaret Thatcher*, vols I and II (London, 2000 and 2003)

Camps, Miriam, *Britain and the European Community: 1955–1963* (London, 1964)

Carrington, Lord, *Reflect on Things Past* (London, 1988)

Carver, Michael, *Out of Step* (London, 1989)

Castle, Barbara, *Fighting All the Way* (London, 1993)

Castle, Barbara, *The Castle Diaries. 1964–1976* (London, 1990)

Chapple, F., *Sparks Fly!* (London, 1984)

Churchill, Randolph, *The Fight for the Tory Leadership* (London, 1964)

Clark, Alan, *Diaries* (London, 1993)

Clark, Alan, *The Tories* (London, 1998)

Clark, William, *From Three Worlds* (London, 1986)

Clutterbuck, Richard, *Britain in Agony* (London, 1978)

Cockerell, Michael, *Live from Number Ten* (London, 1988)

Cockerell, Michael, Hennessy, Peter, and Walker, David, *Sources Close to the Prime Minister* (London, 1984)

Cole, John, *As It Seemed To Me* (London, 1995)

Coleman, Terry, *Movers and Shakers* (London, 1987)

Coleman, Terry, *Thatcher's Britain* (London, 1987)

Contemporary Record, vol 2, no.1, 1988

Contemporary Record, vol 3, no.3, 1990

Contemporary Record, vol 3, no.4, 1990

Contemporary Record, vol 7, no.3, 1993

Contemporary Record, vol 9, no.1, 1995

Courtney, Anthony, *Sailor in a Russian Frame* (London, 1968)

Cowley, Philip, and Bailey, Matthew, 'Peasants' Uprising or Religious War? Re-examining the 1975 Conservative Leadership Contest', *British Journal of Political Studies*, vol. 30, Part 4 (Cambridge, 2000)

Crick, Michael, *Michael Heseltine* (London, 1997)

Critchley, Julian, *A Bag of Boiled Sweets* (London, 1984)

Critchley, Julian, *Palace of Varieties* (London, 1981)

Critchley, Julian, *Heseltine* (London, 1987)

Crossman, Richard, *The Diaries of a Cabinet Minister, vol 1: 1964–66* (London, 1975)

Crossman, Richard, *The Diaries of a Cabinet Minister, vol 2: 1966–68* (London, 1976)

Crossman, Richard, *The Diaries of a Cabinet Minister, vol 3:. 1968–70* (London, 1977)

Davenport-Hines, Richard, *The Macmillans* (London, 1992)

Day, Robin, *Grand Inquisitor* (London, 1989)

Denham, Andrew, and Garnett, Mark, *Keith Joseph* (Chesham, 2001)

Dixon, Piers, *Double Diploma* (London, 1968)

Donoghue, Bernard, *The Heat of the Kitchen* (London, 2003)

Du Cann, Edward, *Two Lives* (Malvern, 1995)

Eden, Anthony, *Full Circle* (London, 1960)

Faber, David, *Speaking for England* (London, 2005)

Falkender, Marcia, *Downing Street in Perspective* (London, 1983)

Family History. Journal of the Institute of Heraldic and Genealogical Studies, vol 4, nos 19 and 20/21, 1966

Faulkner, Brian, *Memoirs of a Statesman* (London, 1978)

Fisher, Nigel, *Iain Macleod* (London, 1973)

Fisher, Nigel, *The Tory Leaders* (London, 1977)

Fowler, Norman, *Ministers Decide* (London, 1991)

Garnett, Mark, and Aitken, Ian, *Splendid! Splendid! The Authorized Biography of Willie Whitelaw* (London, 2002)

Giles, Frank, *Sundry Times* (London, 1986)

Gilmour, Ian, *The Body Politic* (London, 1969)

Gilmour, Ian, *Inside Right* (London, 1977)

Gilmour, Ian, *Dancing With Dogma* (London, 1992)

Gilmour, Ian, *Whatever Happened to the Tories?* (London, 1997)

Goodhart, Philip, *The 1922* (London, 1973)

Goodhart, Philip, *Full-Hearted Consent* (London, 1976)

Goodman, Arnold, *Tell Them I'm On My Way* (London, 1993)

Gordon Walker, Patrick, *Political Diaries 1932–1971* (London, 1991)

Gormley, Joe, *Battered Cherub* (London, 1982)

Griffiths, J. A. G., *The Politics of the Judiciary* (London, 1985)

Griffiths, James, *Pages from Memory* (London, 1969)

Grigg, John, *The History of The Times, vol. VI: 1966–1981* (London, 1993)

Hailsham, Lord, *The Door Wherein I Went* (London, 1975)

Hailsham, Lord, *A Sparrow's Flight* (London, 1990)

Haines, Joe, *The Politics of Power* (London, 1977)

Halcrow, Morrison, *Keith Joseph* (London, 1989)

Harvey, Ian, *To Fall Like Lucifer* (London, 1971)

Healey, Denis, *The Time of My Life* (London, 1989)

Helme, Deborah, *Sir Maurice Laing* (privately printed)

Henderson, Nicholas, *Mandarin: The Diaries of an Ambassador* (London, 1994)

Hennessy, Peter, *Cabinet* (London, 1986)

Hennessy, Peter, *The Hidden Wiring* (London, 1995)

Hennessy, Peter, *The Prime Minister* (London, 2000)

Heseltine, Michael, *Life in the Jungle* (London, 2000)

Hill, Lord, *Behind the Scenes* (London, 1974)

Holmes, Martin, *Political Pressure and Economic Policy* (London, 1982)

Holmes, Martin, *The First Thatcher Government: 1979–1983* (Brighton, 1985)

Horne, Alistair, *Macmillan,* vol II: *1957–1986* (London, 1989)

Horne, Alistair, *Kissinger's Year: 1973* (London, 2009)

Howard, Anthony, *RAB. The Life of R. A. Butler* (London, 1987)

Howe, Geoffrey, *Conflict of Loyalty* (London, 1994)

Hurd, Douglas, *Memoirs* (London, 2003)

Jackson, Robert J., *Rebels and Whigs* (London, 1968)

Jenkins, Peter, *Mrs Thatcher's Revolution* (London, 1987)

Jenkins, Roy, *European Diary: 1977–1981* (London, 1989)

Jenkins, Roy, *Life at the Centre* (London, 1991)

Jobert, Michel, *Mémoires d'Avenir* (Paris, 1994)

Jones, Jack, *Union Man* (London, 1986)

Junor, John, *Listening for a Midnight Tram* (London, 1990)

Kilmuir, Lord, *Political Adventure* (London, 1964)

King, Cecil, *The Cecil King Diary: 1965–1970* (London, 1972)

King, Cecil, *The Cecil King Diary: 1970–1974* (London, 1975)

Kissinger, Henry, *The White House Years* (London, 1979)

Kissinger, Henry, *Years of Renewal* (London, 1999)

Kitzinger, Uwe, *Diplomacy and Persuasion* (London, 1973)

Kyle, Keith, *Suez* (London, 1991)

Lamb, Richard, *The Macmillan Years* (London, 1995)

Lawson, Nigel, *The View from No. 11* (London, 1992)

Lee, J. J., *Ireland 1912–1985* (Cambridge, 1989)

Lees-Milne, James, *A Mingled Measure* (London, 1994)

Lees-Milne, James, *Ancient as the Hills* (London, 1997)

Lees-Milne, James, *Through Wood and Dale* (London, 1998)

Lees-Milne, James, *The Milk of Paradise* (London, 2005)

Leigh, David, *The Wilson Plot* (London, 1988)

Lewis, Geoffrey, *Lord Hailsham* (London, 1997)

Lindsay, T. F., *Parliament from the Press Gallery* (London, 1967)

Lloyd, Selwyn, *Suez, 1956* (London, 1978)

Macmillan, Harold, *Riding the Storm* (London, 1971)

Macmillan, Harold, *Pointing the Way* (London, 1972)

Macmillan, Harold, *At the End of the Day* (London, 1973)

Macmillan, Harold, *The Macmillan Diaries: The Cabinet Years*, ed. Peter Catterell (London, 2003)

Maitland, Donald, *Diverse Times, Sundry Places* (Brighton, 1996)

Major, Norma, *Chequers* (London, 1987)

Margach, James, *The Abuse of Power* (London, 1978)

Margach, James, *The Anatomy of Power* (London, 1979)

Maudling, Reginald, *Memoirs* (London, 1978)

McAlpine, Alistair, *Once a Jolly Bagman* (London, 1997)

McSmith, Andy, *Kenneth Clarke* (London, 1994)

Middlemas, Keith, *Power, Competition and the State*, vol. II (London, 1990)

Millar, Ronald, *A View from the Wings* (London, 1993)

Monnet, Jean, *Mémoires* (Paris, 1976)

Morgan, Austin, *Harold Wilson* (London, 1992)

Mount, Ferdinand, *Cold Cream* (London, 2008)

Nabarro, Gerald, *NAB 1* (Oxford, 1969)

Nicolson, Harold, *Letters and Diaries, 1945–62*, ed. Nigel Nicolson (London, 1968)

Nicolson, Nigel, *Long Life* (London, 1997)

Norton, Philip, and Aughey, Arthur, *Conservatives and Conservatism* (London, 1981)

Norton, Philip, *Conservative Dissidents* (London, 1978)

Nott, John, *Here Today, Gone Tomorrow* (London, 2000)

Owen, David, *Time to Declare* (London, 1991)

Palmer, Bernard, *Gadfly for God* (London, 1991)

Palmer, Bernard, *High and Mitred* (London, 1992)

Parkinson, Cecil, *Right at the Centre* (London, 1992)

Peyton, John, *Without Benefit of Laundry* (London, 1997)

Pimlott, Ben, *Harold Wilson* (London, 1992)

Powell, Anthony, *Journals 1982–1986* (London, 1995)

Preparing for Government: The Conservative Research Department 1929–2009, ed. Alistair Cooke (London, 2009)

Prior, Jim, *A Balance of Power* (London, 1986)

Punnett, R. M., *Front-Bench Opposition* (London, 1973)

Pym, Francis, *The Politics of Consent* (London, 1984)

Raison, Timothy, *Tories and the Welfare State* (London, 1970)

Ramsden, John, *The Making of Conservative Party Policy* (London, 1980)

Ramsden, John, *The Winds of Change: Macmillan to Heath 1957–1975* (London, 1996)

Ranelagh, John, *Thatcher's People* (London, 1991)

Rawlinson, Peter, *A Price Too High* (London, 1989)

Renton, Tim, *Chief Whip* (London, 2004)

Rhodes James, Robert, *Ambitions and Realities* (London, 1972)

Ridley, Nicholas, *My Style of Government* (London, 1991)

Roll, Eric, *Crowded Hours* (London, 1985)

Rose, Kenneth, *Elusive Rothschild* (London, 2003)

Rothschild, Victor, *Meditations of a Broomstick* (London, 1977)

Rothschild, Victor, *Random Variables* (London, 1984)

Roussel, Eric, *Georges Pompidou* (Paris, 1994)

Seitz, Raymond, *Over Here* (London, 1988)

Seldon, Anthony, *Churchill's Indian Summer* (London, 1981)

Seldon, Anthony, *How Tory Governments Fall* (London, 1996)

Sewill, Brendon, *British Economic Policy 1970–1974* (London, 1975)

Shepherd, Robert, *The Power Brokers* (London, 1991)

Shepherd, Robert, *Iain Macleod* (London, 1994)

Shepherd, Robert, *Enoch Powell* (London, 1996)

Shrapnel, Norman, *The Seventies* (London, 1980)

Silver, Eric, *Victor Feather TUC* (London, 1973)

Slater, Jim, *Return to Go* (London, 1977)

Stuart, Mark, *Douglas Hurd* (Edinburgh, 1998)

Taylor, Andrew, *The NUM and British Politics,* vol 2: *1969–1995* (Aldershot, 2005)

Taylor, Robert, *The Fifth Estate* (London, 1978)

Taylor, Robert, *The Trade Union Question in British Politics* (Oxford, 1993)

Tebbit, Norman, *Upwardly Mobile* (London, 1989)

Thatcher, Margaret, *The Downing Street Years* (London, 1993)

Thatcher, Margaret, *The Path to Power* (London, 1995)

Thorpe, D. R., *Alec Douglas-Home* (London, 1996)

Thorpe, Jeremy, *In My Own Time* (London, 1999)

Trethowan, Ian, *Split Screen* (London, 1984)

Vickers, Hugo, (ed.), *The Unexpurgated Beaton* (London, 2002)

Waldegrave, William, *The Binding of Leviathan* (London, 1978)

Walden, George, *Lucky George* (London, 1999)

Walker, Peter, *The Ascent of Britain* (London, 1977)

Walker, Peter, *Staying Power* (London, 1991)

Walter, David, *The Oxford Union* (London, 1984)

Wansell, Geoffrey, *Sir James Goldsmith* (London, 1982)

Watt, D. C., *Personalities and Politics* (London, 1965)

Whitehall and the Suez Crisis, ed. Saul Kelly and Anthony Gorst (London, 2000)

Whitehead, Phillip, *The Writing on the Wall* (London, 1985)

Whitelaw, William, *The Whitelaw Memoirs* (London, 1989)

Wigham, Eric, *Strikes and the Government, 1893–1981* (London, 1982)

Williams, Charles, *Harold Macmillan* (London, 2009)

Wilson, Harold, *Final Term* (London, 1979)

Wilson, Harold, *The Governance of Britain* (London, 1976)

Wilson, Harold, *The Labour Government 1964–1970* (London, 1971)

Worsthorne, Peregrine, *Tricks of Memory* (London, 1993)

Wright, Peter, *Spycatcher* (London, 1987)

Wyatt, Woodrow, *Confessions of an Optimist* (London, 1985)

Wyatt, Woodrow, *Journals, vol I,* ed. Sarah Curtis (London, 1998)

Wyatt, Woodrow, *Journals, vol II,* ed. Sarah Curtis (London, 1999)

Wyatt, Woodrow, *Journals, vol III,* ed. Sarah Curtis (London, 2000)

Young, Hugo, *One of Us* (London, 1989)

Young, Hugo, *The Hugo Young Papers,* ed. Ion Trewin (London, 2008)

Ziegler, Philip, *Wilson: The Authorised Life* (London, 1993)

INDEX